News Reporting and Writing

FOURTH EDITION

News Reporting and Writing

Melvin Mencher
Columbia University

ᴜᴄᴃ
Wm. C. Brown Publishers
Dubuque, Iowa

Book Team

Editor **Stan Stoga**
Developmental Editor **Kathy Law Laube**
Production Editor **Kevin Campbell**
Photo Research Editor **Michelle Oberhoffer**
Permissions Editor **Carla D. Arnold**

wcb group

Wm. C. Brown *Chairman of the Board*
Mark C. Falb *President and Chief Executive Officer*

wcb

Wm. C. Brown Publishers, College Division

G. Franklin Lewis *Executive Vice President, General Manager*
George Wm. Bergquist *Editor in Chief*
Beverly Kolz *Director of Production*
Chris C. Guzzardo *Vice President, Director of Marketing*
Bob McLaughlin *National Sales Manager*
Marilyn A. Phelps *Manager of Design*
Julie A. Kennedy *Production Editorial Manager*
Faye M. Schilling *Photo Research Manager*

Cover photographs, clockwise: (front cover)
NASA, © Melvin Mencher, © James Skovmand/
The San Diego Tribune, (back cover) Y. Nagata/
United Nations Photo, © Larry C. Price/
Philadelphia Inquirer Magazine, © Bob Ivins/The
San Diego Tribune.

The credits section for this book begins on
page 698 and is considered an extension of the
copyright page.

Contents

Preface

News Reporting and Writing, Fourth Edition, proposes to teach the beginner how to become a reporter. Learning to report accurately and to write precisely and vigorously is no simple task. The young man or woman who would join the ranks of reporters must learn and then put into practice principles and concepts that have been developed over the years by men and women who understood that truth is elusive and that its pursuit and capture on paper require mastery of a demanding discipline.

To illustrate these principles, we will spend a lot of time with truth-seekers—another way of describing journalists—on newspapers and broadcast stations as they go about their work. We will accompany a young reporter as she conducts her first interview, and we will watch an experienced reporter cover a racial confrontation. We will overhear a reporter's thinking as she ponders the lead to a story about a city council meeting.

We will join wire service reporters covering a West Coast trip of the president when a young woman breaks out of the crowd, pulls a .45 caliber pistol from her leg holster and tries to point it at the president. We will sit in the press box with reporters covering high school football and major league baseball games. We will join a police reporter as she begins her rounds.

We will eavesdrop on a reporter as he struggles with his lead. We will watch him labor over his story until "little beads of blood form on his forehead," as Red Smith described the agony of the reporter's search for the words that will accurately portray the event. And we will share in the reporter's joy when the story is finished and is given a byline and placed on page one.

In other words, we will be concerned with the processes of reporting and writing—how reporters gather facts from sources and from their observations, how they verify these, and how they put them together in news stories.

The reporters we will be watching work for small newspapers in Iowa and Oregon, and they are on the staffs of metropolitan dailies in Chicago and New York. One reporter writes for a network television station in New York; another covers events for a television station in Columbus, Ohio. We will see how general assignment reporters and the men and women assigned to cover politics, sports, business, the police, city hall, education and other beats do their jobs.

Reporters have much in common. Covering a Rotary Club luncheon speech or the president's State of the Union address, the journalist follows the same basic processes. The general assignment reporter in a town of 25,000 and the AP's White House correspondent share a way of thinking, a set of techniques and an approach to journalism. Once learned, these enable the reporter to discover and to communicate information that all of us need in order to solve our problems and to get along with one another.

We will see that these journalists also share an ethic that directs and gives meaning to their work. The literary critic Northrop Frye could be describing journalistic morality: "The persistence of keeping the mind in a state of disciplined sanity, the courage of facing results that may deny or contradict everything that one had hoped to achieve—these are obviously moral qualities, if the phrase means anything at all."

Mary McGrory, the Washington columnist, described another aspect of the journalist's approach to his or her work in comments she made after interviewing 45 journalists who had applied for Nieman Fellowships at Harvard. She said she found these journalists to have a "great deal of commitment and compassion." Most had a trait in common, she said. "They knew a great deal about what they were doing. They did not think it enough."

The journalists I know—my former colleagues and students, from whom I have shamelessly taken time and borrowed ideas—would shrink at being described as moralists. Yet they are tireless in pursuit of a story and are dedicated to their work. Most of them also have an abiding suspicion of power.

Although adversary journalism is often criticized and sometimes ignored, it is as old as the Republic. In our third century as a nation, we must remember that today's journalists are descended from a colonial press described by the historian Robert A. Rutland as "obstreperous newspapers (that) signalled the rise of a new kind of journalism in America that would not truckle long to any officialdom."

The journalist knows that democracy is healthiest when the public is informed about the activities of captains of industry and chieftains in public office. Only with adequate information can people check those in power. Repression and ignorance are the consequences of unchecked power. Walt Whitman, journalist and poet, described the fragility of democracy and its source of strength this way: "There is no week nor day nor hour when tyranny may not enter upon this country, if the people lose their supreme confidence in themselves—and lose their roughness and spirit of defiance."

Confident, rough and defiant—these are apt descriptions of the journalist. The journalist is also skeptical, independent, tenacious and sensitive but tough-skinned. An accomplished professional, the journalist is forever the student, reading, observing, always honing his or her talent and enlarging his or her mind.

For the fourth edition of *News Reporting and Writing* additions were made to most chapters. The increased interest in ethics has led to some new conclusions in the morality of journalism chapter, and I have tried in the chapter on reporters and the law to keep track of the zig-zag path the courts are taking in their treatment of libel, privacy and other matters that concern us. Increasingly, the courts and governments are leaning on the press, curbing it, blaming it for society's ailments.

The reporting section has been amplified. Greater attention is paid to the reporting process. Instructors have asked for more detail, more examples about the procedure in finding the lead to the story. In Chapter 12 I have tried to show the student how high-quality observations begin with devising tentative themes for the story.

In response to suggestions from readers, I have changed the order of Chapters 14 through 27. I have eliminated the chapter on consumer reporting and given broadcast writing a chapter of its own.

This edition also emphasizes the journalist's need to understand and to use figures, charts and data of various kinds. Government, social and physical scientists and special interests churn out material of this sort daily, and the reporter who can turn the information into news stories is prized. I have added data from a variety of sources. Students are encouraged to localize the material.

Learning how to handle this information is an excellent way for the beginning journalist to be introduced to the art of enterprising copy. Editors want self-starters, men and women who can spot stories on their own.

The press has been hard-put to maintain its traditional independence and freedom of action. The task will be made easier if journalists look to their tradition. Albert Camus, the French journalist and author, was sustained by that sense of his calling during the Nazi occupation of France when he wrote from the underground. Accepting the Nobel Prize for literature in 1957, Camus said: "Whatever our personal frailties may be, the nobility of our calling will always be rooted in two commitments difficult to observe: refusal to lie about what we know and resistance to oppression."

We need to keep these commitments in mind at a time when some of the public tells us it does not believe what we print and broadcast. The fear that our readers and viewers might desert us has led some journalists to counsel caution, to warn against adversary journalism, to suggest that we play down bad news. The frightened should ponder the response of Joseph Pulitzer when his newspapers were accused of sensationalism: "A daily journal is like a mirror—it reflects that which is before it. . . . Let those who are startled by it blame the people who are before the mirror, and not the mirror."

In much of what the journalist does, there is an awareness of the relevance of his or her work to human needs and purposes, for the reporter knows that news represents reality to most people. The reporter is interested in ideas, but avoids the sin of making the concrete abstract.

Journalism "is something more than a craft, something other than an industry, something between an art and a ministry," says Wickham Steed, an editor of *The Times* of London. "Journalists proper are unofficial public servants whose purpose is to serve the community."

My model for this amalgam of artist, sentry, public servant and town crier is Ralph M. Blagden, who taught a generation of journalists their duty and introduced them to the power and splendor of their native language. Ralph's classrooms were the newsrooms of newspapers from New Hampshire to California, where he worked as reporter and editor.

Ralph was my competitor as a state capitol correspondent, and never was there such a mismatch. As a beginning reporter, I reported what people said and did and stopped there. Ralph generously took the youngster in tow and showed him that a good reporter never settles for the surface of the news, that the compelling commandment of the journalist is to dig out the truth. He refused to make reporting divisible: All good reporting is investigative reporting, he insisted.

Long before investigative reporting became the fashion, Ralph was digging out documents and records to disclose truths. His journalism was in the tradition of Joseph Pulitzer and that publisher's crusading editor, O. K. Bovard. Those of us who were fortunate to work with Ralph feel ourselves to be members of a journalistic family whose roots are embedded in a noble tradition.

Benjamin C. Bradlee, executive editor of *The Washington Post,* says of Blagden:

"Ralph taught me to be dissatisfied with answers and to be exhaustive in questions. He taught me to stand up against powers that be. He taught me to spot bullies and resist them. He taught me about patience and round-the-clock work. He taught me about ideals and freedom and rights—all of this with his own mixture of wit and sarcasm and articulate grace. He could also throw a stone farther than I could, which annoys me to this day."

Bradlee, who directed the *Post's* coverage of the Watergate story that earned his newspaper a Pultizer Prize for meritorious public service, recalls his first story for Blagden when he was a young reporter.

"It had to do with the post-war housing mess, and he made me rewrite it 16 times. I've never done that to a reporter, but I suspect I should have. He had a great dollop of righteous indignation, which I learned to admire enormously.

"And of course he wrote with style and punch and clarity."

I recall the first story I covered with Ralph. He had heard that patients in a state hospital for the mentally ill were being mistreated. Some had mysteriously died. We interviewed doctors, nurses, attendants and former patients, and we walked through the wards and corridors of the institution. I learned that second-hand accounts are just a starting point, that direct observation and other techniques of verification are essential, and when we wrote the story I learned the power of the simple declarative sentence. I also learned that journalists can be useful members of society, for after the story appeared and both of us had moved on, the state built a modern hospital to replace that aging snake pit.

Acknowledgments

News Reporting and Writing was written in the belief that journalism is a moral enterprise and that this gives meaning to its practice. The morality of journalism can be taught, as it was by Ralph L. Crosman, Zell Mabee and A. Gayle Waldrop at the University of Colorado. Theirs was a journalism of commitment, compassion and conscience. Those of us who studied with them are forever in their debt.

I am also indebted to my former newsroom colleagues and to my students. They have all contributed to this book, some indirectly, like George Baldwin, my first city editor, and some directly, like Berkley Hudson, one of my former students, whose work is included here. I learned from the young woman who stormed out of my classroom when I said I would not assign her to a certain story because I worried about her safety, and I learned from the copy editor many years ago who had worn down a pencil putting black lines through my copy. "Just show us what the guy did," he told me. "Let the reader draw the conclusions."

For the fourth edition, a number of colleagues made helpful suggestions. They are Earl Conn of Ball State University, Lawrence Day of the University of Kansas, John Griffith of the University of Florida, Marian Huttenstein of the University of Alabama, Robert Logan of the University of Missouri, Lynne Masel-Walters of the University of Houston, John D. Mitchell of Syracuse University, Jeffery Smith of the University of Iowa, Jim Toland of San Francisco State University, and Eugenia Zerbinos of Marquette University.

Wade Doares, the head librarian in the journalism library at Columbia University, and Steve Toth tracked down clippings and quotes with the generosity I have found among librarians who work with journalists. I single them out, but I thank all the librarians who have helped me.

Kay Ellen Krane checked the spelling, syntax and style and made a number of valuable suggestions. She also read the proof and compiled the index.

Journalists are sojourners, and many of those who shared in the preparation of the first three editions have moved on to other jobs. In this fourth edition, I am listing the places from which they dispatched material and suggestions for the four editions.

The following list acknowledges some of the persons who shared in the preparation of this book, but only I bear the responsibility for *News Reporting and Writing:*

Marjorie Arnold
The Fresno (Calif.) *Bee*

Brian Barrett
Office of the New York County
District Attorney

Frank Barrows
The Charlotte (N.C.) *Observer*

Professor Barbara Belford
Columbia University

Professor Joan Bieder
Columbia University

Mervin Block
Freelance television writer

Stewart Bowman
The Louisville *Courier-Journal*

Professor Warren Burkett
University of Texas, Austin

Chris Cage
The Sacramento Bee

Art Carey
Bucks County Courier Times,
Levittown, Pa., and
The Philadelphia Inquirer

Jean E. Collins
Core Communications

Kenneth Conboy
Office of the New York County
District Attorney, Deputy Police
Commissioner, New York City, and
coordinator of the New York City
criminal justice system

Claude Cookman
The Miami Herald

Jonathan Dedmon
Rocky Mountain News,
Denver, Colo.

Stuart Dim
Managing Editor, *The Charlotte*
(N.C.) *Observer* and *Newsday*

Robert A. Dubill
Executive Director,
Gannett News Service

Charlotte Evans
The Bergen Record and
The New York Times

Carol Falk
The Wall Street Journal

Ellen Fleysher
WCBS-TV, New York, N.Y.

Joseph Galloway
United Press International

Steve Gettinger
Corrections Magazine

Mary Ann Giordano
Daily News, New York City

J. J. Gonzalez
WCBS-TV, New York, N.Y.

Joel M. Gora
American Civil Liberties Union

Professor Dean M. Gottehrer
University of Alaska

Sarah Grimes
The Philadelphia *Bulletin* and
the University of Massachusetts
at Amherst

Susan Hands
The Charlotte (N.C.) *Observer*

Donna Hanover
WTVN-TV, Columbus, Ohio

Michael Hiltzik
Courier-Express, Buffalo, N.Y., and
Los Angeles Times

Thomas H. Jones
Night city editor, *Chicago Sun-Times*

Harry Jupiter
San Francisco *Chronicle*

E. W. Kenworthy
Washington Bureau,
The New York Times

Professor Penn T. Kimball
Columbia University

Eric Lawlor
The Houston Chronicle

Lynn Ludlow
San Francisco *Examiner*

Tony Mauro
Gloucester (Mass.) *Times* and
Gannett News Service

John McCormally
Editor and publisher,
The Hawk Eye,
Burlington, Iowa

Frank McCulloch
Executive Editor,
The Sacramento Bee

Julie McDonnell
The Register, Shrewsbury, N.J.

Bill Mertens
The Hawk Eye

Professor Alan Miller
University of Maine at Orono

Dick Oliver
City editor, *Daily News,*
New York City

Robert A. Papper
American University

Sydney Penner
Assistant city editor, *Daily News,*
New York City

Merrill Perlman
The New York Times

Paul Peterzell
Independent-Journal,
San Rafael, Calif.

Professor L. D. Pinkham
Director, Journalistic Studies,
University of Massachusetts
at Amherst

Lew Powell
The Charlotte (N.C.) *Observer*

Ron Rapoport
Los Angeles Times and *Chicago Sun-Times*

Richard C. Reid
Minneapolis Tribune

Elizabeth Rhodes
The Charlotte (N.C.) *Observer*
and *Seattle Times*

Professor Ronald Robinson
Augustana College, Sioux Falls,
S.D.

Mort Saltzman
The Sacramento Bee

Professor A. M. Sanderson
University of South Florida,
Tampa, Fla.

Sydney Schanberg
The New York Times

John Schultz
Columbia University

Donna Shalala
Teachers College, Columbia
University, and Hunter College

Eleanor Singer
Editor, *Public Opinion Quarterly*

H. L. Stevenson
Editor-in-chief, UPI

Professor Herbert Strentz
Dean, School of Journalism, Drake
University, Des Moines, Iowa

Mike Sweet
The Hawk Eye

Jeffrey A. Tannenbaum
The Wall Street Journal

Jim Toland
San Francisco *Chronicle*

Kurt van der Dussens
Vincennes (Ind.) *Sun-Commercial*

Mary Voboril
The Miami Herald

Douglas L. Watson
The Washington Post
and *Baltimore Sun*

Howard Weinberg
Senior producer, "Bill Moyers'
Journal," Channel 13, WNET-TV,
New York City

Ken Wilson
San Francisco *Chronicle*

PART ONE

The Reporter at Work

Photo by Wayne Miller of the *Redwood Record,* Garberville, Calif.

CHAPTER ONE

On the Job

Watching reporters at work, we see that they are:

- Hard working
- Enterprising
- Curious
- Calm under pressure
- Knowledgeable
- Compassionate
- Courageous

Reporters are tenacious in their search for facts that will give their readers and viewers information about events. They work quickly and efficiently against deadlines. They have a passion for accuracy and a determination to dig out all aspects of the story.

```
*AP40--To city editor: Information police
headquarters has a report of an explosion in a
telephone company office at Broadway and 215th
street.

This office covering.
  The AP
DF1213PED
```

Brentwood Parent-Teacher Association discusses raising teachers' salaries $2,000 a year.

United Nations considers sending troops into Middle East.

Springfield City Council candidate opposes city park and recreation bond issue.

Billy Harms leads at half-way point in Indianapolis 500.

Five governors argue about water rights at interstate water compact commission meeting.

F̲ew people see these events. But everyone will be able to read, see or hear about them this evening or tomorrow morning because a reporter is covering the news as it develops. The reporter is the link between the event and the reader, viewer or listener. The public sees the UN debate through a reporter's eyes, hears the candidate's speech through a reporter's ears.

Even when people witness events, they want to savor the experience again and to have details they may have missed. A good news story also will provide interpretations and explanations. Readers want to know how the proposed salary scale for teachers will affect the property tax, whether the mayor opposes the bond issue, what the race driver's winning strategy was.

A tacit agreement exists between the reporter and the public. The reporter does his or her best to give the reader, viewer and listener the truth of the event, and the public presumes that the reporter's account is honestly and fully reported and is accurately written. This agreement is important, for people act on what they read and hear:

The last paragraph of the story on the Brentwood Parent-Teacher Association meeting says parents are invited to a dinner Thursday at the local high school. A Brentwood couple decides to attend.

The Friends of Peace in the Middle East lines up pickets for a march on the UN during its debate. A high school student in Peoria and a retired postman in Tacoma write letters to their congressmen urging action by the United States.

A mother of three, angered by the candidate's position on the park and recreation program, calls friends and asks them to vote against him.

Texas cattlemen wire their governor to turn down the Colorado governor's proposal for water allotments.

Behind these news stories is a man or woman sitting alone at a desk pecking out an account of what has happened. Let us watch some reporters cover the news.

We are in the newsroom of a midwestern newspaper with a circulation of 25,000. The telephone on the city editor's desk rings and after listening for a moment, the city editor calls to a young reporter.

"Bob, the publicity director of the Lions Club has a story."

The caller tells the reporter his club intends to donate some equipment to a city playground next Saturday at 10 a.m. at a ceremony the governor will attend.

The reporter calls the governor's press secretary to check the governor's itinerary in case he is making other local stops. In 15 minutes, he has written a short piece, putting the governor in the lead. He again checks the date, time and location of the ceremony against his notes.

A few minutes later, he is told to cover a fire with a photographer.

An hour later, Bob returns to the newsroom.

An Announcement and a Fire

"It was a small fire, about $7,500 in damages, but there's some good human interest in it," he tells the city editor.

"Don't tell me you've got three columns on a three paragraph fire, Bob," the city editor replies. "What's it about?"

Without looking at his notes, he answers:

"The story isn't the fire but the background. I found out the family bought the house a few months ago, had just remodeled it, and this week the wife went to work to help pay for it. She leaves their 10-year-old boy home with his 12-year-old brother for a few hours every day.

"Well, the 12-year-old wanted to make some money cutting grass. He knows they're short of money. He was filling the lawn mower with gasoline in the garage when the tank tipped over against the water heater. Woosh. Lucky he wasn't hurt."

The city editor thinks a moment.

"Got any good quotes from the older boy?" he asks.

"Yes."

"Well, it sounds as though it's worth more than a couple of paragraphs. But don't make it a chapter in the book, Bob."

At his desk Bob pauses before writing. He can start his story like most accounts of fires he has read.

```
    A fire of accidental origin caused $7,500 in damages to
a dwelling at 1315 New Hampshire St. today.
    No one was injured in the blaze that began in the garage
when the 12-year-old son of the owners, Mr. and Mrs. Earl
Ruman . . .
```

But he is unhappy with this start. This is not the way he described the fire to the editor, he recalls. Then he remembers advice he was given by a reporter: "Every story demands to be told a certain way. Don't impose a form or style on it. The way you write it has to flow from the nature of the event."

The nature of his story was the youngster's good intentions gone awry. So he starts again:

```
    Two months ago, Mr. and Mrs. Earl Ruman moved into a
three bedroom house at 1315 New Hampshire St. It was their
dream house.
    After years of skimping and saving . . .
```

At this rate, he will write the book his editor warned him against, he thinks. Although he wants a dramatic story—one that will build to a climax—he cannot take forever to develop the point. Readers will drift away.

The youngster is the heart of the story, he reasons, and the boy must go into the lead. He tries again:

That seems to be more like it. In 40 minutes, he has the story in good shape, he thinks.

The city editor reads through the copy.

"Yes, it's a sad story," he tells his cub reporter. "Be sadder still if they didn't have insurance to cover their loss."

Bob makes for the telephone on his desk. He remembers another bit of advice: "Don't leave unanswered any questions the reader may have. Don't leave any holes in your story."

Some 1,500 miles to the west, we are in Yosemite National Park. Harry Jupiter, a young reporter from the Fresno AP bureau, leans over a ledge on his stomach, his feet grasped firmly by a park ranger. Several hundred feet below in a pocket of rock is a 17-year-old climber who had found himself stymied while working his way up the face of an almost sheer cliff.

A Daring Rescue

It is morning and the youth has been squatting—knees half bent, back against the wall—on an 18-inch ledge since last night. Had he fallen asleep or tried to change his position, he would have plummeted 1,500 feet to the floor of the valley.

Jupiter is watching park rangers prepare a complicated and daring operation. A group of seven rangers descends from the top of Glacier Point to the farthest spot they can reach on foot. From this ledge, four rangers are lowered by rope to the next ledge. At this point, the rescue party splits again and two men are lowered to a third ledge. From here, a sheer granite wall drops below them for several hundred feet. About a third of the way down on a small niche in the rock squats the object of this daring and dangerous rescue.

Lowering the rope to the youth, the two rangers begin the long and hazardous job of pulling him and then themselves back to the top.

Jupiter has been watching and obtaining information from rangers overseeing the operation. As soon as the youth is hauled up from his precarious perch to the bottom ledge, Jupiter calls in a fresh lead to the continuing story. He tells his office that the youth has been reached and hauled part-way, but there is still a long way to go. It will take hours.

The AP rewriteman tells Jupiter that some newspapers and TV stations are now stating that the youth has been rescued. Jupiter tells the rewriteman that the rescue is not complete and that the youth and four rangers still must be raised by rope a few hundred feet. Anything can happen.

Then Jupiter returns to his ledge.

It is midafternoon and the rescue party still is not out of danger when Jupiter makes another call to the San Francisco office to dictate a new lead.

"Harry, you can't be right this time," the news editor tells him. One of the San Francisco newspapers has a story in print about the youth's rescue and describes him as being in the park hospital.

Jupiter assures his editor that the group is still making the long climb up. "Here's some color on the rescue," he tells the editor. He reads his notes on the reactions of the hundreds of spectators. He describes the tension of the rangers' wives and children watching the rescue.

Then he goes back to the ledge to wait for the group. At last they stagger up. Jupiter dashes to meet them. He discovers that one of the rangers is carrying a camera. Jupiter asks him if he had used it during the rescue. He replies that he had. Jupiter borrows the film. (The photos turned out to be spectacular and were used in papers around the country.)

Jupiter approaches the youth and asks him about his long hours on the ledge. The youngster replies that he never was worried. Lagging behind the main group, Jupiter chats with one of the rangers in the rescue party who tells him, "Boy, was this kid arrogant. He gave us plenty of trouble on the way back up and almost got us killed a couple of times. And you know something, he hasn't so much as said, 'Thanks.'"

Enterprise

Raymond R. Coffey has been sent to cover a student riot on the University of Mississippi campus. Coffey can hear the shouts of the students, but police have closed off the campus. The reporters try one entrance, then another, five in all, and each is blocked.

There is a story behind those walls, and Coffey intends to dig it out.

"Back in my hotel room, I took off my suit," he said later, "put on khaki pants, rolled up the sleeves of my blue shirt, and left the collar open. I left my notebook with other reporters and stuffed a few pieces of paper and a pencil into a pocket."

Resembling a student, he slipped into the campus and gathered material for his story.

A Feature

During the Carter-Reagan presidential campaign, *The Anniston Star,* a 32,000 circulation daily newspaper in Alabama, decided to do a series on people and politics. For the first article, the paper assigned R. Robin McDonald, a new reporter.

"It was my third day on the job," McDonald said, "my second in Clay County. My first day in the county I had spied two old men on the courthouse steps." McDonald learned that they had been watching the political scene from their courthouse vantage point for years. She decided to interview them.

"I found them the second day, ensconced in the old chairs in the courthouse rotunda. I told them it was my second day in the county, my first week in Alabama and I wanted to know about the county. I didn't mention the story

at all. I pulled up a chair and we talked county, family (most of my relatives are from Georgia) and gradually drifted into politics. I didn't pull out a notebook, didn't take notes. We talked for about three or four hours. I mentioned I might want to do a story on them, if they didn't mind.

"I went back to the *Star* where I put down impressions, phrases, bits of conversation, anything I could remember on paper. I went back on Monday and we talked again, this time more directly about politics and how it had shaped their lives. By that time I had built a trust—something necessary for the kind of story I wanted.

"On Tuesday, I simply could ask them in the interview, 'Tell me about . . .' or say, 'Remember when you told me about . . .' and thus get some direct quotes. By that time, I had the old men's trust. So they talked more freely than I think they normally would have to a newcomer and a reporter.

"Then I came back, wrote the stories, using my notes. By that time, I had had a chance as well to talk with the old men's cronies, hear their stories, and watch them move around the courthouse."

McDonald decided to give each of the old-timers a separate piece. Here is how her story about Jack Crawford begins:

ASHLAND—Jack Crawford's been sitting in the rotunda of the Clay County Courthouse for 17 years, and he spots a new face like a bird dog on point. There's no one more delighted than Jack to hook a stranger and talk about Clay County, people and politics—as long as the politics are Democratic.

Crawford, at 75, is proud to say he's a lifelong Democrat. The one time he didn't vote the Democratic ticket, in 1928 when Al Smith ran against Republican Herbert Hoover, he just didn't vote. . . .

Here is the beginning of her piece about Mike Carter:

ASHLAND—Eighty-one-year-old Mike Carter's clear blue eyes and angel smile disguise a spirit of pure devilment. He's Jack Crawford's best friend and for years, he too, has staked out a broken-back, red leather chair in the rotunda of the Clay County Courthouse.

The two of them sit on each side of the main hall, just like watchdogs at the gates of Hades. "We know everybody's business that comes through the courthouse," Carter said recently. "And if we don't, we find out."

Carter, like his cohort Crawford, is always eager to listen to people talking politics.

He's more reticent when it comes to voicing his own opinions on the subject, except to proclaim proudly that the blood in his veins is pure Southern Democrat.

He's voting for President Carter for that reason, but this election doesn't stir his emotions as much as earlier ones. It's not that he's not interested. The stakes to him just don't seem as high as they once might have been. "I am," he said, "living better than I ever did in my life."

Localizing a Wire Story

In a newsroom in upstate New York, the news editor tears a story off a long section of wire service copy and calls out:

"Hey, Anne. Here's a short piece on Bemelmans' death." The news story is about the death of humorist Ludwig Bemelmans in New York City.

"He's the author of those books I read my children," the news editor says. "He was stationed around here in the army, they say. Wasn't the main character named Madeline?" he asks the reporter.

"That's right. I remember my sister reading them to me when I was a kid," she answers. "I'll never forget those first two lines."

In an old house in Paris that was covered with vines
Lived twelve little girls in two straight lines.

"Yes, that's it," says the news editor.

"I'll bet a lot of our readers know the Madeline books. It's a slow day for local news. Why don't we localize the story?" She takes the copy to the city editor, who agrees to localize the wire story.

For her rewrite, Anne needs more information and goes to *Who's Who*. Then she verifies her memory of the first few lines of the book by calling the city library and asking for the children's librarian.

"Are the books still popular?" Anne asks.

"Oh yes," the librarian replies. "They are always in demand, almost as much as Winnie-the-Pooh books. I think parents like them as much as the children."

Anne verifies from the newspaper library the news editor's recollection that Bemelmans had been stationed at a nearby army camp.

Finally, she is ready to write. She lines up her notes and the wire service story on her desk. The news, of course, is the death of Bemelmans. But Anne wants to put a local angle into the lead. She can say that Bemelmans was stationed nearby. But that was a long time ago. She writes:

```
The author of the Madeline books, Ludwig Bemelmans,
died in New York City yesterday . . .
```

But she does not like the beginning—there is no local angle—and she tries again:

```
The author of the Madeline books, beloved by children
here and everywhere, died yesterday in New York City . . .
```

Yes. That is closer. But she has neglected the parents. Another try:

```
The author of the Madeline books, read and loved by
parents and children here and everywhere, died yesterday in
New York City. Ludwig Bemelmans was 64 years old.
```

We leave Anne as she slowly rereads her lead, a corner of her eye on the clock. Pleased, she steps up her pace, for she has only an hour before she has to cover a meeting of the city zoning commission.

TV Covers a Fire

It is Christmas day, and in the newsroom of a television station a teletype is clicking off a story about a fire in a small town in New Jersey. The AP reports that while the family was asleep, a fire broke out and flames raced through the house. Four died. Only two boys escaped.

The news editor scans the story and tells a reporter, "Elaine, take this one on."

On the way to the fire, the reporter and the crew discuss the wire story. Elaine thinks of the questions she will ask, the locations in which the story will be shot.

"When I go out on an assignment I am conscious of the need for pictures," she said later. "I look for things that have an immediate impact, because I have a short time to tell the story—maybe two-and-a-half minutes.

"So I look for the strongest statement in a talk, the most emotionally appealing part of a running story. When I arrive at a story, I want to be the first one to interview the eyewitness, so that the person is still experiencing the event. The emotional facts have to tell the story."

She learned from the fire chief that the surviving youngsters had run to a neighbor's house during the fire. As crews from competing stations arrived, she and her crew approached the neighbor's house through the back yard to avoid being spotted.

"When I spoke to the woman next door, I asked her what happened when the boys burst into her home. She became tense and distraught as she described one boy's face, burned and blackened by the fire," Elaine said.

"On a breaking story, a broadcast journalist usually asks fewer questions than the print journalist," Elaine said. "On this story all I needed to ask the neighbor was two or three questions and let her tell the story."

On the return drive, Elaine structured the script in her mind. She had pictures of the fire scenes and interviews of the neighbor and the fire chief. She worked the script around the most dramatic parts.

Back in the newsroom Elaine wrote her copy and then edited the tape.

Covering Watergate on Deadline

It is a few minutes after 9 p.m. in the Washington bureau of *The Wall Street Journal*. On a television set in the office, President Richard M. Nixon is describing his activities following the break-in at the Democratic headquarters in the Watergate apartment complex. Nixon denies that he agreed to pay the burglars to keep them from revealing who had hired them. Pointing to a large stack of notebooks next to him, the president says he is turning over to the House Judiciary Committee transcripts of tape-recorded conversations he had with his advisors following the break-in.

As the president finishes speaking, *Journal* staffers are writing furiously. The deadline for the late edition was some 15 minutes ago and they have only about 20 minutes until the presses roll.

One of those working on the story is Carol Falk. She recalled later that she had assumed that Nixon had probably quoted the most damaging sections from the transcripts in his television address in order to disarm his critics, who were gaining support for impeachment.

The president's 50-page summary of the transcripts is released the next morning at about 10:30 and Falk finds nothing in them beyond what the president said the night before on television.

"At this point," she recalled later, "I was operating on the theory that the president might really have turned it around and releasing the transcripts could be a big plus for him."

The first edition deadline is 6 p.m. Unless reporters can obtain material quickly from the complete transcripts sent to members of the House Judiciary Committee, the early story will have to be based on the president's version.

Falk decides to pinpoint the key dates by going through the Watergate chronology. When the transcripts become available, sections on these dates will be the first she will examine. March 21, 1973, is one of the most important. On that day, the president met with John Dean and H. R. Haldeman, his close advisors, and ostensibly discussed payments—"hush money"—to the men who had been arrested in connection with the Watergate break-in.

Later in the day, the press associations began to run stories quoting sources who had seen material in the March 21 transcripts—and the story seemed to be changing shape. The material coming in indicated the president's speech and summary were highly selective and did not reflect the material in the transcripts.

"I began to work on a first-edition story based on the president's summary and the contrast with the more damaging reports coming out on the Hill," she says. "I was barely into the second graf [paragraph] when we got our own copy of the transcript from the White House at around 3:30 p.m."

Falk tore out the March 21 section and a colleague and the bureau chief took the rest of the transcript. She spent almost an hour checking the March 21 transcript against the president's speech and his summary. She decided that the transcript did not fully corroborate the president's version, and that conclusion went into her lead. By 4:30 p.m., she had written a lead and several paragraphs. As she turned out her copy, the bureau chief and another reporter were sending material to the desk also. There, the work of the three was stitched together into a single story.

The bureau decided to run long stretches from the transcripts to allow readers to draw their own conclusions. The story began this way:

WASHINGTON—The transcripts of President Nixon's Watergate conversations aren't nearly as clear a portrayal of his innocence as the White House is trying to tell the American people they are.

Although Mr. Nixon conceded that the material would prove embarrassing and ambiguous, the full transcript of one controversial meeting—that of March 21, 1973—includes numerous damaging statements that weren't foreshadowed in the president's confident television presentation Monday night.

For instance, while Mr. Nixon said in his speech that his clear intention at the end of the March 21 meeting was that further payments of hush money to Watergate defendant E. Howard Hunt shouldn't be made, the edited transcript shows him looking favorably on that option very near the end of the session. On page 67 of the 79-page account of that meeting among the President, White House Counsel John Dean and Chief of Staff H. R. Haldeman the following exchange begins, referring to Hunt's demand for money:

President: Would you agree that that's the prime thing, that you damn well better get that done?

Mr. Dean: Obviously, he ought to be given some signal anyway.

President: (expletive depleted) Get it. In a way that—who is going to talk to him; Colson? He is the one who is supposed to know him.

An Investigative Reporter at Work

A few weeks after Cammy Wilson has taken a reporting job with the *Minneapolis Tribune,* her city editor gives her a feature assignment: Spend a day with a woman in a wheelchair to see how handicapped people get around in the city. Wilson accompanies the woman as she goes about her chores, does some shopping and has lunch. At the end of the day, the woman remarks to Wilson, "Isn't it awful how much we have to pay to be taken to the doctor." How much? Wilson asks. "Forty to fifty dollars," she replies.

Wilson senses there is a story here of greater impact than the feature she was assigned to write. Wilson asks the woman if she has a receipt for a trip to the doctor. The woman does.

By the time she has finished her reporting, Wilson has a major scandal laid out: The transportation of the disabled is a multi-million dollar operation in which the poor, the elderly and the handicapped are being billed $40 to $120 for a round trip to a medical facility. Companies are billing at an individual rate even when they take groups from a nursing home or a senior citizen center to a clinic.

Her stories interest the Health, Education and Welfare Department in Washington D.C., and, since Medicaid money is involved, HEW investigates. The Minnesota legislature holds hearings and enacts several laws to regulate the transportation firms.

A couple of weeks later, Wilson is house hunting. In one house, she notices that every item is for sale. From worn-out washcloths to underwear, everything has a price tag. "Has the owner died?" she asks the realtor. "No," he says, "the owner is in a nursing home." "Why is he selling?" "He's not selling it. The conservator is," the realtor replies.

Once again, Wilson thinks she has a story. She learns that the owner, Ludvig Hagen, 86, suffered a fall and was taken to a nursing home to recover. While there, the church that he had named in his will marked the house and all of Hagen's possessions for sale. Wilson begins her story this way:

"4415 17th Ave. S."
"4415 17th Ave. S."
The old man in his wheelchair repeated the address, tears beginning to well.
"I don't have to sell my house. It's paid for."
But his house is for sale. It and all his possessions are part of an estate valued at $140,000. . . .

As a result of the story, the county attorney launched an investigation.

Wilson then looked at probate, the handling of wills and estates by the courts. She learned that the county probate court had appointed a management firm to handle the estates of various people and that the firm had sold their homes for well under the market price to the same buyer, who within six months resold the houses for 50 to 100 percent more than the purchase price.

In the newsroom of a daily newspaper in Maryland, the editor calls the education reporter over to his desk. "Dick, here's something pretty important. The overnight man took these notes from a fellow who said he is the publicity chairman of an organization called the Black Parents Association. See if the outfit amounts to anything, and if it does, let's have some comments. Write it down the middle. It's a touchy issue."

The notes read as follows:

    The Association has just sent a complaint to the state
    board of education. We are disturbed by the use of certain
    books our children are being given in the city's schools and
    school libraries.
        Some of this reading gives the children--black or white
    --a stereotyped view of minority people. At a time when we
    are in danger of becoming two societies, every effort must
    be made to understand each other. Some of the books our
    children are being asked to read do not accomplish this.
    They portray black people as ignorant, lacking in culture,
    child-like, sexually loose, etc.
        We are asking that certain books be removed from the
    library and the classroom--Huck Finn, Manchild in the
    Promised Land and Down These Mean Streets. We intend to add
    to the list.
        "The picture of Jim in the Twain book is that of the
    stereotyped black man of slave days," says James Alberts,
    Association president. "Impressionable children are led to
    think of black people as senseless, head-scratching, comic
    figures. We object to that portrayal of Nigger Jim."
        Alberts said that in 1957 the Finn book was banned from
    elementary and junior high schools in New York City by the
    city board at the request of the NAACP. Later, he said,
    black students at Brandeis University picketed a school
    near the university that used the book. In recent years,
    some cities have removed the book from reading lists. In
    Waukegan, Ill., it was removed on the ground that it was
    offensive to blacks. Dr. John H. Wallace, an educator on the
    Chicago School Board, calls it "the most grotesque example
    of racist trash ever written."
        "If it is to be read, it should be read at home under the
    direction of their parents," Alberts said.
        The group met in Freedom Hall of the Mt. Zion Baptist
    Church tonight.

The reporter goes to his newspaper's morgue (library) to see if there are any clips about the Association. He also looks up the names of the books in case they have been in the news. He finds that the Association was formed in 1955, a year after the U.S. Supreme Court ruling on school desegregation. It has been active in local school affairs. He finds nothing on the books in the morgue but he thinks that he has seen or heard something about one of them.

He telephones the president of the Association to ask if any particular incident provoked the action. The president tells him a parent brought up the issue at a meeting last month. The reporter asks for the name of the parent, but the president has forgotten it.

For reaction from the schools, he looks up the telephone numbers of the city school superintendent, some high school principals and the head of the board of education. If he has time, he thinks he will try to go over to a high school. It would be appropriate to interview black students, he decides. But that may have to wait for a folo (follow-up story) the next day.

He rereads the release. Many readers will know *Huckleberry Finn,* but what about the other books? He will have to find out something about them.

He remembers that when he took a course in American literature, one of his textbooks described *Huckleberry Finn* as the greatest of all American novels. Maybe he will work that in to give the story some balance. He read the book for the course and remembers Jim as a man of dignity. But his reactions certainly are not those a black high school student might have, he concedes. Yes, he will have to talk to students and to their parents as well. He will also have to guard against putting his opinions into the story.

Dick looks under *Twain* in the encyclopedia and to his surprise he finds that the book is properly titled, *The Adventures of Huckleberry Finn.* He had better check the other titles.

Dick looks out the window. He admits to himself he does not like what the Association is doing. It is too close to censorship, he thinks. After all, Mark Twain is a great writer. And people are always objecting to authors: Hemingway, Salinger, Vonnegut, Steinbeck. But Mark Twain? Can a great writer be prejudiced? There's a running debate about Shakespeare's *Merchant of Venice* and Dickens' *Oliver Twist.* He recalls reading a wire story from a city in Ontario, Canada, where some parents asked that the *Merchant of Venice* be restricted to high school seniors on the ground that younger students are vulnerable to the anti-Semitic stereotypes in the play.

He also recalls reading that when Twain was a young reporter in San Francisco he wrote an account of an attack by a gang of young whites on a Chinese man. Several policemen stood by and watched, Twain had written. Twain's story, a straightforward account of the incident, never ran.

The Association may have a point about Jim, but Twain was no racist, Dick is convinced. He remembers a story about a letter Twain wrote to Yale in 1865 that a Yale scholar recently dug up. Twain wrote the dean of the Law School offering to provide financial help to one of the school's first black students. He checks the morgue and finds the story.

"I do not believe I would very cheerfully help a white student who would ask benevolence of a stranger," Twain wrote, "but I do not feel so about the other color. We have ground the manhood out of them, & the shame is ours, not theirs; & we should pay for it." Twain subsidized the student's expenses until he graduated in 1867.

Suddenly, he recalls having read somewhere a reference to one of the books in connection with a censorship case. He asks another reporter if she recalls reading about book censorship recently. She replies that she saw a reference to a book-banning in Long Island, N.Y.

"It was about *Black Boy,* I think, and some books supposed to be anti-Semitic," she says.

He consults The New York Times Index, which his newspaper receives. First, he looks under *Obscenity,* then *Pornography.* There are no helpful entries, but there is a note suggesting the reader check *Books—Censorship.* The third entry turns out to be helpful:

Baltimore, Md, School Board is expected to reconsider shortly Nov 29 decision to ban C Brown's book about life in Harlem, *Manchild in the Promised Land*

His research turns up similar incidents in Wisconsin, Texas and Oregon. *The Reader's Guide* leads him to an article that quotes the American Library Association's report that there were three times as many incidents of censorship in schools between 1975 and 1979 than in the preceding 10 years. Since 1980, the Association says, the rate tripled again with more than 1,000 reported attempts to ban or restrict books in public schools.

He also discovers there was a U.S. Supreme Court decision in the Long Island book-banning. The decision supported the students. Dick finds the story from the *Times* microfilms in the newspaper library. The school board of the Island Trees Union Free School District removed nine books from the shelves of junior and senior high schools on the grounds they were "anti-American, anti-Christian, anti-Semitic and just plain filthy." *Down These Mean Streets* was one of the banned books.

Another entry in the Index sends him to a *Times* story that lists in order most frequently censored books:

Go Ask Alice, a diary of a teen-age girl who fell into drug use and committed suicide. The author is anonymous, supposedly the parents of the girl.
   The Catcher in the Rye by J. D. Salinger, long on the list.
   Our Bodies, Ourselves by the Boston Women's Health Collective.
   Forever by Judy Blume.
   Of Mice and Men by John Steinbeck.
   A Hero Ain't Nothing but a Sandwich by Alice Childress.
   My Darling, My Hamburger by Paul Zindel.
   Slaughterhouse Five by Kurt Vonnegut.
   The Grapes of Wrath by John Steinbeck.
   The Adventures of Huckleberry Finn by Mark Twain.

Dick decides he will have to handle the rest of the story by telephone, and an hour before his first deadline he decides he had better start writing:

```
A local school group, the Black Parents Association,
has asked the city school system to remove three books from
high school libraries because they allegedly present a
stereotyped view of blacks.
```

Too long, he thinks. Dull. Maybe he should try a more dramatic lead:

```
Huckleberry Finn should be banned from high school
libraries, a local black parents organization urged today.
```

Too sensational for this kind of story, he decides, and discards this lead. Another couple of tries, and he hits on something he likes.

```
     A local black parents organization has charged that the
city school system uses books that debase blacks and other
minorities.
     The organization, the Black Parents Association, asked
that the State Board of Education order three books removed
from Freeport school libraries and classrooms. The group
charged that the books present a "stereotyped view of
minority people." The books are: "The Adventures of
Huckleberry Finn" by Mark Twain, "Manchild in the Promised
Land" by Claude Brown, and "Down These Mean Streets" by Piri
Thomas.
     The Association, which took the action at a meeting
last night in the Mt. Zion Baptist Church, said it intends
to add other books to the three it named.
```

Dick realizes he will need to put the reaction of educators up high and that he must quote extensively from the Association statement so that readers have the full flavor of the group's anger.

"Too bad," he says, half-aloud, "we didn't have a reporter there." Then he would have something to work with—the sense of outrage, rebuttals. He puts the luxury of speculation aside and settles down to more writing.

After he has written his story. Dick decides to drive to a luncheonette near the high school where students hang out. He sits at the counter and orders a pizza and a soft drink. Around him, students are talking about a basketball game. Gradually, Dick eases into the conversation. He remarks that the team will have its work cut out for it next week. The students agree.

In a short time, he is chatting easily with three boys. He slowly turns the conversation from sports to school work and asks them about the books they read for English classes. He asks if any one has been assigned *Huckleberry Finn*. One student says he has read the book on his own.

Dick decides that this is the time to identify himself. He asks the student for his reaction to the book, and then tells him about the Association's action. One of the boys calls over some other students in a booth nearby, and soon several students, both black and white, are chatting with Dick. He lets them talk. He does not take out his notebook. He wants them to speak freely. He trusts his memory for this part of the discussion.

One youngster says, "Maybe there are some bad things in those books. But maybe censorship is worse." The others agree. Dick takes out his pad.

"That's interesting," he says. "Mind if I jot that down here?"

They go on talking, and Dick quickly writes down what he has stored in his memory as he tries to keep up with the running conversation.

He asks some of the students for their names. He would like to use them in his piece, he says. Readers will distrust the vague attribution to "a student."

Back in the newsroom, Dick tells his editor about his chat with the students. The editor suggests Dick use the material as the basis for a Sunday interpretative piece. He and Dick discuss other people to interview.

"Maybe you'd better talk to some of the people over at the university," the editor suggests. "They can tell us about efforts to condemn or censor important works."

The Qualities of a Reporter

We have watched nine reporters at work, beginners and veterans, members of small and large staffs. Different as they appear at first glance, they share certain characteristics, and there are many similarities in the way they handled their assignments.

One of the characteristics we notice is the reporter's attitude. He or she is curious. The reporter wants to know what is happening—firsthand. Coffey would not accept the version of officials about the demonstrations on the campus. He had to go in, and he did.

The journalist knows how important tenacity is in getting to the truth. "Let me tell you the secret that has led me to my goal," said Louis Pasteur. "My only strength lies in tenacity."

The reporter has an eye for detail. Journalism can be defined as the practice of the art of the specific. *The Wall Street Journal* Watergate story quotes from "page 67 of the 79-page account," and it gives the exact quotation.

Some might say that journalists are courageous in pursuit of the news, although many reporters would shrug off this description. Yet how else describe the work of Frederick Kempe of *The Wall Street Journal* who spent six days trekking over mountain paths to join the guerrillas in Afghanistan and accompanied them in a raid on a Soviet position? It was obviously courageous for Ellen Whitford of *The Norfolk Virginian-Pilot* to go into an abortion clinic, allow herself to be examined and prepared for an abortion. Whitford wanted to prove what she had learned secondhand, that abortions were being performed on women who were not pregnant. Reporters and photographers have died covering wars and disasters, and every journalist is familiar with harassment. A reporter needs courage to refuse the official version and to ask questions that seem to challenge an official's probity. Reporters question authority, and those in command often dislike being questioned.

The reporter needs courage to face facts and the results of reporting that contradict his or her beliefs. The reporter who covered the Black Parents Association's condemnation of *Huckleberry Finn* had to question his assumptions about discrimination and censorship.

The reporter requires courage to stand by a conviction in the face of pressure from competitive news agencies. Jupiter, knowing that perilous work still lay ahead, refused to go along with the competition's assertion that the youth had been rescued.

The journalist has a commitment to accuracy that encompasses the correct spelling of a name and the refusal to accept unproven assertions no matter how prestigious the authority or expert who makes them.

Stanley Walker, one of the great city editors, was once asked, "What makes a good reporter?"

"The answer is easy," he replied, with a show of a smile around his eyes. "He knows everything. He is aware not only of what goes on in the world today, but his brain is a repository of the accumulated wisdom of the ages." Walker, who helped make *The New York Herald Tribune* into a writer's newspaper, continued: "He hates lies and meanness and sham, but keeps his temper. He is loyal to his paper and to what he looks upon as his profession; whether it is a profession, or merely a craft, he resents attempts to debase it."

**In the Newsroom:
The News Flow**

Before we dig into the business of reporting and writing, let us see how the reporter fits into the newsroom operation. We will learn that decisions about what is covered are made by editors, that what is published is based on balancing the relative importance of the stories against the space available.

We could visit any one of the thousands of newspaper and broadcast station newsrooms of various sizes. Whatever the size of the staff we will find similarities in how assignments are made, how the stories are covered and how they are processed in the newsroom. Our trip takes us to the newsroom of the *Daily News* in New York City. It has a circulation of 1.5 million. We are at the city desk and the telephone is ringing. An assistant editor takes the call and turns to the city editor.

"This fellow says the governor's daughter is going to get a marriage license at 2:30. Maybe we ought to get a picture," he suggests.

The city editor is not enthusiastic.

"We had her announcement a few weeks ago," he says. But he decides they may as well take it. Nothing better may turn up for inside pages. (Nothing does, and the picture will run on page three.)

A courthouse reporter calls about a suit he thinks will make a good story. A 21-year-old woman has won $925,000 from a car-rental company. He is given the go-ahead and is told to slug the story "Suit." (The slug is important, for this is the story's identifying mark.) Usually, the desk will tell a reporter how long the piece should run, but the city editor knows that his courthouse man, an experienced reporter, will hold it to 450 to 500 words.

At 2:45 p.m., a reporter turns in a story about the funeral of Richard Tucker, an opera singer who died in Michigan while on tour. He was one of the world's leading tenors, and the funeral was held in the Metropolitan Opera House. An assistant city editor, who reads through all local copy, looks it over

Tucker's Last Song Played at the Met

By ROGER WETHERINGTON

"Richard's song was ended in mid-course." Those were among the words of farewell to Richard Tucker yesterday at a moving funeral service in the Metropolitan Opera House. As thousands of mourners look on, Tucker was eulogized as not only a great artist, but a good man.

A son of immigrant parents, he was described as devoted to his family and a devout Jew, a man who originally aspired only to be a cantor. But he also became the "Brooklyn Caruso," one of the most famed, durable and beloved of Met stars.

His name was almost synonymous with the house.

Rabbi Alvin I. Kleinerman of the Park Synagogue in Chicago, where Tucker appeared as cantor every year during the High Holy Days, said Tucker had considered his voice a gift from God and he "dedicated it to the Lord."

Rabbi Bordecai Waxman of Temple Israel in Great Neck, L.I., where Tucker worshipped, said the tenor's greatest "moments of song" were not those heard at the Met but those he chanted at the bar mitzvahs of his three sons, now grown. "He poured his heart into those moments when he inducted his children into the Jewish tradition."

The home he shared with Sara, his wife of nearly 35 years, "was rich in Jewish tradition and observance," the rabbi said. "The melodies of the synagogue rang in his ears. Richard's song was ended in mid-course," but "it lives on in many hearts."

Cardinal Cooke, a friend of Tucker's, called him "a man of great religious spirit and deep personal faith in God," a "prayerful man."

Herman Malamood, a cantor and a tenor with the New York City Opera, brought the service to an end in singing the prayer for the dead, "El Mole Rahamin," and the Met's great gold curtain

News photo by Jim Hughes
Soprano Leontyne Price leaves Met after services for Tucker.

closed slowly on Tucker for the last time.

Tucker, 60, died Wednesday, apparently of a heart attack while on a concert tour in Kalamazoo, Mich.

Met spokesmen originally said that they believed his funeral was th efirst held by the Met in its 91-year history. But a check of the archives yesterday showed that services for Leopold Damrosch, the conductor, were hled at the old Met on Broadway at 39th St. in 1885; and services for Heinrich Conried, a Met general manager, were held there in 1908.

Tucker Funeral Service. The *Daily News* is known for its clever and succinct headlines. The news editor scheduled the Tucker services for page five, and no late-breaking stories kicked it off the page for this edition.

for errors. He spots what he thinks is a mistake in a name. He tells the reporter to check whether the first name of a conductor in the story is Leopold—not Walter, as the copy has it. The reporter verifies the editor's recollection.

When the assistant city editor finishes his quick but thorough reading of the Tucker piece, the copy goes to the news desk where the news editor determines where it will be placed in the paper, the size of the headline, and the length of the story. Tucker was well-known and at the editorial conference the story had been scheduled for good play. The news editor indicates on the copy that the piece, slugged "Tucker," is slated for page five. The story then moves to the copy desk where it is closely edited to fit the space and the headline is written.

Early in the day, the city desk had made up a schedule of stories the local staff would work on (see fig. 1.1). One of these, a murder, had broken the day before in the *New York Post*. The *Post* story began:

A 22-year-old American Airlines employee was slain by one of three holdup men in her Bronx apartment early today while her husband, bound hand and foot, lay helplessly in another room.

A reporter in the Bronx was told to dig into the story, which was slugged "Slay." The *News* learns that the victim was a stewardess, which gives the slaying what journalists describe as "class." The death of someone with a glamorous or out-of-the-ordinary job is assumed to perk up reader interest.

The *News* picks up a few other facts the *Post* did not have. The police report that the gunmen had asked for $25,000 and that the woman was slain with a shot from a pistol that was placed against her head. The rewriteman double checks the names, and he learns that the victim's name was Gwendolyn Clarke, not Gwendolin Clark. Also, she was 27, not 22.

The rewriteman, Arthur Mulligan, asks if there are any pictures of the victim. There is nothing available yet, he is told.

"I have a theory on this one," he says. A deskman looks up. "Take it easy," he tells Mulligan. "Remember your theory on the Rainslayer?" (After three holdup victims were murdered during nighttime rainstorms several months before, Mulligan had theorized the killer was the "Roving Rainstorm Robber," who preyed on people when their heads were bent under umbrellas. It was not.)

Mulligan says, "My theory is that it was narcotics. Must be. Who has $25,000 sitting around the house? The guy has no job and drives a new Lincoln Continental. She'd just come in from a run, too."

It makes sense, the city editor agrees and calls his Manhattan police headquarters man to check out the narcotics possibility.

CAREY—Names Joe Hynes and Morris Abrams as special
     nursing home prosecutor and Moreland Commissioner,
     respectively.

PROFILES—of Hynes and Abrams.

NURSE—Nearly half of the 175 nursing homes in city
     could face cutoff of federal funds, according to
     list made available to us.

BERGMAN—files libel suit against Times, Stein et al
     for $1 million.

SLAY—Robbers invade home, slay wife, bind hubby and
     escape with car.

SUIT—Good reader on young woman, blinded and severely
     hurt in car crash in France, living off welfare's
     $154 Month, wins $925,000.

ETHICS—Board rules Lindsay can't appear before city
     agencies for at least 2 years, but Goldin's wife
     can hold $13G museum job.

JOBS—On deadline, city submits proposal for $46.7M in
     fed job funds.

UN—Ralph Bunche Institute report finds incompetence,
     cronyism and nepotism in the folks who work for
     our world body.

TUCKER—Services for the famed tenor held at the Met.

ABORT—Morgy OK's abortion for woman in her 28th week,
     2 weeks late.

AUDIT—Levitt report says city isn't even close to
     coping with fraud in the welfare department,
     citing huge jump in fraudulent checks.

CIVIL—Service News column.

BRIEFS—Etc.

Figure 1.1 City Desk Schedule. This list of stories is made up early in the day by the city editor and is submitted to the managing editor at the early-afternoon news conference at which the various editors discuss the stories in hand and anticipated. This discussion gives the managing editor the information he needs to decide on major play in the morning newspaper.

It is 3:40 p.m. and "Slay" has not yet taken shape. The reporters have not called in. At the news conference, the city editor had suggested that "Slay" might be page one material, and the managing editor gave the story the green light. (Murders are given good play in the *News*. The day before, a knife-slaying in New Jersey was displayed on page one of the *News*. *The New York Times*—the *News'* morning competition—played the story on page 39.)

It is now 4 p.m.—an hour before the copy should be off the city desk—and the activity in the newsroom picks up. Reporters are writing faster, copy is moving to the various desks in greater volume, and the tension increases. Copy should be in the hands of the news editor by 5 p.m., but on big stories the paper can hold until 6 o'clock for the first edition.

At 4:30 p.m., the police reporter in Manhattan headquarters calls in with additional information on "Slay." He reports that the narcotics bureau is looking into the possibility that drugs were involved. Mulligan has enough information to go to work on the story.

Ten minutes later, the picture editor relays information from the police radio, which has been crackling with calls all day. "The police think they've spotted a suspect in that bank holdup where the cop was killed," he says. "They're stopping the subways around 42nd Street and Eighth Avenue."

This could be a good story—a chase for a cop-killer through the New York subway system during the rush hour. But the desk takes the information calmly. Rather than send someone out, the desk calls the Manhattan police reporter—a busy man today—and asks him to pinpoint the search area. He had already started to do so.

At 4:58, Mulligan has the first two takes of "Slay" on the city desk. The city editor changes a couple of words, deletes others. It now reads:

```
Bronx homicide police were puzzled yesterday by
circumstances surrounding the murder of a 27-year-old
American Airlines stewardess who was shot in the head by one
of three men who burst in on her and her husband shortly
after midnight in the couple's apartment.
```

After describing the demands of the three men, the details of the slaying, and giving the address of the victim and how the men got away, the story refers to "speculation by the police that the shooting involved narcotics. . . ."

At 5:01, the police radio carries the information that a man has been picked up in the subway for questioning. Later, he is released. No one is ruffled by the collapse of the story about the search for a cop-killer.

At 5:07, the third take of "Slay" is on the desk. At 5:15, the Manhattan police reporter calls Mulligan and says that the police think there may be a link between the murder of the stewardess and the slayings of two men whose bodies were discovered in the Bronx. One of the victims was stuffed into a steamer trunk, the other was put into a wooden box. An insert is written for "Slay," and a short piece that had been written about the bodies and slugged "Trunk," is killed.

The next day a general assignment reporter, Daniel O'Grady, was assigned to check out the narcotics angle. Police confirmed Mulligan's theory about narcotics, and the lead in Sunday's newspaper read:

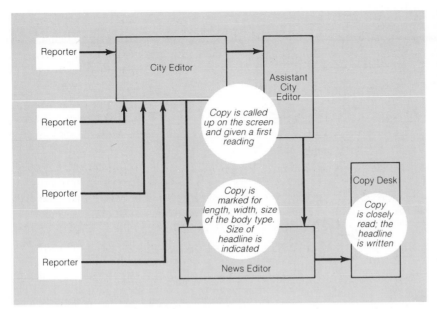

Figure 1.2 Newspaper Newsroom. The newsroom is organized to process stories quickly and efficiently. Copy flows into the newsroom from the wire services (AP, UPI and others) and reporters and is processed by editors. Local stories and copy from the newspaper's bureaus are filed by reporters who are assigned stories by editors. Some reporters—known as general assignment reporters—are based in the newsroom. Others, called beat reporters, are based at the police station, city hall, the courthouse and other locations where news is likely to be found. Their copy is read by the city editor and then assigned to a copy editor for detailed editing. Length of the story, size of type and headline are determined by editors.

A gangland war for control of the lucrative narcotics trade in Harlem and the Bronx reportedly has left six dead in the last two months, including an American Airlines stewardess who, police believe, may have smuggled drugs from the Caribbean for one faction of the all-black mob.

Although work on a metropolitan daily probably will not be the first newspaper job a journalism student lands, most newspapers operate as the *News* does: Assignments are made, reporters cover them and also develop their own stories, copy is turned in under deadline pressure in time to be edited and placed in the newspaper.

A good reporter knows how the newsroom functions and what its requirements are. The reporter is aware of the deadline and operates within its iron grip—a good reporter never misses a deadline. Nor will the reporter give any but his or her best efforts in reporting and writing a story, no matter how inconsequential it may seem.

Journalism is hard work—physically, emotionally and intellectually—and the rewards, particularly for the beginner, are not always immediate and abundant. But most reporters are sustained by the pleasure of creating meaning out of chaos, and by the joy of reporting and writing about events that people are talking about.

Summing Up

Figure 1.3 TV News Operation. Reporters are sent on stories by the assignment editor or his or her assistant. The reporter may tell the story live from a remote, or the reporter may record the report. Recorded scripts can be edited by a producer. Writers are told what stories to write by producers and editors. Unlike newspaper practice—reporters on breaking stories may call them in to rewrite men and women—in television, reporters usually do not phone their stories to writers but work with producers and editors.

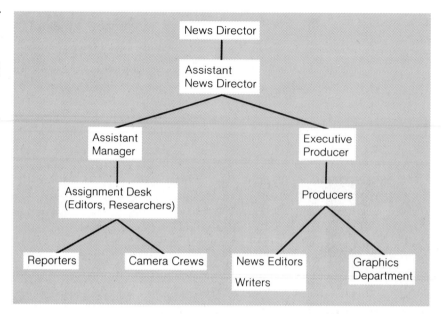

Journalists live in a world of confusion and complexity. Nevertheless, they manage through enterprise, wit, energy and intelligence to move close to the truth of the event and to shape their understanding into language and a form that can be understood by all. The task ahead of us in this book is to develop the reporter's craft and to assist the young journalist to find a personal credo to work by. A reporter who worked her way from small newspapers in New Mexico, Pennsylvania and New Jersey to the AP and then to *The New York Times* says her motto is: "Keep cool but care." This philosophy seems to describe the reporters we have been watching.

Further Reading

Behrens, John C. *The Typewriter Guerrillas*. Chicago: Nelson-Hall, 1977.

Hess, Stephen. *The Washington Reporter*. Washington D.C.: Brookings Institution, 1981.

Kaplan, Justin. *Lincoln Steffens: A Biography*. New York: Simon & Schuster, 1974.

Kendrick, Alexander. *Prime Time: The Life of Edward Murrow*. Boston: Little, Brown, 1969.

Steffens, Lincoln. *The Autobiography of Lincoln Steffens*. New York: Harcourt, Brace and Co., Inc., 1931.

Woodward, Bob, and Carl Bernstein. *All the President's Men*. New York: Simon & Schuster, 1974.

PART TWO

The Basics

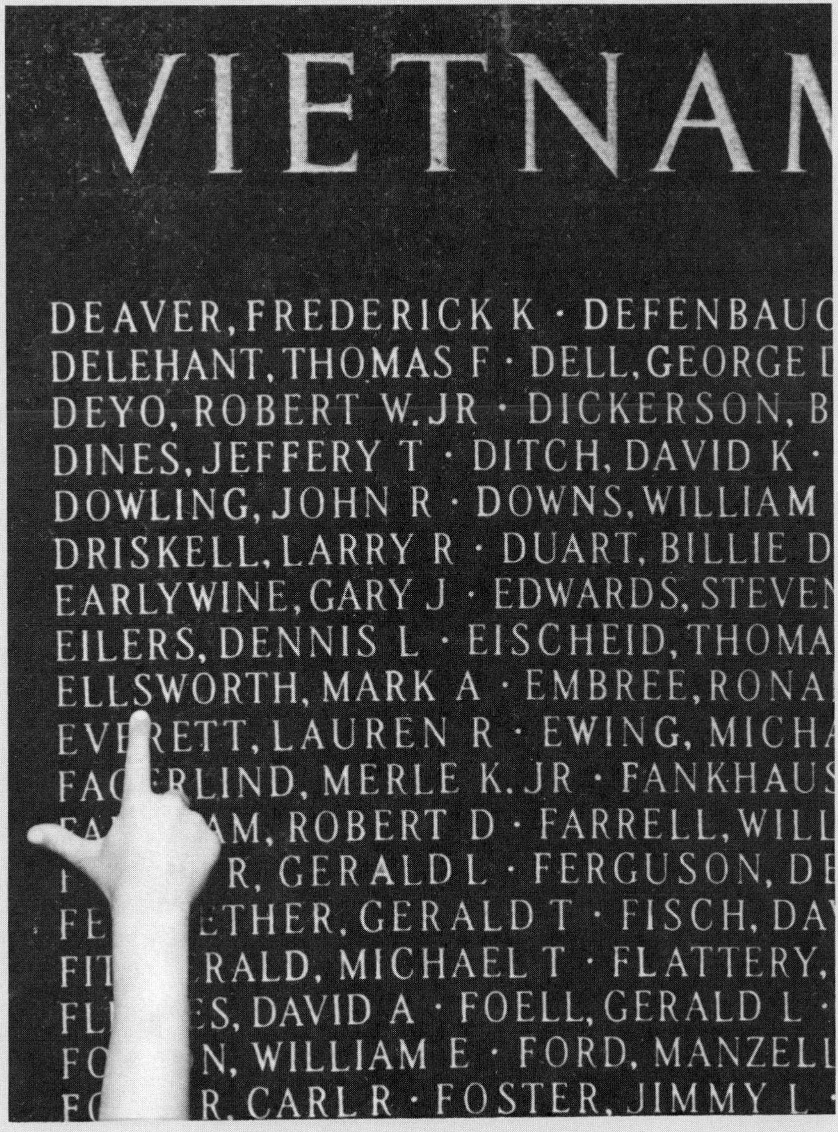

Photo by David Peterson, *The Des Moines Register*.

CHAPTER TWO

Basic Components of a News Story

Preview

News stories are:

- Accurate. All information is verified before it is used.
- Properly attributed. The reporter names the sources of information for the story.
- Balanced and fair. All sides in a controversy are given.
- Objective. The news writer does not inject his or her feelings or opinions.
- Brief. The news story gets to the point quickly.
- Well written. Stories are clear, direct, organized.

Direct observation is the surest way to obtain accurate information. When this is impossible, the story is a second-hand or third-hand account of the event. When important matters are raised in second- and third-hand accounts, the reporter tries to verify the material before using it by seeking out documents and records. When only human sources are available for verification, reporters check the person's reputation for reliability.

If we were to generalize from the work of the reporters we have been watching we might conclude that the reporter:

1. Attempts to report accurately the truth or reality of the event by
    A. Direct observation.
    B. Seeking out authoritative, knowledgeable and reliable human sources and relevant and reliable physical sources that can provide information about the event and its causes and consequences.
2. Tries to write an interesting, timely and clear story. The reporter uses quotations, anecdotes, examples and human interest to make the story vivid.

If journalism needs rules, these points should be the basis of their formulation.

Underlying and directing the application of these rules or guidelines is the reporter's imperative: The story must be accurate.

The highest praise A. J. Liebling, a master reporter for newspapers and *The New Yorker* magazine, could pay a colleague was, "He is a careful reporter," by which Liebling meant that the reporter took great care to be accurate. Although the reporter works under severe space and time limitations, he or she makes every effort to check the accuracy of information through verification and documentation.

Joseph Pulitzer, a towering figure in U.S. journalism, had a cardinal rule for his staff: "Accuracy, accuracy, accuracy." There may be arguments in newsrooms about writing style, about the best way to interview a reluctant source, but there is no debate about errors. A reporter may be tolerated if his writing does not sparkle, but he won't last the week if he makes mistakes in copy.

When the news editor of *The New York Times* spotted a line in a story that described the Canadian city of Sudbury as a "suburb of Toronto," he launched an inquiry. Sudbury is 250 miles north of Toronto. The reporter blamed the source, an FBI agent, but the editor found that no excuse. "It should have been second nature to check," he said. The newspaper ran a correction.

Here's another correction of a newspaper error:

CORRECTION

In last week's edition of the Michigan Chronicle, the story "Fauntroy stirs breakfast crowd," Congressman Walter Fauntroy's grandmother was misidentified. The matriarch was known to Fauntroy family members as "Big Ma," not "Big Mouth" as reported.

Faith Misplaced. When the horse player saw the results in the first edition of *The Washington Post* he resignedly tore up his tickets. Another $18 down the drain. He had played 9-7-6 in a trifecta bet and the newspaper said the winning combination was 9-5-8. Next day he happened to see a later edition, and in that edition the winning combination was given as 9-7-6, with a payoff of $767.40. The better called the sports department and asked for help; the reply was a laugh and "sorry." The moral: Accuracy, accuracy, accuracy. People act on what they read in their newspapers.

The reporter knows that although many people are willing, even anxious, to help, a story based on the reporter's first-hand observation is superior to one based on second-hand or third-hand information. Observation is the journalist's way of obtaining and verifying information.

As Bertrand Russell, the British philosopher, advised students:

Make the observation yourself. Aristotle could have avoided the mistake of thinking that women have fewer teeth than men by the simple device of asking Mrs. Aristotle to keep her mouth open while he counted. Thinking you know, when in fact you don't, is a fatal mistake to which we are all prone.

Despite the air of certainty in the tone of news stories, a close reading reveals that many are not based on the reporter's direct observation. The reporter rarely sees the burglar breaking in, the policy being drafted, the automobile hitting the telephone pole. The reporter obtains information about these events from authoritative sources such as documents and records (police files for the burglary and the accident) and from individuals (policy makers and participants at meetings).

News Filters. First-Hand Account. The story is based on direct observation of the event by the reporter.

News Filters. Second-Hand Account. The story is based on the account passed on by a participant eyewitness.

News Filters. Third-Hand Account. The story is based on information supplied by a source who was told by a participant.

On the Scene. Reporters and photographers are on hand as a medical technician breathes life into a child trapped in a fire. Photo by Don Fontaine, *The Morning Union,* Springfield, Mass.

When the reporter bases his or her story on direct observation, the story is a first-hand account. But when the reporter is not on the scene and information is obtained from those who were present, the reporter's story is a second-hand account. It has been filtered through the source who selects, emphasizes and condenses the original material.

Although the reporter seeks eyewitnesses and participants, some important stories are based on accounts that have been filtered twice before reaching the reporter. For example: An official agency holds a meeting at which the participants are sworn to secrecy. The reporter learns that one of those attending the meeting described it to a member of his staff, who happens to be a good source of news for the reporter. The reporter manages to obtain the staff member's account of the executive's account of what occurred.

News Filters

```
@^CLARO CORTES=
    MANILA, Philippines (UPI)--Thousands of
Filipinos walked through the grounds of the
presidential palace Wednesday for a look at the
compound closed to them during the 20 years Ferdinand
Marcos ruled.<
```

First-Hand Account. Claro Cortes personally watched the celebration.

WASHINGTON (UPI)--Two U.S. aircraft carrier battle groups left Italian ports Wednesday and steamed south toward the central Mediterranean for an expected third round of flight operations off Libya, U.S. officials said.<

FBI agents have established that the Watergate bugging incident stemmed from a massive campaign of political spying and sabotage conducted on behalf of President Nixon's re-election and directed by officials of the White House and the Committee for the Re-election of the President.

The activities, according to information in FBI and Department of Justice files, were aimed at all the major Democratic presidential contenders and— since 1971—represented a basic strategy of the Nixon re-election effort.

During their Watergate investigation federal agents established that hundreds of thousands of dollars in Nixon campaign contributions had been set aside to pay for an extensive undercover campaign aimed at discrediting individual and Democratic presidential candidates and disrupting their campaigns. . . .

—*The Washington Post*

Attribution

The further the reporter is from direct observation, the more concerned he or she is about the accuracy of the report. Accurate and comprehensive direct observation is difficult enough. After the information has been filtered once or twice, only the most foolhardy journalist would stake his reputation on the accuracy of the report. To make clear to the reader that second-hand and third-hand accounts are not based on the reporter's direct observation of the event, the reporter attributes the information about the event to a source.

Here are the first two paragraphs from a story in *The Detroit News:*

For six minutes, a Detroit police operator listened on the telephone as 24 bullets were fired into the bodies of an East Side couple.

But, according to the police, the civilian mistook the shots for "someone hammering or building something" and dispatched the call as a routine burglary.

The lead may give the reader the impression the reporter was at the operator's elbow. But the second paragraph attributes the information to the police.

Attribution actually refers to two concepts:

1. *Statements* are attributed to the person making them.
2. *Information* about the events not witnessed by the reporter is usually attributed to the source of the information.

---

1. Bernstein and Woodward, *All the President's Men.* New York: Simon & Schuster, 1974, pp. 142–44.

Here is a story that contains both types of attribution:

(1) Mayor Stanley Kretchmer said yesterday the city probably could balance its budget this year and next without laying off any workers.

(1) The decision, he said, "depends on a number of factors—the passage of a new tax package, the cooperation of municipal labor unions, general prosperity that keeps revenues high."

(2) At a meeting last week, the mayor told department heads they should consider the possibility of layoffs of about 10 percent of their work force, according to city officials who attended the meeting.

In the following, the first type of attribution is used. All statements are attributed to those making them.

Wayward Car Finds Home

Michael Sellars, 16, was sleeping on the living room floor of his South Side home at about 2:45 a.m. Wednesday when a car crashed through a picture window.

"This big light was in my eyes," he said after receiving a few stitches to close a cut on the back of his head caused by either the car's bumper or flying debris. . . .

Michael's father, Donald, 42, said the accident also woke up the rest of the family in their bedrooms—his wife, Barbara, 37, and his other son, Bobby, 12. . . .

"Bobby said the crash sounded like an atomic bomb," said Donald Sellars.

Michael said: "The driver got out of the car and asked if everybody was okay. . . ."

—*The Milwaukee Journal*

Attribution of Information

Just as no reporter from *The Detroit News* was with the police operator when the call came in, so no member of *The Milwaukee Journal* news staff was sleeping over at the Sellars' home the night the car dropped in. But the car's intrusion is stated as fact, without attribution. We now enter an imprecise area of journalism in which the reporter's guideposts are the policy of the publication or station and the reporter's feeling about the particular story.

Generally, we attribute what we do not observe or know to be factual. Although the reporter may take the information from a police record, the document does not necessarily attest to the truth of the information, only that some source—the police, a victim, the suspect, a witness—said that such-and-such occurred. The reporter will usually attribute the information to this source.

At the Sellars' home, the broken glass, the gap in the house the picture window once occupied, and the presence of the battered automobile would attest to the truth of the fact that an accident had occurred. So would the assertions of the family. To the *Journal* reporter these physical proofs made attribution unnecessary.

Some news organizations like the AP demand rigid adherence to the following policy: Always attribute what you do not see unless it is common knowledge.

Let us examine three stories to see how this policy is carried out. Under each story is the speculation of an experienced reporter about the reasons attribution was or was not used. (Her direct quotes are in parentheses.)

```
      Y165
YMCA
(1) NEW YORK AP--Dr. Jesse L. Steinfeld, former
Surgeon General of the U.S. Public Health Service,
has been appointed chairman of the National YMCA
Health and Physical Education Advisory Council.
(2) Steinfeld is presently professor of medicine at
the University of California at Irvine, Calif., and
chief of medical services for the Veterans Hospital
in Long Beach, Calif.
(3) The advisory council will play an important role
in the setting of future directions of the Y's
nationwide programs, national board chairman Stanley
Enlund said today in announcing Steinfeld's
appointment to the non-salaried post.


1113aED 03-26
```

YMCA:

(1) There is no need for attribution of the appointment because the action is obviously on the record.

(2) Steinfeld's background is taken from records and needs no attribution.

(3) The role of the council is an opinion offered by the chairman of the board and must be attributed to him.

```
      y167
HOTEL FIRE
(1) BRANFORD, Conn. AP--The Waverly Hotel, popular
earlier in the century, was destroyed by a two-alarm
fire today.
(2) The roof collapsed into the heart of the
building. At daylight the burned-out hotel was still
smouldering.
(3) Myrtle Braxton, 73, who lived alone in the
massive three-story building, was reported in fair
condition at Yale-New Haven Hospital suffering from
smoke inhalation.
(4) Officials said the fire was reported by Mrs.
Braxton at 3:41 a.m. They said it apparently started
in the kitchen area where Mrs. Braxton was living
```

after having closed off most of the rest of the
building. She was living there without central
heating or electricity, officials said.
(5) A neighbor said that a large number of antiques on
the third floor were destroyed. Also lost was a huge
ship's wheel from a sailing ship, a centerpiece in the
dining room.
(6) The bank that holds the mortgage said the land and
hotel were worth $40,000 to $50,000.

1124aED 03-26

Hotel Fire:
(1)(2) The condition of the hotel is a physical fact about which the reporter has no doubt.
(3) The attribution is implied here as coming from the hospital.
(4) "Officials," presumably fire department officials, are cited as the authority because only they could have known this. In the second sentence, the
cause is attributed. ("Always attribute the cause of a fire.")
(5)(6) Attribution gives the information credibility.

CBC
(1) The Citizen's Budget Commission, a private
taxpayer's organization, said today that the
proposed city budget of $185 million is more than the
city can afford.
(2) The budget was submitted two weeks ago. Mayor Sam
Puleo described it as an austerity budget.
(3) The Commission said it concluded after studying
the budget that ''significant cuts can be made.''
(4) The $185 million spending plan is up 12 percent
from the current year.
(5) When he submitted the budget, Mayor Puleo said
anticipated revenues would cover the increase. The
Commission is supported by the city's business
community.

CBC
(1) A charge, allegation, or opinion is always attributed, usually at the
beginning of the lead. Here, the Commission is immediately identified as the
source of the allegation.
(2) Background information that need not be attributed since it is part
of the record.
(3) Attribution to the source of the material.

(**4**) Background needing no attribution.

(**5**) Attribute the mayor's statement. ("The last sentence is the reporter's attempt to give the reader the why of the Commission's opposition—it's a taxpayer's group that likes austerity budgets because it means lower taxes. Nice touch.")

"You identify the source of the information in your story," the reporter commented after going through the three stories, "so that if it isn't true then the paper isn't blamed for the mistake, unless your reporting is bad and you misquoted someone, or didn't read the record carefully.

"If you don't identify the source the reader is going to assume that we stand behind the statements because we know they are true.

"My first editor would tell me to give him the source all the time, a person, an organization. If it's impossible to use the source's name, then he wanted it 'spokesman, an official, an official source,' or something similar, although he didn't like that as much as a name."

Identification also helps the reader or listener know something about the source because the name is accompanied by the person's title and occupation and may include age, education and any other personal information relevant to the story.

Look at the following story that came in over the wire:

```
SX22B
     LOMA LINDA, Calif., July 16--Leave the teen-age
drinking problem to the teenager and it will be
solved, says a specialist in classroom instruction on
alcohol.
     Mrs. Viola Eldon, Fresno, Calif., a specialist in
alcoholic instruction, yesterday told the ninth
annual Institute of Scientific Studies on the
Prevention of Alcoholism the teenager is fed up with
the ways adults ''beat about the bush.''
```

It would have helped the reader to know that the "specialist" was also the state director of scientific temperance instruction for the Women's Christian Temperance Union. It is important to include any of the source's affiliations that are relevant to the subject.

When prisoners rioted at the Attica Correctional Facility in upstate New York, many of the news accounts stated that the convicts had slashed the throats of some of the hostages. Some stories also reported as fact that one of the hostages had been castrated. No sources were given for the reports.

A medical examiner later disclosed that most of the deaths of the 11 hostages and 32 prisoners had been caused by rifle and shotgun fire from the 1,000 lawmen who stormed the penitentiary.

In their post-mortems the journalists agreed that they had been swept up by the hostility against the prisoners that developed during the four-day insurrection, and that when an official gave them the information about throat-slashings it seemed to confirm many rumors about convict violence. Some of the convicts had been seen holding knives to the throats of their hostages. Stating without attribution that there had been throat-slashings made the action appear as fact, giving it greater conviction than attributing it would have.

To sum up: Attribution is used to identify the source of the material the reporter has not gathered through direct observation. It is not necessary to attribute matters of accepted, general knowledge.

Warning

Attributing second-hand and third-hand accounts to their sources does not absolve reporters of responsibility for libelous statements in their stories. A reporter for a Florida newspaper reported that a county employee smoked marijuana, and the worker brought suit. "The reporter's own testimony indicated she had relied on second- and third-hand accounts when writing the story," *Editor & Publisher* reported. A jury awarded the employee $70,000. (See Chapter 25 for further discussion of libel.)

Types of Attribution

When the source of information for a story says nothing about being quoted, the reporter can presume that the information is on the record. Sometimes, a source asks to go off the record, and it is up to the reporter to decide whether to accept information on this basis. Once the reporter does so, he or she may not use the material.

Some reporters refuse to accept material with the condition that it may not be used in any form. They may bargain with the source, asking if they can go to another source to obtain confirmation. Or they may ask if the material can be used without using the source's name.

A source may ask to go on background, usually so that the source can provide the reporter with information that will clarify an event or situation. The source cannot be named but may be described as a "city hall official," a "state legislator," or by some other general term. To some sources, background means no direct quotes; others permit direct quotes. The reporter must be clear about the terms of the agreement with the source.

Caution: Many editors refuse to accept copy that contains charges or accusations with no named source. They will not accept attribution to "an official in city hall," "a company spokesman."

The reporter who accepts material with the promise of anonymity for the source or absolute off-the-record status for the information must realize that he is trading the public's need to know for his or her access to information. It is a calculated risk.

Four Types. President Ford's press secretary J. F. terHorst issued these guidelines to White House reporters:

On the Record: All statements are directly quotable and attributable, by name and title, to the person who is making the statement.

On Background: All statements are directly quotable, but they cannot be attributed by name or specific title to the person commenting. The type of attribution to be used should be spelled out in advance: "A White House official," "an Administration spokesman."

On Deep Background: Anything that is said in the interview is usable but not in direct quotation and not for attribution. The reporter writes it on his own.

Off the Record: Information given "off the record" is for the reporter's knowledge only and is not to be printed or made public in any way. The information also is not to be taken to another source in hopes of getting official confirmation.

Background and off-the-record information pose problems for the conscientious reporter because he or she knows that backgrounders can be used to float trial balloons. These stories are designed by the source to test public reaction without subjecting the source to responsibility for the statements. Reporters, eager to obtain news of importance and sometimes motivated by the desire for exclusives, may become the conduits for misleading or self-serving information.

When Vice President Spiro Agnew was facing prosecution for accepting bribes, *The New York Times* ran an exclusive, page one story about Agnew that began: "Vice President Agnew has made up his mind about the next phase of what he calls his 'nightmare.' " After this sympathetic picture of a suffering political leader, the story asserted that Agnew would not resign, would fight for exoneration in the courts and would press his request for a hearing by the House of Representatives. No source was given for the information.

The story made assertions that turned out to be dubious, even false. Attributed to Agnew—who obviously was the source—the comments would have been his responsibility. Stated as they were, the remarks appeared to have the ring of truth.

Agnew's purpose in granting the interview—many Washington reporters were convinced—was to warn the Justice Department and the president that unless he were treated with some leniency he would cause political problems. His lawyers had been dickering with the Justice Department over an arrangement that would enable Agnew to escape prosecution, trial and a possible jail sentence. His lawyer let it be known that Agnew did not want to involve the nation in "a lengthy, bloody, and convulsive battle." At the time, the president was in danger of impeachment and Agnew was in line for the presidency. Agnew had bargaining power, and he used it, reporters believed. The bargaining—behind closed doors and through the agency of the press— was successful. Within two weeks of the story in the *Times,* Agnew resigned and pleaded no contest to a charge of federal income tax evasion. He was not sent to prison.

One of the federal attorneys assigned to the case, James R. Thompson, later to become governor of Illinois, said after seeing the government's case against Agnew, "I've never seen a stronger case of bribery and extortion. If it had gone to trial, I'm sure he would have been sent to jail. He was simply a crook."

In all this, it was clear that the public was not well-served. When a reporter attributes assertions to a source, the reader can assess the accuracy and truth of the information on the basis of the general reliability of the source and his or her stake in the information. Stories without attribution seem to have greater reliability, for the reader usually believes the reporter stands behind the information. When "a White House official," "authoritative sources" and "high officials" are used in lieu of a named source, trust also is generated in the reader.

The lesson for reporters is clear: Avoid commitments not to use names of sources.

Verification

Attributing material to a source does not prove its truth. All a reporter does when attributing information is to place responsibility for it with the source named in the story. Attribution says only: It is true that the source said this.

The reporter who cares about truth is reluctant to settle for this half-step but often is prevented from moving on by deadline pressures and the difficulty in verifying material. If a reporter tried to check every piece of information, most stories would never be written. There are, of course, certain routine verifications a reporter must make:

- Names, addresses and telephone numbers are checked in the newspaper's library, the telephone directory and the city directory.
- Background information is taken from clips in the morgue.
- Dubious information is checked against records, with other sources.

This kind of verification is essential to the reporter's work. Yet error, inaccuracy and fanciful tales creep into the news daily. When Judy Garland died, her death was noted in a syndicated column by Leonard Lyons:

Her end was inevitable, from the day in Chicago's Oriental Theater when George Jessel was to introduce the child singer, Frances Gumm. His tongue resisted the clumsy sound, "Frances Gumm." He suddenly thought of the message he'd just sent to Judith Anderson, who was opening in a Broadway play:

"Dear Judy, may this new play add another garland to your Broadway career."

Jessel therefore blurted the name, "Judy Garland." Then he turned to the child singer waiting in the wings and told her: "Judy Garland . . . That's you, honey."

Even a columnist should tell truths. Had Lyons sought to check the anecdote he might have learned the truth, that Garland was the maiden name of Judy's mother. But that, to be sure, would have ruined his little tale. As it was, he proved the contention of the press critic who observed: "Newspapers never let the facts get in the way of a good story."

The bet was a good story on both coasts. When the Giants and the 49ers met in a National Football League playoff, Mayor Edward Koch of New York wagered a New York deli feast—pastrami, corned beef, dill pickles with corn bread—against Mayor Dianne Feinstein's cracked crab and California wine. The Giants and Koch lost. *The New York Times* reported the food was shipped by the Second Avenue Deli. *The Washington Post* said the Carnegie Deli supplied the sandwiches.

Big deal. Who cares what delicatessen shipped the corned beef and pastrami? Whoa, hold the mayo. We care, as journalists. It's trifles like this that make the reader shake his head knowingly—journalists just can't get the simplest things right.

Causes of Errors

The veteran reporter knows that errors cannot always be avoided. Here are some of the causes of errors:

• Sources can be mistaken. (See news story, "Cuba Has Jailed Mark Rudd . . .")
• Sometimes even the source does not know the whole truth.
• Authorities may have an interest in relating ambiguous, misleading, even erroneous information.
• Even the verifying information can be wrong. Newspaper files sometimes perpetuate an original error. Data and records can be tampered with.

Non-Verifiable Information

The reporter can verify the statement: "The mayor submitted a $1.5 million budget to the city council today." All the reporter needs to do is examine the minutes of the meeting or the budget if he did not attend the council meeting. But he cannot verify the truth of the statement: "The budget is too high (or low)." A city councilman might have indeed stated that he would oppose the budget because it was too large, whereas the head of the Municipal

Cuba Has Jailed Mark Rudd, a Lawyer Says

By SAM ROBERTS

Mark Rudd, the 28-year-old radical still sought for questioning about bombings here and elsewhere across the country, has been jailed by Cuba's regime, an international lawyer said yesterday.

The lawyer, Luis Kutner, said in a telephone interview that he had "no doubt" about the fate of Rudd, a former Columbia University student leader. Kutner said he had had discussions with friends of Rudd, who was said to have smuggled out of Cuba written appeals for help.

According to Kutner, these letters say that Rudd was mistakenly placed in a camp for the rehabilitation of homosexuals after he had been arrested while applying an ointment to cure chapped lips.

The lawyer, who has handled a variety of prominent clients in international law, said he was attempting to make contact with the Cuban authorities to verify Rudd's arrest record and conditions in the prison camp.

Police Here Want Him

Law enforcement officials here said Rudd, from New Jersey, was still being sought on a federal fugitive warrant and on a marijuana-possession charge filed in Buffalo.

The police here also want to question him in connection with a series of bombings — of public and corporate buildings — including Police Headquarters, in mid-1970 — for which the Weather Underground has claimed responsibility.

His former lawyer, Gerald Lefcourt, said yesterday that he last saw Rudd shortly before the issuance of a bench warrant for Rudd's arrest in 1970 for his failure to appear for a trial stemming from the 1968 Columbia riots.

Lefcourt said he had received no indication that Rudd — of others sought for questioning in connection with the Greenwich Village "bomb factory" explosion in 1970 and other blasts — had left the country.

Shortly before he was chosen president of the Columbia chapter of Students for a Democratic Society, Rudd used some saving to pay for a trip to Cuba in 1968. He was said to have returned more enthusiastic than ever about the Castro regime.

Investigators here said that they had no reason to discount the possibility that Rudd had later returned to Cuba, but that hey had no hard evidence to confirm this.

Kutner said he had been approached by people who told him that "Mark is protesting about being sodomized." He said these people were "pretty logical and not hysterical at all."

Mark Rudd
Still sought in bombings

Sources Make Mistakes. The sources for this story apparently took as truth an article about Rudd that had appeared in the *National Lampoon*, entitled "I Am A Prisoner in a Cuban Homo Farm: An Open, Uncensored Letter from Mark Rudd." The newspaper corrected its story the next day.

League might have declared her organization's distress at the "paltry budget that endangers health and welfare projects." We can determine whether the statements were made, but we cannot determine the truth of opinions and judgments.

Despite these obstacles, reporters are obligated to verify their stories whenever possible. Yet squadrons of journalists on scores of papers never bother to go beyond routine checks.

Verification is not the use of another opinion or a countercharge to balance the version of one source with that of another on controversial issues. Journalists should offer several views on controversial matters, and they should seek out the victims of charges. But that is balance, not verification.

When a minister charged that a magazine in use in a public school system in California was Communist-inspired, a *Fresno Bee* reporter balanced the charge with a reply from school officials. He also sought to verify the allegation by checking whether the publication had ever been listed as subversive. The reporter examined several publications that listed so-called subversive organizations and individuals. The magazine was not listed.

Here is how he began his story:

> Rev. August Brustat, a Lutheran minister, has charged the "Scholastic" magazine, which is used in some Fresno schools, with carrying the Communist line to students. But a librarian in Fresno County Free Library and a school official said they can find no evidence the magazine is subversive.

The Techniques of Verification

Sometimes, adequate verification is impossible even when data and records exist. When a reporter is out on a story and under the pressure of a deadline, verification is a difficult task. Political campaigns are especially troublesome because candidates sometimes make serious charges or issue statements to reporters who are on deadline and away from their files.

Verifying Political Charges

The 1964 presidential campaign led journalists to realize, again, that their reporting techniques were limited. They did make significant progress, however, in learning how to cope with serious allegations under deadline pressure.

Sen. Barry Goldwater, the Republican presidential candidate, frequently charged that the Democratic vice-presidential candidate, Hubert H. Humphrey, had an affinity for "socialism." The journalists covering the Goldwater campaign attempted to be careful about such volatile charges. But Goldwater levelled a barrage of charges, sometimes without giving reporters advance copies of his speeches, so that the press corps had time only to listen and dash to the telephone or typewriter. Even bland fare takes time to digest, and the Goldwater charges were hardly the usual fare. Despite their inflammatory nature, the allegations Goldwater was making were often passed on in unverified, unchecked form.

Recalling Goldwater's appearance in Austin, Tex., E. W. Kenworthy of *The New York Times,* one of the reporters on the tour, said he was worried as soon as he walked into the auditorium in Austin. "I knew there was going to be trouble covering the story," Kenworthy said. "He talked fast. The din was terrific. It was impossible—at least for me with no shorthand—to get complete sentences."

The speech was so loaded with allegations, Kenworthy said, that he decided he had to be certain of accurate quotes. Unlike the wire service reporters who had to file their stories as soon as possible, Kenworthy could wait. On the press plane, he checked his notes with other reporters, and when he found many of the quotes did not match, he decided to wait until he could obtain a transcript.

Kenworthy also took time to check the truth of Goldwater's references to Humphrey. He was more fortunate than other correspondents because he had been covering Humphrey's activities and knew Humphrey's positions on many issues.

Also, a fellow reporter on the plane out of Austin had the *Congressional Quarterly's* compendium of quotes by Lyndon Johnson and Humphrey on a wide variety of subjects and their votes. This source, and Kenworthy's own material that he toted in his briefcase, enabled him to refer to Humphrey's positions on the issues that Goldwater had raised.

In his story, Kenworthy reported Goldwater's assertions and followed them with contradictory information based on his own knowledge and on background material.

Four other reporters who were with Goldwater on that Texas swing were asked how they handled the flurry of charges. They confessed they had problems.

Jack Wilson, a Washington correspondent for *The Des Moines Register and Tribune,* said his early deadline meant he had to write about Goldwater's allegation that Humphrey favored admitting Communist China to the United Nations "without trying to get into the question of whether it was true or false."

On a previous story that Wilson had covered about a Goldwater attack on President Johnson, Wilson had precise information about the subject to which Goldwater was referring. Consequently, he said, he was able to write a paragraph in which he explained that Johnson had not said what Goldwater had charged he had said.

Wilson, along with the other reporters, said that it is the reporter's job to verify material.

"But reporters seldom work under ideal conditions, and they must rely on the desk to back them up," he said.

Wilson, in a letter to the author, recalled discussions among the reporters about their campaign coverage:

> Boiled down, it amounted to a fairly general feeling that we could not give an accurate picture of the campaign within the limits of what you might call straight news reporting. We could not, without "editorializing," tell the readers that Goldwater was not getting a strong reaction from the crowds, that he was in some cases boring them.
>
> We couldn't say that some of what he said didn't make sense, in terms of being bad logic expressed in sentences that didn't say anything.
>
> In one of the more blatant cases, when he blamed the fall of Khrushchev on our shipments of wheat, I was able to show indirectly that he was talking nonsense by simply quoting the entire passage verbatim out of the transcript. Even here I probably was taking liberties that would not be allowed a wire service, and even with this additional freedom I didn't feel I had the right to underline the nonsense by saying it was nonsense.
>
> And of course transcripts aren't always available, and the syntax was usually so involved that it would be idiocy to trust longhand notes.

A few newspapers recognized these difficulties and adopted specific policies to cope with them. A spokesman for *The* Louisville *Courier-Journal* described his paper's policy as follows:

> If the truth is readily available, we will put it right in the same story in brackets. If one man misquotes another and we know it is a misquote, we'll put the correct quotation in brackets. We try to correct as we go along, and if it is not readily available, we'll dig. That is sometimes a difficult process because the news breaks fast and many lies carry over before you can catch up with them.

A Vietnam War Story

In a war, the press is partially dependent on official communiqués since so much goes on beyond the reporter's range. When a reporter tries to verify what he is told by military press officers, independent checking can be made difficult.

Nevertheless, some reporters managed to describe the realities of Vietnam, and their versions sometimes differed sharply with those of the Pentagon and the White House.

In August 1973, the United States announced its planes had accidentally bombed the Cambodian village of Neak Luong. The U.S. Embassy told correspondents that the damage was minimal. Sydney H. Schanberg, a *New York Times* correspondent, decided to see for himself and sought air transportation to the village, 38 miles from Phnom Penh, where Schanberg was based. The Embassy intervened to keep him from flying there, but Schanberg managed to find a boat.

Schanberg stayed in Neak Luong a day and night, interviewing villagers and taking pictures. When local authorities learned he had been gathering material, they put him in confinement overnight. But he managed to send his story to his newspaper. Here is how Schanberg's story begins:

> The destruction in this town from the accidental bombing on Monday is extensive.
>
> Big chunks of the center of town have been demolished, including two-story concrete buildings reinforced with steel. Clusters of wood and thatch huts where soldiers lived with their families have been erased, so that the compounds where they once stood look like empty fields strewn with rubble.

Schanberg then quotes the air attaché at the Embassy as saying, "I saw one stick of bombs go through the town, but it was no great disaster." Schanberg goes on to point out that there were almost 400 casualties, and he takes the reader through the village:

> The atmosphere in Neak Luong, on the east bank of the Mekong River 38 miles southeast of Phnom Penh is silent and sad—bewildered at being bombed by an ally. Everyone has lost either relatives or friends; in some cases entire large families were wiped out.
>
> Yesterday afternoon a soldier could be seen sobbing uncontrollably on the riverbank. "All my family is dead! Take my picture, take my picture! Let the Americans see me!"
>
> His name is Keo Chan and his wife and 10 of his children were killed. All he has left is the youngest—an 8-month-old son. The 48-year-old soldier escaped death because he was on sentry duty a few miles away when the bombs fell.
>
> The bombs went down right in the middle of this town from north to south as it lay sleeping shortly after 4:30 a.m. Over 30 craters can be seen on a line nearly a mile long, and people reported others in jungle areas outside the town that this correspondent could not reach.

The story states that a third of the village hospital was demolished and then quotes the Air Force spokesman as saying there was a "little bit of damage to the northeast corner of the hospital" and some "structural cracks" in a wall. Schanberg is like a bulldog that refuses to let his quarry go.

Although the attaché had described a compound for Cambodian Marines that had been destroyed as consisting of "hootches," the *Times* reporter points out that the Cambodians lived with their families in these shacks.

A woman's scalp sways on a clump of tall grass. A bloody pillow here, a shred of a sarong caught on a barbed wire there. A large bloodstain on the brown earth. A pair of infant's rubber sandals among some unexploded military shells.

The colonel is quoted as saying about the reactions of the townspeople, "They were sad, but they understand that this is war and that in war these things happen."

"I do not understand why it happens," said Chea Salan, a 21-year-old soldier who lost relatives and army buddies. "Before, every time we saw the planes coming we were happy because we knew the planes came to help us. Now I have lost heart."

Schanberg's story demonstrates how journalistic guidelines can be used with consummate craftsmanship:

- *Verification*—Assertions are checked against the reporter's observations.
- *Dramatization*—Interviews with those involved personalize the event.
- *Truthfulness*—The detailed and specific observations give a reader the sense of the relationship of the report to truth.
- *Balance*—Both views, the military's and that of the victims, are presented.

Schanberg won a Pulitzer Prize and Sigma Delta Chi Award for his coverage of Cambodia.

The Lessons of Watergate

Had it not been for two young reporters, Carl Bernstein and Bob Woodward, and a few others among the hundreds in Washington, the White House comment that the Watergate break-in was a "third-rate burglary" might have ended the matter. The work of these reporters reminded their colleagues that journalism pivots on the sturdy legs and the skepticism of the reporters who seek verifying material by climbing the stairs, knocking on doors and digging through records.

"It is this personal and independent examination of the event, the verification that gives journalism its credibility over other institutions that make claims to truth telling," wrote two sociologists, Joseph Bensman and Robert Lilienfeld, in assessing journalism in their book, *Craft and Consciousness*.

Verification presumes an active, not a passive, role. The journalist seeks out the truth of the so-called facts. In 1984, 40,000 East Germans moved to West Germany, the biggest wave of legal emigration since the Berlin Wall was built in 1961. This appeared to alarm East German authorities, and they launched a propaganda offensive to discourage a new wave of applicants in 1985. The campaign began with a full-page newspaper advertisement saying 20,000 East Germans wanted to return from West Germany. The advertisement listed the names of 80 people and families and gave their reasons for wanting to go back to East Germany.

New York Times reporter James M. Markham reported all this in his dispatch from Bonn. Then he added: "A spot check of 20 of the family names listed by *Neues Deutschland* (the newspaper) found only two who said they wanted to return to East Germany." Two others said they had not come from East Germany and so "had no desire to move there."

Balance and Fairness

A young reporter, new to the courthouse beat, learned that one of the criminal court judges had placed a man with a long criminal record on probation. Despite the seriousness of his latest crime, an armed robbery, the defendant was not sentenced to prison. The reporter, conscious of the community's anger at the growing crime rate, dug into the story. He obtained the details of the defendant's criminal record from a source in the police department. He spoke to the district attorney who prosecuted the case.

The piece he handed in the following week was heavy on factual detail, and the reporter was proud of his work. However, he had one hole—a big one—which the city editor spotted immediately.

"Where's the judge in this?" he asked the reporter. "Didn't you ask him why he did it? Around here we give both sides, always."

The story made the judge appear incompetent or worse, whereas he may have had a valid reason for not sending the criminal to prison. He should have been asked why.

Although readers and listeners often tell pollsters they do not believe what they read in the newspapers and what they hear on radio and television, most people act on this information. Reporters try to give reliable and balanced accounts so people have adequate information for their actions.

A council member says that businesses will be driven from downtown into suburban shopping malls unless property taxes are lowered. If the reporter can find a spokesperson who justifies the present rate, he or she will do

State Senator Pushes Computers

SALESMAN'S FATHER
Sen. J. Ebb Duncan

'I have not been in state government long, but it seems most unusual to me that a state senator accompanies a marketing representative on a sales visit.'

—Bill Oliver

'It is not news to me that my son works for Univac. I made a statement that my son works for Univac before a joint meeting of the House and Senate Appropriations committees, the public, and the press.'

—Sen. J. Ebb Duncan

Fair Play. The statements in italics preceding this story in the *Atlanta Constitution* emphasized the senator's reply as well as the charge.

so in order to balance the council member's position. During political campaigns, editors try to balance—in some cases down to the second of air time or the inch of copy—candidate A and opponent B.

Balance is important. But some journalists contend that balance does not mean they must station themselves precisely at the midpoint of an issue. If candidate A makes an important speech today, the speech may be worth page one play. If, on the same day, opponent B repeats what he said yesterday or utters nonsense, the newspaper or station is under no obligation to balance something with nothing. A journalism of absolute balance can add up to zero. Balance is a moral commitment and cannot be measured by the stopwatch or the ruler.

The same common sense should be applied to matters that require fair play. Should candidate A make a serious accusation against opponent B, fairness requires that a reporter seek out B for a reply. The targets of charges and accusations should always be given their say, and the reply should be placed as closely to the allegation as possible.

When charges are made for which no documentation is offered, the reporter is required to say so, as high in the story as possible. In a wire service story from South Africa, a Johannesburg newspaper was quoted as saying that the South African government had donated $3.9 million to the presidential campaign of Gerald Ford. The story carried Ford's denial. But it also stated, in the second paragraph, that the charges had been made "without supporting evidence." Those were the reporter's words.

At the end of his 1984 presidential campaign, Ronald Reagan said there had been a federal deficit in every year since World War II. After quoting Reagan, Lou Cannon, White House reporter for *The Washington Post,* added: "According to budget documents Mr. Reagan sent to Congress earlier this year, there have been eight budget surpluses during this period, five of them during Democratic administrations."

A reader complained to the *Post,* "Why is Cannon debating with the president? Why doesn't he just report what the president says?" Sam Zagoria, the newspaper's ombudsman, replied that the *Post's* standard of fairness says, "No story is fair if it consciously or unconsciously misleads or even deceives the reader. So fairness includes honesty—leveling with the reader." Zagoria said Cannon was right, that "the added facts were necessary for completeness."

When Emotions Get in the Way

Lack of balance and the absence of fairness are often inadvertent. Since writing is as much an act of the unconscious as it is the conscious use of controlled and disciplined intelligence, the feelings of reporters crop up now and then.

In describing an official the reporter dislikes, a reporter might find himself writing, "C. Harrison Gold, an ambitious young politician, said today. . . ."

Or, writing about an official the reporter admires, that reporter might write, "Gerald Silver, the dynamic young state controller, said today. . . ."

It is all right for a young man or woman to be "ambitious," but when the word is used to describe a politician, it can have a negative connotation. On the other hand, the "dynamic" politician conjures up an image of a young man hard at work serving the public. Maybe the reporter is accurate in these perceptions. Maybe not. The reporter's job is to let the reader draw conclusions by writing what the politician says and does.

Here is part of a press association story in which the reporter's feelings about East Germany emerge in the choice of adjectives and adverbs:

```
LEAD EAST GERMANY
     BERLIN, Oct. 7--East Germans dutifully trooped
to the polls today to cast ballots in a no-contest
election. . . .
     The Communists used well-oiled propaganda
techniques to create an atmosphere of excitement and
significance for the voting.
     Bands of heavily-indoctrinated youngsters
paraded through the city streets at 6 a.m. blowing
horns to wake their elders to go to the polls. The
streets were strung with red banners proclaiming
``trust in our candidates'' and ``our voice for the
nation of peace.''
     Goateed Walter Ulbricht and his wife Lotte were
handed bouquets of carnations and red roses as they
ceremoniously cast their votes at a polling station
in a walled and guarded section of East Berlin.

HZ 568 PED
```

This approach to foreign news is sometimes referred to as "nationalism in the news." Professor Lawrence D. Pinkham of the University of Massachusetts describes it as "patriotic prose."

One of the best preventives for imbalance and lack of fairness is the advice a senior copy editor gave a young reporter. Peering up from his desk where he was vigorously slashing the young man's work, he said, "Eschew adjectives."

Danger exists any time a reporter departs from the recital of observed fact. Similes and metaphors can cause trouble because their use sometimes leads the reporter to inject his or her feelings into a piece. One reporter wrote, "Looking as though he would be more comfortable in a scarlet bowling shirt than in the delicately plaid business suit he wore, State Assemblyman Louis Montano faced tenants from the end of a long table." The imagery ran away from the reporter's good sense and decency. The sentence implies that the legislator was more suited to bowling than lawmaking. Montano, like others written about by the press in disparaging ways, has little rejoinder. He could write a letter to the editor. But the damage has been done.

Balance and Fairness for Broadcasting

The print journalist is morally bound to balance and fairness, but the First Amendment gives him the freedom to be as irresponsible as he wishes. Not so the broadcast journalist who is bound by legal requirements set by the Federal Communications Commission (FCC). The fairness doctrine requires broadcasters to meet standards of "fairness" and "balance" in their programming. The reasoning behind this requirement is that there are a limited number of stations on the public airwaves—unlike the unlimited possibilities for newspapers and magazines. Stations are required to present competing views and ideas about issues that affect the public.

The FCC also requires broadcasters to give a "right of reply" to the subjects of personal attack on radio and television.

Unless the broadcaster gives both sides of an issue and grants a person the right to reply within seven days of the attack, the station is subject to a fine. Persistent or serious violations can be cause for the revocation of the station's license.

The constitutionality of these requirements has been attacked by some broadcasters who contend that the regulations are inconsistent with the First Amendment, but the Supreme Court has held them to be constitutional.

Objectivity

Unfair and unbalanced journalism might be described as failures in objectivity. When journalists talk about objectivity, they mean that the news story is free of the reporter's opinion or feelings, that it contains facts and that the account is by an impartial and independent observer. Stories are objective when they can be checked against some kind of record—the text of a speech, the minutes of a meeting, a police report, a purchase voucher, a payroll, unemployment data, or vital statistics. An objective report contains material that everyone would agree is based on fact. Stories are objective when material in them is borne out by evidence. The reporting of facts that can be verified is the mainstay of journalism in the United States.

If the reader wants to weep or laugh, write an angry letter to a congressman or send money to the Red Cross for tornado victims, that is his or her business. The reporter is content to lay out the facts. Objective journalism is the reporting of the visible, what people say and do.

In the 1950s, social and political problems that had been proliferating since the end of World War II began to cause cleavages in society, and reporters found their methodology—objective reporting—inadequate in finding causes and fixing responsibility.

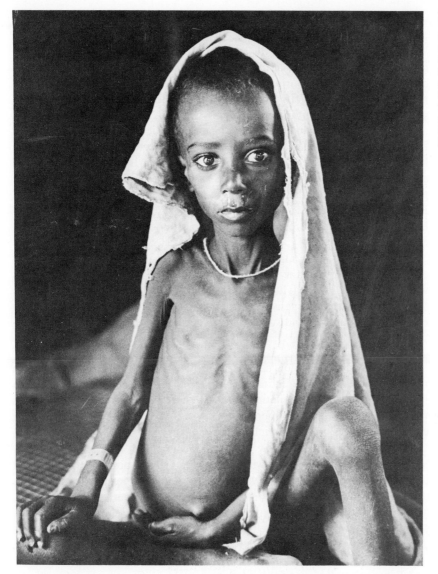

Journalists were concerned about the attention they had given Joseph McCarthy, the Wisconsin senator whose charges of Communist conspiracies had been given front-page play over the country. Their tortured self-analysis led them to assume collective responsibility for the senator's power. They realized it was not enough to report what McCarthy had said—which was objective reporting. McCarthy had indeed made the charges. But many were found to be false.

Journalists asked themselves whether they had a responsibility to go beyond mere transcription of what people say and do. They found they were waiting for events to develop, the authority to speak out. They did not venture into areas that are not discernible or not measurable. They did not seek the depths of the iceberg, but settled for the observable tip. That kind of journalism, with little predictive capacity, is unable to fulfill journalism's role of supplying the public with information on which to base decisions.

Journalists reported the announcement of policies and programs, but infrequently examined the consequences for those affected. The monitoring was left to the bureaucracy, taxpayer organizations, other special interest groups and a few journalists. Journalism failed to alert the public to the problems of poverty, racism, inequality and the domestic consequences of the Cold War. It seemed to be committed to institutions rather than to people and to have a built-in bias toward established authority, presumed to be rational, disinterested and responsive.

Elmer Davis, a courageous radio journalist, pointed to the limitations of objective journalism in the 1950s. He described the frustrations of reporters who knew officials were lying, but were unable to say so in their stories.

Davis advised journalists that they had to walk a tightrope between irresponsible objectivity and subjectivity. He said bare facts were not enough.

Adjustments

Another broadcast journalist, Edward R. Murrow, who had moved from radio to television, pioneered in-depth reporting. He sought to make television journalism more than a bulletin board with news for the middle class. In his work in the 1950s, Murrow demonstrated passion and conviction along with curiosity and journalistic discipline.

Davis, Murrow and a few print journalists gave a broader scope to objective reporting. Journalists—with their unique non-partisan perspective, and their commitment to democratic values, accurate observation and truth—began to see how they could provide insights for the public and for policy makers. To do so more effectively, they knew they had to change some of their traditional practices. Underlying their conviction that change was needed was their assumption that journalists are publicly useful men and women.

The Commission on Freedom of the Press in the late 1940s (see *A Free and Responsible Press. A General Report on Mass Communications: Newspapers, Radio, Motion Pictures, Magazines, and Books,* pp. 21–22) had told journalists that they are most useful when they give "a truthful, comprehensive, and intelligent account of the day's events in a context which gives them meaning. . . . It is no longer enough to report *fact* truthfully. It is now necessary to report the *truth about the fact*."

Journalists began finding ways to work themselves away from the constrictions that the Commission had said impeded truth-telling. One of their responses was to look behind the breaking news story for causes, to find those with the authority to speak about possible consequences.

Viewing the urban crisis as having its roots in the problems of race and class, journalists began digging into official releases and statements by authorities. Learning about the previously invisible worlds of blacks, the Spanish-speaking, youth and women, journalists made analyses of their own, putting their intelligence as well as their craft to work.

Journalists sought to give an added dimension to their stenographic function by examining the background of assertions and the cause of actions, and by looking for the "truth of the fact." This kind of journalism, demonstrated in the coverage of Watergate and in Schanberg's reporting from Vietnam, moves the reader, listener and viewer closer to the truth, which is something more than the mere accumulation of observable data. These are the stars that provide guidelines as we navigate toward the destination of truth. But they can never fully illuminate our passage. They require context, meaning. The journalist took on this task, which developed at the same time that colleges began to train large numbers of journalists. The new objectivity required knowledgeable practitioners.

Brevity

In our generalization about the reporter's job at the outset of this chapter, we pointed out that the news story is succinct. The tersely told story is admired by editors and by busy readers and listeners. Here is a two-paragraph story that says a great deal although it contains only four sentences:

JOHANNESBURG, South Africa, Nov. 8—The bodies of 60 victims of an accidental dynamite explosion a mile and a half down a gold mine 100 miles southwest of Johannesburg were brought to the surface today.

Of the dead, 58 were Basuto tribesmen from Lesotho, chosen for the dangerous job of shaft-sinking, or blasting a way down to the gold-bearing reef. The two others were white supervisors. The black Africans will be buried in a communal grave tomorrow.

—*The New York Times*

All creative activities are based on the art of omission. In architecture, the twentieth century has been marked by structures that follow the dictum: Less is more. Economy of expression is the hallmark of the artist.

When Beethoven was struggling with the music to his opera, "Fidelio," he realized that the leisurely pace of the music did not meet the demands of the theater, and for years he pared down his work. David Hamilton, the music critic, describes Beethoven's effort as a "ruthless piece of self criticism . . . Beethoven expunged balancing phrases, trimmed decorative expansions, excised anything that did not move forward, eventually achieving the terse urgency that now marks the opera's crucial scenes."

In eliminating large sections of his music, Beethoven rejected three overtures he had written. One, "Leonore No. 3," became one of the most popular pieces in the orchestral repertory. Despite its obvious beauty and power, Beethoven found it unsuited to his opera.

Joseph G. Herzberg, an editor on several New York City newspapers said: "Newspapering is knowing what to leave out and condensing the rest."

Too often, beat reporters and specialists write more than is necessary because they forget they are writing for general readers, not for their sources. The reporter covering new transplant technology for a newspaper cannot go into the kind of detail that a reporter for the *Journal of the American Medical Association* must in his story.

But stories can be too brief. A copy editor can always remove excess material. He cannot add essential detail and background that an overly brief report ignores.

Selectivity

The way out of the dilemma of being brief but not writing telegrams is through Herzberg's advice, which can be summed up in one word—selectivity. Brevity is a function of selectivity—knowing what to leave out. The ability to select essential facts from the welter of material that the reporter gathers comes with experience.

Selectivity also involves the use of language that makes the point succinctly. Edna Buchanan, the police reporter for *The Miami Herald,* began her account of a record-breaking week of violence in Dade County this way:

Dade's murder rate hit new heights this week as a wave of violence left 14 people dead and five critically hurt within five days.

A couple of paragraphs compared these figures with murder figures of previous years, and then Buchanan summarized most of the deaths:

In the latest wave of violence, a teen-ager's throat was cut and her body dumped into a canal. A former airline stewardess was garroted and left with a pair of scissors stuck between her shoulder blades. Four innocent bystanders were shot in a barroom gun battle. An 80-year-old man surprised a burglar who battered him fatally with a hammer. An angry young woman who "felt used" beat her date to death with the dumbbells he used to keep fit. And an apparent robbery victim was shot dead as he ran away from the robbers.

A natural tension exists between the editor and the reporter over the issue of brevity. The desk, confronted with ever-decreasing space and time, wants shorter stories. The reporter, excited by the event and driven by a compulsion to tell the full story, wants more time and more space.

Buchanan advised young *Herald* reporters, "For sanity and survival, there are three cardinal rules in the newsroom: Never trust an editor, never trust an editor, never trust an editor."

Some editors contend that if Genesis can describe the creation of the world in a thousand words then no reporter needs any more than four pages of copy for any event of human dimension. But some events are so complex that only an extended account will do. Important stories often require scene-setting and background that consume time and space. The guide for the length of stories is: Make it brief but complete.

Clarity

The executives of 40 daily newspapers in Iowa and journalism instructors at the state's three journalism schools were asked to rank certain characteristics considered most important for beginning reporters. Both groups put the ability to write clearly and interestingly first.

Clear prose follows comprehension. That is, the reporter must be able to understand the event before he or she can explain it clearly and succinctly. Clarity follows analysis. No reporter can successfully handle a story without putting his or her intelligence to work first, and then applying the art and skill of writing. You cannot clarify what you do not understand.

Clarity is enhanced by simplicity of expression, which generally means short sentences, short words, coherence and logical story structure. We shall be looking at these in detail in Chapter 7.

Human Interest

To make certain his story is read, the journalist must recount events in ways that substitute for the drama of the personal encounter. That is, the reporter must bring these events to life in the telling. One of the ways the journalist does this is to tell the story in human terms. Reporters personalize and dramatize the news by seeking out the persons involved in the event. Human interest is an essential ingredient of news.

A change in city zoning regulations is dramatized by pointing out that now low-income families can move into an area that had been effectively sealed off to them by the previous two-acre zoning rule. A factory shutdown is personalized by talking to workers who must line up at the unemployment office instead of at a workbench.

Here is how a story about the state's approval of a new bus line began:

The working people who serve Astoria's suburban homes no longer have to wait on street corners for a ride in a friend's car.

The state public service commission yesterday granted the Johnston Bus Co. permission to make round trips from the city to six stops in the suburbs.

Johnston had petitioned for permission, citing the difficulty domestic workers and others had in commuting to their jobs. The company presented petitions bearing 185 signatures to the state commission.

In a story about chemicals polluting the Hudson River and ruining the fishing industry, Barry Newman of *The Wall Street Journal* begins:

GRASSY POINT, N.Y.—In the gray-shingled shack at water's edge, four fishermen sit playing cards around an old kitchen table, ignoring the ebb tide laden with the spring run of shad. The wall is hung with foul-weather gear; rubber boots are piled in the corner. On the refrigerator door somebody has taped up a newspaper clipping about the awful chemical in the fish of the Hudson River.

"I do my fishing from the window here," an old man says, looking off to the quiet hills on the east bank, three miles across the river from this small valley town.

"No nets for me this year," another man says. "No pay," says the third. And the fourth: "A lot of trouble, this."

Responsibility

Ted Williams was one of baseball's greatest players. The Boston Red Sox outfielder won six batting titles over a span of 17 years and was one of the few to win the Triple Crown twice, leading the league in 1942 and in 1947 in batting, runs batted in and home runs. To many baseball fans, he was heroic. To some sports writers, he was, as Roger Kahn put it, "a pill."

It was possible for readers to know the real Williams because, Kahn says, when nine writers covered Red Sox games "it was impossible to conceal" the truth about Williams. "If one writer courted The Thumper by refusing to report a tantrum as news, another inevitably seized the tantrum as news. Regardless of each reporter's skill, an essential, imperfect system of checks and balances worked. If you cared enough about Williams, and I did, you could find a portrait that was honest by consensus."

But many of the Boston newspapers that covered Williams are gone, as are others in many cities. There are fewer than 50 cities with competing daily newspapers. This means that the responsibility for truth-telling falls on fewer shoulders. It falls, in most U.S. cities, in fact, on a single reporter, for most local news events are covered by only one journalist.

Responsibility is not a visible part of a news story. It is an attitude that the reporter carries to the job. It encompasses all the components we have discussed in this chapter.

Responsibility is the reporter's commitment to the story, to journalism and to the public. Responsibility demands of the reporter that the story be accurate, fair and balanced, that it be so clear anyone can understand it.

Nothing in the law requires a reporter to be responsible. In fact, journalists sometimes flinch at the word. The reason for their discomfort is that some people and some organizations use the word as a club with which to beat journalists when the newspaper or station presents material they dislike.

Journalists testily reply that they can be as irresponsible as they like. That's understandable, and it is true. But beneath the surface, every reporter, every editor understands that journalism is a moral enterprise, that theirs is a calling practiced with honesty and diligence within the limits of truth and time.

Writing

Finally, a word about the writing. A news story may be accurate, properly attributed, balanced and fair, objective and brief. The reporter may be compassionate and understanding, may have carried out his or her tasks with responsibility. The story may have something interesting and exciting to say. But unless it is written with some skill, the reader or listener will not bother.

Good writing—direct and clear, simple and straightforward—is an important component of the story. Good writing avoids clichés and redundancies. It does not strain for effect. It does not call attention to itself but to the story it tells.

Further Reading

Bensman, Joseph, and Robert Lilienfield. *Craft and Consciousness*. New York: John Wiley and Sons, 1973.

Commission on Freedom of the Press. *A Free and Responsible Press*. Chicago: University of Chicago Press, 1947.

Liebling, A. J. *The Press*. New York: Ballantine Books, 1961.

Schiller, Dan. *Objectivity and the News: The Public and the Rise of Commercial Journalism*. Philadelphia: University of Pennsylvania Press, 1981.

Siebert, Fred S., et. al. *Four Theories of the Press*. Urbana, Ill.: University of Illinois Press, 1956.

PART THREE

Writing the Story

Photo by John Shearer.

CHAPTER THREE

What Is News?

Preview

Reporters have established a set of news values to help them determine the newsworthiness of events. The values are:

- Impact or importance of the event.
- Timeliness of the event.
- Prominence of the people involved in the event.
- Proximity, the closeness of the event to readers and listeners.
- Conflict.
- The unusual, bizarre nature of the event.
- Currency, the interest people have in the situation.

Most stories combine two or more of these news values. At least three-fourths of all stories fall into the general categories of consequence (impact, importance, significance) and interest (unusual, strange, bizarre).

News is relative. What is used and how it is used are affected by a variety of factors such as the amount of advertising on a given day, the volume of important news, advertising pressures, the nature of the audiences the newspaper, magazine or station is trying to reach and the nature of the medium.

W e have discussed several essentials of journalism—accuracy, attribution, verification, balance and fairness, objectivity, brevity, clarity, human interest, and responsibility. These elements are the reporter's guides to reporting and writing the story. But what leads the reporter to the events worth reporting? Among the cascade of events the reporter encounters in a work day, which should be singled out for attention?

How does the courthouse reporter leafing through a dozen civil complaints decide which is the newsworthy document? How does the police reporter determine which of the score of arrests is noteworthy? After determining that an event or idea is worth reporting, how does the reporter decide whether to write two paragraphs or seven? How does the broadcast journalist know a story is worth 60 seconds at the start of the 6 p.m. newscast or 10 seconds toward the end? If journalism can be described as the art of selection, then what guidelines does the journalist use in practicing selectivity?

If we go back to the beginning of formal news communication we learn that what we read, see and hear today is not much different from the material in the daily bulletins posted in the Roman Forum and what was later printed in gazettes and newsbooks.

Realizing that Roman citizens needed to know about official decisions that affected them, Julius Caesar posted reports of government activities in the *Acta Diurna*. In China, the T'ang dynasty (618–906 A.D.) published a gazette—handwritten or printed by wood block—to inform court officials of its activities. The more immediate predecessor of the newspaper was the handwritten newsletter, containing political and economic information, that circulated among merchants in early sixteenth century Europe.

The first printed newsbook, published in 1513 and titled *The trewe encounter,* was an account of the Battle of Flodden Field. The Anglo-Scottish wars of the 1540s provided printers with material for more newsbooks.

During the seventeenth century, news sheets spread to the business centers of Europe, reporting news of commerce. In this country, as historian Bernard Weisberger has pointed out, the newspaper "served as a handmaiden of commerce by emphasizing news of trade and business."

To this day, much of our news is about the actions of government and business, and our journalism continues to stress the drama of war and other calamities.

A major difference between these old information carriers and modern journalism is that the news media—newspapers, magazines, television, and radio stations—aim at such a diverse audience that many different kinds of news are in a single issue or newscast. Editors look for a balanced news report to appeal to a wide audience, for economic survival depends upon holding the mass audience.

Day and Bennett

The newspaper editors of the nineteenth century understood the need to appeal to a large audience to stay in business, and their acumen led to definitions of news that hold to this day. The papers in the large cities were printing news for the newly literate reader of the working class. One of the first penny papers—inexpensive enough for working people—contained the ingredients of popular journalism. In 1833, the first issue of Benjamin H. Day's *New York Sun* included a summary of police court cases and stories about fires, burglaries and a suicide. Other stories contained humor and human interest.

Several years later, James Gordon Bennett—described by historians as the father of American yellow journalism and the originator of the art, science and industry of newsgathering—used the recently developed telegraph to give the readers of his *Herald* commercial and political news to go along with his reports of the everday life of New York City, its sins and scandals. His formula of news for "the merchant and man of learning, as well as the mechanic and man of labor" guides many editors today.

Know the Audience. When Barney Kilgore took over *The Wall Street Journal* it had a circulation of 32,000. Twenty-five years later, the circulation exceeded a million. "Don't write banking stories for bankers," he instructed his staff. "Write for the bank's customers. There are a hell of a lot more depositors than bankers."

Pulitzer

Day and Bennett followed the tastes and appetites of their readers, but they also directed and taught their readers by publishing stories they deemed important. This blend of entertainment, information and public service was stressed by Joseph Pulitzer, who owned newspapers in St. Louis and New York. He, too, gave his readers what he thought they wanted—sensational news and features. But Pulitzer was not content with entertainment. He also used his news staff for his campaigns to curb business monopolies and to seek heavy taxes on income and inheritance. In 1883, Pulitzer charged the staff of his New York *World* with this command:

> Always fight for progress and reform, never tolerate injustice or corruption, always fight demagogues of all parties, never belong to any party, always oppose privileged classes and public plunderers, never lack sympathy with the poor, always remain devoted to the public welfare, never be satisfied with merely printing news, always be drastically independent, never be afraid to attack wrong, whether by predatory plutocracy or predatory poverty.

Pulitzer and his editors understood that newsmakers seek to shape the news into forms suitable to them. Pulitzer cautioned his staff to go beyond the handout and the interview, to dig under the surface for the news. Otherwise, he said, the public is ill-served.

Today's Editors

Modern editors overseeing newsrooms humming with the latest electronic wonders use many of these nineteenth century concepts of news. If asked, they would also agree with the definition of news offered by Charles A. Dana, who ran the *New York Sun* from 1869 to 1897. Dana said news is "anything that interests a large part of the community and has never been brought to its attention before."

One of Dana's editors contributed the classic comment, "If a dog bites a man, it's not news. If a man bites a dog, it's news."

Another enduring definition of news was offered by Stanley Walker, a Texan gone East to success as city editor of *The New York Herald Tribune* in the early 1930s. He said news was based on the three W's, "women, wampum, and wrongdoing." By this he meant that news was concerned with sex, money and crime—the topics people secretly desired to hear about.

For the mass media today, Walker's definition holds true, although their stories about women and sex are likely to be concerned with patterns of divorce, sexual liberation and feminism; stories about money will include analyses of the local economy and of the community's tax structure; and crime stories will include opinions on the age at which a juvenile should be treated as an adult offender.

In the mid-1970s the United States had been through three crises: A war in Vietnam that wound down with guilt and defeat for many Americans; the Watergate scandals; and the realization that some political, social, and economic experiments of the 1950s and 1960s that had been hailed as solutions to international conflict, racial tension and unemployment had failed.

It was not surprising, then, to see a shift in the criteria used to determine the news. Av Westin, the executive producer of the American Broadcasting Company's "Evening News" program, said Americans wanted their news to answer the following questions: Is the world safe? Are my home and family safe? If they are safe, then what has happened in the last 24 hours to make them better off? Is my pocketbook safe?

Another trend developed in the late 1970s and carried into the following decade. A UPI survey of its daily newspaper subscribers found that editors not only wanted more pocketbook stories but escape as well. Reflecting the interests of their readers, the editors asked for more entertainment in the form of copy about lifestyles, leisure subjects and personalities.

In the 1980s the pocketbook of the middle class became a major news topic: interest rates, taxes, investments, the budget deficit. In Ronald Reagan's second term, the intensification of international dangers led to more coverage of arms talks, terrorism, nationalism. Editors were trying to answer the question: Is the world safe?

The importance of these criteria used by editors and producers should not be underestimated. Westin's news judgment directly affected what 11 million persons knew about the day's events. The majority of the "Evening News" viewers would not read, or would only glance at, a newspaper the next day. Their knowledge of what was happening was confined to the 15 or 20 stories that Westin was able to cram into the 22 minutes of news allotted for the half-hour program.

Reporters follow the guidelines of their editors and publishers. Reporters also form agreements among themselves on what constitutes news. Thus, at any given time, news in the mass media is similar. The differences occur in the writing and the presentation. Except for the news of local events, the 11 p.m. television newscast in Kansas City and the morning newspaper in Houston will not be appreciably different in their selection and emphasis of national and international news.

Summing up these definitions of news, two general guidelines emerge:

• News is information about a break from the normal flow of events, an interruption in the expected.

• News is information people need in order to make sound decisions about their lives.

How does a reporter or editor determine what events are so unusual and what information is so necessary that the public should be informed of them?

Timeliness. An early-morning fire in a hotel in Paterson, N.J., brought residents to windows, screaming for help. Thirteen died in the blaze. The three in this photo by Rich Gigli of *The Record* were rescued.

News Values

The following seven factors determine the newsworthiness of events and ideas:

Impact: Events that are likely to affect many people. Here, journalists talk about significance, importance, the kinds of information that interest people or that journalists decide the people need to know to be informed. A postal workers' strike will be covered in detail because everyone is affected by the delivery of mail. A campaign for Congress will receive attention in the candidate's district, since journalists consider it essential that voters know the candidates' positions before voting.

Some news that has considerable impact in one community may be unimportant in another. To residents in Milwaukee, a November cold snap has little impact because cold weather in that month is hardly an interruption in the expected. But when 40-degree weather was forecast for St. Petersburg, Fla., many of whose residents had fled northern winters, it was front page news under a large headline.

Timeliness: Events that are immediate, recent. The daily newspaper and the hourly newscast seek to keep readers and listeners abreast of events, to give them a sense of immediacy. Thus, broadcast news is written in the present tense, and most leads on newspaper stories contain the word *today*. No matter how significant the event, how important the people involved, news value diminishes with time. André Gide, the French novelist, defined journalism as "everything that will be less interesting tomorrow than today."

Rocky Mountain News

DENVER, COLORADO
© Tuesday, January 28, 1986

EXTRA

25¢

SHUTTLE EXPLODES

All 7 in Challenger crew die after liftoff

ASSOCIATED PRESS

The fireball that signaled disaster for shuttle mission 51-L occurred only 1 minute, 15 seconds after liftoff from Kennedy Space Center. NASA officials said there were no apparent problems at the time.

Impact. This extra sold 67,000 copies, and a reprint the next day sold 125,000 copies. On television, stations showed the explosion of Challenger over and over to millions of viewers.

The communication media are commercial enterprises that sell space and time on the basis of their ability to reach people quickly with a highly perishable commodity. The marketplace rewards a fast news carrier. Although newspapers place less emphasis on speed than do the electronic media, a newspaper that offers its readers too much rehashed news will not survive. Radio, which was being prepared for its funeral when television captured a large segment of the listening audience, staged a comeback with the all-day, all-news stations.

Timeliness is important in a democracy. People need to know about the activities of their officials as soon as possible so they can assess the directions in which their leaders are moving. Told where they are being led, citizens have an opportunity to react before actions become irreversible. In extreme cases, the public can rid itself of an inefficient or corrupt official. For their part, officials also want quick distribution of information so that they can have feedback from the public. This interaction is one of the reasons the Constitution protects the press. Without the give-and-take of ideas, democracy could not work.

Timeliness is also the consequence of advertising necessities. Since most businesses are based on the quick turnover of goods, advertisements must appear soon after goods are shipped to stores. The news that attracts readers to the advertisements must be constantly renewed.

Prominence: Events involving well-known persons or institutions. When the president trips disembarking from an airplane, it is front-page news; when a city councilman missteps, it is not worth a line of print. A local banker's embezzlement is more newsworthy than a clerk's thievery, even when the clerk has stolen more. When Michael Jackson sprains a thumb while working on a Walt Disney movie, it is network news. Names make news, goes the old adage, even when the event is of little consequence.

In 1884, an American poet, Eugene Field, was moved by the journalism of personalities, and wrote:

> Now the Ahkoond of Swat is a vague sort of man
> Who lives in a country far over the sea;
> Pray tell me, good reader, if tell me you can,
> What's the Ahkoond of Swat to you folks or me?

Dick Harwood of *The Washington Post,* commenting on the coverage of the president's part in a congressional campaign, discussed the journalistic yearning for important persons.

> We salivated over the Republicans last fall for one reason only—the president was out campaigning for them. No matter that he had very little to say that was significant or unpredictable at the whistlestops along the way. No matter that he *did* very little beyond waving at crowds. No matter that there was little or no evidence that what he said or did affected a single vote, the mere fact that he was out there was page one news in *The Washington Post.* What he was doing was

"important," we told ourselves, because presidents are "important" men. That kind of circular reasoning frequently affects our news judgments. . . . It says something about our sense of values and about our perspectives on the world. . . .

Despite Field's gentle poke and Harwood's salvo, journalists continue to cater to what they perceive as the public's appetite for newsworthy names.

Proximity: Events in the circulation or broadcast area. People are interested in, and affected by, activities close at hand. A city ordinance to require licensing of dogs in Memphis, Tenn., would be of interest to that city's residents, of some interest to Nashville, Tenn., residents, and of little interest to dog owners in Butte, Mont.

If 42 people die in an airplane crash in the Andes and one of the passengers is a resident of Little Rock, the news story in Little Rock will emphasize the death of the local resident. This process is known as *localizing* the news. (See page 66.)

People also feel close to events and individuals with whom they have emotional ties. Newspapers and stations in communities with large Catholic or Jewish populations will give considerable space and time to news from the Vatican or the Middle East. When the space shuttle Challenger exploded in 1986 and sent seven crew members to their deaths the *Amsterdam News,* a weekly in New York City with a predominantly black readership, headlined on page one the death of the black astronaut who was aboard.

Economic interests can bridge distances, also. As the ownership of common stocks became more widespread in the United States, the annual report of the American Telephone & Telegraph Company became almost as important in the shoptalk of Jackson, Miss., businessmen as the state's annual cotton yield. Every major newspaper had to make room for the daily closing prices of the New York Stock Exchange. A newspaper in Mankato, Minn., will devote staff time and news space to crop reports and the livestock and grain markets. If the newspaper in an agricultural area has a correspondent in Washington, much of his time will be devoted to covering the Department of Agriculture and the committees dealing with farm matters.

Conflict: Events that reflect clashes between people or institutions. Strife, antagonism and confrontation have provided stories since people drew pictures of the hunt on the walls of their caves. Man's struggles with himself and his gods, a Hamlet or a Prometheus, are the essentials of drama. The contemporary counterparts are visible to the journalist whose eye is trained to see the dramatic—an official who must decide whether a proposed highway should go through the homes of a dozen families, a parents' movement that seeks changes in the reading list that high school authorities have adopted.

Eternal Conflicts. The writer George Steiner identifies "five principal constants in the condition of man"—age against youth, society against the individual, men against women, the living against the dead and men against the gods.

Proximity. *The Times-News* of Twin Falls, Idaho, emphasizes local and state stories on its front page. The newspaper serves an eight-county area in south-central Idaho. "Our emphasis is on what's going on in the state, region and community," says Managing Editor Stephen Hartgen.

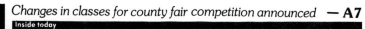

Changes in classes for county fair competition announced — **A7**

Inside today

Oklahoma! on stage - B1

Chen takes lead at U.S. Open - C1

The Times-News

25¢

80th year, No. 171 | Twin Falls, Idaho | Friday, June 14, 1985

Causa paid for 26 Idaho legislators' trips

Copyright © 1985
By Magic Valley Newspapers

By DEAN S. MILLER
Times-News writer

TWIN FALLS — Causa, the activist arm of the Rev. Sun Myung Moon's Unification Church, has sent at least 26 Idaho legislators on all-expense-paid trips to Los Angeles, Salt Lake City and Denver since the Legislature adjourned in March, The Times-News has learned.

The trips apparently represent the first time a sizable group of state legislators from anywhere in the country has attended the church's anti-communism seminars.

On April 15-18 at the Pacifica Hotel in Los Angeles, 16 Idaho legislators were among 350 people at Causa's three-day conference on communism awareness.

On May 13-16 at the Salt Lake City Sheraton Hotel, six Idaho legislators attended a similar conference. Two had attended before. On June 3-6, six Idaho legislators stayed at the Clarion Airport Hotel in Denver at the expense of the Unification Church for another of the conferences.

The legislators were invited along with ministers and opinion leaders from Idaho.

"We were their guests all the way," said Sen. Atwell Parry, R-Melba, Wednesday. "Quite a chunk of the money comes from the Unification Church," Parry said. He said the legislators were told that Causa is also funded by "large corporations and large churches" but he did not know the names of any.

"Paul Victor (a Twin Falls Causa supporter) was the one that was instrumental in getting me to go," Parry said. "I have to admit it (the Unification Church connection) made me nervous at first," he said.

Victor confirmed he had arranged for the legislators to attend the conference.

Parry said his misgivings were put to rest when he heard the workshops on Causa's perception of the threat of communism.

Parry said he was a co-convenor at the Salt Lake City conference after he attended the Los Angeles conference.

"Not at any time was there any pressure, any mention of the Unification Church," Parry said.

Causa USA president Phillip Sanchez said in a Thursday phone conversation that at the conventions, Causa shows a documentary film called "Truth Is My Sword" which tells about the Koreagate influence peddling scandal hearings in which Unification Church second-in-command Colonel Bo Hi Pak was implicated.

Rep. L. Gene Winchester, R-Kuna, said the legislators were also told in the film of Rev. Moon's life story. Moon is currently serving a federal prison term for federal income tax violations.

Winchester said he was told Causa has a target figure of 40,000 people nationally it wants to attend the conferences this year.

Sanchez said that number would be impossible since the average attendance at the conferences is 350 people.

Rep. JoAn Wood, R-Rigby, said Wednesday she

• See LEGISLATORS on Page A2

Unification Church active in Idaho political arena

TWIN FALLS — The Rev. Sun Myung Moon's Unification Church has cropped up a number of times in Idaho politics since 1983.

Most recently, the Times-News has discovered that a number of Idaho legislators have been flown to communism awareness conferences sponsored by Causa, an activist arm of the Unification Church.

Another Unification Church-sponsored group, the Freedom Leadership Foundation, flew a member of the staff of Sen. Steve Symms, R-Idaho, to Central America for meetings with government officials in Honduras and Guatemala in May of 1984.

And, in August of 1984, the Times-News reported that Unification Church members were selling copies of former Rep. George Hansen's book "To Harass Our People." Hansen's book has a chapter dealing with alleged Internal Revenue Service harass-

• See CAUSA on Page A2

Pool vote recount ordered

By ANNETTE CARY
Times-News writer

TWIN FALLS — Fifth District Judge Daniel Hurlbutt has ordered a recount of votes cast in the April 23 bond election to raise money for a Twin Falls city swimming pool.

The first count came up eight votes short of the two-thirds majority needed to pass the $700,000 bond.

The recount is set for Wednesday at 3 p.m. in the city police station, says City Attorney Shane Bengoechea.

The same precinct workers who counted the ballots April 23 will be asked to conduct the recount, Bengoechea said.

Hurlbutt is requiring that the recount be completed before June 31. Lance Clow, the co-chairman of the Twin Falls Citizens Pool Committee, will be responsible for the first $200 of the recount's cost, Hurlbutt has ordered. If it costs more, the city will pay the rest of the costs.

Hurlbutt's decision followed an informal hearing in the judge's office Wednesday, Bengoechea said.

Both sides had already agreed in a stipulation entered in the case that there were irregularities in the election and a recount should be held. They had also agreed to the payment plan that Hurlbutt ordered.

Precinct 6 took a half hour longer than any other prcinct to count votes, the stipulation says. Also, several residents who were qualified to vote were turned away from the polls, it says.

The City Council agreed, after the April 23 vote, that a recount should be made. However, officials at the state attorney general's office said a recount should follow a court action.

The vote was the city's third effort to pass a bond for a new city swimming pool, after the old one at Harmon Park crumbled beyond repair. The April 23 vote was for a $1.2-million outdoor pool at Harmon Park.

Times-News photo/ANDY ARENZ

A field aflow

Gary Griffith swings his shovel alongside him as he surveys irrigation flow to a pea field west of Twin Falls. Griffith, an irrigator and tractor driver for Colner Farms Inc., made sure the pea, grain, bean and hay fields under his watch received their proper share of water on a recent warm and dusty afternoon.

$9 million more may go toward 'hopper spraying

By KENNETH A. BROWN
Times-News writer

TWIN FALLS — Actions by Idaho's congressional delegation may make an additional $9 million available for grasshopper spraying in the state, the offices of Sens. Steve Symms and Jim McClure announced Thursday.

Wednesday, the House passed a supplemental appropriations bill which allots an additional $10 million for grasshopper spraying.

Originally, $10 million had been appropriated by the Department of Agriculture for grasshopper spraying in the Western states.

The Animal Plant and Health Inspection Service predicted Thursday that all of its $10 million spraying budget will have been spent in Idaho and Utah by the time spraying finishes on Friday.

Originally the department had predicted that only $2 million would be required for spraying in the state.

The Senate action pushed by Symms and McClure could add an additional $9 million to the spraying program by re-directing money already appropriated to the Department of Agriculture.

Orginally, the Senate had agreed to appropriate $19 million to the Agriculture Department if the Secretary would make $10 million of that available for grasshopper spraying.

Symms and McClure are now trying to get Secretary of Agriculture John Block to commit the remaining $9 million of the original appropriation to the grasshopper spraying program.

Thursday it looked "very promising" that the Secretary would make the additional $9 million available for grasshopper spraying in Idaho, according to Trent Clark, a staff assistant for Symms' office in Washington.

Similar action has been going on in the House, according to Kelly Olson, a staff aide with Rep. Richard Stallings' office.

In addition to the $10 million approved in the House's supplemental appropriations bill, Olson said Stallings and other house members have been pressuring the Department of Agriculture to transfer funds from the Commodities Credit Corporation to the spraying program.

The corporation, which buys surplus crops through default, has funds available for pest eradication.

The catch, Olson explained, is that funds from the Commodities Credit Corporation are traditionally used only on pests which can be eradicated.

While the spraying program cannot eliminate the grasshoppers, Olson said Stallings believes that when the present emergency merits changing the guidelines.

So far increased funding for the grasshopper

• See SPRAYING on Page A2

Father of teen rapist nabbed, charged with 2 child sex offenses

By BONNIE BAIRD JONES
Times-News writer

TWIN FALLS — The father of a 15-year-old boy who was sentenced Monday on a rape charge was arrested by Twin Falls police Thursday on two sex charges.

Robert Allen Morris Sr., 45, 345 4th Ave. W., Apt. 2, in Twin Falls, was charged with lewd and lascivious conduct with a minor and with a crime against nature. Both alleged offenses involve an 11-year-old boy, police reports show.

A complaint filed with police said the alleged acts occurred in January and had occurred previously over the past eight years.

The victim told police Morris forced him to engage in oral sex and other acts on numerous occasions, including the most recent — last January — when Morris came to his home while his family was away.

The suspect's 15-year-old son, Robert Allen Morris Jr., was given a life sentence six months ago, after he pleaded guilty to the charge involving the rape of a 16-year-old girl in a cave in Rock Creek Canyon.

The judge retained jurisdiction for a six-month period, and on Monday the younger Morris, who was treated as an adult in the case, returned to court and was given a 10-year probation.

Part of the probation period will be spent at the Youth Service Center in St. Anthony, in custody of the Department of Health and Welfare.

The youth's father will be arraigned on the two felony counts today. Investigating officers said because of the Idaho law that requires a rape victim to be a female, the older Morris cannot be charged with rape.

A number of other states have updated the rape statutes to include male victims, police noted, while Idaho still requires a female victim other than the wife of the suspect in order to constitute a rape charge.

Noh predicts more education funding

By MARILYN HAUK ESSEX
For The Associated Press

BOISE — A state senator is predicting that the Republican-controlled Idaho Legislature will be more generous in funding education during the 1986 session.

But Sen. Laird Noh, R-Kimberly, told the Idaho Association of School Administrators Thursday that education reform will be one of the major issues facing Idaho lawmakers as Republicans try to elect a GOP governor. Lt. Gov. David Leroy, a Republican, and former Democratic Gov. Cecil Andrus are considered likely candidates in the 1986 Idaho governor's race.

That race "puts pressure on the majority party to perform," said Noh, who co-chairs an interim legislative committee studying home education.

The home-school recommendation likley will be structured so that requirements aren't prohibitive to parents who sincerly want to educate their children at home, Noh said.

Noh said he wishes lawmakers could have done better during the last session, when legislators passed a $304 million public education bill. State Superintendent Jerry Evans had requested more than $330 million.

The appropriation was not enough to fund a teacher career ladder program or salary increases.

Noh said the Legislature's failure to appropriate more money to education reform was partly due to freshman legislators who proceeded cautiosly during their first session.

Although Noh is predicting more education dollars in the next session, he couldn't offer a specific amount. " 'How much?' That's the question," he said.

Noh also told school administrators that "the office corps" should be subject to the "same scrutiny as the foot soldiers."

Idahoans should be sure they're promoting the "best and the brightest" to positions of responsibility, he said.

Noh said he has had problems getting background information on school superintendents.

A random check of what degrees are held by school officials showed 40 percent with diplomas in physical education, he said. Noh said that's a situation that's "maybe good, maybe bad," but nevertheless needs to be examined.

Noh also called for a parternership rather than "dictatorship" between school administrators and teachers. "There's reasons why we get unions and there's reasons why unions become militant."

On the home education issue, Noh said the state shouldn't place such strict restrictions that the program becomes impossible.

Rules that apply to other Idaho students, such as the C average requirement and 90 percent attendance rule, likely wouldn't apply to home-school pupils, he said.

State education support at a high, says analyst

BOISE (AP) — A legislative financial analyst says state support for Idaho education is nearly at an all-time high, even though higher education is receiving a smaller share of state funds.

Mark Falconer told a legislative study committee on Thursday that in the new state budget starting July 1, education will take 74.6 percent of all general state revenue.

That's second only to the 74.7 percent allocated in 1981, Falconer said. But higher education will receive about 15 percent of the money, down from a high of 18 percent in 1978.

A legislative study committee on higher education opened hearings Thursday morning. Cochairman Sen. Terry Sverdsten, R-Cataldo, said the first meeting would be

• See EDUCATION on Page A2

Although critics of the press condemn what they consider to be an over-emphasis on conflict, the advance of civilization can be seen as an adventure in conflict and turmoil.

The Bizarre: Events that deviate sharply from the expected and the experiences of everyday life. The damage suit filed by an Albuquerque couple because the club they had rented for their wedding reception was occupied when they and their 200 guests arrived stands out from the dozen other suits filed that day.

In 1970, when an all-white jury awarded a black man $70,000 in damages, the racial angle was played up in the wire service story:

Police Victim Gets $70,000

CHICAGO, June 17—An all-white jury awarded $70,000 in damages yesterday to a black man who said that two policemen had violated his civil rights by beating him after they stopped him on a traffic charge. . . .

Nowadays, it is not unusual in most parts of the country for a white jury to make awards to black plaintiffs, and such a story would probably not be put on the transcontinental wires of the press associations.

Currency: Events and situations that are being talked about. Occasionally, a situation of long standing will suddenly emerge and become newsworthy. As the historians might say, it is an idea whose time has come.

The poor have always been with us, and remain so. In the early 1960s President Kennedy called attention to their plight, and President Johnson declared a "war on poverty." Newspapers responded by covering health and welfare agencies, by going into ghetto areas. Television produced documentaries on the blighted lives of the poor. Twenty years later news of the poor, not much less numerous, was replaced by coverage of gentrification and the lives of yuppies (young, urban professionals).

In the mid 1980s stories of missing children leaped onto news pages and the television screen. Milk cartons and shopping bags were used to tell of the plight of these children. Congress mandated the National Center for Missing and Exploited Children, whose director estimated 1.5 million children disappear every year. Actually, the FBI reported, the figure is well under 100,000. Most people reported missing return home within days; 97 percent of those reported missing are home within a month.

Newspapers and broadcast stations will sometimes make discoveries of their own and push them so that they become current. When a newspaper decides that some facet of community or national life is worth intensive coverage, it may assign a reporter or a team of reporters to dig into the situation. The result, usually a number of stories, is called a campaign or a crusade. Much of this news has a steamroller effect and further news is developed because of the currency of the theme or issue.

Events Combine News Values

Few events fall solely into a single category. Most newsworthy events are combinations of these guidelines.

At least three-fourths of all stories journalists write fall into these categories:

- Consequence—News that has consequences for large numbers of people. (Impact, importance, significance.)
- Interest—News that is unusual, strange, entertaining.

These guidelines do not tell us that one of the most enduring stories is the tale of how humanity prevails. How we live now is a story few readers have ever been able to resist. Also, these guidelines do not tell us how news values change. Nor do they give us any hints about the realities of the newsroom—its pressures and its politics.

News Is Relative

News is a relative concept. What is news changes with geography, demography and time. At the turn of the century, fewer than 115,000 men and women were in college. Now, more than 50 times as many students attend college, and newspapers assign reporters to cover the colleges in their areas on a regular basis.

Even the so-called essential guidelines change. For years, human interest was considered one of the basic criteria in assessing the news value of an event. The feature story, with its focus on individuals and their foibles, was a fixture in almost every newspaper. This led to a wild assortment of trivia in the news.

Today, the emphasis is on presenting the human element in all events whenever possible. A budget story is personalized by showing the consequences of the new property tax to homeowners, apartment dwellers and the merchants who may have to raise their prices as taxes increase. Changes in the school curriculum are made interesting by describing what John and Jane will be reading in the third grade next fall. *The Wall Street Journal* has been influential in the trend toward personalizing the news. A typical *Journal* story will begin with several paragraphs about an individual—perplexed, hard-pressed, triumphant or defeated—and bring in the news peg after personalizing the issue through an individual.

Pictures and Print

Watch the local evening news on television. Compare the placement and time given each news item in the broadcast with the play each receives in the newspaper. Some of the news that is emphasized on television is given routine treatment in the newspaper, and some newspaper stories receive slight mention in newscasts. Obviously, some news is better suited to the newspaper than to television, and television is better able to capture some events than the newspaper.

Television technology and the audience demand pictures, which leads television to lean heavily on action. As Richard Salant, president of Columbia Broadcasting System News, put it, "You see more fires on local television than you do in the newspapers because fires look better on television."

Whereas the newspaper reader can decide not to read some stories on the basis of the headline or the lead, the television viewer and radio listener must sit through the news items that distress or bore him, turn off the set or change the channel. The broadcast editor is thus faced with a potentially flighty audience and is careful not to lose it with too much detail or too many complicated ideas. Reporters for the electronic media understand the needs of radio and television and respond to them in their reporting, writing and editing.

In a newspaper, the space allotted for news usually depends on the amount of advertising that is sold. Unlike radio and television, which have nonexpandable time slots for newscasts, a newspaper may run 32 pages one day and 48 the next, when department stores place their white-sale advertising. A story that would run half a column on a day when the news hole is tight would be given a full column when ample space is available.

On any given day, the news flow may be slow. That is, important stories simply may not be breaking. On days like these, events that would be ignored on busy news days are covered.

Advertising and News Flow

Advertising Pressures

After a Connecticut newspaper printed a front-page story about a kidnapping at a shopping center, the merchants at the center demanded a meeting with newspaper management. They told the publisher that the newspaper's survival depended on the economic health of local business but that such stories would drive shoppers elsewhere. The newspaper replied that crime was always covered by the newspaper and that no individual or group could be given special treatment.

Such confrontations are infrequent, but when they do occur the response of the journalist is usually that advertiser intrusion in news policy is intolerable. Nevertheless, media managers are conscious of the feelings and needs of their advertisers, and this awareness affects news decisions. The recognition that advertising lubricates the media may mean that the newspaper or broadcast station will assign a new staff member to general assignment rather than to consumer reporting. The Connecticut editor who was criticized by his advertisers may put the next shopping center crime on page three instead of page one.

After *The Charleston Gazette* ran a series of articles indicating that local automobile dealers and garages were engaged in dishonest practices, advertising by auto dealers declined. Don Marsh, the editor of the West Virginia daily newspaper, said the advertising department had not complained. The department knew it "wouldn't have done any good," the advertising manager remarked.

Marsh named the companies that had stopped advertising and those that had continued to advertise.

Marsh admitted that advertising boycotts and threats can be and have been "an effective muzzler. Lose an account because of a story?—madness. Ask any publisher of a struggling paper whether he would prefer an exposé of a county official or the continued placement in his columns of the county's advertising. His answer is inevitable."

A newspaper is as independent as its finances permit, Marsh concluded. The *Gazette* is strong enough to be independent, he wrote. "Ask any car dealer."

The pressure to please advertisers sometimes does lead to stifling the news. *The Wall Street Journal* reported such a case.

The story has its origin in the seizure of 1.5 million cans of soup produced by Bon Vivant of Newark, N.J. The federal Food and Drug Administration acted after a man died and his wife was paralyzed as the result of drinking the company's vichyssoise. The soup contained bacteria that cause botulism, a crippling and often fatal disease. But not all the cans were seized and destroyed. Years later, a University of Wyoming student spotted the cans on the shelf of a Laramie food store, and the city's environmental commissioner dashed over to pick them up. He turned them over to the state department of agriculture, which issued a press release advising consumers that the soup had turned up and warning them not to eat it if they had any at home. The local newspaper ignored the story.

Only after the local radio stations and television stations in Cheyenne and Denver ran the story did the local newspaper print an item, on page three. The name of the store was not mentioned.

Asked what had happened to the story, the newspaper's managing editor is quoted in the *Journal* as answering:

"I think you could say this was one of those cases where the advertising department did have some influence over a news story. We're a small town and we have to react differently from the big cities. We can't just run out and say, 'My God, everybody, John Shuster's selling poison soup.' We didn't want to prejudice his business."

The advertising manager didn't want the story to run, said the managing editor. "So it didn't," he said.

At one of the local radio stations, the news director, Ralph Swain, who was also an instructor in journalism at the University of Wyoming, energetically dug into the story, identifying the store so that people who shopped there would be careful and "so we wouldn't cast suspicion on the other stores that hadn't sold Bon Vivant." Following his 6 p.m. newscast, the store cancelled its advertising with the station. According to the *Journal,* Swain said he was cautioned about future stories on the soup and that his reporting led to his dismissal.

A reporter for the *Trenton* (N.J.) *Times* was fired because he inserted background material into a press release his editor had told him to run without any changes. The release was from an advertiser. After the dismissal had led to a barrage of criticism of the newspaper, the publisher apologized, but the reporter was not rehired. A quarter of the reporting staff quit in disgust.

Soft on Cigarettes

Elizabeth Whalen, the executive director of the American Council on Science and Health, was asked by *Harper's Bazaar* to write an article with the title, "Protect Your Man from Cancer." Her article began with the link of smoking and cancer. When the editor saw the article he told a copy editor, "Christ, Jane, I can't open this article with smoking." She moved the material to the end "so it wouldn't jump in the face of every cigarette advertiser."

Whalen was told the cutting was based on her "frequent mention of tobacco and the fact that they (the magazine) ran three full-page cigarette ads each month."

Some publications do not succumb to the pressures of cigarette advertisers. *The Charlotte Observer* carried a 20-page special report titled, "Our Tobacco Dilemma." The state's farmers grow two-thirds of the tobacco used for cigarettes, and North Carolina workers manufacture more than half of the almost 700 billion cigarettes made in the United States each year. Tobacco, the state's leading cash crop, brings in $1 billion a year to growers.

Yet the *Observer* did not shrink from putting under the title of its special section this headline:

N.C.'s top crop; part of our lives but bad for health

Lifeblood. "Survival is at stake and there is no time to lose," said the publisher of the *Daily News* in 1986 when a major New York City department store announced it would close. The store, Gimbels, spent $10 million a year on *News* advertising. No newspaper relies on circulation revenue as a major source of income.

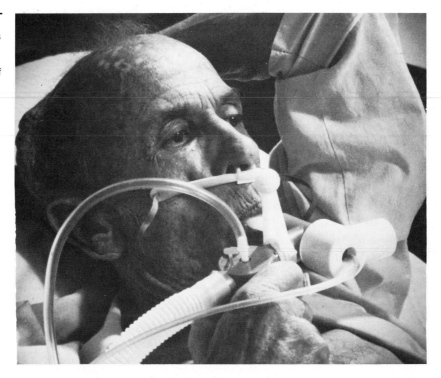

Five Packs a Day. Although *The Charlotte Observer* serves farmers who grow two-thirds of the tobacco used to make cigarettes, it ran this picture of a victim of "smoking-caused emphysema" in a section entitled, "Our Tobacco Dilemma." Photo by Mark B. Sluder.

On the front page next to a picture of a tobacco warehouse was a photograph of James McManus, 62, a former painter and paperhanger, a five-pack-a-day smoker. He was pictured with the tubes from his oxygen tank attached to his nose and mouth. "McManus speaks only with difficulty and needs an oxygen tank to survive," the paper states. He has "smoking-caused emphysema."

The tobacco industry outspends all other national advertisers in newspapers and is second to the transportation industry in magazine advertising. The tobacco industry spends more than $1 billion on advertising cigarettes, about $25 a smoker per year.

In a story on the consequences of this huge advertising budget, *The Wall Street Journal* reported that the financially weak publications are subject to pressure from the tobacco companies. When a reporter for the *Twin Cities Reader* in Minneapolis covered a press conference announcing the Kool Jazz Festival, sponsored by Brown & Williamson, he inserted a list of famous jazz artists who had died of lung cancer. The reporter was fired the next day. If a cigarette advertisement should run near an obituary or close to a story about the effects of tobacco on health, then the company is given a "make good," or free ad, the *Journal* reported.

Advertisers can elevate the performance of a newspaper, too. Increasingly, large retailers are more interested in the quality of readership than quantity. They seek publications with an upscale readership—well-educated, middle-income men and women interested in news of substance. This is the reason *The New York Times,* with half the readership of the *Daily News,* sells twice as much advertising as the *News. The New York Post,* a sensational newspaper with about the same circulation as the *Times,* has about 5 percent of the total advertising in New York City.

In 1983, the *National Enquirer* decided to change its contents to attract more and higher quality advertisers. Once a gossip and celebrity publication with stories such as one about a baby born singing like Elvis Presley, the *Enquirer* attracted mail-order houses that advertised breast enlargers and lucky rabbits. Then the *Enquirer* began to emphasize service stories—diets, coping with husband or wife, caring for pets. In two years, it increased its national advertising by 44 percent. Tide, Kraft, Johnson Wax and Mr. Clean coexist with the mail-order houses now. The *Enquirer* continues to have credibility problems, however. A poll released in 1986 showed that 14 percent of the public rated the weekly as "believable" or "highly believable" whereas *The New York Times, USA Today* and *The Wall Street Journal* all ranked higher than 70 percent.

The politics in the newsroom can affect the news. The power structure, which puts the reporter close to the bottom of the power hierarchy, places decision making in the hands of editors, publishers and news managers who rarely see the events the reporter writes about. Yet they often have firm ideas about how stories should be written, and the reporter is tempted to go along to get along. Some publishers and station owners have pet projects—a favored charity, the downtown business mall—and these will be given special attention. Political and social cronies may be granted time and space disproportionate to their actual news value.

Ideology sometimes determines what is printed. Reporters and copy editors are proud of their independence, particularly of the distance they put between the newsroom and the editorial writer's alcove. But the ideological commitments of the newspaper sometimes seep into the newsroom and affect what is covered and its play.

From Gossip to Diets

Yuppies. In its pitch to advertisers, *USA Today* says its readers are "credit card users . . . heavy movie viewers . . . frequent travelers . . . young, affluent professionals . . . they represent almost 80 percent of frequent alcoholic beverage consumers."

Newsroom Politics and Ideology

Castro Narrowly Escapes Drowning
Too Bad! Too Bad! Too Bad! Too Bad!

When Fidel Castro had a swimming accident, the *El Paso Times* ran this headline.

The Sins of Omission

These pressures work in two directions—what is used and what is tossed out. A publication or station can be assessed as much by its wastebasket as by its columns and newscasts, for the sins of omission are as serious as those of commission. Reporters and editors are affected by common assumptions and the tide of public opinion. As a consequence, the divergent idea or the unusual person may not be assessed with the same criteria applied to the accepted and the expected.

Some editors favor certain types of news—political stories, features, hard news—and give less attention to other kinds of news. The commitment of a newspaper to a large statehouse staff may mean a lot of news from the state capitol, even at the expense of important international news, because people on the payroll must be put to use.

When the regime of Ferdinand Marcos of the Philippines was on the verge of collapse, Dan Rather was in Texas to begin a week of reports on the U.S. farm crisis. The farm story had been heavily promoted by CBS. In weighing the news values, the network decided to give as much time to the farm story as to the end of Marcos' long and dictatorial presidency. The decision was, to many, a nod to promotion rather than to news.

The Audience

Reaching Out. Newsmakers have the audience in mind, too. Political leaders in Washington try to appear on the Sunday news programs because they are the basis of Monday morning newspaper headlines, and they like the morning news programs because many people watch them and the questions usually are not difficult. The "MacNeil-Lehrer News Hour" on PBS is not popular because the 2–4 million households that watch are considered a small audience. "We usually send them lower-level officials," said a Reagan administration official.

The nature of the audience is an essential factor in determining what is covered and how events are reported. News directors of non-commercial television and radio stations lean heavily on analysis and venture into advocacy journalism, whereas the commercial stations with their mass audiences stay close to so-called objective, event-oriented reporting. Reporters for special-interest magazines and alternative newspapers are less sensitive to the needs of the mass audience than are the reporters for daily newspapers.

Newspaper readership studies have shown that young people are interested in stories about music and entertainment and that as they grow older, marry, and purchase homes they become more interested in local news. Stories about taxes, schools and local politics interest older readers, as do stories about food, health and medicine.

Reporters and editors learn to anticipate the responses of their audiences to a subject. Sometimes, the guesswork leads to a disproportionate amount of news about what readers already know or want to hear confirmed and to oversimplification. A steady diet of this kind of journalism can become a self-fulfilling prophecy, developing readers and listeners who distrust the different and fear the new.

The economics of stations and newspapers affect coverage. A small station may not have the resources to cover many events in the community. It may rely on sources other than its staff—publicity handouts and releases, the press associations, volunteers—and rewrite news from the local newspaper, which usually is able to muster more reporters than the local radio or television station. Short-handed newspaper staffs rely on the telephone, a poor substitute for on-the-scene coverage.

Policies and traditions also determine how news is covered and what is reported. Many newspapers are satisfied with being publications of record. That is, they will cover the formal activities of their communities. The kind of journalism that results from this policy is described as event-oriented, since it leans heavily on meetings, speeches, accidents and disasters, crime and other overt activities. It is a denotative journalism, pointing to what has happened, and it is a fairly inexpensive and non-controversial journalism.

The strong publisher determined to influence public policy through his or her newspaper has just about disappeared. But ownership still influences how news is covered and what is published. Without the spur of competition, the monopoly newspaper may become lazy, sitting back to await news rather than going out to dig it up. It may ignore what Benjamin C. Bradlee, executive editor of *The Washington Post,* describes as the "special responsibilities" of the monopoly newspaper: "to listen to the voiceless; to avoid any and all acts of arrogance; to face the public with politeness and candor."

The chain newspaper might be light on local news, which is expensive to gather, and heavy on wire news and syndicated material, which requires only editing. An anonymous home office concerned with the profits of the chain may direct the editor of the local newspaper to the bottom line on the ledger rather than to the local news hole figures. The editor may not be willing to run the story that would provoke local advertisers or the major employer in town.

The chains are swallowing newspapers at such a rapid rate that three of five newspapers are now within one of the 170 groups. In 1985, chains had 77 percent of daily newspaper circulation. The chains defend group ownership by contending that the financial strength of groups gives local editors greater resources to risk offending the local power structure. But Ben Bagdikian of the University of California, a press critic, disagrees with this optimistic view of chain ownership. He sees the ever-present need for profits precluding the development of quality journalism.

Economics and
News Policies

The Influence
of Owners

"There's real danger that the number of distinguished papers will decline, because they're part of chains now, too, and the pressure is on them to produce dollars," Bagdikian says.

In a 10-day period in 1986, two respected family-owned newspapers were sold to chains: Gannett bought *The Courier-Journal* and *Louisville Times,* and the Times Mirror Corp. of Los Angeles bought *The Sun* and *The Evening Sun* in Baltimore.

A Sociologist's Perspective

News, says Herbert J. Gans, a sociologist who writes about journalism, is "mainly shaped by the size of the news hole, news organization budgets, information available from news sources and newsmakers and by 'media considerations'—for example, television's need for dramatic tape or film."

David Altheide, a sociologist at Arizona State University, contends that for television the availability of visuals determines the type and extent of coverage of an event. Visuals, he says, are part of a "format" or "news code," which he defines as the "rules and logic underlying the use of time and space by network personnel." Newspapers, magazines and radio also use formats or codes.

The Personal Element

Impersonal and objective as some journalists would like to make the determinants of news, much of journalism is based on selection, and choice is a highly personal matter. It derives from the reporter's professional background, his or her education and the intangible influences of family and friends. Even more elusive are the decisions that have their origin in the arena where ambition and conscience battle.

Vague as these influences may be, the reporter must cope with them. Fortunately, the reporter's handiwork is tangible. Once the heat of reporting and writing has cooled, the reporter can examine the story. Then, alone or with a trusted friend or colleague, the reporter can try to pinpoint the reasons for decisions. This self-questioning—directed by some of the principles we have discussed in this chapter and those in Chapter 27 where the morality of journalism is discussed—is part of the journalist's continuing education.

Bagdikian, Ben H. *The Media Monopoly*. Boston: Beacon Press, 1983.

Fry, Don. *Believing the News*. St. Petersburg, Fla.: The Poynter Institute for Media Studies, 1985.

Gans, Herbert J. *Deciding What's News*. New York: Pantheon Books, 1974.

Roshco, Bernard. *Newsmaking*. Chicago: University of Chicago Press, 1975.

Schudson, Michael. *Discovering the News*. New York: Basic Books, 1978.

Westin, Av. *Newswatch: How TV Decides the News*. New York: Simon & Schuster, 1983.

Further Reading

CHAPTER FOUR

The Tools of the Trade

Preview

Journalists use a variety of tools to do their job. These include the devices that are necessary to reporting and writing and a variety of reference works and sources that bolster stories—the Freedom of Information Act, clippings, data bases, census and other data from official agencies and from polls. The journalist must:

- Master the VDT, tape recorder.
- Understand how to use basic references.
- Observe newsroom requirements.
- Know public-record laws.
- Feel at home using mathematics, analyzing graphs and tables.
- Understand how the computer can help analyze information for stories.
- Be able to conduct and interpret a public opinion poll.

Careful reporters check spellings and meanings of which they are unsure against the dictionary. Usage is checked in the stylebook. Quotations from written works are verified in Bartlett's Familiar Quotations. To help them analyze information, reporters apply mathematical procedures to data for easier and quicker comprehension by readers and viewers.

The computer allows reporters to obtain background material from the newspaper library and from data bases, and certain equipment permits reporters to send stories from any location.

Journalists use several kinds of tools. There are the instruments with which they shape the raw material of their reporting—the pencils, pads, tape recorders, typewriters, video display terminals. There are the reporting devices—the telephone, reference materials and such analytic tools as mathematics and polling techniques. Then there is the special language the journalist uses to communicate with co-workers.

Learning the language is essential, as the apprentice electrician finds out the first day on the job when he is told to get a bucket of volts, or the chemistry student who is immortalized in the couplet:

> Johnny was a chemist; Johnny is no more.
> What Johnny thought was H_2O was H_2SO_4.

Hugh Mulligan, a long-time AP reporter, recalled what happened when a news editor did not know the meaning of a certain word in the journalist's special vocabulary—*overhead:*

> The paper in Walsenburg, Colo., was going to press. In those days the PMs wire closed at 3 o'clock and they were anxious to know who won the Indianapolis 500. They messaged the AP bureau in Indianapolis and the bureau said it would send the result to them by Western Union, which of course was "overheading," and the bureau message read: "Will overhead winner of Indianapolis 500."
>
> And we had the famous headline: WILL OVERHEAD WINS INDIANAPOLIS 500. They even concocted a little story to go with it.
>
> They said he was so far behind that his name didn't even appear in any of the previous stories.

A glossary of journalism terms is provided in the back of the book. When in doubt about any term, consult it. You may want to pencil in comments and additions.

Unlike the reporter's vocabulary, the tangible tools are supplied by the employer.

The VDT (video display terminal) is used on most newspapers. Reporters work at the keyboard, which relays electric impulses to the computer. The story is visible on the screen. Printouts can be made from the stored material.

A pad with a hard back like a stenographer's notebook is best for note-taking. The stiff backing makes jottings clear, and the spiral binding keeps notes in order.

The tape recorder is a necessity for the radio reporter, optional for the print reporter. The tape recorder is useful in covering speeches, formal interviews, symposia. It is an aid in stories requiring precise quotes, but it cannot substitute for the reporter's patterning—determining the structure of the piece. The broadcast journalist may not tape the voice of the source without asking permission.

The telephone is a basic tool of the trade. It allows reporters to gather information quickly under deadline pressure and to reach sources too far away for personal interviews. Some reporters have become experts at pulling information from reluctant sources by telephone. But the telephone cannot substitute for the face-to-face interview.

The electronic revolution may alter telephone use by reporters in the field. The cellular phone and the computer, powered by battery, allow reporters to send in their stories from any location. It also permits quick information retrieval in the field. The system can be placed in a briefcase.

The Tangible Tools

The Intangibles. Some say the most important tools of all for the journalist are ingenuity, tenacity and a cool head.

When President Kennedy was shot in Dallas, Merriman Smith, the UPI reporter, leaped from the press car and grabbed the only available phone. The AP reporter, hemmed in by others in the back seat, made it to the phone late and tried to wrestle it from Smith, who hugged it to him and curled into a ball.

This gave the UPI the beat on the assassination and the Pulitzer Prize went to Smith.

Equipped. Notepad and tape recorder at the ready, William Cohan of the *News & Observer* in Raleigh, N.C., covers a school board meeting. Photo by Jonathan Wiggs.

Obtaining detailed information by telephone can sometimes be difficult because of the similarities of sound when names and other key information are spelled out. To cope with this, various phonetic alphabets have been adopted. The armed forces use Alpha for A, Bravo for B, etc. The alphabet in table 4.1 has been used by telephone systems in training operators. It uses common first names for most of the letters.

The microcomputer allows reporters to make charts, graphs, and diagrams to blend into their written accounts. With the microcomputer it is possible for even the smallest newspapers and stations to expand their use of visual material produced in the newsroom.

The electronic revolution has even spawned magazines and newsletters that are available only through a terminal—on-line journalism.

The hardware for users now is available for under $300.

Newsroom Habits

Here are some suggestions for the development of sound newsroom work habits:

- Be punctual.
- Observe the deadlines, yours and those of others.
- Conform to office dress and appearance standards.
- Be courteous to sources and co-workers—colleagues, telephone operators, receptionists, janitors, interns.
- Adhere to the chain of command.
- Read the newspaper and watch and listen to news programs every day.

Table 4.1 Phonetic Alphabet for Telephone Use

A—Alice	H—Harry	O—Olive	V—Victor
B—Bertha	I—Ida	P—Peter	W—William
C—Charles	J—James	Q—Quaker	X—X-Ray
D—David	K—Kate	R—Robert	Y—Young
E—Edward	L—Lewis	S—Samuel	Z—Zebra
F—Frank	M—Mary	T—Thomas	
G—George	N—Nellie	U—Utah	

- Do not:
Ask editors unnecessary questions.
Break office conventions.
Interrupt persons on deadline.
Vanish from the office.
Telephone family or friends from the office.
Write memos explaining why you missed or blew a story.
Complain about an assignment.

Basic References

On the desk, every reporter has at least two volumes—a dictionary and the city telephone directory. Reporters always verify a questionable spelling. The dictionary is also used to check whether a word has the shade of meaning intended. Since editors conclude that a reporter who misspells is a lazy reporter—and some even have the notion that spelling ability and intelligence are synonymous—the reporter who ignores the dictionary is inviting trouble.

Some newspapers have cross-indexed directories, a listing of telephone numbers by address. This directory is invaluable on a late-breaking story when the reporter cannot go to the event and needs details from the scene.

A few reporters have a small library on or near their desks—a one-volume American history, an atlas, a thesaurus and a world almanac. If these are not within arm's reach, the reporter should know where they are in the newsroom.

Every reporter should know how to use these references:

- The World Almanac.
- The Reader's Guide to Periodical Literature.
- The New York Times Index.
- Bartlett's Familiar Quotations. Who penned: "How do I love thee? Let me count the ways."? Had a Chicago journalist consulted Bartlett's, the newspaper might have been spared embarrassment. The quotation was

Sound-Alikes. Make no assumptions about the words you hear on the telephone. This appeared in *The Charleston* (W. Va.) *Gazette:*

"The second, a whimsical number titled 'London Derriere,' was heralded by Karr as his salute to St. Patrick's Day."

Actually, Karr, the soloist, had commented whimsically that the Irish took London out of the name so as to call the song "Derry Air."

Stylebook. No matter how well-written, no story can gain reader acceptance if it contains inconsistencies in spelling, capitalization, punctuation and abbreviation. If the reporter writes 10 West Fourth Street in one place and 79 W. 5th St. in another paragraph, the reader wonders whether the reporter is equally sloppy with the facts. The stylebook gives the rules or guides to use to assure consistency. See the Stylebook on page 651.

used under a large page-one picture of a couple sitting on a statue of Shakespeare in a Chicago park—with attribution to William Shakespeare. (If you do not know the author, look it up.)

• The National Zip Code & Post Office Directory. For locating cities in states and for finding the ZIP code.

• City directory. Several firms produce directories, which are invaluable references for information about persons living in the community. A typical entry will have the following information: correct full name, occupation and employer, complete street address including apartment number, husband's or wife's name and initial, homeowner, whether the person is retired, whether husband and wife are employed, whether the person is a student. Most of the directory firms include a street directory so that the reporter can find the name of the resident and his or her telephone number from a given address. Some directories are based on telephone numbers; given a number, the reporter can find the name of the telephone subscriber. The directory companies also make up classified business directories that list, at no charge, all businesses.

• Who's Who in America contains biographical information about 72,000 living North Americans and is an essential source for basic information about leaders in social, economic, cultural and political affairs. Biographical information is supplied by the person listed. Other biographical directories are published by the same firm, Marquis Who's Who Inc., including regional directories and those based on the biographee's profession. For biographies of long-dead persons, the Dictionary of American Biography is useful. For persons who have died within the last several years, back volumes of Who's Who can be consulted or Who Was Who or back volumes of Current Biography.

• Source book and futures book. Every reporter keeps a current address book of names, titles, addresses and telephone numbers from his or her beat. A date book or date pad listing future assignments and appointments—called a futures book—is also necessary.

• Stylebook. The new reporter should have the newspaper's or station's stylebook handy.

• Maps. Some reporters keep in their desks or have quick access to the city map or street directory and a mass transit map. A Rand McNally road atlas for the U.S., Canada and Mexico can be useful.

• Grammar. Deep in a drawer and consulted on the sly by a few journalists is a grammar, high school or college variety. Some reporters never do learn how to punctuate the question in a quote within a quote or the possessive of *Jones*. Grammatical errors can be embarrassing.

The list of references is endless. Some reporters make a habit of browsing through the *Congressional Record,* the daily account of congressional debate and activity. *The Federal Register,* another federal daily publication, lists the

Ms. Makes News. When *The New York Times* finally added *Ms.* to its stylebook its decision became news coast to coast. The newswire of Reuters reported: "After 15 years of sometimes heated debate with feminists over its style," the newspaper conceded "Ms. has become part of the language." The *Times,* the story reported, "is considered the leading arbiter of newspaper style in the United States."

actions of federal agencies, executive orders of the president and a variety of other actions. One area of special interest to journalists is the publication of petitions and forms of relief granted to special interests.

Government agencies have a variety of forms that groups and individuals file that are useful in investigative work. When the Sun Newspapers of Omaha investigated Boys Town and found that despite pleas of poverty the nonprofit organization had a $209 million investment portfolio, it relied on Form 990 that the institution filed with the Internal Revenue Service. Tax-exempt organizations file details of their finances on the 990.

To obtain Form 990, write the Disclosure Officer at the local IRS district office, giving the name of the organization, and mention that the newspaper or station will pay for copying expenses. Private foundations are exempted from disclosure.

The reporter's basic newsroom reference is, of course, the morgue or library. No story should be written without first checking the morgue. In many newsrooms, what used to be newspaper clippings are now electronic impulses; material can be retrieved and shown on the terminal screen.

Data Bases

When a Russian airplane shot down a Korean airliner, newspapers and stations needed background information—fast. Some were able to have the material on their screens within minutes by using a data base. The data base is an electronic library that is accessible through on-line computers. In this case, the reporters and editors searching for background typed in the words *Korean Air Lines*. The data base computer scanned thousands of stories for the words and in less than a minute a list of articles was available.

There are three kinds of data bases:

- Full texts of news stories, magazine articles and documents.
- Bibliographic material that refers to magazine and newspaper articles, government reports and scholarly articles. Some bibliographic data bases provide only references, and others give summaries of the articles as well as the references.
- Numeric data bases contain census data, statistics and a variety of demographic material.

Rapid Growth. By the end of 1986, there were more than 3,200 data bases available through 490 on-line services. The number of data bases is growing at the rate of 35 percent a year.

Vu/Text, which claims it is the "nation's largest full text newspaper databank," gives its clients access to *The Washington Post, The Boston Globe, The Philadelphia Inquirer* and other newspapers. Nexis stores the full texts of 25 newspapers and wire services and almost 100 magazines and newsletters. Medline has about 4 million records and is a major source for biomedical material. For its story on herpes and a drug for the disease called Lysine, *The Providence Journal* used Medline. ERIC has almost half a million citations on education, and Lexis is a legal data base. For a story on a large company, a business reporter used a Dow Jones data base to obtain the SEC 10-K form on which businesses list ownership, finances and other information.

The data base can be expensive—$35 to $200 an hour—and mostly larger newspapers subscribe. Reporters whose newspapers do not have access to a data base usually can find some place in town with access. University and college libraries do data base searching; a law firm may be on Lexis.

Census Data

Census data provide much more than the national head count. Since the Bureau of the Census breaks down its count into census tracts of around 4,000 persons, vast amounts of information are available to the local reporter such as people's jobs, incomes and educational attainments. There is information about how many married women are living with their husbands, how many households are headed by females, median and average family incomes. The housing census has information about the types of dwellings in which people live, their bathing facilities and plumbing.

The reporter who wants to track social change in his or her community will find census data essential. Working mothers, children in nursery school, shifts in family patterns and demographic changes—data on all this are available. Reporters have used census data to find pockets of the elderly and concentrations of ethnic groups. Changes in the racial makeup of neighborhoods can be charted with census data.

For a story about the housing stock in the community, the reporter can find the number of houses that lack toilets, private baths and hot water. The number of persons living in housing units (density) can also be determined.

By analyzing who lives in a representative's district, it is possible to indicate how he or she is most likely to vote or to determine the pressures exerted on the legislator on public housing, Social Security and other social issues.

Printed census reports are available at public and university libraries and at many local, state and federal agencies. An investment of about $100 will purchase all the reports for a state. More detailed information is stored on computer tapes, and this, too, is available. Colleges and universities often have the tapes. If not, the Bureau of the Census, U.S. Department of Commerce, can help in locating the nearest tape center.

The Census Bureau makes a national population count every 10 years. It also conducts other counts continuously. The Bureau takes more than 250 sample surveys a year to monitor trends in employment, population growth, fertility, living arrangements and marriage patterns. It makes surveys of a number of activities every five years, including housing, agriculture, business, construction, government, manufacturing, mineral industry and transportation.

For information on what the census covers, write: Public Information Office, Bureau of the Census, Washington, D.C., 20233.

Family Income. The Census Bureau study of median family income in 1985 revealed:
White families—$29,152
Hispanic families—$19,027
Black families—$16,768

Death and Disease Data

Some of the best-kept official records are those for disease and death. Doctors, clinics and hospitals are required to keep scrupulous records, and these are sent to city and county health offices, which relay them to state and federal agencies.

Table 4.2 Infant Mortality Rates for Major Cities

City	Total	White	Black
Average	11.2	9.7	19.2
Baltimore	17.5	11.1	20.9
Boston	11.5	8.9	16.4
Chicago	17.7	11.2	24.9
Cleveland	16.5	14.5	18.2
Columbus	12.5	11.0	17.7
Dallas	12.4	10.6	16.5
Detroit	19.8	11.4	23.1
Houston	13.0	12.0	17.1
Indianapolis	14.9	12.4	22.0
Jacksonville	12.8	11.7	15.1
Los Angeles	12.8	10.8	22.2
Memphis	17.5	9.4	23.1
Milwaukee	12.7	10.6	16.6
New Orleans	17.6	9.2	21.0
New York City	13.6	11.8	17.3
Philadelphia	17.0	12.6	21.9
Phoenix	13.7	12.6	25.7
San Antonio	10.7	10.7	10.6
San Diego	10.4	9.8	20.2
San Francisco	11.3	13.2	17.7
San Jose	10.1	10.3	13.0
Washington, DC	19.3	11.6	21.3

The rate is calculated per 1,000 live births. Figures are for 1983 and are from the Mortality Statistics Branch, Division Vital Statistics, National Center for Health Statistics.

Since this information has been carefully kept for many years, it can provide the journalist with an insight into community health standards and care. In fact, infant mortality rates are sometimes described as the measure of a society's civilization. See table 4.2.

Reporters can compare their community's health care with that of cities of similar population. Internal comparisons can also be made since most local health agencies break the city into health districts. Middle-class districts can be compared with low-income districts, white with non-white. Age of mothers is also on record, and an enterprising reporter might find a relationship between teen-age pregnancy and infant mortality.

Table 4.3 Syphilis

	States			Cities	
	Average	29.0		Average	65.0
1	Florida	76.4	1	Atlanta*	221.3
2	Texas	70.6	2	San Francisco	201.2
3	Louisiana	66.0	3	New Orleans	167.5
4	Georgia	57.8	4	Newark	161.5
5	Mississippi	55.1	5	District of Columbia	158.0
6	South Carolina	49.8	6	Dallas*	138.3
7	New York	43.9	7	Miami*	137.2
8	California	43.5	8	Houston	124.1
9	Alabama	34.5	9	Charlotte	118.8
10	Maryland	29.9	10	Corpus Christi*	112.1

Number of cases per 100,000 population.
*County data or equivalent.

One reporter noticed a short wire story reporting that Atlanta had a higher rate of syphilis and gonorrhea than any other city and that there were more than 875,000 reported cases of gonorrhea in the nation and almost 70,000 cases of syphilis during the year. The source was the Disease Control Center and the dateline was Atlanta, Ga.

To find out how his city ranked in these diseases (which local doctors had described as being at epidemic proportions), he wrote the Center for information. Tables 4.3 and 4.4 contain figures for 1984.

For morbidity reports on notifiable diseases—sexually transmitted diseases, tuberculosis, childhood diseases—write or call:

Disease Control Center
Atlanta, Georgia 30333
(Phone: 404 329-3761)

For data on death such as infant mortality rates write:

Scientific and Technical Information Branch
Division of Operations
National Center for Health Statistics
3700 East-West Highway
Hyattsville, Maryland 20782
(Phone: 301 436-8500)

Table 4.4 Gonorrhea

	States			Cities	
	Average	374.8		Average	760.0
1	Georgia	743.2	1	Atlanta*	2554.4
2	Delaware	666.6	2	District of Columbia	2476.8
3	South Carolina	666.1	3	Baltimore	2220.0
4	Maryland	659.4	4	St. Louis	1871.4
5	Tennessee	654.9	5	Newark	1863.1
6	Alaska	616.2	6	Memphis*	1779.0
7	Alabama	578.8	7	New Orleans	1713.7
8	North Carolina	567.8	8	Charlotte	1567.4
9	Louisiana	554.4	9	Cleveland	1520.2
10	Mississippi	506.6	10	Richmond	1492.9

Number of cases per 100,000 population
*County data or equivalent

Public Records

Reporters should know just what records are available to them on their beats. Among the many records usually accessible to the public are:

Assessment and tax records, deeds, property transfers.

Records dealing with licenses—restaurant, dog, liquor, tavern and the many other business and professional licenses.

City engineer's records—streets, alleys, property lines, highways.

City building permits, variances.

Automobile ownership.

Election returns.

Articles of incorporation. Some states do not require officers to file their names; most do. Partnerships.

Bills and vouchers for all governmental purchases. Copies of the checks (warrants) paid out for goods and services.

Minutes of city council, county commission meetings. All appropriations, budgets.

Most records in judicial area—indictments, trials, sentences, court transcripts.

Wills, receiverships, bankruptcies.

Most police records on a current basis. There are limits to arrest records.

Reporters sometimes discover that public records are denied to the public and to reporters. A check of the law helps to open them up. Half the states have "sunshine laws" that require records be available for public examination.

For information on legislation in the House or Senate, call 202 225–1772.
For information on when a bill was signed or vetoed, call 202 456–2226.
For tapes of proceedings on the floors of Congress:

	Senate	House
Democratic	202 224–8541	202 225–7400
Republican	202 224–8601	202 225–7430

To obtain documents from the Government Printing Office, write:

Superintendent of Documents
U.S. Government Printing Office
Washington, D.C. 20402
(202 783–3238)

Freedom of Information Act

Access to one of the vast areas of information—federal records—had been limited until Congress enacted the Freedom of Information Act in 1966. The act, and important amendments in 1975, unlocked millions of pages of federal documents. The FOIA states that the public has the right to inspect any document that the executive branch possesses, with nine exceptions. These exceptions prevent reporters, or anyone else, from examining income tax returns, secret documents vital to national defense or foreign policy, intra-agency letters and other sensitive material.

The 1975 amendments give the federal courts the power to review classified documents to make sure that they are properly classified, and they put a limit on the time an agency can take to reply to a request.

The *Mercury-News* in San Jose, Calif., used a Freedom of Information request to the FBI to obtain material that revealed that President Reagan had been an FBI informer in the late 1940s. The documents obtained by the newspaper identified Reagan as "T-10" and said that he and his first wife had "provided the FBI with names of actors they believed were members of a clique with a pro-Communist line." The *Mercury-News* also learned from FBI files on the author John Steinbeck that the FBI had tracked Steinbeck for years because of his involvement with labor causes. Steinbeck wrote *The Grapes of Wrath,* which won the Pulitzer Prize for literature in 1940.

To use the act, find out which agency has the records sought. A guide is the *U.S. Government Manual,* which may be obtained from the Government Printing Office. Ask for Stock Number D22–003–00424–8. Requests usually should be sent to the Freedom of Information Office of the agency. No reason need be given for the request for information, but it sometimes makes the request easier to handle if specific information is requested. Charges are usually nominal. The reporter may ask for charges in advance of any work by the agency.

The letter should state that the request is being made "under the provisions of the Freedom of Information Act, 5 U.S.C. 552." See Appendix B for the request procedure and a sample letter.

Under Attack. The Reagan administration forcefully attacked the FOIA and sought revisions to what William Safire, a *New York Times* political columnist, says is legislation that "has done more to inhibit the abuse of government power and to protect the citizen from unlawful snooping and arrogant harrassment than any legislation in our lifetime."

State Laws

Most states have enacted open records and open meetings laws. Usually, these laws presume that everything public and official is open with stipulated exceptions. Most denials of requests for records fall into these categories:

1. *Confidential records.* Those records that are exempted by federal or state law such as income tax returns, health and welfare files on individuals.
2. *Privacy.* Records that would allow an unwarranted invasion of an individual's privacy. (Officials have less right of privacy than private individuals.)
3. *Collective bargaining negotiations.* Disclosure of present or imminent actions in these areas could impair discussions.
4. *Trade secrets* that might injure a person or firm in a competitive situation.
5. *Records compiled for law enforcement agencies* that would impede a fair trial, endanger the life or safety of an agent or an informer.
6. *Inter-agency memoranda and intra-agency reports* except statistics, policies and instructions to the staff.
7. *Examinations and evaluations* that will be used again in assessing job applicants.

The states' open meetings laws exempt executive sessions that are concerned with collective bargaining, imminent legislation, the medical, financial or credit records of a person or corporation and any matters made confidential by state and federal law.

Mathematics for the Reporter

The UPI dispatch read:

> The average American who lives to the age of 70 consumes in that lifetime the equivalent of 150 cattle, 24,000 chickens, 225 lambs, 26 sheep, 310 hogs, 26 acres of grain and 50 acres of fruits and vegetables.

A Nevada newspaper reader who saw the story was puzzled. That seemed like a lot of meat to consume in a lifetime, he thought. He consulted his butcher who estimated the dressed weights of the various animals. They came up with a total of 222,695 pounds of meat. The reader wrote the UPI that he then did some figuring. He multiplied 70 years by 365 days to find the total number of days in the person's lifetime. The figure was 25,500 days. He divided the total meat consumption of 222,695 pounds by the number of days. "That figures out to a whopping 8.7 pounds of meat a day," he wrote.

The UPI retired the reference work from which the item was gleaned.

We live in an age of quantification. Everyone shoots figures at us. Take the police reporter. Looking over the annual report of the police department, he is awash in a sea of data. One figure seems to stand out. The number of arrests for violent crimes declined from 22,560 two years ago to 17,030 last year. That seems a sharp drop, so he decides to make it the lead of his piece. He tells his city editor his plan, and the editor cautions him: "Don't give us the raw numbers in the lead."

The reporter knows what his editor wants, a percentage decrease. By subtracting 17,030 from 22,560, the reporter obtains the decline last year. He puts his subtraction over the original figure, 22,560, to obtain the percentage drop, almost 25 percent. Not only is the percentage easier for the reader to grasp, it makes a good headline.

"An estimated 50 million Americans smoked 600 billion cigarettes last year," the story about a local anti-smoking measure said. The city editor looked up and called the reporter handling the story to the desk.

"Let's put this and a lot of the other figures into some understandable terms," he told the reporter. "In this case, why not follow the sentence with one that says, 'This means the average smoker lit up so many cigarettes a day.' "

Back at his desk, the reporter makes a few simple calculations: 600 billion cigarettes smoked a year ÷ 50 million smokers = 12,000 cigarettes per smoker a year.

We want average daily use, so we make the next calculation: 12,000 cigarettes a year ÷ 365 days = 32.87 cigarettes per smoker a day.

The reporter rounds that off to 33 . A reader can see the smoker crumpling up a pack and smoking halfway through a second pack for his daily dose. This is more graphic than the millions and billions, which depersonalize the story.

Since 1970, when the first electronic editing terminal was placed in the newsroom of *Today* in Cocoa, Fla., newspapers and the UPI and the AP have replaced reporters' typewriters and editors' pencils with video terminals. Some of the smaller newspapers have two or three terminals. *The Sun* in Baltimore has more than 75, *The New York Times* more than 300.

The terminal is an electric typewriter keyboard with an 11-inch television screen that replaces copy paper. As the reporter types a story on the keyboard, the story appears on the screen and is recorded in a central computer, called a controller. All the terminals in the newsroom are wired to the controller, and copy stored there can be called back by reporters or editors. The reporter can make changes by moving the copy with some of the keys (called scrolling) and by using other keys to erase letters and words. Copy editors also insert or delete material by using these keys. Paragraphs can be moved around with equal ease.

Newsday's computer allows reporters to use the keyboard for mathematical figuring—it adds, subtracts, multiplies and divides. It can also be used to store the telephone numbers of sources as well as their names and addresses.

The Electronic Newsroom

Some reporters say that the computer has made for better stories, if for no other reason than that the computerization of the newsroom has speeded up the process of producing a newspaper. A reporter has more time to write the story since deadlines can be moved back. The time-consuming process of setting stories in type is replaced by the reporter's own hand; with the VDT, the reporter has copy ready for editing and for photocomposition.

The computer is also used to store and retrieve information. Newspaper libraries and data banks provide reporters with vast amounts of information at a touch of their fingers.

Computer-Aided News Stories

The computer can be used to help pattern and analyze large quantities of information. It is especially helpful with polling data. In a presidential race, information from 1,300 people about their preferences—along with age, party, education, race, religion, address and other demographic data—is fed into a computer. The reporter can determine quickly how those over 45 say they would vote, the party loyalty factor, how those with a college education say they will vote and so on. Usually, such polls also ask for information on specific issues— the person's feelings about abortion, the death penalty, a nuclear freeze. The computer will feed out information on what percentage of those against abortion would favor the Democratic candidate, for example.

When the 1980 census data became available, *Newsday* fed demographic information into its computer and was able to show how black and Hispanic ghetto areas were growing in predominantly white sections of Long Island.

The Philadelphia Inquirer has used its computer to check the performance of judges, analyzing how judges treated white defendants and black defendants accused of the same offense.

In Florida, *The Miami Herald,* the Orlando *Sentinel Star* and the *St. Petersburg Times* joined to computerize campaign contributions to Florida officials. Each time a politician seeking a statewide office reports a contribution—a requirement of Florida law—the contributor's name and amount goes into the data base in the Florida State University computer that the newspapers use. The computer checks the name of the campaign donor against the names of previous contributors, directors of Florida corporations, registered lobbyists, real estate brokers and others likely to be interested in a friend in the state capital.

"The politician who regulates banks in Florida (the comptroller) has received contributions from people connected with banks whom we would have failed to identify that way without the computer's help," said Patrick Riordan of the *Herald.* "I wrote about a bank that had six of its nine directors and two of its officers make donations. That wasn't evident in the paper forms filed."

Many contributors, he found, cloaked their affiliations. But the computer turned up their relationships once the names were fed into it.

The Arizona Daily Star in Tucson used a software program called dBase II to analyze fatal traffic accidents. The analysis helped the newspaper to decide to support a bond issue on street lighting.

Since many governmental units now have computers, reporters have access to an enormous range of information. The police reporter can find out quickly the precincts with the highest percentage of violent crime and then obtain data on unemployment and welfare in the same areas. This information can then be fed into the newspaper computer to find correlations. Some officials will give reporters their computer printouts for use by the newspaper.

The federal government also makes computers, computer tapes and computer printouts available to reporters. The U.S. Census Bureau sells tapes at nominal cost.

The computer is being used on a number of newspapers to store the newspaper library. This allows a reporter who is working on a story about a candidate for mayor, for example, to call up on the VDT screen all the clips on the candidate.

TV Revolution

The new technology has had considerable impact in the television newsroom as well. With portable earth stations that can send a signal from a news location to a satellite that beams the signal to TV sets, television is able to cover with great speed a wide variety of events. "It's no longer unusual," said Ted Koppel of ABC News, "to have a local station in Chicago have someone reporting from the Middle East, or a station in Texas have someone reporting from Mexico. Local newscasts are starting to look a great deal like the nightly network newscasts."

Television equipment is getting lighter, quicker, easier to move, said Richard Wald, senior vice president of ABC News. Events that had been difficult or too expensive to cover are now accessible to even the smaller stations.

Home Information Retrieval

News, as well as other information, can be delivered on request to the home. The delivery of text and graphic messages on the computer monitor is the subject of experimentation in almost 100 areas around the world.

The users of such a system can call up on their home terminals a vast array of information in addition to news—sports, stock market closings, travel conditions, weather, display advertising and more.

"We can update the information constantly so people don't have to wait for the traditional newspaper," says an official of a videotex firm. Viewers have access to 3,000 pages of information every 24 seconds on these systems.

The Systems

Videotex is described as "two-way interactivity." That is, the person using the modified television set or computer in the home can request news, weather information, sports results, or advertising from a central computer where information in the form of pages is stored and requests are processed. Videotex uses two-way cable or telephone lines.

Teletext is "one-way interactivity." With this system, the viewer uses a special decoder to intercept the pages he or she wants. The teletext system gives the appearance of interactivity, but it is actually a one-way transmission of data. Teletext uses over-the-air broadcasting or cable TV.

Cable news or **cable text** is the system some newspapers and cable companies are using to send out news, sports, weather and stock market information to homes hooked into the cable. The channels offer written text, graphics and advertising on a regular schedule. News is often provided by newspapers and delivery by the cable station.

Hailed as a new way to deliver the news, videotex and teletext have fallen short of expectations. "People thought videotex was going to be an electronic newspaper," said Reide Ashe, the head of Viewtron. "It's something else, but we're not sure what yet." Viewtron, the Knight-Ridder cable system, lost more than $50 million in trying to find out what it was, and in 1986 decided to call it quits, shortly after the Times Mirror folded its Gateway videotex service. Time Inc. spent more than $30 million on a 5,000-page satellite-delivered cable teletext service in 1982 and then ditched the project. It found people in test homes had little interest in the service. Also, decoders were too expensive. Decoders cost from $300 to $1000. When they cost $10 or $20, the systems may become successful, says Paul Bortz, a consultant in the field.

Public Opinion Polling

The news was about the budget, taxes and the battle between Congress and the president. The political season was warming up also. Would the people support or repudiate the president in the congressional elections?

In the past, the answer derived from taking the public pulse was hardly convincing. Reporters would chat with political leaders, those supposedly perceptive insiders with delicate olfactory nerves attuned to the mildest of political breezes. Some voters might be interviewed. The result might be interesting reading, but it had no predictive value whatsoever.

Now, the science of polling and surveying gives the journalist a surer hand to reach into areas of coverage that had been handled with impressions and conjecture.

Polls are used for a variety of stories. The well-designed poll can tell a reporter with a fair degree of accuracy not only what people think of a president's performance but also whether a proposed school bond issue is popular in a middle-class section of the community or what types of day care are favored by working mothers. Polls have been used to determine whether Catholics approve of abortion, how people feel about the death penalty, what blacks think of affirmative action. *The New York Times* even ran a poll that established that 87 percent of 3- to 10-year-olds believe in Santa Claus.

Realizing the value of polls and surveys, many newspapers and television stations have hired pollsters and polling organizations. The reporter is still essential, for the poll can only supply the information. The reporter must make the poll into news. To do this, he or she must understand how polls work and their possibilities and limits.

The poll is a systematic way of finding out what people are thinking at a given time. It can provide a fairly accurate stop-action photo of a situation. This does not mean that all polling data given the journalist should be taken at face value. There are some inherent problems in polling, and there are pollsters whose purpose is to sell their clients. Reporters who understand polls know what to accept, what to discard. Reporters who are overwhelmed by data, who believe there is some mystery about figures, will be victimized, just as they can be misled by any public relations gimmick.

Polls are "able to establish with great accuracy the extent to which an opinion is held, and they can successfully predict behavior over the short run," writes Sheldon S. Wolin of the Department of Politics at Princeton University. "Once the period is extended," he cautions, "the reliability of the findings diminishes rapidly."

There are hundreds of polling organizations and firms. The majority are local groups that conduct marketing surveys. The big firms—Gallup, Harris, Roper and others—handle commercial clients, too, but are best-known for their political polls and surveys which, although they are not too profitable, give the organizations considerable publicity. It is this political polling that so often finds its way into newspapers and news broadcasts. During a political campaign, as much as one-third to one-half of the news is about the public's reaction to a candidate or an issue.

Unfortunately, the emphasis on predicting winners, on who's ahead rather than on interpreting the data leads to the waste of huge amounts of fascinating material about how people are voting and why, whether some groups—blacks, Jews, Irish Catholics, Swedes, farmers, government employees—have switched their traditional allegiances, for example.

The Gallup Poll found some interesting vote patterns in the Reagan-Mondale election: 64 percent of male voters said they voted for Reagan, whereas 55 percent of the female voters voted for him; 61 percent of the voters with a college education voted for Reagan compared with 49 percent of those with a grade school education; the traditionally Democratic South gave Reagan his largest vote, 63 percent, of any region; Reagan received almost half (48 percent) of the vote from union families.

The Gallup Poll forecast a 59–41 percent Reagan victory, and the Harris Survey predicted a 56–44 percent result. In the election Reagan received 59 percent of the vote.

Although reputable pollsters pretest their questions to make sure they test precisely what the pollster desires, ambiguities do creep in. Reporters should always examine the questions behind the polling data to make sure that they are clear and, for polls conducted for private clients, to ascertain whether they are loaded.

Sometimes, polling on the same issue by different pollsters may lead to slightly different results because of the way questions are worded. The interpretation of words by pollsters may also be controversial. During the Nixon administration, the White House objected to the way the Harris organization evaluated its polls of Nixon's public rating. The Harris polls asked people to rate the president's performance as excellent, pretty good, fair and poor. It counted fair and poor replies as negative assessments. The White House complained that *fair* was a positive word.

Types of Polls

The first check a reporter makes of polling material is a determination of how the poll was conducted. There are a variety of ways to elicit information from the public, some of them unreliable, some less reliable than others.

The coupon poll is just about worthless. People are asked to clip, fill out and mail a coupon that appears in the newspaper. The results are distorted because the person who goes to all that trouble—including paying for postage—is usually someone with strong feelings about the subject and hardly representative of the general population.

The call-in poll, in which readers or viewers are asked to express their sentiments about an issue by telephoning the newspaper or station, is subject to the same criticism as the coupon poll. When the San Francisco *Chronicle* conducted a call-in poll on the death sentence, it headlined the results on page one. Not surprisingly, three-fourths of those calling favored the death penalty. The newspaper did tell its readers that the poll had limited value. In the 12th paragraph of the story, the reporter wrote:

> The Chronicle Poll is not designed scientifically, for it does not use the standard sampling techniques that major opinion surveys use. It does, however, provide readers with an opportunity to express their opinions on topics of current interest.

The straw poll is no more reliable, although some newspapers have been using this technique for many years. For a straw poll, a person hands out ballots at one or more locations. People then drop their ballots into a box at the spot. It is difficult to keep the straw poll from being over-represented by the people in the one or two locations selected—usually supermarkets, factory gates and the like. The *Daily News,* which conducts straw polls for New York and national elections, uses a professional pollster to organize its straw locations.

The man-in-the-street poll is probably the most frequently used technique to gather opinions at the local level. Newspapers and stations without access to their own polling apparatus will send reporters out to interview persons about a candidate or an issue. Those who have had to do this kind of reporting know how non-representative the persons interviewed are. Reporters may seek out persons who look as though they can supply a quick answer, those who do not need to have the question explained to them. Reporters may stay away from those who are poorly dressed, members of minority groups.

These polls can be used so long as the story says precisely what they are—the opinions of a scattering of people, no more than that, no more scientific than astrology. The sample of people interviewed in such polling is known as a "non-probability sample," meaning that the conclusions cannot be generalized to the population at large.

A good poll, says Professor Penn T. Kimball of the Graduate School of Journalism at Columbia University, who was associated with the Harris organization, should be done at night and over weekends, not just during the day. Also, he says, it is best to poll persons in their homes rather than on the street. "The point is that a sound sample is based on home addresses from which flow census data, voting statistics and other vital information for interpreting the data," he says.

Some polls are conducted this way, by home interviews, and they are usually more reliable than the catch-as-catch-can polling techniques of the straw poll or man-in-the-street interviews. Polling by telephone is done to save time and money, although many Americans do not have phones. There is some debate over the relative merits of the telephone poll vs. the door-to-door poll.

To reach its conclusions about how well adults around the country thought the president was handling his problems, *The New York Times*/CBS Poll spoke to 1,422 persons by telephone. At first glance, this seems madness. To pass off the opinions of fewer than 1,500 people as representative of more than 100 million adults seems folly. Yet if the sample is selected carefully, the questions properly put, the results stated fairly and completely, and the interpretations made with discernment, a sample of around 1,500 persons can reflect accurately the opinions of people across the country with a margin of error of about 3 percentage points (see Appendix B, "Public Opinion Polling Checklist").

The Literary Digest Disaster

You would think that a poll that asked the opinions of well over two million persons would be accurate. But the most disastrously wrong election prediction relied on 2,376,523 replies and was 20 percent off.

In 1936, the *Literary Digest* set out to forecast the presidential contest between Franklin D. Roosevelt and Alf Landon. The *Digest* selected names from telephone subscriber lists and automobile registration lists and mailed out straw ballots to 10 million persons on the lists.

This was a classic example of quantity over quality. The numbers were huge, but the persons selected were hardly a good sample of the voting population. The poll was taken during the height of the Depression, when few persons could afford a car or a telephone. The sample thus was tipped toward persons who were likely to favor the conservative candidate, Landon, rather than the candidate who was campaigning for social and economic reforms, Roosevelt. This is just the result the *Digest* obtained: A Landon victory.

Roosevelt easily swept into office, carrying every state but Maine and Vermont.

Telephone polling is still with us. Television stations ask people to call in their votes on a variety of issues. When used for an indication of voter sentiment, however, the polls are biased against the same kind of voter overlooked in the *Literary Digest* poll—the poor. The reason: The telephone company charges 50 cents a call to record a vote or viewpoint. (Also, non-voters are not screened from voters, and usually there is no limit on the number of calls a person may make.)

Projecting Elections. By using a combination of exit polling, votes in key precincts and general raw vote data it is possible to project an election winner before all the polls have closed. The television networks have used this technique with considerable success.

In exit polling, key precincts are selected and interviewers told to talk to every fifth or tenth person. Data is collected about age, sex, race, political affiliation and attitude on issues as well as the way the person voted. The general information also allows the pollster to indicate trends, such as how blacks or women voted and why.

The Sample

Obviously, if a small group is to speak for the many, that group must be carefully chosen so that it is representative of the larger group. The key word here is representative.

If we want to know what people think of an incumbent governor, we can interview voters and non-voters. But if we want to know whether people will vote for him for re-election it is common sense to interview eligible voters, those who have registered. But we cannot stop there. If we went out in the daytime to supermarkets, laundromats and parks where mothers gather with their young children our sample would be skewed heavily toward women. That would be a non-representative sample since men constitute a large percentage of voters.

Samples are selected in a number of ways. *The New York Times*/CBS Poll sample of telephone exchanges was selected by a computer from a complete list of exchanges around the country. The exchanges were chosen in such a way that each region of the United States was represented in proportion to its population.

Once the exchanges were selected, the telephone numbers were formed by random digits. This guaranteed that unlisted as well as listed numbers would be included in the sample.

The making of this sample demonstrates how pollsters try to eliminate the human factor from the choice of those who will be interviewed. The concept of a good sample is that it should give everyone in the population we are trying to learn something about a chance to be included in our poll. This is what is meant by the term *random sample*. To the average person, the word *random* usually means haphazard, without plan. Pollsters use it to mean that the sample guarantees that any of those in the larger population group have as good a chance to be polled as anyone else in that group.

Once the sample has been drawn, it is then weighted to adjust for sample variations. In the *Times*/CBS Poll of the president's popularity, the sample consisted of 445 persons who told the pollsters making the calls that they were Democrats, 482 who said they were Republicans and 495 who said they were independents. For the opinions of Republicans, the sample was adequate. But to reflect the opinions of the general population, using the breakdown in the sample would over-represent the Republicans. To reflect the known proportion of party members in the voting population, the groups of voters were then weighted by party identification.

The poll also weighted the results to take account of household size and to adjust for variations in the sample relating to religion, race, age, sex and education. This weighting was done in accordance with what is known of the characteristics of the adult population from the results of the last election, the proportion of men and women in the population, census figures on nationality, religion, income and so on. The raw figures are adjusted to eliminate distortions from the norm.

Despite our first inclination to think that the more persons interviewed the more accurate the results will be, the statistical truth is that it is as much the quality of the sample that determines the accuracy of the poll. After a critical number of interviews have been conducted, little additional accuracy is achieved by huge quantities of additional interviews. Results based on a good sample successfully interviewed are adequate for most purposes. After all, polls say no more than at the time the poll was taken, this is what people said they would do, or this is what they said they were thinking.

The numbers can be too small to provide an accurate indication of public opinion. In 1986, *The New York Times* reported President Reagan had an approval rating among blacks of 56 percent. That struck even the politically unaware as strange. It turned out that only 110 blacks had been interviewed—a margin of error of about 10 percentage points. An ABC News/*Washington Post* poll in the same period found 63 percent of blacks disapproved of Reagan's handling of the presidency, and 56 percent thought of him as a racist. This poll contacted 1,022 black men and women—less than a 4 percent margin of error.

Winners and Losers

Journalists must be careful about their tendency to heed the demands of readers and listeners for definitive opinions and for winners and losers. A poll can only state what people say they are thinking or how voters say they will vote at the time they are polled, and sometimes even then the opinions and races are too close to call.

Journalists should remember: People change their minds; polls cannot guarantee that behavior will be consistent with intentions.

Reputable pollsters know just how far they can take their data. But they are often under pressure to pick winners in election contests. When pre-election polls indicate a 60–40 percent breakdown, a pollster feels at ease in choosing the winner. But when an editor, reflecting the desire of readers and listeners, asks for a choice in a 44–42 race with 14 percent undecided, then trouble lies ahead.

Although editors and broadcast producers tend to be most interested in the top of the poll—who's ahead—most of the significant material in the poll usually is found in why the candidate is ahead or behind and how the candidate is faring with certain groups. This can make interesting and significant news. There may be a good story in the candidate who does well with a certain religious group and poorly with another because of his or her stand on abortion or prayer in schools.

Preparing Copy

Students preparing stories on typewriters should use the copy editing symbols in figure 4.1 to correct copy.

Copy Editing Symbols

Spell out	The (PHA) is pushing for the extension, viewing	The Pittsfield Housing Authority is pushing . . .
Transpose	it as the final link in its urban|road|renewal|	. . . urban renewal road
Begin new paragraph	network.⌊If undertaken, the city is planning	network. If undertaken, the city . . .
Delete letter	to work in conjunction with a neighbo(u)rhood	. . . a neighborhood
Restore marked-out or hard-to-read material	revitalization program for the three-block area *that is* ~~that is~~ affected.	that is affected.
Change to lower case	The S̸tate and F̸ederal governments would pay	The state and federal governments would pay
Separate words	for|the road work.	for the road work.
Abbreviate	The (Pittsfield Housing Authority) says that	The PHA says that
Insert	five houses would be taken by the proj‸et with	. . . by the project with
Spell out	a possibility that as many as ⑧ more would	. . . eight more would
Delete material; close up	have to ~~eventually~~ come down.	have to come down.
Indent for paragraph	⌊The finite takings involve buildings at 90	The finite takings . . .
Capitalize	summer st., 83 and 90 Union St., and 88 and 95	Summer St., 83 and 90 . . .
Run in, or bring copy together	Bradford St. ⏋ ⌞Of the five, only one is a single-family home.	Bradford St. Of the five, only one is a single-family home.
Punctuation	The others are multiple‾family dwellings. ‸	. . . multiple-family dwellings.

Figure 4.1

Preparing Copy for Print on the Typewriter

A. Use copy paper, newsprint or some other non-glossy paper; triple space; leave adequate margins left and right.

B. Make a carbon of all your work. Retain the carbon.

C. In the upper left-hand corner of the first sheet of all assignments, place your name, slug of story, news source, and date. Thus:

Goldstein
PHA-attended
2/25/87

D. Begin one-third down the first page. Write on one side of the paper only.

E. If the story consists of more than one page, write "more" at the bottom of the page, circle it. On the next page, place your name, "2", and slug at top left of the page. Thus: "Goldstein-2-PHA."

F. End each page with a paragraph, not in the middle of a sentence.

G. Do not correct mistakes by backspacing and writing over. Cross out and retype. Never write over. Use copyediting symbols to make changes.

H. Never divide words at the end of the line. Hit margin release and continue, or cross out and begin word anew on next line.

I. Keep copy clean. Retype hard-to-read sections and paste over.

J. Do not write more than one story on each sheet of paper.

K. Follow the stylebook.

L. End stories with end mark: 30, # or END.

M. When finished, fold all pages together, in half, copy on the outside, reporter's name in the upper left.

VDT

Because most newspapers do not use typewriters, students should be prepared to handle the VDT.

Briefly, the terminal consists of a keyboard and screen. Raw copy is typed into the terminal on the keyboard. Before the story is typed, the reporter must enter various typesetting parameters. The parameters are instructions on size of the type, line length, typeface and spacing.

Copy is typed into the machine continuously. The computer or the disk justifies lines automatically. When the reporter makes a mistake, the cursor is used—a movable block of light that can be placed anywhere on the screen to make insertions, deletions and corrections.

As the story is typed, it is read on the screen. When the reporter has a long story, the previous material is stored in the computer or disk and can be recalled for examination by the reporter's scrolling the story (moving the type up or down on the screen). A list of computer terms and their definitions is included in the glossary at the end of the book.

Barzun, Jacques, and Henry F. Graff. *The Modern Researcher.* New York: Harcourt Brace Jovanovich, 1985.

Huff, Darrell, and Irving E. Gers. *How to Lie With Statistics.* New York: Norton, 1954.

McCormick, Mona. *The New York Times Guide to Reference Materials.* New York: Times Books, 1985.

Meyer, Philip. *Precision Journalism.* Bloomington: Indiana University Press, 1973.

Williams, Frederick. *Reasoning With Statistics.* New York: Holt, Rinehart and Winston, 1968.

Further Reading

CHAPTER FIVE

The Structure of the News Story

Preview

Planning precedes writing. Reporters see the news story as an organized whole; each paragraph is placed to suit a purpose. Even while reporting their stories, reporters try to visualize what they will write, especially the beginning of the story, the lead. The lead contains the subject or theme of the story and gives the story its structure, because the story is built on this theme.

News stories have a linear structure:

• The beginning includes a summary of the most important material. It tells the reader what to expect.

• The remainder of the story—the body—amplifies, buttresses, gives examples and explains the beginning. It also contains background and secondary material.

First the idea. Then the words.

As the young reporter struggled with his story he recalled this advice that his city editor had given him the day before. He had written the obituary of a Denver banker in 45 minutes and had been proud of his speed. But the editor had said that the story was disorganized. Then, the editor had offered him the advice about writing. Remembering the editor's comment, the reporter read his story carefully. Yes, he was writing without a firm idea of what he wanted to say and how it would fit together.

Suddenly, he was struck by what he had just told himself: "What do I want to say? Where do I put it?" No one, not even his city editor, had told him that. But that was the key to putting his notes into some kind of structured shape.

• What do I want to say?
• Where does it go?

This reporter's discovery is made all the time by young journalists. Usually, it is followed by another revelation, that the news story form or structure is simple and that most stories fit into this structure:

- The lead.
- The material that explains and amplifies the lead.
- The necessary background.
- The secondary or less important material.

The city editor's advice about thinking before writing has been offered to generations of students. As an essay in the *Fifth Reader,* a grade school textbook of the 1880s, puts it: "In learning to write, our first rule is: '*Know what you want to say.*'" (The italics are those of the author of the essay, Edward Everett Hale, the Boston clergyman who wrote the short story, "The Man Without a Country.") Hale had a second rule: "Say it. That is, do not begin by saying something else which you think will lead up to what you want to say."

Every writer who has written about the writer's craft—whether journalist, poet, novelist or critic—has understood these first principles of writing. George Orwell, the British journalist and novelist, was concerned that the English language was being endangered by unclear thinking. In an essay, "Politics and the English Language," he wrote that the first question scrupulous writers ask themselves before writing is: "What am I trying to say?"

In *The Elements of Style,* the "little book" that generations of college English students have used, authors William Strunk Jr. and E. B. White begin their section on writing this way: "Choose a suitable design and hold to it." They continue: "A basic structural design underlies every kind of writing. . . . The first principle of composition, therefore, is to foresee or determine the shape of what is to come, and pursue that shape."

Henry James, the American novelist, said without form "there is absolutely no substance." Form, he wrote, "*takes,* holds, and preserves, substance—saves it from the welter of helpless verbiage that we swim in as in a sea of tasteless tepid pudding, and that makes one ashamed of an art capable of such degradations."

Sometimes plans change. While writing, a reporter will develop new ideas, and the original plan has to be discarded. But even then a new plan should be substituted.

Essential as a plan would seem to be, many reporters start to write without one in mind. As a result, their stories exhibit one of the most common faults of journalistic writing—disorganization or lack of focus. Henry Fairlie, a British journalist, calls this deficiency "shapelessness." He attributes it to "an intellectual inability, on the part both of the reporter and copy editor, to master the story." This mastery, Fairlie says, must be put to use "before writing." Planning requires thinking the story through first.

As one journalism teacher has been telling his students for two decades: "You can't write if you can't think." Ambrose Bierce, a newspaperman and author of *The Devil's Dictionary,* described good writing as "clear thinking made visible."

The Basic Idea

Almost all writing is based on an observation, an emotion or an opinion that the writer wants to communicate. This basic idea may be put at or near the beginning of the piece as it usually is in a news story, or it may be tacked on at the end, as is a request for money for the flight home at Christmas in a student's letter to his or her parents. The basic idea is *always* there.

The news story has a beginning that sets out the basic idea or theme and a body that elaborates and explains the theme. In the language of journalism, the story's theme—its most significant fact or facts—is stated in the lead. Thus, when reporters attempt to form ideas for stories, they search for the lead of the piece. Fairlie describes the importance of the lead this way: "Every journalist who has ever struggled with [a lead] knows why it can take so much effort. It is as important to him as to the reader. Writing it concentrates the mind wonderfully, forcing him to decide what in the story is important, what he wants to emphasize, and can eventually give shape to the rest of the story as he writes it."

The hunt is not ended when the writer corners the lead, however. The reporter still has to identify material that explains, supports, buttresses and amplifies the lead before he or she can begin to write. Since most news events consist of more than the important action or actions singled out in the lead, the reporter also has to identify the secondary material that will have to be included.

Planning the Single-Element Story

A story that consists of one important action or is based on one major fact or idea is a single-element story. Also known as the single-incident story, it is the story handled most often by beginning reporters. The story requires:

- Lead.
- Explanatory and amplifying material.
- Background (if necessary).
- Secondary material (if any).

Story	Analysis

Thieves Get 36 Batteries

Thieves who entered a Charlotte auto parts store stole 36 Delco batteries, police were told yesterday.

Crowell Erskine, 49, manager of the Piedmont Auto Exchange at 410 Atando Ave., told officers the store was broken into between 5 p.m. Tuesday and 8 a.m. Wednesday by thieves knocking a hole in the rear wall of the one-story brick building.

Erskine said the batteries were valued at $539.18.

—*The Charlotte Observer*

1. The lead focuses on the basic idea, the theft of a batch of batteries. The reporter knows the reader opens the newspaper each day with the question: *What* happened today?

2. The reporter answers what he thinks will be the logical questions a reader might ask: *Where* did the break-in occur? *When* did it happen? *How* was it done? The answers to these questions explain and amplify the lead.

3. Background is provided. The reporter knows the reader will want to be told the value of the goods stolen.

Let us suppose that the break-in occurred in the police department's property room at headquarters. Then the lead would emphasize *where* the theft occurred. If the theft took place in broad daylight while shoppers thronged the streets, this fact—*when* the theft occurred—would go into the lead.

Had the thief scaled a 15-foot wall to gain entry, *how* the theft was managed would be placed in the lead.

If the thief left a note in the store apologizing for his act and saying he needed the money to pay medical bills for his sick wife, *why* the theft occurred—according to the thief—would be put into the lead.

The most important element always forms the basic idea for the lead. To find that basic element, the reporter anticipates the questions the reader will ask, and then goes about answering them. These questions have been summarized as *who, what, when, where, why* and *how*—the Five W's and an H.

A student was assigned to interview the chairman of the local United Way Campaign, which was in the middle of a fund drive. The reporter knew that the campaign issued weekly reports, and he thought that the midpoint of the drive might be a good time to check progress. Here is the story he turned in:

Burying the Lead

```
    The local United Way Campaign today issued its second
weekly report in its current campaign to raise $750,000 for
next year's activities.
    Tony Davis, the campaign chairman, said that donations
in the first two weeks had exceeded last year's fund raising
at a similar time.
```

> "We've collected $350,000, and that's about $25,000
> ahead of last year," Davis said. "Thanks to the work of our
> downtown volunteers, the local merchants have been
> canvassed more thoroughly than ever before, and their gifts
> have been very generous."
> The month-long drive seeks funds for 28 local
> organizations, including the Big Brothers, Senior Citizens
> House, and a new program to aid crippled children.

The story is clear but it has a glaring fault: What should have been the basic theme for the lead was placed in the second paragraph. Occasionally a reporter will intentionally delay the lead, usually for dramatic effect. This was no such instance. The most significant fact the student reporter gleaned from his reporting was that the campaign was running ahead of last year's receipts. And since this is a straightforward or spot news story, it should have gone in the lead. Given this advice by his instructor, the student wrote another story beginning this way:

> The United Way Campaign to raise $750,000 is running
> ahead of last year's drive at the midway point.
> Tony Davis, the campaign chairman, said today that in
> the first two weeks of the month-long fund drive $350,000
> had been collected. That is $25,000 ahead of last year's
> collections at this time.
> "Thanks to the work of our downtown volunteers, the
> local merchants have been . . ."

The same set of facts was given to a reporting and writing class. Here are some of the leads that emerged:

> Tony Davis, the chairman of the United Way Campaign,
> reported today that the fund drive is running ahead of
> schedule.

> The United Way Campaign has collected $350,000, which
> is $25,000 ahead of last year's drive at this time.

> Local merchants were credited today with helping to
> push the United Way Campaign closer and faster toward its
> goal of $750,000.

In each of these leads, the basic idea is the same: Collections are ahead of last year. This was the most important element and it had to be the basis of the lead, which determines the story's structure.

When five persons died at a fertilizer plant in Columbus, Ohio, the local newspaper and broadcast stations gave it saturation coverage. The next day, the story was still alive, and Donna Hanover of WTVN-TV in Columbus, who anchored the noon report, wrote this script. The news elements were the autopsy underway at the time of the newscast and the condition of two critically injured firemen.

A TV Story

```
INLAND PRODUCTS        DH/dn                    7/1 noon
                       Autopsies are underway at this
Silf: 40               hour on five victims of poison gas
A roll                 who died late yesterday afternoon
                       at Inland Products Corporation.
                       Two firemen who attempted rescues
                       are still in critical condition.
                       The accident apparently began when
                       an employee who was fixing a pump
                       fell 15 feet into a sludge pit
                       containing animal carcasses used
                       in making fertilizer. Three other
                       employees attempted rescues, not
                       realizing that bacteria in the
```

rotting carcasses were apparently
producing deadly hydrogen sulfide
gas. The first fireman into the pit
also died from the gas, which acts
like carbon monoxide, except that
it kills almost instantly. Inland
Products still refuses to comment
on the accident.

Storytelling

Hanover put at the beginning of her script the two news elements she considered most important. This is the structure for most stories of breaking news events—the most important action right at the beginning. Increasingly, reporters are using the storytelling structure. Here, the reporter begins with an example or an anecdote and then moves into the significant action.

Modern buildings of glass and steel mark the downtown section.

But the city's business is conducted in an old brick building that many residents liken to a warehouse.

Last night, city officials went shopping for a new city hall. They looked at a modern 10-story office building. . . .

The third paragraph contains the news element, the lead idea. The first two paragraphs relate a little tale. Nothing wrong with that.

But suppose the reporter is covering a fire in city hall that led to two deaths. This story must begin with the news of the deaths. That news cannot be delayed. The story's form or structure takes its shape from the nature of the event. Let's examine the story structure for spot news stories like the city hall fire.

The Wall Street Journal Formula

Here is a story structure the *Journal* uses:

Anecdote—Begin with an example or illustration of the theme.

Explicit statement of theme—The lead. It should be no lower than the sixth paragraph.

Statement of the significance of the theme—Answers the reader's question: Why should I be reading this?

Details—Proof, elaboration of the theme.

Answers to reader's questions—Why is this happening? What is being done about it?

The single-element story may contain several themes or ideas, but in this type of story the reporter decides that only one is worthy of the lead. A story of this kind may have the following structure:

Single-Element Story Structure

- Lead: Idea A.
- Explanatory material. Elaboration of Idea A.
- Secondary material. Sub-themes B, C, D, E.
- Background.
- Further elaboration of Idea A.

Short pieces written this way usually can be cut after the lead or two paragraphs, and longer pieces can be cut after a few paragraphs.

Multiple-element stories can be similarly edited because we write them the same way as the single-element story. The difference is that we place more than one basic idea high up in the story.

An event that has two or more major ideas or themes calls for a multiple-element story. The structure of the multiple-element story is:

Multiple-Element Story Structure

- Lead: Idea A, Idea B.
- Explanatory material. Elaboration of Idea A, Idea B.
- Secondary material. Sub-themes C, D, E, F.
- Background.
- Further elaboration of Idea A, Idea B.

Every multiple-element story may not be structured precisely in this order, but these five components invariably are included in the multiple-element story.

Here are 12 paragraphs from an election story that appeared in the *Daily News*. Seemingly complex, the story has a simple structure that is based on the two major story ideas: A. Rejection of the bond issue; B. Republican control of the Legislature.

Two-Element Story

Gov. Hughes Loses Bonds & Legislature

by Joseph McNamara

(1)   New Jersey Gov. Richard J. Hughes took a shellacking all around in yesterday's statewide election. The voters rejected the $750 million bond issue proposal on which he had hung much of his political prestige, and the Republicans gained control of both houses of the Legislature.

(2)   Hughes, who had warned during the campaign that if the bond issue were defeated he would ask the Legislature in January for a state income tax and sales tax to meet the state's financial needs, announced early today that he "may have to do some rethinking" about the size of the need. And he made it clear that the "rethinking" would increase his estimate of the amount required.

(3)   "I accept the verdict rendered by the people," he said in a written statement.

(1) The lead contains a colloquial phrase in the first sentence that the reporter felt would attract readers. The second sentence summarizes the two themes, A and B.

(2–8) These seven paragraphs refer to theme A. In 2, the reporter gives a possible consequence of the loss of the bond issue.

(2–8 cont.) In any election, vote tallies are essential, and the reporter supplies them in 5 and 6, which set up a good example in 7 of the extent of the governor's shellacking. In 8, the reporter gives a bit of background to A.

(9) Secondary information about other items on the ballot.

(10–12) Elaboration of theme B. Examples of specific races are given.

Behind from the Start

(4) The bond issue proposal, which was broken into two questions—one on institutions and the other on roads—trailed from the time the polls closed at 8 p.m. With the count in from 4,238 of the state's 4,533 districts, the tally early today was:

(5) Institutions: No. 868,586; Yes, 736,967.

(6) Highways: No. 866,204; Yes, 681,059.

(7) As a measure of Hughes' defeat, in the Democrats' Hudson County stronghold—where the Governor had hoped for a plurality of 150,000—he got only a 100,501 to 64,752 vote in favor of the institutional bonds and 93,654 to 66,099 in favor of the highway bonds.

(8) He had promised that if the bond issue were defeated, he would go before the Legislature in January and ask for a state income tax and a state sales tax to meet the state's obligations.

(9) Four other referendums had no great opposition, and passed easily.

They were on voter residency requirements, a tax break on farm land and a change in exemptions from the ratables to the finished tax for both veterans and the elderly.

(10) The Republicans have controlled the State Senate for the last half century, and smashing victories yesterday in crucial Essex, Burlington and Camden Counties increased their majority—which had shrunk to a hairsbreadth 11-10—to two-thirds.

(11) Democrats swamped in the avalanche included Gov. Hughes' brother-in-law Sen. Edward J. Hulse of Burlington County. He was unseated by Republican Edwin B. Forsythe who ran up a convincing 6,000-vote majority.

(12) In populous Essex County, Republican C. Robert Sarcone defeated Democrat Elmer M. Matthews—who conceded shortly after 11 p.m. without waiting for the final count. And in Camden County, Republican Frederick J. Scholz unseated incumbent Joseph W. Cowgill. . . .

Three-Element Story

The following is an example of a story that begins with a three-element lead. The reporter would have singled out one element for the lead had she felt that one was the most important of the three. She decided the three were of equal importance.

Study Links 3 Factors to Heart Ills

By Jane E. Brody

(1) The lead has a three-part theme: A study concludes that smoking, A; overweight, B; and physical inactivity, C, increase risk of heart disease.

(2) Brody tells the reader the source of the material, where it came from, and then gives more information about theme A.

(3) More detail on A.

(4) Here she jumps to C, physical inactivity. It might have been better to have followed the A, B, C order.

(5) More on physical inactivity.

(1) A new study conducted among 110,000 adult members of the Health Insurance Plan of Greater New York has once again demonstrated that smoking, an overweight condition and physical inactivity are associated with a greatly increased risk of death and disability from heart disease.

(2) The study, published yesterday in the June issue of The American Journal of Public Health, reported that men and women who smoke cigarettes face twice the risk of suffering a first heart attack as do non-smokers.

(3) The annual incidence of first heart attacks among pipe and cigar smokers was also found to be higher than among non-smokers, but not as high as among cigarette smokers.

(4) Men who are "least active," both on and off the job, are twice as likely as "moderately active" men to suffer a first heart attack and four times as likely to suffer a fatal heart attack.

(5) Men who were classified as "most active" showed no advantage in terms

of heart attack rate over men considered "moderately active." The authors reported that other differences between active and inactive men, such as the amount they smoked, could not account for their different heart attack rates.

(6)   The heavier men in the study had a 50 percent greater risk of suffering a first heart attack than the lighter-weight men. An increased risk was also found among women who had gained a lot of weight since age 25.

(7)   None of the differences in risk associated with weight could be explained on the basis of variations in smoking and exercise habits, the authors stated.

(8)   The incidence of heart attacks was also found to be higher among white men than among non-whites and among Jewish men than among white Protestants and Catholics. But the heart attack rate among Jewish women was not markedly different from that among non-Jewish women.
—*The New York Times*

(6) Brody moves on to theme B, overweight.

(7) More on B; its relationship to A and C.

(8) Brody considered this secondary information.

Some reporters might have found a lead in the information Brody places in the last paragraph. Although most events have obvious leads, a number do not. News judgment is essential on multiple-element stories, and judgments differ. Brody was on target. The last paragraph is secondary.

Brody's story also illustrates another basic guideline for structuring a story: Put related material together.

Story Units

In organizing their stories, news writers move from one theme to another in the order of the importance of the subjects or themes. The lead is elaborated first, and then the next-most-important theme is stated, and then elaborated and explained. The rule of thumb is: Put everything about the same subject in the same place.

When his editor explained the rule to Dwight Macdonald, a journalist and critic, his first reaction was, "Obviously." His second, he said, was, "But why didn't it ever occur to me?" His third was, "It was one of those profound banalities 'everybody knows'—after they've been told. It was the climax of my journalistic education."

The Inverted Pyramid

The story structure of the examples in this chapter—important elements at the beginning, less important at the end—has for decades been taught to students as the "inverted pyramid" form. The term is somewhat misleading. An inverted pyramid is an unbalanced monolith, a huge top teetering on a pin-point base. It is a monstrous image for journalists, for the top of a story should be deft and pointed. If the student can discard the picture of this precariously balanced chunk and remember that all it means is that the most important material is usually placed at the beginning of the story and the less important material placed at the end, all is well.

The news story takes its shape from the requirements and limitations of the craft as measured by the clock—a silent but overwhelming presence—and the available space for copy. Given these realities, most stories must be written in such a way that they can be handled quickly and efficiently. If the 10 inches of available space suddenly shrinks to eight, there is no problem. The news story structure makes it possible to cut the bottom two paragraphs in an instant without losing key information.

If the only justification of the standard news story form were its utility to the people writing and editing the news, it would not have stood up over the years. The form has persisted because it meets the needs of media users. The readers of news usually want to know what happened as soon as the story begins to unfold. If it is interesting, they will pay attention. Otherwise, they turn elsewhere. People are too busy to tarry without reward.

Sometimes the pleasure may come from suspense, a holding of the breath until the climax is revealed deep in the story. When the reporter senses that this kind of structure is appropriate for the event, a delayed lead will be used.

Research tells us that structure can help increase the viewer's and reader's understanding of the story and his or her involvement in it. For those who stay with the story from beginning to end, the start and the conclusion seem to be the best-remembered portions of the piece. Now that page layout can be more accurately designed, the reporter can put a kicker or summary at the end of a story without worrying that it might be squeezed out.

News forms may be said to be utilitarian or pragmatic, in the tradition of the hustle and bustle of American life. But there is also an aesthetic component in the standard news form that its detractors sometimes fail to detect. If the expression "form follows function" implies beauty in the finished work, then the news story is a work of art, minor as it may be. The news story does meet the demands of art: It reveals a harmony of design.

Story Necessities

Take any event and play the reporter's game. What are the necessary facts for an automobile accident story, a fire story, an obituary? Let us say an automobile hits a child. What must the story include? It will have to contain the child's name, age and address; the driver's name, age, address and occupation; the circumstances and location of the accident; the extent of the child's injuries; the action, if any, taken against the motorist. Any other necessities?

Given an assignment, the reporter has in mind a list of necessities for the story—any story. The necessities guide the reporter's observations and direct the questions he or she will ask of sources. But there can be a problem.

Unless the reporter can spot the significant differences, one accident story will be like another, one obituary like a dozen others. The reporter on the "automobile hits child" story tries to discern the unusual aspects of the event that should be given priority: Was the youngster playing? If so, was he or she running after a ball, playing hide-and-seek or jumping rope? Was the child looking for a dog, cat, younger brother? Was the child crossing the street to go to school? If seriously injured, how badly was he or she hurt? Will the youngster be able to walk normally?

Once the reporter has thought about the necessities of stories he or she is assigned and then seeks out the facts that differentiate this story from others like it, the story is on its way to being organized. The final step is to single out the important or unique element and then construct a lead around it. There is no simple formula for determining what should go into the lead. The criteria for news we developed in Chapter 2 are helpful. Basically, news judgment is an exercise in logical thinking.

When a fire destroys a hotel worth $3 million and takes 14 lives, the reporter focuses the lead on the lives lost, not the destruction of the hotel, no matter how costly. The reporter reasons that a life cannot be equated with money. But if no one was killed or hurt in the fire, then the significance may well be that it was a costly structure, not a three-story hotel for transients that had seen better times. If there were no injuries and the hotel had some historical interest, the lead might be that a landmark in town was destroyed by fire. Finally, if no one had been hurt and the hotel was a small, old building like many others in town, the fire would rate only two or three paragraphs.

The thinking process that underlies writing news stories is precisely the same as the thinking process that guides reporting. Reporting and writing are inextricably bound together, and properly done they provide the ingredients for the well-organized story.

Let us visualize a reporter assigned to the education beat who is told to check a report that public school teachers may not report for work next fall. When she was given the assignment, the reporter thought of several essential questions:

- Is the report true?
- How many teachers are involved?
- What are the reasons for the strike?
- When will the decision be made whether to strike?
- What are the responses of authorities to the threat?
- What plans are being made for the students should there be a strike?

The answers to these questions and other observations made during her reporting were the building blocks for the story. The reporter knew what her lead would be from the minute she received the assignment—the possibility of a teacher strike and schools not opening. She had a simple formula for finding the lead: What do I know today that I did not know yesterday and that everyone would like to know?

Covering a Strike Threat

These are the first few paragraphs of the story she might have written:

Teachers in all 15 public schools in the city today
threatened to strike next September unless they are given
an 8 percent wage increase in next year's contract.

Spokesmen for the local unit of the American Federation
of Teachers, which represents 780 Freeport school
teachers, said the strike threat will be presented to the
City Board of Education at Thursday's negotiating session.

"Without a contract that contains pay levels
reflecting the increased cost of living, we will not report
for work in September," said Herbert Wechsler, the
president of the local unit. "No contract, no work."

If the Thursday session led to no resolution of the issue, the reporter's
story would begin this way:

The possibility of a strike of public school teachers
next September loomed larger today when six hours of
contract talks failed to settle the wage issue.

The teachers' union seeks an 8 percent pay increase
over the current pay levels for next year's contract. The
school board has offered 4 percent.

The non-stop discussion between the union and the city
school board failed to produce a settlement, said Herbert
Wechsler, the president of the local unit of the American
Federation of Teachers. The union, which represents the
city's 780 public school teachers, issued its strike threat
Tuesday and presented it formally at today's session.

Joseph Foremen, the state superintendent of education,
who is attending the contract talks at the invitation of
both sides, said:

"The two groups are widely separated. We need a
cooling-off period. Unless one side or the other makes some
kind of concession, we may have no teachers in the schools
Sept. 9. And a concession is the last thing on their minds
now."

Anyone who watched the education reporter in the newsroom as she wrote her story might conclude that news writing is not difficult. She walked into the newsroom, put her notes on her desk and started to write. Occasionally, she looked at her notes. It seemed effortless.

Appearances are deceiving. A lot of work went into the story. As a reporter of some 30 years' experience on a California newspaper put it to a beginner, "Those of us who survive work on our stories from the minute we get the assignment." The work the reporter was talking about takes the form of projecting at each level of reporting and writing the story as it will appear in its final form.

Reporters try to visualize their stories at these stages:

- Immediately on receiving the assignment.
- While gathering material at the event.
- Before writing.
- During writing.

It is time to examine the most important step in the writing process—creating the lead.

Scanlan, Christopher, ed. *How I Wrote the Story*. Providence, R.I.: **Further Reading** Providence Journal Co., 1983.

Snyder, Louis L., and Richard B. Morris. *A Treasury of Great Reporting*. New York: Simon & Schuster, 1949.

Wilson, Ellen. *The Purple Decades: A Reader*. New York: Farrar, Straus and Giroux, 1982.

CHAPTER SIX

The Lead

Preview

The lead gives the reader an idea of the story to follow. There are only two types of leads:

• Direct: This lead tells the reader or listener the most important aspect of the story at once. It is usually used on breaking news events.

• Delayed: This lead entices the reader or listener into the story by hinting at its contents. It usually is used with feature stories and is increasingly being used on news stories.

Keep the lead under 35 words whenever possible and follow the subject-verb-object sentence structure for clarity.

The effective news story lead meets two requirements. It captures the essence of the event, and it cajoles the reader or listener into staying awhile. The first calls for the use of disciplined intelligence. The second calls on the reporter's art or craftsmanship. For the writer, the proper lead helps to organize the story.

> We slept last night in the enemy's camp.
> —By a correspondent for the *Memphis Daily Appeal,* after the first day of the Civil War Battle of Shiloh.

> Millionaire Harold F. McCormick today bought a poor man's youth.
> —Carl Victor Little, UP, following McCormick's male gland transplant operation in the early twenties. UP's New York Office quickly killed the lead and sent out a sub (substitute lead).

> The million-to-one shot came in. Hell froze over. A month of Sundays hit the calendar. Don Larsen today pitched a no-hit, no-run, no-man-reach-first game in a World Series.

—Shirley Povich, *The Washington Post & Times Herald,* on the perfect game the Yankee pitcher hurled against the Brooklyn Dodgers in 1956.

"I feel as if I had been pawed by dirty hands," said Martha Graham.
—Walter Terry, dance critic of *The New York Herald Tribune,* after two members of Congress denounced Graham's dancing as "erotic."

What price Glory? Two eyes, two legs, an arm—$12 a month.
—St. Clair McKelway, *Washington Herald,* in a story about a disabled World War I veteran living in poverty.

Snow, followed by small boys on sleds.
—H. Allen Smith, *New York World-Telegram,* the weather forecast.

These leads defy almost every canon decreed by those who prescribe standards of journalistic writing. The first lead violates the rule demanding the reporter's anonymity. The UP lead is in questionable taste. Povich's lead has four sentences and three clichés. Terry's lead is a quote lead, and McKelway's asks a question—both violations of the standards.

Yet, the leads are memorable.

They work because they meet the requirements of lead writing: They symbolize in graphic fashion the heart of the event, and they entice the reader to read on. Here are two leads from New York City newspapers that appeared the morning after the mayor announced his new budget. Which is better?

Mayor Lindsay listed facilities for public safety yesterday as his top spending priority for next year, shifting from his pledge of a year ago to make clean streets his first objective in capital expenditures.
—*The New York Times*

Mayor Lindsay dropped his broom and picked up the nightstick yesterday, setting law enforcement facilities as the top priority in the city's construction plans for the coming fiscal year.
—*Daily News*

The business of luring the reader into a story is hardly confined to journalistic writing. Andrew E. Svenson, the prolific author of many of the Nancy Drew, Bobbsey Twins and Hardy Boys juvenile books, said that the trick in writing is to set up danger, mystery and excitement on page one, and force the child to turn the page. He said he had rewritten page one as many as 20 times.

The Old Testament begins with simple words in a short sentence: "In the beginning God created the heavens and the earth."

Plato knew the importance of the first words of a written work. "The beginning is the most important part of the work," he wrote in *The Republic.*

Editors sometimes tell their staffers they want a "grabber" in the lead, something that will take hold of the readers or listeners and keep them pinned to the newspaper or the set.

The lead also serves the reporter. It forces a structure on the piece. Once the reporter decides which fact or facts will go into the lead, the story automatically takes shape. The lead material must quickly be amplified and buttressed. Secondary facts must be placed farther down in the story.

New Yorker writer John McPhee says, "The first part—the lead, the beginning—is the hardest part of all to write. I've often heard writers say that if you have written your lead you have 90 percent of the story." But that's not easy, he says.

"You have tens of thousands of words to choose from, after all—and only one can start the story, then one after that, and so forth. . . . What will you choose?" McPhee asks.

There are many facts as well, and before the words can be selected, the facts must be sorted out. How does the reporter select the one or two facts for a lead from the abundance of material he or she has gathered?

Beginning reporters find lead writing their most troublesome task. A beginner looking over the six leads that begin this chapter might despair of ever becoming a journalist as he compares them with his handiwork. No need to worry. With practice, most journalists do learn to write good, better and then arresting leads.

Finding the Lead

The thinking process involved in lead writing often begins with the reporter's asking himself or herself:

1. *What* was unique or the most important or unusual thing that happened?
2. *Who* was involved—who did it or who said it?

After these questions have been answered, the reporter seeks words and a form that will give shape to the responses. This leads to three more questions:

3. Is a direct or a delayed lead best? (Does the theme of the story go in the first sentence or somewhere within the first six paragraphs?)
4. Is there a colorful word or dramatic phrase I want to work into the lead?
5. What is the subject, and what verb will best move the reader into the story?

The five questions are simple enough. The answers, however, can be so difficult that a reporter with years of experience may halt in the middle of a story, suddenly aware the story is going off in the wrong direction, that it has lost its focus. The reason is that the reporter failed to answer the first two questions properly.

The most common mistake of the beginning reporter is to bury the lead so that the story backs into it. Sent to cover a speech in which a sociologist says teen-age pregnancy is costing the U.S. billions of dollars a year, a newly minted reporter began his story:

> A Harvard sociologist studying teen-age pregnancy gave a speech last night to more than 200 students and faculty members in Hall Auditorium.

The reporter had failed to ask himself the first of our five questions. It was hardly unique, important or unusual for a sociologist to address a college audience. Not until the third paragraph did the reporter reach the news point—the high cost of such births.

Here is a lead a reporter wrote about a congressional race. He thought he had answered the first two questions.

> Replies of Rep. Ronald A. Sarasin and William R. Ratchford, candidates in the Fifth Congressional race, to a Connecticut League of Women Voters questionnaire were released today.

He did include *what* had happened and *who* was involved. But he did not make his answer to the first question sufficiently specific. What did they say in their replies? The reporter might have reached this answer in the story, had his editor let him continue. But the editor pointed out that voters want to know the opinions and positions of their candidates quickly in stories about politics. Such events do not lend themselves to delayed leads.

A better lead for the political story might have been:

> Ronald A. Sarasin and William R. Ratchford, candidates for Congress in the Fifth District, agree that the deficit is the major domestic issue facing the nation.

The next paragraph might have included the background information that the reporter had mistakenly put into his lead:

> Their positions on the budget and on other issues were released today by the Connecticut League of Women Voters. The League had sent its questionnaires to all major candidates for office.

The subsequent paragraphs would expand the deficit theme and introduce other material from the replies of the congressional candidates and others.

Lists of Leads

Beginning journalists often are offered lists of leads. They are told about the who, what, where, when, why and how leads; the anecdotal, clause, gag, shotgun and quote leads. And a score of others.

This categorizing may be useful for a research project, but the lists are of little use to the working reporter. No reporter looks at his or her notes and thinks, "Well, this looks like a *who* lead here. Or maybe it's a *what* lead."

What ran through the mind of the reporter who wrote this lead?

> NORFOLK—Charley Greene has hit the roof in an effort to prove that he isn't six feet under.
> —*The Virginian-Pilot*
> (Norfolk, Va.)

Is that a *who* or a *what* lead? What is the difference and who cares? The reporter learned that a retired Navy warrant officer had not been receiving his retirement pay because the government thought him dead. The situation seemed humorous enough for feature handling. Then the reporter played with some words that would express the plight of a man caught in coils of red tape. The reporter decided on a delayed lead.

There are only two types of leads, direct and delayed.

Direct Lead

This type of lead is the workhorse of journalism, the lead that is used on most stories. The direct lead focuses on the theme of the event in the first paragraph. The surest way to test a reporter's competence, editors say, is to see whether his or her leads on spot news events move directly to the point and are succinct and readable.

Here are some direct leads:

> A local couple was awarded $150,000 in damages yesterday in Butte County Court for the injuries they suffered in a traffic accident last March.

> Guy Barton Rhodes, an organist with the First Methodist Church for 45 years, died at his home at 33 Raritan Ave. He was 91 years old.

> Another in a series of snowstorms is expected to hit the Sierra today.

The direct lead need not be dry and factual. Here's a direct lead by Aljean Harmetz of *The New York Times* to a business story, which we usually think of as a dry subject to be written as such:

Two veteran motion picture industry executives were chosen today by the board of Walt Disney Productions to head the troubled company a mouse built.

The direct lead answers the reporter's first two questions—what happened and who was involved?—in the first sentence of the story. To write a direct lead, the reporter must have a firm grasp on the specifics of the event, for this is the core of the direct lead. The reporter also must put in the lead when the event occurred (usually *today*), a source and the location of the event, when relevant:

Three firefighters were injured and 41 families were evacuated when a fire roared through a six-story building at 204 Union Ave. today, police said.

Delayed Lead

The delayed lead is most often used on features and news features, the kinds of stories that are not about developing, running or fast-breaking events. The delayed lead usually seeks to set a scene or evoke a mood with an incident, anecdote or example. Increasingly, the delayed lead is being used on all types of newspaper stories, not only on features, for the delayed lead offers the reporter much more latitude in telling a story.

Here is a delayed lead on a feature about a man who runs a demolition company. It was written by AP Newsfeatures writer Sid Moody:

> Jack Loizeaux is a dentist of urban decay, a Mozart of dynamite, a guru of gravity. Like Joshua, he blows and the walls come tumbling down.

Notice that the reader does not know from this lead just what Jack Loizeaux does—the delayed lead does not reveal essential information to the reader. That is one of its attractions.

The UPI put this delayed lead on a news story that could have taken a direct lead—the passage by the House to extend daylight saving time two months:

> WASHINGTON—The House wants to add a little daylight to the dark and dreary days of March and April.

Here is how an investigative reporter for the *Chicago Tribune* began a series of articles exposing corruption in Chicago's ambulance services:

> They are the misery merchants and they prowl the streets of our city 24 hours a day as profiteers of human suffering. . . .

Heidi Evans of the *Los Angeles Times* began her story about the aftermath of a traffic accident this way:

> Robert Trueblood is alone.
> His wife, Pamela, and their three young children were killed Tuesday night when an allegedly drunk driver veered his vehicle across the center divider and collided with their car two blocks from their Fullerton home.
>
> After two restless nights and an anguished day of retelling the tragedy to friends and relatives, Trueblood tried to preoccupy himself Thursday by going to work but found himself haunted by memories of the family he cherished.

Just any incident or anecdote will not do for the delayed lead. The lead must be consistent with the news point, the theme of the story. It must lead the reader straight to the heart of the story. Notice how John Rebchook of the *El Paso Herald-Post* takes this delayed lead to the news point in the fifth paragraph, the current status of the drive to collect unpaid traffic fines. Rebchook illustrates his point about unpaid traffic warrants by using in his lead a specific driver who has avoided paying:

Example

In less than three miles, Joseph L. Jody III ran six stop signs, changed lanes improperly four times, ran one red light, and drove 60 mph in a 30 mph zone—all without a driver's license. Two days later, he again drove without a driver's license. This time he ran a stop sign and drove 80 mph in a 45 mph zone.

For his 16 moving violations—the first 13 committed on Sept. 20, 1982,—Jody was fined $1,795.

He never paid. Police say that Jody has moved to Houston. Of the estimated 30,000 to 40,000 outstanding traffic warrants in police files, Jody owes the largest single amount.

Still, Jody's fines account for a small part of at least $500,000 owed to the city in unpaid traffic warrants.

News point (Theme)

In February, Mayor Jonathan Rogers began a crackdown on scofflaws in order to retrieve some $828,000 in unpaid warrants. As of mid-March, some $368,465 had been paid.

A Feature

A reporter assigned to find out whether women served on the boards of the city's major firms found that although some of the nation's big industries had been naming women to their boards, most local companies—metal manufacturers, paint firms and others—had no women on theirs. She began her story this way:

```
    The scene is the deeply-carpeted boardroom of one of
the city's major industries.
    Community leaders, an educator and business executives
file into the room. They take their seats at a large, highly
polished table and prepare for the business at hand.
```

```
    All is ready for a meeting of the board of directors,
and everything is in place.

    The session looks like any other formal meeting, except
for one aspect: It is an all-male affair. There are no women
on the board.
```

The story begins leisurely. The first four paragraphs set the scene. The fifth paragraph states the theme:

```
    Although the city's population is more than half
female, women constitute a small fraction of the boards of
almost all the city's industries.
```

A direct lead could have been written from the information in the fifth paragraph:

```
    Few women serve on the boards of the city's major
industries, a survey by this newspaper revealed today.
```

This lead would be acceptable to some editors. But it is not too imaginative. Also, it has a sense of immediacy that is inconsistent with the nature of the event being described. Probably there have been no women on most boards for some time, perhaps forever. The delayed lead is more appropriate than the direct lead.

Here is the beginning of a story from *Editor & Publisher:*

The young black woman awaiting her turn with *Boston Globe* interviewers for 15 minutes looked at the white woman skeptically.

"Would you mind if I cut ahead for just a minute?" the white woman asked. "I need to run in for just a moment."

A stare met the request before the black woman answered with a sigh and a disbelieving "Uh-huh."

The point of the story, which was about a Black Journalists Jobs Fair, was that editors found the quality of minority applicants to be excellent. The delayed lead used by *E & P* hardly sets up the theme of the story.

Given the opportunity, a reporter will try to featurize a straight news story by putting a delayed lead on it. At first glance, the death that police reporter Robert Popp of the San Francisco *Chronicle* saw in the police file seemed routine. But rewriteman George Williamson, copy editor Jim Toland and Popp turned it into a sad tale. Here is their story:

Small Boy's Big Loss to Drugs

Johnny B., 6, awoke at a pre-dawn hour yesterday and saw his fully clothed mother lying on the floor next to the bed they shared in the Roy-Ann Hotel at 405 Valencia street.

Her nose was bleeding badly. Johnny got up, found some tissues, and wiped her face clean. Then he went back to sleep.

When he awoke again at 8:30 a.m., Anne B., 25, was still on the floor. Her face was covered by new blood.

Johnny dressed himself neatly—as usual—and groomed his Dutch boy haircut before going downstairs to tell the hotel clerk about his "sick" mother.

The coroner's office later determined that she had died from an overdose of an undetermined drug.

Johnny recounted that the night before, two men had visited the studio apartment in the Inner Mission District. He said he asked one man why he was using a rubber cord to make his arm veins bulge, and the man responded that he was taking a blood test.

The men left some time after Johnny went to bed.

Postscript: Jim Toland had given students in his news writing class at San Francisco State University the facts taken from the police report. One student, curious to see if there is such a place as the Roy-Ann Hotel, drove by. She found the *Chronicle* had misspelled the name of the hotel. It was the Royan.

The Wall Street Journal for years emphasized the human-interest lead in which a news event is personalized through the use of people directly involved in or affected by the event.

When Anthony Ramirez of *The Wall Street Journal* wrote his story about the admissions policies of selective colleges and universities, he decided that a delayed lead would be appropriate. In his first paragraph, he plunges the reader into the deliberations of a college admissions committee. Gradually, he works his way to the point of the piece in the fourth and fifth paragraphs:

DURHAM, N.C.—It's a sunlit Thursday morning, and around a long wooden table, a college admissions committee squints at thick books of computer printouts and argues about a black high-school senior with much promise but bad grades.

One of 12 children from a Detroit ghetto family, he wants to attend Duke University here, but his case perplexes admissions officials. Although they want to admit more blacks, this young man ranks in the bottom fifth of his class, and his scores are just average on the Scholastic Aptitude Test, which is said to measure college potential. "He's scary," mutters Edward Lingenheld, Duke's admissions director. Yet the Massachusetts prep school that the student is attending on an affirmative-action scholarship is one of the best private schools in the country. It backs him strongly, saying his character and leadership ability are outstanding.

After a few minutes of sharp debate, the committee, swayed mainly by the school's praise, decides to accept him. He is one of more than 6,800 high-school seniors who want to get into Duke's freshman class next fall. Only 1,000 will make it.

Every year, elite colleges and universities get tens of thousands of applications from anxious high schoolers throughout the nation—and launch a painstaking selection process that most other schools don't bother with. By mid-April, the colleges tell most of their applicants that they aren't getting in. Watching the admissions committee's deliberations here at Duke for a few days shows the sifting and sorting that lands some students in the college of their choice, and leaves others—often with almost identical grades and test scores—rejected.

Like other selective institutions, Duke wants a "diverse" student body. The reasoning is that a kind of gumbo of top students who are different, either in the lives they have led or the talents they possess, produces opportunities for learning that books don't provide. To admissions officers, getting the right mix requires the work of reasonable people trying to judge reasonably. To high schoolers and their parents, the process can often mean apprehension and mystery, followed by disappointment. . . .

In her story for *USA TODAY,* Barbara S. Rothschild describes a sex therapist's boo-boo with this delayed lead:

There may finally be a question that embarrasses Dr. Ruth Westheimer. It's about the accuracy of her book.

Teens who read the new sex book co-authored by the USA's best-known sex therapist could get more than they asked for.

A baby, perhaps.

First Love: A Young People's Guide to Sexual Information, by Dr. Ruth and education professor Nathan Kravetz, has a major error on page 195.

In a chapter on contraception, the $3.50 books says it's "safe" to have sex the week before and the week of ovulation.

It should read "unsafe"—since those are the times a woman is *most* likely to become pregnant. . . .

News Magazines

The delayed lead is a favorite of *Time* and *Newsweek.* Since they are read after their readers have seen the news on television or read about it in their local newspapers, a different writing style must be used lest readers decide they cannot afford to pay twice for the same information.

The news magazines emphasize drama, interpretation, explanation and background in their stories. But few stories contain more information than the wire service and newspaper stories that moved the day the event broke. The magazines just do what they consider to be a better job of writing, and much of the dress-up is based on the delayed lead.

Here is the UPI's lead for morning newspapers when Ronald Reagan defeated Walter Mondale for the presidency:

```
WASHINGTON (UPI)--President Reagan piled up a
landslide election victory yesterday, narrowly
missing a 50-state sweep and generating such coattail
strength that Republicans could gain working control
of Congress.
```

Four days later, when *Time* and *Newsweek* were delivered to their subscribers, not a soul among them looked into their magazines to find out who had won the big race. They read the story anyway, to recapture the drama, to relish their man's victory, to suffer defeat once more. Here are *Time*'s and *Newsweek*'s leads. Decide for yourself whether they say much more than the UPI lead.

Time:

For an utterly predictable election, it managed to generate surprising suspense and even a bit of tension at the very end. Not about who would win, of course, or even whether Ronald Reagan would win re-election by a historic landslide. The verdict came almost the moment the count began: a resounding yes.

Newsweek:

It was the night that Ronald Wilson Reagan became Mr. America. In a star-spangled blowout, the American people reaffirmed their identification with his can-do confidence, his patriotic pride, and their vote transcended party and ideology: it was more than 52 million Americans roaring "Thank you!" to a president who had made the country feel good about itself. That was the message of the electronic scoreboard: the numbers that showed Reagan burying Walter Mondale by a margin of 59 to 41 percent—winning a record 525 electoral votes and sweeping everything except the District of Columbia and Mondale's stubbornly, but barely, loyal Minnesota.

The Dangers

The Wall Street Journal's narrative style has influenced papers across the country, but its news style sometimes has spread by contagion rather than by healthy example. The delayed lead requires a talented hand. Moreover, it cannot be used on just any story.

In an attempt to sell minor pieces to their editors, ambitious reporters use delayed leads on straight news stories. Some reporters play with delayed leads when they are unable to write a direct news lead. By taking the narrative or chronological approach or by focusing on an individual, they hope that the reader will somehow figure out just what the news point is.

Editors are aware of these tactics.

"We don't go for long scene setters," says Jerry Gold of *The New York Times,* which has a rule that when a reporter uses a delayed lead the reporter must tell the reader what the story is about by the fourth paragraph.

The delayed lead has a couple of offspring, the blind lead and the combo lead.

Leads that tell little or are vague are known as blind leads, and they can repel as well as attract. Here is a lead that has become a classic because of this duality:

Unwise were the flies that plagued Keshoprasad Varma when he was shaving 10 years ago.

—*AP*

The Blind Lead

It is a lead, an editorial in *Life* magazine said, that has "added a bijou to the great lead sentences in the museum of journalism. Curators will doubtless classify it with the blind, indirect or up-the-dark-stairs type of lead popular in the *New York Sun* in Frank Ward O'Malley's time. But in our opinion it transcends this category and belongs with those which convey just enough information to make further reading either impossible or absolutely necessary."

The story, by the way, was about a patent for a new fly trap.

The Combo Lead

Some reporters have mastered a technique that combines the direct and delayed lead and has elements of the blind lead. The story begins with a few general sentences. Then the reporter hits the reader with a karate chop. Edna Buchanan, police reporter for *The Miami Herald,* is partial to this kind of lead:

The man she loved slapped her face. Furious, she says she told him never, ever to do that again. "What are you going to do, kill me?" he asked, and handed her a gun. "Here, kill me," he challenged. She did.

On New Year's Eve Charles Curzio stayed later than planned at his small TV repair shop to make sure customers would have their sets in time to watch the King Orange Jamboree Parade. His kindness cost his life.

Buchanan covered a story about an ex-convict, Gary Robinson, who pushed his way past a line at a fried-chicken outlet. He was persuaded to take his place in line, but when he reached the counter there was no fried chicken, only nuggets, whereupon he slugged the woman at the counter. In the ensuing fracas, a security guard shot Robinson. Buchanan's lead was:

Gary Robinson died hungry.

Buchanan says her idea of a successful lead is one that could cause a reader who is breakfasting with his wife to "spit out his coffee, clutch his chest, and say, 'My god, Martha. Did you read this?'"

For her lead on a story about a man who died when some of the condoms that were used to hold cocaine began to leak in his stomach, Buchanan wrote:

His last meal was worth $30,000 and it killed him.

Buchanan's exploits are described by Calvin Trillin in a profile, "Covering the Cops," in the Feb. 17, 1986 *New Yorker.*

Roundups

A roundup is a story that joins two or more events with a common theme. Roundups often take multiple-element leads. They are often used for traffic accidents, weather, crime stories. When the events are in different cities and are wrapped up in one story, the story is known as an "undated roundup."

Torrential rains in Missouri and Kansas left five persons dead, hundreds homeless and crop losses of more than $1 million.

Teachers in 11 states walked picket lines yesterday for more money and other demands. Nearly one million children thus had an extended summer vacation or dawdled the hours away in understaffed schools.

—*UPI*

Let us listen to a reporter as she mulls over the notes she has taken at a city council meeting.

Deciding on a Lead

There were 13 items on the agenda. Well, which were the important ones? I'll circle them in my notes—

- General traffic program to route heavy trucks to Stanley Street and keep Main for lighter traffic.
- 56 stop signs to be bought.
- Paving program for Kentucky Street that will later fit into the bypass.
- OK'd contract to White Painting Co. to paint City Hall. $28,000.
- Hired consulting firm for traffic study.

Four of them seem to deal with traffic. Should I put them into a summary lead? Or should I pick out the traffic truck route or the traffic study? They seem equally important, so maybe I'll play with a summary lead. I'll drop the stop signs way down and then go into the painting contract.

She writes:

> The City Council today took three significant actions
> to cope with the city's downtown traffic congestion.
> The Council:
>
> 1. Approved the employment of Rande Associates, a
> consulting firm from Burbank, Calif., to make a study of
> traffic patterns.
> 2. Called for bids on paving 12 blocks of Kentucky
> Street, which is planned as part of a downtown bypass.
> 3. Endorsed the city traffic department's proposal to
> route heavy vehicles to Stanley Street before they enter
> Main Street.

At this point, some doubts assail the city hall reporter. She remembers that the truck traffic issue has been argued for several months. Downtown merchants complained to the mayor about the truck traffic, and Stanley Street homeowners petitioned the Council to keep the trucks away. The local newspaper and radio station have editorialized about it. In her haste to structure a complicated story, her news judgment went awry, she thinks. She writes:

> The City Council today decided to route truck traffic
> to Stanley Street and away from downtown Freeport.

The reporter is pleased with the lead she has written. But then more doubts. Maybe the overall pattern is more important than the single item about Stanley Street. After all, she thinks, the Council's three major actions will affect more people than those involved in the Stanley Street situation. She decides that she needs some advice and she walks over to the city editor. She shows him both leads.

"That's a tough one," he tells her. "Sometimes you flip a coin. Why don't you use your first lead and move up the third item, the one on Stanley Street, and put it first in the list. I like your conclusion in the lead that the actions were significant."

If we look closely at the two leads the city hall reporter prepared, we notice that the single-element lead about the routing of truck traffic to Stanley Street denotes a specific action the council took. The summary lead about the council taking three "significant" actions to "cope with" traffic congestion is, as the city editor remarked, the reporter's conclusion or interpretation. The *Daily News's* summary lead on the New Jersey election in Chapter 5 also contains an interpretation, that the governor "took a shellacking all around in yesterday's statewide election." Editors allow experienced reporters to interpret the news.

Most weak leads are the result of poor writing. Almost as many are the consequence of inadequate reporting. Consider this lead:

```
Barbara Elizabeth Foster, 19, St. Mary's University
sophomore, will be queen of the city's Rose Festival.
```

Immediately, the city editor knows he is in for a tedious trek through the copy. The reporter failed to single out an interesting characteristic of the new queen to add to her age and year in school, common identifying factors. Glancing through the copy, the editor notices that her mother was named Maid of Cotton 25 years ago. At the end of the story, there is a fleeting mention that her father enjoys gardening.

The editor runs his fingers through thinning hair. Masking his exasperation, he circles two sections and suggests to the reporter that there just might be a lead in the mother-daughter relationship and that a logical question to have asked the new queen was whether her father grew roses. Without good reporting no story can shine, much less be complete.

Next, to the fourth and fifth of our five guides to writing leads. The fourth question the reporter has to answer is: Is there a colorful word or dramatic phrase that I want to work into the lead? The ability of the reporter to answer the question often depends on the reservoir of words the reporter has accumulated.

In 1979, Florida conducted the first execution in the United States in a dozen years in which a person was put to death against his will. Capital punishment had not only been considered by several federal courts, it had involved the nation in a debate about the morality of such punishment. How best to put the Florida execution into words? Here is the lead Wayne King wrote for *The New York Times:*

STARKE, Fla., May 25—The state of Florida trussed Arthur Spenkelink immobile in the electric chair this morning, dropped a black leather mask over his face and electrocuted him.

The choice of the verb "trussed" is inspired. Not only does it mean to secure tightly. Its second definition is "to arrange for cooking by binding close the wings or legs of a fowl."

Caution: During the thinking that precedes writing, a word or a phrase will pop into the reporter's head, and the decision is made instantly that it must go into the lead. Now and then, however, the choice points the reporter to dead ends. Although the word or phrase may be inappropriate for the lead, it clings tenaciously to the reporter's consciousness, and it clogs thinking.

The fifth guide takes us directly into the construction of the lead—the selection of the subject and verb for the lead.

The basic construction of the lead should be subject-verb-object, S-V-O. That is, the lead should begin with the subject, should be closely followed by an active verb and should conclude with the object of the verb.

The S-V-O structure has an internal imperative: It directs the reporter toward writing simple sentences, which are sentences with one main clause. This kind of construction keeps leads short, another major requirement for a readable beginning.

Here are two leads consisting of simple sentences.

State Rep. Jack Campbell wants to run
for governor.
—*The Albuquerque Tribune*

S = Campbell; V = wants; O = to run.

SAN FRANCISCO—A federal judge
has ordered the City of San Francisco to
hire 60 women police patrol officers within
the next 32 weeks.
—*UPI*

S = judge; V = ordered; O = San Francisco.

Not every lead lends itself to a simple sentence structure. But even leads made up of complex and compound sentences have at their heart the S-V-O news kernel.

The S-V-O construction is the staple of journalistic writing. Three-fourths or more of the sentences a reporter writes follow this pattern. Most direct news leads—whether for print or broadcast—have this construction. It parallels the usual pattern of discourse and conforms to the command: "Write as you talk." Also, the S-V-O construction is functional. It is consistent with the thinking pattern of the reporter as he or she structures the lead. It is the most direct way of answering the first two questions the reporter asks when trying to find the lead: What happened? Who was involved?

Variety Is Possible

Although the S-V-O guideline may seem rigid, it does permit a variety of styles. Let us look at several leads written the night of a heavyweight championship fight:

```
BULLETIN
CHICAGO, Sept. 25 (UPI) SONNY LISTON KNOCKED OUT
FLOYD PATTERSON IN THE FIRST ROUND TONIGHT TO WIN THE
HEAVYWEIGHT CHAMPIONSHIP OF THE WORLD.
        M950ct
```

CHICAGO, Sept. 25—Nobody got his money's worth at Comiskey Park tonight except Sonny Liston. He knocked out Floyd Patterson in two minutes six seconds of the first round of their heavyweight title fight and took the first big step toward becoming a millionaire.

—Robert L. Teague,
The New York Times

CHICAGO, Sept. 25—Floyd Patterson opened and closed in one tonight. It took Sonny Liston only 2:06 to smash the imported china in the champ's jaw and, thereby, record the third swiftest kayo in a heavyweight title match—a sudden ending that had the stunned Comiskey Park fans wondering wha' hoppened. The knockout punch was there for everyone to see. It was a ponderous hook on Patterson's jaw. But the real mystery was what hurt the champ just before that; how come he suddenly looked in trouble when Liston stepped away from a clinch near the ropes?

—Leonard Lewin,
The Daily Mirror

CHICAGO, Sept. 25—Sonny Liston needed all of two years to lure Floyd Patterson into the ring and only two minutes, six seconds to get him out of it in a sudden one-knockdown, one-round-knockout at Comiskey Park last night.

—Jesse Abramson
The Herald Tribune

CHICAGO, Sept. 25—It was short, sweet and all Sonny Liston here tonight. The hulking slugger with the vicious punch to match his personality teed off on Floyd Patterson, knocked the champion down and out at 2:06 of the first round and won the world heavyweight championship without raising a bead of sweat on his malevolent countenance.

—Gene Ward,
Daily News

All the reporters agreed on the news angle or theme—Liston's quick knockout of Patterson. The thinking of these reporters was along the S-V-O line:

S = Liston; V = knocked out; O = Patterson.

The first lead, written for the UPI, whose reporters are told to remember that there is a deadline every minute, has little more than the S-V-O structure in the lead. Written within seconds of the ten-count, the story was designed to meet the needs of newspapers and broadcast stations on deadline.

The other reporters, who worked for New York City newspapers when the city had four morning dailies, were under less pressure and were able to fashion more distinctive leads. Some put personal observations and their interpretations into the leads—a practice permitted byline reporters.

Four Essentials

Looking back at the direct news leads in this section, we can generalize about their essentials.

First, we notice that each lead has something *specific* and *precise* to tell the reader. The reporter moved directly to the heart of the event.

Next, the *time* element is almost always in the lead. Then, there is usually a *source* of the information or action, and the source is often identified. And finally, the *place* of the action is often included.

Keep It Short

When a reporter writes a lead, he or she must navigate between divergent currents. One pull is toward writing a longer-than-average sentence as the lead must be precise and must offer significant information. The other is toward a short sentence, since short sentences are more readable than long ones. The long sentence may be difficult to grasp; the short sentence may be uninformative or misleading.

There is no outright prohibition against long leads, but good long leads are difficult to write. They must have rhythm, symmetry and balance. Only experienced writers can successfully handle long leads. Here is an example of a good long lead from an article about Rockefeller Center, "The City Where Nobody Lives," by Joe Alex Morris:

> The most magnificent city in America is an irregular block of limestone, steel, glass and masonry snugly set into a dozen acres of solid rock, with its foundations anchored sixty-eight feet below the surface and its towers rising 850 feet toward—and frequently into—the clouds. Nobody lives there.
>
> —*Saturday Evening Post*

Notice the short second sentence, which balances the longer first sentence. The content of the two sentences also offers the reader a contrast in ideas.

Leads should adhere to a 30–35 word limit whenever possible, for visibility as well as readability. Long leads occupy so much of the narrow newspaper column that they appear forbidding. For broadcasting, all sentences tend to be short for quick comprehension.

Reporters have several techniques to keep leads short. The most fundamental method is the relentless removal of all but essential material. The adage about placing the answers to the Five W's and an H in the lead is journalistic history, although it may be helpful to the beginner struggling to shape a story. The experienced reporter will pick the single most important or most compelling element.

A common but unnecessary space-and-time consumer is the precise time—11 a.m. today or the redundant 11 a.m. this morning or 12 midnight. Unless the exact time is essential to the story—tax returns must be postmarked before midnight—*today* is sufficient. Unnecessary attribution also wastes space.

Placing and Condensing Attribution

Should attribution go at the beginning of the lead or at the end? If a title or descriptive phrase is long, how can the reporter keep the material from cluttering the main point? The answers are provided by an editor who spent many years breaking in young reporters at *The New Mexican,* a daily newspaper in Santa Fe, N.M.: "Remember that the basic sentence structure is subject, verb, object. So the subject, the source of the lead, usually should go first when it is necessary to carry attribution in the lead. Also, I want to know immediately who's talking. It makes a difference whether a local druggist or the mayor says that the mill levy should be lowered. You would not write a lead this way:

```
City taxes are much too high and must be lowered as soon
as possible, Albert Quigley, owner of the Owl Drug Store and
former city councilman, said today in a Rotary Club
luncheon address.
```

"You wouldn't do it this way because the reader has to go almost to the end of the lead before he realizes that it's old Al Quigley, that constant complainer, sounding off again," the city editor says.

"Now to the second point. Suppose you're covering the Rotary luncheon and we have a speaker in town from Chicago, Dr. Robert Cohen, a physician who's done cancer research. He says it's necessary that middle-aged men and women have annual checkups. Dr. Cohen is unknown among our readers. But we must tell the reader who he is so that his statements are authoritative. We could write it this way without his name in the lead:

```
A cancer specialist said today . . .
```

"Or if the paper prefers more specific attribution and is not worried about a slightly longer lead, we could write:

```
The head of the cancer clinic at a Chicago hospital said
today . . .
```

Unlike this editor, some editors prefer attribution at the end of the lead, unless the source is as important as what is said. This would reverse the S-V-O structure. For reporters, the argument is theoretical; they do what their editors demand.

Keep It Fresh

The journalist may roam the world for ideas and stories, but his time dimension is a narrow confine—the few hours of his news day. The journalist moves through the world of today. Such is his anxiety about old news that his writing has been parodied in this lead for an obituary:

```
John Smith was dead today. He died yesterday.
```

Leads of this sort do appear in newspapers, and they occasionally run on the wires of the press associations. Here is a lead that was sent over the wires of one of the press services:

```
INDEPENDENCE, MO., Oct 10-William Sermon today
was no longer mayor of Independence.
    In a short, prepared statement, Sermon told the
city council last night he wanted to resign because of
''ill health''. . .
```

In this story, the present tense could have been used, or the present perfect, or the future tense: . . . is no longer. . . . has resigned. . . . Or more imaginatively: . . . has decided to forgo budget battles for a fight against ill health. Or: Independence will have to find a new mayor.

Follow-Up Stories

The task of updating or freshening stories is not difficult with continuing events. Usually, it is possible to find an authority to comment on a new development or to track down people affected by a new program or policy. Causes and consequences are useful for leads on follow-up stories.

> Service and maintenance workers were returning to their jobs today following a vote to end a 10-day strike against three Baltimore-area hospitals.
> —*The Baltimore Sun*

Disasters are updated without difficulty. If the cause of the airplane crash is unknown, investigators can be asked about the progress of the inquiry. If there were serious injuries, the condition of the victims can be checked, and if there are additional fatalities, a new death toll can be used as the basis of the lead.

Second-Day Leads

Delayed leads are often used to freshen day-old stories. The reporter finds a new angle that lends itself to narrative telling and the story gradually works back to the fact that the event occurred yesterday. These stories begin like this one about a baseball game:

> Preacher Stowe knew he was heading for a long, hard day's work when he had to borrow his roommate's pants.
> "The hotel mislaid my luggage, and in order to make the bus to the stadium I had to borrow a pair of pants," Stowe said. "I knew right then there would be trouble."
> There was.

The two-word sentence is the transition or tie-in paragraph to the news:

Stowe lasted four innings last night. He was shelled from the mound after giving up four runs. The Red Sox defeated the Tigers 9–2.

Most fans knew the score before reading the newspaper, and they enjoyed the little tale, which we presume came from the experience of Preacher himself and not from the imagination of the club's public relations man.

Whenever possible, a new fact is put into a second-day lead. Or else a fact that was not mentioned prominently in the original story is put into the lead—when appropriate.

The second-day lead can be stretched to absurdity, particularly when the end becomes the means, when the purpose of the updating is word play. Some reporters become so adept at rewriting leads that they can fool experienced editors into believing old news is new. They will dig out a secondary fact of no great consequence and fluff it into importance with clever writing.

Overnight Leads

Sometimes an overnight lead—a lead on a story for early editions of afternoon newspapers that usually contains no new information—is overly imaginative. The overnight desks of the press associations usually have to fabricate a dozen overnight leads a shift, and sometimes the creative juices flow abundantly. Here is an overnight lead fashioned by a rewriteman in the Miami bureau of one of the press associations:

MIAMI, FLA., Jan 8—Five thousand chickens are clucking around homeless today.

Their home, the longest chicken coop in Dade County, burned down last night.

Firemen say the chickens, smarter than horses, which sometimes stay in a burning barn, fled the coop immediately. None was fried.

Damage was estimated at $25,000.

Whether this is the thirteenth lead turned out by a rewriteman suddenly wearied of inventing overnight leads for a dozen stories, or whether this is the height of the art is up to the reader to decide. In either case, it is a classic.

Make It Readable

A reporter handed in this lead:

    The city planning office today recommended adding a
    section to the zoning code regulations on classification
    for residential use of property.

The editor puzzled over it and then instructed the reporter to simplify the lead and to say specifically what the proposed section would do. The reporter tried again.

> The city planning office today recommended that
> property zoned for two-acre, one-family dwellings be
> rezoned to allow the construction of cooperative apartment
> houses for middle- and low-income families.

The city editor looked this over and seemed pleased. "Let's take it a step further," he said. "What's the point of the recommendation? To change the code so people can move into that wooded area north of town near the Greenwich Estates section. Let's try to get people into the lead." The reporter returned in 10 minutes with these two paragraphs:

> Low- and middle-income families may be able to buy
> apartments in suburban areas north of the city.
> This is the intention of a proposal made today by the
> city planning office. The recommendation to the city
> council would rezone property in the area from the present
> restrictions that permit only single-family dwellings on
> two-acre lots.

In this process of writing and rewriting, the reporter went from a jargon-loaded, impenetrable lead to one that stated succinctly and clearly what the proposed regulation was intended to bring about. Accuracy was not sacrificed for simplicity and readability.

Readability stems from the ideas that make up the sentence, the order in which they are presented and the words and phrases chosen to give the ideas expression:

Ideas—When possible, the lead should contain one idea. "The sentence is a single cry," says Sir Herbert Read, the British critic and author, in his *English Prose Style*. Too many ideas in a sentence make for heavy going. Also, the idea selected should be easy to grasp; complexities should be simplified.

Sentence Order—The S-V-O construction is the most easily understood. "Reduced to its essence, a good English sentence is a statement that an agent (the subject of the sentence) performed an action (the verb) upon something (the object)," says John Ciardi, an American teacher and poet.

Word Choice—Since the lead moves on its subject and verb, the choice of nouns and verbs is essential for readability. Whenever possible, the subject should be a concrete noun that the reader can hear, see, taste, feel or smell. It should stand for a name or a thing. The verb should be a colorful action verb that accelerates the reader to the object, or makes him pause and think. It is not so much the presence or absence of the verb that matters, but the choice between a transitive and an intransitive verb, the American teacher and critic E. F. Fenollosa points out.

Where to Put When. Placing the when of the story— *today, tonight, yesterday*—in the lead often poses a problem. It should go next to the verb, in most cases after the main verb:

So-so: Gov. Susan Mc-Cormick today said she. . . .

Better: Gov. Susan Mc-Cormick said today she. . . .

Leads to Running Stories

It is 4:27 p.m. on a Saturday in March. Twelve jurors file into the jury box in a courtroom in the federal courthouse in San Francisco. The jury foreman hands an envelope to the court clerk who slits open the envelope, takes out the verdict form and hands it to the judge.

Guilty.

After 12 hours of deliberation, Patricia Hearst—the 22-year-old daughter of the publisher of the San Francisco *Examiner* and a granddaughter of William Randolph Hearst, the founder of the vast Hearst publishing empire—was found guilty of armed bank robbery and the use of a gun to commit a felony.

The verdict ended the most intensively reported trial since Bruno Hauptmann was tried for kidnapping the Lindbergh baby more than 40 years earlier. Reporters from over the world—400 of them—had converged on the courthouse, drawn by the Hearst name and the incredible story of an heiress who had been kidnapped by a revolutionary political group and who then had joined it in crime. The picture of her holding a submachine gun during a bank robbery was used all over the world.

Most of the reporters in the courtroom had only minutes to catch the early editions of their Sunday newspapers. Radio, television and wire service reporters had to react immediately. The world was waiting for the news.

Despite the tremendous pressure on these reporters, they met their deadlines. Although some reporters only called in the single word "Guilty" over the telephone, full stories appeared. The reason: *B copy.*

"Lead Hearst," one shouted into a telephone, and dictated:

Use of B Copy

    SAN FRANCISCO--Patricia Hearst was convicted by a
    federal court jury this afternoon of armed bank robbery and
    the use of a gun to commit a felony.

Then the reporter hung up. He knew that the desk would put this on B copy, the background material that the reporter had written and dictated that morning while the jury was deliberating. His B copy had begun this way:

```
    The verdict ended a 39-day trial in which 66 witnesses
had testified and 1,000 exhibits had been entered.
    Miss Hearst had testified that she had helped a
revolutionary political group rob the Sunset branch of the
Hibernia Bank in San Francisco on April 15, 1974. She said
she had done so on the threat of death.
    Miss Hearst's testimony was considered by a jury of
seven women and five men, who heard Federal Judge Oliver J.
Carter tell them yesterday that they alone had to decide the
key issue at the trial: Had Miss Hearst acted as a willing
participant in the bank robbery?
```

For the next edition, the reporter wrote an *insert* to go after the lead and before the B copy. The insert contained the courtroom drama as the verdict was returned.

Don't Write Writing

Immersed in words, the reporter is tempted to write writing, to make meaning secondary to language. This is fine when a Dylan Thomas plays with words, but it is dangerous for a journalist, whose first allegiance is to straight-forward meaning. Word play can lead to flippancies such as this lead from a wire service.

```
    JACKSONVILLE, Fla.—Like jus-
tice, the new judge of the Duval County
Court is blind.
```

Some reporters seem to think that using a direct quotation in the lead or injecting *you* into the lead makes for classy writing. They're wrong. Editors consider this weak writing, and when you are tempted, consider this lead and imagine the editor's explosion when it popped out on his screen:

```
    Now you don't have to go to a doctor to find out whether
you are pregnant. Test kits can be bought over the counter.
```

Good journalism is the accurate communication of an event to reader, viewer or listener. As Wendell Johnson, a professor of psychology and speech pathology at the University of Iowa, put it, "Communication is writing about something for someone . . . making highly reliable maps of the terrain of experience." Johnson would caution his students, "You cannot write writing."

Ask Me No Questions.
"The Achille Lauro is docked safely in Port Said this morning. But where are the hijackers? Have they already gone free?"—TV newscast.

"You're asking *us*? We tuned in to find out."—Mervin Block in the *RTNDA Communicator*, May 1986.

"Why not skip the question and go straight to the news?" says Block.

The temptation to make writing an end instead of the means is enormous. Janet Cooke, a feature writer for *The Washington Post,* could not resist. She wrote a moving story about Jimmy, an 8-year-old heroin addict in the Washington ghetto. The Pulitzer Prize jury was impressed and gave her its feature writing award for 1981.

Background information about Cooke distributed by the Pulitzer office aroused the suspicions of a newspaper which checked her claims that she had graduated from an elite women's school in the East—she had not—and that she spoke several foreign languages—she did not. It emerged that her story was also a fabrication. There was no 8-year-old heroin addict named Jimmy.

"I did not want to fail," she said in a television interview after she had been exposed. There is an undercurrent at the *Post* of "competitiveness and the need to be first, to be flashiest, be sensational."

She was stripped of her Pulitzer Prize and fired by the *Post,* but the damage had been done. Journalism had been tarnished in its efforts to maintain public trust.

The reporter who puts writing first on his or her priority list will achieve notoriety of a sort, if he or she is clever enough. Such fame is fleeting, though. Editors and the public eventually flush out the reporter whose competence is all scintillation.

This is not a red light to good writing. In fact, the fashioning of well-written stories is our next objective. We have only skimmed the subject of the writer's art. Now for the plunge.

Further Reading

Howarth, W. L. *The John McPhee Reader.* New York: Vintage Books, 1977.

Murray, Donald. *Writing for Your Readers.* Chester, Conn.: The Globe Pequot Press, 1983.

Roberts, Gene, and David R. Jones. *Assignment America.* New York: Quadrangle/Times Books, 1974. (An anthology of good writing by correspondents for *The New York Times.*)

CHAPTER SEVEN

The Writer's Art

Well-written stories have these qualities:

• They show the reader the event or individual through anecdotes, quotations and examples.

• They contain quotations and human interest high in the story that sum up the situation or the person the story is about.

• The language is precise, clear and convincing.

• Sentences are short. Transitions take the reader smoothly from one theme to another.

• The writing style is appropriate to the event.

Good writing depends on thorough reporting that turns up relevant information. The information is organized in a story that moves smoothly from beginning to end. The story flow is aided by the use of transitions and the narrative structure. Language is simple and direct.

W hether three-paragraph item or Sunday feature article, the news story is carefully constructed. We have discussed some of the rudiments of the well-crafted story:

The structure. The lead states the essential elements of the event. The body amplifies and expands the lead.

The content. Facts, derived from direct observation or reliable sources, are accurately presented by showing and telling the reader or listener what happened, who was involved, when and where it happened, and the causes and possible consequences of the event, its how and why.

Stories that contain these elements will satisfy readers because logical order and the precise and economical use of language are pleasing. But more is expected of the reporter. The news story should be well written.

Readers and viewers are not passive recipients of news. They demand that it be presented in an interesting way or they will move on to another story or station. This means that the information, the content of the story, must be carefully chosen and the writing must be carefully crafted.

The well-written story is clear, easy to follow, easy to understand. Good writing helps the reader to see the event the reporter is trying to describe. George Orwell said, "Good prose is like a window pane."

The window pane, unlike the stained glass window, does not call attention to itself. Good writing does not shout for attention. It calls attention to the people in the story, the event, the information.

There is a saying that great writers are born, not made. If so, it is unlikely that a course or a textbook can impart the gift that separates journalists like Mike Royko, Jimmy Breslin or Jack Nelson, from the many capable reporters on newspapers, magazines and broadcast stations. Still, it is possible to learn to write well. It is also possible that during the learning process latent talents will emerge. The sudden discovery of the power and the beauty of words has transformed many young men and women into acceptable if not accomplished writers.

For years, journalistic writing had the reputation of being bad writing—a reputation probably well deserved. This kind of writing was best described by the city editor of a California newspaper as "basic hack minimum." Nowadays, more than the minimum is required. Genius, no. Craftsmanship, yes. Editors want reporters who can tell truths with a flair.

The men and women who write for a living work at learning their trade. They have an "idea of craft," as the English scholar Frank Kermode put it, the drive toward "doing things right, making them accurate and shapely, like a pot or a chair." To sharpen their craft, journalists read writers who inspire them to move beyond themselves and who teach them the skills they always must be polishing. And they write.

The writers that journalists talk about as part of their tradition—an Ernie Pyle, Red Smith, Ernest Hemingway—wrote incessantly.

Hemingway read five hours a day, and he wrote and rewrote. He wrote, he said, 39 versions of the ending of *A Farewell to Arms,* a luxury no journalist is granted. But editors complain that reporters too often are satisfied with their first versions. Smith often was surrounded by a snow mound of rejected leads. As gifted as he was, he would rip out a dozen different tries, ball them up and miss the wastebasket. While in his 70s, the poet Carl Sandburg remarked, "All my life I have been trying to learn to read, and to see and to hear. If God lets me live five years longer, I hope to be a writer."

Every writer is familiar with the agony of chasing elusive words. The writer knows that words can be brought to life only by strenuous and continued work. The aim is perfection of expression, the absolute fit of words to the event. Walt Whitman described the writer's goal this way:

> A perfect writer would make words sing, dance, kiss, do the male and female act, bear children, weep, bleed, rage, stab, steal, fire cannon, steer ships, sack cities. . . .

Creative workers and craftsmen know that the path to individuality begins with emulation. In teaching students at the Royal Academy about their study methods, Joshua Reynolds, an eighteenth century English painter, advised: "The more extensive your acquaintance is with the works of those who have excelled, the more extensive will be your power of invention, and the more original will be your conceptions."

Journalists read fiction, poetry and other journalists to master style and technique, to learn the tricks of the writer's trade. Poet or police reporter, the writer struggles to find words and phrases to match his observations. When Hemingway covered the police court for the *Kansas City Star,* he would take his notes home and work over them hour after hour to simplify the testimony of witnesses until, in a few words, he had captured the essence of the evidence. He would always use the words he had heard in court. This practice, as much as the influence of Ezra Pound and Gertrude Stein, may have been responsible for Hemingway's objective prose, what the critic Maxwell Geismar called "his famous flat style: the literal, factual description of the 'way things are.'"

This style, more brother than cousin to journalism, is evident in the ending to *A Farewell to Arms.* Frederic has just pushed the nurses out of the room where Catherine has died. He wants to be alone with her:

> But after I had got them out and shut the door and turned off the light it wasn't any good. It was like saying good-bye to a statue. After a while I went out and left the hospital and walked back to the hotel in the rain.

The Reporter's Task

"The recognition of truth and the clear statement of it are the first duties of an able and honest writer," writes Hal Boyle, for many years one of the AP's top reporters. "The problem of good writing doesn't vary whether a man is writing a good novel or a good news story. He must look at the situation, find the kernel of truth he is seeking and record it in a durable book or a newspaper which, proverbially, will be used to wrap fish tomorrow."

Although the poet W. H. Auden was describing the poem, his definition applies to the news story as well: "Firstly, it must be a well-made verbal object that does honor to the language in which it is written. Secondly, it must say something significant about a reality common to us all, but perceived from a unique perspective."

Unlike the novelist and the poet, the journalist cannot spend hours searching for the truth, much less the right word. No other writer is asked to commit words to paper with such speed, under such pressure. All the more reason, then, for the journalist to follow those whose struggles have cleared paths toward good writing.

We might start with Tolstoy who, in describing the strength of his masterwork *War and Peace,* said, "I don't tell; I don't explain. I show; I let my characters talk for me."

One of the reporter's first writing rules might be: Show, don't tell. Telling makes the reader passive. Showing engages him by making him draw the conclusions, see the significance of the facts the writer presents. Good writers let the words and actions of the participants do the work. John Ciardi elaborates on Tolstoy's advice: "Make it happen, don't talk about its happening."

When the reporter makes it happen, the reader moves into the story. The reporter disappears as middleman between the event and the reader.

Covering the funeral of a child killed by a sniper, a reporter wrote, "The grief-stricken parents wept during the service." Another reporter wrote, "The parents wept quietly. Mrs. Franklin leaned against her husband for support." The first reporter tells us the parents are "grief-stricken." The other reporter shows us the woman's grief.

In a movie review, Stanley Kauffman of *The New Republic* writes: "We are told later that he (George C. Scott) is a cool man—which, presumably, is why his wife left him—but we are only *told* it; it's characterization by dossier, not by drama."

In a three-sentence paragraph, Sam Blackwell of the Eureka (Calif.) *Times-Standard* shows us a lot about teen-age romance in the 1980s:

> They had met cruising the loop between Fourth and Fifth Streets in Eureka. She fell in love with Wes' pickup truck, then fell in love with Wes. Wes gave her an engagement ring the day she graduated from high school.

Louis Lyons, a Boston newspaperman and later curator of the Nieman Foundation for journalists at Harvard, never forgot the lesson his night editor taught him. "When I was a cub reporter I had a story to do on the quarterly report of the old Boston Elevated system, whose history then as now was a nearly unbroken record of deficits," Lyons recalled. "This time they were in the black. I knew just enough to know how extraordinary that was.

"I wrote: 'The Boston Elevated had a remarkable record for January— it showed a profit. . . .'

"The old night editor brought my copy back to my typewriter. He knew I was green. In a kindly way, quite uncharacteristic of him, he spelled out the trouble.

"He pointed out that the word remarkable 'is not a reporting word. That is an editorial word.'" Then he advised Lyons to write the story so that the reader would say, "That's remarkable."

**Good Quotes
Up High**

The reporter is alert to the salient remark, the incisive comment, the words of a source that sum up the event or that will help the reader to visualize the person who is speaking. Also, a person's words help to achieve conviction, the feeling of truth. After all, if these are the words of a participant, the reader reasons, the story must be true. The higher in the story the quote appears, the better, although good quote leads are rare.

Notice the use of the poignant remark of the child in the second paragraph of this story:

Mary Johnson, 9, lay alongside the bodies of her slain family for nearly two days. She believed she, too, would die of the bullet wounds inflicted by her mother.

But Mary lived, and told ambulance attendants on her way to the hospital yesterday: "Don't blame mother for the shootings."

In an interview with an opponent of the U.S. government's policies in El Salvador, a reporter used this quote high in her story:

"Why are we on the side of those who are killing the nuns?" he asked.

Reporters have an ear for the telling quote. In a story about the record number of murders in Miami-Dade, Edna Buchanan of *The Miami Herald* quoted a homicide detective as saying, "In Dade County, there are no surprises left." Bodies are regularly fished out of the bay by beachcombers and fishermen. Buchanan wrote: " 'It's kind of a nuisance when you plan to do your research on the reef,' fumed Professor Peter Glynn of the university's Rosentiel School of Marine and Atmospheric Science."

**Human Interest
Up High**

A working rule for reporters: Try to place as close to the lead as possible the high quality example, incident or anecdote that spotlights the theme of the story. Often, this will be something about the persons involved in the event. Events become newsworthy because of their connection to human beings. When delayed leads are used, the human interest incident begins the story. With direct leads—which often stress the formal aspect of the event—the human-impact illustration or example should be close to the lead.

We are all a little like Alice (of *Alice's Adventures in Wonderland*). " 'What is the use of a book,' thought Alice, 'without pictures or conversations?' " The reporter lets the anecdotes serve as his pictures, and the quotations are his conversations.

Chicagoan, 15, wins $5,000 as champion of video game

WASHINGTON — (UPI) — Zap! Crunch! Swoosh!

With his eyes riveted on the TV screen and his hands dancing over a control stick, 15-year-old Andy Breyer of the Chicago area scored 142,910 points Saturday to win the world championship of the popular Asteroids video game.

Breyer, of Arlington Heights, Ill., beat out 17 other finalists from around the world to win the first-place prize of $5,000 from the competition's sponsor, Atari Inc.

"I don't like Asteroids that much," Breyer later told reporters, much to the chagrin of Atari officials standing nearby.

Well, what about that other popular Atari game, Space Invaders?

"That's kind of boring," Breyer replied.

The sponsors cringed.

A sophomore at Buffalo Grove High School, Breyer said he began playing video games about two years ago and bought a video game system with money he received for his bar mitzvah.

How much money have you spent playing these games at arcades?

"Oh, about 50 cents at the most. I don't like to waste my money on this stuff."

The sponsors faded into the crowd.

Breyer said he began playing Asteroids about three weeks ago, and practiced about five hours a day to get ready for the competition. He had only scored more than 100,000 points twice before. His all-time high is around 157,000.

"I don't think I could play any better than I did today," he said. "I would say at least 75 per cent of it is luck."

The youngster said he probably will use his prize for college tuition.

The second place winner was Gary Wong, 18, of San Francisco, with a total 128,780 points, and third place went to Dirk Mueller, 18, of Hamburg, West Germany, with 123,540 points. Wong got $3,500, Mueller $2,500.

The contestants played two games each.

The game consists of a player directing a space ship in the middle of an asteroid belt and using the ship's ray guns to blow up the asteroids before they hit and destroy the ship.

Breyer described his winning technique:

"I stay in the middle, then I go up left diagonally for just a fraction of a second and shoot all of the asteroids on the left side and then I shoot the right side. I don't like to use hyperspace."

After some prodding by the sponsors, Breyer said he did like their Football and Missile Command video games.

Do you feel like a champion?

"No, not really," the Asteroids champ replied. "I'm going to put the game away for a while and do something else."

The competition was staged in a room decorated to resemble a TV game show studio. One of the finalists, who had come all the way from Singapore, was unable to leave his hotel room because of an upset stomach.

Seventeen TVs, with computer games attached, were lined up in front of the dimly lit room. In the background was a mural of a Martian landscape, and music included themes from the movies *Superman* and *Star Wars*.

The master of ceremonies introduced each contestant game-show style and advised the audience "you're going to see some real guts ball play here."

Mark Twain's Principles

Before we invoke any more writing rules, let us listen to what a master craftsman, a former reporter, said about writing.

Mark Twain had volunteered to read the essays submitted by the young women at the Buffalo Female Academy for a writing contest. He was delighted by what he read, and in his report to the Academy he pointed out the virtues of the two prize essays. He described them as "the least artificial, least labored, clearest, shapeliest and best carried out."

The first prize essay "relates a very simple little incident in unpretentious language," he said. It has "the very rare merit of *stopping when it is finished*." (Twain's emphasis.) "It shows a freedom from adjective and superlatives, which is attractive, not to say seductive—and let us remark, in passing, that one can seldom run his pen through an adjective without improving his manuscript.

"We can say further that there is a singular aptness of language noticeable in it—denoting a shrewd facility of selecting just the right word for the service needed, as a general thing. It is a high gift. It is the talent which gives accuracy, grace and vividness in descriptive writing."

Good writing has four characteristics. It is:

- *Accurate:* The language fits the situation. This is Twain's "accuracy of wording," "using just the right word."
- *Clear:* Through proper use of form and content, the story is free from vagueness and ambiguity.
- *Convincing:* The story is believable. It sounds true.
- *Appropriate:* The style is natural and unstrained. In Twain's words, "unpretentiousness, simplicity of language . . . naturalness . . . selecting just the right word for the service needed."

The categories are not islands unto themselves. Causeways connect them. If we write that a congressman "refuted" charges that his proposal will cause unemployment, when he actually "denied" the charges, the language we use is inaccurate. As a consequence, the story is not clear. When we quote persons as they use the language—not in the homogenized dialogue that passes for the spoken word in too many news stories—the language is appropriate and our stories are more likely to convince readers they are true.

Let us examine each of Twain's principles. Before we begin, a reminder and a qualifier.

The reminder: A great deal of work is done before the reporter writes. The observing, note-taking and thinking that precede writing shape the story. The writing gives form and direction to ideas the reporter already has in mind. Good journalistic writing is the result of good reporting and clear thinking. Clever writing cannot conceal a paucity of facts, stale observations or insensitive reactions to people. But bad writing can nullify superior reporting.

The qualifier: In the rest of this chapter—and in other chapters, too—rules, formulas and injunctions are presented. They are offered as guidelines, as ways to get going. They should not be considered inviolate laws. But it is best for the beginner to accept them for the time being, until his or her competence is proved. After this apprenticeship has been served, the experienced reporter can heed Anton Chekhov's comments about writing in his play *The Seagull:* "I'm coming more and more to believe that it isn't old or new forms that matter. What matters is that one should write without thinking about forms at all. Whatever one has to say should come straight from the heart."

Love That Word. Two *New York Times* reporters with nothing better to do one slow night asked the newspaper's Information Bank to find out how often the word *controversial* had been used in a recent two-week period.

The computer came back: 30 times—for several political figures, a fumble by a football player, a new building in Portland, Ore., a new album by Linda Ronstadt, a stamp honoring St. Francis of Assisi. The *Times'* in-house *Winners & Sinners* commented: "W&S would be hard pressed to cite a word that tells less, yet appears more often, than *controversial.*"

The city editor of a medium-size Iowa daily stared at the lead in disbe-lief. A reporter who had covered a city commission meeting the night before had written that the commission adopted a controversial resolution "with one descending vote." The proper word is *dissenting,* the city editor informed his errant reporter.

Accuracy

Without accuracy of language, the journalist cannot make the story match the event. The obvious way to check words for accuracy is to use the dictionary. But reporters who misuse language often do so without knowing it. They could be saved from embarrassment by widening their reading. Watching good writers put words to work might jar some journalists to the realization that their vocabulary is uniquely their own.

The handwritten manuscript of *The Great Gatsby* reveals that F. Scott Fitzgerald ruthlessly eliminated long sections of beautiful writing because they interfered with the story's flow. He worked unceasingly to find the accurate word, replacing *looked* with *glanced* in one place, changing *interrupted* to *suggested* in another. Fitzgerald knew Tolstoy's rule, "Show, don't tell." He eliminated sections that told the reader about his characters and instead let the action and dialogue do the work.

Hemingway's writing was simple, but it was not simplistic. He shaved language to the bone, but at no sacrifice to meaning. This required hard work. He was asked why he had rewritten the ending to *A Farewell to Arms* so many times. "Was there some technical problem?" he was asked. No, Hemingway replied, the problem was not that complicated. It was "getting the words right."

An accurate vocabulary also comes from the development of a feel for words, for the way people use the language, which may differ from dictionary usage. "The true meaning of a term is to be found by observing what a man does with it, not by what he says about it," says P. W. Bridgeman, a physicist. Journalists use words that correspond to specific objects and identifiable feel-ings and ideas. When the journalist writes about the state treasurer's annual report, he is describing a specific person who has issued a document that can be examined. But when the reporter takes it upon himself to describe the re-port as *sketchy* or *optimistic,* he is moving into an area in which there are no physical referents. He may use such words in an interpretative story, but only if he anchors them to specific facts and figures.

Use Words With Referents

Words such as *progress, freedom, patriotism, big business, militant, radical* and others like them cause trouble because they float off in space without being anchored to anything specific, concrete or identifiable. Re-porters will quote sources who use these words and phrases, but they ask sources to explain just how they are using these vague terms.

Unwary reporters can become participants in brainwashing the public by using vague language. When an oil company distributed a press release announcing the construction of an "oil farm" outside a Massachusetts town and the reporter dutifully wrote in her lead that the "oil farm will occupy a tract southeast of the city," the reporter was not only using language inaccurately, she was helping the oil firm obscure the truth. The so-called "farm" was to be used for oil storage tanks, which have a grimy image. A farm, with visions of white barns and green pastures, is what the oil company wanted readers to imagine so that potential opposition would be diverted. *Farm* as used here is a euphemism.

Euphemisms

When Congress was discussing taxes, it sought to soften the impact of that dread word by substituting the words *revenue enhancement*. In Northern California, where marijuana is a major agricultural product, the polite term for its cultivation is *cash-intensive horticulture*. When a pleasant word or phrase is used in place of one that may be grim, the substitute is called a euphemism.

Some journalists may consider themselves compassionate for letting euphemisms slip by. After all, what is the harm in permitting people who work with convicts to describe them as the *consumers of criminal justice services?* What, for that matter, is wrong with *senior citizens* for older people or *sight deprived* for the blind? Surely, these euphemisms hurt no one.

Killers and Costs. The State Department stated that it would no longer use the word *killing* in its reports on human rights. In its place, the department said, will be "unlawful or arbitrary deprivation of life."

Allen H. Neuharth, head of the Gannett newspaper chain, had a unique way of talking about a price increase for *The Detroit News*. "Sooner or later," he said, the *News* "will give readers the opportunity to pay for their products what they are worth."

Actually, they do damage us because they turn us away from reality. They blur the truth. If the journalist's task can be reduced to a single idea, it is to point to reality. Words should describe the real, not blunt or distort it.

The absurdity of substituting an agreeable or acceptable expression for unpleasant language was demonstrated several years ago by a Chicago police reporter who was covering a rape. He was reminded by his desk of the newspaper's prohibition of what the publisher considered earthy language. *Rape,* he was told, was taboo. In his second paragraph, he wrote, "The woman ran down the street screaming, 'Help, I've been criminally assaulted! Help, I've been criminally assaulted!' "

During the Vietnam War, the violence and carnage were softened by euphemisms. Worse, words were used for propaganda purposes, and the press fell into line. *Destruction* became *pacification. Destroy* became *save,* as in the classic statement of an officer, "We had to destroy the town in order to save it."

Don't Fear *Said*

These misuses of the language are dangerous shoals on which many reporters have run aground. If we could mark the reefs that threaten writers, the most dangerous would be where reporters have gone under while fishing for synonyms for the verb *to say*. Let it be said at once, loud and clear, the word *said* cannot be overused for attribution. If tempted to replace it with *affirmed, alleged, asserted, contended, declared, pointed out, shouted, stated* or *whispered,* see the dictionary first. Better still, recall Ring Lardner's line: "Shut up he explained."

If neither the dictionary nor Lardner work, try Donald Barthelme's short piece, "Snap Snap," in his collection *Guilty Pleasures,* (New York: Dell Publishing Co., 1976), pp. 31–37. Barthelme leafed through *Time* and *Newsweek* one summer and found a fascination for *snap, cry,* and *warn:*

> "Ridiculous!" snapped Hollywood's Peter Lawford. . . . (*Newsweek,* June 21.)
> "Adolescent," snapped author Ralph Ellison. . . . (*Time,* June 25.)
> Americans are "abominable," Russell snapped. . . . (*Time,* June 25.)

Sixteen snappers appeared in *Time* in June and July, fewer in *Newsweek.* The criers included an Egyptian, a Brazilian and Cuba's Castro (twice in *Time,* June 18 and June 25). "Strongman Castro nearly always cries in newsweeklies," writes Barthelme. "Sometimes roars. He has been heard to snort. But mostly cries."

Generally, it is wise to avoid fishing for synonyms. Writing in which the same word appears and reappears may seem uninspired and dull to the writer. It is not to the reader. Consider the experience of the reporter who wrote a piece about the major export of a Central American country, the banana. As he looked over his copy, he noticed the word banana in the lead, then in the second sentence. In the fourth sentence, banana was replaced by fruit. But there in the fifth, it loomed up again. Hardly a paragraph was free of the word, which by now he had come to hate. But what to use in its stead?

Suddenly, he hit upon it. "In Costa Rica, the elongated yellow fruit is harvested on both coasts."

The journalistic world has long forgotten what this creative journalist wrote, but the phrase "elongated yellow fruit" has come to represent a type of stilted and silly writing that journalists should shun.

This does not mean the news writer should steer clear of words and phrases that help to make writing picturesque or dramatic. In an interview, a reporter quoted an official of a peace organization as saying, "55,000 young Americans came home in rubber bags" from the Vietnam War. That image hits the reader more effectively than saying 55,000 were killed.

Beware of Synonyms

Facts First, Words Second

One of the impediments to accuracy stems from the reporter's unceasing desire for the story that will perk up the reader. The desire is healthy, but it can lead to the selection of words—as well as facts—that are more colorful and exciting than the event merits. Reporters sometimes are so stimulated by the urge to be creative that they separate their language and their stories from the reality that inspired them. As writers, they feel an occasional liberty with facts and language may be granted them. In his novel *The Deer Park,* Norman Mailer describes the lure of a well-crafted story for a movie director, Charles Eitel. Mailer indicates the corruption of such temptation: "The professional in Eitel lusted for the new story . . . it was so beautifully false. Professional blood thrived on what was excellently dishonest."

Inaccurate writing often stems from finding the words and phrases first, then hanging on to them despite the facts. Every writer is carried away by the beauty and incisiveness of his or her writing. But just as the broadcast journalist should never use the camera as an end in itself, so the print reporter must not use words as an end. The objective is to communicate information accurately, not to display technical brilliance with the zoom lens or tape splicer, not to play with words. Technique has its place; its proper role is to aid in accurate communication. As Pauline Kael, the movie critic, put it: "Technique is hardly worth talking about unless it's used for something worth doing."

Caution. Red Smith, the peerless sportswriter, said of journalism: "The essential thing is to report the facts; if there is time for good writing as well, that's frosting on the cake."

Spelling

A few words about the bane of the copy editor, the misspelled word. A word incorrectly spelled is a gross inaccuracy. It is like a flaw in a crystal bowl. No matter how handsome the bowl, the eye and mind drift from the sweeping curves to the mistake. A spelling error screams for attention, almost as loudly as an obscenity in print. Intelligent reporters—good spellers or bad spellers—use the dictionary. Many editors associate intelligence with spelling ability because they consider the persistent poor speller to be stupid for not consulting the dictionary—whatever his or her native intelligence. See Appendix A, page 665.

The saying has it that doctors bury their mistakes and architects cover them with ivy. Journalists have no such luck. Their blunders are forever committed to public view:

So There. When Harvard awarded Andrew Jackson an honorary degree, John Quincy Adams boycotted the ceremonies, describing Jackson, known as the people's president, as "a barbarian who could not write a sentence of grammar." To which Jackson replied: "It is a damn poor mind indeed which can't think of at least two ways to spell any word."

Argentina Says Its Ready for Peace or War
—Tribune–Eagle
(Cheyenne, Wyo.)

Blind Girl servives first round of bee
—Gazette
(Indiana, Pa.)

The words and phrases the journalist selects must be put into a setting, into sentences and paragraphs that make sense to readers. Proper words in proper places, is the guide. "If you're going to be a newspaper writer you've got to put the hay down where the mules can reach it," said Ralph McGill of the Atlanta *Constitution*. Although he ranged over subjects as complex and touchy as race relations and foreign affairs, McGill wrote for ordinary people. His journalism was never vague. A reader of the King James version of the Bible, he learned early the strength, vigor and clarity of the precise word in the simple declarative sentence.

"A word fitly spoken is like apples of gold in pictures of silver," McGill said of the journalist's craft, quoting from Proverbs in the Old Testament. We know several ways to make these pictures—these sentences and paragraphs—clear to our readers.

First, there are the essentials of grammar and punctuation. In grandfather's day, students stood at the blackboard and diagrammed sentences. They broke sentences down into nouns, verbs, pronouns, adjectives, adverbs, prepositions, conjunctions and interjections. From there, they went into phrases—verbal, prepositional, participial, gerund and infinitive. Then they examined clauses—main and subordinate. This is the way they learned how sentences are constructed. In most schools today, the only grammar students learn is taught in foreign language classes. For a journalist, this is inadequate training.

One way the beginning journalist can cope with this inadequacy is to invest in a handbook of grammar. It will not only solve grammatical problems quickly, it will also expand the student's writing range. Some journalists stick with a limited style because it is all they can handle. No matter what the story, it is written with the same flat sentence structure the reporter used on the blues-singer interview yesterday and the bus-truck collision the day before that. See Appendix A on page 665, for a guide to grammar.

Clarity

Make Sense. In his *Red: A Biography of Red Smith*, Ira Berkow says Smith was influenced by his journalism teacher at Notre Dame, John Michael Cooney, who often began class by intoning: "Let us pray for sense." A former student said Cooney wanted "no jargon, no gobbledygook. He liked to see a sentence so definite it would cast a shadow."

Grammar

Five Fatal Flaws

After reading through dozens of freshman compositions, Loretta M. Shpunt, an English teacher at Trinity College in Washington, D.C., said she seriously considered buying a red ink pad and a set of rubber stamps that read:

NOT A SENTENCE
"IT'S" EQUALS "IT IS"
"ITS" IS POSSESSIVE
DANGLING PARTICIPLE
"I" BEFORE "E" EXCEPT AFTER "C"

Punctuation

Punctuation is the writer's substitute for the storyteller's pauses, stops and changes in voice level. The proper use of punctuation is essential to clarity. Misuse can change emphasis or meaning.

> She could not convince him of her innocence, however she tried.
> She could not convince him of her innocence; however, she tried.

We know that readers pause at the ends of sentences and paragraphs. These short interruptions in the flow of the story help the reader absorb what he or she has read. Broadcast copy needs even shorter sentences. Short as these stops are, they are important for comprehension, particularly to the listener, who cannot reread something unclear to him. Even Gertrude Stein, the author of non-stop prose ("Rose is a rose is a rose is a rose."), came to recognize the value of the period. In *Lectures in America* (Boston: Beacon Press, 1957), p. 217, Stein said:

> When I first began writing, I felt that writing should go on, I still do feel that it should go on but when I first began writing I was completely possessed by the necessity that writing should go on and if writing should go on what had colons and semi-colons to do with it, what had commas to do with it, what had periods to do with it. . . .
>
> What had periods to do with it. Inevitably no matter how completely I had to have writing go on physically one had to again and again stop some time then periods had to exist. Besides I had always liked the look of periods and I liked what they did. Stopping sometimes did not really keep one from going on, it was nothing that interfered, it was only something that happened, and as it happened as a perfectly natural happening, I did believe in periods and I used them. I never really stopped using them.

Sentence Length

Spurred by an anxiety to cram facts into sentences, some inexperienced reporters write block-busters that send the reader down line after line in increasing confusion. When you spot a sentence running three lines or more, think of the self-editing of Isaac Babel, a Russian writer whose short stories are highly polished gems:

> I go over each sentence, time and again. I start by cutting all the words it can do without. You have to keep your eye on the job because words are very sly. The rubbishy ones go into hiding and you have to dig them out—repetitions, synonyms, things that simply don't mean anything.

Before I take out the rubbish, I break up the text into shorter sentences. The more full stops the better. I'd like to have that passed as a law. Not more than one idea and one image to a sentence.

A paragraph is a wonderful thing. It lets you quietly change the rhythm, and it can be like a flash of lightning that shows the landscape from a different perspective. There are writers, even good ones, who scatter paragraphs and punctuation marks all over the place.

The maxim that each sentence should, if possible, carry only one idea has been assumed to be an injunction limited to journalism. Not so, as we see from Babel's comment. The fact is, good journalistic writing is based upon the principles of good writing. Journalism is a part of the world of letters.

The press associations have concluded after a number of studies that one of the keys to readable stories is the short sentence. Here is a table distributed by the UPI:

The Shorter The Better

Average Sentence Length	Readability
8 words or less	Very easy to read
11 words	Easy to read
14 words	Fairly easy to read
17 words	Standard
21 words	Fairly difficult to read
25 words	Difficult to read
29 words or more	Very difficult to read

This table refers to average sentence length. One sentence after another under 17 words would create a staccato effect. Readers and listeners would feel as though they were being peppered with bird shot. The key to good writing is variety, rhythm, balance. Short and long sentences are balanced. A long sentence that is well written can be as understandable as an eight-word sentence, if it is broken, usually by punctuation, into short clauses and phrases.

There are events whose nature dictates a relaxed style with long sentences. A public official retiring after 45 years of work with the state attorney general's office recalls in an interview the gradual evolution of civil rights. The story—told leisurely with rolling, conversational sentences—is written with a style far different from the short-sentence style employed to describe a bank holdup. This is a matter of appropriateness of style, and we shall go into it in more detail later. But it is important to point out here that although we want short sentences, the nature of the event determines how we tell the story.

A Pulitzer Prize Story: Workings of the Brain

Here is the beginning of the first story in a series by Jon Franklin that won the 1985 Pulitzer Prize for explanatory journalism for *The Evening Sun*. The word count in these 12 sentences runs: 16, 24, 34, 9, 13, 18, 14, 21, 19, 5, 13, 21. The average sentence length is 17 words, standard reading fare. Notice the way Franklin varies the length of his sentences to set up a rhythm—long, short. The longest sentence in the sample—the third, 34 words—is followed by a short sentence—nine words.

Since the days of Sigmund Freud the practice of psychiatry has been more art than science. Surrounded by an aura of witchcraft, proceeding on impression and hunch, often ineffective, it was the bumbling and sometimes humorous stepchild of modern science.

But for a decade and more, research psychiatrists have been working quietly in laboratories, dissecting the brains of mice and men and teasing out the chemical formulas that unlock the secrets of the mind.

Now, in the 1980s, their work is paying off.

They are rapidly identifying the interlocking molecules that produce human thought and emotion. They have devised new scanners that trace the flickering web of personality as it dances through the brain. Armed with those scanners, they are mapping out the terrain of the human psyche.

As a result, psychiatry today stands on the threshold of becoming an exact science, as precise and quantifiable as molecular genetics. Ahead lies an era of psychic engineering, and the development of specialized drugs and therapies to heal sick minds.

But that's only the beginning: The potential of brain chemistry extends far beyond the confines of classic psychiatry.

Many molecular psychiatrists, for instance, believe they may soon have the ability to untangle the ancient enigma of violence and criminality.

Use Short Words and Human Interest Words

Two other writing devices can help to make sentences clear—the number of syllables in the words used, and the use of human interest words.

Long words should be used infrequently. One study advises no more than 150 syllables for every hundred words. Obviously, no reporter can or should count syllables. The point is that short words are best.

Participles add unnecessary syllables to sentences. Not only that, they turn sentences around, as in this lead:

```
    Expecting heavy traffic over the July 4th weekend, the
state police today assigned all available manpower to duty
over the three-day weekend.
```

It would take no great effort to make the lead conform to the S-V-O construction and to eliminate extra syllables. With a few pencil marks, clarity can be achieved:

```
The state police today assigned all available men to
duty for the three-day July 4th weekend to handle the heavy
traffic that is expected.
```

The use of human interest words also helps to make writing clear and interesting. These words range from the simple *you, your, his, her, me, mine, my,* to proper nouns and the names of familiar persons and subjects. It is better to write *the pansies* than *the plants, the Stones* than *a rock group.*

Some reporters have trouble writing short sentences because they cannot handle transitions, the links between sentences and paragraphs. Because these reporters have no mastery of the device that enables a writer to move smoothly from sentence to sentence, their tendency is to think in large clots of words. The journalist with fingertip control of transitions thinks in smaller sentence clusters.

Transitions

There are four major types of transitions:

1. **Pronouns.** Use pronouns to refer to nouns in previous sentences and paragraphs:

Dr. Braun began teaching history in 1927. *He* took *his* Ph.D. that year. *His* dissertation subject was the French Impressionists.

2. **Key words and ideas.** Repeat words and ideas in preceding sentences and paragraphs:

He has been accused of being an *academic purist. Those words* make him shudder.

"*Academic purist* is made to sound like an epithet," he said.

3. **Transitional expressions.** Use connecting words that link sentences. A large array of expressions function as connectors. Here are most of the major categories of conjunctions and some of the words in each category that can be used as transitions:

Additives—Again, also, and, finally, furthermore, in addition, next, thus, so.

Contrasts—But, however, nevertheless, instead, on the other hand, otherwise, yet.

Comparisons—Likewise, similarly.

Place—Adjacent to, beyond, here, near, opposite.

Time—Afterward, in the meantime, later, meanwhile, soon.

He tried twice to obtain permission to see the paintings in the private museum. *Finally,* he gave up.

Dr. Braun's *next* project centered on the music of Berlioz. *But* his luck remained bad. An attempt to locate a missing manuscript proved a *similar* failure.

In the meantime, he continued his study of Spanish so that he would be able to do research in Spain.

4. **Parallel structure.** Sentences and paragraphs are linked by repeating the sentence pattern:

No one dared speak in his classes. *No one* ventured to address him in any but the most formal manner. *No one,* for that matter, had the courage to ask questions in class. His lectures were non-stop monologues.

Transitions emphasize the logical order of a news story. But they cannot create coherence where there is none. Transitions are used after the reporter has planned his piece by blocking out the major sections. Transitions link these blocks as well as the smaller units, the sentences. Transitions are the mortar that holds the story together so that the story is a single unit.

Logical Order

A news story should move smoothly from fact to fact. When natural sequence is disrupted, the story loses clarity. Here are two paragraphs from a story in an Oklahoma daily newspaper:

"There is nothing new in the allegations," Bartlett said. "We've heard them all before."

"When we first heard them we thought there was nothing to it, but then we had a second look," Tillman said.

Although the first paragraph is closed by a quotation mark, which means that the speaker (Bartlett) is finished, most readers jump ahead to the next quote and presume that Bartlett is still talking. They are jolted when they find that Tillman is speaking. The solution is simple: When you introduce a new speaker, begin the sentence or paragraph with his or her name.

Jumps in time and place must be handled carefully to avoid confusion.

NEW YORK (April 13)—A criminal court judge who last month ruled that a waiter had seduced but not raped a college student sent the man to jail for a year **yesterday** on a charge of escaping from the police after his arrest.

On March 19, Justice Albert S. Hess acquitted Phillip Blau of raping a 20-year-old Pembroke College student. The judge said a man could use guile, scheme, and be deceitful, but so long as he did not use violence, rape did not occur.

At that time, women's groups protested the decision.

"Despite the protests of outraged feminists who demand your head, or other and possibly more appropriate parts of your anatomy," the judge told Blau **yesterday,** "I shall punish you only for crimes of which you have been found guilty."

The changes in time are clearly indicated at the start of the second and third paragraphs. From "yesterday" in the lead, the reader is taken to "March 19" in the second paragraph, and is kept there in the third paragraph by the transition "At that time" that begins the paragraph. When the quote begins the fourth paragraph, the reader is still back in March with the women. Midway through the paragraph the reader realizes the judge is speaking and that he spoke yesterday. The jolts in time and place could have been avoided with a simple transition paragraph:

In sentencing Blau **yesterday,** Justice Hess commented on the protests. He said: . . .

This may seem to be nitpicking. It is not. The journalist knows that every sentence, every word, even the punctuation marks must be carefully selected. For the reader does read from word to word, and is pushed, maneuvered, teased, sped and slowed through the story by the way it is written. Major disturbances of logic and order in the story confuse readers, just as a quick jump cut on television destroys the continuity of the event for the viewer.

Logical order is based upon the organizing concept that the reporter selects. The most frequently used organizing principle is chronology, a narrative device that is particularly useful on dramatic longer pieces.

Telling Stories. "The basis of good *Time* writing is narrative, and the basis of good narrative is to tell events (1) in the order in which they occur; (2) in the form in which an observer might have seen them—so that readers might imagine themselves at the scene."—a *Time* editor.

"The White Rabbit put on his spectacles. 'Where should I begin, please your majesty?' he asked. 'Begin at the beginning,' the King said, very gravely, 'and go on till you come to the end; then stop.' "—*Alice in Wonderland.*

Some critics of journalistic writing scoff at what they consider the absurdity of a news story whose climax is presented in the headline, then in the lead, and again when the story builds to a climax, already twice-told. These critics are not disturbed by hearing *Carmen* for the third time; nor do they balk at rereading *Hamlet*. No news story can match the brilliance of a work by Bizet or Shakespeare. But people do read interesting stories even when they know the outcome, whether it be from having seen it themselves, from the headline and lead, or from seeing last night's 11 o'clock news account.

Avoid Jargon

Beginning writers sometimes try to impress their editors with their grasp of their beats by using the specialized language of the field they are covering. The effort is wasted. Few readers know what these words mean.

For those who would like to master jargon, here's a list that made the rounds of newspapers in Colorado:

Personal Jargon Generator

	1st digit	2nd Digit	3rd Digit
0	Long Range	Conceptual	Alternatives
1	Comprehensive	Facilitating	Objectives
2	Community	Regional	Interface
3	Ecological	Functional	Capacity
4	Schematic	Infrastructure	Analysis
5	Infill	Transportation	Matrix
6	Inter-Related	Open-space	Mitigation
7	Coordinated	Esthetic	Densities
8	Integrated	Planning	Relationships
9	Multi-Phase	Impact	Coefficient

Select any three-digit number. Apply it to the list above. Insert the phrase in copy when confused about the facts. If your editor is savvy, try it on friends. If they treat you with greater respect, drop them. They are too easily impressed.

Long Stories

No matter how badly organized a short news story may be, readers will suffer through it if the information is essential. But no one will tarry on a disorganized longer piece. Coherence, focus and organization are essential to the feature, the analytical or interpretative article and certainly to the magazine article.

Here is the beginning of a story, "On Chuck Hughes, Dying Young," Barnard Collier wrote for *Esquire*. The transitions involving the characters have been marked. The underlinings (references to Hughes), circles (Butkus) and rectangles (doctors) in the first four paragraphs show how Collier has kept his central figure (Hughes) and the two minor figures (Butkus and the doctors) on stage. These provide human interest. They lace in and out of the paragraphs, moving the action forward in a continuous flow:

In the fourth quarter of the Sunday-afernoon pro-football game on TV, a twenty-eight-year-old Detroit Lion named Chuck Hughes dropped dead of a heart attack on the fifteen-yard line in front of the gathering of millions of Americans.

You did not know right away he was dead, but you knew something was very wrong. The cameras showed a close-up of Dick Butkus of the Chicago Bears standing over him and waving in a scared and frantic way for the referees and then for the doctors on the Lions bench. A player must wave for the referees before the doctors can come out on the field or it is a violation of the National Football League rules. A player might be lying there faking an injury to stop the clock. The Lions were behind by five points and they needed a touchdown before the clock ran out in order to win. But an incomplete pass had already stopped the clock, so Chuck Hughes had no reason to fake. He must have looked very bad off to Dick Butkus, because you knew that Butkus is mean and ornery when he is out there on the football field and doesn't normally come to the aid of an injured man who is not on his team.

The doctors ran out and started moving around too fast. You knew from looking at it on TV that this wasn't just a man with the wind knocked out of him. He was too still. Nothing of him moved. The doctors were working too hard. Instead of just loosening his pants like they do when a man is down with the wind knocked out, they went for his chest and mouth.

One doctor was pounding on Chuck's chest with his fist, and the other gave mouth-to-mouth breathing. This football player was not going to get bravely to his feet and walk off the field under his own steam, hanging from the shoulders of the trainers and dragging a leg. This man was not just injured. You knew

After this description of the on-the-field scene, Collier moves the reader. He writes, "Chuck's wife, Sharon, was in the stands." Then he describes her reaction to her husband's collapse. Collier's intention in this story is not to describe a football player's death but to tell us about Hughes' life as an athlete, beginning with his childhood in Texas. To move from Sharon in the stands to this background, Collier uses a transitional paragraph: "She kept thinking about their marriage and how much Chuck was in love with football." This is followed by a paragraph that begins: "When Chuck was a little boy in Breckenridge, Tex., he carried a football around with him nearly all the time." We are now moved into a chronology of Hughes' life.

Conviction

Some people find the news they read, hear and see as unconvincing as some of the advertising that accompanies it.

"What's the real story?" reporters are asked, as though they were prevented from revealing the truth by powerful advertisers or friends of the publisher or station manager. These pressures rarely influence reporters. More often, the pressures of time and the inaccessibility of documents and sources impede truth-telling, and just as often, reporting and writing failures get in the way of the real story. Let us examine the components of a news story that is accurate and complete and that is credible:

Reporting:

1. Relevant factual material from personal observation and physical sources.

2. Authoritative and knowledgeable human sources for additional information.

3. Significant and complete background information.

Writing:

1. Simple language.
2. Illustrations, examples and quotes that document the lead.
3. Human interest.
4. Appropriate style.

Let's examine each of these.

Relevant Material

As we have seen, writing depends on the facts the reporter unearths. The journalist will use details just as any writer does—to build a picture that shows the full extent of what is going on and that convinces us of the truth of the account. The journalist—whose eye catches the color of the trees felled in the disease eradication program and the tears of the child whose puppy takes third place instead of first at the dog show—convinces the reader he is an accurate observer and that his account can be trusted.

The journalist is conscious of the backdrop, the scene. It may be that the news conference took place in the mayor's office, that the rescue was made in a calm sea at dusk. Then the particulars: The mayor spoke seated at his desk, with seven microphones from radio and television stations in front of him and a dozen journalists in attendance; the Coast Guard boat was manned by six seamen and an officer.

A journalism teacher, a veteran of many years on small-town and big-city newspapers, still shudders at his recollection of the night he was sent out to the suburbs by a San Francisco newspaper. Fumes from an unvented heater had poured through a house, killing the entire family. Only the dog survived. The reporter gathered the relevant information—names and ages of the victims, occupation of the father, approximate time of death, schools the children attended, how long they had lived in the house, whether the vent was legal, even the name of the dog (taken from its collar). Racing to a pay phone to make the final edition, he was dictating the story when he was stunned by the rewriteman's question: "What kind of house was it? Wood? Stucco? Brick?" The reporter had no idea, and there was no time to dash back to the house to find out.

Details should be relevant to the story's theme or mood or they waste space and divert the reader. The political profile of a major presidential appointee in a national news magazine described him as: "neat, careful, conservative, reverent, industrious, polite without pretension, but incredibly smooth and self-controlled, always keeping his distance, maintaining the inner core of his being inviolate and locked. . . . He generates great sincerity in avoiding the direct answer, although he is by nature decisive and succinct."

Some of these details resemble the comments a college admissions officer might make after interviewing a high school senior. Others indicate the reporter is possessed with extrasensory perception that allows him to penetrate his subject's "inner core." We want to know the official's record and his opinions on issues, not whether he is neat or sincere. Who can tell whether he is sincere? Reporters are always relearning that their judgments and inferences about human nature are as fallible as a teen-ager's opinions of his parents.

Details and More Details. When reporting a murder, Edna Buchanan says she wants to know "what movie they saw before they got gunned down.

"What were they wearing? What did they have in their pockets? What was cooking on the stove? What song was playing on the jukebox?

"I always ask what the dog's name is, what the cat's name is."

Here are the first four paragraphs of a speech story:

This country must return to law and order if America's free institutions are to survive, Lexington businessmen were told Monday night.

And, it is the responsibility of businessmen on the local level to educate Americans, particularly the youth, in the importance of these free institutions and what they mean.

Speaking at a general membership meeting of the Greater Lexington Area Chamber of Commerce, Dr. Kenneth McFarland, author, educator and businessman, said that the current situation must be turned around.

"We can no more co-exist with this than we can co-exist with a cancer," he said. "We've got to take the handcuffs off the police and put them back on the criminal where they belong."

These are serious statements, and we wonder who is making them. We are given the source's background in the third paragraph. Later in the story he is referred to as a "master's degree candidate from Columbia University." But the identifying material raises more questions than it answers: Author of what? Educator where? What kind of business? Does he own or manage the business? Why is a doctor studying for a master's degree? Or if he holds a Ph.D., why the need for a lesser degree?

Since the story is so vague about the qualifications of the source, readers will be reluctant to accept his analysis. He may have been qualified, but the story does not give his qualifications.

One of the reasons readers and listeners find some news unconvincing is that the sources that journalists use are officials or so-called experts who have not experienced the situations they are describing. A story about unemployment that quotes only officials and data is inadequate. Unemployment is more than figures released by an official sitting at a desk. It is men and women standing idly on street corners or waiting in anterooms for job interviews day after day.

It is, of course, easier for a reporter to call an official for material than it is to seek out people affected by events. The result is educational stories written without interviewing students, public health stories that lack comments from those who use clinics and emergency rooms—stories that lack completeness and conviction.

In an AP story about the Army's pleasure over an unusually heavy crop of volunteers, the "story cited every factor except the main one: The economy was down, unemployment up, and enlistments always rise under those circumstances," said Jack Cappon, AP's general news editor.

An event that is not placed in context lacks meaning. Context can provide the how and why of the event. As Cappon put it:

> In news writing, nothing is more basic than making sure that any event, speech, situation or statistic is reported in sufficient context to fix the meaning accurately.

Most of the time we do it right: A story about relaxed marijuana penalties puts it in the framework of current figures for offenses and convictions. A Moscow dispatch about Russian-American trade talks harks back to the collapse of an earlier trade agreement in December.

Simple Language

Whoa. Good writers use similes and metaphors—carefully. An imaginative student wrote of an airline that was going broke:

The nuts and bolts of the organization chewed their nails all week under a shroud of uncertainty.

Four writing components add to the readers' and listeners' conviction that the story is accurate and complete, that it is credible.

One of the journalist's justifications for his privileges is that he fashions his stories for all people so that they can understand events and act immediately. Even the most complex idea must be taken to the people if it is an idea that affects them. This can be done. One of the biggest best sellers in this country's history was a political treatise, *Common Sense,* by Thomas Paine. Within three months of its publication in 1776, 120,000 copies were sold in the Colonies, whose population was about 2.5 million. Today, a book selling as well would reach 10 million readers in this country. Paine used the language of the people. He began his pamphlet: "In the following pages I offer nothing more than the simple facts, plain arguments, and common sense."

The good reporter is firmly rooted in the language of the common people, which, because it is comprehensible, has the ring of conviction.

Illustrations, Examples and Quotations

Wallace Stevens, the insurance company executive who wrote poetry that influenced a generation of poets, commented with some incredulity about events that were swirling around him: "In the presence of extraordinary actuality, consciousness takes the place of imagination." Fact has supplanted fiction.

Why, then, is so much journalism dull and unconvincing? One of the answers is that journalists sometimes do not use in their stories what they see and hear. They paraphrase good quotes. They explain instead of letting the example show the reader.

Here are two paragraphs from a book by Studs Terkel, *Working: People Talk About What They Do All Day and What They Think of While They Do It*. Terkel, a radio reporter based in Chicago, interviewed a 14-year-old newsboy, Terry Pickens:

> I don't see where being a newsboy and learning that people are pretty mean or that people don't have enough money to buy things with is gonna make you a better person or anything. If anything, it's gonna make a worse person out of you, 'cause you're not gonna like people that

don't pay you. And you're not gonna like people who act like they're doing you a big favor paying you. Yeah, it sort of molds your character, but I don't think for the better. If anybody told me being a newsboy builds character, I'd know he was a liar.

I don't see where people get all this bull about the kid who's gonna be president and being a newsboy made a president out of him. It taught him how to handle his money and this bull. You know what it did? It taught him how to hate the people on his route. And the printers. And dogs. . . .

No paraphrase or summary would have the impact of Terry Pickens' own words. For that matter, few psychologists with their understanding of the problems of adolescence and growth can express so succinctly and convincingly—and with such emotion—the realities of the working world. Journalists can.

Talk about extraordinary actuality: Who could imagine a nine-year-old boy holding up a bank? It happened, and the AP story combined quotations and observations to convince the reader of the youngster's daring. The last paragraph shows the reader that the bandit might be cool, but that he is still a little boy. Here is part of the story:

The pint-sized bandit first entered the consumer loan department of the bank about 11:20 a.m. Wednesday and told an employee: "This is a holdup."

Told he was not in the banking section, he left without protest, to reappear moments later in the proper area.

"This is a holdup," the young bandit repeated for teller Yvonne Patterson, brandishing his weapon anew and peeking over the counter.

"Don't press any buttons. Just give me the money in the drawer."

"He was very calm, like a little man, and she looked at him and thought it was a joke," Police Officer Robert McQuade said later.

However, eventually convinced he meant business, Miss Patterson handed over the $118 in currency.

The boy left, but just before going out the door to Sixth Avenue, he held the bills above his head and jumped up and down triumphantly, police said.

When the Virginia State Bar Association voted to admit its first black member despite a determined effort by some senior members to block the move, a news story quoted a Richmond lawyer as praising the applicant as a "commendable person with a high standing as a lawyer." Then the story quoted him as adding, "But he is a Negro and therefore I am opposed to accepting him as a member of this association. . . . I have a good many Negro friends, but I don't invite any of them to my home or club to socialize with me."

In three sentences, the reporter crystallized an aspect of race relations by letting one of the participants in the relationship speak.

Telling Trifles. The British novelist John Galsworthy said that the secret of a good description is the significant trifle— a seemingly inconsistent remark, an unusual word, a slip by a witness. The alert reporter catches these. Freud could be said to have constructed psychoanalysis on the principle of the significant trifle.

The best advice she received from an editor, a reporter remarked, was:

"Follow every generality with a specific."

Every story has a logical structure, she said. When a council member says next year's budget will set a record high, the reporter asks how high that will be, what the amount will be. And that is how it is written:

Riggio said next year's budget will "be a record high." He estimated it would amount to more than $125 million.

Another example:

Miles said, "Lombardi was wrong when he said winning is everything."

It is more important to develop the athlete's sense of fair play and his or her love of sport, the coach said.

A UPI story from Knoxville, Tenn., about Joey Maxim, describes his descent from a light-heavyweight champion to a second-rate wrestler. The reporter quotes Maxim as saying about his former fight manager, "He probably doesn't want to see me any more—afraid I might want to borrow some money." That one quote tells us a great deal about Maxim, the manager and the boxing business. When a reporter hears a statement like that, he perks up. He senses that here, in a few words, is a summary of the situation. The same excitement rushes through a reporter when he or she spots an incident that will illustrate the event.

Sarah Grimes covered juvenile court in Philadelphia. Overworked and understaffed, the court was unable to cope with the cases before it. Also, the judges were generations away from the reality of street life. Here are some sections of a story Grimes wrote to show the distance between the court and the young offenders. A judge is speaking to two boys in court:

"You should stand still and be respectful when approached by a police officer. Then the officers will respect you. . . .

"I imagine they roughed you up a little bit, huh? I'd have given you a couple of good ones, too, before I took you in.

"In the old days, we used to have Irish policemen and we'd get it over the legs and then we'd get it again at home when the police took us to our fathers.

"We didn't call it police brutality then, and I'm concerned about the disrespect shown here for the policemen. . . .

"The next time you see a policeman, think positively. You can even say, 'Officer, what can I do for you?' The police are paid to protect us. When I see them I feel safe.

"You work, you pay taxes, the police are there to protect you."

Caution: Important as quotations are, it is improper to put into direct quotation what has been heard second or third hand. This device, used by imaginative reporters influenced by the New Journalism, is unethical. Reconstructed quotes are best left to the novelists.

Illustrations and examples can become symbols of ideas and events. When a reporter was covering a long and complicated discussion by the city council that led nowhere, she recalled that during the desultory debate, the mayor had built a pyramid with paper clips and matches. She wrote this into her story to illustrate his reaction to the discussion.

As we saw earlier, the two press associations consider the use of human interest words and incidents to be important elements in readability. Human interest also is essential to credibility. Readers who see people in news stories are likely to believe the stories.

When a reporter returned with a videotaped feature about a local store that was selling books, posters, pictures and other material based on television's "Star Trek," his editor praised his enterprise. The film concentrated on the material sold. There was little about the customers, the "Star Trek" fans.

"We missed," the editor said. "We should have followed a customer around and used him as the center of the story."

Frederick C. Othman, a veteran reporter for UPI, advised reporters to put as many personal references as possible into each sentence, "meaning he, she, King George, uncle, boy, girl or any such word describing a human being. The more such words, the more interesting the story."

Here is some more advice from Othman: "If a gent wears a dark-brown coat, say it's chocolate-colored. Not only is that descriptive, but it gets food into the story. Any word connoting food adds interest value.

"Tell about the taste of things and, especially, smells. Both good and bad. Take the man smoking a Turkish cigarette; it smells like burnt chicken feathers. Say so."

Othman worried that stories about ideas and things would bore readers. He said, "Don't write about ideas, or even things, but about the people who have the ideas, or who build (or break) the things."

In 1945, when Othman's advice was distributed to United Press reporters, the world had undergone a catastrophic war whose origin lay in the racial and political theories of Adolf Hitler. The tens of millions who died in the gas chambers and concentration camps and on the battlefield were tangible proof that ideas must be the subject of journalism, even when they cannot be animated.

Actually, most ideas can be dramatized and personalized by putting them into human terms. The simplest way to do this is to show people affected by these ideas, or, as Othman suggested, to infuse the article with the personality of those advancing or opposing the ideas and theories.

The Human Touch. This photograph of Vietnam veterans seeking to reach out to their dead comrades combines two elements of good writing—details (the names of the dead) and human interest (the two veterans at the Iowa Vietnam Veterans Memorial). Photo by David Peterson of *The Des Moines Register.*

Sometimes reporters fail to personalize events that easily lend themselves to human interest. When a puppy fell into the shaft of an abandoned well in Carlsbad, N.M., the rescue operation became a front page story in many newspapers. One press service story that used the name of the puppy, Wimpy, was widely preferred to the competition's story that lacked the pup's name.

As we have seen so often, no amount of good writing can compensate for inadequate reporting. William Burroughs, the novelist, said of the writer: "Generally speaking, if he can't see it, hear it, feel it and smell it, he can't write it."

Compare these versions of the same story:

All doctors hope their patients never have occasion to use the Poison Control Center recently established in the emergency room of the Community General Hospital. However, it should be reassuring to citizens, particularly parents, to know the center exists for use in an emergency.

Springfield is one of only eight cities in the state which have official "recognized" centers to handle poisoning cases. The other seven cities are. . . .

A frantic mother called her physician and cried that her two-year-old had been at the oven cleaner. The child's lips were smudged with the liquid.

The label said poison. What should she do?

Her call set in motion a series of checks and other calls. In a short time her physician knew precisely what chemicals were in the cleaner, which were poisonous, and what should be done.

The child was treated and beyond a few small burns on the lips and tongue the baby is doing well.

This happened the other day, and it was the first case for the Freeport Poison Information Center in the Community General Hospital.

The journalist who wrote the second piece did a better job of writing because his reporting was superior. Also, he contributed a greater public service because the picture he painted of a mother and child is etched in the minds of parents. The second story is also more appropriate to the event. That is, the material is consistent with the nature of the event being reported—what the Center does.

The style of the second piece is consistent with the event. The average sentence length of the first five sentences, which describe the poisoning incident, is between 11 and 12 words. The next three average 21 words because the reporter was seeking to give an air of calm after the frenzy of the incident. This brings us to the fourth and last of our guidelines for good journalistic writing.

Appropriate Style

Every event has its own tone, texture and pace that good reporters try to reflect in the way they write their stories. The way a story is written is known as its style. An understanding of style might start with Cicero, the Roman statesman and orator: "Whatever his theme he will speak it as becomes it; neither meagerly where it is copious, nor meanly where it is ample, not in this way where it demands that; but keeping his speech level with the actual subject and adequate to it."

This congruity between theme and speech is what the journalist means by fitting the story to the event. Cardinal John Henry Newman in his book *The Idea of a University* said, "Matter and expression are parts of one; style is thinking out into language."

In a review of Lillian Ross' *Reporting,* the reviewer, James F. Fixx, says that Ross in her stories shows how reporting can be made into an art. She "somehow makes commonplace things interesting, but she never overdramatizes, never gains falsely heightened effects through dishonest juxtaposition or phony cuteness." He continues:

> The result is an uncommon steadiness of tone that seldom lets her writing sink either into banality or that shrieking, supercharged prose that, in the hands of some journalists, makes the reader wonder whether life could ever have been all that exciting. Miss Ross's style is, in fact, a manner of reporting that all but eliminates the reporter.

In this story of a murder, the short sentences reflect the starkness of the event:

Fight for Hat Cited as Motive in Boy's Slaying

Sixteen-year-old Kenneth Richardson was killed Thursday over a floppy brown hat, police said.

"It was just a plain old hat," Metro Homicide Detective Hugo Gomez said.

Richardson was wearing it. Someone tried to take it. Richardson refused.

Others entered the fray. The youth ran. They chased him.

"It was a running and shooting type thing. They were shooting directly at him," Gomez said.

Richardson still had the hat when taken to International Hospital, where he died in surgery, Dade's 554th homicide this year.

He was shot in the parking lot of the Miami Gardens Shopping Plaza at 12:15 a.m., soon after the nearby Gardens Shopping Skating Center closed for the night, police said.

No arrests have been made.

"They were all Carol City kids," Gomez said. "There was talk of several guns."

About 25 youths were in the area at the time, police say. "But there was nothing but the dust settling when we got there," Gomez said.

—*The Miami Herald*

Since journalists are obliged to tell their stories briefly, they must choose words that count, words that quickly and efficiently paint pictures. The story is most effective when the journalist selects words in which the denotative and connotative meanings, the explicit and implicit meanings, mesh.

During New York City's financial crisis in 1975, the city appealed for federal aid. President Ford brusquely said no, that the city's profligacy and incompetence had caused its fiscal misery and that it had to put its house in order itself. Pondering the story on the president's refusal, William Brink, the managing editor of the *Daily News,* cast about for the five or six words he could fit into the *News'* page one headline for the story. He tried:

FORD REFUSES

AID TO CITY

The headline was dull, and the top line was half-a-unit too long. He tried again:

FORD SAYS NO

TO CITY AID

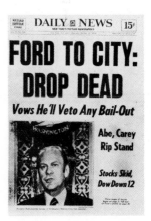

This fit, but it was as dull as the first. Brink recalls that in the back of his mind was the idea that "Ford hadn't just declined to help us. He had, in effect, consigned us to the scrap heap." He then wrote two words on a piece of copy paper. After a few moments, he put three other words above them.

The headline was instantly famous. Television news stations displayed it that night, and *Time* and *Newsweek* ran it in their summaries of the city's plight. It not only presented the information succinctly (denotative), the headline also suggested the president's disdain for New York (connotative). The headline was appropriate to the subject.

The key to appropriateness and stylistic excellence is a wide vocabulary and a sensitivity to language that will guide word choice. For instance, when the treasurer of a large utility is convicted of taking $25,000 in company funds, a reporter can write:

- The *employee* was xxx.
- The *official* was xxx.
- The *executive* was xxx.

Each noun has a different connotation. *Employee* would be appropriate for a lower-ranking worker. Although he is an *official* of the company, the word usually is used in connection with public officials. *Executive* seems most appropriate.

Let us look at some verbs:

- He *pilfered* $25,000 xxx.
- He *took* $25,000 xxx.
- He *appropriated* $25,000 for his own use.
- He *embezzled* $25,000 xxx.
- He *stole* $25,000 xxx.

Pilfered seems to trivialize the event. *Took* is prosaic: we *take* a rest, *take* cream in our coffee. *Appropriated* suggests an official action: Congress *appropriates* funds. *Embezzled* and *stole* are strong words and probably the best to use.

Word Play

Some reporters play word games in their leisure moments. They make lists of synonyms: wound, laceration, gash; mistake, error, boner, blunder, blooper; car, automobile, limousine, jalopy, hot rod, vehicle; went, trotted, ran, scampered, scurried. Each suggests, implies, connotes a slightly different meaning.

Reporters are not reluctant to borrow from their notes in English courses. The use of words whose sounds imply the object or action being described is a useful writing device.

- He *babbled* into his beard.
- The knife *slashed* through the fruit.
- The snake *slithered* through the grass.
- He *drooped* in the heat.

This stylistic device is onomatopoeia. Journalists also borrow metaphor, simile, even hyperbole when it suits their purpose and when it is appropriate to the event.

Good writing is anchored in control. Sometimes the words take off on their own:

Thoughts flew like spaghetti in his brain.

But what teachers don't seem to know is that they are compounding the same insult by their timorousness at being checked out while they are at the controls of their classroom, and while they are wielding the educational scalpel upon their students.

"Marvin," she hissed.

The muscles on his arms rose slowly, like a loaf of bread taking shape.

The Stylist

Style is, Alfred North Whitehead wrote, the best way "to attain your end and nothing but your end." Whitehead said that style, a sense of the appropriateness of the work, is "an aesthetic sense based on admiration for the direct attainment of a foreseen end, simply and without waste . . . with style the end is attained without side issues, without raising undesirable inflammations. . . ."

The stylist is prized in every newsroom, just as an individual style is valued in every field. Yet reporters often are unimaginative in their selection of facts, and their writing is uninspired. A vapid writing style begets stereotyped observations and vice versa. Compare these two stories about Memorial Day. Which one is more appropriate to the event?

Topeka Reminded of Debts to Dead

An Army general officer and a Navy lieutenant commander reminded Topekans of their debt and responsibility to America's war dead in two Memorial Day services Tuesday morning.

Brig. Gen. John A. Berry, commanding general of Fort Riley, spoke to representatives of 18 veterans organizations at ceremonies at Mount Hope Cemetery.

Earlier, Lt. Cmdr. John G. Tilghman, U.S. Navy Reserve, talked briefly at services on the Topeka Avenue Bridge.

"It is good for us to gather this morning to think of—and thank—those men and women who gave their lives in wars past that you and I may have the full benefits and privileges and responsibilities of our American heritage," said Cmdr. Tilghman.

"Many men in World War II and the Korean War did not always understand all the causes behind the war in which they fought, but they were sure they wanted those of us at home to continue to enjoy the birthright and heritage which is ours, and gave their lives that we might do so.

"You and I must realize our responsibilities in making sure our children and those to come in future generations will be sure of the same promise.

"Today, thousands are fleeing from those who would take away their birthright and their heritage. You and I may someday join their flight unless we get off the fence and take a stand for that which is right—morally right and right patriotically."

Tilghman told his audience protection of its heritage may not always be in combat dress and on a battlefield.

—The State Journal

Fresno Rites Honor Fallen War Heroes

Walk with me early this Memorial Day through the Liberty Cemetery before the ceremonies begin and a thousand feet scatter the dust over these quiet gravestones.

Here are the dead of many of our nation's wars.

A Flag flutters beside each grave and flowers grace them all. No one is forgotten.

Some died in uniform. Others, like Sergeant William J. Dallas of the 2nd Tennessee Infantry in the Spanish-American War, went to war and returned to live a long life—80 years long.

Many stones stand upright, their marble veined with the passage of time. What stories lie behind some of these stones? The passerby cannot tell. The inscriptions simply say:

Michael O'Connor, US Navy, Spanish-American War. Or, in the Civil War section: Isaac N. Ulsh, Company B, 13th Kansas infantry.

Other markers do tell their stories:

Jack T. Martin, Jr., 1922–1942, USS Langley, Lost At Sea.

James S. Waggoner, CEM, USN, USS Kete, 1917–1945, Lost At Sea.

Sergeant Keith A. Matthew, 877th Bomber Squadron, USAAF, 1918–1945, Lost At Sea.

Two Petersons

Side by side are these two:

T. Sergeant Maurice Peterson, 9th Air Corps, 330th Bomber Group, 1917–1944, Ploesti, Roumania.

Sergeant Sterling Peterson, Airborne Infantry, Company B, 1919–1944, Normandy, France. . . .

The sun rises higher and friends and relatives of the dead come bearing flowers.

Families come and decorate graves with snapdragons, roses, stocks, hydrangea, marigolds and others. While the adults place the flowers, the children roll in the grass and shout to one another.

Then the ceremonies begin.

Veterans organizations march to the cemetery, and the Colors are massed at the War Veterans Memorial Shaft.

"Let us pray that we may always honor those who have given the last full measure of devotion to their country," Dean Emeritus James M. Malloch says.

"Let us pray that the United States may ever be the land of the free and the home of the brave and the advocate of peace in the councils of nations."

Pay Tribute

At the Belmont Memorial Park, military units stand at attention while tributes are paid to the dead.

Mayor C. Cal Evans reminds the quiet crowd Memorial Day has a new significance, paying "homage to the heroes of peace as well as to the heroes of war."

The main speaker, Legislative Commissioner Ted C. Wills, says:

"Although the bodies of our loved ones are consigned to the earth, their souls have winged their way to the Father in Whose house there are many mansions, where, for all eternity, theirs will be the fullness of joy."

The oratory is carried to the treetops and fades away and the soldiers march off.

—*The Fresno Bee*

The first story is like dozens of Memorial Day stories. The oratory, while perhaps passionately uttered, has little emotional impact because it ignores those the event commemorates—the victims of war. The second story teeters on the edge of sentimentality in the lead, but soon settles into understated narrative that seeks to match the solemn nature of the event.

The recent antecedents of the journalist's relaxed, non-stilted writing style are the non-fiction novel of the 1950s and the New Journalism of Tom Wolfe and others in the 1960s. In a *Wall Street Journal* review of an anthology of Wolfe's works, *The Purple Decades: A Reader,* Ellen Wilson describes Wolfe's inspiration for this new way of writing:

In the early Sixties, Tom Wolfe went to the New York Colosseum to cover a Hot Rod and Custom Car show, and came back with the New Journalism. As he tells it in the introduction to "The Kandy-Kolored Tangerine-Flake Streamline Baby," he felt frustrated by his inability to recreate the atmosphere of the show, with its "nutty-looking, crazy baroque custom cars, sitting in little nests of pink angora angels hair," in standard journalese. He needed a style flexible and uninhibited enough to capture everything a straight news story would miss: the carnival atmosphere and the thoughts and emotions of the participants.

He came up with a style incorporating slang and contemporary speech patterns, stream of consciousness and abrupt switches in perspective. The first step was painstaking research and close attention to detail. After that, he was free to select from the novelist's whole bag of tricks.

Actually, good, free-wheeling writing did not begin with the New Journalists. Jimmy Cannon, Red Smith, A. J. Liebling, Ernie Pyle and scores of other journalists were writing imaginatively before many of the New Journalists were born—without the invented dialogue and other non-journalistic tricks. Even the weather story had its Bard, H. Allen Smith, who took a couple of minutes a day to write a one-sentence forecast. Here are a few:

> This is a nice day.
> This would be a good day to be off on.
> Dubious day, good for fog, smog and grog.
> Snow will flur today.

Edwin A. Lahey of the *Chicago Daily News* was a reporter's writer. Here's a lead to a story Lahey sent his paper after covering a Senate committee meeting:

WASHINGTON—The Senate Rackets Committee produced evidence today to show how Teamster President Dave Beck drove a pickup truck through the union treasury.

Reading for Writers One way to develop a distinctive style was suggested at the outset of this chapter: Read the masters. Whom shall the journalist read? Begin with this advice in Sir Herbert Read's *English Prose Style:*

> The great strength of the English language lies in its splendid array of transitive verbs drawn both from the Anglo Saxon and Latin. Their power lies in their recognition of nature as a vast storehouse of forces. . . . Shakespeare's English is immeasurably superior to all others. . . . It is his persistent, natural and magnificent use of hundreds of transitive verbs. Rarely will you find an *is* in his sentence. A study of Shakespeare's verbs should underline all exercises in style.

Abraham Lincoln, who had little formal schooling but wrote forceful, compelling prose, read Shakespeare and the Bible.

Few journalists realize how much they owe the King James Bible. Almost every virtue of the prose style the journalist uses can be traced to its influence: direct simplicity, exactness and economy of language, rapid pace, even the S-V-O construction. The writings of John Bunyan, Emily Brontë and scores of others were influenced by the Bible. Peter Abràhàms, a South African black author, said he had a teacher who "whenever I used big words or made clumsy and almost meaningless sentences, sent me to the Bible. I read the Bible and I saw."

This is no place to make a plea for taking up the Bible. But look at these sentences and consider the possibility of some extracurricular reading:

- For many are called, but few are chosen.
- Who is this that darkeneth counsel by words without knowledge?
- We all do fade as a leaf.
- Man shall not live by bread alone.
- A word spoken in good season, how good it is.
- The rich rules over the poor, and the borrower is the slave of the lender.
- How forcible are right words.
- Let thy words be few.

Gilbert Millstein, a network television newswriter after jobs with *Time* magazine, *The Saturday Evening Post* and *The New York Times,* recommends reading 19th and 20th century American fiction: Hawthorne, Melville and Nathanael West. Of West's novels he said:

> For example, any television newswriter who reads *Miss Lonelyhearts* or *The Day of the Locust* by Nathanael West would find in them an economy and vividness of language achieved without adjectives that would surprise the life out of him. I would offer those two books as

models for any person who wants to write factual news. The economy of *Miss Lonelyhearts* is unbelievable. There isn't a single word that could be dropped. The same is true for *The Day of the Locust.* But young people appear not to read these kinds of books anymore.

All reporters have favorite authors and books that influenced them. Fred L. Zimmerman, an editor with *The Wall Street Journal,* recommends Shakespeare, Ibsen, Dostoyevsky, Joyce, the plays of O'Neill and Arthur Miller, and the modern American authors, Updike, Capote, E. B. White, Salinger and Styron. He has read and reread Hemingway's *The Sun Also Rises,* Steinbeck's *The Grapes of Wrath,* John O'Hara's short stories and James Agee's *A Death in the Family.*

Among the magazines, reporters recommend *Time* and *Newsweek* and the monthlies, *The Atlantic* and *Harper's.*

They also read *The New York Review of Books, The New Republic, Commentary, The New York Times Book Review, The New Yorker* and *National Review.*

Story Length

Everyone agrees that the shorter the sentence the clearer it is. Some extend the reasoning to the story itself. They argue:

Given: People have less time than ever for their newspapers. Not only are they busy pursuing leisure activities, there are plenty of other sources of information, such as radio, television, cable, weekly newspapers, the freely circulated shoppers, magazines.

Therefore: Catch the reader on the run with short news stories. Cut and cut some more.

More: Events have become so complex that people despair of understanding the world around them. Moreover, they feel information has little utility since they are powerless to effect change as the result of what they have learned. Thus, not only write short stories; make them simple. Short and simple is the rule.

Yes and no: The most successful newspapers in the nation run long stories—*The New York Times, The Wall Street Journal, The Washington Post,* the *Los Angeles Times, The Philadelphia Inquirer* and others. Their editors contend that some stories cannot be shortened without losing essential material. Readers seem to associate truth with the length of a story, which is not difficult to understand since the more space the writer has the more facts he or she can present to document the theme.

Proper length is determined by news value, not by editors' theories about readability. However, the reality for the reporter is that stories are written to the editor's command. After hearing the reporter describe the information he or she has gathered, the city editor tells the reporter how much to write. Sometimes, the two disagree, the reporter usually trying to persuade the editor that the story is worth more. Although the editor has the power in the newsroom, no reporter need defer without a battle if he or she is convinced of the story's value.

Write, Write and Rewrite

Much of what has been said in this chapter has presumed a rational, disciplined approach to news writing. Sometimes, diligent thinking and careful planning are of no avail. The right lead will not come; the exact words lurk just beyond our reach; sentences stumble over each other; and the whole business looks a mess.

Then—only minutes before the edition closes or the newscast is to go on—the story comes together. The theme of the piece is clear. There it was, hiding in the fourth graf. And there, that quote in the fifth graf, the perfect second graf. We toss out 50 lines. Adrenalin flows and the words fly. Everything fits. On deadline, too.

Every writer has gone through this scene. Sean O'Faolain, the Irish writer, points out that ideas sometimes become clear "by, and only by, the very act of writing."

Some reporters can function only under this kind of pressure. Given a day to do a story, they dilly-dally until the deadline is an hour off. Then they can write. True enough, they rarely miss their deadines. But the wear and tear they undergo, and the anxiety they inflict on their editors, is frightening to behold. Better to develop good writing habits now, gradually and without too much pressure, so that on-the-job writing most often is a calm, deliberate process. That means writing, seeing your mistakes and rewriting.

With practice, writing comes easier and is accomplished more quickly. Speed is important. No matter what his or her gifts may be, if the reporter cannot put words on paper before the deadline, he or she will not hold the job.

Breslin, Jimmy. *The World According to Breslin.* New York: Ticknor & Fields, 1985.

Clark, Roy Peter, ed. *Best Newspaper Writing for (year).* St. Petersburg, Fla.: Poynter Institute for Media Studies, (year). (annual anthology)

Clark, Roy Peter, ed. *Improving Newswriting.* St. Petersburg, Fla.: Poynter Institute for Media Studies, 1982.

Ross, Lillian. *Reporting.* New York: Dodd Mead & Co., 1981.

Terkel, Studs. *The Good War: An Oral History of World War Two.* New York: Pantheon, 1984.

Terkel, Studs. *Working: People Talk About What They Do All Day and What They Think While They Do It.* New York: Pantheon, 1972.

CHAPTER EIGHT

Features and Long Stories

Preview

Features are written to entertain. The feature writer lets the actions and comments of the personalities carry the story. Most features follow this structure:

- Beginning—Usually a delayed lead, an incident, example or anecdote that illustrates the point of the feature.
- Body—Additional incidents, quotes, examples, background and the news peg.
- Ending—Clincher or climax that sums up the person or situation.

Long stories usually are written to provide readers with information about a complicated idea or situation.

- Reporting—Develop the theme as quickly as possible so that material can be gathered that is relevant to the theme.
- Structuring—Organize notes under the main theme (lead) and the subthemes. Organize notes in the order the story will take.
- Writing—Find a tone or style and a point of view appropriate to the theme. Use ample quotes, incidents, anecdotes and action to keep the story moving and the reader interested.

THE FEATURE

Some editors say there are three types of news stories. Although there are no precise lines that can be drawn to separate the three, they can be distinguished as follows:

Spot news story—Contains material of such significance that it must be reported immediately to the public.

News feature—Uses information that supplements the spot news, usually by providing the human element behind the breaking news event or by giving background through interpretation and explanation.

Feature—Aims to entertain through the use of material that is interesting but not necessarily important.

Coverage of spot news takes up most of the news budget of newspapers and broadcast stations. But an increasing amount of time and space is being given over to features.

The feature has had a reputation much like Canadian mining stock, slightly suspect. Although it has worthy antecedents in the satire and parody of poets and essayists who used the pen to attack individuals in public and private life, the feature has been approached gingerly by many editors. Most editors have subscribed to the philosophy of Richard Draper, who wrote in his Boston *News-Letter* in the 18th century that he would use features only when "there happens to be a scarcity of news." Nevertheless, the allure of the feature always has been irresistible.

Nineteenth century conservative editors reacted with distaste to the features published by the penny press from the 1830s to the Civil War. Directed to the working class being enlarged by the country's industrial revolution, these inexpensive newspapers ran stories about domestic tragedy and illicit sex, stories that editors like Horace Greeley found unworthy of the mission of journalism. When he established the *Tribune* in New York in 1841, Greeley announced that his newspaper would avoid the "immoral and degrading Police Reports, Advertisements and other matters which have been allowed to disgrace the columns of our leading Penny Papers." But Greeley was soon running some of the material he had condemned in his competitors' newspapers.

The feature story was a weapon in the great circulation wars between Pulitzer and Hearst in New York at the turn of the century. Crime stories, sports, society, science news—all of it embroidered with sensational details often as much invented as factual—were used to attract readers. This type of feature became synonymous with Yellow Journalism.

The Hearst newspapers were perhaps the most successful of the sensational and flamboyant papers of their day. W. A. Swanberg in the biography *Citizen Hearst* describes them:

> They were printed entertainment and excitement—the equivalent in newsprint of bombs exploding, bands blaring, firecrackers popping, victims screaming, flags waving, cannons roaring, houris dancing and smoke rising from the singed flesh of executed criminals.

In the days of Front Page journalism—see Ben Hecht's book *Gaily, Gaily,* which is about Chicago journalism around 1910, when the philosophy was never to let the facts get in the way of a good story—the feature writer's job was to wring tears from the bartender, smiles from the policeman, and gasps of wonderment from the tenement dwellers. The tales of the city as spun out by the feature writers of the day were long on drama, short on fact.

Screamer. A reporter for one of the Hearst newspapers described a typical Hearst newspaper as "a screaming woman running down the street with her throat cut." The Chief, as Hearst was known, had the man fired.

As the United States grew to world power and its citizens had to confront the consequences of World War I and then a pervasive depression, some of the press graduated to more serious pursuits. The feature came to be seen as too frivolous for the responsible newspaper. Newspapers that held on to the old formulas declined in popularity. The Hearst chain dwindled from 22 newspapers to eight.

In 1947, when Joseph G. Herzberg, city editor of *The New York Herald Tribune*, put together a series of essays by *Tribune* staffers for the book *Late City Edition*, not one of the 29 chapters was devoted to the feature story.

Now Thriving

Nevertheless, the feature is alive and well. First, editors discovered that serious journalism does not have to be tedious. They rediscovered the fact known to the Greek playwrights 2,300 years ago, that almost all events have a human dimension. Indeed, it is the human aspect of the event that makes it worth communicating. In his play *The Frogs,* Aristophanes has the playwright Euripedes say, "I made the drama democratic. I staged the life of every day, the way we live."

In addition to this humanizing of the news—usually through the news feature—editors found that an unvarying diet of seriousness will be rejected by the mass audience. To reach that audience, the newspaper or broadcast station must present a variety of news, the same variety that marks our lives. There is a time to think about economic problems and a time to laugh at someone's humorous predicament. The news must include a story about a family affected by a teacher's strike (news feature) along with a story that reveals how furniture wholesalers show off their new line to prospective buyers (straight feature).

Recognizing the maturity of the feature, in 1978 the advisory board to the Pulitzer Prizes created a new category, feature writing. The guideline is: "For a distinguished example of feature writing giving prime consideration to high literary quality and originality, one thousand dollars ($1,000)."

Nowadays, editors see only a fine line between news and features. Lew Powell, of *The Charlotte Observer,* says, "The distinctions between news and features are increasingly blurred these days.

"Features are busting out of the back-of-the-book ghetto and changing the way stories are written throughout the paper. The old 'Mayor Harris said today . . .' kind of straight news story is just as likely to begin with an account of a testy exchange between the mayor and a councilman or with an analysis of how the mayor's statements fit in with his re-election campaign or with his previous statements."

A well-trained journalist can handle any kind of story in the manner the event demands. If the situation calls for a light touch, the reporter can churn out a feature. If the event is serious, demanding the careful recitation of facts, data, dates, dollars and cents, then the reporter knows how to adjust his or her style to the requirements of the straight news story.

On most newspapers and stations, reporters are expected to do double duty, handling spot news and features. But on some, particularly the larger papers and stations, a few reporters are regularly assigned to handle features.

Some young reporters say they prefer to write features rather than hard news because the feature is easier to handle. This is the blather of the uninformed. The momentum of the news event carries most spot news stories. True, it is not easy to learn to organize a tight news story, and the skill to devise succinct leads that quickly take the reader to the news point is not easily mastered. But the feature writer must carry these burdens and more.

The feature is an exception to some of the rules of reporting and writing, and this imposes on the writer the task of pioneering in each piece, beginning anew to find form, a story tone, the appropriate words and the telling scenes for this particular story. Readers demand more of feature writers than of straight news writers, and so do their editors.

The few rules for feature writing cut to the heart of writing itself: **The Rules**

- Show persons doing things.
- Let them talk.
- Underwrite. Let the action and the dialogue carry the piece.
- Keep the piece moving. This requires a plan that gives the piece a beginning, a middle and an end.

Few reporters have ever gone wrong by making the individuals in their stories carry the action. This requires a discerning eye and a discriminating ear. The telling action and the illuminating quote must be caught if the feature is to tell us something about ourselves or others.

Showing people doing things and letting them speak requires that the reporter be on the scene of action. Jim Warren of the *Lexington Herald-Leader* accompanied Glenna Allen of the Frontier Nursing Service as she made her rounds in the eastern Kentucky mountains. His story begins this way:

HYDEN—The road that snakes up from Coon Creek is hard-packed dirt in some places and bottomless mud in others, all of it pitted with cavernous potholes.

Slide one way and you hit a mountain wall; slide the other and you go off a cliff into space.

Driving is tricky, especially when a mountainous coal truck—in this case a Tennessee Orange Mack with a full load of bituminous coal—looms around a blind curve.

Glenna Allen handled the situation with skill that comes from long practice, steering her battered tan Toyota almost to the drop-off at the right edge of the road. . . .

Backwoods Nurse. For his story about Glenna Allen of the Frontier Nursing Service, Jim Warren watched her negotiate muddy roads, walk up long hills and take medical supplies to those unable to make it to towns with doctors. Photos by Tom Woods II of *The Lexington Herald-Leader.*

Warren lets Allen talk:

"My mother hates it that I'm doing this," Miss Allen said with a laugh. She left Dayton, Ohio, to work in the mountains. "She thinks I'm going to get myself killed by a rattlesnake or run over some cliff, and she keeps asking when I'm coming home. . . ."

Subjects. Look around you, suggests Jimmy Breslin, Pulitzer Prize winning columnist.

"Notice the women eating alone at night, the people without friends."

Loneliness, Breslin says, is one of the country's major problems, especially for women.

When reporters were assigned to cover the opening of an off-track betting parlor in a suburb of New York City, most of them were content to report such obvious facts as the size of the crowd and the name and address of the first bettor on line. Leonard Levitt of *Newsday* resisted the routine and did some checking about the 62-year-old grandmother who was first in line. He refused to settle for the obvious. As good feature writers know, snappy writing cannot sustain the under-reported feature.

Through interviews with the woman, her husband and children, Levitt learned that she was a chronic gambler who bet $50 and $100 a day. Her husband told Levitt, "It was hard when the kids were growing up. I used to hold three jobs." The woman told Levitt, "My husband doesn't approve of my betting. Neither do my kids. None of them bets. But they love me." In these few quotes, a family's tragedy is unfolded.

The feature writer also sees the absurd and hears the preposterous. In his piece about the Southern Furniture Market in High Point, N.C., where the new styles in furniture are previewed each year, Lew Powell tells us about Dr. Samuel Dunkell, "psychotherapist and author of the bestselling 'Sleep Positions.' " Just to make sure we know this event is hardly the stuff of which significant news is made, Powell sets the mood in the first paragraph:

Today in Washington reporters are awaiting Koreagate revelations. In Memphis, the latest on Elvis. In Minneapolis, the Billy Graham audit. In High Point we're crowded into a mattress showroom waiting for the inside poop on sleep positions.

From the serious to the silly. Powell does this in a few sentences. The words "inside poop" tell the reader that what follows is going to be fun. And that's what Powell provides:

Enrico Caruso slept with 18 pillows. Neil Sedaka rubs his feet over each other. The late Hannah Arendt, author of "The Origins of Totalitarianism" and not someone you'd expect to be spilling this kind of stuff, favored the "water wings" position.

And have we got a photo opportunity for you! As Dunkell discusses the "royal" position, the "flamingo," the "mummy," the "sphinx" and the "swastika," model Norma demonstrates. Her yellow sleepshirt keeps riding up, ensuring undivided attention. When she's joined by a male model for the "hug" and "spoon" position, a sockfooted TV cameraman clambers onto an adjacent Maxipedic for a better angle.

"Republicans sleep face down, Democrats on their backs," Dunkell says. Scribble, scribble. "Surprisingly few people fall out of bed—perhaps 20 percent in their lifetime." Scribble, scribble. . . .

The feature writer must see universals as well as aberrations. What is there about this soccer player, that pianist, this dancer with dreams that strike chords common to all of us? The feature writer knows that great writers inspire us to see ourselves, in Tolstoy's Natasha, Fitzgerald's Nick Carraway and Melville's Captain Vere. The feature writer must be open to human experience. An art critic said of Rembrandt, he "rejected nothing human." Neither must the feature writer.

Most of us are curious. As youngsters, we took apart the kitchen clock. Later, we experimented with the forbidden; and as adults we wonder about each other's lives. What are we missing? What are the others doing? The feature writer understands this curiosity and envy and gives us some answers.

Frank Barrows, a sports writer for *The Charlotte Observer,* decided to do a piece about the acrobatic young men and women who lend color and excitement to the moments between plays and the intermissions between periods. Barrows followed the cheerleaders at Clemson University as they prepared for an October game. Barrows knows that many people wonder what kind of youngsters these are who will spend hours doing calisthenics to prepare for their brief hour upon the stage. Are they really the empty-heads some presume them to be? He interviews one of the cheerleaders:

A Tale of Cheerleading

George Langstaff lounges at Sourdough's Sandwich Emporium, a subs-and-beer hangout near campus and talks cheerleading. . . .

"You'd think," he drawls flatly, "cheerleaders would be real outgoing people, willing to do crazy stuff anytime, just to get attention. That's what you'd think, isn't it? Well a couple of us were kicking that around a day ago and we figure the people we've got for the most part are quiet. They're not true introverts—but they need something to help them climb out of themselves. It's easy to cut loose when 12 others are there. And they want to cut loose once in a while. So they're cheerleaders." He shrugs. "I think I'm like that."

Barrows' quotes sound authentic. He knows that the people in feature stories must be made realistic. We accept the cardboard cutouts that straight news stories make of our officials and others in public life. The characters in features must be individuals. After all, this is why they are being written about—it is their individuality that makes them interesting. And so much the better if the writer has a style of his or her own. This individual touch brings joy to an editor's heart. Confronted by the dull prose of much local and wire news copy the feature is like the single rainbow trout in a creel of brown trout.

Feature stories must be written with care, for they can be held for days, sometimes weeks, until space opens. (At *The Wall Street Journal,* features are called "evergreens" in recognition of their perpetual freshness.)

Planning

To Barrows, careful planning of the feature is essential. He says:

"Simply because a feature is not written to be cut from the bottom—as a news story might be—does not mean that the material can be randomly set down on paper.

"For a feature to be something other than puffery, you must do the type of serious preparation and thinking that lead to organization. For instance, you might not want to put all the straight biographic data in one place."

Barrows knows that such material is usually tedious. Beginners tend to bunch up background. More experienced hands break up background like biographical material and place bits and pieces into the moving narrative.

For example, Barrows says, when a reporter comes to a place in the story where he or she is showing how the person's hometown influenced his life, that is the place to put something about the person's birthplace and a few other routine details. In other words, the necessary background is spotted into the ongoing story.

Another fault of beginners is the leisurely pace they set at the outset of the piece, as though they are feeling their way toward the theme of the story.

"Too often in features the writer does not tell his reader soon enough what he or she is writing about," Barrows says.

Look at how Eric Lawlor of the *Houston Chronicle* slides the reader right into his piece about a truck stop outside town. He sets a scene in the first paragraph, pulls us into the restaurant in the second paragraph, and in the third paragraph we meet a waitress who introduces us to a dialogue that gives us a good idea of what's going on:

The truck stop on the North Freeway is ringed with rigs. Trucks glide past one another with the grandeur of sailing ships: 16-wheel galleons bearing—not spices from the Indies or gold from the New World—but auto parts and refrigerators.

Truckers weave as they enter the restaurant; like sailors on shore leave, they are still finding their legs.

Tina Hernandez, an 18-year-old waitress here, serves an order of ham and eggs.

"Where are my grits?" asks the recipient.

"You don't get grits unless you ask for them," she tells him. "If you want grits, you gotta say, 'I want grits.' "

If this sounds unnecessarily acerbic, it's not, in fact: Tina and her customers are actually fond of one another. An affection that masquerades as good-natured abuse.

"Give me a bowl of split-pea soup," says a man whose face looks curiously flat. Perhaps someone sat on it. "Is there any meat in there?"

"There's meat in there all right," says Tina. "The problem is finding it."

"How are you and Billy (not his real name) doin'?" he wants to know.

"We don't talk anymore," says the waitress. "He got scared. Just checked out."

"Oh, I don't believe that. I'll bet you are goin' out and just don't want anyone to know about it."

"I'm tellin' ya: that man is scared of women."

"Maybe, he just doesn't like YOU," offers Myrtle, another waitress.

At a nearby table, a driver is telling a colleague about a recent fling.

"I had to leave her finally because she was so cold-blooded. You could get pneumonia sitting next to a woman like that."

With the arrival of new telephone directories, bells ring in the memories of many editors, and they respond by assigning a reporter to do a feature on the entries. Here's how Mary Voboril of *The Miami Herald* began her piece:

Lyons and Tigers and Bears and 293 Foxes are ensnared in the White Pages of the new edition of the Greater Miami Telephone Directory, the annual gift from that mythical matriarch known as Ma Bell.

A record 1,679 pages contain every listed human customer from Faye Aaker to Vladimir Zzzyd—plus corporate clients with such names as the Aaaaaall Together Escort Service, My Refugee Market and Your Island Dream.

The 700,000 customers in the area can Dial a Maid, a Meal, a Translator or a Jewish Story, but it still takes a long-distance call to New York City to Dial a Joke.

Have a message for Garcia? Good luck—there are 40 columns of them.

There are Blacks and Whites. Laurel and Hardy. Salt and Pepper. Sainte and Sinner. Manet and Monet. A Kitchen but no Sink. Lots of Gays and a few Straights. A Freud, a Jung—and, in the two-volume Yellow Pages, 10 columns of psychiatrists.

Southern Bell spokesman Don Mathis is unsure which is the most common surname in the directory these days. His betting still is with Smith, though Gonzalez may be closing in—if it hasn't already taken over.

Southern Bell's hired help began distributing the first of three million telephone books Friday and will be unloading 80,000 to 120,000 of them a day for the next two to three weeks. . . .

In another feature story, this one about a school for bartenders, Lawlor gets down to business at once, taking the reader into the classroom in the lead:

Using All the Techniques

K. C. Stevens is explaining the difference between a godfather and a godmother.

"To make a godfather," she tells her class at the Professional Bartenders School, "use amaretto and scotch. A godmother, on the other hand, combines amaretto and vodka."

Then Lawlor steps back for a few paragraphs to let the reader survey the scene, telling us something about the teacher and her students:

K. C., a onetime barmaid, has been teaching people to mix drinks for four years now.

"I didn't want to find myself at the age of 40 wearing orthopedic shoes behind some crummy bar," she says. "Being a bartender is a young person's game."

Her class nods agreement. If that isn't to exaggerate this barely perceptible movement of heads. This is a pretty lethargic group. They slump at the school's mock bar as if drink had ravaged them. They wouldn't look out of place in Pompeii.

It's hard to imagine these people doing anything as animated as tending bar. Indeed it's hard to imagine them doing anything as animated as standing up.

K. C., a good soul, is inclined to agree.

"A lot of them are spaced off somewhere," she says. "I was telling a couple of them just this morning, 'Look, you're gonna have to put more time into studying.' But once they get the picture, things usually work out. Many people come in here expecting to party. They don't realize there's a lot of work involved."

From the first sentence, the reader is as hooked on this story as an alcoholic is on gin and tonic. This is the object of the writer who seeks to entertain readers—grab them and keep them reading. Move the reader along with quotes and action.

Lawlor goes on:

That's putting it mildly. To qualify for certification, these students must memorize 150 cocktail recipes and learn to mix as many as eight drinks in no more than 10 minutes. That's 75 seconds a drink. Try it sometime. It's not easy.

This is a class of six—three males, three females. Two of the guys are about 45; the others are in their early 20s.

One kid looks hardly old enough to drink. Another is barely visible when she goes behind the bar.

At what stage in this 40-hour program will these people begin to resemble bartenders?

"Early next week," says K. C. "This crowd is just starting out, but come Monday, you won't recognize them. And by the time they finish, well, you'd think they'd been bartenders all their lives."

"For the first couple of days, I just tell them to relax, to take it easy until they can find their way around."

For the moment, these incipient bartenders wander about like wraiths. They blink at the bottles ranked eight deep in front of them and handle their glasses as if they were live grenades. Movements are clumsy—so many bulls in so many china shops. Glasses are filled until they overflow; drink is sloshed onto counter tops; garnishes roll onto the floor.

K. C. is now taking them through Lesson 6: Hot Toddy, Hot Buttered Rum and Irish Coffee.

"Put these on your recipe cards," she says. "They're served where it's cold and snowy." It's 93 degrees outside. "They're not popular down here," she goes on, "but go up North, and they'll run you crazy."

The young blonde in the class yawns.

"But Irish coffee is popular most places. You'll get lots of sweet old ladies weighing 400 pounds ordering them instead of cheesecake. They don't know that cheesecake has only 400 calories; Irish coffee's got 750.

"Irish whiskey is fairly potent," she warns, "I want all of you to see how much I put in this cup." The cup passes from hand to hand, and student after student peers inside. It might have been the Holy Grail.

"And now we're going to talk about customer service." K. C. continues. "We're going to talk about money. And let's not forget what keeps us in this business: It's the money; the green stuff.

"If you can hook someone on your Irish coffee, he's going to come back for more. And he's going to tell his friends about you, and they'll tell their friends. And how do you do that? How do you personalize a drink?"

"With a garnish," someone says. K. C. looks gratified. It's the answer she'd been looking for. And more important, a sign of life.

This story has already run 750 words, almost a full column of type, and there is more to come. But few readers will quit now. Why? If we can answer the question perhaps we will make a start toward understanding what makes a good feature.

First, the subject is interesting. Even if you can't tell a Hot Toddy from a Hot Buttered Rum—and care less—you wonder about these people who stand behind bars and are able to throw together scores of different concoctions from the amazing array of bottles behind the bar.

But even the most interesting subject in clumsy hands will be dulled. Lawlor knows what he is doing. Let's analyze his craft.

The story moves quickly.

The quotations are vivid.

The characters interact. They talk, do things.

Tone and Style

In any discussion with feature writers, the words *tone* and *style* always come up. A feature writer uses one tone—one kind of voice—for a piece about a classical guitarist, another for a guitarist with a rock group. Tone is established by selection of facts, quotes, illustrations, by word choice, length of sentences, even by the length of paragraphs. The rock musician may be quoted in short, one or two sentence paragraphs to match the rock beat, whereas the classical musician's quotes may run on longer to give the reader the sense of the sonority of classical music.

The profile of a businessman who crashes big parties will have a humorous cast to it, whereas the profile of a survivor of the Holocaust who recalls the concentration camps will be written in somber grays, the sentences running longer than those in the profile of the businessman. The verbs will be different. The piece about the businessman will have crisp action verbs. The rule about avoiding the intransitive verb *to be* may be broken in the Holocaust piece in a deliberate effort to underplay the reporter's writing and to allow the source's recollections to carry the piece.

Duck Talk. When the Houston Community College system sponsored a waterfowl seminar, Eric Lawlor of the *Houston Chronicle* located a master duck caller and let him tell his story: "You've got to tell those ducks what they want to hear," says Jimmy Goddard. "Talk to them the way you'd talk to your lady. Say, 'I love you honey; please come on back. . . .' You have to mean everything you say," he explains. "Nothing alive spots a fraud faster than a duck. . . . You must be able to tell a duck's mood. I watch that bird. If he's happy, I'm happy. I tell him, 'If you'll just come on down here, the two of us can have a fine old time.' That's if he's happy. If he's lonesome, then you have to be lonesome. Ask him if he'd like to cry on your shoulder." Photo by Steve Veckert, the *Houston Chronicle*.

Les Mueller of *The Lexington Herald-Leader* visited Dorothy and Troy Ramey 17 years after they had received a telegram from the Army informing them of the death of their son Tommy in Vietnam. The grief remains, and Mueller shows it to us through the words of the parents:

"I've raised nine and I love all of them," said Ramey, 65, "but Tommy—it's like somebody went out in my flower garden and cut the biggest and prettiest one I had. He was one of the most lovable young 'uns. . . ."

Ramey, who suffers from two mining-related lung diseases, shook his head.

"It was a useless war," he said. "There was no profit in it for anybody. It just left a lot of mothers and fathers like us. It caused us to look down on our own government."

Mueller asks Ramey to recall their son's childhood. Like their other children, he helped tend crops and cattle in the bottomland below their home.

"He was the most timid little boy," his father said. "He grew up blond and sweet and handsome, but he was always so humble."

Features usually have a strong ending—a summary of the point of the piece or another incident or quotation to highlight the theme. One technique, which Mueller uses here, is to begin and end on the same theme:

The Beginning

In Troy Ramey's kitchen there is a straight-backed chair where he once sat every afternoon before leaving for work. He would sit there, with his miner's lunch bucket on the table, sip coffee and look through the kitchen window at a large oak tree in the yard.

Looking at that tree gave him so much pleasure, he said, that he sometimes began an unconscious whistle, soft and low. "I was happy."

Ramey doesn't sit there anymore, nor does he whistle. The tree itself is dead now. It began dying, he said, about the same time two soldiers came to his back door and told him his son Tommy had been killed in Vietnam.

The Ending

The dead oak tree still stands outside the kitchen window, bare and stark now in the spring sunshine.

Troy Ramey says he sometimes thinks about cutting it down, but that's about as far as he got. When you've loved something for a long time, he said, it's hard to let it go.

The Monster

The new field of neuroscience interested Jon Franklin, chief science writer for *The Evening Sun* in Baltimore. Franklin had been talking to Dr. Thomas Ducker, chief of neurosurgery at the University of Maryland Hospital, about brain surgery, and Ducker had agreed to call him the next time he planned an especially difficult surgical procedure. When Ducker called, Franklin set out to follow the story of Edna Kelly, who was afflicted with what she calls her monster, a tangled knot of abnormal blood vessels in the back of her brain. She was born with the malformation but in recent years the vessels had ballooned inside her skull and were crowding out the healthy brain tissue.

Kelly agreed to be interviewed, and she allowed Franklin to use her name. She also permitted Franklin to watch the surgery. Ducker agreed to cooperate.

Here is how the first story in Franklin's two-part series begins:

In the cold hours of a winter morning, Dr. Thomas Barbee Ducker, University Hospital's senior brain surgeon, rises before dawn. His wife serves him waffles but no coffee. Coffee makes his hands shake.

Downtown, on the 12th floor of the hospital, Edna Kelly's husband tells her goodbye.

For 57 years Mrs. Kelly shared her skull with the monster. No more. Today she is frightened but determined.

It is 6:30 a.m.

"I'm not afraid to die," she said as this day approached. "I've lost part of my eyesight. I've gone through all the hemorrhages. A couple of years ago I lost my sense of smell, my taste, I started having seizures. I smell a strange odor and then I start strangling. It started affecting my legs, and I'm partially paralyzed.

"Three years ago a doctor told me all I had to look forward to was blindness, paralysis and a remote chance of death. Now I have aneurisms; this monster is causing that. I'm scared to death . . . but there isn't a day that goes by that I'm not in pain and I'm tired of it. I can't bear the pain. I wouldn't want to live like this much longer." As Dr. Ducker leaves for work, Mrs. Ducker hands him a paper bag containing a peanut butter sandwich, a banana and two fig newtons. Downtown, in Mrs. Kelly's brain, a sedative takes effect.

Franklin's intentions are made clear at the outset. This is to be a detailed account of the confrontation of a skilled surgeon and a woman in desperate need. Franklin takes the reader into the operating room:

Now, at 7:15 a.m. in Operating Room 11, a technician checks the brain surgery microscope and the circulating nurse lays out bandages and instruments. Mrs. Kelly lies still on a stainless steel table.

A small sensor has been threaded through her veins and now hangs in the antechamber of her heart. Dr. Jane Matjasko, the anesthesiologist, connects the sensor to a 7-foot-high bank of electronic instruments. Wave forms begin to move rhythmically across a cathode ray tube.

With each heartbeat a loudspeaker produces an audible popping sound. The steady pop, pop, pop, pop isn't loud, but it dominates the operating room.

Dr. Ducker enters the operating room and pauses before the X-ray films that hang on a lighted panel. He carried those brain images to Europe, Canada and Florida in search of advice, and he knows them by heart. Still he studies them again, eyes focused on the two fragile aneurisms that swell above major arteries. Either may burst on contact.

The one directly behind Mrs. Kelly's eyes is the most dangerous, but also the easiest to reach. That's first.

The first story ends at 11:05 a.m. Ducker has managed to find and clip off one of the two deadly aneurisms. The next article begins with Ducker peering into the neurosurgery microscope in search of the second. The going is slow, dangerous.

At 1:06 p.m. there is trouble and Ducker worries that his patient's heart has been slowed too many times. He decides not to continue. If she recovers, he says, he will try again.

If she survives. If. If.

"I'm not afraid to die," Mrs. Kelly had said. "I'm scared to death . . . but . . . I can't bear the pain. I wouldn't want to live like this much longer."

Her brain was too scarred. The operation, tolerable in a younger person, was too much. Already, where the monster's tentacles hang before the brainstem, the tissue swells, pinching off the source of oxygen.

Mrs. Kelly is dying.

The clock in the lounge, near where Dr. Ducker sits, says 1:40.

"It's hard even to tell what to do. We've been thinking about it for six weeks. But, you know, there are certain things . . . that's just as far as you can go. I just don't know. . . ."

He lays the sandwich, the banana and the fig newtons on the table before him neatly, the way the scrub nurse laid out instruments.

"It was triple jeopardy," he says, finally, staring at his peanut butter sandwich the same way he stared at the X-rays.

"It was triple jeopardy."

It is 1:43, and it's over.

Dr. Ducker bites, grimly, into the sandwich.

The monster won.

Franklin holds the reader in suspense until the jolting final sentences. The three sentences are short, quick—consistent with the abrupt end of Mrs. Kelly's life. Franklin was awarded the Pulitzer Prize in 1975 for the feature story, the first time a Prize was given in this category. You might want to go back to our four rules for writing the feature and note in the margins of the sections from Franklin's pieces where he follows these guidelines.

The News Feature

Franklin's story is a news feature, a story designed to throw light on a subject by emphasizing the human element. Peter R. Kann, a *Wall Street Journal* reporter, found that the facts and figures used in a *Journal* news story about Bangladesh were inadequate to explain that country's misery and despair. He decided on some vignettes and a highly personal approach in a news feature that begins:

DACCA—Bangladesh may well be the world's poorest and most hopeless nation.

An article yesterday reported on some of Bangladesh's many economic and political problems. But facts and figures don't do justice to misery and despair, and so this article offers some voices and vignettes from the land that cruelly, but all too aptly, has been described as "an international basket case."

The Nun's Tale

An Irish nun is visiting Bangladesh, staying at a Christian hostel in Dacca. On her second evening in the city, she steps outside for a breath of air and finds an emaciated baby deserted on the door-step. She takes the baby in, feeds it, doctors it, bathes it, and then goes out searching for the mother, who is nowhere to be found.

The next morning the nun finds a second starving baby lying in the street in front of the hostel. So she takes the second baby in. Then she goes off to the local police station to report the missing babies and to seek advice.

That advice is to put the babies back in the street or, the police officer says, you will find four more babies tomorrow.

"What on earth am I to do?" the nun says later in the day. "Am I to put them out to starve?"

The Doctor and His Wife

The news feature usually has its origins in some news event. When Carl Hiassen of *The Miami Herald* dug into the court case involving a doctor and his millionaire wife, he came up with a tale of greed preying on loneliness. His story begins:

To Dr. Edward Gordon, love meant never having to say he was out of money.

Six years ago, the solicitous Miami Beach physician married a patient who was worth more than $8 million. Her name was Elizabeth Buffum, and she was a lonely alcoholic.

With Gordon, she stayed lonely and she often stayed drunk. She just barely stayed wealthy.

Today, as lawyers doggedly try to retrieve her scattered fortune from all over the globe, the former Mrs. Gordon lies in a Fort Lauderdale nursing home, permanently brain-damaged. Relatives say her life was destroyed by four ruinous years as the doctor's wife. They say it wasn't a marriage, it was a matrimonial Brink's job.

"Unbelievable," says one son, Peter Beaumont. "It's sort of a classic: elderly lady with lots of bucks heads down to Retirement City and gets fleeced by local doctor."

It began as a September love affair. He was 62, silver-haired and single, with a new medical practice in Florida. She was 60, a bit overweight and twice divorced, given to irascibility and depression. . . .

The lead is inviting. Nobody, every writer knows, ever tires of reading about love, money and violence. Hiassen is using Stanley Walker's description of the three basic elements of news—women, wampum and wrongdoing.

The second and third paragraphs are like the coming attractions at a movie, or the come-on advertising on television. The reader is given a summary of the story's most dramatic facets.

The fourth paragraph drives home the theme: A woman ruined by her marriage. And in the fifth paragraph, a quote is used to sum up the theme.

The Feminization of Poverty

The national figures startled Jan Lovell of the *Globe-Gazette* in Mason City, Iowa: 75 percent of the poor in the U.S. are women and their children. By the year 2000, just about all of those living in poverty will be women and their children. Thought of as an urban problem, poverty does reach beyond the city limits. Lovell wanted to see whether rural America, specifically northern Iowa, was affected.

She interviewed 50 women and their children and dug into the data and read studies on the subject. She decided to tell the stories through the women and their children.

"Each of the major stories focuses on individual women and their families to make the problems real and tangible for the reader," Lovell says. The first story in the series begins this way:

Nancy's 18-month-old daughter suffered frostbite in December's sub-zero temperatures while they were waiting to catch a bus in Mason City.

They had to take a bus because Nancy couldn't afford to buy gas for the car that week.

•

After some 11 years on welfare, Hampton resident Pauline received training so she could get a job and support herself and her two young daughters.

Despite the training, she only made about $7,000 in her full-time job in 1983. That was supposed to cover house payments, taxes, insurance, utilities, food, clothing and all other expenses for the family.

And Pauline's hours were recently cut back because business has been slow.

"You're damned both ways," she says. "It's out of the frying pan and into the fire."

•

Lois' husband had always been the breadwinner of the family because he did not want his wife to work outside the house.

So Lois took care of the children and the household chores. Then her husband became ill and spent several years shuttling in and out of the hospital. Lois was forced to go job-hunting while in her mid-40s.

She worked as a waitress at various Mason City businesses, but quit work after 15 years to care for her ailing husband. He died about 13 years ago and Lois, now 79, lives on Social Security benefits from their lifetime of work—$271 per month.

Lois is thankful for good health but fearful of major emergencies.

•

The series was a finalist in the APME's annual contest for outstanding public service journalism.

Mary B. Lhowe of *The Journal-News* in Rockland County, N.Y., wrote a series of news features on the plight of the handicapped, mentally ill and retarded whose state support for education is terminated when they turn 21. For many of these young adults who are turned out of the schools and workshops, there is no place to go. This became Lhowe's theme: No Place to Go: The Agony of Aging Out. Her first story begins with an overview and in the fifth paragraph Lhowe gives an example:

Nancy, Pauline and Lois are just three of an escalating number of North Iowa women living in poverty. They are statistics in the startling national trend over the last decade called the "feminization of poverty."

Turning Away the Handicapped

For most people, the 21st birthday is cause for celebration, but for handicapped people in New York, it is often a swift kick into an ominous future.

At that birthday—the beginning of adulthood in the eyes of the law—care in homes or schools for handicapped children can suddenly end as state funding for tuition is cut off:

Families that had refused to place their children in lifelong public institutions, where costs are covered regardless of age, discover a frightening shortage of group homes or day treatment centers for adults.

The situation can provoke acts of desperation, particularly from older parents terrified about the uncertain future of their dependent son or daughter after their own deaths.

When Marcia Lehevan of Monsey was told last summer that her 21-year-old retarded and autistic son had to leave a residential school because of his age she threatened to take him and "go to a motel and we'll both go to sleep."

The school, which had treated Scott Lehevan in his late teens without the heavy use of drugs for the first time in his life, agreed to let him stay a few months longer. The effect was to buy time, putting off the inevitable search for an opening in an adult home, a slot that is notoriously hard to find.

Lhowe's series was also recognized by the APME.

Feature Ideas

The feature writer makes journalism out of daily experience. Shopping in a supermarket, the reporter notices the stacks of candy and gum and other small items near the checkout counter. A story idea pops up, and others. Listen to the reporter think:

How important is impulse buying? How do merchants determine what goes on the bottom shelves, on the top shelves? How much do people spend on junk food? What is junk food anyway? Do students really spend a lot of money on such items? How much do Americans spend on potato chips, soda?

And there the reporter's train of thought halted. In the files, the reporter finds that annual per capita consumption of soft drinks was 40.3 gallons in 1984. Retail sales amounted to $28.1 billion. Soft drinks overtook coffee in 1975 and milk in 1976. At the rate people are drinking soft drinks the per capita consumption of water (now at 58 gallons) will eventually be surpassed.

The reporter then does some arithmetic, translating the gallons into quarts and into glasses. He finds annual consumption of soft drinks in 1984 was 430 cans or bottles a year. Dividing by 365 the reporter gets a little more than a can or bottle a day for every man, woman and baby in the land. Now, he will talk to local bottlers to localize his piece.

Avoiding the Pitfalls

The feature writer who botches a story suffers the agonies of those who make public spectacles of themselves. As the feature is widely read, when it fails it collapses in full view. In the newsroom, colleagues excuse the spot news writer's failures more readily. After all, breaking news is written under pressure of deadline before all the facts are in. The feature writer has plenty of time to report and write and usually is given enough space.

The following suggestions are from a dozen feature writers around the country:

• Single-source stories are not as good as multi-source stories. No one cares to read about the author who talks about his life unless his personal account is supplemented by interviews with fellow writers, critics, his family, friends, even some readers.

• Do not have such a love affair with quotes that you fail to paraphrase routine material. Worse: Do not use quotes chronologically from the interview as a prop for failing to organize the piece. Good features can be written that are almost all quotes, but the quotes in many of these stories are usually rearranged.

Land Mines on the Way to a Good Feature

• Overwriting: Often the result of trying too hard for effect. Sometimes the result of inadequate reporting.

• Overreporting: One good anecdote or quote that proves or illustrates each point is enough.

• Concern for the subject. Be fair and give an accurate, complete and balanced account. Do not be overly concerned with what the subject will think of the piece.

• Bogging down in background: Look for the highlights of the career, the situation. A year-to-year, or day-to-day account fogs the point, bores the reader.

• Lack of guts: If everyone says your subject is a tightwad but still a charming guy, say so. Give the full profile, blemishes and beauty marks.

- Know what you are going to say and the tone in which it is to be said before starting. Otherwise, the story will never get off the ground.

- Develop an enthusiasm for the piece. Sometimes features are marred by an objectivity that keeps the reader at a distance. "The idea of a feature is to involve the reader," a reporter said. "But this is often taken to mean good craftsmanship through colorful writing. That's not enough. In many features, the writer needs to take a point of view, not simply to say, 'Look at this guy who was put into an institution for the retarded at the age of six, and when he was 18 some worker in the place saw that the kid wasn't retarded at all but had a learning disability.'

"The writer of this kind of piece has to be indignant at the tragedy. How can you be objective about this kind of inhumanity? A reader should be moved to indignation—not by the reporter's sounding off. We don't want that. But this kind of piece has to have the kind of facts and a story tone that gives a strong sense of human waste and bureaucratic inefficiency."

- Make sure the story has a good plot and is unusual enough to hold our interest. This means the central idea should have possibilities for drama, conflict, excitement, emotion.

- Don't tell us when you can show us people doing things.

A Short Feature: A Man Beset

A feature story need not be long. By making every word count, a reporter for *The Fresno Bee* captured the mood of a man with a problem:

Ben Karp is a patient man. Like most of us he can shrug off life's little onslaughts in hopes of a better day.

But Karp has been shrugging and dodging and hoping for six months now, and his patience finally snapped. He called the *Bee* and asked for a reporter to see him at his general merchandise business at 1837 Mariposa Street.

"Very important," he said. On the scene, Karp whipped off his hat, pointed a slightly trembling finger at a brownish spot the size of a half dollar on it and then wordlessly pointed skyward.

There, cooing happily and roosting comfortably in corners and on window sills, were pigeons. Dozens of pigeons.

"I've called the mayor, the public works commissioner, the health department," Karp said. "They promised me to do something. Nothing is done. It's ruining my business. People don't like to walk in here past that line there.

"I'd like to get a shotgun and scare them off. But you can't shoot a gun in the city. The health department says it can't do anything because it can't prove pigeons carry disease. The humane society says I can't trap or poison them. The mayor's office says he was going to have a meeting on it. Nothing happened.

"This is bad for the city, I tell you. Thousands of people go in and out of the bus depot and they see this and I hear them say to each other, 'Fresno can't be such a clean city. Look at this.'

"I don't blame people for not wanting to come into the store. What can I do about it?"

And Karp looked up at his feathered friends and shrugged.

THE LONG STORY

Newspapers have responded to the clear advantage of broadcast journalism in covering the spot story by emphasizing reporting in depth. This has meant that newspaper reporters need to be able to handle series of stories and depth pieces that run more than a column. Broadcast journalists who do documentaries also must master the techniques essential to handling the long piece.

A simple recital of events is not enough for the long story. Readers, viewers and listeners will not waste time on a lengthy story or documentary unless the reporting has developed insights for them and the writing is a cut above the pedestrian prose often accepted in the short news story written under pressure. The story also must be well-organized. It must carry the reader through a long journey.

When John McPhee, whom many consider one of the best reporters in the country, was at *Time* he wrote many of the magazine's longer pieces. "Each had to have a beginning, a middle and an end, some kind of structure so that it would go somewhere and sit down when it got there," he said.

The Reporting

"The first point about reporting a depth story," says Jeffrey Tannenbaum of *The Wall Street Journal*, "is that it usually requires a lot of work. For a profile of Rockefeller University, I conducted at least 20 interviews in person, and the typical interview lasted 90 minutes. I also did several more interviews by phone and read a great deal of background material from the Rockefeller files and from news clips."

The long story, he says, "is an interplay between the specific and the general." By "general" he means the themes that the reporter has selected as the basis of the piece. A story about a breaking news event may have one or two themes. The long story may have half a dozen. "Specific" refers to the material that amplifies, explains and buttresses the themes.

"For every generalization or theme in the story," Tannenbaum continues, "there should be specific illustrations to buttress it. This means the reporter has to identify his or her themes and then must dig out the proof for them. The more specific and colorful the details that are used as proof or buttressing material, the more effectively the generalization or theme will be brought home to the reader."

Proof and buttressing material can consist of anecdotes, quotations, observations and pertinent background. But before the reporter can gather these, he or she must determine the heart of the story, its main point or major theme. Like all experienced journalists, Tannenbaum tries to sketch out his theme as soon as possible. This may come before any reporting is done, or soon after the reporting begins. It can come from a tip, an editor's assignment, the reporter's hunch. Or it may simply be the logical step following a series of developments on a beat.

Tannenbaum's theme for the Rockefeller piece was that the institution's scientific freedom was being threatened by changes in its financial status. "From that point on, I pressed in interviews for material—the more colorful the better—to buttress my theme. I needed to show how wealthy Rockefeller University once was and how it was now comparatively less well off. I needed to show in detail the problems that had developed as a result. At the same time, I still had to convey a sense of what Rockefeller is like and what its accomplishments are.

"For each key point, I want two things: Good quotes stating the point and colorful illustrations, anecdotes, examples," he says. "I knew exactly what I was looking for from each subsequent interview subject."

In the reporting, additional themes often will develop, and these, too, must be buttressed with specific quotes, illustrations, data and anecdotes.

In a story Tannenbaum did for the *Journal* about violence in junior and senior high schools, his main point or major theme, his news peg, was that school violence is increasing:

Acts of violence—shootings, beatings, rapes and strong-arm robberies—are cropping up with unnerving frequency.

This sentence occurred in Tannenbaum's third paragraph. Like many long pieces, Tannenbaum's began with a delayed lead. He began the piece with the most telling of the illustrations his reporting turned up:

In a second-floor washroom at Franklin D. Roosevelt Junior High School in Cleveland, four pupils recently cornered a 15-year-old classmate, Kenneth Wagner, and authorities say the foursome executed him by firing six rifle bullets into his head.

Tannenbaum used other incidents to illustrate the themes in his story. At Nottingham High School in Syracuse, N.Y., when black students and white students were fighting in the cafeteria, the principal tried to restore order. He was cracked over the head from behind with a chair.

Statistics are essential in a story of this sort. They provide conviction. Tannenbaum found government data that showed a seven-fold increase in pupil attacks on teachers and a two-and-a-half-fold increase in pupil attacks on other students.

The *Journal* wants reporters to include a "significance paragraph" high in their stories, a few sentences telling the reader why this story is important. (*Journal* reporters call this the "nut" paragraph, and the term has spread to other newsrooms.) Tannenbaum wrote that as a result of "growing violence, students in a number of cities face not only the increased possibility of being physically harmed but also near certainty that the quality of their education will suffer."

The idea that school violence affects learning needed buttressing, and so Tannenbaum sought out an authority to shore up the conclusion, and he wrote:

> An atmosphere of violence, says Richard T. Frost, director of urban studies at Syracuse University Research Corp., which has studied violence in the schools for the U.S. Office of Education, "mortally threatens the capacity of some schools to educate anybody."

If the story describes a problem, the reporter must find out what is being done to solve it. Tannenbaum learned that school security forces are being increased, city police in some cities are assigned to school grounds, and changes in the curriculum are being made with student participation.

Organizing the Story

The major difficulty writers have with the long story is controlling its several themes and ideas, the half dozen building blocks that must be arranged in logical and interesting order. It is not easy. McPhee says he goes "nuts trying to put it all in focus."

McPhee's first step is to structure the piece by typing up his notes and organizing them by subject or theme. He types the themes on index cards and tacks them to a bulletin board. Some reporters spread their cards on a flat surface. The story is plotted by arranging the cards in the order that seems best for the story.

By attaching the notes to the appropriate cards with the thematic material, the reporter has the story laid out in a form easy to scrutinize and to rearrange if necessary. This physical arrangement tends to give the reporter a sense of control over the story, and control of themes and reporting detail is the key to mastering the long piece. The long article must move logically and coherently from beginning to end, from idea to idea.

The system of organizing copy suggested here may not work for every reporter. Some reporters can keep a plan in mind as they write. Others need only to jot down a few words to remind them of the themes and the order in which they will be handled. "Strange as it may seem to the beginner anxious to set words to paper, structuring the story challenges a reporter's creative talents as much as the writing. What's most absorbing is putting these stories together," says McPhee. "I want to know where I'm going from the start of the piece. It's my nature to want to know."

The following system is useful to organize the long article:

1. Identify all themes. Summarize in a sentence or two.
2. Place each theme on a separate index card. Put the cards in the order that the themes will follow in the story.

3. Cut up notes by theme and place them next to cards. Reread and again arrange cards and notes in the order in which they will be written.

4. Look through the cards for the major theme that will serve as the lead or the integrating idea for the article. Write on card.

Writing Preparations

As the notes are lined up (Step 3), a reporter may discover that he or she does not have adequate documentation or illustrative material to buttress some of the themes. More reporting will be necessary.

Good reporters check their notes at this stage for the high-quality quotes and illustrations that can be placed high up in the various sections of the story. One might be used to begin the article if the piece lends itself to a delayed lead. Some reporters use a colored pencil or pen to mark these high-quality quotes, anecdotes and incidents so that they call out for use.

Caution: Resist the temptation to use a dramatic quote or telling incident simply because it is attention-getting. The material must illustrate the theme it accompanies. If the fit is loose, put the example with a more appropriate theme or toss it out, however much work went into digging it up, however exciting the material.

Remember: Keep clearly in mind or in view the major theme for the piece (Step 4). Toss out any material that is irrelevant to this integrating idea.

Changing Directions

Once the story is organized, do not assume that the structure cannot be changed. If the piece does not seem to be flowing properly, shift some of the elements around.

Some of the other problems that come up are:

• A theme has too much material to organize. *Divide it into sub-themes that can be handled more easily. Consider dropping, or at least drastically subordinating, some themes.*

• A theme is too minor to be worth the space being given it. *Blend it into another theme or discard it.*

• The transition from one theme to another is awkward. To go from one theme to another smoothly, *reorder the themes so that the linkage is more natural.*

• A long block of background material does not move; it impedes the flow of the article. *Break up this background, history, explanatory material and blend sections into the narrative.*

Look at this paragraph in a long article about an evangelist:

The search for miracles is virtually an American tradition. Throughout American history and literature, "the quest"— for hope, for answers, for reasons and fulfillment—has been a pervasive theme. In the 18th century. . . .

This could be the beginning of a long historical section. But the reporter, Mary Ann Wallis, is aware that she must keep the reader in the present, with the faith healer, Bishop Bryant in Yonkers, about whom she is writing. After another paragraph of history, she writes:

> But the hope of fulfillment through re-ligion and a longing for miracles has al-ways been a consistent example of the American quest. Bishop Bryant's revival service, with its thick stifling air of expec-tation, was a symbolic microcosm of this American theme. . . .

The Writing

The poet Ezra Pound spoke disparagingly of those who "seem to think that a man can write a good long poem before he learns to write a good short one, or even before he learns to produce a single good line." The same could be said of the reporter who attempts a long article. The art and craft for doing the shorter piece must be under the reporter's control first. McPhee trained for his long-article writing by mastering his craft at *Time*.

"I must have written 200,000 words a year," he recalls. "Writing teaches writing."

Every writer hews to his or her craft every day. Students have fewer writing demands on them than the professional journalist and thus must impose writing quotas on themselves—500 to 1,000 words a day, even if the writing is for a personal journal. Such discipline is not easy. Tongue slightly in cheek, McPhee says that sometimes he ties himself to his typing chair with a sash.

Basketball players and pianists practice. So should writers. As Norman Podhoretz, an editor and writer, says, "Articulateness on paper is a gift which does not differ in principle from the gift of physical coordination we call athletic skill; like muscle, it needs to be exercised not only in order for it to develop but because it exerts a pressure of its own on the possessor to use it, to keep working it out, and to no special purpose beyond the pleasure of feeling it function as it was meant to do."

A Television Documentary

Everyone who sets words on paper for a living goes through the anxieties of cutting back, of discarding quotes, of tossing out details that get in the way of the theme and that impede the flow of the story. But this cannot be done until the theme is clearly identified. Let us watch the producer of a television documentary as he tries to focus on a theme for his subject, the decline of many of the country's older cities, and then makes changes in his script.

The deterioration of the inner city has had the attention of planners, politicians and journalists since the 1950s. If the city is civilization, then the troubles afflicting the city cores of Sacramento, Denver, Detroit, Cleveland,

Philadelphia, Boston, Baltimore, St. Louis, New York and dozens of others threaten a way of life—cultural, commercial, educational, religious. For in the cities are the opera houses and philharmonic halls, the factories and the offices, the schools, and the churches and the cathedrals. The city gives a center to life.

To make journalism out of this national phenomenon is no easy task. The decline is the result of complex social, political and economic forces. Reporters with a national audience cannot write about all the cities in trouble. They must make one or two illustrate the plight of the many. They must draw from the tangled problems of many cities their common elements and then find a city that symbolizes most of these elements.

When Howard Weinberg, a producer of "Bill Moyers' Journal" on the Educational Broadcasting Corp. network decided to look at the problems of the inner cities he cast about for some central themes and a city to symbolize them.

Weinberg first defined the scope and limits of his piece. He then settled on a point of view. His idea was to show the forces, especially racism, at work in causing neighborhood deterioration.

"I went to Chicago," Weinberg says. "My associate and I spent a week there, interviewing realtors, mortgage bankers, open housing leaders, community leaders, journalists, government officials and others on the south, west, north sides of Chicago."

When he returned to New York he felt frustrated. He had no idea how he would tell such a complicated story in half an hour. Tentatively, he decided to use the neighborhood of Austin on the west side where black and white community groups had organized to preserve and improve their neighborhood. Also, a woman organizer, Gale Cincotta, lived in Austin, and Weinberg wanted to have a person as a focus for the program.

"In discussions with Bill Moyers, I was forced to rethink and refine my outline," he says. In looking back at his original outline, Weinberg found he had written, "It is beginning to be understood in communities of the inner cities that deterioration is not an accident, it is the inevitable result of a lack of faith. Expect deterioration—and you'll get it."

This idea of a self-fulfilling prophecy kept coming back to Weinberg, and he continued to do more reporting. Gradually, a theme and a strong point of view emerged. "It became clearer that 'redlining' was the story I wanted to tell, not the FHA abuses, not the efforts to relocate blacks in the suburbs or to 'stabilize' a threatened neighborhood."

Redlining takes its name from the red circles banks and other lending agencies reportedly draw on maps around neighborhoods that the lenders decide will not be given mortgage money because they believe it is deteriorating. The practice makes it difficult for residents to improve their homes or for buyers to come into the neighborhood. Further deterioration results.

Weinberg was struck by the material he turned up in his reporting. "A savings and loan association was licensed to serve a neighborhood—and clearly, it was not doing that when it openly admitted that it received 80 percent of its deposits from its neighborhood and reinvested 20 percent in its neighborhood," Weinberg says.

Weinberg visualized the booming suburbs—which the savings of inner city residents were helping to build—and the deteriorating inner city. This would make for dramatic pictures.

He decided to shift the main focus from Austin to Rogers Park, which was beginning to go the way of Austin. Here is how the script of "This Neighborhood is Obsolete" begins:

BILL MOYERS: The skyline of Chicago thrusts a handsome profile above the shores of Lake Michigan, suggesting the serene self-assurance of a city and its architecture, its wealth and its power and its tolerance for new ideas in urban living. But opulent skylines point up and away from the reality in their shadows. And in Chicago, as in every large American city, the grand vista is misleading.

Out beyond the soaring, secular temples of commerce, before you reach the shopping centers of suburbia, the future of Chicago is being decided every day in less spectacular surroundings: in neighborhoods where drugstores and delicatessens, taverns, laundromats, barbershops, and small churches on treelined corners express a lifestyle in danger of extinction.

For the way the economic game is played these days, these neighborhoods hardly have a chance. There's a profit in moving people out and hang the human cost.

In the next half hour, we'll look at two Chicago neighborhoods where the neighbors are fighting back.

I'm Bill Moyers.

This neighborhood is obsolete.

The people who live here don't think so, but some of the banks and savings and loan associations do. They stopped lending money because they believe the community's deteriorating and the risk is too great. But without money to improve people's homes or to give them a chance to buy another, the decay speeds up and the fear becomes a self-fulfilling prophecy.

In this and similar neighborhoods in Chicago, people accuse the savings and loan associations and the banks of redlining. Redlining means an entire geographic area can be declared unsuitable for conventional loans and mortgages. A redline is, in effect, drawn like a noose around a neighborhood until for want of good housing the working and middle classes are driven to the suburbs and the neighborhood is left to the very poor.

A side effect of redlining is something called disinvestment. You probably haven't heard of that term before. I hadn't until I came here. Disinvestment is a process of collecting deposits in one neighborhood and investing them somewhere else. The lending agents say it's necessary to spread the risk, but it leaves a neighborhood like this short of capital and hope. Gasping for its very life.

The people who could afford to, move on. And that's what the savings and loan associations would like to do. After they've helped to build up the suburbs and make them affluent and attractive, they want to move there, too, or at least to open a suburban branch. Only then does an old neighborhood like this discover where its money has gone, but by then it's too late.

MARY LOU WOLFF: This federal savings and loan is the largest savings institution in the state of Illinois. It's the leading savings and loan that sets the tone for the rest of savings and loans that will not give us money for our neighborhoods. Okay? The savings and loan industry has got to take us seriously. We are not kidding around. . . .

Like much good journalism, the documentary and the campaigns of local stations and newspapers had results. The month after the Moyers documentary, the Illinois Savings and Loan Commissioner issued a regulation against redlining. The regulation prohibits savings and loan associations from refusing to lend money in a neighborhood because of its age or changing character. The following year, Congress passed two pieces of legislation to end redlining by banks.

Notice that Weinberg had to reduce his ideas to the dimension of his program. Like the writer of a 300-word story or a 30-second news item, he had to focus on a single theme and toss out all extraneous material. The journalist never escapes the chore of boiling down material, of eliminating anything not related to the theme.

That basic theme can always be expressed in a simple sentence or two. David Belasco, the American theatrical producer, once remarked, "If you can't write your idea on the back of my calling card you don't have a clear idea."

Freelancing Articles

Some writers prefer to work on their own rather than to work for a news organization full time. These writers are known as freelancers. Some do this full time, and others use free-lance writing to supplement their income. The free-lance market is competitive: Freelancers compete with each other and with the staffs of the publications for which they hope to write. Here are some suggestions about developing markets for free-lance articles by Wilmer C. Ames, Jr., who has written articles on a free-lance basis and is on the staff of *Sports Illustrated:*

1. Read the magazine for at least the previous six issues before submitting anything, even a query letter, to familiarize yourself with its style, its contents, how many articles are written by staff writers and freelancers. This will also tell you how much space is allotted to a particular subject.

2. Study the masthead. Determine which editors handle which sections and subjects. Once you do get an assignment this will help you to know what the particular editor expects in a story. This will also indicate which editor has the most power on the staff (something that is important when a freelancer's story is competing against a staff writer's).

3. It is best to send a query letter the first time around. This should be written as carefully as one would write the finished article. In fact, all of your basic research will probably have been completed by the time you compose the query letter.

4. The most difficult job when breaking into a magazine is to find an article idea that an editor or a staff writer has not come up with. Your idea should lend itself to the magazine's format, and should not be so timely as to necessitate immediate publication. Make it newsworthy, but make sure it can sit in-house until there is space to run it.

5. Treat everyone courteously. Most secretaries are important to an editor—they sometimes not only screen unsolicited manuscripts, but also unwanted phone calls. When your letter or copy comes in there are many things they can do with it. The better they feel about you, the more quickly and gently your copy will be handled.

6. It is important to know the style of the magazine in order to make sure that your piece will fit in. Don't worry, initially, about showing your style. The most important thing is that your piece fit the magazine. After you've gained some recognition as a competent writer, then you can take liberties with your copy.

7. Part of your job is to be more thorough than a staffer. Do all of your homework before talking to an editor about a piece—*you* have to sell him on your knowledge and your abilities.

8. Be neat. An editor may say he doesn't mind typos in your copy, but you never know who will see it and pass judgment on it.

9. Call in periodically after the assignment has been completed. Volunteer to make any changes, to help with the research, and to assist in any way you can. While you're writing, check in with the editor and let him know how the story is developing.

10. Don't fight making changes on your first few articles—at least until an editor respects your abilities and knowledge.

11. Expect to be asked to rewrite. Initially you may find it difficult fitting into a magazine's style.

12. Always be prompt. The only thing a freelancer has, initially, is his or her reputation, and the most important part of that reputation is dependability. If there is a problem, notify the editor well in advance. The managing editor is depending upon the senior editor and the senior editor is depending upon you. If the M.E. gets angry with the editor, the editor will get angry with you. A freelancer always has the most to lose.

13. Most magazines are ethical organizations and will give you the opportunity to write the article and then to rewrite it if necessary. They will not steal your idea or assign it to a staff writer. If you fail to deliver what they need, they may then pay you and assign your idea to someone else.

14. Maintaining contact and staying in touch with "your" editor after a story is completed is important. There are many others out there who also want to appear in print, so it is important that the editor have you at the top of the list.

> **Get it in Writing.** The pleasures and pitfalls of freelancing are described by Melissa Ludtke Lincoln in an article, "The freelance life," in the September/October 1981 *Columbia Journalism Review*. She suggests that freelancers try to obtain a written contract—or at least an agreement—that covers the following:
> - The date the article is due.
> - The length of the story.
> - The amount of payment—due on acceptance—or the kill fee.
> - The amount for expenses.
> - The right to look over the proofs to permit correction of errors.

Further Reading

Buchwald, Art. *You Can Fool All of the People All the Time*. New York: G. P. Putnam's Sons, 1985.

Halberstam, David. *The Powers That Be*. New York: Alfred A. Knopf, 1979.

Mitchell, Joseph. *McSorley's Wonderful Saloon*. New York: Grosset & Dunlap, 1943.

Moffitt, Donald, ed. *The American Character: Views of America from The Wall Street Journal*. New York: George Brogiller, 1983.

Swanberg, W. A. *Citizen Hearst*. New York: Charles Scribner's Sons, 1961.

Swanberg, W. A. *Pulitzer*. New York: Charles Scribner's Sons, 1967.

CHAPTER NINE

Broadcast Writing

Preview

Broadcast stories are written to be understood quickly and easily. Radio and television writers:

- Use everyday language.
- Write short sentences that follow the S-V-O sentence structure.
- Use one idea to a sentence.
- Use the present tense as often as possible.

Broadcast news writers usually confine their stories to one major theme, and their language is simple and direct.

In addition to writing local news stories, radio news writers rewrite into broadcast form news they obtain from the news wires of the AP, UPI and other services. The material is compressed, sentences shortened and tenses changed.

Television journalists must cope with a complex technology that emphasizes the visual. Writing and news judgment often are based on the available pictures.

Importance. A Roper Organization for the Television Information Office found that television is the primary source of news for 64 percent of the population and the only source of news for 46 percent.

A 1985 *Wall Street Journal* study of the time people spend on information products found:

TV 252 minutes
Radio 124
Newspapers 31
Magazines 15

Broadcast news takes its form and its format from the fact that it is written to be read aloud by newscasters and to be heard or seen by listeners or viewers. This means that stories are written to rules considerably different from those for print journalism. Copy is prepared differently and stories are shorter.

Tune in a radio station and time the items on a newscast. Watch the evening news, stopwatch in hand. Most of the tell stories—stories read by an anchor or reporter without tape—are short, two to five sentences running 10 to 30 seconds. Most stories run fewer than two minutes. If all the news on a half-hour newscast were to be printed, it would not fill two-thirds of a page of a standard-size newspaper.

Broadcast news serves a purpose different from the newspaper. Its intent is to provide the public with basic information quickly and succinctly. The broadcast writer's job is to get the story idea across clearly and precisely,

without the detail. To communicate the day's events in such succinct pulses to an audience that cannot read or hear the material again, the broadcast journalist follows a special set of guidelines.

Like the jockey or the weight-watcher who must think twice about every slice of bread, the broadcast journalist has to examine every idea and every word. Too many words and the story may squeeze out another item. Too many ideas and the listener or viewer may be confused. Broadcast newswriters set their writing rhythm to a series of near-inflexible rules: Keep it tight. Write simple sentences. Keep one important idea to a sentence. If attribution is needed, begin with it. The story logic must be precise. Every expressed idea must flow logically and cleanly into the next.

Rewriting the Wires

Much of radio's national and international news is rewritten from the news wires. The wire stories are condensed and simplified. On television, most of the brief items—the tell stories—are also taken from the wires and re-written. Let's see how this is done.

First, let's compare the news and radio wire versions of the same story. On the left is the beginning of a story from the news wire, and on the right is the radio version, which was less than a third the length of the news wire story. The stories were moved by the AP's Newark bureau.

News Wire

TRENTON, N.J. (AP)--
PEOPLE CHARGED WITH
POSSESSING MARIJUANA
CANNOT CLAIM AS A DEFENSE
THAT THEY NEEDED THE
ILLEGAL DRUG FOR MEDICINAL
PURPOSES, THE NEW JERSEY
SUPREME COURT RULED MONDAY
IN A 4-3 DECISION.

ONLY WASHINGTON, HAWAII
AND THE DISTRICT OF
COLUMBIA RECOGNIZE A
MEDICAL NECESSITY DEFENSE
IN DRUG POSSESSION CASES,
ACCORDING TO ATTORNEYS IN
THE NEW JERSEY CASE.

IN ISSUING ITS DECISION,
THE STATE'S HIGHEST COURT
REVERSED A 1984 APPEALS
COURT RULING THAT SAID
MICHAEL TATE, A 23-YEAR-
OLD QUADRIPLEGIC, COULD
PRESENT TO A JURY THE
ARGUMENT THAT HE HAD NO
REASONABLE CHOICE BUT TO
SMOKE THE DRUG.

TATE, WHO BROKE HIS NECK
IN A 1980 DIVING ACCIDENT,
WAS ARRESTED IN MARCH 1983
AT HIS MANALAPAN HOME AND
CHARGED WITH POSSESSION OF
MORE THAN 25 GRAMS OF
MARIJUANA. THE CHARGE
CARRIES A MAXIMUM PENALTY
OF SIX MONTHS IN JAIL OR A
$500 FINE.

TATE HAS SAID HE SMOKES
MARIJUANA BECAUSE IT
RELIEVES CHRONIC MUSCLE
SPASMS WITHOUT CAUSING THE
HARMFUL SIDE EFFECTS OF
SOME PRESCRIPTION
DRUGS. . . .

Radio Wire

(TRENTON)--THE NEW
JERSEY SUPREME COURT SAYS
PEOPLE CHARGED WITH
POSSESSING MARIJUANA
CANNOT CLAIM AS A DEFENSE
THAT THEY NEEDED THE
ILLEGAL DRUG FOR MEDICINAL
PURPOSES.

THE STATE'S HIGHEST
COURT WAS DIVIDED FOUR-
THREE AS IT REVERSED A 1984
APPEALS COURT RULING. THE
LOWER-COURT RULING SAID A
23-YEAR-OLD QUADRIPLEGIC
COULD PRESENT TO A JURY THE
ARGUMENT THAT HE HAD NO
REASONABLE CHOICE BUT TO
SMOKE MARIJUANA.

MICHAEL TATE, WHO BROKE
HIS NECK IN A 1980 DIVING
ACCIDENT, WAS ARRESTED IN
MARCH 1983 AT HIS
MANALAPAN HOME. HE WAS
CHARGED WITH POSSESSION OF
MORE THAN 25 GRAMS OF
MARIJUANA, WHICH CARRIES A
MAXIMUM PENALTY OF SIX
MONTHS IN JAIL OR A 500
DOLLAR FINE.

TATE SAYS HE SMOKED
MARIJUANA BECAUSE IT
RELIEVED CHRONIC MUSCLE
SPASMS WITHOUT CAUSING THE
HARMFUL SIDE EFFECTS OF
SOME PRESCRIPTION DRUGS.

THE SUPREME COURT RULED
THAT THE STATE LEGISLATURE
HAD CONSIDERED AND
REJECTED THE DEFENSE OF
MEDICAL NECESSITY WHEN IT
CLASSIFIED MARIJUANA AS A
CONTROLLED DANGEROUS
SUBSTANCE. . . .

The radio news writer has changed tenses in the lead and moved a secondary element, the 4-3 vote, to the second paragraph. Attribution was placed first in the radio wire version. The radio wire account does not include the second paragraph of background from the news wire story.

Now let's watch Mervin Block rewrite a UPI piece into a 20-second tell story for network television news. Here is the wire copy Block had before him:

```
    ROUEN, France (UPI)--Police have arrested a
disgruntled employee who admitted he tried to slowly
irradiate his boss to death by planting three
radioactive discs under the driver's seat of his car.
    Guy Busin, an executive at a nuclear rod
treatment plant, is the world's first known intended
murder victim by use of nuclear waste.
    Noel Lecomte, 27, who was arrested Wednesday,
told police Busin ''was always questioning me and
bothering me'' and confessed that he decided to kill
him by exposing him to nuclear radiation.
    Busin was Lecomte's supervisor at the Nuclear
Treatment Center in La Hague near the Channel Coast,
the world's largest plant for the treatment of
nuclear fuel rods.
    Busin has been under medical observation since he
found the intended radioactive murder weapon in his
car more than a month ago. Doctors say he apparently
suffered no ill effects from the material except
extreme fatigue.
    Lecomte told police he was alone in the plant one
night in either May or June of 1978 when he stole three
nuclear discs used to move nuclear fuel at the plant,
and planted them under the driver's seat of Busin's
car.
    Busin found the discs March 21, eight months
after they were planted.
    He said he had not used the car for five months
because it had been damaged in an accident that
occurred when he was returning home from a wrestling
match.
    ---------=
    UPI 05-10 02:46 aed=
```

Here is Block's story:

```
    French police say that a worker in a nuclear plant has
admitted trying to kill his boss by planting radioactive
discs under the driver's seat of his car. The worker
explained that he was angry because the boss irritated him.
So he decided to irradiate the boss. But the boss discovered
the deadly discs in his car. He seems to have suffered no
harm, except for extreme fatigue.
```

Here is how Block says he thought the story through:

I start off by establishing the location of the event with "French police." I wouldn't use the name of the town because if I did use it, what would it mean to listeners? They wouldn't know where it is, and if I had to tell them, I would be taking up valuable time.

The second paragraph of the UPI story says the executive was the world's first intended murder victim by use of nuclear waste. I avoid all absolutes and superlatives: the first, the biggest, the highest, the most, the least. How would anyone know? Who keeps track of that?

I wouldn't use the name of the executive, nor of the suspect or his age, or the name of the plant or the site. Incidentally, *site* is a word to avoid in broadcasting because it can be confused with *sight* and *cite*.

The story was of no great significance but was used because of its bizarre nature. This gave Block some liberty to featurize the piece. "If I were writing it today with more time," Block said, "I would restructure it. I think the script would have been improved if I had put the two sentences, 'The worker explained . . . irradiate his boss', at the end of the item."

"Newsbreak"

"Newsbreak" runs on the CBS television network several times a day. In less than a minute, several major stories are read. One day, Block compressed seven wire stories into 50 seconds. Here is his script (left) and his explanation of how he wrote some of the items:

```
A former
employee of the
Westchester
Stauffer's Inn,
near New York
City, was
arrested today
```

Rather than start a story with a place name, ''In White Plains, New York,'' I always try to fix the place up high but unobtrusively. In the fifth line, I wrote ''outside,'' then realized that ''near'' is closer and shorter. I

and charged with setting the fire that killed 26 corporate executives last December.

didn't use his name because he was an unknown and his name wouldn't mean anything to anyone outside White Plains, which is largely unknown itself except as the site of a Revolutionary battle.

The government's index of leading economic indicators last month rose slightly, one-point-four percent. The increase reversed three straight months of declines.

To save words, I didn't say the U.S. Department of Commerce issued the statistics. It's sufficient to say ''the government.'' I originally wrote, ''rose slightly last month.'' Then I caught myself, remembering Strunk's rule to ''place the emphatic words of a sentence at the end.''

Pennsylvania Congressman Raymond Lederer said today he's resigning because of his conviction in the Abscam scandal. Just yesterday, the House Ethics committe called for his expulsion.

Again, a story that a newspaper might give hundreds of words. But newscasts don't have the luxury of roominess. I didn't have space for his party affiliation, his hometown or the particulars of his crime. I did try to put the news in perspective by writing a second sentence. (In my haste, I left an ''e'' off ''committee.'' When not under pressure, I spell it with ease.)

A British truck driver admitted today he was the ''Yorkshire Ripper,''

This is a simple, straight-forward, no-frills account of a dramatic development in a sensational story. But there's no need here for any supercharged

pleading guilty to manslaughter in the deaths of 13 women. By not pleading guilty to underline{murder}, Peter Sutcliffe could be sent to a hospital for the criminally insane--and not prison.

language to ``sell'' the story. (As architect Ludwig Mies van der Rohe used to say, ``Less is more.'') My second sentence gives the ``why'' for his plea. I underlined ``murder'' because I thought it was a word the anchor should stress. (Some anchors welcome this. In any case, in the pressure-cooker atmosphere of a network newsroom, the stress is usually on the writer.)

Israeli warplanes swept into action over Lebanon for the fourth straight day, bombing Palestinian guerrilla bases just across the Israeli border.

This one-sentence story does not provide details, of course, but there's no time for details. Details are secondary. Most listeners, I suspect, aren't even interested in details. Anyway, casualties and the extent of damage are usually in dispute. If I'd had word of many casualties-- and I didn't--I'd have said so.

Voice-Over Videotape

Television writing is complicated by the need to write to visuals. Block was told to write a lead-in and 20 seconds of voice-over videotape for the "CBS Evening News" from this wire service story:

CRESTVIEW, Fla. (AP)--Tank cars carrying acetone exploded and burned when a train loaded with hazardous chemicals derailed here today. Thousands were evacuated as the wind spread thick yellow sulfur fumes over rural northwest Florida.

Only one injury was reported. A fisherman trekking through the woods near the wreck inhaled some of the fumes and was hospitalized for observation.

Oskaloosa County Civil Defense director Tom Nichols estimated that 5,000 people had fled homes or campsites in the 30-square-mile evacuation area, which included several villages and about half of Blackwater River State Forest.

```
``It's a rural area and houses are scattered all
through it,'' said Ray Belcher, a supervisor for the
Florida Highway Patrol. ``It's about half woods, half
farms.''
    Civil Defense officials put the approximately
9,000 residents of nearby Crestview on alert for
possible evacuation as approaching thunderstorms
threatened a wind-shift that would push the fumes in
that direction. . . .
```

Block was writing "blind" in the tape. That is, he did not have access
to the videotape his copy would refer to. Block recalls his thinking:

First, I see the dateline, Crestview, Fla., and I know that in writing
for broadcast I have to put the dateline up near the top in as unobtrusive
a way as possible. It has to be done deftly.

When I started writing for broadcast, I was told by one of the editors
that it's inadvisable to begin a story by saying, "In Crestview, Florida
. . ." The editor told me that was a lazy man's way of starting a story.
In London today . . . in Paris today. . . . He didn't say never. But in 90
or 95 percent of the cases, it's best not to begin that way.

We see in the first line of the AP story that one of the trains is
carrying acetone. My reaction is that most people don't know what
acetone is. That probably is a reflection of my ignorance. If we were to
use it on the air, it could sound like acid-own. In any case, there's no
need to identify the chemical, or any of the chemicals, perhaps. The most
important element is the explosion and the evacuation.

In the second paragraph of the story, it says that only one injury was
reported. I didn't mention the injury. It seems slight. The third
paragraph gives the name of the county. In writing news for broadcast
you have to eliminate the details and focus on the big picture.

In my script, beginning with the second paragraph, there is silent film,
and I had to write 20 seconds of voice-over. As so often happens, I had
no chance to see the videotape in advance, so I had to write in a general
way without getting specific. I made an assumption at this point, and
although it's dangerous to assume, I have seen so many derailments on
TV films or tape that I figured the opening shot would be of derailed
cars. So I presumed my paragraph covering the tape of the accident
would be appropriate.

I was looking for facts in the AP story that would be essential in my
script. As you can see, my script consists of about a five second lead-in
and 20 seconds of voice-over for the tape. Within the tight space, I can
use only the most important facts because a script cannot consist of a
string of dense facts.

Incomprehensible. Mark R. Levy and John P. Robinson of the University of Maryland contend that "the average viewer fails to understand the main points in two-thirds of all major TV news stories . . . people who say TV is their main source for news are among the least well-informed members of the public."

On the basis of their research they recommend:

Simplifying: TV "too often uses language and concepts that are outside the viewer's normal vocabulary."

Slowing down delivery: They clocked Dan Rather at 200 words a minute.

Longer pieces: "Telling fewer stories at greater length" will help the viewers, most of whom "aren't paying all that much attention in the first place."

Information redundancy: "Viewers often need to hear and see the same information more than once to understand it." Headlines at the outset and teasers just before the breaks help.

Simple, clear graphics. Video and script must be "explicitly reinforcing."

So-what test. Tell the viewer why the story is important.

Their suggestions are made in an article "The 'huh?' factor: untangling TV news" in the July/August 1986 *Columbia Journalism Review.*

Here is the script as Block wrote it:

```
mb              A tank car
DEAN            explosion in the
                Florida Panhandle
                today led to the
                evacuation of about
         ⑦      five-thousand people
                from their homes.

SIL/VO          The explosion was
:20             one of several that
                ripped through 18 cars
                that derailed at
                Crestview, Florida.
```

```
Several were carrying
toxic and explosive
chemicals.
Because of the
danger of various
fumes and the
chance of further
explosions,
officials ordered
the evacuation of
one-fourth the
population of the
county.
      ⃝
```

Block rewrote the piece for another television news program:

```
     Several railroad tank cars blew up in northwestern
Florida today, causing the evacuation of about five-
thousand people. The cars were carrying hazardous
chemicals near Crestview, Florida, when they derailed,
exploded and burned. Thick yellow sulfur fumes spread over
the area, and one man was hospitalized. If the winds change,
thousands more might have to be evacuated.
```

He prefers the second version because "northwestern Florida" locates the accident more clearly than the "Florida panhandle."

From our window into the thinking of a broadcast newswriter, we can generalize about writing for the ear.

Write short, simple sentences. Use everyday language. Make the structure of most sentences conform to the S-V-O rule. Keep one idea to a sentence. Here are some other guidelines and examples:

- Begin sentences with a source, with the attribution, if needed:

WRONG: The city needs new traffic lights, the mayor said.

RIGHT: The mayor says the city needs new traffic lights.

- Avoid introductory phrases and clauses:

WRONG: Hoping to keep the lid on spiraling prices, the president called today for wage-price guidelines for labor and industry.

RIGHT: The president is calling for wage-price guidelines to keep prices down.

- Use ordinary, one-syllable words whenever possible:

WRONG: The unprecedented increase in profits led the Congress to urge the plan's discontinuance.

RIGHT: The record profits led Congress to urge an end to the plan.

- Use vigorous verbs. Avoid adjectives and adverbs:

WEAK: He made the task easy for his listeners.

BETTER: He simplified the task for his listeners.

WEAK: She walked slowly through the mud.

BETTER: She trudged through the mud.

- Use the active, not the passive, voice:

WEAK: He was shown the document by the lawyer.

BETTER: The lawyer showed him the document.

- Use familiar words in familiar combinations.
- Write simply, directly. Omit useless words.

The writer should test his or her writing by reading it aloud. Not only will the reading catch sounds that do not work, it will reveal whether a newscaster can read one idea in a single pulse. The newscaster must be able to breathe, and each breath closes out an idea.

Simple, direct writing can be elegant. This is the language of Mark Twain, Dickens, and Edward R. Murrow. Here is a lead by Charles Kuralt, a correspondent for CBS television who was doing a piece about exploitation of the environment.

> Men look at hillsides and see board feet of lumber. Men look at valleys and see homesites.

Use a phrase to indicate someone is being quoted—as he said, in his words, as he put it.

> WRONG: He said "We need protective tariffs."
> RIGHT: As he put it, "We need. . . ."
> As he told the Senate, "We need. . . ."
> In his words, "We need. . . ."

Sentence Structure and Language

Clarity? A television newscast included this lead to a major story: "A 44-year-old mother and nurse was found stabbed to death by her daughter in the basement of their home on Rush Road." Was she stabbed to death by her daughter or stabbed to death and then found by her daughter? The listener can't go back and reread the sentence. Also, "mother" is unnecessary since the sentence mentions her "daughter."

Place titles before names. Spell out most numbers. Do not use initials for agencies and organizations unless they are well known, such as FBI and CIA. Use contractions for informality. Paraphrase quotations unless they are essential or unusual. Keep sentences to fewer than 20 words.

Tenses

The anchoring tense for broadcast copy is usually the present or the present perfect tense:

Present

```
    The state highway department announces a six million
dollar improvement program for farm-to-market roads.
```

Present Perfect

```
    The state highway department has announced a six
million dollar improvement program for farm-to-market
roads.
```

When the present tense is used in the lead, the story usually continues in that tense. When it is impossible to put the lead in the present tense because the event clearly is not new, then the present perfect tense is used. The story then shifts to the past tense to indicate when the event occurred:

Present Perfect

```
    A federal judge has issued a temporary order stopping
efforts to put a reservist on active army duty because he
refused to shave off his beard.
```

Shift to Past

```
    A federal judge yesterday gave the army ten days to
answer a suit filed by the American Civil Liberties Union.
```

Following the past tense, the story can shift back to the present perfect or even to the present tense if the writer believes the situation is still true or in effect. The AP radio story continues:

Past

```
    The ACLU filed the suit on behalf of a high school
teacher, John Jones of Bristol, Rhode Island.
```

Shift to Present

```
    The suit asks the court to declare unconstitutional a
regulation forbidding beards and claims the teacher was
marked absent from several drills that the suit says he
attended.
```

But shifts from the present directly to the past sound silly, as in this piece from the radio wire of one of the press associations:

Present

```
    The New Jersey Taxpayers Association says a recent
government report shows the state's per capita property
taxes are the highest in the nation.
```

> The association <u>reported yesterday</u> that only
> Massachusetts had a higher property tax average than New
> Jersey.

The writer would have been better off had he used the present perfect in the lead and then shifted to the past:

> The New Jersey Taxpayers Association <u>has reported</u> that
> a recent government. . . .

> The association <u>said</u> yesterday that only
> Massachusetts. . . .

Sometimes, the future tense works best. Go back to the first example in this section and try this:

> The state highway department <u>will spend</u> six million
> dollars on an improvement program for farm-to-market
> roads.

Some events are too complex to plunge into immediately. Or there may be a confusing array of personalities or numbers. The listener then has to be set up for the theme of the piece.

NEWSPAPER LEAD: As Gov. Alfred Caster neared the end of his seven-day working vacation aboard a riverboat today, his aides said that he was unconcerned about some editorial criticism that he had become an absentee governor whose administration was adrift.

BROADCAST LEAD: Some newspaper editorials have criticized Governor Caster as an absentee governor. They have contended that his administration has gone adrift. Today, his aides aboard a riverboat with the governor said that the criticisms don't bother Governor Caster. He is nearing the end of his seven-day working vacation on the boat.

The broadcast lead may read like an old enemy of the newswriter, the lead that backs into the story. But this is precisely what some broadcast stories require—a gradual buildup to the nub of the event, as though the story were being related to a friend.

When a major Soviet KGB officer who had defected to the West decided to redefect, newspaper accounts began this way:

WASHINGTON—Vitaly Yurchenko, a KGB officer described as one of the most senior Russian officials ever to defect to the West, announced today that he was returning to the Soviet Union.

This kind of lead would not do for television. Here is how Peter Jennings began his account of the event on ABC's "World News Tonight":

> There has not been anything like it in modern espionage. A Soviet KGB agent who we were told had defected to the US this summer, suddenly appeared before reporters at the Soviet embassy in Washington this evening and said he hadn't defected. He'd been kidnapped.
> Moreover, that he has now escaped. And Vitaly Yurchenko. . . .

Notice that the agent's name does not appear until the breathtaking news has been presented. The sentences come in pulses, and though they may not pass muster on paper, they do tell the story when read aloud.

Broadcast Reporting

Let's look at how reporters for broadcast stations work. First, we will go to a local all-news radio station.

Each evening, the news director makes up an assignment sheet for reporters for the next day. The editor goes through the futures file, notes of continuing stories and consults the wire services' schedule of stories. About 6 a.m. reporters begin to check with the editor for their assignments.

In the field, the reporters, who are equipped with tape recorders, may each cover three or four stories—a feature, a running news story from city hall, a talk by a congressman and a traffic accident that tied up a major artery. For each, the reporter calls the editor who decides whether the reporter should go on live or is to be recorded.

If live, the editor places the reporter on a newscast in progress. If recorded, the reporter talks to an aid who makes sure the material is being recorded properly by an engineer. The recording, called a cart, is labelled by slug and time and given to the editor.

Radio reporters cannot rely on pictures and therefore supply much of the descriptive material for their stories. Quotations from their interviews are essential to give the listener a sense of immediacy and participation. The radio reporter develops a keen ear for the high-quality quote, the quotation that sums up the situation. The rest is ruthlessly discarded.

The television reporter works within the same limited time boundaries but has a more complicated technology to cope with. Television reporters try to plan coverage because of the difficulty in moving equipment.

One of the most important tasks of the television journalist is to ask the right questions. Like the radio reporter, the television reporter has to move quickly to the heart of the news event. Long questions, questions that call for a yes or no answer, complicated questions—these are taboo. The good interview is made by the good answer.

Since tape can be edited, the reporter can ask a question again if the answer is too long or complicated.

Cover shots (see glossary) may be needed to cover the sound track. If the story is about nutritious breakfasts, a cover shot of people shopping for cereal might be appropriate. Words and pictures must always blend.

The feature or timeless piece may include an interview, voice-over silent tape, or tape with sound of an event and the reporter summarizing the event. The few minutes that the story runs may be the result of days of planning and hours of shooting, writing and editing.

For a story on a new reading program in the city schools, an interview with the superintendent of schools may set out the intent of the curriculum change. Additional interviews would allow viewers to hear the specific plans of teachers. School children would be interviewed. Locations might include classrooms, the teachers chatting about the program at lunch, the superintendent in his office.

Wide shots to establish the event and the usual array of medium, closeup and cutaway shots will be taken to build a coherent picture story to go along with the reporter's narration and interviews.

When the script is put together, and if there is time, script and tape may be shown to a producer, who may choose to change either picture or script yet again before the story is aired.

Stories for newspapers usually follow the inverted pyramid—most important material at the beginning, least important at the end. But for longer broadcast pieces, the form is a circle because the ending usually restates the beginning.

Interviews must be short and to the point and represent the essence of the source's thinking or emotions. The three or four minutes of tape may become not much more than a 15-second sound bite.

Reporting and Writing To Tape

The television writer's task is to marry natural sound, visuals, interviews and the reporter's words. Sometimes the writer muffs the opportunity. In a piece about a cloistered order of nuns who vow perpetual silence, the reporter wrote a narration with no pauses. He wrote about silence but never stopped talking. In effect, the viewer could not hear the silence. The event would have been captured had he stopped talking in some places, a few seconds at a time, to allow viewers to hear the clatter of knives and forks at a silent dinner, the footsteps of nuns in darkened hallways. The story should match the event.

Packaging Short News Features

Let's accompany a television news student, Cathy, as she puts together a news feature. The story is about a program designed to prevent children from committing crimes when they grow up. Cathy has an interview with the psychologist who developed the program. She also has filmed the children in the program as they talk to the psychologist and play. Cathy has interviews of the children's reactions to the program.

After a few hours on the scene, Cathy and her camera crew leave with about 40 minutes of tape. Cathy has to block out the story, which she starts doing on her way back to the station. Here are her plans:

> Cathy will tell her editor to start with pictures of the children in a circle for 20 seconds while in her script she will give some facts about the project.
>
> Then a 20- to 30-second sound bite from the psychologist explaining the "substitute family" technique. As he talks about the substitute parents, the editor will show pictures of the children and parents greeting each other affectionately.
>
> Then she will write a short transition into the interviews. She thinks that to get into this section she will pose the question, "But does the program work?" and have three or four short interviews with the answers.
>
> She'll close with a good quote from the psychologist for 20 seconds and then her own wrap-up from the scene to answer questions she feels have been left unanswered. By her calculations, the spot will run from 2:30 to 2:45, just what the producer wants.

Interviewing

Much of what Cathy did was the result of planning. For her interviews, she devised questions that sought to get to the heart of the story quickly. Interviews have to be kept short, to the point. This requires gentle but firm direction by the reporter. Here are some guidelines:

1. Don't ask questions that can be answered yes or no.
2. Don't ask long, involved questions—the subject might not understand what you want him or her to answer, and the goal is to let *him* or *her* explain, not to do all the explaining yourself.

3. Don't suggest answers to interviewees.

4. Build on the subject's answers—don't ask questions just because you prepared them. Listen to his or her answers and ask questions about what he or she says.

5. Develop a sense of timing. Cut in if the subject starts to be repetitive or long-winded. Don't cut the subject off just when he or she is about to say something important.

6. Make the subject comfortable before shooting the interview.

a. Describe the general area your questions will cover, but don't tell the subject exactly what they will be. The first, spontaneous response to a question is often the truest.

b. Explain the setting—which mike the subject should speak into and so on. But tell him or her to look at *you* or other questioners—not the camera—unless he or she is going to show the audience how to make a soufflé or do something else that requires more direct communication between speaker and audience.

c. Chat easily to dispel any nervousness prior to the interview. Show an interest in the subject's area so he or she will gain confidence.

d. Don't act like you know it all—or you will look foolish when the truth comes out. But *prepare,* so you *do* know enough so that your subject feels you understand what he or she says. Learn as much as you can about the interviewee and the topic beforehand.

e. Know what you are looking for. Most short news items must be carefully focused because of time limits.

7. Stay on one topic if possible.

8. Adjust the tone of the questions to the interviewee's experience. A politician may need to be pushed, asked tough and direct questions.

9. If the subject tends to be long-winded, tell him or her ahead of time that answers should be kept as short as possible.

No reporter can anticipate what a source will do, and no one can prepare fully to handle spontaneous events. When John A. Ferrugia was a reporter for KCMO-TV in Kansas City, Mo., he investigated the sale of flood-damaged cars by Allstate Insurance Co. He asked the firm for interviews with officials—without fully disclosing the nature of his story. Ferrugia told Allstate he wanted to find out how the company handled claims following the flood.

Ferrugia had found that open titles were passed on to used-car dealers and that this enabled the dealers to fill in company names and make it appear as though the cars had been sold directly to them. Thus, purchasers had no idea the automobiles were damaged. Many people over the country bought the cars at premium prices as they appeared to be in good shape.

"Well into the interview, we asked the company official to explain the company role in auto claims. He outlined it, and at that point we laid out material that contradicted everything he said," Ferrugia said.

"Cut the cameras," the official suddenly said, and stood up and left.

As a result of the KCMO series, six companies were forced to reclaim flood-damaged cars from across the country.

Copy Preparation

Copy is written to give the newscaster as much help as possible. The rules for copy preparation differ from station to station. Some require the slug in the upper left-hand corner and the time the story takes to run above it. The date is lower left.

Copy for television is written in the right half of the paper. The left-hand column is kept open for instructions. Some stations also ask that radio copy be written this way.

Depending on the size of the typewriter characters, a line of 45–50 units will take two and one-half to three seconds to read. By keeping lines to the same length, it is easy to estimate the time it will take to read the story without the use of a stopwatch.

End each page with a full sentence. Better still: End on a paragraph. Do not leave the newscaster hanging in the middle of a sentence or an idea as he or she turns the page. Keep paragraphs short.

Each page should be slugged. For pieces running more than one page, each page should be numbered, and the writer's name should appear on all pages.

Place the word *more,* circled, at the bottom of stories of more than one page, and use a clear, large end mark when finished.

Some stations require copy to be written in capital letters for easier reading, although studies have shown that all-capital text is more difficult to read than cap-and-lower-case. For television, visual directions should be written all caps.

Electronic News Delivery

In some cities, the all-news radio stations have a counterpart in all-news and information cable television channels. The news on these channels is displayed in written form on the screen, sometimes with still pictures. The stories are tightly written, many no more than 40 or 45 words and are known by a variety of titles: cable news, cable text, or teletext. Many of these news services are cooperatives, ventures between newspapers and cable television companies. Most accept advertising, and some offer color. Often, background music is played as the news is flashed on the screen.

Newspapers and cable companies decided to finance home-delivered news and information text because of their belief that people are as willing to accept information from a screen as from a newspaper. In 1967, three of four people surveyed said they read a newspaper every day. In the 1980s, one of those three had stopped daily newspaper reading; only two of four said they read the paper daily.

Newspapers have adjusted to changing times by supplying news, and sometimes personnel, for news on the screen. Large and small newspapers and newspaper chains have arranged with cable television companies to carry news text on the screen. Viewtron, owned by the Knight-Ridder newspaper chain, spent millions on its system. The *Mail-Sun* newspapers in Sheldon, Iowa, operates a limited community access television channel that it leases from a local cable company.

The Mail-Sun Cable News offers 26 pages of video text that includes a community bulletin board of coming events, school lunch menus, advertisements and news.

Some studies have shown only lukewarm public interest in video text, and in 1986 Viewtron announced it would terminate the system. People prefer entertainment—horoscopes, video games—in this form. The result has been a decline in the number of cable news operations.

Writing Cable News

The screen, or page, holds eight to a dozen lines, depending on the system. The Mail-Sun has a small screen. Each line has 32 characters, and most stories run for one page. A page remains in the screen, "dwells" there, for 14 to 17 seconds.

Most news is rewritten from the local newspaper that operates the cable news channel. All stories are written tightly. "Anything that takes more than three minutes to read, they'll ignore," said Mary Lou Forbes when she was the executive editor of The Source, a videotex firm owned by *The Reader's Digest*.

Selection or news judgment is essential in stripping stories down to their essentials. Short newspaper stories are boiled down to one to three sentences for cable news. Longer pieces may run two or three paragraphs.

Most copy that the Mail-Sun Cable News carries runs one sentence long:

```
    A special ASSIST meeting to inform rural and town
residents of the continuing farm financial conditions will
be held at 7:30 tonight in the Wansink Center of Handicap
Village.
```

Some cable news operations use headlines, and others capitalize the first two or three words of the text:

```
TAX INCREASES of $95 billion over the next 3 years are
called for in a compromise budget OK'd Wednesday night by
the Senate Budget Committee.
```

Notice that the number three is not spelled out and "OK'd" is used instead of approved. Such compression is essential. The original wire story ran almost 500 words; the cable news version ran 45 words. Cable news does not follow the stylebook rules, and it does not use attribution as often as newspapers.

Usually, the cable news writer will take the lead of the newspaper story, simplify it in the S-V-O construction and let it go at that.

Broadcasting Skills

The *Washington Journalism Review* asked broadcasters about the ingredients for high-quality television reporting. Here are some replies from the February 1985 issue:

Bob McFarland, Washington bureau chief, NBC News—"In this business, going live is what we get paid for. When all hell breaks loose, you have to have that ability to stand in front of a camera and communicate. . . . The best correspondents in the world are masters of the short, declarative sentence with few modifiers and clauses."

Don Hewitt, executive producer, "60 Minutes"—"It is a combination of being able to find out and being able to communicate what you found out."

Ed Turner, executive vice president, Cable News Network—". . . well-grounded in the English language, to have a sense of fairness and balance and to be absolutely tireless because it requires long, long hours. . . ."

Lane Venardos, executive producer, "CBS Evening News"—"The single most important thing is the kind of writing skill that is more than just writing to pictures; it is involving the visual material in the fabric of the story itself."

Tom Pettit, executive vice president, NBC News—". . . looks matter . . . basic journalistic skills that reporters in other media should have—the ability to find a story, get a story, write it very well and turn it in on time."

James Bellows, executive producer, ABC News—"Curiosity is the first important thing and then determination."

William Lord, executive producer, ABC "World News Tonight"—"The heart of excellence is the ability to write well."

Broadcast or print, the basic skills are the same—digging out the story and writing it clearly and interestingly.

Terse and Tight. On one of the evening news programs of ABC's "The World News Tonight" with Peter Jennings, there were 15 news items. Six were packages, the longer pieces, and nine were brief tell stories. Of the six packages, four ran two minutes, one three minutes and one six minutes. The tell items ran 25–30 seconds each. Average sentence length: 14 words.

Arlen, Michael J. *Living-Room War.* New York: Viking Press, 1969.

Epstein, Edward Jay. *News From Nowhere: Television and the News.* New York: Vintage, 1973. (The Arlen and Epstein books are critical examinations of television news coverage.)

Gates, Gary Paul. *Air Time.* New York: Harper & Row, 1978. (This book examines CBS News.)

Hewitt, Don. *Minute by Minute.* New York: Random House, 1985. (Hewitt is the executive producer of "60 Minutes.")

Sperber, Ann M. *Murrow: His Life and Times.* New York: Freundlich Books, 1986.

PART FOUR

Reporting Principles

Photo by Scott Caraway

CHAPTER TEN

Gathering the Facts

Preview

The reporter's job is to gather information that helps people to understand events that affect them. This digging takes the reporter through the three layers of reporting:

- Surface facts: press releases, handouts, speeches.
- Reportorial enterprise: verification, investigative reporting, coverage of spontaneous events, background.
- Interpretation and analysis: significance, causes, consequences of event.

The reporter always tries to observe events directly rather than to rely completely on sources, who often seek to manipulate the press. One of the common tactics of sources is the media event, an action staged to attract media attention. Reporters cover the event but explain the staging.

Verification, background checking, direct observation and enterprise reporting amplify and sometimes correct source-originated material. Reporters are allowed to interpret events when necessary.

T he reporter is like the prospector digging and drilling his way to pay dirt. Neither is happy with the surface material, though sometimes impenetrable barriers or lack of time interfere with the search, and it is necessary to stop digging and to make do with what has been turned up. When possible, the reporter keeps digging until he or she gets to the bottom of things, until the journalistic equivalent of the mother lode—the truth of the event—is unearthed.

The reporter, like the prospector, has a feel for the terrain. This sensitivity—the reporter's nose for news or street smarts—helps. In addition, the reporter has access to some tangible guides.

First, the reporter knows that his observations generally are more reliable than those of most sources, who have not been trained to see and hear accurately. Nor do some of these sources have the reporter's motivation—the revelation of truth.

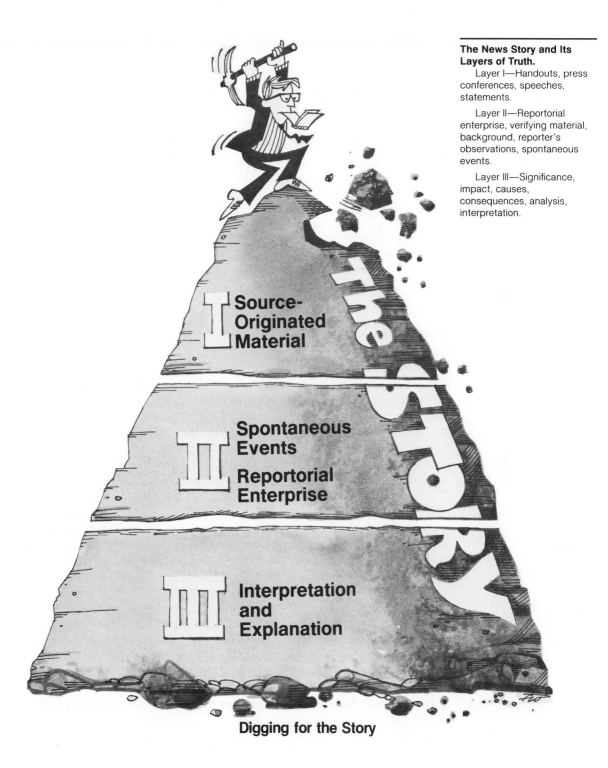

The News Story and Its Layers of Truth.

Layer I—Handouts, press conferences, speeches, statements.

Layer II—Reportorial enterprise, verifying material, background, reporter's observations, spontaneous events.

Layer III—Significance, impact, causes, consequences, analysis, interpretation.

I Source-Originated Material

II Spontaneous Events
Reportorial Enterprise

III Interpretation and Explanation

The STORY

Digging for the Story

When forced to rely on someone else's observations, the reporter uses various tests for determining the reliability of the source. When the reporter must use second-hand or third-hand accounts—or when he doubts his own observations—he knows where to look for verifying materials.

As the journalist goes about his work of digging up information, he is guided by an understanding of the nature of reporting:

> Reporting is the process of gathering facts—through observation, reasoning and verification—that when assembled in a news story give the reader, viewer or listener a good idea of what happened.

The reporter's job is to look beneath the surface for the underlying reality. Lincoln Steffens, the great journalist of the muckraking period, said the reporter's task is "the letting in of light and air." Many reporters base their work on the same conviction that guided Steffens. Their job is to seek out relevant truths for people who cannot witness or comprehend the events that affect them.

Layer I Reporting

Layer I reporting is the careful and accurate transcription of the record, the speech, the news conference. Its strengths and its limitations are those of objective journalism.

Layer I is the source for the facts used in most news stories. Information is mined from material that originates with and is controlled by the source. Fact gathering at this level of journalism may involve going to the mayor's office to pick up a transcript of the speech he is to deliver this evening or it may involve calling the mortuary holding the body of the child who drowned last night. The stories based on these facts rely almost wholly on information the source has supplied.

Fact gathering at Layer 1 is the journalistic equivalent of open pit mining. The reporter sinks no shafts into the event, but is content to use the surface material, some of which is presented to him by public relations specialists and press agents. Much of the reporter's task is confined to sorting out and rearranging the delivered facts, verifying addresses and dates and checking the spelling of names. Most stories appearing in newspapers and on radio and television are based on source-originated material.

Manipulation by Source

News organizations, as well as sources, thrived under the arrangement implicit in Layer I journalism. Material for news stories could be obtained quickly and inexpensively by the newspaper or broadcast station. In a sense, the success of Layer I became its undoing. As the mass media, particularly television, became the dominant dispensers of experience in American life, sources sought to manipulate the media for their purposes. They realized that press releases and announcements unaccompanied by visual material of events would not merit more than 20 seconds on most newscasts, if that. Only a newsworthy announcement could break into television's preoccupation with action. As a result, sources learned to stage events for the press that resembled spontaneous events (Layer II), but were, in fact, as much under the control of the source as the press release and the prepared speech. These staged events also are known as media events or pseudo-events.

The press shares responsibility for the development of the fabricated event. The press could use the stories and pictures of the first female window washer in San Francisco, even if the event had been dreamed up to publicize the availability of rental space in a new office building. By providing the media with an endless stream of events, the managers of staged events enable the 11 p.m. news to be different from the 7 p.m. news and the afternoon newspaper to take the morning news a step further. The flow of contrived events feeds the insatiable news maw, for the public has been conditioned to demand vivid, dramatic news with every newscast and edition. Television stations—creating and responding to the demand—devised news programs with titles such as "Eyewitness News" and "Action News."

Following a presidential State of the Union speech, Russell Baker of *The New York Times* asked one of the president's advisers "if it was not mostly a media event, a nonhappening staged because reporters would pretend it was a happening."

"It's *all* media event," the adviser replied. "If the media weren't so ready to be used, it would be a very small splash."

Daniel J. Boorstin, the social historian, originated the term *pseudo-event* to describe these synthetic occurrences. He says that a "larger and larger proportion of our experience, of what we read and see and hear, has come to consist of pseudo-events." In the process, he says, "Vivid image came to overshadow pale reality." His book (see *Further Reading* at end of chapter) opens with this short dialogue:

> ADMIRING FRIEND: "My, that's a beautiful baby you have there!"
>
> MOTHER: "Oh, that's nothing—you should see his photograph."

Boorstin says the pseudo-event has these characteristics: "It is not spontaneous, but comes about because someone has planned, planted or incited it. . . . It is planted primarily (but not always exclusively) for the immediate purpose of being reported or reproduced. Therefore, its occurrence is arranged for the convenience of the reporting or reproducing media. . . . Its relation to the underlying relativity of the situation is ambiguous. . . ."

Pseudo-Events

PR and the News. In their book, *PR: How the Public Relations Industry Writes the News* (New York: William Morrow and Company, 1985), Jeff and Marie Blyskal estimate that 40 to 50 percent of all news stories originate in public relations firms. They conclude that "whole sections of the news are virtually owned by PR." These firms plant stories in the press, which helps sell goods.

The authors quote the Coleco public relations executive who was behind the Cabbage Patch doll selling job: "When Bryant Gumbel or Jane Pauley . . . says, 'Here's the season's hottest item,' it means more to consumers than if Coleco says the same thing. The credibility that achieves far outweighs an advertisement."

Political Manipulation

The orchestration of events for public consumption is most evident in politics. Needing maximum public attention, politicians often resort to media manipulation. In 1972, at the Republican convention, the stage managing was just about total. Because President Nixon was certain of renomination, Republicans faced a publicity problem: How could reality—the routine renomination of the president—be made exciting? If there were no drama, how then would the White House press managers keep the public tied to the television screen and how would they be able to provide the raw material from which reporters could fashion their stories?

The GOP's solution was to override reality with a staged event of enormous dimension. The White House wrote a 50-page scenario for the convention, a full script that called for "impromptu remarks" from delegates, "spontaneous" shouts of "Four more years," and allotted—to the minute—screams of enthusiasm. At the moment the president would be renominated, the chairman was instructed to attempt "unsuccessfully" to quell the "spontaneous" cheering.

The document fell into the hands of the press. *The Wall Street Journal,* among others, ran news stories on how the White House had organized the convention for television viewers. As the *Journal's* reporter put it in his story, the "convention was perhaps the most superorganized ever . . . the delegates' only function during the formal proceedings was to serve as a necessary backdrop for the TV show."

The reporter, Norman C. Miller, went offstage and tried to dig up the real story—Layer II. He interviewed delegates, watched a pep rally for Republican women and found no one had showed up at the "Poor People's Caucus."

A dozen years later, the press fretted about President Reagan's use of television in his re-election campaign. Reagan exploited the fact that as president he commands the attention of reporters. The result was that he received considerably more coverage than his opponent, Walter Mondale. Chris Wallace, the White House correspondent for ABC News, said Reagan "very skillfully" wrapped "his campaign in what appears to be a new wave of good feeling about the country." The result was that "attacks against him are made to seem unpatriotic."

This is the criticism the Reagan administration levelled against the press, that its coverage of Reagan revealed a lack of patriotism. The press was unable to cope with Reagan's draping the flag about his campaign, his administration, his policies. Reporters knew they were being used, but as Dudley Clendinen of *The New York Times* said in a news analysis, "The assumptions about what is presidential, what is political and what is hype remain clouded."

Switch. Some events, like labor strikes and demonstrations, are carefully planned by their sponsors. Often, however, they slip away from the control of their planners and the reporter is covering a Layer II event.

Media managing has flourished at the state and local levels, too. An article by Richard Kotuk in the *Village Voice* describes how a state legislator used the media. Accompanied by a television crew and newspaper reporters the legislator's publicity man had alerted, the assemblyman drove to a farm on Long Island that was supposedly exploiting migrant workers. After unsuccessfully seeking comments from workers, the camera crew decided to film the assemblyman in action. Here is a concluding section of Kotuk's story of his day with the press and politician:

Then the CBS crew set up just outside the camp, but with the shanties, the kids, the wash on the line in the background. The interview—CBS: "Why are you here?" Stein: "This is a national disgrace! (Motioning to the rotting cabins behind) These people work hard. We're not asking for anything for them for free. They deserve a decent wage." CBS: "What do you hope to accomplish here?" Stein: "I want to get the Legislature to act on workmen's compensation for them, unemployment insurance. And I want a guarantee that the local authorities won't intimidate the United Farm Workers. We want to keep the pressure on. We want the people to know these horrible living conditions exist." The cameras clicked off. Stein mopped his brow.

Riding back to the city, Stein told me: "This situation has existed for the last several decades. No local authorities, including Duryea, have made any attempt to deal with it."

I wrote dutifully, then put away my pen. Stein turned to his aide. They talked politics. Bobby, Teddy, Lindsay, Herman B., and all the fiery questions of the game.

"I want to keep plugging on this," Stein told me. "I want to keep the pressure up for the migrants."

But later, Orin said softly to Stein: "This is just a one-shot deal isn't it? I don't want to keep driving out to the island."

"Yes," Stein said, "we can't spend any more time out there."

The city was close, traffic got heavy, Andrew Stein began to think of other things. . . .

Reporting the Manipulation

News reporters handling stage-managed events rarely do what Miller and Kotuk did, even when the staging is the most significant or interesting aspect of the event. There has been an unwritten agreement that such events are treated as legitimate news. And to some extent they are, even though the photos are posed, important statements are repeated for the television crews that missed them the first time around, and the entire event is set up to sell something. When reporters heard that Joe Namath, a quarterback for the New York Jets, would have an important announcement at a press conference the next day, they showed up. Namath had just turned down a lucrative offer to jump to another team in a rival league. Would he announce a new contract with the Jets? Fans across the country wanted to know about the plans of the most colorful quarterback in action. What they were told was that Namath was signing a multi-million dollar contract with a cosmetics firm.

Though they knew they had been taken, most reporters mentioned the name of the firm. One of the few who did not was a sports columnist for *The Press* in Asbury Park, N.J., who advised his readers that if they wanted the name of the firm they could call Namath's agent, and he printed the agent's telephone number.

When Pelé, the Brazilian soccer star, agreed to play for the New York Cosmos, the team arranged a press conference for Pelé's contract signing. The event obviously was legitimate news: Pelé, the best-known soccer player in the world, had led the Brazilian national team to three world championships and then retired. He was to be paid $4.7 million, making him the highest-paid team athlete in history at the time. H. L. Stevenson, editor-in-chief of the UPI, describes the scene for the *UPI Reporter:*

In a dark-paneled room adorned with 18-inch beer steins and stuffed antelope heads, more than 300 persons showed up, twice the capacity of the place. There were scores of interlopers. A large contingent of foreign reporters, nearly a dozen television stations or networks and one man from *Advertising Age.* Pelé promotes Pepsi-Cola in his spare time.

The bedlam that resulted went something like this:

11:00 a.m.—There is no sign of Pelé at the announced hour. "You knew about Pelé before you knew that a soccer ball was black and white," says Ron Swoboda, the former New York Met now doing television sports.

11:05 a.m.—Two large trays of hors d'oeuvres placed in the middle of the room. Few pay attention to the Pepsis in silver ice buckets around the room.

11:10 a.m.—Hors d'oeuvres gone. Pepsis remain. Bar still busy.

11:20 a.m.—"The armored car bringing him had a flat tire," a sports writer quips.

11:35 a.m.—Clive Toye, general manager of the Cosmos, enters waving contracts in red folder.

11:37 a.m.—"Down, down, down, down," TV cameramen shout at the still photographers.

11:40 a.m.—"Ladies and gentlemen," booms Toye, "now the legend, the great one, the king." Pelé, in a black brocade suit, enters flashing a "V" sign. He smiles—sometimes shyly, sometimes broadly—all the time.

11:41 a.m.—Pelé starts signing the contracts amid continuing shouts from the mob of photographers. "Let's not get anyone killed," pleads a Cosmos official. "Please, gentlemen, be calm."

11:45 a.m.—Punches are thrown between American and South American television cameramen in the crush in front of the ceremonial table. Cameras turn from Pelé to record the fight, a draw.

11:50 a.m.—Still photographers are ordered to the rear of the room. They refuse. "O.K., gentlemen, unless you move back we'll have to leave this platform," threatens Cosmos official. The photographers grin, and agree to sit or kneel on the floor.

11:55 a.m.—Pelé signs more papers for the TV cameras. His attractive wife kisses him on right cheek. More shouts of "down, down, down" from the cameramen.

12:03 p.m.—"It is like a dream to be here," Pelé says in Portuguese, his first words. "You can spread the news all over the world that soccer has arrived in America." Someone in the rear drops a glass.

12:07 p.m.—"I had a dream that one day the United States will be known for soccer," he says in response to a question about his coming out of retirement. Pelé says he feels he can help and that Brazil would be proud of its contribution to the game. He is sincere. Is there another athlete who can say the same thing with a straight face?

12:12 p.m.—There had been speculation he would get up to $9 million for three seasons, with the Cosmos. True? "The money is no problem," Pelé says. "You made the confusion in the press."

12:13 p.m.—"Well, you solve the confusion for us," a reporter yells. Pelé ducks the question, saying his contract is a "package" that includes promotional fees and exhibition games. "I don't want to discuss money at this time," he adds. Another glass shatters somewhere in the packed room.

12:15 p.m.—Pelé, asked to say a few words in English, responds: "Listen, I don't speak well in English. But after three months, you come and I make an interview with you."

12:30 p.m.—Pelé leaves clutching a soccer ball and still smiling. Radio Free Europe man says his tape recorder has vanished.

Now, read the story the UPI sent out on its wires:

NEW YORK (UPI)--Pelé, the greatest ambassador the game of soccer has ever known, came out of retirement Tuesday to join the New York Cosmos, insisting he's not doing it so much for the $4.7 million he'll be paid, but because he had a dream he could help popularize the sport in the United States.

Edson Arantes do Nascimento, known the world over as Pelé, was more than a half hour late signing his Cosmos contract at a news conference which sometimes had overtones of pure bedlam.

When he finally was able to speak, Pelé said:
``Everybody in life has something to do, a mission, a
goal. The only country in the world where soccer is
unknown is the United States. I had a dream that some
day soccer would become known in the U.S., and that's
why I came out of retirement.''

Pelé spoke primarily in Portuguese through an
interpreter, Julio Mazzei, during a wild session at
the famed ``21 Club'' in midtown. At one point the
conference was temporarily halted while cameramen
from rival television networks got into a fist
fight as they jockeyed for a better shooting
position. . . .

Although the story did capture some of the atmosphere, the in-house
account of the staging as well as the signing is more interesting because it
describes the signing and it also reveals something of the social phenomenon
known as a news conference.

Dangers of Layer I

When reporting is confined to Layer I, the distinction between journalism and public relations is hard to discern. The consequences for society
can be serious. Joseph Bensman and Robert Lilienfield, sociologists, explain
what the consequences can be:

When "public relations" is conducted simultaneously for a vast
number of institutions and organizations, the public life of a society
becomes so congested with manufactured appearances that it is difficult
to recognize any underlying realities.
As a result, individuals begin to distrust all public facades and retreat
into apathy, cynicism, disaffiliation, distrust of media and publication
institutions. . . . the journalist unwittingly often exposes the workings of
the public relations man or information specialist, if he operates within a
genuine journalistic attitude.

Tom Wicker of *The New York Times* says the press has been weak—
because of its concentration on Layer I—at picking up new developments before they have become institutionalized, acquired spokesmen, and their sponsors have learned to stage media events to attract attention.

Correctives

The journalistic attitude the sociologists discuss requires that the reporter make his own observations whenever possible and verify the information supplied him when observation is not possible. Properly reported, an event
then would reveal behind-the-scenes stagecraft. Far from being an unwitting
exposé of the public relations person's work that the sociologists describe, the
story would be like Miller's or Kotuk's, an intentional description of the orchestration.

Some staged events do produce news—Pelé's signing, the civil rights demonstrations across the South in the 1960s, picketing by the local teachers union. And certainly the dozens of news stories that are based on source-originated material—such as the text of the mayor's speech, and the details the mortuary supplies about the child's death—are legitimate news. But the reporter must always ask about Layer I information whether it reflects the truth of the event and whether reportorial enterprise is needed to supply the missing facts and relevant background.

Sometimes restraint is necessary because of the motives of the orchestrators. This was the conclusion of some journalists following the hijacking in 1985 of a TWA airliner in Lebanon. Shiite terrorists killed one American and took the crew and 39 passengers prisoner in Beirut. The terrorists held press conferences at which some of the passengers dutifully, or fearfully, mouthed Shiite propaganda. Television used it all, feeding what many experts on terrorism describe as "the theater of terrorism." The intent of these people, say the experts, is to thrust their extremist propaganda on the world, as *The New Republic* put it. The magazine commented:

> Access to the media is one of the benefits of terrorism. . . . And just as surely as the cost of terrorism must be raised, the benefits must be reduced. The media can do this on their own, without any peril to the First Amendment. Legitimate limits should be set on the kind of coverage given to terrorists . . . media restraint would take away an incentive for terrorism.

The transition from Layer I to Layer II can be seen at a press conference. The reading of a statement provides the source-originated material (I). The give-and-take of the question and answer period is spontaneous (II). When the source declines to answer questions, the reporter should understand that he or she is back in Layer I, dealing with material controlled by the source.

Layer II Reporting

When the event moves beyond the control of its managers—press relations experts, publicity men and women, sources—the reporter is taken into Layer II. Reporters should not wait to dig into the information supplied by the source. The reporter must show some enterprise rather than act as a passive receptacle for facts. Even simple events should be examined critically. The unchecked story at any level may carry errors.

Going from I to II

The reporter who seeks verification from a second source that the governor will appear at the Lions Club ceremony is moving into Layer II. So was the reporter who, after she was told by the police that the hotel was robbed at 5:46 a.m., checked the newspaper to determine the time of sunrise that day. The check enabled her to write: "The holdup man left the hotel in the early-morning darkness."

When they have time, reporters verify source-originated material. The investigative reporter, whose work is based almost wholly on material gathered through enterprise, digging and checking, operates within Layer II. The investigative reporter exposes what other reporters accept as reasonable and logical explanations and assertions. The reporter who writes that the state purchasing agent has awarded a contract for a fleet of automobiles to a local dealer is engaged in Layer I journalism. The investigative reporter who digs into the records to learn that the contract was awarded without bids is working at the second level.

When an official of a city struck by recession recommends a city-financed plan that he says will increase employment, the reporter will ask him for precise details. Who helped draft the plan? Why should the city act? What will be the reaction of private business? Those questions belong mostly in Layer I reporting. Then the reporter will check the data the official has supplied. He will also look into the program the official said has been working in another city in the South. This checking is the kind of work that moves the reporter into Layer II.

Finally, the reporter will seek comments from other city officials about the feasibility of the proposal and its prospects for adoption. Untold numbers of stories have been written about proposals that went nowhere because they were badly drafted or were introduced or recommended by people with no influence. Local newspapers usually play up a legislator's proposals or his intentions, but give no attention to the fact that he is a freshman with no influence, a member of the minority party, or that the committee chairman has vowed never to let such legislation move through his committee.

Reality. A. J. Liebling, a master reporter, would say, "You have to climb the stairs," meaning that reporters worthy of their vocation should seek out the news. Dusko Doder, *The Washington Post*'s Moscow correspondent, says that Soviet officials realize the real news lies in the daily lives of ordinary people. Doder, considered one of the best foreign correspondents working, said the Kremlin keeps reporters cooped up in one building, only partially so the government can keep an eye on them. The other reason "is to keep us from seeing how sad life is here. They're terribly concerned about what America thinks. They don't want us to get robbed or to see people standing in line. But out *there* is the real story—what the trends are, what the mood is, whether life is getting better or worse."

With the Guerrillas in Afghanistan

Following the Russian invasion of Afghanistan, reporters tried to pierce the news blackout of the war by trekking over mountain paths into the beleaguered country. In 1985, Frederick Kempe of *The Wall Street Journal* spent six days walking to join a guerrilla group. He wanted to know more about the Afghans, he said, "about what they wanted, how the guerrillas operated, whether the resistance could survive." He accompanied Afghan guerrillas on an attack mission. (Layer II)

Kempe admired the courage and determination of the Afghans, but his on-the-scene observations led him to conclude that the guerrillas faced near overwhelming problems in their fight for freedom.

Street Kids. Reporter Gail Roberts of *The Sun-Bulletin* in Binghamton, N.Y., had heard stories about young people making their homes on streets, in basements and in parks. Rather than rely on city officials to describe the situation, she sought out the street people themselves. They told her they managed to survive by selling sex, fencing stolen items and asking for handouts. Photo by Frank Woodruff, *The Sun-Bulletin*.

If we look back at the reporters at work in Chapter 1 we can see how often journalists move from Layer I to II:

• The reporter who went on the campus to see the demonstrations for himself rather than accept handouts.

• Carol Falk, a general assignment reporter in *The Wall Street Journal*'s Washington bureau, did not accept the president's version of the tapes but read the transcripts before reaching any conclusions.

• Much of the work Dick did on his story about the Black Parents Association after receiving the handout from the group was on his initiative. The group did not name the authors of the books it sought to remove from the schools. Dick inserted the names. He also gave the plots of the novels, and he interviewed the students for their reactions. Most important, he supplied background.

• Cammy Wilson's investigative stories in the *Minneapolis Tribune* were carried out entirely in Layer II.

The reporters we saw at work moved beyond merely relaying information originated and controlled by a source. Each checked the information, supplied missing facts, explained complicated details. None of these efforts is the activity of a reporter content to gather facts at Layer I. This is only the beginning.

Investigative Reporting

The reporter who digs soon finds his or her appetite whetted for the kind of information that such digging produces. Reporters who hear about strange doings in the athletic department of the local university do some checking. In time, a major scandal is unearthed. Such checking and digging led to a Pulitzer Prize in local reporting for Clark Hallas and Robert B. Lowe of *The Arizona Daily Star* for their investigation of the University of Arizona athletic department.

When Judy Johnson of *The Anniston Star* heard some people in an Alabama community were having trouble getting credit from banks and finance companies she decided to investigate. She spent months examining records of mortgages and land transfers. "I compiled them into lists year by year, looking for patterns, building a history," she said.

She talked to people affected by these practices. Through the years of borrowing from a local businessman, one woman had accumulated $50,000 in loans. Among her loans was $3,400 for a four-year-old car she and her husband had bought from his used car lot. When new, the model she bought would have cost a little more.

Johnson showed how the poor, who cannot obtain credit from large lending institutions, are victimized by private lenders. Her series won national recognition.

Abortions and Dust Cloths

"Are you going to perform an abortion?" Ellen Whitford asked the doctor who was standing over her after completing a pelvic examination. Whitford, a reporter for *The Virginian-Pilot* in Norfolk, had gone to the clinic to investigate statements women had given her of unusual activities there. Whitford was not pregnant, but the doctor indicated he was going to do an abortion.

Whitford had the proof she needed—that the clinic was performing unnecessary abortions—and her series of stories about the clinic led to the George Polk award for local reporting. Other Polk awards have gone to a television team from KPRC-TV in Houston for exposing home improvement contractors who were performing slipshod work and charging inflated prices. When the homeowners, many of them poor people, could not meet the payments their homes were seized. Reporters Rick Nelson and Joe Collum's work led to an official investigation of the con artists and a halt to the foreclosures.

James Dwyer of *The Dispatch* in Hudson County, N.J., found something strange on his check of the bids made to sell materials to a vocational school. Some seemed to be typed on the same typewriter. Also, he noticed that the

Work. David Halberstam, a Pulitzer Prize-winning reporter and author, says that reporting means "doing homework, reading, or going through the clips or going to the library, doing four interviews instead of two, eight interviews instead of four, in preparation."

prices for ladders, dust cloths, shovels and other items were high. Even when purchased in quantity they were higher than those in hardware stores. For example, the school paid $564 for ladders that local stores sold for $189.

Dwyer tried to locate the firms that made the bids. He could not find them. He visited the school and found enough dust cloths to keep the school's furniture glowing for a couple of centuries. He theorized that the agent through whom the goods were sold had invented bidders, and using these fake firms to enter high bids, his firm was awarded the contracts. A minute check of files revealed his theory to be true, and a grand jury took over.

Handling the Handout

"Don't be a handout reporter," Harry Romanoff, a night city editor on the *Chicago American* would tell young reporters. One of Romanoff's charges was Mervin Block, who recalls an encounter with Romanoff:

"I remember his giving me a fistful of press releases trumpeting movie monarch Louis B. Mayer's expected arrival at the Dearborn Street Railroad Station. An hour later, Romy asked me what time Mayer's train would be pulling in. I told him, and when he challenged my answer, I cited the handouts: one from the Santa Fe, one from Mayer's studio (MGM), and one from his destination, the Ambassador East Hotel. All agreed on the time. But that wasn't good enough for Romy.

" 'Call the stationmaster and *find out*.' "

Reporters ignore Romanoff's warning about being a handout reporter at their peril. Go back to Chapter 2 where we saw that *The Washington Post* and *The New York Times* named different delicatessens as the source of the sandwiches that the mayor of New York sent west. The cause of the confusion: A handout.

The handout named the Carnegie Deli as the supplier. But a *Times* reporter checked before rewriting the release. She found the supplier was the Second Avenue Deli. The *Post* did not check.

When food chains in Chicago announced price cuts on thousands of items, the Chicago newspapers bannered the stories on their front pages. One such headline:

Inflation Breakthrough—Food Prices to Drop Here

—Chicago Sun-Times

Despite the rash of stories about how the shopper "may save 15% in price battle," as one paper said in a headline over one of its stories, consumers were actually paying more on a unit, or per-ounce, basis.

The Chicago commissioner of consumer affairs demonstrated that the city's consumers were being misled by the store announcements and consequently by the newspaper stories that took the handouts at face value. Many of the items that were reduced in price were also reduced in weight. Peanut clusters went from 72 cents a packet to 69 cents, an apparent saving of 3 cents. But the packet went from 6 ounces to 5¼ ounces. With a little arithmetic, a reporter could have figured out that this was actually an increase of six cents a packet. Some items were publicized because they stayed at the same price "despite inflation," according to the handouts and the stories. True enough. A 30-cent can of beef stew was still 30 cents. But the new can contained half an ounce less than the old can.

When 53 school children and their teachers were felled by creosote fumes in a Paterson, N.J., school, the school officials said the fumes were non-toxic. Other newspapers accepted the school officials' version and described the fumes as "noxious chemical vapors" and "nontoxic fumes." Rita Jensen of the *News* had a feeling the school authorities would try to minimize the situation, and so she checked with independent sources, the hospital and fire department. Jensen's check determined that the fumes were toxic.

    Bob Greene, a prize-winning investigative reporter at *Newsday,* has a reputation for asking the necessary, if impolite, questions. He advises reporters to demand the file instead of having it read to them, and to check comments and statements for factual content before printing them.

Asking Questions

When a reporter moves from the first to the second level of reporting, he often discovers that his reporting has uncovered facts that contradict what he had been told by a source. We saw in Chapter 2 how E. W. Kenworthy of *The New York Times* used information from his files to clarify and correct assertions made by a presidential candidate. Here is another example of Kenworthy's work, a paragraph from a story about Sen. Edward Kennedy:

Correcting the Source

> Edward Kennedy thereupon launched into a speech on medical care for the aged, declaring that while the Republicans in the Senate had opposed it, "every Democratic Senator voted for it," a statement not borne out by the Congressional Record.

Kenworthy did not wait for or seek another source to deny Kennedy's assertion. He corrected it on his own, in the same story in which the misstatement was made.

    A city planner from San Francisco commented in an interview in a journal that a portion of Sixth Avenue in New York City should have been dug up and an underground traffic-way constructed to make way for a plaza. The reporter who rewrote the interview for *The New York Times* interjected an observation of his own, that during the interview the planner "was not asked to explain how Sixth Avenue could go underground without driving the Sixth Avenue Subway further underground." Sweeping statements should have some grounding in reality. If they do not, the reporter is obligated to shoot them down.

The Alternative Press

Some of the impetus in the movement away from total reliance on sources to trust in the reporter came from the small newspapers and magazines that proliferated during the 1960s. Known as the alternative press, these publications offered news that seemed to come closer to the truth than did many of the stories published by the commercial press. The reporters for these publications understood what Murray Kempton, a veteran political reporter and writer, meant when he said: "One of the big mistakes people who write for newspapers make is to assume the participants, speaking to them as reporters, are telling them the truth."

The commercial press was quick to use these techniques. Gradually, the press associations changed, too. Newspapers that had to rely for national and international news on the press associations were complaining that competing newspapers and broadcast stations with special correspondents and access to such syndicated news services as The *Los Angeles Times/Washington Post* and *The New York Times* News Services were doing a better job of reporting the news than were the wire services. A shift had to be made away from total reliance on Layer I reporting.

Politics and Public Affairs

The coverage of politics and public affairs often tests a reporter's ability to move into Layer II, for candidates and officials seek to set the agenda for public discussion. That is, they prefer to select the issues and to discuss these on their terms. They prefer to avoid embarrassing or politically dangerous subjects. When that cannot be done, they deflect or blunt the tough questions.

In politics and the area of public policy, the news media have replaced the traditional political institutions. The Social Science Research Council reports, "Elections are now waged through the mass media, which have supplanted the political parties as the major intermediary between the office seekers and the electorate."

Officials turn to the media to mold public opinion in order to win support for their policies. If the press permits itself to be used as a megaphone, the office seeker and the official are able to manipulate public opinion.

The Watergate tapes, documents and hearings and trials turned up a vast amount of press-related information that shows how the Nixon administration sought to exploit the press's penchant for color, drama and personalities, and its willingness to settle for appearance rather than significance. An incident involving the appointment of a party spokesman during the 1972 campaign underlines the necessity of Layer II journalism, the need to dig into the event to determine its full meaning rather than to settle for what social historian Boorstin describes as the "vivid image."

To win "those outside middle America," particularly the youth vote, the deputy director of the president's re-election campaign, Jeb Magruder, proposed that a young Nixon assistant, Martin Anderson, be used as a party spokesman. A memo that Magruder sent to H. R. Haldeman, the White House chief of staff, makes it clear that Magruder understood the appeal Anderson would have to journalists, as well as to young voters.

"Who better than Marty Anderson can 'turn on' young people about draft reform?" Magruder wrote. "Young Metroamerica won't listen to Mel Laird, but they will to Marty Anderson, not because Marty's any more liberal (he probably is less liberal than Laird) but because he's got more *hair,* a Ph.D., a sexy wife, drives a Thunderbird, and lives in a high-rise apartment."

In the margin of the memo, Haldeman noted: "*Absolutely.* Really work on this."

This is, in its most unsophisticated form, the kind of political image-making Boorstin describes as "reducing great national issues to trivial dimensions."

The press has matured sufficiently to catch obvious attempts to exploit its weaknesses.

The general failures of political reporters and the inadequate coverage of the 1968 and 1972 presidential campaigns were cited by Wes Gallagher, AP president and general manager, in a letter he sent to all AP staffers in preparation for the 1976 campaign.

"We should not accept without challenge any political promise which is not detailed as to how it will be carried out. If the candidate cannot or refuses to answer questions, we should clearly state so in the story—a warning flag to the reader that the whole promise may just be hot air." In short, Gallagher was telling AP reporters that unless they report at Layer II they fail to inform their readers.

Reagan and the Press

"By and large," said Gary Schuster, White House correspondent for *The Detroit News,* "everything you get out of the White House day after day is staged." Ann Devroy, the White House correspondent for Gannett News Service, said that the "president has a tendency to say things that get him into trouble, so the more they keep him away from the press, the less opportunity for him to get into trouble."

Lou Cannon, *The Washington Post*'s White House correspondent, described Reagan as being "cocooned" by his managers. These aides, said ABC White House correspondent Sam Donaldson, have a "basic contempt" for the press. John W. Kole, who covers Reagan for *The Milwaukee Journal,* said Reagan's managers may have accomplished "the most successful news management job in American history." And in 1986, the Society of Professional Journalists, Sigma Delta Chi, report card on presidential freedom of the press gave Reagan an F on government and White House openness in eight of 10 categories.

What to do? Most reporters have made the manipulation and secrecy a story, describing the president's use of the media to reach the public directly, without the interference of reporters with questions. Some reporters made journalism out of the press conferences held next to helicopters. The intention was obvious: No one could hear Reagan's replies. "We're all in the position of trying to be lip readers," said Devroy.

Caution: Journalists cannot expect public support for their anger at being denied access to public figures. "The press in America is operating in an environment of public opinion that is increasingly indifferent—and to some extent hostile—to the cause of a free press in America," George Gallup, the pollster, concluded after measuring public attitudes toward the press. He found that 37 percent of his respondents said curbs on the press were "not strict enough," whereas 32 percent said they were "about right," and only 17 percent said they were "too strict." The others had no opinion. Harris surveys have found a majority say that the press has no right to be present at all trials, search warrants of newsrooms are justified and that journalists should not be warned before a search.

A reason for this anti-press sentiment may be found in another set of questions Gallup asked. The poll found that only 24 percent of those asked knew "what the First Amendment to the U.S. Constitution is or what it deals with." Less than half, 42 percent, of the college educated answered correctly.

Barriers and Breakthroughs

The reporter is flooded with Layer I-type information. He cannot discard all of it, for he knows that the official must have access to the public. That is, statements, handouts and press releases must be reported faithfully so that the public is informed of the actions of its officials. Once this Layer I reporting is completed, there may be little time for enterprise.

Another impediment facing the reporter who wants to dig beneath the surface is the reluctance of some officials to cooperate. After the reporter has allowed a source access to the public, the public has a right to access to the official. But what does the reporter do when a source prefers to keep the reporting at Layer I?

Reporters have a few techniques to make sources responsive to the public's need to know. When a source will not come to grips with legitimate questions about public events and issues, the reporter can follow Gallagher's advice to AP reporters—state that the source "refused to answer" a particular question or that he "did not explain his answers." Other sources can be asked to comment on the issue and on the source's silence. When there is demonstrable falsification, the reporter is free to indicate this. Another device is the use of background material to supply needed information.

People are not content with knowing only what happened. They also want to know how and why it happened, what it means and what may occur as a result—causes and consequences. Sometimes, this explanatory information is not immediately available to the journalist, and the only fact gathering that can be done is at Layers I and II. But when the story is important and the material can be dug up, reporters should mine Layer III, the area of interpretation and analysis.

Layer III reporting tells people how things work and why they work that way, or why they don't work. Such reporting moves beyond telling us what people did yesterday and what they say they will do tomorrow (Layer I). It is the journalist's way of helping people understand complex events. Layer III reporting is analytical. It may move beyond the recital of fact into the subjective area of judgment and inference. Obviously, this kind of journalism requires reporters who have command of subject matter along with their mastery of the craft skills.

When James Toland of the *San Francisco Chronicle* heard some editors talking about the problems in Northern Ireland he was disturbed to hear them reduce that country's bloody strife to a conflict over religion. He thought that if reasonably intelligent people had such scant knowledge of the situation, the public must be even less well informed. That set him off on several weeks of research and resulted in an article that was given a full page display.

Toland blended history, current events and interpretation. He wrote, "The divisions in Ireland are more complex than can be explained by issues of religion or a map-line splitting six northern counties from 26 southern counties. Many factions exist: native Irish, Ulster Scots, British soldiers, Unionist and Nationalist political parties, and Catholic, Presbyterian and Episcopal churches."

A tangled web of population imbalance, discrimination, conflicting value systems and inherited conflict mark the struggle that over the past 14 years has left 2,400 dead and 19,000 injured, he wrote.

The AP story from Chicago began:

William Rodriguez trudged home through rain and snow and wee-hour darkness.

He was only 23, in good health and known as a happy-go-lucky fellow.

Yet he would be dead before sunrise. . . .

Rodriguez had purchased rat poison on his way home from work, and as he walked he ate the poison. How? Why? the AP asked and assigned two reporters to find out. Their digging turned up the answer—easy credit. Rodriguez owed about $700 to merchants for furniture, clothing, a television set.

He couldn't meet the payments and the creditors were threatening to tell his employer.

The story galvanized the city's enforcement agencies. Rodriguez had been sold low-grade merchandise and had been given credit at usurious rates. The legislature reacted by lowering interest rates. The law is known as the "Rodriguez Law."

In wire stories reporting Argentina's invasion of the British-controlled Falkland Islands, reporters gave the necessary added dimension to the spot news report with sentences like this one from an AP story:

> The invasion came at a time of increasing domestic trouble for the Argentine government, and the issue of the islands' sovereignty has always been a patriotic rallying point for the country.

The AP story said that Argentines celebrated the invasion whereas "only last weekend Argentines had demonstrated against the junta's economic policies."

When the New Jersey state legislature passed a bill banning state Medicaid payments for abortions, it ignored nine federal district court decisions in eight states that ruled similar bills were unconstitutional. The reason for the legislators' action was described in this Layer III sentence from *The New York Times:* "Approval of the measure reflects the influence of the Catholic Church, which opposes abortion, in New Jersey: About 55 percent of the state's registered voters are Catholic."

The battle over the need for interpretative reporting has long been over, although some newspaper and broadcast station editors are adamant about its dangers and rarely permit it. Dangers there are, but the risks are only slightly greater than those inherent in other areas of journalism. The benefits to the reader outweigh these risks.

Interpretation Essential

Compare these two short pieces that were published when the Middle East erupted in war in 1973. The first is Layer I journalism; the second paragraph of the second is Layer III journalism:

KARACHI, Pakistan, Oct. 7—Prime Minister Zulfikar Ali Bhutto, today condemned "Israeli aggression" and reaffirmed Pakistan's support for the Arab countries in messages to the presidents of Egypt and Syria.

According to an official spokesman in Islamabad, Mr. Bhutto also sent a message to Secretary General Waldheim of the United Nations, expressing Pakistan's concern over the outbreak of hostilities.

NEW DELHI, Oct. 7—An Indian Government spokesman declared today that Israel's "intransigence" caused the outbreak of hostilities. India's sympathies are "entirely with the Arabs whose sufferings have long reached a point of explosion," he added.

Behind India's traditional pro-Arab position in any outbreak of fighting in the Middle East is believed to be her awareness of the importance of Arab votes in

He reminded Mr. Waldheim of the Security Council's responsibility for peace in the area.

Mr. Bhutto discussed the Middle East situation with Arab ambassadors in Islamabad. Later he held separate meetings with the Iranian and Turkish ambassadors.

the United Nations on the question of Kashmir. For more than 25 years Kashmir has been the subject of a territorial dispute between India and Pakistan, a Moslem country.

The New Delhi story adds a dimension that the reader needs to understand India's motivation. This addition explains the "why" of the event. When explanation and interpretation are lacking, the reader is left with questions.

One device reporters use to add interpretation to their news pieces is simple enough. They ask a source to size up the situation. Sometimes the how and why of the event may be so elusive that no single explanation is sufficient. Then the reporter must talk to several sources to find a range of explanations and cross-explanations, analyses and cross-analyses. This kind of reporting will give the reader or listener alternatives on which to base his or her conclusions.

In Warrentown, W. Va., 63 indigent mothers were sterilized with their permission. Reporters were sent to the city to do follow-up stories. Here are the headlines over two of these folos in New York City newspapers:

Necessary Risks

Town in Uproar Over Sterilization

Virginians Calm On Sterilization

Troublesome as interpretative reporting can be, reporters have little choice but to try to explain the events they cover. Walter Lippmann, one of the few original thinkers about American journalism, observed that during the 1930s with the advent of the New Deal "events started happening which were almost meaningless in themselves. It was the beginning of the era when Why became as important as What, when a Washington correspondent left his job half done if he only told what happened and failed to give the reasons and hint at the significance." Journalism has no rule that what Washington reporters can do is prohibited to local reporters.

While editor of *The Christian Science Monitor,* Erwin Canham weighed the pros and cons of interpretative journalism: "News interpretation, with all its hazards, often is safer and wiser than printing the bare news alone. Nothing can be more misleading than the unrelated fact, just because it is a fact and hence impressive. Background, motives, surrounding circumstances, related events and issues all need to be understood and appraised as well as the immediate event. . . .

"Interpretation requires integrity and knowledge and understanding and balance and detachment."

Putting I, II and III to Work

Let us watch a reporter mine these three layers for his story.

City Planner Arthur calls the local stations and newspaper to read to reporters a statement about a new zoning proposal. The release contains facts 1, 2 and 3. At the newspaper, reporter Bernard looks over the handout, tells his city editor that 1 and 2 are of no news value but that 3—elimination of two-acre zoning north of town—is important and worth exploring in an interview with Arthur. The editor agrees and assigns Bernard to the story.

Before leaving for the interview, Bernard checks the newspaper library for a story about a court decision he recalls that may be related to the proposed regulation. He telephones another city official and a real estate developer to obtain additional information. With this background and Arthur's statement, Bernard begins to develop ideas for questions. He jots down a few, 4, 5 and 6.

During the interview, City Planner Arthur repeats 1, 2 and 3. Reporter Bernard asks for more information about 3, the elimination of the minimum two-acre requirement for home building. Bernard also brings up his own subjects by asking questions 4, 5 and 6. New themes develop during the interview, 7, 8 and 9.

Back in the newsroom, Bernard looks over his notes. He sees that his hunch about 3 was correct—it was important. Arthur's answer to question 5 is newsworthy, he decides, and fact 7—the possibility of low- and medium-cost housing in the area—that developed during the interview, may be the lead, especially since the broadcast stations will probably not have it. Bernard needs comments on the impact of 7 from developers. A couple of calls and the possible consequences—10—emerge. The developers confirm their interest in building inexpensive housing. Looking over his notes, he spots background from the morgue—11—that is now relevant and also will go into the story.

Some Practical Advice About Reporting

- There is a story behind almost any event. Remember it was a third-rate break-in in a Washington building that began the Watergate revelations and ended in the resignation of a president.
- Always check all names in the telephone book, the city directory and the morgue to make absolutely sure they are spelled correctly.
- Follow the buck. Find out where money comes from, where it is going, how it gets there and who's handling it. Whether it is taxes, campaign contributions, or donations, keep your eye on the dollar.
- Be counter-phobic. Do what you don't want to do or are afraid to do. Otherwise you'll never be able to dig into a story.
- Question all assumptions. The people who believed the emperor was clothed are legion and forgotten. We remember the child who pointed out his nudity.
- Question authority. Titles and degrees do not bestow infallibility.

The story will contain facts 3, 5, 7, 10 and 11. Bernard decides he will fashion 7 and 10 into a lead, and he worries about how to blend 11 into the story at a fairly early stage without impeding the flow of Arthur's explanation. Background is important, but sometimes it is difficult to work smoothly into the story. He writes this lead:

```
A proposed change to eliminate the two-acre zoning
requirement for home building north of town could open the
area to people who can afford only low- and medium-cost
housing.
```

Well, Bernard thinks, at least it's a start.

Referring back to the layers of the news story, we can see that Bernard's story will consist of the following:

Facts	Layer
3	I
5, 7, 11	II
10	III

Bernard has used almost all the techniques reporters have at their command to gather facts for stories. He was given information by a source. Then he used the newspaper library—a physical source—for background. He then interviewed his original source—a human source—and made independent checks by calling up additional sources.

Further Reading

Boorstin, Daniel J. *The Image: A Guide to Pseudo-Events in America.* New York: Atheneum, 1961.

Crouse, Timothy. *The Boys on the Bus.* New York: Random House, 1973.

Hersey, John. *The Algiers Motel Incident.* New York: Knopf, 1968.

McGinniss, Joe. *The Selling of the President 1968.* New York: Pocket Books, 1973.

Weir, David, and Dan Noyes. *Raising Hell: How the Center for Investigative Reporting Gets the Story.* Reading, Mass.: Addison-Wesley, 1983.

CHAPTER ELEVEN

Building and Using Background

Preview

Reporters are always at work building two kinds of background knowledge:

• General—The overall knowledge that the reporter takes to the job. It is based on wide reading and general experience. This type of background helps to put the news into context.

• Specific—The specialized information that helps the reporter cope with his or her beat. It includes, for example, the way the city judicial system is structured, one judge's preference for jail sentences and another's for probation.

A command of background allows the reporter to see connections among facts and incidents, and this grouping of material often leads to stories that are more revealing than the bare recital of the breaking news event.

The reporter is expected to know a lot. An error, a missing fact or a misinterpretation cannot be explained away by the reporter.

Demanding as this may seem, it is the lot of the professional that he or she be unfailingly certain in performance. The doctor is expected to identify the ailment that plagues the patient. The attorney is a compendium of the law. The teacher is a wise, unfaltering guide who takes students through the complexities of phonics, irregular French verbs and William Blake.

But we know they are all fallible. Doctors misdiagnose, and sometimes their operations fail. Lawyers lose cases through incompetence and ignorance. Teachers are human, too, like the grade school teacher who assigned her class the task of writing sentences containing words from a list she supplied. One youngster, whose father had taken him to a baseball game the day before, chose the word "cap," and he wrote: "Catfish Hunter wears a cap." The teacher returned the boy's paper with the sentence corrected: "A catfish hunter wears a cap."

Should the teacher have known Catfish Hunter was a baseball player? Well, perhaps we do make excuses for teachers, as well as for doctors and lawyers. But we do not excuse the journalist who errs through ignorance.

Should the journalist really be expected to know everything? "Yes," replies Murray Kempton, journalist and author. "When you're covering anything, and you're writing about it at length, you use everything you know. And in order to use everything you have to be interested in an extraordinary range of things."

In Mark Twain's *Sketches,* he describes his experiences as a newspaperman in "How I Edited an Agricultural Paper." Twain is telling someone that little intelligence is needed to be a newspaperman:

Twain's and Mencken's Complaints

> I tell you I have been in the editorial business going on fourteen years, and it is the first time I ever heard of a man's having to know anything in order to edit a newspaper. You turnip! Who write the dramatic critiques for the second-rate papers? Why, a parcel of promoted shoemakers and apprentice apothecaries, who know just as much about good acting as I do about good farming and no more. Who review the books? People who never wrote one. Who do up the heavy leaders on finance? Parties who have had the largest opportunities for knowing nothing about it. Who criticise the Indian campaigns? Gentlemen who do not know a war whoop from a wigwam, and who never have had to run a foot race with a tomahawk, or pluck arrows out of the several members of their families to build the evening camp-fire with. Who write the temperance appeals, and clamor about the flowing bowl? Folks who will never draw another sober breath till they do it in the grave.

H. L. Mencken, a journalist whose prose skewered presidents, poets and bartenders with equal vigor, used some of his most choice execrations to denounce his fellow journalists. In an editorial in the *American Mercury,* October 1924, he wrote:

> The majority of them, in almost every American city, are ignoramuses, and not a few of them are also bounders. All the knowledge that they pack into their brains is, in every reasonable cultural sense, useless; it is the sort of knowledge that belongs, not to a professional man, but to a police captain, a railway mail-clerk or a board boy in a brokerage house. It is a mass of trivialities and puerilities; to recite it would be to make even a barber or a bartender beg for mercy. What is

missing from it is everything worth knowing—everything that enters into the common knowledge of educated men. There are managing editors in the United States, and scores of them, who have never heard of Kant or Johannes Müller and never read the Constitution of the United States; there are city editors who do not know what a symphony is, or a streptococcus, or the Statute of Frauds; there are reporters by the thousand who could not pass the entrance examination for Harvard or Tuskegee, or even Yale. It is this vast ignorance that makes American journalism so pathetically feeble and vulgar, and so generally disreputable no less. A man with so little intellectual enterprise that, dealing with news daily, he goes through life without taking in any news that is worth knowing—such a man, you may be sure, is as lacking in true self-respect as he is in curiosity. Honor does not go with stupidity. If it belongs to professional men, it belongs to them because they constitute a true aristocracy—because they have definitely separated themselves from the great masses of men. The journalists, in seeking to acquire it, put the cart before the horse.

Well, that was years ago. Journalists are now college-trained, often in schools of journalism (a hopeful sign, Mencken said in the same editorial). Yet what are we to make of the current generation, one of whose representatives wrote in a college newspaper about a presentation of *The Merchant of Venus,* instead of *The Merchant of Venice?*

And what can we say to the journalism student who wrote of the sculptor Michel Angelo?

Should the journalist be expected to know the plays of Shakespeare, the world of art and the names of baseball players? Would it terrify would-be journalists to suggest that the answer has to be yes?

This storehouse of knowledge is the reporter's background. As Kempton, Twain and Mencken suggest, it should be kept full and constantly replenished—if such a feat is possible. The reporter needs to have at his or her fingertips a wide assortment of information, and more. Not only does the reporter need to know dates, names, policies made, policies defeated, what leads the best-seller list and what agency makes the list of the 10 most-wanted criminals. All of this has to be put into some kind of schematic, some kind of pattern or the reporter will eventually see himself or herself in the sad comment of T. S. Eliot, "We had the experience but missed the meaning."

The term *background* has three meanings:

A reporter's store of information. This knowledge may be amassed over a long period or picked up quickly in order to handle a specific assignment. Without background knowledge, a reporter's fact gathering can be nondirected.

Material placed in the story that explains the event, traces its development and adds facts that sources have not provided. Without background, a story may be one-dimensional.

Material a source does not want attributed to him or her. It may or may not be used, depending on the source's instructions.

Reporters have a deep and wide-ranging fund of knowledge. Much of this stored information concerns processes and procedures: the workings of the political system; the structure of local government; arrest procedures; government finance. The good reporter is aware of the past and its relation to the present. The *Dred Scott* and the *Brown* v *Board of Education* Supreme Court decisions are kept in mental drawers, ready for use. When a speaker refers to the New Deal, the reporter knows what he means.

The knowledge of how things work can turn a routine assignment into a significant story. When a reporter for a Long Island newspaper was sent to cover a fire in a plastic factory, she noticed that the plant was located in a residential zone. On her return to the office, she told her editor, "I've got the information on the fire, but I want to check out why that factory was built there in a residential zone. Was it zoned industrial when the factory was built, or did the company get a variance?" The reporter knew that variances—exceptions to general zoning patterns—are sometimes awarded to friends or supporters. Though the reporter was not a city hall reporter or a specialist in covering real estate, she knew about zoning through her overall understanding of city government. Her curiosity and knowledge led to a significant story.

When Joe Munson, a photographer for *The Kentucky Post* in Covington, Ky., was covering the Indianapolis 500 the daring tactics of a driver caught his eye. Munson knew that there is an imaginary line that race car drivers must follow around bends in order to keep their cars under control.

"I noticed driver Danny Ongais straying six inches from that imaginary line and I suspected he was destined for a crash," Munson recalled.

"So I kept my camera focused on him."

Munson was ready when Ongais lost control and his car cracked into the wall. Munson was able to run off 20 shots of the fiery crash. One of them took first place in the sports category of a National Press Photographers Association regional competition.

A frequent criticism of U.S. journalists is that although their mastery of the journalistic craft is unexcelled, their general knowledge is limited. American journalism lacks a tradition of scholarship, critics contend.

The Contents of the Storehouse

More than Writing. "The vocabulary of a writer is his currency but it is a paper currency and its value depends on the reserves of mind and heart which back it."—Cyril Connolly.

Casualty at the Indy 500.
Photographer Joe Munson of *The Kentucky Post* had noticed that the driver of this car was cutting turns too closely. He kept his camera trained on driver Danny Ongais and was able to take several shots of this crash.

Knowing the Records

Such knowledge is important because it is the bedrock on which news stories are built. The American philosopher John Dewey said, "We cannot lay hold of the new, we cannot even keep it before our minds, much less understand it, save by the use of ideas and knowledge we already possess." Irving Kristol, a writer on social and political affairs, says, "When one is dealing with complicated and continuous events, it is impossible to report 'what happened' unless one is previously equipped with a context of meaning and significance."

Marcia Chambers, who covered the Criminal Courts Building for *The New York Times,* scored many exclusives because she had mastered the procedures of the criminal justice system. Chambers used files, records and background for a piece she did on the arrest of a mass-murder suspect. Without the background material, the arrest story would have had some interest but little significance. Here is her description of how she went about digging up the information for her story:

"On the day Calvin Jackson was arrested, I covered the arraignment where the prosecutor announced that Jackson had been charged with the murder of one woman and had 'implicated himself' in several others. At the time, we wanted to find out more about Jackson's prior criminal record, but given the hour—5:30 p.m.—we couldn't get the information. In a sidebar story that appeared the next day, Joe Treaster, the police reporter, said Jackson's previous arrest had occurred 10 months before. But the disposition of the case, the story said, was unknown.

"From my experience, I knew that nearly all cases are disposed of through plea bargaining, the process whereby a defendant agrees to plead guilty in exchange for a lesser charge. Several weeks before I had obtained from the Office of Court Administration data that showed that last year only 545 out of 31,098 felony arrests went to trial, including drug cases.

"On Monday, at 10 a.m., I went to the court clerk's office. My premise was that Jackson's last arrest, like the thousands of others that pass through the criminal court system, had probably involved plea bargaining, a reduction of charges and a minimal sentence.

"From the docket book, I obtained the docket number of the mass-murder case, and since case records are public information, I asked the clerk for the case. I took it to the side of the room, and quickly copied the file that contained information about his previous arrests." (In addition to carrying change for phone calls, reporters should carry at least two dollars in change at all times for the copying machine.)

"On Tuesday, having obtained the dates of Jackson's previous arrests from the rap sheets, I checked the docket book again, obtained the cases and copied them.

"At about 2 p.m., I called my desk to say I thought I had a good story. I had a general outline, but said I was uncertain whether it would be ready to go that night. I left the courthouse and went to the *Times*.

"First I went to the law library at the *Times* to check the Penal Code and Criminal Procedure Law. I knew from the complaint that Jackson had been charged with two felonies in his prior arrests, which had been delineated on the court papers by statute number. From the law books I learned the maximum sentence for each crime. In this case, the original charges were "C" felonies, punishable by up to 15 years in prison.

"By 3:30 p.m., I was still missing information, I wanted to talk to the victim who had pressed the charges against Jackson and his two accomplices on his last arrest, but a check at the Park Plaza Hotel where he lived, and where a half dozen of the murders had occurred, turned up the fact that the complainant had moved out four months before and left no forwarding address or telephone number.

"I wanted to talk to the judges involved. Two were unreachable; one was on the bench.

"At 4:30 or 5 p.m., I told my editors the status of the story. We decided that while it was important to speak to the participants, the records clearly spoke for themselves. The decision was made to write the story at about 5:15 p.m., for a 7 p.m. deadline.

"After I finished writing, a young intern came over to my desk and said to me, 'Boy, that was a good leak.'

"I was startled by his comment and told him how the story came about. His statement indicated to me one of the major failures of journalism today— an over-reliance on leaks and insufficient attention paid to enterprise."

Suspect in Slayings Once Got 30 Days Instead of 15 Years

By Marcia Chambers

Calvin Jackson, who is said by the police to have "implicated himself" in the murder of at least nine women, was arrested in Manhattan 10 months ago on felonious robbery and burglary charges that could have sent him to prison for 15 years, an examination of court records disclosed yesterday.

Instead, the 26-year-old former convict was sent to jail for 30 days after the felony charges against him and two others were reduced to misdemeanors.

He had pleaded guilty in plea bargaining in Criminal Court to the lesser charges, which arose from the robbery last November of a young man, a resident of the Park Plaza Hotel, where Mr. Jackson lived and where six of his alleged victims were killed.

Mr. Jackson's experience is no different from that of thousands of others who yearly pass through the city's court system.

In 1973, the year of Mr. Jackson's last arrest, there were 31,098 felony arrests in Manhattan, according to the crime analysis unit of the Police Department. Of these, only 545 cases went to trial on the original felony charges, including possession or sale of narcotics.

Four out of every five of the 31,098 felony arrests were subject to plea-bargaining and were disposed of at the very outset of the court process—at arraignment before a Criminal Court judge or at a subsequent hearing. That is what happened in the Jackson robbery case. . . .

—The New York Times

A Background Check

Reporters often have to make a background check of an individual, sometimes simply as a matter of routine, sometimes because they suspect the person of hanky-panky.

- The first stop is the clips in the file. Make notes of friends and foes that come up in the reading.
- Next, the county courthouse. Check civil and criminal files to see whether the individual is a plaintiff or defendant. Check under names of businesses with which the individual may be associated. Look for judgments and settlements. Federal tax liens are on file here as well.
- Check real estate transactions, mortgages, liens. Check the probate court.
- If business names turn up, check these with the secretary of state's office in the state capital to obtain names of company officials and check those names in civil dockets at the courthouse and the grantor-grantee files of real estate transactions.

This material was provided by Tim Weiner and Bill Marimow, who do investigative reporting for *The Philadelphia Inquirer.* Detailed information is available in the *Reporter's Handbook* of the Investigative Reporters and Editors organization. (See *Further Reading.*)

- Next, to the federal courthouse to check the individual and businesses and other individuals whose names have turned up. Check the bankruptcy and tax court files.
- Look into public records held by other state and federal agencies—Small Business Administration, economic development agencies, SEC filings, campaign contributions (if a public official).
- Compare the individual's lifestyle and living costs with his or her income. The person's mortgage, costs of educating children and other fixed costs can be estimated.
- Interview all adversaries, opponents, people who have some reason to dislike the person.
- Finally, interview the individual. If the person refuses, talk to his or her attorney or top aides, and as a last resort send the person a registered letter requesting the interview and explaining what you would like to discuss.

Reporters with ample background knowledge do not embarrass themselves or their editors by blundering in print or on the air. Witness these bloopers, the result of a lack of specific knowledge:

Specific and General Knowledge

> In one of her columns, Harriet Van Horne referred to Canada as having a "tough and happily homogeneous population. . . ." (The columnist ignored the large Indian and Eskimo populations and the almost six million French-speaking Canadians, who have their own schools in an officially bilingual country. Not only is the country not homogeneous, the French and English-speaking Canadians are hardly happily ensconced together. Many of the French-speaking people contend they are second-class citizens, which led to a separatist movement in the province of Quebec.)

> When the basketball coach at Boston College accepted the head coaching job at Stanford, a CBS sports announcer said that the coach had "followed Horace Mann's advice to go west." (The advice is attributed to Horace Greeley, founder and editor of *The Tribune:* "Go west young man." Horace Mann was an educator.)

> In a feature on food served during the Jewish holidays, a reporter for the *Press-Enterprise* in Riverside, Calif., described Yom Kippur as "marked by rich, indeed lavish meals." (Yom Kippur, known as the Day of Atonement, is the most solemn of all Jewish holy days and is observed by fasting.)

During a televised National Basketball Association game, a player let the man he was covering drive past him for a basket. The player looked disgusted with himself, and from the broadcast booth the sportscasters could see his lips moving. "What do you think he's saying, Bill?" one asked his colleague, Bill Russell, one of the great defensive stars in basketball and the first black coach in the NBA.

Russell replied, "I know how Walt feels. I can hear him muttering a four-syllable word." Russell's colleague laughingly corrected him: "You mean four-letter word, Bill." Slowly, deliberately, Russell said, "No, I mean four-syllable word."

There was a long pause, a smothered gasp, and then a commercial. (Russell's long playing career had given him a vast store of knowledge about the game, from strategy to the obscenities players use in moments of futility.)

General knowledge can be accumulated by reading widely, but all knowledge does not come from books, and the academic community does not have exclusive access to knowledge. The young men and women who are determined to be journalists are alert to the world around them. They listen closely to people and observe them carefully. They welcome new ideas, new ways of seeing events. They are interested in history, current affairs, and the things that make people and organizations tick. They speculate about what motivates people; they wonder about the role of money in society, and they are interested in how geography, history and the weather affect what people think and do. Although they are present-oriented, they know something of the past. They learn by going to roller rinks and museums, from talking to third-graders and pensioners, by watching fishermen and street vendors.

Pairing Facts

Good reporters collect stray pieces of background that often have no particular use at the moment. Sooner or later, another bit of information will come along that when paired with the first will make a good story.

For example, a reporter who made it his business to look in on the state penitentiary every few weeks was talking to a guard one day when an old man walked by. He was an inmate with a long record, a farmer with an inability to earn an honest living, the guard said. Swindler, thief and bad-check artist, he was always in trouble, and now he was in the pen for life. A few weeks later, the reporter was chatting with the warden about another prisoner from Albuquerque. Despite a long record of violent crime, he was in for an eight-year term, which meant he would be out in a little more than half that time.

The disparities in sentences interested the reporter, but he did little with the information. Such disparities were not new to him. Well-to-do defendants were never convicted for drunken driving but instead were allowed to plead to reckless driving charges; the poor were usually convicted of drunken driving. He had done a story on that. The short prison terms imposed on white collar criminals was also an old story.

Every so often, the reporter would go through the penitentiary's records of the arrests, convictions and sentences of the inmates for possible features. One day, while leafing through the record book, he noticed that the farmer had been sentenced under something called the "habitual criminal law," which required stringent sentences for frequent offenders. Other convicts were also sentenced under the same law, but there was no consistency in sentences. The reporter's interest was piqued.

The convict with a long record of serious crimes was not sentenced under the habitual criminal law. Putting these facts together, he wrote a series of articles pointing out that judges and district attorneys over the state were ignoring and misapplying the habitual criminal law so that of the 72 frequent offenders in the state penitentiary who should have been sentenced under the law, only 14 were doing time under its provisions.

Many Prosecutors and Judges Ignore New Mexico Habitual Criminal Laws

(New Mexico has a stringent law concerning habitual criminals. But a Journal survey has shown that it is being consistently ignored by law enforcement officers. This is the first in a series of articles on this important law.)

SANTA FE, Jan. 4—New Mexico's habitual criminal laws, which were designed to increase punishment for the frequent offender, are ignored, inconsistently used, and misunderstood by many of the state's law enforcement officers and judges, a study of official records disclosed today.

Although the laws are clearly mandatory and require district attorneys to bring charges under the act when they can be applied, few district attorneys follow the statutes.

The habitual criminal laws apply to persons who have been found guilty of more than one felony.

Yet of the 72 men now behind bars at the state penitentiary who have committed three or more felonies, only 14 were sentenced under the habitual criminal act. The number of second offenders who could have been sentenced under the law but were not were too numerous to check.

In a few cases where men have been convicted under the law, district judges have handed down illegal sentences and have not applied the law consistently.

For some time the legal profession has been aware of these facts, but little has been done either to repeal the laws or to make them work fairly.

The habitual criminal act was passed in 1929 and establishes a table of increased prison sentences for law violators who have committed more than one felony. . . .

—*The Albuquerque Journal*

Always Use Background

Few stories are complete without some background information. Reporters who disregard this advice do so at the peril of inadequately informing their readers and listeners. Events have causes and consequences.

The third paragraph in the following short item from *The New York Times* gives meaning to the story. Without this background, readers would have been deprived of possible motivation:

Negro Business Aid Group Backs Carswell Nomination

WASHINGTON, April 4—An organization called N.E.G.R.O. has taken a full-page advertisement in tomorrow's edition of *The New York Times* to endorse the nomination of Judge G. Harold Carswell to the Supreme Court.

N.E.G.R.O., an acronym for National Economic Growth and Reconstruction Organization, Inc., gives technical aid to black entrepreneurs to help them establish businesses.

The advertisement was signed by the group's president, Dr. Thomas W. Matthew, a New York neurosurgeon. Earlier this year, Dr. Matthew was pardoned by President Nixon after he had served two months of a one-year sentence for income tax evasion.

The Mind Fixers

The series was 11 years in the making. When Jon Franklin of *The Evening Sun* in Baltimore covered a news conference in 1973 about the discovery of the brain receptor, he made a discovery of his own: "I knew then—partly hunch and partly because I saw the handwriting on the technical walls—that I had found the story of my life."

The problem was that the field was difficult to understand. Also it had "unpleasant philosophical implications about who we were and how we worked—that we were basically mechanistic beasts." But he went ahead anyway, and it took more than a decade for him to gather enough background so that he could write understandably about the highly technical subject.

"It was an incredible writing problem, requiring the crafting of dozens of different metaphors and explanatory techniques," he said. In 1982, he gave it a shot. He tried to put together an explanation of brain chemistry that was understandable to the layman. When he finally wrote "30" on his computer he had 30,000 words. For two years he whittled away, and in 1984 he had 3,000 words.

This encouraged him to go on, and the result was a seven-part series called "The Mind Fixers" that led to the Pulitzer Prize for 1985 in explanatory journalism, a new category. Franklin's control of the background of his subject is obvious:

"We're out-and-out materialists," says Daniel C. Dennett, professor of philosophy at Tufts University, summing up a Johns Hopkins scientific conference on the issue.

Or, in the blunter words of one neuroanatomist, "The brain is an organ; it produces thoughts the same way the kidney produces urine."

If that attitude outrages some philosophers and priests, the scientists themselves are unperturbed.

A little philosophical discomfort, they say, is a small price to pay for a new science capable of curing the mental diseases that afflict perhaps 20 percent of the population and constitute a major drain on the gross national product.

And scientists such as Dr. Candace Pert, a key figure in brain chemistry at the National Institute of Mental Health, say the mechanistic view is in fact the most humanitarian one.

She argues that thinking of the mind as something spooky and apart has historically led to judgmental attitudes toward the insane.

"It's sad, but even today, this far into the 20th century, mental illness is not even totally talked about. It's still considered something ugly, something to hide. People are ostracized.

"But people who act crazy are acting that way because they have too much or too little of some chemicals that are in their brains. It's just physical illness! The brain is a physical thing!"

Further Reading

Lewis, Anthony. *Gideon's Trumpet*. New York: Random House, 1964.

Steel, Ronald. *Walter Lippmann and the American Century*. Boston: Atlantic Monthly Press, 1980.

Ullmann, John H. *Reporter's Handbook: An Investigator's Guide to Documents and Techniques*. New York: St. Martin's Press, 1983.

CHAPTER TWELVE

Finding, Cultivating and Using Sources

Preview

Reliable sources are essential. There are two basic types of sources.

• Physical sources, which consist of records, documents, reference works, newspaper clippings, direct observations.

• Human sources, which consist of authorities and people involved in events. They are often less reliable than physical sources because they may have interests to protect, are untrained observers and sometimes tell reporters what they think the reporter wants to hear. When using human sources, find the person most qualified to speak—an authority on the subject, an eyewitness, an official.

Some of the dangers that reporters face in using sources are: writing for the authorities who are the reporters' sources rather than for the general reader; using people as sources who have impressive credentials but whose subject knowledge may be skimpy; trusting printed material that may contain errors.

J ournalists depend so much on their sources it is an axiom that a reporter can be no better than his or her sources. These sources include officials, spokesmen, participants in events, documents, records, tape recordings, magazines, films and books. The quality of the reporter's story depends on the quality of the sources.

Reporters spend a lot of time looking for and cultivating people who can become sources and contacts. A county courthouse reporter in California estimates that he spends a couple of hours a day chatting and just passing time with his sources. He also chats with guards, secretaries, elevator operators. He describes these as contacts, people who can lead to a story with a tip. An elevator operator tipped him off about a well-known businessman who had been summoned by a grand jury and was taken to the jury room by a back elevator.

During his first weeks covering Congress for *The Wall Street Journal,* Fred L. Zimmerman learned that finding and cultivating sources and contacts was essential.

"If you can establish a friendly relationship with a committee chairman's secretary, she will tell you where he can be found in a hurry," Zimmerman says. "Or she will put you through on the phone sometimes when she wouldn't do it for a reporter she doesn't know. It's impossible to cover Congress well unless a reporter works hard at establishing good relations with dozens of these people whose names never get into the newspaper."

There are two kinds of sources, human and physical. The distinction between the two, and their relative reliability, was nicely put by Sir Kenneth Clark, the British writer and critic: "If I had to say who was telling the truth about society, a speech by the Minister of Housing or the actual buildings put up in his time, I would believe the buildings."

The difference is often on the reporter's mind, for even though much of his or her work depends upon interviews, the reporter seeks physical evidence whenever possible. This kind of material includes newspaper clippings, books, records and documents as well as the reporter's direct observation.

The coverage of an assassination attempt against President Ford illustrates the importance of the physical evidence provided by direct observation. During his visit to Sacramento, Calif., Ford was to walk from his hotel to the state capitol where a crowd was awaiting him. In the hotel, Richard Lerner, a UPI White House correspondent, looked out the window and debated whether to join the president. He was exhausted after 20 hours of tracking Ford, and he knew that two other UPI reporters would be walking the few hundred yards with Ford to the capitol. On the other hand, perhaps he should test the recent promise of the president's press secretary that the Secret Service would allow reporters to stay close to the president.

In one of those blindingly lucky decisions reporters make, Lerner says he figured, "What the hell, I'm going to tag along."

When a young woman, Lynette "Squeaky" Fromme, pulled a .45 caliber pistol from a leg holster, Lerner was only eight or ten feet away. He saw the woman, the gun and an agent grabbing the woman before she could shoot.

Later, the Secret Service told the press that the gun had never been higher than the woman's mid-thigh. But Lerner had seen the gun come near her waist, and he also saw the president spot the gun before the Secret Service agents had.

"Ford moved on his own, I'm certain of that," Lerner says. "I was startled and froze on the spot. By then the Secret Service had seized the woman and there was a scuffle going on for the gun."

Lerner recovered quickly and sprinted about 200 yards back to the hotel. He called his Washington bureau and began dictating a bulletin and his eye-witness account. The AP had reporters close to Ford, too, but they had not seen the pistol in the woman's hand. Along with other reporters, the AP had to await the official version. The wait cost the AP much of the newspaper play because editors around the world had the UPI bulletin on their desks before the AP story began to move. Not only were other stories late, they did not have the conviction that direct observation carries.

Let us examine these two types of sources in detail.

Human Sources

A person with information the reporter needs for a story or for background is called a source. Sources include the woman who saw an airplane fall short of the landing strip, and Deep Throat, the informant who cooperated with *Washington Post* reporters Woodward and Bernstein on their Watergate investigation. The stockbroker friend of a reporter on the business beat who explains complicated financial matters is a source, although his name may never appear in a story.

Here is how Arthur L. Gavshon, the diplomatic reporter for the AP, defines a source in an article on sources in the *AP World Magazine:*

> To me anyone on the inside of any given news situation is a potential source. But they only turn into real sources when they come up with a bit, or a lot, of relevant information. In writing thousands of stories over the years I have been helped in varying degrees, by prime ministers, even a president or two, members of cabinets, politicians, diplomats, doormen, police officers. . . .

Gavshon says he finds sources anywhere and everywhere. He develops his sources "just as you would get to know a friend and nurture a relationship in everyday life (always assuming you can live a normal life as a newsman!)—through the exercise of patience, understanding and a reasonable capacity to converse about shared interests."

Sometimes, if sources seem inaccessible, Gavshon uses two techniques to open their doors:

> There's nothing quite like trying the direct approach through normal channels as a start. . . . My own private way of establishing a line to someone really worthwhile has been to suggest a meeting for the purpose of writing a profile-cum-interview with the person. Few public people find it in them to resist that sort of thing.

Media Manipulator. The news conference was crowded with reporters and television crews as Dr. Josef Gregor announced that he had distilled cockroach hormones into a pill so potent it would make people immune to ailments as diverse as acne and menstrual cramps. His study group, the "Metamorphosis," distributed the literature to eager reporters.

More recently, at another packed news conference, a man named Joe Bones announced that he had formed the Fat Squad to serve as watchers for people who needed help to diet. For a fee of $300, the Squad was prepared to use physical force if necessary.

The Fat Squad story was carried on network television and in *The Washington Post, Philadelphia Inquirer, Miami Herald* and many other newspapers.

Gregor-Bones is Joe Skaggs, a teacher of media communications. Skaggs says he stages hoaxes to show how careless the media are in checking sources. "Aren't they also susceptible to more dangerous manipulation?" he asks.

(*The New York Times* did not use the Fat Squad story when a reporter, who checked with Joe Bones after the conference, told his editor that it sounded fishy.)

Murder. ''We've been exploited, we've been assaulted, we've been murdered,'' the Salvadoran Indian told a reporter-photographer team from the Sierra Vista (Ariz.) *Herald-Dispatch*. Photo by T. J. Lynch.

Contacts Pay Off. A summer barbecue came to a sudden end for reporter Diane Goldie when she was ordered by beeper phone to rush to a Jersey City police station where an officer had shot another police officer. Unable to change clothes—her deadline was little more than an hour off—she raced to the station, only to be informed of a press blackout. Goldie telephoned a friend on the force who passed her the police report. Photo by Linda Cataffo.

Sources need not be directors of companies, mayors or congressmen. The city hall reporter knows that the town clerk who has served a succession of mayors has a comprehensive knowledge of the community and the inner workings of town government. The courthouse reporter befriends law clerks, court stenographers and security guards. Business reporters cultivate switchboard operators, secretaries, the mailroom help.

Reporters have gone out of their way to do favors for their sources. At one newspaper in California, the reporters who handle obituaries send birthday candy and flowers to the mortuary employees who call to report the deaths of important people. A death called in near deadline means the newspaper or station telephoned first will have that much more time to write the obituary. A difference of two minutes can be the difference between making or missing the last edition or the 6 p.m. newscast.

Some reporters cultivate sources by reversing the news-gathering process. One Midwestern newsman says that instead of always asking sources for news, he puts his sources on the receiving end. "I see to it personally that they hear any gossip or important news. This pays off. When I want news, I get it," he says.

The source needed for information on a single story need not be cultivated with the care reporters lavish on sources essential to a beat. But courtesy and consideration are always important. In speaking to a source for the first—and perhaps the only—time, the reporter identifies himself or herself immediately and moves to the questions quickly. A different pace is necessary for the source essential to a beat. Gavshon cautions:

> Don't ever rush things. Don't make the ghastly mistake of thinking only in terms of tomorrow's headline. . . . One-night stands rarely satisfy anybody.

Keeping the Source

The source is the reporter's life blood. Without access to information through the source, the reporter cannot function. The reporter is just as necessary to most sources, for without the journalist the source has no access to the public. Most sources need public reaction to their ideas and policies.

Out of this mutual need a source-reporter relationship develops: The source will provide the reporter with information and will brief him or her on developments. In return, the reporter will write a fair account of the material.

As events become more complex, the reporter's dependence on sources increases. Briefings to explain complicated information are essential. When a reporter learns of a probable future event, such as the presentation of the municipal budget to the city council, he or she may ask a source for background so that the difficult story can be written without deadline pressure. The courthouse reporter who learns through the grapevine that the grand jury is about to return an indictment against the city clerk will ask the district attorney for a briefing, promising not to break the story before the indictment is returned. Sources usually are happy to comply, because they prefer an accurate story to a rush job.

Some reporters score exclusives by rushing into print with tips and by disregarding embargoes. Sources eventually freeze out such reporters. It can be risky to go ahead with a story before the facts are confirmed or verified. Writing a story on an indictment before it has been returned, for example, can lead to disaster for a reporter. It has become common practice among prosecutors to threaten to indict the subject of an investigation so that he or she will inform—*turn* is the prosecutor's word—on a bigger target. The Watergate inquiry was replete with examples of this tactic. Gullible reporters, or scoop artists, can be used by prosecutors to help turn a person.

Protecting Sources

Sometimes reporters have to protect a source's identity. An investigative reporter learns from a police officer that a convict serving a life term for murder was convicted on perjured police testimony. In return for the tip about the frame-up, the reporter must promise not to name his source.

In half the states, the reporter can make this promise because shield laws protect confidential sources. All states have some kind of protection, but in some states, a reporter who tries to protect a confidential source may face contempt charges and jail. State press associations usually distribute pamphlets about reporters' rights.

Protection of another kind can also be troublesome to reporters. Sometimes a reporter is reluctant to hurt or embarrass the source with a tough story. Walter Lippmann said there must be a "certain distance between the reporter and the source, not a wall or a fence, but an air space." Once a friend becomes an official, he said, "you can't call him by his first name anymore." Often the reluctance to criticize stems from the fear that a critical story may dry up the source.

After the newspaper *Newsday* ran articles critical of President Nixon, the newspaper was excluded from the president's trip to China, and the presidential press secretary refused to speak to the newspaper's White House correspondent for three months. President Johnson forbade his press secretary to give any information to a reporter for the *St. Louis Post-Dispatch* because Johnson felt the reporter's questions at press briefings had been too aggressive. Good reporters are willing to sacrifice favors from this kind of source.

Still, reporters protect certain sources. The reason: Without some sources, the reporter cannot function. Jack Anderson, a Washington columnist who specializes in inside information, states his philosophy as follows: "We will give immunity to a very good source as long as the information he offers us is better than that which we've got on him."

The young reporter has still another problem that sometimes leads to the overprotection of sources. Mixing with the kinds of people the reporter had once only read about or seen on television—governors, congressmen, movie stars, generals—can be a heady affair. As a consequence, the reporter may lose objectivity. Veteran reporters suffer from another form of this ailment. They become source-oriented. Forgetting that they are responsible to the general reader, they write copy for their source's approval.

Important as human sources are, they are not the most reliable. The beat reporter finds that his sources often have interests they wish to protect, programs and ideas they want to push, enemies they want to hurt.

The Washington Post reported that outgoing President Jimmy Carter had planted a recording device in Blair House while incoming President Ronald Reagan and Nancy Reagan were staying there. When Carter protested, the *Post* apologized and said its source had been in error. Some reporters concluded that the source was out to embarrass Carter.

The reporter who has to rely on transient sources for quick information on a breaking story knows that most people are notoriously inaccurate. A woman who says she saw an airplane crash "in a ball of fire" may not be relaying what she saw but what she has seen on television and in movies over the years.

An eyewitness can seduce a reporter by the sheer drama of his or her story. Instead of being enthralled, the reporter should be cautious, for his knowledge of human nature should tell him that most people seek attention and tend to overdramatize events.

Erving Goffman, the sociologist, says everyone is a performer trying to put his or her stamp of individual identity on things. Individuals find it hard not to exaggerate their observations or feelings when they know that the more dramatic they are the more likely they or their remarks will appear. Also, having seen what is used on television newscasts, people tend to give the reporter what they think the reporter wants. This phenomenon is one reason for the stereotyped responses of most people interviewed at breaking news events. People also remember selectively, recalling mostly that which fits their preconceived notions or that which they find pleasant.

How can the reporter test the source's reliability? Sources essential to a reporter's beat should be selected because of their knowledge of the subject, their contacts, and their reputations for intelligence and honesty. Here are some measures of reliability for transient sources:

Was the person an observer of the incident, or did he or she hear about it from someone else?

Is the person a competent observer? An airline employee would be a better source for information about an airplane crash than a student or a salesperson.

Can the source supply precise details that have the ring of truth and seem consistent with the facts?

Tall Tale? The student had been sent to Atlantic City to do a story on compulsive gamblers. She interviewed pawnshop owners to find out what gamblers pawn to stay in action. "Gamblers will do anything to keep gambling," the story quoted one owner. "One time a fellow pulled out three of his back, gold-filled teeth in the store. My ex-husband gave him the pliers. We had to sit here and bang out the enamel." Great quotes. But true?

False Credentials

Sometimes reporters use sources because of who or what they are, not because of what they know. Most people tend to believe those in authority. The greater the title or position, the higher the social position, the more prestigious the alma mater, the more faith people have in the expert or authority. This is known as the "hierarchy of credibility"—the higher on the scale the authority is, the more believable he or she is thought to be. When the journalist surrenders to this tendency, he or she allows those in power to define events and situations.

Reporters must be careful to use sources only within their area of expert knowledge. Asked questions within the narrow range of their expertise, sources are useful. A banker can talk about banking, a general about the strategy and tactics of war. But it is dangerous to rely on a banker for comments on the nation's economy or on a general as an authority on international affairs. They may be less useful than the lesser-known labor department area representative or the assistant professor of international affairs at a local college.

A reporter's best sources are those who have demonstrated their knowledge and competence as accurate observers, interpreters and forecasters of events. Reporters should drop sources who are proved wrong in their observations and assessments, whether they served in the president's cabinet, ran a multi-million dollar import business or graduated *summa cum laude* from Harvard.

Testing Steady Sources

Before the reporter decides to depend on an individual as a steady source of information, a simple test can be made of that person's reliability. The reporter can corroborate facts from other sources, physical as well as human. The individual's recollections can be checked against reference works or news clippings. If the potential source is found to be inaccurate, he or she is dropped. Sources should be evaluated periodically, particularly after a change in jobs. The city manager may lose effectiveness as an authority on certain topics after he becomes executive secretary of the local real estate board.

Sometimes the information necessary for a story is so complicated that no one person can know everything about the situation. In these situations, a second source is essential.

During *The Washington Post's* Watergate investigation, when the reputation, if not the survival, of the newspaper hung on the reliability of sources, a corroborating source was always sought so that all the facts lacking physical evidence were attested to by at least two individuals.

Gavshon uses a fairly simple device to test reliability. "My own rough-and-ready rule is to test out the new-found source with questions to which I already know the answers."

Despite all these tests, the reporter must keep in mind that he or she is relying on someone else, and that fact alone makes the story vulnerable. No reporter can ever feel certain that another person's observations are as accurate as his own or that the person lacks bias or self-interest.

Physical Sources

The range of physical information is enormous. Physical sources are limited only by the reporter's imagination and knowledge of their existence.

Many reference resources are free to the journalist: the law library of the district attorney or the nearby law school; the public and private libraries in town whose librarians delight in visits or calls from journalists; the files of local and state agencies in town, and the considerable resources of the nearby college or university. Many of the larger state educational institutions have on their campuses various state-supported and private programs for governmental studies that are well-stocked with materials for stories as well as for background. Master's and doctoral theses make good sources for copy.

One reporter who leafed through the office copy of the *Congressional Record* each week often turned up interesting stories about area congressmen. A couple of thousand miles from their constituents, the congressmen apparently felt free to say what they might not tell local reporters. Once the reporter happened on a congressman's eulogy for Generalissimo Francisco Franco, the Spanish dictator. The piece drew considerable comment from the congressman's constituents.

Blind Spot. In his study of Washington reporters, Stephen Hess found the journalists he interviewed used no documents in almost three-fourths of their stories. "When newspaper and television reporters are given more time to do stories, they simply do more interviews," Hess says.

All Sources Are Not Equal

As we have seen, good reporters prefer the physical source to the human source. But not all physical sources are of equal reliability. The annual tables of vital statistics are more reliable than the city official's summary introducing the tables. The World Almanac is more reliable than a newspaper clipping of the same event, for the Almanac is usually the work of professional researchers, and the news story may have been written in a hurry before all the facts were in. Although reporters know they make mistakes, they sometimes use other reporters' work as the basis of their stories and the results can be embarrassing.

Veneration for Print

Journalists have a tendency to venerate the printed word, no matter what its source, perhaps because the journalist spends his or her life so close to words on paper. Whatever the reason, the journalist's esteem for the somber black characters of print can be misplaced. In fact, print sometimes solidifies an original error. Once a story is written and filed in the newspaper morgue, it is difficult to correct.

Here is the chronology of a printed error that was given added circulation because the journalist, Tom Wicker of *The New York Times*, assumed that the published word was true:

A Memorial Day column detailing the problems of Vietnam war veterans stated that 500,000 of them had attempted suicide. This statistic was derived from an article in *Penthouse* magazine. The author of that article obtained it from a pamphlet of Twice Born Men, a veterans' group in San Francisco, now defunct.

That organization's former director, Jack McCloskey, says he got the figure from the National Council of the Churches of the U.S.A. The council disavowed any knowledge of the statistic, which must therefore be considered unsupported. Its publication in this space is regretted.

The figure 500,000 should have seemed preposterous on its face. But reporters sometimes are influenced by their attitudes. Wicker may have been predisposed to believe the figure because of his opposition to the Vietnam War.

As for photographs, everyone knows by now that pictures can distort, if not lie. Camera angles, close-ups and the time appropriated to incidents in film or on tape can emphasize irrelevancies or capture an atypical moment.

The Spy Who Wasn't

Art Jester of the *Lexington Herald-Leader* used physical and human sources to puncture the dramatic story of a public speaker, Col. John Cottell, who passed himself off as having served as a spy for the British and told tales of being parachuted behind Nazi lines, being imprisoned in Moscow's dreaded prison, Lubyanka, and being the model for John Le Carré's novels, *The Spy Who Came in From the Cold* and *Tinker, Tailor, Soldier, Spy.* He gave 70 to 75 talks a year at $2,500 each.

The tales were just too dramatic, Jester felt, and he started to dig. His conclusion in a copyrighted story by the newspaper: "Much, if not all, of his story is fiction."

• Le Carré denied any knowledge of Cottell. "I'm getting fairly irritated by the man. I've never heard of him, and there's no question of him being the basis of characters in my work. He is either mad or a fraud."

• Cottell said he was in a spy exchange at the Berlin Wall in 1957. The Wall was built in 1961.

• He claimed he was an ordained Anglican priest, and in his talks he often wore clerical garb. An Anglican bishop Jester contacted said: "Cottell has no connection with this diocese and we believe him to be a fraud." In answer to Jester's questions, Cottell acknowledged that he only holds a mail-order ordination certificate from the Universal Life Church Inc., which sends out certificates to anyone who mails a fee.

• His birth certificate listed him as two years younger than he claimed, which would have made him 16 years old when, he asserted, Winston Churchill dispatched him to parachute behind German lines in World War II.

Oops. The judge seemed to be poking fun at a handicapped defendant. According to the newspaper story, his opinion stated that the man, who had one leg, "hasn't a leg to stand on." Ann Landers printed the story with an irate letter from a reader who accused the judge of making fun of the handicapped. The judge spotted the Landers column and he responded. He did not write the opinion, he said, but wrote the dissent. As for the defendant, he had two perfectly good legs. In her defense, Landers wrote that "when I read an article in a newspaper I assume that the facts are correct."

The Paper Trail. Much can be learned by tracking a person through the many documents he or she leaves behind. Such searches are described as following the paper trail. The trail is enormous: birth certificate, hospital records, school records, real estate transfers and purchases, marriage and death certificates. The major areas for inquiry are newspaper clippings, the courts, reference works and government agencies.

Let us accompany four reporters as they work with various kinds of sources for their stories. The first story is the type that puts reporters on their mettle, the late-breaking event that must be handled quickly and accurately.

How Reporters Use Sources

The story takes us to a New Jersey newsroom where a reporter is making late police checks, which consist of calling area police departments not personally covered by the police reporter. Here, the reporter must rely on human sources. There is little opportunity to examine police records.

A Fatal

Police reporters often turn up good stories because the police are the first to know of accidents, crimes, public disturbances and other deviations from the normal run of community life. The reporter was told that a car had plowed into a motorcycle at a stop light and the two young people on the motorcycle were killed. The driver was arrested three miles down the highway and charged with drunken driving. The reporter knew this was a big story, but little time remained before the last edition closed. The rule in the newsroom, she remembered her editor telling her, is simple: "In baseball, if you get your glove on the ball and don't handle it cleanly, it's an error, no matter how hard it's hit to you. If you get a story before deadline and don't have it written for the next edition, you're not a reporter."

She had seen several baseball games in which fielders managed to touch a ball but were not given errors when they failed to throw the batter out. But she had not called that to her editor's attention. She knew better.

She quickly learned the names of the victims and the driver and the location and circumstances of the accident. Knowing that the investigating officers were still writing their report, she asked if they were available at the station. She knew they would have details she needed, especially about the chase for the driver. She then called the mortuary to obtain background about the victims. Mortuaries will usually have the exact spelling of the victim's name, age, address and occupation. She glanced at the clock to see whether she had time to call the parents of the victims for more precise information. Also, relatives often are on hand to help out, and they might be able to tell her something about the deceased youngsters. But she decided that first she would try the clippings to see if the victims' names were in the newspaper library.

During her interviews with the investigating officers, one of them mentioned that this was the third motorcycle accident in the last month, and she had noted that on her pad for a quick check in the library, too.

The check of the library disclosed this was actually the fourth motorcycle accident in the county, one of the others having been fatal to a young man. The clippings also turned up a story about the young woman who had been killed. She was the daughter of a prominent local family, and the story indicated she used a middle name, which was not in the reporter's notes.

The reporter then decided she should try to locate the parents of the man who had died in the accident. She realized that she had decided not to make those calls because of her distaste for intruding on the family's tragedy. At some newspapers, reporters do not have to make such calls, she recalled a colleague telling her, but that was not the case at this one. The younger sister of the man answered the telephone and was able to supply some details about him.

The reporter used physical and human sources. One of the keys to the story was her knowledge that the investigating police officers might be at the police station writing up the report of the accident. She knew that the best sources are those close to the scene. Although they had not seen the accident, they had arrived quickly and had conducted the investigation. The names of the officers would add authenticity to the story.

With her notes and the library clippings in view she began to type, some 20 minutes before the last edition would close. She knew she had time because she had been organizing her notes as she was reporting.

A Shooting

Although reporters sometimes use the telephone when they should be on the street talking to people or at meetings observing the give-and-take of open debate, there are times when direct observation is impossible. We have just seen a reporter handle a fatal accident by telephone. When the deadline is imminent and the source or the event is more than a short walk or trip away, the only recourse is the telephone.

Using the telephone can be an art. Properly used, it is a boon to reporting. Let us watch a television news reporter cover a shooting 50 miles north of her station, WKTV in Utica, N.Y.

Early one fall evening, Donna Hanover was told by a cameraman that he had picked up a police report that two persons had been shot in separate incidents as they drove past an Indian encampment near the town of Big Moose. Hanover knew immediately this was a big story. Some Mohawk Indians had moved onto state-owned land in the Adirondack Mountains six months before and had refused to leave.

Hanover's major problem was her impending deadline and the distance to Big Moose. Her newscast was at 11 p.m., which gave her no time for the trip up, reporting and the return trip. She had to use the telephone.

By 10:15 p.m., her calls to the state police had turned up little information—a few details on the shooting and the names and ages of the injured. Apparently both were wounded by shots fired at the cars in which they were riding. Hanover then called a medical center near Big Moose to check the condition of the victims, a 22-year-old man and a 9-year-old girl. She also hoped to learn something more about the incident. She was told that the young man had been taken to a hospital in Utica and that the girl was on her way.

She asked for information about the relatives of those who were injured and a hospital attendant gave her the name of the injured man's father. "I then called information for the home telephone number, hoping that some member of the family would have stayed at home in Big Moose," Hanover said.

She was lucky. The father was not there, but the victim's brother answered her call, and he had been riding in the car with his older brother at the time of the shooting.

This piece of good fortune enabled Hanover to use an eyewitness, a better source than someone with a second-hand account. He told Hanover that they had been fired at twice by the Indians. The first time they had missed. But on the return trip, the car had come under heavy fire and his brother was hit in the shoulder.

The girl was in a car that passed by the Indian encampment a few hours after the boys were fired on. The Indians fired at the vehicle as it was disappearing down the road. One bullet entered the trunk, went through the rear seat and struck the girl in the back.

As a result of her calls, Hanover was able to make the 11 o'clock news with a report of the incident. She did not have all the information she needed, but she did have the interview, information from the state police, the condition of the 22-year-old and the name of the 9-year-old girl who was also injured. (See figure 12.1.)

The next day, with plenty of time, Hanover and two photographers drove to Big Moose to do an on-the-scene report. She interviewed the injured man's brother again, this time in front of a camera, photographed the damaged automobile and interviewed local residents and the state police.

"The interview with the brother was important," Hanover says, "because he was a primary source. The police report wasn't, and our job is to give our viewers the best and most accurate information about what has happened." The interview also added an essential ingredient for television news—visual identification.

DH

INDIANS

A 22 YEAR OLD MAN AND A 9 YEAR OLD GIRL WERE INJURED TODAY IN TWO SEPARATE SHOOTING INCIDENTS ON BIG MOOSE ROAD NEAR EAGLE BAY. STEPHEN DRAKE OF INLET, NEW YORK, IS IN THE INTENSIVE CARE WARD OF ST. LUKE'S MEMORIAL HOSPITAL IN SATISFACTORY CONDITION. HIS BROTHER, 20 YEAR OLD MICHAEL DRAKE, WAS WITH HIM WHEN HE WAS SHOT, AND EXPLAINED WHAT HAPPENED. MICHAEL SAID THE TWO WERE DRIVING DOWN BIG MOOSE ROAD WHEN THREE SHOTS WERE FIRED AT THEIR VEHICLE BY *WITHOUT WARNING* A GROUP OF THE INDIANS WHO xxx MOVED ON TO THE LAND ABOUT SIX MONTHS AGO. THE *DRAKES* KEPT DRIVING UNTIL THEY WERE OUT OF RANGE, AND SPENT ABOUT 20 MINUTES AT BIG MOOSE LODGE. ON THE WAY BACK, AT 5:30, *AGAIN WITHOUT WARNING,* THEY CAME UNDER HEAVY FIRE AT THE SAME SPOT. STEPHEN, WHO WAS DRIVING, WAS HIT IN THE LEFT SHOULDER. MICHAEL SAID THERE WERE ABOUT 15 MEN, AND THAT AT LEAST FIVE OF THEM WERE ARMED WITH RIFLES AND SHOTGUNS. AFTER THE DRAKES WERE OUT OF RANGE AGAIN, MICHAEL TOOK OVER THE WHEEL. STATE POLICE HAVE SET UP A ROADBLOCK ACROSS THE BIG MOOSE ROAD TO PREVENT ANYONE FROM ENTERING THE AREA. xxxx xxxxxxxx MICHAEL'S PARENTS, ALLAN AND AUDREY DRAKE, OPERATE DRAKES INN ON ROUTE 28 ABOUT 6 MILES FROM BIG MOOSE. THE BUSINESS IS A FAMILY OPERATION IN WHICH THE FIVE CHILDREN PARTICIPATE, AS DOESN STEPHEN'S WIFE, ELLEN. MICHAEL DRAKE SAID THAT THE INDIANS HAVE NEVER BOTHERED HIM BEFORE, BUT THAT *TWO* xxx CUSTOMERS HAVE REPORTED BEING FOLLOWED, PULLED OVER, AND WARNED TO STAY OFF INDIAN LAND. *AT DRAKE'S INN* MICHAEL SAID THE INDIANS OCCASIONALLY STOP FOR GAS, BUT RARELY INDULGE IN CONVERSATION. xxxxxxxxxxxx STEPHEN DRAKE WAS TREATED AT AN OLD FORGE MEDICAL GROUP BEFORE BEING TAKEN TO ST. LUKES. ALSO TREATED AT OLD FORGE AND THEN ST. LUKES WAS *A NINE YEAR OLD GIRL* WHO WAS RIDING *IDENTIFIED AS APRIL MADIGAN*

2-

WITH HER FAMILY ON BIG MOOSE ROAD, AFTER DINING AT BIG MOOSE LODGE. SHE WAS REPORTEDLY IN THE BACK SEAT WHEN THE CAR WAS FIRED ON.

A Command Post has been set up at the Eagle Bay Firehouse. State Police have been brought in from Tupper & Saranac Lake as well as from the surrounding area.

Major, Robt Charland, Commander of Troop D, is currently at the scene, heading the investigation.

10-28-74   dh

Figure 12.1 A Shooting.
The script for the shooting incident was written under deadline pressure. Hanover was still bringing the story up-to-date at air time.

"I always try to make the viewers feel close to the scene, to make them feel they were there as it happened," says Hanover.

One patrolman was photographed indicating bullet holes in the car. The Indians were not available for interviews. Later, they told her they had been shot at and were returning the fire.

Her script began:

New York state police are manning roadblocks near Eagle Bay and are escorting cars on Big Moose Road where two people in passing cars were shot Monday. Nine-year-old April Madigan of Geneva, New York, is in critical condition at St. Luke's Memorial Hospital Center. . . .

We turn from these spot news stories to a story that began with a chat between college classmates.

Jeffrey A. Tannenbaum, a reporter with *The Wall Street Journal,* was in the newsroom when a call came in from a friend, Ralph Sanders, one of Tannenbaum's classmates at Columbia University. Sanders, who is blind, told Tannenbaum he was active in an organization called the National Federation of the Blind and that the group was planning a demonstration. Sanders said that the blind were tired of being denied rights granted to sighted people.

Sanders suggested the demonstration would make a good story. Sensing a broader story than the coverage of an event that was being staged for the media, Tannenbaum arranged to have lunch with Sanders.

"I was fascinated with the possibility of writing a story about the blind comparable to early stories on the civil rights movement," Tannenbaum says. "In the course of a long interview, Sanders provided the theme for the story. I used it in the sixth paragraph of the finished story.

"What I needed to do after the interview was to document the central thesis. I needed to find examples of ways in which blind people are discriminated against. And I needed to find cases of discrimination in which blind people were militant."

Sanders provided some sources and examples of militancy. Tannenbaum found other examples by calling organizations of the blind. He learned about the alleged discrimination by checking with social agencies and human rights commissions. He was able to find more than a dozen examples of discrimination.

"As a rule of thumb," Tannenbaum says, "I like to have half-a-dozen highly readable, colorful, to-the-point examples in a story. Each one should illustrate a different aspect of the general problem, buttressing the main theme but not duplicating one another."

He checked with people who might have another point of view on what the blind had charged was discrimination. Tannenbaum says, "More than fairness is involved here; a good reporter knows that the best stories are multidimensional. Conflict and controversy do make a better story, but they also accurately reflect reality."

Tannenbaum now had sources with specific complaints and incidents. He had a feeling an incident at a Washington, D.C., airport described by Keith and Elizabeth Howard would be well up in his story, perhaps the lead.

He interviewed the head of Sanders' organization and a blind professor of American history at Seton Hall College in New Jersey, who provided an excellent quote that gave an overview. He consulted some references for data about the blind. He had now interviewed 40 people and was ready to write.

THE WALL STR

© 1975 Dow Jones & Company

VOL. CLXXXVI NO. 7 ★ ★ EASTERN EDITION THURSDAY, JU

New Crusaders

Angry Blind Militants, Seeking 'Equal Rights,' Try Tougher Tactics

Sightless Stage Walkouts, Sue Landlords, Bosses, Reject 'Excessive' Pity

The Fight With Sky Glider

By JEFFREY A. TANNENBAUM
Staff Reporter of THE WALL STREET JOURNAL

Keith and Elizabeth Howard were all set to board an Allegheny Airlines flight from Washington, D.C., to Philadelphia. The airplane wasn't fully booked. Yet an airline official suddenly insisted they must take separate flights.

The reason: The Howards are both blind.

The couple say they were told the pilot didn't want more than one blind passenger on the flight because he assumed that blind people might cause a safety problem or require extra service. While his wife went on ahead, the 43-year-old Mr. Howard waited for the next flight.

Far from being helpless nuisances, the Howards both successfully manage their own lunch counters in Washington. They angrily protested to Allegheny, which confirms their story. Allegheny apologized, and says that Ransome Airlines, which operated the flight under contract, has changed its policies to prevent a repeat of the incident. But the Howards figure their problems are far from over. They say the airline incident was typical of the "common discrimination—a normal thing" that society practices almost routinely against the blind.

But nowadays, blind people like the Howards are moving with increasing fervor to protest such discrimination. They are voicing complaints, turning to the courts and even staging strikes and demonstrations. As a result, employers, landlords and businesses generally are finding they must either change their policies or face protests and lawsuits.

"A Dash of Leprosy"

"Society will give charity to the blind, but it won't allow us to be first-class citizens," charges Ralph W. Sanders, president of the Arkansas unit of the National Federation of the Blind. "Like the blacks, we've come to the point where we're not going to stand for it anymore," he adds.

Ironically, this militancy occurs at a time when conditions for the blind are improving significantly, particularly in the realm of jobs. Several states in recent years have approved broad

What's News—

* * *

Business and Finance

OIL'S EXPORT PRICE was cut by Ecuador in what may be the first major crack in the oil cartel's pricing structure. Ecuador's cut was through a reduction in the income-tax rate charged oil companies.

(Story on Page 3)

* * *

A tax on most crude oil and refined petroleum products of up to three cents a barrel was proposed, as expected, by President Ford to help pay for damages caused by oil spills.

(Story on Page 3)

* * *

A Honduran commission urged steps to nationalize the concessions and property of units of United Brands and Castle & Cooke to increase that country's participation in the banana-export business.

(Story on Page 2)

* * *

Developing nations' efforts to negotiate new international agreements fixing commodities prices will be resisted by the U.S., a top Treasury official said.

(Story on Page 2)

* * *

General Motors is being countersued by a former dealer for $33 million in connection with a tangled series of criminal and civil cases involving alleged warranty fraud. Separately, GM said its supplemental benefit fund for laid-off employes could soon resume payouts for a brief period.

(Stories on Page 4)

* * *

Ford Motor confirmed that it quietly paid for repairing about 69,000 rust-damaged 1969-73 models even though normal warranties had expired.

(Story on Page 4)

* * *

Great Atlantic & Pacific Tea reported a $6.5 million loss, less than predicted, for its May 24 first quarter; a year earlier it earned $10.3 million.

(Story on Page 4)

* * *

International Paper's second quarter earnings slid 37% to $47.2

World-Wide

A MIDEAST AGREEMENT isn't "anywhere near," Kissinger said.

The Secretary of State, beginning a European trip during which he will meet with Israeli Prime Minister Rabin, said reports that an Egyptian-Israeli accord had been all but wrapped up are "totally wrong." Hearst Newspapers quoted Egyptian President Sadat as indicating that basic terms of a new interim Sinai agreement had been worked out. But Prime Minister Rabin said some key issues remain to be settled.

Sources suggested that an agreement would involve an electronic surveillance system, operated by the U.S., to warn of any attack through the Gidi and Mitla mountain passes in the Sinai.
Rabin conferred with West German Chancellor Schmidt in Bonn, who urged the Israeli premier to take advantage of the current chance for a settlement with Egypt. Kissinger arrived in Paris and will meet with Soviet Foreign Minister Gromyko in Geneva before seeing Rabin Saturday in Bonn.

The Palestine Liberation Organization said in Beirut that it had failed to win the release of an American Army colonel kidnapped last week. It said the colonel was being held by two radical Palestinian groups that don't belong to the PLO. The deadline the abductors set for the U.S. to meet their ransom demands passed.

* * *

A TURKISH-ARMS COMPROMISE was offered to the House by Ford.

After meeting with 140 House members, the President proposed legislation partially lifting the ban on military aid that was imposed after Turkey used U.S. weapons in invading Cyprus. Under the plan, undelivered arms already paid for by Turkey would be shipped and more weapons could be bought for cash, but Turkey wouldn't be eligible for grants. Ford would report to Congress every two months on arms sales and on the chances for a Cyprus settlement.

The three leading House opponents of arms for Turkey weren't invited to the meeting with Ford. One of them, Rep. John Brademas (D., Ind.), denounced the proposal as a fraud.
Speaker Carl Albert predicted the House would approve Ford's plan. The Senate last month voted 41-40 to end the arms embargo. Turkey has demanded that negotiations on the status of U.S. bases begin next Thursday if the embargo hasn't been lifted by then. It wasn't known whether Turkey would accept Ford's compromise.

* * *

PORTUGAL'S ARMED FORCES will form local units bypassing political parties.

The writing was relatively painless, he recalls. "A well-reported story—one reported logically with a central theme in mind—tends to write itself." He began with the Howards in a delayed lead and presented the theme in his own words in the fifth paragraph, then in Sanders' words in the sixth paragraph.

The next two paragraphs were perspective, background. Originally, he had the blind professor's quote lower in the story, but he remembered the guideline that good quotes should be put up high in a story and he raised the quote as high as he could.

"While writing, I realized I needed to do more reporting. For instance, in writing about the blind seeking jobs I decided to add a paragraph putting credibility into the claims of the blind that they can handle jobs, which is hard for most sighted people to believe. So I called back a source and got some more information."

Then the story moved to the copy desk. "An editor sharpened some of my transitions and, as editors often do, axed several paragraphs to make the story shorter. He also asked me some questions that enabled him to improve the background paragraphs. A good editor is helpful since a reporter can become so close to a story that he doesn't see ways to simplify it."

Tannenbaum's story is known as an enterpriser—it originated with the reporter. From the outset, he had an idea of the theme. He was able to line up his sources, persons who would illustrate through their experiences the two parts of his theme—militancy and discrimination. Authoritative sources were used to give some overall perspective to the theme—the college professor, a state insurance commissioner, lawyers.

Because Tannenbaum's story did not have the immediacy of breaking news, he was able to spend some time on it. Such stories can be run at any time and are known as time copy. Our fourth story is also time copy.

Does Johnny Read?

The reporter, Mullins, is told by his city editor to find out whether people are reading as much as they used to—a vague assignment, but Mullins thinks he knows what his editor has in mind. The editor has talked so often about television and the "deficiencies of the young" that Mullins gathers he wants to know if youngsters can read as well as they used to. The reading scores in local schools have been steadily declining in recent years, and the editor has played up those stories.

"If you find out anyone is still reading, tell us what he's reading," is the editor's parting comment as Mullins leaves. He visits bookstores and talks to clerks, and he chats with librarians.

Trend Stories. Mullins' story was based on his editor's sense of a national trend or situation. Good local stories often are developed from trends at a regional, state, even international, level. A large amount of reference material is available on almost any topic a reporter looks into for a trend story.

Editor & Publisher and *The Washington Journalism Review* regularly list trade organizations that make information available to the press. Governmental agencies such as the Department of Commerce have considerable information available to the public.

When a reporter noticed in a wire service story that the number of poor had increased from 29 million in 1980 to 35 million in 1983, he decided to do a local folo. Income figures for his state were obtained from the Department of Commerce's State and Metropolitan Area Data Book, and to check on Social Security payments to the elderly he consulted the annual supplement to the Social Security Bulletin. Census data for his city further refined the material. For general background, he checked what others had written through the Reader's Guide to Periodical Literature.

In one library, he notices some youngsters chatting at a table near the window. Unobtrusively, he moves over to listen.

"What did you find out about the clipper ships?" one of the boys asks another. A few minutes later, a girl asks the boy next to her if he knows when the first transcontinental railroad was completed. Apparently they are doing research for an assignment on transportation. Mullins asks one of the boys, and he is told the work is for an honors history class in one of the local high schools. That is worth noting, Mullins decides.

As he passes three boys, he glances at the books they are reading—Jack Kerouac's *On the Road,* Hermann Hesse's *Demian,* and a book that appears to be about race car driving, judging by its title. That, too, goes into Mullins's notes. Suddenly, it strikes him that this is just what he needs to be doing, that he has been relying too heavily on human sources and not enough on his own observations. He knows that sources often will tell reporters what will make them or their organizations look good, and yet he has been relying on interested sources—librarians and bookstore owners and their clerks—instead of physical sources.

He decides to make his observations the basis of the story.

Mullins strolls around the library. As he passes one shelf, he observes that most of the books, which bear numbers ranging from 200 to 300 on their spines, are hardly used but that a few are well worn. The well-read books are on eastern religions. He jots down their titles, and he makes a note to look into that by talking to the librarian. She might have some of the titles of books that have been borrowed frequently.

The physical evidence seems to show that youngsters on school assignments are major library users as are older people with time on their hands. The older readers congregate around the newspaper rack, and much of their borrowing and reading is among the historical romances, adventure novels and mysteries. Considerable activity by all age groups focuses on the how-to books that offer instruction on investments, gardening, home repair and sex.

As a result of these observations, Mullins is able to supplement what he has been told by the people he had interviewed. His story is a blend of physical and human sources, the one supplementing the other. By adding his observations of the people in the library, he is able to inject human interest into his story. He *shows* his readers the students and adults using books, newspapers and magazines. He uses titles of books, names of readers.

To summarize the work of the reporters we have been watching, we can make these generalizations:

- Use direct observation whenever it is possible.
- When it is necessary to rely on second-hand accounts, use high-quality published sources, records and documents and the most knowledgeable and authoritative human sources available.
- Stay with the central character(s) or source(s) of the event you are covering—the speaker, the performer, the witness, the official.
- Line up ahead of time, or have in mind, human sources who can provide official or authoritative versions: police, fire chief or marshal, press secretary, spokesmen, authorities in the field. Stay close to them. But remember: The official version is not always the correct one.
- Use insiders whose information will serve as a check on official accounts.
- Know the limitations of human and physical sources.

Further Reading

Downie, Leonard J. V. *The New Muckrakers*. Washington, D.C.: New Republic Book Co., 1976.

Sigal, Leon V. *Reporters and Officials*. Lexington, Mass.: D.C. Heath, 1973.

CHAPTER THIRTEEN

Making Sound Observations

Preview

To make the reliable and relevant observations that are essential to the news story, the reporter must:

• Know what readers and listeners are interested in and what they need to know.
• Find a theme for the story as early in the reporting as possible.
• Look for the dramatic, the unusual, the unique aspect of the event that sets it apart from other events like it.

Reporters face limitations to their fact gathering. Time is always too short; it is not always easy to find good physical vantage points to see the event; failing to devise a workable theme, reporters chase events to dead ends. Sometimes, the information they obtain seems too incredible for belief and they miss a significant story.

In addition to the standard methods of reporting, journalists use unobtrusive observation (the identity of the reporter is unknown to those being observed) and participant observation (the reporter becomes part of the event being reported).

The Congo was torn by civil war. Because the war had serious international implications, the United Nations dispatched a peacekeeping force and sent Secretary-General Dag Hammarskjold to the African republic to try to arrange a cease-fire.

At dusk, reporters at the Ndola airport in Northern Rhodesia awaiting Hammarskjold's arrival saw a plane land and a fair-haired man emerge. The reporters, who had been held behind police lines a hundred yards away, ran to file bulletins on the secretary-general's arrival. Anticipating Hammarskjold's next move, the press associations soon had stories describing Hammarskjold's conferring with President Moise Tshombe about a cease-fire. Many of these stories ran in early editions of the next day's newspapers.

But the man the reporters saw disembark was not Hammarskjold. He was a British foreign affairs official on a fact-gathering tour. At the time the reporters were filing their stories, Hammarskjold was aboard another plane that was to crash in a forest 10 miles north of Ndola, killing the secretary-general and the others on board. It took eight hours for the UPI to correct its erroneous story and four more hours for the AP.

How did it happen? The UPI reporter told his boss later, "I saw a man I thought looked like Hammarskjold. Other reporters claimed they were sure it was. After comparing notes, we all agreed to file stories."

The incident, which occurred in 1961, reveals some of the problems reporters face in covering spot news stories. One is obvious. To make sound observations, the reporter has to see and hear the event clearly. In this case, the reporters did what reporters do when their observations are uncertain and they are under pressure.

Because the man was light-haired and his build approximated that of the secretary-general, the reporters jumped to the conclusion that he was Hammarskjold. This violated the reporter's maxim, "Beware of inferences. Do not jump from the known to the unknown."

To guard against individual error, they checked with each other and formed a consensus. The result, as we have seen, was an egregious blunder, a classic of journalistic incompetence.

The difficulty in covering events often causes journalists to consult each other for reassurance, and this leads to what is known as herd or pack journalism. Reporters tend to chat about the lead, the credibility of the source, the reliability of the documentation they have been offered. They seek agreement in resolving the uncertainties. Should anything go wrong, the reporter can always point to his colleagues' reporting.

The life of the loner is difficult, even when his or her copy is accurate and revealing. The editor may query the reporter, asking why his copy is so different from that of other reporters. Editors find security in unanimity.

Although the loner may be doing the job well, he or she may grow weary of the call-backs and decide to join the pack. There is group pressure against the reporter who does not go along. Because no reporter can be everywhere, everyone is expected to lend a hand at filling in his or her colleagues. Also, no reporter wants to be beaten by an enterprising competitor. The line between herd journalism and legitimate cooperation is difficult to draw, but most reporters usually will share routine stories and keep enterprisers and exclusives to themselves.

Making sound observations—more difficult than it seems—begins with an understanding of how the reporter works, the methods he or she uses in searching out relevant information for the task of truth-telling.

"Seeing as a Whole"

In his short story "The Murders in the Rue Morgue," Edgar Allen Poe has his character C. Auguste Dupin expound on the art of observation as he goes about solving the grisly murders of Madame L'Espanaye and her daughter, which have stumped the Parisian police. He dismisses the way the police work:

"There is no method in their proceedings, beyond the method of the moment. . . . The results obtained by them are not unfrequently surprising, but, for the most part are brought about by simple diligence and activity. When these qualities are unavailing, their schemes fail."

Although hard work is essential to good reporting, lots of footwork is not enough. A method is essential. Dupin says that the detective makes "a host of observations and inferences. So, perhaps, do his companions; and the difference in the extent of the information obtained, lies not so much in the validity of the inference as in the quality of the observation. The necessary knowledge is of *what* to observe."

In other words, the vacuum-cleaner collector of information wastes time. Dupin says the proper method is to follow "deviations from the plane of the ordinary." This is how "reason feels its way, if at all, in its search for the true. In investigations such as we are now pursuing, it should not be so much asked 'what has occurred,' as 'what has occurred that has never occurred before.' "

Dupin talks of seeing the "matter as a whole." This, too, is excellent advice for the journalist, for the reporter is like the detective. Every assignment is a mystery to be unraveled. To observe, to analyze; to synthesize, to pattern the observations—to do this the journalist must have a method, and the method begins with seeing the matter as a whole as quickly as possible. This gives the reporter an idea of what to look for, what to observe. Dupin talks of "educated thought." We will examine the way to such thinking.

Relevant Observations

The reporter on assignment is confronted by a flood of facts. A meeting can last two hours, cover seven different topics and include four decisions. A speaker may deliver an address containing 4,500 words. To handle these stories, the reporter may have at most a column for each story, about 750 words, or 90 seconds on a newscast.

There are three major guidelines to selecting relevant facts:

1. *Know the community:* Develop a feeling and understanding of what readers need and want to know.

2. *Find the theme:* Carefully identify the theme of the story so that facts that support, buttress and amplify the theme can be gathered.

3. *Look for the drama:* Develop a sensitivity to the unique, the unusual, the break from the normal and routine.

We saw in Chapter 2 that facts that are relevant to readers in one section of the country may be unimportant to readers in another area and that the story that fascinates some readers may bore others. The reporter must know what interests his readers or viewers. This news sense is part intuition, part common sense and part knowledge acquired from living and working in the community.

Know the Community

Reporters who move from one area to another often have trouble adjusting to their new readers and listeners. The story is told about the veteran reporter for a Chicago newspaper who decided to forsake the big city for a more relaxed life in Texas. He accepted a job as the city editor of a west Texas daily newspaper. One day a fire broke out in town and the reporter's blood stirred in the city editor. He decided to go out on the story himself.

On his return, he battled out a story, Chicago style—dramatic and well-written. The managing editor was pleased with his city editor's handiwork, but for one hole in the story.

"How much water did they use to put out the fire?" he asked. In parched west Texas, that fact was as important to readers as the number of fire units answering the call would have been to Chicago readers.

Our second guideline is based upon the form of the news story, which places certain demands on the reporter that he must satisfy in his fact gathering. We know that the story consists of the statement of a central theme or idea (the lead) and the elaboration of that theme or idea (the body). The reporter must find the theme quickly so he or she can ask the relevant questions and make the appropriate observations—a time-consuming task.

Find the Theme

When the Salvation Army dispatched 4,000 of its soldiers to New York City to do battle against "sin and evil," a reporter for *The New York Times* accompanied some of the troops through the streets. Impressed by the work of the Army men and women, the reporter decided to emphasize their dedication and singled out this detail in her account to illustrate her theme:

"The Army believes in total abstinence," a young soldier was saying to a disheveled-looking man, whose breath reeked of alcohol. "You are the temple of the Lord and if you destroy yourself, you're destroying Him."

"Am I?" the older man asked, as they stood in front of the entranceway of the Commodore. "No, I'm not."

"Sure you are," the soldier replied, resting his hand on the man's shoulder. The man reached out his hand, too, and began to cry. So did the Salvation Army soldier.

This approach—confining observations to the theme—is not unique to journalism. All writing that is intended to communicate information is written with the theme clearly in mind. Irrelevant details are gravestones marking dead writing, despite the apparent liveliness given by the flood of detail.

When the theme is determined, the reporter focuses on observations relevant to that theme. This does not mean that facts contrary to the theme are discarded. If the reporter discovers facts that contradict the basic idea, then the idea is discarded and a new theme is adopted. In this way, the reporter is like the scientist whose conclusion can be no stronger than his or her evidence.

Of course, some events will have secondary themes. The same rule about gathering only material that buttresses the theme applies to the secondary ideas.

Devising Themes

Experienced reporters almost always have a theme or tentative idea of the story as soon as they receive an assignment or at the outset of a story they enterprise. If a reporter is sent to cover a fire in a college dormitory, the reporter immediately thinks of deaths and injuries and the cause as the theme or possible lead. If the assignment is about the rescue of a drowning man, the lead could be the courage or ingenuity of the rescuer. Six youngsters die in an automobile accident; the reporter cannot help but immediately think of alcohol and drugs or speeding.

These themes or ideas tell the reporter "what to observe," to use Poe's language. They guide the reporter in asking questions, in doing background checks. In short, they allow the reporter to structure the reporting.

The theme or idea is also fairly broad. It is the idea that instinctively comes to a reporter's mind when given an assignment. It throws a broad shaft of light on the subject. But reporters want to focus in on their stories. They need the pencil-light penetration of the subject in order to find, again in Poe's words, "the deviations from the plane of the ordinary," which is actually one of our definitions of news. (In Chapter 3 we defined news as "a break from the normal flow of events, an interruption in the expected.") It is also our third guide to making relevant observations.

The reporter can spot these deviations, these interruptions in the expected by knowing a lot and by keeping his or her mind in a state of alertness. The ordinary event fits into what our experience and knowledge tells us is routine. The extraordinary shouts out for attention. As Poe put it, "To observe attentively is to remember distinctly." Alertness means a readiness, an openness, a reaching out for the significant, the novel. It means making use of what the reporter sees and hears, and what he or she tastes, smells and feels.

Look for the Drama

Learning to distinguish the break from everyday routine seems simple. But to the reporter covering his tenth fire, his thirty-third ball game and his third board of education meeting this month, events seem to settle into a familiar pattern. Spotting the differences between this fire, this game, this meeting and the others is difficult. After all, most people cannot differentiate the Delicious from the Jonathan, the Jersey from the Holstein. To them, all apples are alike and all cows are just cows.

Science in the Newsroom. O. K. Bovard, the great editor of Pulitzer's *St. Louis Post-Dispatch*, was said to take a scientific approach to news. He would advance a theory or hypothesis on the basis of a bit of information and then prove or disprove it. He said he and his staff used the approach "all day long in this room. The imaginative reporter does it when he refuses to accept the perfunctory police view of the mystery and sets himself to reason out all the possible explanations of the case and then adopts a theory for investigating the most likely one."

Mourner. The sting of defeat bites deeply. The story may be as much the personal saga as the score. Photo by Greg Lovett.

The reporter has to learn to look at the world through the eyes of the child, who views everything as new and different. At the same time he applies to the world the discerning eye of the wise elder, who can differentiate the significant from the meaningless, the dramatic from the routine. The reporter is ever alert, always ready to use his or her experience.

Red Smith, a sportswriter who covered so many baseball games he lost count, explained the basis of his artistry: "Every ball game is different from every other ball game—if the reporter has the knowledge and wit to discern the difference."

When Gustave Flaubert, the French novelist, was teaching Guy de Maupassant to write he told the young man to pick out one of the cab drivers in front of a railway station in Paris and to describe him in a way that would differentiate him from all the other drivers. To do so, Maupassant had to find the significant details that would single out that one man.

Individuality

Experienced reporters usually agree on the theme of the stories they cover. Beyond that, each reporter puts his or her individual stamp on the story. Some of that individuality comes from writing style. Much is based on the particular observations the reporter makes. What is relevant to one reporter may be irrelevant to another.

When Homer Bigart, the winner of two Pulitzer Prizes and one of the country's great reporters, was sent to cover the military trial of Lt. Willam Calley, who had been accused of murdering civilians in the My Lai massacre during the Vietman War, Bigart observed how Calley was brought into court. He placed this observation against his observations at another army officer's trial and he wrote:

> Although he had just been found guilty of twenty-two murders, Calley was treated far more gently than was Army doctor Captain Howard B. Levy four years ago after receiving a sentence for refusing to give medical training to Green Berets on the grounds that the training would be used unlawfully in Vietnam.
>
> Unlike Levy, Calley was not handcuffed and left the court unfettered. An officer explained: "His conduct has been exemplary throughout and he'll continue to be treated as an officer."

Bigart's editors at *The New York Times* apparently considered his references to the Levy trial to be irrelevant, for the section read simply:

> Lieutenant Calley was not handcuffed when driven to the stockade.

Whose judgment was better, Bigart's or his editors? Bigart's reference to the Levy trial provides the reader with some idea of the intense feeling of the military against the peace movement—of which Levy was a symbol—and its consideration for the accused murderer of civilians, a career army man.

Accurate Observations

The reporter sent to a nearby city to cover the debut of a local singer is seated in the orchestra among the staid patrons of the opera. He hears only polite applause after the singer's first major aria as Florestan. If he had been seated high in the opera house he would have heard the vigorous applause of the younger opera goers and the knowledgeable standees. What, then, is the audience reaction?

The lesson: When in doubt, move about. Find a variety of perspectives, if possible and if it makes sense for the story. On breaking news stories, vantage point is often out of the reporter's control. In organized events, like the opera, the reporter can control his location.

Wrong Turn

A reporter decided to visit the site of the World War II reception center where he had been inducted 40 years before, which was now being used by a national research laboratory. In his story in *The New York Times,* the reporter described the "barracks-like buildings with no windows" and "locked gates" that reminded him of his feelings as a young soldier.

A laboratory employee, puzzled by the description that bore no relationship to the laboratory, followed the reporter's route as outlined in the story. The reporter, it turned out, had made a wrong turn off the parkway and had driven to the back entrance to a racetrack. The "barracks-like buildings with no windows" were stables.

In moving about, reporters sometimes must shoulder their way to the front of the crowd. A reporter for a college newspaper was unable to find a seat near the front of the lecture she was assigned to cover and took a place in the back of the room. The lecture was on political satire, and the speaker seemed to be explicit in his summary. The reporter wrote this lead:

> "Political satire of today stinks,"
> Dennis Quinn, assistant professor of
> English, said at yesterday's Poetry Hour.

A few days later, the newspaper received a letter from Professor Quinn. With some restraint, he wrote that he had actually said, "Political satire is practically extinct." The *University Daily Kansan* printed his letter, and despite the reporter's embarrassment she stayed in journalism and went on to do distinguished work as an AP correspondent in Vietnam and elsewhere.

The incident also illustrates the necessity of checking—when possible—unusual quotations with the source and others who heard them if the reporter is unsure of what has been said. No source should be permitted to back down from a strong statement, but sometimes reporters cannot hear well and need to verify what they think they have heard.

When a fact is so unusual, a story so implausible, the reporter should pause.

Editors attending a luncheon at a convention of the American Society of Newspaper Editors were astonished when they saw Fidel Castro, the guest of honor, reach across the table and swap plates with the president of the Society.

Had one of them acted on that astonishment at the 1961 banquet and done what reporters are supposed to do—ask why—the editor might have been informed that Castro feared assassination. And had the editor not laughed

Swimming Mice. The *Asbury Park Press* reported sewage effluent was being tested by placing "mice and shrimp" in the liquid for four days; if half survive, the effluent is considered harmless.

No, no, the source of the story moaned when he saw the article in the New Jersey newspaper. "I said 'mysid shrimp,'" he told the managing editor.

Facts That Need Investigating

that off but checked into Castro's assertion, that editor might have changed history. For in 1975, the Central Intelligence Agency admitted that during the administrations of presidents Eisenhower, Kennedy and Johnson the United States government had indeed tried to murder Castro.

A book by Deborah E. Lipstadt, a historian at the University of California at Los Angeles, maintains that many newspapers refused to publish reports of the Nazi Final Solution because the reports of death squads and gas chambers were "beyond belief." (See "Further Reading" at end of chapter.) If the newspapers and radio had been less skeptical of the reports of refugees, she writes, they might have had an accurate description of Hitler's rise to power and his policies. Even when faced with government reports of Nazi atrocities, the press maintained a "persistent incredulity," says the author. The accounts of eyewitnesses seemed too horrifying to be believed.

Lipstadt holds the press "ultimately as culpable as the Government" for failing to report on the Holocaust. She does recognize a few journalists, among them Edward R. Murrow, who did spot the dangers of Hitler early and were inclined to believe what happened later.

The Holocaust, the Castro incident, the Watergate burglary point to an unseen dimension of reporting. Although the reporter is guided by logic, he must be open to the most implausible facts and observations. Time after time reporters find aberrant facts and extraordinary observations and put them aside as too unusual for further examination. No observation should be dismissed—no matter how outlandish it seems—without at least a quick check.

Incredible. No one could believe it, and so the story was ignored by journalists—except for Arthur Howe of *The Philadelphia Inquirer.* Howe found the IRS had mishandled one of every three tax returns in 1985 at a cost of $300 million.

In Atlanta, a worker flushed returns down a toilet. In Memphis, complicated returns were destroyed. Despite IRS denials, the story was true. Howe won the 1986 Pulitzer Prize for national reporting for the stories.

Limitations of the Story

Although we may agree that the reporter's task is to continue the search for relevant facts until the theme is adequately supported, we also must admit that the search can never be completed, that there are facts beyond the reporter's reach. Just as a map can never be the complete guide to a territory, so a news story is rarely the definitive statement of reality.

Here are some of the obstacles reporters face:

- The source the reporter could not locate.
- The record, document or newspaper clipping that was missing.
- The incident the reporter could not see or hear properly.
- The facts the source would not divulge.
- The material the copy editor cut out of the story.
- The reporter's own limitations.
- The book or magazine the reporter failed to read. Yesterday's newspaper left unread beyond page one.

Reporter's Equation.
Truth = Story + X.

X represents the obstacles the reporter can never completely overcome.

Add to this formidable list the reporter's slavery to the tyrant of time. The clock is the journalist's major obstacle to truth-telling. Unlike the historian or the sociologist, who face few daily or weekly deadlines in their work, the journalist submits to the requirements of publication and air time while still seeking to present a complete account.

Although the journalist tends to give the public a sense of truth in his or her accounts, limited observations permitted by the allotted time result in only an approximation of the event. This is one reason reporters often look back at stories they have written. They want to see whether they should give the story another go, to tidy up loose ends and to present facts they did not have when the story was written.

Complex events require the time to find relationships that link seemingly disparate events. The reporter may find that the newspaper or station will not provide time. Discouraged, the reporter sometimes settles for a rudimentary form of truth, the recital of what sources declare (Layer I journalism), which is truth of a sort.

The journalistic style also may obstruct truth. The journalist is required to tell a story in simple, dramatic, personalized prose. Some important events are prosaic, some abstract. The reporter who seeks to make these events—usually ideas, trends, concepts—come alive may distort them by using too many exciting details that are colorful but irrelevant or misleading. For years, the news magazines specialized in this kind of detail. Their correspondents sent in the name of the wine the diplomat drank, how many cigarettes he smoked during a tense hearing. The significance of the event often was lost in the human-interest trivia.

Go With What You've Got. Asked about the many predictions and assertions in the Evans and Novak newspaper column that were wrong, Rowland Evans said:

"I think every reporter who's got a reputation for decency and honesty has every right to print this as a probable thing. You might ask, 'Why didn't you check it out at State, the CIA, DIA, people in Moscow, Britain and France?' That's a valid question. The answer is, you can't—you don't have time. By the time you checked it all out, the idea would be dead and buried."

The Reporter as Intruder

The act of reporting can itself be an impediment to accurate observations. Walter Lippmann characterized the journalist as a "fly on the wall," a detached observer whose presence does not affect the event being observed. But if reporting requires close-at-hand observation, scrupulous note-taking, photographs, or tape, how unobtrusive can the reporter be? The fly descends and buzzes around the event.

We know what happens when a television crew arrives at an event. Drones become animated. Reserved people begin to gesticulate. Reality is altered.

At a political rally in Central America, a reporter noted the calm, almost serene atmosphere. Even when a speaker released a dove from the center of the plaza, the crowd was hushed. Then the television and still photographers arrived, and the event suddenly took another shape. A few fists were shaken.

A Cuban flag was unfurled for the photographers, and revolutionary slogans were shouted into the recording equipment. When the photographers departed, the rally returned to its placid pace. In the next day's newspaper, accompanying the reporter's story of a quiet protest against United States policy, was a shot of what seemed to be a fist-shaking mob.

Even the reporter's pencil and paper can distort the event. Every reporter experiences the trying moment when, after chatting with a source to put him or her at ease, it is time to reach for a pencil and notepad. In an instant, the mood changes. The simple tools of the reporter's trade have spooked the source.

Unobtrusive Observation

This type of reaction can be avoided by non-reactive or unobtrusive observation, methods that have the merit of allowing the reporter to be a fly on the wall. Let us follow a reporter as he uses this reporting technique.

Among the dozens of reporters gathered in central California to attend a Republican state conference was a reporter who wanted to prove to his editor that he could handle politics. The newspaper's political reporter was assigned to the main political story. The reporter we are following was to do sidebars.

Unlike the other reporters at the convention, our man was unknown to the delegates. He was able to mix freely, smiling and shaking hands with delegates. He knew he was being mistaken for a young delegate, and when one of the central committee secretaries told him there was an important meeting, he went along with her. They walked into the meeting together, and he sat near her, apparently doodling absent-mindedly on a pad in front of him.

All day long he moved in and out of caucuses, meetings and powwows. He heard Orange County delegates denounce the president, a Republican, as a liberal, a spendthrift, an enemy of the party's conservative principles. He listened as deals were made to try to attract the labor and minority votes.

His story, played prominently on page one, was exclusive and other newspapers were forced to quote from it. Republican leaders were chagrined. Our young reporter was jubilant.

The week before when another political group—a national organization of right-wing partisans—held a convention, the reporter had plumped down in a soft chair in the lobby of the hotel and listened. He had heard delegates talk about bringing back the gold standard, the threat of communism from minorities, the radicalism of the labor movement and the dangers of sex education in the public schools.

Many reporters justify eavesdropping if the public interest is served by disclosure, particularly if the event involves public bodies and officials. A city council meeting surreptitiously held in a downtown hotel may be covered by a reporter hovering in a hall, ear to the door or eye to the keyhole. Public officials have no right to do public business in private, and the reporter is willing to risk appearing undignified—even unethical—if that is what he must do to dig out the news.

Reporters have hidden in closets, rented hotel rooms next to politicians, even used hidden tape recorders in order to dig out the news.

Some journalists condemn this kind of reporting. Their criticism stems   **Ethics Debated**
from their concern about widespread intrusions into privacy by insurance firms, credit investigators and the federal government, which has poked into people's lives through wiretaps and mail openings. What right, then, should the journalist have to do what it is his business to expose as a violation of privacy?

The journalist who uses unobtrusive observation, and more devious means of fact gathering, defends his prying into private as well as public affairs on the ground that the story—the search for truth—justifies the means if the story reveals wrongdoing or aids the public in decision making. As for a check on the prying journalist, he would have none but his conscience. "Let me use my judgment," he says. "I will not use material irresponsibly."

Opponents of the ends-justify-the-means argument contend that the reporter cannot adopt methods he condemns in others, that he cannot set himself apart from the rules that apply to others.

The concerned journalist seeking to do his or her job but confused by the conflicting opinions might find some guidance from a debate that occurred in the pages of *Society* magazine following the publication of an article, "Tearoom Trade: Impersonal Sex in Public Places," about homosexual activity in public men's rest rooms.

The author, Laud Humphreys, a sociologist, posed as a voyeur interested in homosexual activity. The homosexuals accepted him and stationed him outside the rest room as a "watchqueen," a lookout to warn of the police or other intruders.

"I played that part faithfully," he writes in the January 1970 issue. By peeking in the window, he was able to observe the activities of the men. When they left, he took down the numbers of their automobile license plates and learned their identities. A year later, he interviewed 50 of the 100 men of whom he had a record.

The Defense and the Criticism

Anticipating criticism of his method of observation, Humphreys defended his work on what he wrote were three ethical assumptions:

1. The social scientist should not avoid an area of research because it is difficult or socially sensitive.
2. He should "approach any aspect of human behavior with those means that least distort the observed phenomena."
3. He "must protect the respondents from harm."

Humpreys' second item is a restatement of Lippmann's fly-on-the-wall concept and a defense of unobtrusive observation. But the articles and their author's defense were shrugged aside by one of his critics, Nicholas von Hoffman, a columnist, who attacked the methods of observation as an invasion of privacy. As for the argument that the information served a good purpose, von Hoffman wrote, "Everybody who goes snooping around and spying can be said to have good motives. . . . No information is valuable enough to obtain by nipping away at personal liberty."

In reply, two editors of the magazine, Irving Louis Horowitz and Lee Rainwater, defended Humphreys on these grounds:

1. People have a right to "learn the truth" about themselves and each other.
2. The article served a "socially constructive purpose" in helping readers to understand deviant behavior and the activities of the police in this victimless crime.
3. Such research is consistent with the social scientist's "demystification of human life and culture."
4. The "tearooms" were public rest rooms on public land.

Balancing the right of privacy with the public's need to know, the editors cited information gathered by the Census Bureau, health and welfare departments and other agencies that collect information for the common good but intrude on privacy.

The link between the journalist's unobtrusive observation and Humphreys' methods is close. Journalists who use this technique may therefore want to ponder the objections to and the defense of the method. A guideline: For private activities, think twice; for official activities held in private, act in the public interest.

Journalistic ethics are discussed further in Chapter 27.

Workout with Fonda.
Reporter Mary Voboril of *The Miami Herald* asks actress Jane Fonda a wide range of questions while taking part in Fonda's exercise class. Photo by Bruce Gilbert.

Another research method—participant observation—also links social science and journalism strategies. An Oregon reporter who managed to fold his six-foot frame into a third grader's seat at school was a participant observer. The reporter who worked as a telephone operator and then wrote a series of articles based on her observations was basing her stories on personal experience. At the simplest level, a reporter can spend a day with a meter reader, a public health nurse. Mary Voboril of *The Miami Herald* took an exercise class with actress Jane Fonda.

In participant observation—the opposite of unobtrusive observation—the reporter discards his or her role as the uninvolved, detached observer and joins the activity of the person or group he or she is covering. The newspaperman who became a third grader for a story participated in the children's school work, ate lunch with them and played ball at recess. The school children took him for a friend, a bit older and awkward about some things, but a companion nevertheless. They talked to him as an equal. His relationship with the students enabled him to gather material that the usual interview and observation techniques would not have revealed.

Participant Observation

William Foote Whyte, in his classic study of an Italian-American slum, *Street Corner Society,* (Chicago: The University of Chicago Press, 1943), talks about the difference between the traditional perception of what is news and the reality of the way people live, which particpant observation allows the reporter to view:

> If the politician is indicted for accepting graft, that is news. If he goes about doing the usual personal favors for his constituents, that is not news. The newspaper concentrates on the crisis—the spectacular event. In a crisis the 'big shot' becomes public property. He is removed from the society in which he functions and he is judged by standards different from his own group. This may be the most effective way to prosecute the lawbreaker. It is not a good way to understand him. For that purpose, the individual must be put back into his social setting and observed in his daily activities. In order to understand the spectacular event, it is necessary to see it in relation to the everyday pattern of life. . . .

Whyte learned how to be accepted by the street corner people. "If you ask direct questions, people will just clam up on you," he writes. "If people accept you, you can just hang around, and you'll learn the answers in the long run without even having to ask the questions."

When Whyte used some obscenities to try to gain acceptance, one of his new friends advised him, "Bill, you're not supposed to talk like that. That doesn't sound like you." Whyte had to be careful about influencing the group he was observing. "I tried to be helpful in the way a friend is expected to be helpful." The results of his observations allowed the reader to have a moving picture of the street corner society, not the still photograph that the brief glimpse allows.

The Live-In

Journalism students at Columbia University do participant observation in an assignment known as the Live-In, which sends students into homes and workplaces. To move closer to their sources, students have tutored addicts in drug rehabilitation centers and children in schools. They have slept on the floors of mission houses in the Bowery, in sleeping bags at a residence of the Catholic Workers and on cots in emergency shelters.

Students have walked the beat with police officers, gone on home visits with social workers and accompanied ambulance drivers on their calls. These experiences were not one-shot affairs. They met the policeman's family, talked to the welfare mother's children and went into wards to talk to patients.

Charles Young, a white, middle-class student from Wisconsin, did his Live-In in a junior high school in West Harlem in New York City. Young is waiting for the assistant principal in his office. The room is filled with students. Young describes the scene at the beginning of his Live-In:

Gus Marinos, known simply as "Marinos" to everybody, a Greek immigrant in his twenties with dazed but kindly eyes beneath his Coke-bottle glasses, returns to his office on the fourth floor. The room erupts with a deafening chorus of his name.

"MAH-*REE*-NOS! HER FINGERNAILS BE POISON!" a girl screams, holding up her scratched right hand.

"So die," says Marinos, examining some smudged papers on his desk.

"WHY 'ON'T CHEW DIE!"

"You wanna go home?"

"YEAH, BUT CHEW CAN'T TELL ME HER NAILS AIN'T POISON!"

"So go home."

"HER NAILS GOT DIRT AN' SHIT IN 'M!" The girl leaves with a pass home.

"MAH-*REE*-NOS!" another girl demands, "GIMME A PENCIL!" He hands her a pencil from his desk. "I 'ON'T WANT NO PENCIL LIKE THAT! I WANNA BLACK PENCIL!"

"This *is* a black pencil."

"I MEAN A YELLOW PENCIL THAT WRITES BLACK!"

"We don't sell those here."

"I 'ON'T WANT TO BUY NO PENCIL! I WANT CHEW TO GIMME IT!" She grabs the pencil from his hand and in the process drops a text book. "NOW SEE YOU MADE ME DONE DIRTY MY BOOK!"

"I made you done what?"

"DIRTY MY BOOK!" She leaves for class.

These girls read an average of two years below the national norm for their grade level (slightly ahead of the boys), but the ghetto has already taught them how to get what they want from life: yell until somebody gives it to you. The lesson is apt, because when they are graduated in three years or so, they won't be equipped to do anything anyway.

That these girls (all sent to the office for disciplinary reasons) want something is obvious. What they want is less obvious and increasingly important as the market for unskilled labor dries up.

The first step in finding out what they want is learning a new vocabulary, some of which would be useful to define here. To "come out your mouth" is to communicate. "On time" is an adjective or adverb of approbation meaning you have done something according to socially accepted procedure. "On cap" is synonymous with "in your head," referring to intelligence. . . .

Young interviewed the assistant principal in charge of discipline, who, he writes, "carries a cane in one hand and a leather whip in the other when she wades into a group of warring Dominican and Puerto Rican youths."

His description continues:

She resembles an army tank—solid, low-to-the-ground, unstoppable, paradoxically maternal.

She is in fact known as the mother of the school. Teachers speak with awe of the dedication that brings her to the otherwise deserted building on weekends and vacations. Students speak with equal awe of her omniscience. Because they trust her, she knows exactly who is pushing what drugs and who is fighting with whom.

Standing at the main entrance to the building at 3 o'clock one Friday afternoon in anticipation of a gang fight, Williams catalogues a gathering of a dozen or so Puerto Rican school alumni.

"That one is on parole now. . . . That one is pushing. Look at his station wagon. . . . That one has a sawed-off .38 in his pocket. We'd tell the police about it, but it will pass fifty hands by the time they can react. . . ."

On Thursday, one of their little brothers dropped a piece of chalk from the fourth floor that hit a Dominican on the head. In the ensuing melee, another Puerto Rican was badly cut on the arm with a broken bottle. The Puerto Ricans seek vengeance.

Having no stake in the matter, the blacks are blasé and leave the area immediately. They've seen it all before and even the prospect of serious violence is a bore. The Hispanics gather in groups along the sidewalk and buzz with rumors, with more energy than they have shown all day in class.

Williams crosses the street and puts her arm around one of her former students who has an Afro bigger than the rest of his body. She makes small talk for a couple of minutes, then kisses him on his pock-marked cheek as the gang scatters off down the street. A group of Dominicans, observing the enemy from a block away, disappears to its lair on 133rd Street.

The aborted fight is typical of junior highs anywhere in that the participants seem willing to do battle over nothing. What is frightening is that the involved alumni range in age from 16 to the mid-twenties. They never grew up, just became better armed. They are the fruit of the American system of education.

"Even five years ago they at least expressed an interest in college," says Williams back in the dormitory-room-sized office which she shares with three other school officials and usually seven or eight students who have been thrown out of class. . . .

Young befriended a bright young black student in the school. After Young graduated and went to work for *Rolling Stone,* he decided to look up the youngster for a story for the magazine about his dream of becoming a basketball star. He found the youth in high school, playing basketball, struggling with his classes, and still filled with hope. Young's piece, "Above 125th Street: Curtis Haynes' New York," begins:

I'M GROWIN' PLANTS ALL THE TIME," says Curtis Haynes, pouring half a glass of water over a geranium. The floor and window ledge of his bedroom are covered with leafy pots. "Plants are everything. They give us oxygen and food. They also a home for insects." He brushes an aphid off a leaf. "Insects gonna inherit the earth."

He continues the tour of his room—recently painted electric blue by his mother—by pulling a picture off a shelf full of basketball trophies. Judging by his fleeting eyes and reticent tone of voice, he doesn't know what to make of me—a pale, white, 26-year-old, bearded magazine editor with thick glasses from a myopic childhood of too much TV watching and book reading in Madison, Wisconsin. Nor do I know what to make of him—a handsome, ebony-skinned, 16-year-old, short-haired high-school student with sharp vision from a childhood spent on the basketball courts of Harlem. "This my brother, Footie," he says, holding a blurred photograph of a teenager bearing a strong resemblance to Curtis. "Remember, remember, remember. . ." is inscribed around the margins. "We named him that because he had such big feet," he says. Curtis' Pro Ked basketball shoes equal my own 11½ Adidas—and I am 6′ 2″ while he is just 5′ 10″. "He died in a fight two years ago. Puerto Rican friend got in an argument at a party and the other dude pulled a gun. My brother jumped between them. I never go to parties no more."

The concept of the Live-In is based on the work of anthropologists such as Margaret Mead and Oscar Lewis and the psychiatrist and author Robert Coles. They spent considerable time with the people they were observing. In describing the field work that went into her book *Coming of Age in Samoa,* Mead wrote:

> I concentrated on the girls of the community. I spent the greater part of my time with them. I studied most closely the households in which adolescent girls lived. I spent more time in the games of children than in the councils of their elders. Speaking their language, eating their food, sitting barefoot and cross-legged upon the pebbly floor, I did my best to minimize the differences between us and to learn to know and understand all the girls of three little villages on the coast of the little island of Tau, in the Manua Archipelago.

Concerned by the direction of journalism toward centers of authority, reporters realized that they were observing only one facet of life. A concentration on the formalities of life—its ceremonies, meetings, announcements—was not helping them describe the reality of human experience. They became anxious to develop techniques that enabled them to expand their reporting. Sarah Grimes, a reporter in Philadelphia, said after she had been covering the juvenile court for a year, "I wonder why so many reporters insist on quoting people in positions of power rather than observing people who are affected by power."

She listened closely to the young defendants in court, and she sought to understand the effect of the system on youngsters by talking to them. One day she learned that an 11-year-old boy—who was brought into court in handcuffs—had been held in a detention center for nine months although he had not committed a crime. He was a runaway. Grimes asked to talk to the youngster, who had been sent to foster homes after his parents were judged neglectful. He had not liked the foster homes and had run away. Here is part of the story she wrote:

"Jones, Jones," the guard's voice could be heard as he walked up and down the cell-block. Amid a few undistinguishable low grumblings behind the rows of bars came a small, high voice. "Yes, that's me."

Johnny was brought out to an ante-room. No longer crying, he sat with downcast eyes in dungarees and a gray sweatshirt. Quietly and slowly he answered questions.

He wished he had somebody to bring him soap because the institutional soap gives him a rash. He would like to leave YSC (Youth Study Center) and would go "any place they send me."

How does it feel to be handcuffed? In a barely audible voice, he answered: "It makes me feel like a criminal."

It is a natural step from this kind of reporting to participant observation, for the only way the reporter can understand some situations is to experience them. Without this personal experience, some reporters contend, the people they write about become cardboard figures.

These reporters who contend that journalism has not dug deeply enough into the lives of people would agree with Chekhov's observation in his short story "Gooseberries":

We see the people who go to market, eat by day, sleep by night, who babble nonsense, marry, grow old, good-naturedly drag their dead to the cemetery, but we do not see or hear those who suffer, and what is terrible in life goes on somewhere behind the scenes. Everything is peaceful and quiet and only mute statistics protest: so many people gone out of their minds, so many gallons of vodka drunk, so many children dead from malnutrition. And such a state of things is evidently necessary; obviously the happy man is at ease only because the unhappy ones bear their burdens in silence, and if there were not this silence, happiness would be impossible. It is a general hypnosis. Behind the door of every contented, happy man there ought to be someone standing with a little hammer and continually reminding him with a knock that there are unhappy people, that however happy he may be, life will sooner or later show him its claws, and trouble will come to him—illness, poverty, losses, and then no one will see or hear him, just as now he neither sees nor hears others. But there is no man with a hammer. The happy man lives at his ease, faintly flutterd by small daily cares, like an aspen in the wind—and all is well.

Some reporters see themselves as the man with the hammer.

Problems of Involvement

But participant observation also entails some problems. In addition to the possibility that the reporter's presence may affect the event, the participant observer can become too deeply involved with his or her sources, risking the possibility that feelings may precede responsiblity to the facts.

Participant observation has also been criticized as exploitation of the source. After all, the journalist is using the lives of people as the basis of a story, which, if it is good, will lead to the reporter's acclaim, help him win a pay raise and possibly a promotion. But the alcoholic, the addict, the welfare mother, the assembly-line worker and the police officer are not reimbursed for their contributions. They enhance the career of the reporter, and usually little is done about the problems that overwhelm some of these people.

The journalist James Agee agonized over prying into the lives of Southern sharecroppers and their families. He and the photographer Walker Evans were assigned to do an article on cotton tenantry, the system by which farmers worked the fields of landowners in return for a share of the crop less what is advanced to them for seed, living quarters and tools. The sharecroppers were poorer than dirt poor, for not even the earth they tilled was theirs. The magazine article was not published, but in 1940 the work became a book, *Let Us Now Praise Famous Men.* Agee knew the justifications for his intimate observations, but they did not console him. Early in the book, he describes his reservations:

> It seems to me curious, not to say obscene and thoroughly terrifying, that it could occur to an association of human beings drawn together through need and chance and for profit into a company, an organ of journalism, to pry intimately into the lives of an undefended and appallingly damaged group of human beings, an ignorant and helpless rural family, for the purpose of parading the nakedness, disadvantage and humiliation of these lives before another group of human beings, in the name of science, of "honest journalism" (whatever that paradox may mean), of humanity, of social fearlessness, for money, and for a reputation for crusading and for unbias which, when skillfully enough qualified, is exchangeable at any bank for money (and in politics, for votes, for job patronage, abelincolnism, etc.). . . .

In rebuttal to these criticisms, reporters who use the technique say that public awareness is increased by stories about the lives of people. They say this awareness can lead to reform by involving the public emotionally in the situations described by the reporter.

Also, participant observation can help correct the detachment that can lead to callousness. A student who said he considered drug addicts weak and worthless conducted a Live-In with a young female addict. The woman's daughter was being put up for adoption because her mother had been judged unfit to raise her. The woman's agony at the prospect of losing her daughter—which the student felt intensely—led him to do a series of revealing articles about the city's adoption laws.

The experience of participant observation allows the reporter to step outside routines and familiar environments to achieve new insights.

The methods that lead to better stories also help the reporter to avoid another trap—the tendency to stereotype. Stereotyping is a natural human process, all the more understandable in a reporter working under pressure. Stereotyping permits the journalist to simplify complex events and to communicate them to an audience in easily understood terms. Forgetting that life is endless variety and change, some reporters look at the world through a kaleidoscope that is never turned. As a consequence, their observations reflect only a narrow, static vision. We will examine these stereotypes and the feelings and ways of thinking that determine how reporters look at events in Chapter 16.

Further Reading

Agee, James. *Let Us Now Praise Famous Men.* Boston: Houghton-Mifflin, 1960.

Lipstadt, Deborah E. *The American Press and the Covering of the Holocaust, 1933–1945.* New York: The Free Press, 1985.

CHAPTER FOURTEEN

Interviewing Principles

Preview

There are two kinds of interviews:

• News interview—The purpose is to gather information that will explain an idea, event or situation in the news.

• Profile—The focus is on an individual. A news peg often is used to justify the profile.

For effective interviews of both types, reporters prepare carefully, and they ask questions that induce the source to talk freely. Questions are directed at obtaining information on a theme that the reporter has in mind before beginning the interview. If a more important theme emerges, the reporter develops it with questions related to the new theme.

The reporter notes what is said, how it is said and what is not said. If the source refuses to comment, the reporter can demand answers of sources who are public officials if the questions relate to their official activities. For other sources, an open-end question that induces the subject to chat may be used to lead up to the probing questions. Sources are encouraged to keep talking by the reporter's gestures and facial expressions.

In the stadium locker room, the half-dressed athlete was stuffing his warm-up suit and track shoes into a battered black bag. Seated on a bench nearby, a young man removed a pencil and a notepad from a jacket pocket.

"I'm from the paper in town," the young man said. "You looked sharp out there. Mind if I ask you some questions?"

The athlete nodded and continued his packing.

"First time you've been to this part of the West or this city?" the reporter asked. Another nod. This was not going to be easy, the reporter worried. The sports editor had told him to make sure he brought back a good story for tomorrow's paper, the day the National Association of Intercollegiate Athletics would begin its annual outdoor track meet at the local college. The tall, lithe young man standing in front of the bench was a world record holder in the hurdles, the editor had said, and worth a profile for the sports section.

The reporter tried again. "What do you think of our town?" The athlete seemed to see the reporter for the first time.

"I don't know anything about this town," he replied. "I'm here to run. I go to the East coast, the West coast, here. They give me a ticket at school and I get on a bus or a plane and go. My business is to run." He fell silent.

Rebuffed, the reporter struggled to start the athlete talking again. In the 20-minute interview, the hurdler never really opened up.

Back in the newsroom, the reporter told the sports editor about his difficulties. They seemed to begin with his first question about whether the athlete had been to the town before, he told his editor. His boss was not sympathetic.

"First, you should have checked the clips and called the college for information about your man," the editor said. "That way you could have learned something about him, his record or his school. That might have been used to break the ice. Or you could have asked him about the condition of the track, something he knows about."

Then the editor softened. He knew that interviewing is not easy for young reporters, that it can be perfected only through practice.

"I think you have a good quote there about the business of running," he told the reporter. "Did you get anything else about the places he's been? That could make an interesting focus for the piece."

Yes, the reporter said, he had managed to draw the hurdler out about where he had been in the last few months. With the editor's guidance, the reporter managed to turn out an acceptable piece.

This incident illustrates the four principles of interviewing. They are:

- Prepare carefully whenever possible.
- Establish a relationship with the source conducive to obtaining information.
- Ask questions that induce the source to talk.
- Listen and watch attentively.

Since much of the daily work of the journalist requires asking people for information, mastery of interviewing techniques is essential. The four principles underlie the various techniques the reporter uses. Clearly, the sports writer's troubles began when he failed to prepare by learning about the athlete he was to interview. Lacking background, the reporter was unable to ask questions that would draw out his source. Furthermore, he had failed to establish a rapport with the hurdler, so that the session was more like dentistry than journalism, with the reporter painfully extracting bits and pieces of information from an unwilling subject. Fortunately, the reporter had listened carefully so that he managed to salvage something from the interview.

If we analyze news stories we will see they are based on information from three kinds of sources: physical sources, such as records, files and references; the direct observations of the reporter; and interviews with human sources. Most stories are combinations of two or three of these sources.

News and Sports. Bryant Gumbel, a former sportscaster, is co-host on the NBC "Today" show, where he has proved himself a skilled interviewer, a talent he developed covering sports. He compared news and sports interviewing:

"There are more similarities than differences between news and sports coverage. In both cases the people who you're talking to want to give you the predictable locker room statements and talk about the 'team effort.' If you do your homework, and ask what you think are intelligent questions, then you get something more out of them."

If we had been able to watch a reporter sent to cover the governor's address at a party fund-raising dinner, we would have seen the reporter cover the speech (direct observation) and then question the speaker and some of the guests (interviews). Before and after the event, the reporter consulted clippings from the newspaper library (references) for additional material. Thus, the speech story contains material from the three kinds of sources.

The Interviewer's Ground Rules

Both parties in an interview have certain assumptions and expectations. Generally, the reporter expects the interviewee to tell the truth and to stand behind what he or she has told the interviewer. The interviewee presumes the reporter will write the story fairly and accurately. Both agree, without saying so, that the questions and answers mean what they appear to mean—that is, that there are no hidden meanings.

Having said this, we must admit to the exceptions. As we have pointed out, sources may conceal, evade, distort and lie when they believe it is to their advantage. The reporter must be alert to the signs that indicate a departure from truth.

The rules that govern the reporter's behavior in the interview can be detailed with some certainty. Reporters, too, conceal, mislead and, at times, lie. A few reporters justify these practices, but most would agree the reporter should:

1. Identify himself or herself at the outset of the interview.
2. State the purpose of the interview.
3. Make clear to those unaccustomed to being interviewed that the material will be used.
4. Give the source an idea of how much time the interview will take.
5. Keep the interview as short as possible.
6. Ask short, specific questions the source is competent to answer.
7. Give the source ample time to reply.
8. Ask the source to repeat or to clarify complex or vague answers.
9. Read back answers if requested or when in doubt about the phrasing of crucial material.
10. Insist on answers if the public has a right to know them.
11. Avoid lecturing the source, arguing or debating.
12. Abide by requests for non-attribution, background only or off the record should the source make this a condition of the interview or of a statement.

Reporters who habitually violate these rules risk losing their sources. Few sources will talk to an incompetent or an exploitative reporter. When the source realizes that he or she is being used to enhance the reporter's career or to further the reporter's personal ideas or philosophy, the source will close up.

Sources also risk trouble when they exploit the press. Reporters understand that their sources will float occasional trial balloons and give incomplete, even misleading, information. But constant and flagrant misuse of the press leads to retaliation by journalists.

Types of Interviews

The major story on page one of a September issue of *The Hawk Eye* in Burlington, Iowa, is about a three-alarm fire that destroyed a two-story building that housed an automobile sales agency and a body repair shop. The reporter interviewed several people for information to supplement his observations. Here are the people he interviewed and a summary of their comments:

- The owner—15 cars destroyed; exact loss as yet unknown.
- A fire department lieutenant—The building could not have been saved when firefighters arrived. They concentrated on saving the adjoining buildings.
- An eyewitness—"I didn't know what it was," the story quotes her as saying of the fire. "It just went all at once. I seen it a-burning and I was scared to death."
- The fire chief—The state fire marshal will investigate the cause of the fire.

Although the reporter was not present when firefighters battled the fire during the early morning hours, the interviews with the lieutenant and the eyewitness give his story an on-the-scene flavor. Since these interviews help to explain the news event, we describe them as news interviews.

Another locally written front page story also relies on a news interview. A head-on automobile crash on Iowa Route 2 near Farmington took the life of a Van Buren County woman and caused injuries to four others. Although no source is quoted, the story is based on information from a call to the Iowa Highway Patrol.

Next, let us look at another type of interview story, the profile or personality interview. Shortly after her graduation from journalism school, Mary Ann Giordano was assigned by *The Bergen Record* in New Jersey to interview a high school English teacher who had been involved in a dispute with his school administration over articles in the student newspaper of which he was the adviser. The *Record* had run news stories on the conflict. Giordano was to profile the teacher. (See story on next page.)

We have described the two types of interviews:

1. The news interview, which develops information about an idea or an event that is the focus of the story.

2. The profile or personality interview in which an individual is the focus of the story.

The strong and quiet voice

A teacher's story

By Mary Ann Giordano
Staff Writer

He is the most unlikely looking rebel. Graying and middle-aged, scholarly and low-key, James Williams Downs resembles a college librarian or a junior-college humanities professor whose motto might be, "Happiness is never making waves."

Profile

Actually, Downs has been in the middle of turmoil and controversy for two years at Pascack Valley High School in Hillsdale, where he teaches junior and senior English.

Last year, he became embroiled in a censorship dispute with the administration after he allowed the school newspapers to publish articles on teen-age pregnancies and growing marijuana.

It was a matter of principle to Downs, but it cost him his job as the paper's adviser, his two journalism classes, and his health. This year, he was one of 10 teachers cut down by the budgetary ax, but managed to save his spot, thanks to a tenure technicality.

Students and friends say Downs never really looks for the trouble, that he is simply a man of principle. "I don't believe in blind obedience," Downs agreed in his quiet but emphatic way. "There's things I like to express my mind about."

Not the type

His readiness to express himself was developed over the years as a Harvard undergraduate, a drill-press operator, a private-school headmaster. The experiences have led Downs to believe in not giving up, even if the stand leads to a lot of trouble.

But if there is a classic type of "troublemaker" or "controversial figure," the 52-year-old Downs seems not to fit.

As one former student described him, "he lacks dynamics. He's not vocal enough." A soft, Midwestern twang can still be detected in his even, steady voice, revealing his Indiana upbringing. But when he wants, his words are sharp and emphatic. He chops the air with his right hand to punctuate his meaning. And the honesty and ease of his expression sometimes border on the daring.

"Throughout life, it seems there. . . .

News Interview. New York City mayor Ed Koch's new policy on rebuilding the city's infrastructure (bridges, roads) is the subject of an interview by radio and newspaper reporters. Photo by Leslie Jean-Bart.

Rarely does a reporter cover an assignment without asking someone for information. A city clerk may be asked to verify an election result for a story about the next mayoral election, or a lawyer will be asked for background about a suit he has filed in the county courthouse. In the course of the day, a reporter may interview a dozen or more people for the stories on which he is working. Usually, these are quick question-and-answer sessions conducted over the telephone.

When a reporter talks about doing an interview, usually he is referring to a more extended session with one or more sources that will form the basis of a story. These long sessions can be news or personality interviews, depending upon the purpose of the piece.

The extended news interview can provide readers and listeners with interpretation, background and explanation. When Douglas Watson, a *Washington Post* reporter, was covering the extortion and tax evasion trial of a Baltimore County official, he heard the testimony of a stock manipulator who was a confessed white collar criminal and political fixer. Watson was told that the witness was being held by United States marshals in a special facility while testifying for the government. Watson learned there were several of these facilities—known as "safe houses"—and he decided to do a story about them. After the trial, he spent several hours talking to officials.

The News Interview

"In the interviews, I learned about other interesting and unreported aspects of the organization besides 'safe houses,'" Watson said. "One of the Service's activities is giving new identities to people who had been government witnesses. This enables them to start new lives in another part of the country."

Here is how Watson's story begins:

"Restricted Area—U.S. Govt. Training Center," says the sign on the barbed wire-topped fence surrounding a barracks at Ft. Holabird on the edge of Baltimore.

The sign doesn't say it, but the barracks is one of several "safe houses" that the U.S. Marshal's Service operates for the special care and feeding of very important prisoner-witnesses such as Watergate conspirator E. Howard Hunt, political saboteur Donald Segretti and stock manipulator Joel Kline.

Three to five "safe houses" have been in existence around the country for about a year, usually holding about 50, mostly white collar, "principals," as they like to call themselves. They are federal prisoners who usually were involved in organized crime and who are considered too valuable as government witnesses or too endangered by threats to be incarcerated in the usual prison. . . .

The news interview can emphasize an aspect of a continuing story that the reporter considers to have been overlooked or neglected. When the debate over nuclear weapons heated up, Jimmy Breslin of the *Daily News* interviewed I. I. Rabi, one of the nuclear physicists who built the first atomic bomb.

Breslin wondered if Americans weren't too casual about nuclear weapons. A master journalist, Breslin let Rabi speak:

"You're a Queens Catholic. Get on your knees and pray," Breslin quoted Rabi.

"Nuclear weapons are entirely beyond the people in our government today. It doesn't take much to know that."

Rabi recalled that during the 1980 Reagan-Carter debate Carter had talked about his daughter Amy's concern over nuclear weapons. "The newspapers said it was stupid," Rabi said. "I never did. It was the little girl who was going to be killed. . . .

"In Washington, they never think of what could happen to the American people. I'm sorry for the American people. . . . The government acts as if it were on drugs. A high. They talk about what they can do to Russia and they forget us. I pay our government to worry about me.

"Nations are now lined up like people before the ovens of Auschwitz, while we are trying to make the ovens more efficient."

Rabi is quoted extensively because he has something to say, and he says it well. Young reporters are often surprised at how eloquent the subjects of their interviews can be. Let them talk; let them tell their stories, for, as someone remarked, journalism is really just storytelling.

The Profile

The profile should be seen as a mini-drama, blending description, action and dialogue. Through the words and actions of the source, with some help from the reporter's insertion of background and explanatory matter, the character is illuminated. Profiles should include plenty of quotations.

The major ingredients of the profile are:

- The person's background (birth, upbringing, education, occupation).
- Anecdotes and incidents involving the subject.
- Comments by the individual relevant to his or her newsworthiness.
- The reporter's observations.
- Comments of those who know the interviewee.
- A news peg, whenever possible.

Interviewing only the source will lead to a thin, possibly misleading story. When a young *New York Times* reporter turned in a piece about an alcoholic nun who counsels other similarly afflicted nuns, the story did not move past Charlotte Evans, an editor.

"As it stands," Evans told the reporter, "all you have is a moderately interesting interview with Sister Doody. You sat in a chair, and she sat in a chair and you had a chat. That's not very good, considering the story material.

"Did you talk to any nuns in treatment or just out of it?

"Where is the anguish, the embarrassment, the guilt?

"It doesn't sound as if you had done any real reporting, digging, pushing. Where are the people, the quotes, the color?"

For her profile of Les Brown, a black preacher and radio personality, Itabari Njeri of *The Miami Herald* talked to other ministers, a community activist and the directors of the local chapters of the Urban League and the National Association for the Advancement of Colored People, as well as to Brown. Assessments of Brown diverged widely:

"I will not allow anyone to manipulate or prostitute the black community, and that is what Les Brown is doing to the nth degree," an Urban League official said. The activist had a different view:

"He is different . . . he's got guts. He is a challenge to the traditional black leaders here."

Most profiles have some relationship to news. A television personality has just won an award. A college student has solved a problem puzzling mathematicians for years. A community organizer is involved in a racial conflict.

When Giordano was assigned to profile the English teacher who had been criticized because of his devotion to his students' freedom of expression, she said she decided on several "reporting areas."

"I watched Downs in action with his students. I immediately sensed his warmth and communication, the easy-going and relaxed feelings between them. Instincts are not always correct, but unless I immediately learn otherwise, I try to follow my feelings as a hypothesis for the story."

She interviewed other teachers and found that Downs was well liked and respected. "Like the students, they felt Downs was a good man, a courageous man and an inspiration to them." She also interviewed his former students, administration officials, and Downs himself. She was surprised "that a man so close to being fired would still remain unafraid to speak out.

"I watched Downs very closely during the interview. His features—his grayness, his tiredness, his restrained, gentlemanly nature—told me a lot about him. I noticed his clothing, the way he spoke. When he spoke, he chopped at the air with his hands to emphasize a point. I jotted all this down and included much of it in the story.

"I had to keep reminding myself as I wrote that the story was a personality profile, not a biography. Writing, rewriting and cutting, I finally put the story together the way I wanted."

Her advice for doing profiles: Take your time with the story. Keep your eyes open for revealing details. Talk to as many people as possible. Do not ignore negative instincts, but wait to draw conclusions.

Lew Powell, who has written many profiles for *The Charlotte Observer,* begins his work by gathering background about the subject. Powell first goes through the newspaper's clippings.

"I make notes on things I'd like to know more about," he says. "I keep an eye out for quirks and holes in the public image that I can follow up.

"In the interview, I ask a ton of questions. For one long piece about a husband and wife who own a Charlotte radio station, I had three interviews with them, and I had telephone interviews with probably 20 people who have known them at one time or another. The interviews with other people can provide anecdotes and illustrations as well as facts the source may have forgotten or doesn't care to remember.

"You strike out a lot this way, but every now and then you hit a real gem.

"I look for little glimpses of the subject, incidents that will make people who know the subject say, 'Ah, that's Stan, all right.'"

Reporting and Writing the Profile

Preparing and Doing. Benedict says that she prepares by reading everything she can find about her subject. "People who are interviewed a lot get tired of the same old questions. You want to stand out as an interviewer to get a good story, and that depends on preparation and intelligence," she says. She writes down questions and takes her list with her, consulting it now and then to make sure she has forgotten nothing important.

In the interview, she gently guides her subject after establishing his or her trust. "Don't interrupt too much, and don't challenge too early so the person is on the defensive," she says. "Don't talk too much."

See the subjects in their homes to observe their taste, clothes, objects on walls and desks, which can be revealing, she says.

Stay with the person as long as possible, and observe the person closely for habits, mannerisms, how he or she moves, sits, drinks coffee, answers the phone, speaks to others.

Live-In. A useful technique for the profile is the modified Live-In, staying with the subject while he or she goes about a day's activities. Wayne Miller of the *Times-Standard* in Eureka, Calif., accompanied a sheriff's deputy, Richard Mayton, on the rounds of his beat, an area, Miller says, that is two-thirds the size of Rhode Island. He listens to the deputy chat with the people in isolated mountain cabins, and he lets the officer chat about his work, which takes him into tense areas:

> His beat is part of the infamous "Emerald Triangle." It is marijuana country, but it is also retirement country for many. Today, Mayton is headed for Burr Valley to check on a retired couple named Johansen.
>
> "I try to check on the retired people once a week," he says as he brings the vehicle to a stop at a locked

gate. Off to the left is a single residence with a sign that reads, "LOMITA POP. 5."

> They grind their way uphill over a single-lane dirt road that shakes and rocks the car.
>
> "These people don't have the freedom they once had," Mayton says, emphasizing the word freedom. "This is the season when the older people are afraid to get out of their houses because it's harvest time.
>
> "But they see my patrol vehicle and it makes them feel better knowing that I'm here."

Miller watches Mayton chat with the Johansens, and he interviews Mayton's boss, the sheriff, who says of his deputy that he has an ability to work with people, "is comfortable working alone and is a sensitive individual." Photos by Wayne Miller.

Blending the Two Types

As reporters sought to personalize news stories, the line between the news interview and the profile began to blur. When the UPI questioned the editors of more than 100 daily newspapers about how to improve its wire stories, many of them said that more news stories should have a human angle.

The editors were telling the UPI that their readers wanted the same kind of human element in stories about political, economic and international affairs that the UPI had been putting into many features. For example, when flood waters had surged through several Southern states, the UPI had assessed its effects by describing one family's suffering. The UPI's night lead began:

HATTIESBURG, Miss., Feb. 25 (UPI)—"We ain't never had too much, but we've never been this bad off."

J. W. Creel Jr., 47, a mechanic who has been struggling since before Christmas to stretch his $30 weekly unemployment compensation checks over the needs of himself, his pregnant wife and nine children, sadly surveyed his chattering brood at the Red Cross shelter in the Hattiesburg Community Center.

The Creels, and thousands like them, are the victims of disastrous floods ("Worse than 1900," one old gentleman commented) that are sweeping broad areas of southern Georgia, Alabama, and Mississippi.

The Creels lost everything but the clothes they wore.

Creel said he left his rented home briefly Wednesday to see the flood waters and returned to hear "the kids hollering at me. 'Daddy, water's coming in the house.'

"It was up to my knees," he said. "They were trying to sweep it out but I told them it wasn't no use to sweep and to grab the young 'uns and get out of there."

After a few more paragraphs about the Creel family, the story concentrated on the straight news.

This kind of journalism—the smooth blending of news and personality interviews in a single story—requires information for the factual description of the event and material to provide a lively or moving account of the people involved or affected by the situation. *The Wall Street Journal* has mastered this technique. The key to success with this type of story lies in fusing the thoughts or experiences of the individual with the news event. Here is the beginning of a *Journal* story about stormy economic times for Newfoundland fishermen:

BAY BULLS, Newfoundland—Cyril Mulcahy has seen some lean years in his 51 years of fishing, but he laments that "this is one of the worst."

It's late afternoon and Mr. Mulcahy is baiting fish hooks with pieces of squid in preparation for a full day of cod fishing tomorrow. At dawn, he will be several miles offshore in a 26-foot open boat setting his lines with the hope of catching enough cod so that he and his only crew member will each bring in $50 for a 12-hour working day. And that "would be a good day," he says. "I've been out days when I couldn't make $5."

Mr. Mulcahy, like most of the other older men in this tiny coastal village, has been fishing since he was a young boy, following a way of life that has been traditional in Newfoundland for 350 years. But Mr. Mulcahy, now 61 years old, sees himself as an endangered species. "The way things are, there's no youngster taking it up anymore. The youngest man fishing here (in Bay Bulls) now is 40."

These opening paragraphs do the job of giving the reader a taste of the fisherman's life, Mulcahy's own background and an indication of the problems he and other Newfoundland fishermen face. The next two paragraphs mark the shift to the situation—the news peg—that prompted the story. Notice how the first sentence serves as a transition to the news:

Canadian employment statistics would certainly back him up. There are about 15,000 fishermen in Newfoundland today. That's several hundred fewer than a year ago and about 4,400 fewer than in 1968. Most of these are known as "inshore" fishermen who ply the Atlantic waters with nets or lines in small boats within a few miles offshore. Almost all of them have watched the size of their catches decline steadily over the past several years.

The main reason for their plight: overfishing, or more precisely, overfishing by fleets of foreign trawlers. The trawlers travel thousands of miles to fish in these waters, especially in the 80,000-square-mile Newfoundland Grand Bank. They seek mainly groundfish, such as cod, haddock and flounder, that are found close to the ocean floor. . . .

The Mini-Profile

When Mark Patinkin and Christopher Scanlan were assigned to profile the black community in Rhode Island for *The* Providence *Journal-Bulletin,* they focused on individuals—the people who symbolize the facts and figures they were gathering.

For one of their stories, about the high rate of unemployment among blacks, they talked to a black man who was looking for work:

Voices: Stephen Gordon on Unemployment

Match the Event. Note how the writers of these mini-profiles let their subjects speak. They adhere to the rule: The story should match the nature of the event. In this case, the event is people talking about their lives. What more natural, then, for the story to include many quotations.

"I felt like everything I was trying to build was worthless," said Stephen Gordon. "I was back at the bottom. Quite a few times, I'd just break down and cry. I couldn't even get a job on a garbage truck. I felt less than a man."

Stephen Gordon, 27, sits in the darkness of his kitchen in a Newport housing project, speaking of being black and jobless.

Back from Vietnam in 1971, he had gone through three years of the hardest of times. He had no high school diploma. He had no job. He had two children. His family survived on welfare.

Then came a federal job program that reached out and gave him hope, gave him training as a welder. He was a tradesman. For nine months, he strove to build the good life.

He was fired. He appealed the firing to the State Human Rights Commission, which found the company guilty of racial discrimination. That was two years ago, but the case remains on appeal. Meanwhile, Gordon went on unemployment, then welfare. He remembers the feeling.

"My inspiration was destroyed again," he said. "It was the same old rut."

Recently, he climbed out of the rut by finding a job as a cook in a Newport inn. For other black adults in the state, joblessness remains chronic.

Unemployment among Rhode Island blacks is higher than for any other group. There were 8,880 blacks in the labor force in 1976, and state figures show, 11 percent were unemployed, compared to an overall state rate of 8 percent.

There are the thousands more the statistics don't mention.

There is hope in the black community, and with the careful use of quotes and the selection of incidents, the reporters showed success:

Voices: Ed Blue on moving up

"I wanted the good life," said Ed Blue. "I wasn't going to settle. I figured, I'm a citizen, I'm a taxpayer. I have as much a right as anybody else. Just give me a chance."

Twenty-eight years ago, Ed Blue came to Rhode Island with a suitcase and $300, another poor black immigrant from a small town in the South. Today he is the state's chief bank examiner and lives with his family in the state's wealthiest suburb, Barrington. Barbara, his wife, is running for Town Council.

For most blacks, Rhode Island has not been a place of opportunity. It wasn't for Ed Blue either. It was a place of slammed doors.

They slammed as soon as he got out of college. One large retailer put an "X" on his application for a clerk's job. He demanded to know why. The interviewer admitted it was to mark black applicants. Next he went to a bank. The bank told him he'd never be anything more than a guard.

Ed Blue saw other blacks told the same thing and saw them accept it. Don't bother, they told him, you won't make it, they won't let you make it. Blue would not accept that. "I was new here," he recalled, "I figured hell, I'll give it a shot. I'm going to break that down."

He put his shoulder against the door and he pushed hard. And when it finally gave, and a higher door slammed, he broke that one, too. He did it, he said, by proving he was so qualified they had no choice but to hire him. Ed Blue made it because he believed in Ed Blue.

"This is one of the things I've instilled in my children," he said, "Don't say you can't. I don't want to hear 'You can't.'"

For their report on crime in the Providence ghetto, they interviewed a prostitute:

Voices: Debbie Spell on hustling

"Being a hooker is all I know," said Debbie Spell. "It's how my mother supported me. That's all I seen when I was a kid, broads jumping into cars. Put me in a factory and I just couldn't hack it."

In poor neighborhoods, where unemployment and welfare rates are high, many blacks turn to hustling to survive. Debbie Spell turned to prostitution. Although she is 20, she looks 15. She is already the mother of three children. She normally works on Pine Street in Providence, where most of her customers are white.

"If it wasn't for them, then I wouldn't have food for my kids," she said, "or Pampers for my baby." Nor would she have her color television and living-room furniture.

"I'm not proud of it," she added, "but it's the way I make a living. Why should I work in a factory for $100 a week when I can make that much on a Thursday night?"

Although blacks make up only 3.4 percent of the population in Rhode Island, they make up 24 percent of the population at the Adult Correctional Institutions and 7.5 percent of admissions to state drug abuse programs.

In Providence, blacks account for about 10 percent of the population, but a much higher percentage ends up in the city's arrest books. Last year, of the 243 juveniles Providence police arrested for major crimes, 37 percent, or 90, were black. As blacks get older, their arrest percentage grows. In 1977, of the 470 adults Providence police arrested for major crimes, 48.7 percent, or 229, were black.

Short as these pieces are, they say a great deal by letting those directly involved tell their stories. The quotes reveal frustration, anger, futility, possibilities.

The story about Debbie Spell has a tragic epilogue. A year after she was interviewed, she was arrested on charges of assault and loitering for prostitution. Two days after her arrest, she hanged herself in the shower room of the prison.

Scanlan returned to the streets Debbie walked to find out more about this woman who became a hooker at 12, was a drug addict, had three illegitimate boys, and was dead at 22.

Scanlan admits he was worried when he went out to interview Debbie's friends. He was concerned about how a prying reporter would be treated.

Follow-up to a Tragedy.
Reporter Christopher Scanlan of *The* Providence *Journal-Bulletin* interviews prostitutes who were friends of a young woman who hanged herself after her arrest on prostitution charges. Photo by Andy Dickerman, *The* Providence *Journal-Bulletin*.

"What I found were two grief-stricken women who told me an illuminating story about life on the streets," he said. His interview with Debbie's prostitute friends begins:

PROVIDENCE—It's a little after 5 on a Friday afternoon. Pine Street, between Pearl and Portland Streets, is a desolate stretch littered with broken glass, where young women wait on the sidewalks for men who drive slowly by to stop and pick them up for a few minutes of sex.

This part of South Providence was where Debbie Spell used to wait, too—until last Wednesday when the police arrested her. On Friday, she hanged herself at the Women's Prison in Cranston.

Maurine sits in the doorway of a vacant building, a tired-looking woman in her early twenties, wearing shorts and a halter top.

"Sometimes it's not even worth the money to me," she said. "I got stabbed three times. I got busted in the face with a bottle. Just crazy guys. I told the police, but they didn't do nothing. I even got his plate. They still didn't do nothing. They said, 'If that's the type of life you want to lead, you got to take the bitter with the sweet.'"

Last summer, Debbie Spell told a reporter that she was a prostitute because the money was good. But times have changed, Maurine said.

"Hmph," she snorted when a reporter told her what Debbie had said. "Ain't no money here. Too many girls now. Some girls bring their little sisters down here, underage girls, 11 or 12 years old, some of them."

A young man approached and slowed his car.

"Wanna go?" Maurine asked halfheartedly. He looked at her, shook his head and drove on.

Another young woman came up. A few minutes before, Tammy had been dropped off by a trick, and now she was back on the corner. She said she was Debbie's best friend. On her way to Pine Street, she learned that Debbie was dead. She spoke bitterly, her voice husky with grief, sharp with anger. Tears shone in her eyes. Like Maurine, she did not want her real name used.

"This was Debbie's life, right here on Pine Street," Tammy said. "This is all of our lives, right here."

She too was bothered by all the younger girls on the streets, but for a different reason.

"They don't know what they're getting into," she said, "This is no game. It's just step up and make money. But they don't know that yet." A man stopped his car at the corner. She talked to him for awhile, leaning on his car door, but he, too, drove away. . . .

Tom Wolfe, one of the founders of so-called New Journalism, said that the new journalists derived their techniques from the realistic novelists who used:

Realistic Dialogue and the Commonplace

- Full dialogue. ". . . realistic dialogue involves the reader more completely than any other single device. It also establishes and defines character more quickly and effectively than any other single device."
- The third-person point of view. This required interviews with people involved in events, asking about "thoughts and emotions, along with everything else." The first-person story based on the reporter's point of view was "irrelevant to the story and irritating to the reader."
- Everyday activities.

Much of the work of the new journalists appeared in magazines, but the techniques had a lasting effect on newspaper reporting and writing. The profile was expanded to include the personal lives of public figures, and reporters looked into the lives of individuals who seemed to typify a class or a group of people. In their work, journalists were granted greater freedom. Barriers were lifted on subject matter and reporters were encouraged to write their stories imaginatively.

Stories on the Human Plight

Newspapers and television stations began to concentrate on the human condition—the plight of the family around the block, the girl next door. Parents wanted to know why their children were turning away from them and toward friends. Instead of developing values from the family, children were taking on the outlook of their peers. What happened to marriage, parents wondered. And what about acceptance of homosexuality as a lifestyle?

Parents worried about what their children were learning in grade school. They wondered whether social mobility was leading to a new value system in which they had little faith.

Into the arena stepped the reporter, ready to ask questions on behalf of a concerned public. Across the country, editors wanted interviews with sociologists and psychologists, homosexuals, unmarried couples, women running group sessions, psychiatrists, college dropouts. The working man and woman were rediscovered and made the subject of interviews.

Sensitive Topic. Reporter Berkley Hudson caused controversy in the community with these stories about homosexuals in Bend, Ore.

THE BULLETIN **Lifestyle**

Central Oregon homosexuals dream of freedom

If you are a homosexual in Central Oregon, you probably lead a secretive existence.

Traditionally, and especially in America, theological, medical, and legal theorists have considered homosexuals to be deviants who should be shunned and kept in society's skeleton closet with the other minorities and aberrant types.

However, this view is changing. In recent years, homosexuals, along with other groups, actively have sought and partially have gained "liberation."

Yet, in Central Oregon, homosexuals still dream of freedom, as blacks have dreamed of equal job and housing opportunities.

"There is no such thing as a Christian homosexual. They could change and become a Christian," Rev. Rex E. Blott, presiding minister of the Bend Jehovah's Witnesses, said without hesitation.

The minister quoted from the Bible, Romans 1:26-27, which reads:

"God therefore handed them over to disgraceful passions. Their women exchanged the normal practices of sexual intercourse for something which is abnormal and unnatural. Similarly the men, turning from natural intercourse with women, were swept into lustful passion for one another.

"Men with men performed these shameful horrors, receiving, of course, in their own personalities the consequences of sexual perversity."

Rev. Leopold O'Riordan of St. Francis of Assissi Catholic Church, Bend, said homosexuals can be Christians, but like other problems, such as kleptomania, homosexuality needs to be overcome.

In the field of psychology, the debate continues, with the views of Sigmund Freud gradually being shaken. Freud said homosexuality is an incurable mental illness and perversion.

His theory of an Oedipus complex stated a child may develop homosexual tendencies after becoming strongly attached to the parent of the opposite sex and rejecting the other parent. Also, an overprotective parent combined with an absent or brutal parent may contribute to a child becoming homosexual, he said.

The Freudian view prevailed for more than 50 years. Only this April, the American Psychiatric Association (APA) decided to uphold its board's decision to drop homosexuality from the group's listing of mental diseases.

The organization now considers it a mental illness only when homosexuals "are bothered by or in conflict with or wish to change their sexual orientation."

This year a study, which has become a book — "Male Homosexuals: Their Problems and Adaptations," by psychiatrists Martin Wienberg and Colin Williams — found male homosexuals not under psychiatric care to be as psychologically adjusted as other males.

This survey, taken of 2,437 men in Denmark, the Netherlands and the United States, recommended an end to legal and social harassment of homosexuals. It said the United States was the most anti-homosexual of modern Western nations.

The professors are continuing the work of Dr. Albert Kinsey, of Indiana University, who in 1948 said 40 to 50 per cent of the male population had experienced a homosexual situation and psychiatry should reassess its idea that persons should conform to a particular sexual standard.

The 1974 survey, which included 1,067 American men, said 67.8 per cent of homosexuals still attempt to hide their sexuality from heterosexuals.

But more than half disagreed with the statement, "I wish I were not a homosexual."

Twenty-eight per cent said they would like to give up homosexuality and 27 per cent said they weren't sure. Seventy-six per cent said they were happy or pretty happy and about the same number said they weren't depressed, anxious or ashamed of being homosexual.

In Deschutes County, Charles Whitchurch, a psychiatric social worker, says the few homosexuals who seek help from him have problems not with their homosexuality but with living in a small town and having to be discreet and not as free as if they were in a large city.

"Married homosexuals have the problem of leading a double life, being bisexual. They have a similar problem as someone who is cheating on his wife," he said.

"Homosexuality in a small community is still a scary thing. Our country works on the national average mentality. If you don't have 2.5 kids, aren't mortgaged on house and car, aren't white, Protestant, Catholic or Jew, then you don't fit," said Jim Henson, director of the Deschutes County Family Counseling Center.

In Oregon, no law prohibits consenting persons over 18 years old from engaging in homosexuality, according to Warren West, Deschutes County assistant district attorney. However, he said there are laws against solicitation in public places or homosexuality involving adults and those who are under 18 or mentally incompetent.

A bill which would have made it illegal to discriminate against homosexuals in the areas of jobs and housing died last year in an Oregon Legislature committee. That bill proposed a law similar to ones existing in Seattle, Wash. and San Francisco, Calif.

———————

It's 10:30 p.m. in a Bend tavern one night last week. At the bar, all six stools are occupied. The male customers laugh and drink and joke with each other and the barmaid.

One man throws a verbal barb to another at the end of the bar. The target of the barb, who is a homosexual, replies, "You better watch out, I've got my broomstick parked outside."

(Later, he says, "Everybody knows fairies ride brooms.")

"Oh, I thought you were going to hit me with your purse," the joker counters, and everyone laughs.

Less than 10 months ago, that homosexual, Ricky (not his real name), had written in his diary on Nov. 30, 1973: "At one time Central Oregon wasn't big enough for both of us (Ricky and his father). I have returned not in vengeance or contempt, but to live my life in my own way."

"Not just as a gay, but as a proud gay. And not afraid to admit the fact. Why live a lie and be something you're not or what somebody else wants you to be?...be yourself open and freely."

Ricky, one of the estimated 11 million homosexuals in American, says it has taken him many months to be accepted by his friends with whom he now jokes about his homosexuality. His story and brief profiles of several other area homosexuals accompany this article.

Ricky:

'. . . I realized chicks weren't the thing for me'

Ricky was born and has lived in Central Oregon for most of his 25 years, except for a brief period in the Navy and short stints working in Portland and Seattle.

"When I was 15 or 16, I realized chicks weren't the thing for me. I had a lover (male) down the street, but when we were 16, a girl broke us up. I went with her for two or three years. That was very frustrating," Ricky recalled.

In his diary, on Nov. 5, 1972, Ricky — who now works for a restaurant in the area — wrote: "Remember you at that age? What a crazy mixed up kid you were. Kept trying to change from gay life to hetero. Each time you changed, the more dissatisfied you became. And not just with women. You became that much more disgusted with yourself.

"Even became suicidal. Then you tried, almost succeeded, if...your ex-wife's son, 16 years old and damn good looking, hadn't of pulled your body from the surf. The tide was going out and nobody would've missed you."

After being dismissed from the Navy for a nervous condition related to problems with his homosexuality, Ricky went to Portland and became very successful in his job there.

He "came out" (a gay term for publicly asserting one's homosexuality) and joined the scene there with lavish parties and old, rich "sugar daddies" cruising in their sleek, fancy cars, looking for young homosexual partners.

In Portland, Ricky was married to an older woman for six months. The marriage was a "social" marriage for tax purposes and to maintain appearances of being "straight" or heterosexual.

Returning to Central Oregon, he worked in various restaurants and "quit" at one after the boss accused him of making sexual advances toward another male employe.

Ricky said, "I don't mess around on the job. That's a no-no."

Although Ricky spent several years learning to cope with his sexuality, he feels comfortable now as a homosexual. He enjoys his job and sees a positive future in it.

Ricky's boss knows he's gay.

His relations with his family, who still live here, have varied. Now, he considers the situation good. He again is thinking of marrying to maintain the apppearance of being heterosexual.

"To a certain extent, I'm a recluse. But I have a very pleasant life," Ricky said.

He likes the slow, unhurried pace of Central Oregon and puts most of his energies into his job.

After quoting verbatim, Romans 1:26-27, Ricky — who grew up as a member of the Christian Church — said the Bible's hostile view toward homosexuality is outdated.

Another portion of his diary, on Nov. 30, 1973, reads as follows, "Even though I feel I have no family, the fond memories linger...Thank you, God, for giving patience and understanding, not to mention that great gift only you can give — love."

Barbara:

'It's like we belong in another country . . .'

When Sue and Barbara moved eight months ago from the Willamette Valley to Central Oregon, someone scrawled on the door of their home: "Fairies wear boots."

This greeting was a harbinger of many experiences they would have in Bend.

On several occasions in bars, they have been ridiculed for being "queers" and mocked with obscene jokes about their homosexuality.

Twice, Sue (not her real name) has been denied a change of job location by her employer.

She describes herself as a professional and says, "I don't want to force the issue by being identified."

She said her homosexuality is the unofficial reason given for the transfer denials.

"Right now I would like people not to think of me as gay or straight, man or woman, but that I do a job well," she said.

We would just as soon see a people world," instead of one segmented sexually, racially and religiously, said Sue, who is 27 and grew up in the Pacific Northwest.

"I don't want to be snickered at or hear dirty jokes said behind my back at work and loud enough so I can hear them. I'm tired of explaining myself to people. I just want to go some place and to live. And if people don't accept me, to hell with them," Sue said.

Barbara, who lived in various places as her father traveled around the world in the Army, said she is not unhappy in Bend, but she couldn't live here for any prolonged periods.

She said, "Compared to our other friends, we haven't had much trouble, though."

Barbara (not her real name either) is 25 and works for a motel in the area. She and Sue have lived together for more than three years. They consider their relationship unusual among lesbians. Both regard themselves as monogamists.

"I don't feel I need to have children to make my life complete," Barbara said.

It we could just find some friends here," she says.

They know one married couple besides the people they know at work. They say the unfriendliness they feel in Bend stems from their being outsiders and homosexuals.

"It's like we belong in another country. And people think that we don't vote and we just are perverted with our whips and chains" Barbara said.

Sue, who deals with the public in her job, said once when working she approached someone who said, "Here comes that dirty queer again."

Sue said, "If you don't have hair down to your waist and big boobs, you're not a woman."

Barbara said, "I believe in God. I'm not a Christian Scientist but I lean towards that. God is love and that's all he knows. He can't condemn love when it doesn't hurt anybody. I don't feel we're perverted. I can't say because I'm a queer, I'm going to hell."

David:

'I think being homosexual is a positive thing'

Although David Buscemi knows Bend doesn't encourage homosexuality, he isn't reluctant to reveal his name. He came here in July with the man he's been living with for six years.

They left a tiny New Hampshire town after pressure was applied because they were activist homosexuals. Their trouble began when they handed out pro-homosexuality leaflets which said, in part: "Gay is not tragic. Gay is OK."

David's partner, Gene, which is his actual first name, was born in Bend and has lived here most of his life. He's 31 and was married but has been separated for six years. He has several children who live with his wife.

"I can see why gays would want to be discreet in Bend," David, 25, said. "The feeling here is of masculinity, with loggers and cowboys. I really feel self-conscious about being gay in Bend."

David, a native of Groton, Mass., attended Syracuse University for two years and later the University of Washington, where he met Gene.

Although David bitterly recalls being harassed as a youngster, he said, "I think being a homosexual is a positive thing. I think as far as our relationship goes, we're pretty free and easy. It's sensitive."

David said Gene is more radical than he because Gene grew up repressed in the Bend environment and he has reacted to that.

"I hope some of my children are homosexuals," Gene said. "Homosexuals should recruit more homosexuals because we're not going to make anymore."

"We're into gay liberation," said Gene, who graduated from Bend High School and now is a carpenter.

"My favorite thing is to go up to people on the street and ask them if they want to go to bed with me. The only reason people shun it, is they're afraid they might like it."

"There is a myth of homosexuals being milktoasts. That's why radical action, even shooting pigs who are down on homosexuals, would be good. Homosexuals are going to come out soon," Gene said.

Henry:

'There is quite a bit of cruising going on . . .'

Henry, a homosexual, came temporarily to Oregon. He is college educated and works with a film company recently in the area.

Henry says the "gay scene" in Central Oregon is far removed from the glittering, gay discotheques such as Le Jardin in New York, or San Francisco's sauna baths or Hollywood's bizarre, bisexual parties.

Henry isn't his real name.

"Knowing the way people feel here in Bend, there is a certain degree of paranoia about revealing my name," he said.

People fear homosexuality because, he says, "if everyone were homosexual, there would be no human race."

"The only woe of being gay in Bend is it's hard to meet people. There are more closet cases here than any other place I've been," Henry said.

Despite that, he said, "There is quite a bit of cruising going on around here."

Cruising is a subtle tango of the eyes which occurs among gays in several after hours bars in the area. Cruising is a necessary part of the game, Henry said, because only 15 per cent of homosexuals are identifiable by outward appearances.

Henry, however, has been reluctant to indicate his gayness in bars here.

"There is baiting in small towns. Also, if a gay here were afraid I would expose him, it might come to the point where he might kill me," he said.

During a recent two-week period, Henry said he met more than a half dozen gays who were cruising.

He said people in small towns should be more tolerant of homosexuals, for there is no reason to fear them sexually.

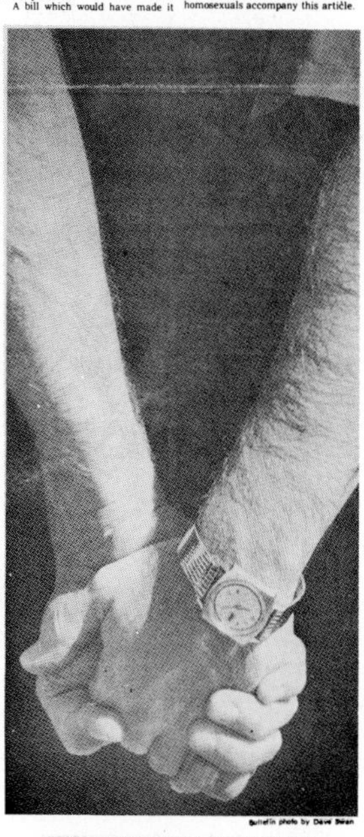

Stories by Berkley Hudson

Berkley Hudson, a reporter for *The Bulletin* in Bend, Ore., wrote several stories that revealed aspects of community life of which most residents were unaware. The metropolitan press and network television had been carrying news and features about homosexuality as a lifestyle, but Hudson realized that little had been written about the lives of homosexuals in small- and medium-sized cities.

To meet homosexuals, Hudson ran a classified advertisement in *The Bulletin* inviting them to discuss "the joys and woes of being gay in Central Oregon" and promising confidentiality. The word was soon around town about what Hudson was up to. Bend was not sure it liked the idea. Several residents protested in letters to the editor, and two Jehovah's Witnesses visited Hudson in the newsroom to try to dissuade him. Hudson turned the visit to good use; the visitors inspired him to do a story on the sect.

Hudson received about 10 replies to his advertisement, and he selected two single men and two couples—one male couple, one female couple—for his interviews. Each interview lasted two to four hours. One interviewee would meet Hudson only in out-of-the-way places. Only one let Hudson use his real name. Most feared loss of jobs and community ostracism.

"Since I'm not gay, that caused a slight problem," he recalled. His sources were unsure of his motives and his understanding of their problems. But his obvious sincerity established a rapport that led to a reciprocal openness.

The Bulletin devoted an entire page to Hudson's stories. There were more letters, including a few that contained the page from *The Bulletin* with the word "GARBAGE" scrawled across it, about 20 telephone calls and a few personal visits. More than a year after the article appeared, some people in town still shunned him. However, the response was not all negative. Some callers and letter writers praised Hudson's reporting.

Hudson continued to seek out stories about people with divergent life-styles. If we could have followed Hudson from the time he developed his ideas for these stories through his interviewing, we would have noticed his careful preparations and the warm relationships between him and his sources. His questions were designed to elicit relevant information, and he listened more than he talked.

Preparations

Fred Zimmerman of *The Wall Street Journal* has these suggestions for reporters about how to prepare for an interview:

1. Do research on the interview topic and the person to be interviewed, not only so you can ask the right questions and understand the answers, but also so you can demonstrate, clearly but unobtrusively, to the interviewee that you cannot easily be fooled.

2. Devise a tentative theme for your story. A major purpose of the interview will be to obtain quotes, anecdotes and other evidence to support that theme.

3. List question topics in advance—as many as you can think of, even though you may not ask all of them and almost certainly will ask others that you do not list.

4. In preparing for interviews on sensitive subjects, theorize about what the person's attitude is *likely* to be toward you and the subject you are asking about. What is his or her role in the event? Whose side is he on? What kind of answers can you logically expect to your key questions? Based on this theorizing, develop a plan of attack that you think might mesh with his *probable* attitude and get through his *probable* defenses.

Research

A. J. Liebling, a master reporter who moved from the newspaper news-room to *The New Yorker* magazine, is quoted in *The Most of A. J. Liebling,* edited by William Cole: "The preparation is the same whether you are going to interview a diplomat, a jockey, or an ichthyologist. From the man's past you learn what questions are likely to stimulate a response."

Research begins with the library's clippings about the subject matter of the interview. If the topic has more than local importance or if the interviewee is well-known, The New York Times Index and Facts on File may have a reference that can be useful. The Reader's Guide to Periodical Literature also may list a magazine article about the topic or the person who is to be interviewed. For personality interviews, Who's Who in America and other biographical dictionaries can be consulted. Persons who know the interviewee can be asked for information, also.

These resources provide material for three purposes: They give the reporter leads to specific questions, they provide the reporter with a feel for the subject, and they provide useful background for the story.

In the best of all possible worlds for the reporter, all sources love to talk, and they speak openly and to the point. Strange as it may seem, reporters sometimes realize these dreams. Television cameras seem to make people talkative, as does the prospect of seeing one's name in print. Sometimes the urge to talk wells up from a need that lies deeper than the desire to be seen on television. People occasionally have a compelling desire to share an experience or to call attention to a topic that requires exposure.

Arthur L. Gavshon, the AP's diplomatic reporter, says that one of his first good stories after he had been assigned to the diplomatic beat came when Britain was administering Palestine. Jews who were fleeing Europe were entering Palestine in violation of the British limitation on Jewish immigration. The Arabs were pressuring Britain to stop the flow from Europe, and the Jews were anxious to flee the Continent where so many of their relatives and friends had been killed by the Nazis.

"Daily, I checked unhappy government men for their solution to a situation of deep sadness. Then, by chance, I saw a three-line newspaper report that said that the Royal Navy battleship *Vanguard* had sailed from Malta to Haifa," he says.

Gavshon knew that warships do not venture into dangerous areas without orders. He made several checks with his sources and was able to write that Britain was about to mount an air-sea blockade to halt the stream of Jews into Palestine.

Gavshon says he was able to score this exclusive because "some officials were ready to reveal a plan they did not much like."

For most interviews, some questions can be prepared ahead of time. Often, but not always, they are asked early in the interview. In a personality interview, the reporter will want to know the vital data about the source—age, address, education, jobs held, family, and so on. Some of these may not seem necessary since the clippings and references may contain such material. But people move and change jobs, and clippings can be wrong. Also, questions about these are non-threatening and relax the interviewee.

Harold Ross, the brilliant and eccentric former newspaperman who founded and edited *The New Yorker,* slashed in exasperation at the pages of profiles and interviews that lacked vital data. "Who he?" Ross would scrawl across such manuscripts.

The reporter must also identify the source sufficiently to provide the reader or viewer with reason to give credence to the source's comments.

As obvious as these questions about identification may be, the beginning reporter may want to jot them down before setting out on an interview. Otherwise, the reporter may be embarrassed by having to call the source later for basic information. In her first week at *The Daily Register,* Shrewsbury, N.J., a journalism school graduate was sent to interview an Austrian organ maker

Asking Questions

Abrasive? Not He. Some viewers find the questions of Sam Donaldson, ABC's chief White House correspondent, abrasive. He defends his tough, boring-in style:

"There's a perception that I'm always asking some rude or confrontational question. That's absolutely wrong. I'm not trying to make the president say something foolish or trip him up. But I think it's proper to ask him a question that confronts him with the critics of his policy."

The Basic Questions

who was installing a new organ in the United Methodist Church in nearby Red Bank. All went well until the reporter and the photographer were on their way out of the church. At the door, the photographer whispered to her. She looked crestfallen and ran back into the church.

"I had forgotten to ask the builder how old he was," she says.

Sometimes a reporter will ask a question that is of little news value in order to break the ice with an interviewee. These lead-in questions must be carefully chosen. The politician, athlete or diplomat usually expects to be queried about relevant matters and has little time for chit-chat.

Once the reporter moves into the serious business, he or she must ask questions that are aimed at revelation, disclosure and insight for the reader or listener. These questions, sometimes called leading questions, are designed to turn up material that will enable the public to learn something that has been unknown or that will clarify material that had been unclear.

Leading Questions

Most questions follow what the reporter perceives to be the nature or the theme of the assignment. A reporter calls the state highway patrol and hears about a fatal accident nearby. Automatically, the reporter knows that he or she must find out who died and how and where the death occurred. The same process is at work in the more complicated interview.

A reporter is told to interview an actor who had been out of work for two years and is now in a hit musical. The reporter decides that the theme of the story will be the changes the actor has made in his life. He asks the actor if he has moved from his tenement walkup, has made any large personal purchases and how his family has reacted to his suddenly being away most nights. These three questions lead the actor to talk at length.

On another assignment, the reporter is to interview a well-known singer-composer. The reporter decides to ask about the singer's experiences that led him to write songs that call attention to war, poverty, sexism and racism. "Bread," says the singer in answer to the first question the reporter asks. "Money," he explains. There is a good market in such songs. The reporter then quickly shifts themes and asks questions about the economics of popular music and the singer's personal beliefs.

Open-End and Closed-End Questions

When the sports writer asked the hurdler, "What do you think of our town?" he was using what is known as an open-end question that could have been answered at length. The sports editor's suggestion that the reporter ask the athlete about the condition of the track would have elicited a specific response—fast, slow, or slick—as it was a closed-end question.

The open-end question does not require a specific answer. The closed-end question calls for a brief, pointed reply. Applied properly, both have their merits. Two months before the budget is submitted, a city hall reporter may ask the city manager what he thinks of the city's general financial situation—an open-end question. The reply may cover the failure of anticipated revenues to meet expectations, unusually high increases in construction costs, higher interest rates and other factors that have caused trouble for the city. Then the reporter may ask a closed-end question, "Will we have a tax increase?"

As we have seen, reporters often begin their interviews with open-end questions, which allow the source to relax. Then the closed-end questions are asked which can seem threatening to a source if asked at the outset of the interview.

Television and radio interview programs usually end with a closed-end question because the interviewer wants to sum up the situation with a brief reply.

The reporter who asks only open-end questions should be aware of their implications to the source. To some sources, the open-end question is the mark of an inadequately-prepared reporter who is fishing for a story.

Some television reporters seem to have a tendency to ask open-end questions, even when a specific one is more appropriate. A Chicago TV reporter in an interview with orphans asked a youngster, "Do you wish you had a mother and father?" The most famous of all these open-end questions that poorly prepared TV reporters ask is, "How do you feel about . . . ?"

Good questions are the result of preparations, and this goes well beyond reading the local newspaper and chatting with authorities. Reporters who hold themselves to these narrow confines usually are able only to operate in a linear fashion. That is, today's coverage is built on yesterday's newspaper stories and the council meeting of the day before. Good stories—informative journalism—often are spurred by the question that breaks the chain of events. Remember Copernicus. All he asked was what would happen if the sun and not the earth were the center of the universe, and centuries of linear thinking shot off into a new plane.

Asking the Tough Questions

Sometimes a young reporter finds that posing the right question is difficult because the question might embarrass or compromise the interviewee. There is no recourse but to ask.

Oriana Fallaci, an Italian journalist famous for her interviews, says that her success may be the result of her asking the world leaders she interviews questions that other reporters do not ask.

Soft on Riggins. When Joe Namath, a former star quarterback, made his debut as a sportscaster for ABC's Monday night football game he was criticized for his interviewing technique. "He stayed away from the tougher issues," a *New York Times* sports writer commented. In Namath's interview with John Riggins, a Redskins fullback, Namath failed to ask about Riggins' holdout, his recent arrest for being drunk in public and his behavior at a Washington dinner when he said to a justice of the Supreme Court, Sandra Day O'Connor, "Loosen up, Sandy baby." Namath's contract was not renewed.

Interviewing the Klan.
Reporter Peter Francis of *The Stockton Record* questions two leaders of the Ku Klux Klan about their plan to organize California chapters. Bill Wilkinson (with cigar), KKK national leader, and George Pepper, head of the California Klan, said their program of promoting racial segregation was attracting new members "every day." Although Wilkinson refused to shake his hand when they were introduced and both men were wary, Francis was able to draw them out about their plans for California. Photo by Rich Turner, *The Stockton Record.*

The High Road. On the television interview program "Face the Nation" Fred Graham asked Muhammad Ali how he squared his Muslim beliefs with his reputation as a womanizer. Ali glared at Graham for a long moment and replied, "I thought this was going to be one of those high-type programs."

"Some reporters are courageous only when they write, when they are alone with their typewriters, not when they face the person in power. They never put a question like this, 'Sir, since you are a dictator, we all know you are corrupt. In what measure are you corrupt?' "

Remarkably, heads of state, kings and guerrilla leaders open up to Fallaci. One reason for this is her obvious courage. She lets her sources know that the public is entitled to answers to her questions. She will not be treated impolitely or with indifference. When the heavyweight champion boxer Muhammad Ali belched in answer to one of her questions, she threw the microphone of her tape recorder in his face.

Another reason for her effectiveness is "her talent for intimacy," as one journalist put it. "She easily establishes an atmosphere of confidence and closeness and creates the impression that she would tell you anything. Consequently, you feel safe, or almost safe, to do the same with her," writes Diana Loercher in *The Christian Science Monitor.*

In her interview with Henry Kissinger, the U.S. secretary of state at the time, Fallaci had him admit that his position of power made him feel like the "lone cowboy who leads the wagon train alone on his horse." His image of himself as the Lone Ranger caused Kissinger later to say that granting Fallaci the interview was the "stupidest" act in his life.

In *All the President's Men,* Bob Woodward describes his telephone call to Kissinger to ask whether the secretary of state had placed wiretaps on his aides. Woodward explains to Kissinger that he had been told by sources in the FBI that Kissinger had done so.

Kissinger paused. "It could be Mr. Haldeman who authorized the taps," he said.

How about Kissinger? Woodward asked.

"I don't believe it was true," he stated.

Is that a denial?

A pause. "I frankly don't remember."

Woodward reminds Kissinger that his sources said that Kissinger had personally authorized the taps.

A brief pause. "Almost never," he said.

Woodward suggested that "almost never" meant "sometimes." Was Kissinger then confirming the story?

Kissinger gets excited and tells Woodward that the questioning is like a "police interrogation."

"If it is possible and if it happened, then I have to take responsibility for it . . . I'm responsible for this office."

Did you do it? Woodward asked.

There is no hesitation here. Woodward gets right to the point.

Kissinger did not like the questioning and called Woodward's boss, Benjamin Bradlee. He told Bradlee that it was "almost inconceivable" that he had authorized the wiretapping, hardly a denial. (He had.)

When a reporter accompanied Sen. Don Nickles on a speech-making tour of Oklahoma towns he noticed that Nickles was being praised as a conservative who was tough on federal spending. Yet in Eufaula Nickles announced "good news" from Washington, a commitment of federal funds for a new housing project.

The reporter then asked if the Republican senator's approach was consistent—condemning government spending and welcoming it. Nickles' answer: He will vote against federal housing funds but so long as they are available, "I will try to see that Oklahoma gets its fair share."

The quote ends the story, and the reader is left to decide whether the senator is a political realist or an opportunist.

Some reporters gain a reputation for asking tough questions. They waste no time on preliminaries. When Jack Anderson, the Washington columnist whose specialty is political exposés, calls a congressman, the politician knows that he is unlikely to be asked for the text of a speech he is to give in Dubuque. Anderson is after meatier game.

Still, there are questions that few reporters like to ask. Most of these concern the private lives of sources—a city councilman's recent divorce, the mental retardation of a couple's son, the fatal illness of a baseball player. Some questions are necessary, some not. The guidelines for relevance and good taste are constantly shifting, and reporters may find they are increasingly being told to ask questions that they consider intrusive. This is the age of intimacy.

Often, this uneasiness stems from the anticipation that the source may be hurt or embarrassed. Yet, reporters who dislike asking these questions because they would prefer to spare sources anguish are sometimes surprised by the frank replies to their questions. A reporter for *Newsday* was assigned to follow up an automobile accident in which a drunken youth without a driver's license ran a borrowed car into a tree. One of the passengers, a 15-year-old girl, was killed. In doing his follow-up story, the reporter discovered that most of the parents were willing to talk because, as one parent said, the lessons learned from the accident might save lives.

Making Sources Talk

The early stage of the interview is often a feeling-out period for the source and the reporter. The interviewee balances the hazards and gains for him or his organization in divulging the information the reporter seeks, and the reporter tries to show the source the rewards the source will receive through the disclosure of the information—publicity, respect, and the feeling that goes with doing a good turn.

When the source concludes that the risks outweigh the possible gains and decides to provide little or no information or is misleading, the reporter has several alternatives. At one extreme, the reporter can try to cajole the source into a complete account through flattery—or by appearing hurt and surprised. At the other extreme, the reporter can demand information. If the source is a public official, such demands are legitimate because officials are responsible to the public. The reporter can tell the source that the story—and there will be some kind of story—will point out that the official refused to answer questions. Usually, the source will fall into line, for he eventually realizes he needs the press more than the press needs the source.

If the source is a public official, he or she cannot escape a question with the plea of ignorance. A city controller, whose job it is to audit the financial records of city agencies and departments, told a reporter he had no idea whether a bureau had put excess funds in non-interest bearing bank accounts. Told by the reporter it was his business to know that and that the story would state so, the controller supplied the information.

Stephen P. Morin and Dan Stets of *The* Providence *Journal-Bulletin* revealed that committees of the Rhode Island state legislature hire 20 lawyers and that many of them do little for their $4,000 to $6,000 a year. The jobs are usually awarded through patronage.

Accompanying their story revealing the expenditures was a sidebar that shows Morin trying to make one of the lawyers talk:

How Did You Get Your Job, Mr. Marzilli?

Frederic A. Marzilli has been legal counsel to the Senate's Health, Education and Welfare Committee since January 1981. He served as counsel to the Judiciary Committee the year before that.

Reporter Stephen P. Morin asked him how he got his job:

A. Ah, I'm trying to think if I got a letter indicating that I wasn't going to be rehired for Judiciary. Ah, I don't know. I don't even have a file. I had one when I was in Judiciary, but I don't keep a file no more.

Q. I'm incredulous.

A. What does that mean?

Q. It's hard for me to believe that you don't know how you got selected for a job that pays $6,000.

A. Well, again, I don't think it's a job.

Q. What is it then?

A. A contract. It's no different than a garbage company. I'm not an employee. I'm a contractor. Look, I'm not trying to give you a tap dance.

Q. Work is a job, isn't it? Whatever you do is a job, right?

A. Right.

Q. How did you hear about this job?

A. I know how the General Assembly works. I was an intern for two years. I was a member of the Model Legislature. I go down there a lot. It wasn't something I was unfamiliar with.

Q. Do you know legislators?

A. Ah, yes.

Q. Are you related to anybody?

A. No. Definitely not. Nepotism is a bad word.

Q. How about cronyism?

A. Ah. I don't call it cronyism.

Q. Well how were you selected? Do you know Rocco Quattrocchi?

A. I know him. We've been involved in politics before.

Q. Is he your godfather? Do you have a godfather?

A. No.

Q. No one recommended you for the job?

A. I'll be candid with you. I don't want to be singled out. I don't know whether to . . .

Q. Why don't you just speak honestly? That would relieve your problems. How did you get the job?

A. I think, because of my previous experience down there. I think that point is valid.

Q. Previous experience doing what? Being a lawyer?

A. No, no. Knowing how the General Assembly works.

Q. You're saying you did not make any phone calls asking for this position?

A. Oh, I inquired. I inquired as to what the proper steps were for getting a job. I sent a resume and sent out an application, and I think I gave it to Jerry Mosca (Angelo Mosca Jr., head of Legislative Council). I wanted to work at Leg. Council.

Q. Legal counsel (to the committee) is second best?

A. I guess. They didn't say to me, 'If you don't want this, you want this job?' I went down and tried to talk to him (Mosca), but he's a real tough guy to get in touch with, and I'm trying to remember if I got a call from Rocco's secretary or not. I know it wasn't by mail. I know it was Christmastime, 1980.

Q. She gave you a Christmas present?

A. Christmas present? Boy, are you tough. I like reporters.

Q. Essentially Rocco selected you?

A. Yeah, I would say that was a fair estimate.

Q. Thanks.

A. Listen. Take it easy on me, will you?

Sometimes a source will seem to talk freely but will cover the important material with a layer of unimportant information. When this happens it is worthwhile to encourage the source to talk on. The reporter listens, occasionally asking a simple question. Emboldened by the rapt attention of the reporter, who is studiously taking notes, the source may begin to exaggerate or fabricate. These assertions duly noted, the reporter may suddenly appear puzzled by statements that, he informs the source, contradict what the source had said earlier or what is known as fact. Given the opportunity to pull back gracefully, the source may do so by giving the reporter the desired information. If the source does not, the reporter says that he has no alternative but to print the source's fabrications and accompany them with the evidence that contradicts or corrects the statements. Confronted by the implicit threat to make the source look silly, evasive or duplicitous, the source often agrees to supply the necessary material.

These techniques may appear unethical to the uninitiated. Properly applied to public officials, they are justified by the public's need to know and the obligation of journalists to hold officials accountable to the public.

Wendell Rawls Jr., who has worked for *The Tennessean* in Nashville, *The Philadelphia Inquirer* and *The New York Times,* says of interviewing:

> Don't tell people what you know. Ask questions. Then back off. Use diversion. I love to do that—talk with people about things you're not there to talk to them about. You ask a question that may be very meaningful. Then you move away from it. I do it sometimes even if the person doesn't get particularly fidgety, because I don't want him to think that I think what he has told me is necessarily important to me. I'll move to another question and say, "What is that on the wall? That's an interesting sort of. . . ." Whatever. Anything that will divert him, and he will start talking about that. And then maybe ask two or three questions about junk, and then come back and ask another very pointed question.

Letting the Source Talk

The assignment was a delicate one—to interview Archbishop Valerian D. Trifa, the 69-year-old head of the Rumanian Orthodox Church in America who was trying to find a country to accept him after he agreed to be deported during his trial on charges that he lied about his part in crimes against Jews in Rumania during World War II. Howard Blum of *The New York Times* let Trifa turn the interview into a two-hour rambling conversation.

Trifa denied taking part in any pogroms against Jews, said he had not been helped by the Vatican to enter the United States and seemed assured that although he had spent two years trying to find a country that would accept him his search would end successfully.

Blum dropped a question: "Why do you think you were deported?" Trifa pushed back in his chair, seemingly angry, and began to talk heatedly. He brought up the Holocaust, that his deportation was the result of people reviving the period during the Nazi era when six million Jews were killed. He said that "all this talk by the Jews about the Holocaust is going to backfire. . . . Be it legislative or whatever, against the Jews." Blum asked him what he meant by "whatever."

Trifa raised his voice. "I don't want you to say Bishop Trifa is saying people will kill Jews because of what was done to him. No sir. I am just saying 'whatever.' That something will be done."

As for the deaths of Jews in the Holocaust, Trifa said he had no idea whether they were killed. He needed no prodding now. "I do know that not a single Jew was killed in Rumania. At least not because he was Jewish. Statistics prove that." Blum pointed out in the next paragraph that 300,000 Jews were killed in Rumania. Blum asked about articles in a newspaper Trifa edited, whether they were anti-Semitic.

"They were not anti-Semitic. They were anti-Jewish. And they were true," the Archbishop said.

Blum allowed Trifa to indict himself. "You throw a few questions out, making them more specific each time," Blum said. "When the net got quite tight, the subject started beating against it. When he started flaying away, he trapped himself. Or at least some of the people who read the interview thought so."

Rare is the reporter whose persuasiveness is so overwhelming or whose charm is so overpowering that he or she is never told, "No comment." Reporters must then resort to techniques and devices that will nudge information from unwilling sources. One *Wall Street Journal* reporter says if he fails to convince the source that revelation will benefit him, he remarks that he already knows the other side of the issue and that "no comment" will mean that only the other side will be reported.

The reporter can open up silent sources by telling them that they will be quoted as saying "no comment," which might lead people to believe they are hiding something. Some reporters tell "no comment" sources that they will keep trying to dig up the information, and when they do they will make it a point to include the silent source's "no comment." Few sources want to be embarrassed this way.

Reporters know there is more than one source for a story. A reporter assigned to find out about local automobile sales made no headway with the local dealers. Obviously hit hard by flagging sales, they did not want to admit that all was not well. The reporter was at sea and told his editor the story could not be broken. The editor suggested he check the motor vehicles department and the tax office. In many cities, new car sales are recorded for fee and tax purposes. Once the reporter had the basic data, the local automobile dealers opened up.

Handling
"No Comment"

Another technique is to tell the source that although the available information is incomplete the station or newspaper will have to run it anyway. The source is told that with his help the story will be more accurate.

"One of my sources will never tell me anything if we start from scratch on a story," a business reporter said. "But he will talk if I have something. Sometimes I bluff that I know more than I really do," he said.

Investigative reporters are masters of the bluff. During the Eisenhower administration, Jack Anderson heard that private attorneys who had lost cases before various commissions suspected political fixes. (A reporter's maxim: When investigating suspicious deals, talk to the losers.)

Anderson learned that Commissioner Richard Mack of the FCC had promised his decisive vote to an applicant before the commission proceedings began. The applicant, considered the least qualified of the four applicants by the FCC examiner, had hired an attorney to lobby his case. The attorney, Thurman Whiteside, was a friend of Mack and a notorious fixer.

Anderson found out that Whiteside controlled a trust fund. "I was half satisfied he was using this as a funnel for payments to Mack, but I had no proof," Anderson recalls in his book *Confessions of a Muckraker* (New York: Random House, 1979). He called Mack

. . . and tried to con the truth out of him before he could get his defenses straight.

After giving him the nerve-jangling news that I was Jack Anderson of Drew Pearson's office, I bluffed, 'I have an accountant who is prepared to testify that Whiteside has paid you money from the Grant Foster trust. I'd like to hear your side of it.'

There was a moment of dead air as Mack fell for the bait and groped for a way to reconcile the irreconcilable. 'Those were only loans,' he ventured, not seeming to realize that even in sweetening up the transactions he was admitting to the impermissible offense—taking money under any guise from an attorney in the Miami television case.

Mack dug himself into a deeper and deeper pit as he tried to parry Anderson's educated guesses. By the time the interview was over, Anderson had confirmed his suspicions: Mack was on the take.

Anonymous Sources

Sometimes a source will allow material to be used on the proviso it is not attributed to him. When the information constitutes an attack on an individual, it should be handled carefully. People who criticize others should be asked by the reporter to stand by their words rather than to hide behind the reporter, who must assume responsibility for the story with no source.

When it is necessary to promise anonymity make sure that the source cannot be identified in the story. The reporter cannot have it both ways—promising anonymity and making it possible for the reader or viewer to identify the person.

A murderer in a California prison was promised a fictitious name in the story in return for information about prison gangs. In his story, the reporter identified his informant as a former gang member, "a six foot seven inch murderer named Tom Danforth who is now locked in a protective custody unit at Tracy because he informed on his murder partner."

After the article had appeared, the reporter's editor received a letter from the prisoner, who wrote, "I am the only six foot seven inch ex-gang member who is at Tracy. I am also the only six foot seven inch ex-member who is in here for informing on his crime partner. That really points right at me. . . .

"The gang menace may not be real to you but to us who know, it is as real as the paper I am writing on.

"I have a family on the streets and I have had to tell them to move again because the Family know where they are, and thanks to your article they now have to hide and sneak to work. I should have known better than to talk to that guy, but I really did think he would keep his word, but then what is another Black convict dead or his family dead."

To sum up, here are some guidelines for interviewing suggested by Zimmerman:

Guidelines for Questioning

1. Almost never plunge in with tough questions at the beginning. Instead, break the ice, explain who you are, what you are doing, why you went to him or her. A touch of flattery usually helps.

2. Often the opening question should be an open-ended inquiry that sets the source off on his or her favorite subject. News rarely comes out of this kind of question. Its value is to get the person talking, to set up a conversational atmosphere, and to provide you with important clues about his or her attitude toward you, the subject and the idea of being interviewed.

3. Watch and listen closely as he talks. How is he reacting? Does he seem open or secretive? Maybe interrupt him in the middle of an anecdote to ask a minor question about something he is leaving out, just to test his reflexes. Use the information you are obtaining in this early stage to ascertain whether your pre-interview hunches about him were right. Use it also to determine what style you should adopt to match his mood. If he insists upon being formal, you may have to become more businesslike yourself. If he is relaxed and expansive, you should be too, but beware of the possibility the interview can then degenerate into a formless conversation over which you have no control.

4. Start through your questions, usually in an arranged order, to lead him along a trail you have picked. One question should logically follow another. Lead up to a tough question with two or three preliminaries. Sometimes it helps to create the impression that the tough question has just occurred to you because of something he is saying.

5. Listen for hints that suggest questions you had not thought of. Stay alert for the possibility that the theme you picked in advance is the wrong one, or is only a subsidiary one. Remain flexible. Through an accidental remark of his you may uncover a story that is better than the one you came for. If so, go after it right there.

6. Throughout the interview, keep reminding yourself that when you leave, you are going to do a story. As he talks, ask yourself: What is my lead going to be? Do I understand enough to state a theme clearly and buttress it with quotes and documentation? Do I know his or her full name and title? Do I have enough information to write a coherent account of the anecdote he just told me?

7. Do not forget to ask the key question—the one your editors sent you to ask, or the one that will elicit supporting material for your theme.

8. Do not be reluctant to ask an embarrassing question. After going through all the preliminaries you can think of the time finally arrives to ask the tough question. Just ask it.

9. Do not be afraid to ask naive questions. The subject understands that you do not know everything. Even if you have done your homework there are bound to be items you are unfamiliar with. The source usually will be glad to fill in the gaps in your knowledge of the subject. So do not try to seem omniscient.

10. Get in the habit of asking treading-water questions, such as "What do you mean?" or "Why's that?" This is an easy way to keep the person talking.

11. Sometimes it helps to change the conversational pace, by backing off a sensitive line of inquiry, putting your notebook away, and suddenly displaying a deep interest in an irrelevancy. But be sure to return to those sensitive questions later. A sudden pause is sometimes useful. When the subject finishes a statement just stare at him, maybe with a slightly ambiguous smile, for a few seconds. He often will become uneasy and blurt out something crucial.

12. Do not give up on a question merely because the subject says "no comment." That is only the beginning of the fight. Act as if you misunderstood him and simply restate the question a little differently. If he still clams up, act as if he misunderstood you and rephrase the question again.

On the third try, feign disbelief at his refusal to talk. Suggest an embarrassing conclusion from his refusal and ask if it is valid. Later, ask for "guidance" in tracking down the story elsewhere, or suggest non-attribution, or get tough—whatever you think might work.

13. Occasionally your best quote or fact comes after the subject thinks the interview is over. As you are putting away your notebook and are saying goodbye he often relaxes and makes a crucial but offhand remark. So stay alert until you are out the door.

Zimmerman acknowledges that his list is long. His advice to the novice: "Pick the techniques you think you can use and then practice them. Eventually, they'll become so natural you won't have to think about them."

Further Reading

Capote, Truman. *In Cold Blood*. New York: New American Library, 1971.

Fallaci, Oriana. *The Egotists*. Chicago: Henry Regnery Co., 1968.

Garrett, Annette. *Interviewing: Its Principles and Methods*. New York: Family Association of America, 1982.

Kadushin, Alfred. *The Social Work Interview*. New York: Columbia University Press, 1983.

(*Note:* The books by Garrett and Kadushin, which are used in schools of social work, are excellent guides for journalists.)

CHAPTER FIFTEEN

Interviewing Practices

Preview

A successful interview depends on:

• Questions that put the source at ease, show the source the reporter knows the subject and elicit information that supports the story's themes.

• Role playing by the reporter. The reporter may adopt a personality with which the source feels at ease. Usually, the reporter is himself or herself—efficient, direct, unemotional.

• Patience and accurate observations. The reporter lets the source talk without interruption while observing the physical surroundings and any revealing interactions between the subject and third parties.

Sources respond to interviewers they consider trustworthy and competent. They pick up cues about the reporter from the reporter's appearance, behavior and the questions the reporter asks.

When A. J. Liebling interviewed the jockey Eddie Arcaro, the first question he asked was, "How many holes longer do you keep your left stirrup than your right?"

"That started him talking easily, and after an hour, during which I had put in about twelve words, he said, 'I can see you've been around riders a lot.'

"I had," Liebling said later, "but only during the week before I was to meet him." In his preparations, Liebling had learned that most jockeys on counter-clockwise American tracks help balance their weight and hug the rail by riding with the left stirrup longer than the right. A rail-hugging journey is the shortest distance from start to finish.

Careful preparations such as Liebling's enable the reporter to establish an open, friendly relationship with the source, who usually is complimented that the reporter took time to learn something about him and what he does. But no matter how carefully a reporter may prepare, it is impossible to predict the mood of the source or the feelings a particular question will generate.

Starting Off Right

Liebling recalls going to a Washington, D.C., hotel early in World War II to interview General John J. Pershing for a profile. Pershing had been commander of the American Expeditionary Forces in World War I, and Liebling thought he might have worthwhile comments on the outbreak of fighting in Europe. "I did everything I could to get the old man to loosen up, including some pretty obvious flattery," Liebling writes in "Interviewers" in *The Most of A. J. Liebling*.

" 'When they started to cut down the Army after the Armistice in 1918, General,' I said, 'you were against it, weren't you, because you foresaw this new European crisis?'

"The old boy looked at me in an angry, disgusted manner and said, 'Who the hell could have foreseen this?' "

Usually, it is not necessary to spend much time on the preliminaries with sources the reporter knows. But people who are infrequently interviewed—the atomic physicist in town for a lecture at the university, the engineer sent out by his company to survey the area north of town for industrial development—must be put at ease.

Reporters use all sorts of techniques to start interviews. One reporter usually glances around the source's home or room as soon as he enters. He tries to find something about which he can compliment the source. Before one interview, he noticed an ivy growing up one wall of the source's office.

"How do you keep the leaves against the wall?" he asked. "Magnets and small clasps," she replied, and talked about her plants for several minutes.

One cause of trouble can be the reporter's misreading the source's willingness to be led. Some sources take over the interview situation, and if they supply the needed information, the reporter should be willing to assume the passive role. Most sources, unaccustomed to being interviewed, need guidance in the form of suggestions, leading questions, encouraging gestures and facial movements. Sometimes the reporter takes control of a domineering personality and the interview is unsuccessful.

Who's In Control?

A source may dominate the interview and intentionally or inadvertently avoid the issue in which the reporter is interested. The source may be at ease, even talkative, in such a situation. But the reporter must wrest control, subtly if possible. Control need not be overt. Indeed, a reporter bent on demonstrating that he or she is in charge will fail to achieve the balance of listening, watching and guidance that is necessary for the successful interview.

A source may allow the reporter to direct the interview on the strength of the reporter's reputation or his experience with the reporter. Some first-time sources consider reporters to be authority figures and become submissive. Generally, cooperation and a willingness to be guided depend on the source's immediate reactions on being confronted by the reporter. Some of the questions that the source may ask himself or herself are:

- Why is the reporter talking to me?
- What is her purpose? Is she here to hurt, embarrass or help me?
- What sort of story does she intend to write?
- Is she competent, or will she misunderstand and misquote me?
- Is she mature, trustworthy?
- Is she bright enough to grasp some of the complexities, or should I simplify everything?
- Will I have to begin at the beginning, or does she seem to have done her homework?

Sources answer these questions from the cues they pick up from the reporter's clothing, looks and behavior as well as from his or her reputation, conversation and questions.

Appearance and Behavior

One afternoon a journalism student cornered an instructor.

"Professor X (and here he named the journalism school's senior professor) told me I had better get my hair cut," the student said. "He said I would offend people I'm sent to interview."

The student's hair was long. "Have it cut and stop worrying," the instructor replied. "Most of the people you will be interviewing will be very proper people."

The student plunged deeper into gloom. "But it will ruin my love life," he said.

The instructor and the student thought over the problem, the student in deep despair.

"Why not have it trimmed, and see what happens?" the instructor suggested.

The student took an inch or so off his locks and had no further trouble with Professor X. Nor, presumably, did his love life suffer, for there were no further anguished visits from the young man, who, after graduation, became a long-haired and successful rock music critic for *The Village Voice*.

A few years later, when the hirsute look had become common on assembly lines and in offices and faculty clubs, the issue became women in pants. And so it goes: Youth expresses its independence through dress and grooming. And traditionalists—who usually are the majority and always in authority—take offense and condemn the new ways, until sometimes they join in and the fad becomes a trend and later a tradition. Until then, reporters in the vanguard risk offending sources, most of whom are traditionalists in politics, social activities, business and education.

A carefree, casual attitude and dress can tell a source that you, the reporter, do not take him or her seriously. Along with hair and dress, tone of voice, posture, gestures and facial expressions convey messages to a source. Anthropologists say that what people do is more important than what they say, and the first impressions the reporter conveys with his or her dress, appearance, posture, hand and facial movements may be more important than anything the reporter may say.

A reporter can choose his or her garb, practice speaking in a steady, modulated voice and learn to control the hands. But age, race, sex and physical characteristics are beyond the reporter's control, and some sources are affected by these.

The attitude toward women has changed considerably over the past 20 years, but some men in authority still find it difficult to address a woman as an equal. The worlds of government and finance are male-dominated and many men have attitudes toward women formed from their relationships with their secretaries, switchboard operators, mothers, sisters, wives and daughters. As a consequence, women reporters sometimes find male sources are either cold and distant—possibly because they are uncomfortable being questioned by a woman. Or the source may be excessively friendly or protective—possibly because of a sense of *machismo* or paternal interest.

Where there is identification with the reporter, the source is much more likely to speak freely than he or she is with an interviewer of another sex, race, religion or age. People feel comfortable with those who are like them.

Most small- and moderate-size news staffs are dominated by young reporters, and it may well be that the prejudice among sources against youth is the most pervasive. Youth must prove itself. And until a source is sure that a young reporter can be trusted, the source may be uncooperative.

Reporters can contribute to polluting the interview atmosphere. Reporters have prejudices and biases that can impede their work. One of the most common prejudices among the young is intolerance of the elderly.

Because of these limitations, some social scientists—and a few reporters—distrust the material they gather in interviews. In their book on unobtrusive observation, Eugene J. Webb, et al., maintain:

> Interviews and questionnaires intrude as a foreign element into the social setting they would describe; they create as well as measure attitudes; they elicit atypical roles and responses; they are limited to those who are accessible and will cooperate. . . .

Although no reporter would surrender the interview, some reporters prefer to use physical sources—records, documents and their own unobtrusive observations—as primary sources.

Equals. In "The Gentle Art of Hunkering," which appeared in the July/August 1986 issue of *Mother Earth News,* Bill Wodraska advises newcomers to the country how to ask their neighbors for aid, advice and information. Wodraska's suggestions are appropriate for reporters conducting interviews.

". . . rid yourself of any notion that you're 'bringing yourself down to the level of the local people.' True, you may be better educated, more widely traveled and perhaps even wealthier than your new neighbors. *But you're the one going to them for help and advice, not the other way around.* . . .

"The speed with which you walk up to him, the expression on your face, whether you're smiling or not, your posture, and the way you hold your arms all speak volumes about your intentions toward him. . . .

"It won't hurt to introduce yourself with a smile and a 'Good morning, Mr. Hopkins.' . . . Then you'll want to observe the universal rapport-breeding ritual of brief chitchat about the weather and the crops.

"These preliminaries serve not only to break the ice but also to give you an idea of Ed's reaction to your approach. If he's sullen, cold and defensive, you'll have to work on building a warmer climate before popping your question. . . .

"What judgment Ed will make of you will depend, at least in part, on *how* you talk during this meeting and those to come. Your voice needs to be low, slow, modulated and friendly . . . not brisk or clipped. . . .

". . . your query or request ought to be as specific and well thought out as you can make it."

Role Playing

Sent to interview a pioneer developer of the polygraph, a reporter sensed that the man was easy-going and relaxed. In an attempt to be humorous, the reporter's opening remark was, "You're described as the country's leading polygraph expert. That's a lie detector, right?"

The interviewee suddenly stiffened. "If that's all you know, I'm going to call your city editor and have him send someone else over," he said. The reporter apologized, adopted a matter of fact approach, and the interview was conducted satisfactorily for both of them.

Another reporter sent to interview a retired state department official decided that the official was so forbidding that by acting naive and a little helpless she might break the ice. "I see you have just returned from Rio de Janeiro," she said. "That's in Brazil, on the coast, I believe."

The distinguished former ambassador peered at the reporter from under thick, white eyebrows. There was a long silence. The reporter decided to drop that gambit.

Both reporters were intelligent and had carefully prepared for the interviews, but they had decided to appear naive to open up the source. They were role playing, and although their interviews skirted disaster, role playing is generally successful if the reporter acts out a role appropriate to the source and situation. Experienced sources expect a neutral, business-like attitude from their interviewers. Sources who are unaccustomed to being interviewed respond best to the stereotypical journalist they see on television or in the movies, the knowledgeable expert. Some talk more freely to the opposite type, the reporter who confesses he or she needs help from the source.

Obviously, the best role for the journalist is the one he or she fits most comfortably, which for most journalists is the impersonal, unemotional and uninvolved professional. Sometimes, the reporter finds he or she must become involved or the story will slip away. When one reporter was assigned to cover the rush week activities at a local college, she was struck by the depression of the young women who were rejected by sororities. She felt she was unable to break through the reserve of the young women until she remarked to one of them, "I know how you feel. I went through the same thing in school."

From Friend to Authority Figure

Reporters can adopt the role of friend, confidant and companion when sources appear to need boosting-up before they will talk. When a source indicates he will cooperate only if he is sure that certain benefits will accrue to him, or his cause, the reporter may have to appear to be an authority figure, someone sufficiently powerful and prestigious to bring about such benefits.

Antonio Madrid, 44, and George Montes, 37, both serving time for narcotics transportation in separate cases, said employment prospects were dismal because they couldn't even fill out a job application.

Both, in the words of Montes, jumped "at a chance for quick, easy money" in the sometimes lucrative drug trade. Neither is a career criminal.

"If I had a good education or been able to get into a good trade, I wouldn't have got into this trouble," said Montes, reading from a typewritten statement he said he spent six hours composing. Montes, who has served 11 months of a six-year sentence, recently completed the basic literacy program and is now enrolled in courses to obtain a high school diploma.

As a youngster Montes thought he wanted to become a lawyer, he said, but he dropped out of school during the 6th grade in Los Angeles.

In another interview, Alonzo Riggsbee, 28, said his mother was as frustrated as he was with his elementary school teachers in Washington, D.C. He dropped out in the 9th grade.

Riggsbee tried the education program at the federal prison in Lexington, Ky., when he was doing time there. But he didn't gain from the program because "They wouldn't take the time to work with me . . . ," he said.

After he was transferred to La Tuna, he started to improve after only one week in the program, he said.

Prison Interview. E. Patrick McQuaid, a reporter for the *El Paso Herald-Post* went behind bars to interview prisoners in the La Tuna Federal Penitentiary literacy program. His interviews and research revealed a high rate of illiteracy among the inmates. (Part of one of his stories appears at the right.) Photo by John Hopper, *El Paso Herald Post.*

(Excerpted from one of a series of articles by McQuaid in the *El Paso Herald-Post.*)

Some stories require pressing sources to the point of discomfort, or implying a threat should they fail to respond. Journalism often becomes the business of making people say things they would prefer to keep to themselves. Many of these things are properly the public's business, and the reporter who shifts roles from friend to authority figure or threatening power figure may justify his role as being in the public interest.

The line limiting how far a reporter can go before role playing becomes unethical is difficult to draw. Is there a line between the prohibition against a reporter posing as a coroner to speak with the widow of a murder victim and feigning ignorance in an interview? If there are no outright prohibitions against the latter behavior, then what does it do to the morale of the reporter? Does it generate a contempt for sources, for the reporter and his or her work?

One well-known Washington reporter said she did not mind letting a senator pat her on the fanny if it meant he would be more inclined to give her a story—an attitude many of her female colleagues find abhorrent. But is that much different from some role playing considered to be proper?

Limits to Role Playing

There are other questions. How well, after all, can a reporter assess a source so that role playing is useful? We saw how two reporters failed. Even psychiatrists admit to no special ability to make lightning diagnoses.

Reporters usually are best off when they are themselves—once they determine who they are—and then modify that behavior as the situation seems to demand. When John McCormally, editor of *The Hawk Eye,* went to Cuba with a group of journalists, he studied television reporter Barbara Walters for a story he planned to write. In his story, he wrote:

Does she use the fact that she is a woman? people ask. Of course she does. Just as I'm using my "old country editor" routine to try to outwit the big city boys; and Marty McReynolds of UPI uses the fact that he's an old Latin hand, and Joe Klein that *Rolling Stone* is a former underground sheet these revolutionaries ought to appreciate. You use what you've got in this rat race. But if that's all you've got, you're nothing.

Looking and Listening

Every story that makes a reader or viewer take notice contains sights and sounds the reporter has captured with such precision that the people in the story come alive. Behind the carefully chosen words of the story are the reporter's accurate and precise observations. These observations center on the person and his or her words and radiate outward to include the source's immediate surroundings.

Watching carefully and listening attentively, the reporter is able to reconstruct on paper the scene that unfolds before him. Here is *New York Times* reporter John Corry's description of George Balanchine, the choreographer:

He is, nonetheless, a slender, attractive man with high cheek bones, a chiseled face and a slight scimitar of a nose. Most often he looks as if he were about to be surprised, and if a caricature were to be done of him it could very well look like a bemused chipmunk.

Listening to Balanchine instruct the company in a rehearsal, Corry caught him in full swing:

"No, you don't do 1, 2, 3; you do 1, 2, 3, 4 . . . Just once through because I don't even know what it is, I forgot . . . Slow, slow, slow . . . It's easy, chata-chata-cha . . . You know, like shish kebab when you put it on a spit, you want to see every side. . . .

"Now you walk this way, da-da-da . . . The man needs the woman, or else how does he know what to do? . . . And now I have to go left . . . AH, THAT'S GOOD, GOOOOOD."

You are entering the office of the chairman of the English department. You had telephoned to ask if you could interview him about the department's plans to cope with the increasing numbers of high school graduates who arrive on campus poorly trained in reading and writing. He had told you to drop in about 3 p.m.

As you enter, you notice two pictures on a wall and some books on his desk. He also has books in a floor-to-ceiling bookcase against one wall. These impressions do not particularly concern you because this will be a news interview focused on the situation, not the individual. Nevertheless, the setting could provide an occasional break in the recital of facts.

The chairman is worried, he says, about the growing numbers of students unable to understand college-level material. The chairman pauses often in his answers and occasionally goes to a shelf to take down a book that he reads to amplify a point.

"A friend of mine calls this the cretinization of American youth, and I used to laugh at him," he says. He reads from a copy of *McGuffey's Readers*. "This kind of material is now at the high school level," he says. "I wonder if anyone cares." He then reads from a Wordsworth poem that he says used to be memorized in grade school. No more, he says.

As the interview proceeds, you notice that the chairman is toying with what appears to be a battered cigarette lighter. You wonder whether to ask about it.

Suddenly, you decide that the interview should include more than the plans of the department to offer more courses in remedial writing and grammar. The story will include the chairman's personality as well as his plans and ideas. That will help to personalize it, to make it more readable.

Quickly, you re-examine the office to make note of the artists of the prints, the titles of the books on the desk, and you ask about the ancient cigarette lighter. (You learn that the lighter is a World War II memento the chairman uses to relieve tension; he is trying to stop smoking.)

As the chairman talks, you note his mannerisms, his slow speech, his frequent stares out the window. A student enters the office and asks for permission to drop a course, and you watch him persuade the freshman to give the course another week.

Noticing the family pictures on the chairman's desk, you ask for their identities. Smiling, the chairman complies, then says, "You must be a believer in Whitehead's remark that genius consists of the minute inspection of subjects that are taken for granted just because they are under our noses."

You make a note of that, too, more for yourself than for the story.

Back in the newsroom, the editor agrees that the story is worth two columns, and he sends a photographer to take a picture of the chairman.

The Careful Observer

Details, Details

The reporter was acting in the best reportorial manner by noting specific details of the setting and the interviewee's mannerisms as well as watching for any interaction with third parties. In looking for details, the reporter was seeking the material that gives verisimilitude to an interview. Here is a *Time* correspondent's report about Jacqueline Kennedy in Hyannisport during the Kennedy presidential campaign:

> Jackie settled back into a huge flowered arm chair, draped a striped beach towel over her knees, and spread out a vast clutter of paint tubes, palette brushes, a glass of water, a glass of rosé wine (left from dinner), a cup of coffee, a jar full of L&M cigarettes, and pulled an immense easel with a half-started painting to a spot between her and the TV screen. . . .

On Target. When a *Baltimore Sun* reporter turned in a story about a murder, a copy editor asked him, "Which hand held the gun?" The question is asked in newsrooms nowadays when a reporter writes a story that lacks precise details.

There are least 10 concrete details in this short passage, and these specifics help to project the reader into the Kennedy vacation home.

It was not enough to say that the chairman toyed with a cigarette lighter. The reporter wrote of the "World War II-vintage lighter that he fingered to remind him of his no-smoking pledge." The reporter did not write that the chairman had read from an elementary school reader used in U.S. schools generations ago. He gave the book's title. The reporter did not merely quote the chairman when he spoke about the low scores of entering freshmen on the English placement test. The reporter noted the dejected slope of the chairman's shoulders, and he checked the school to obtain the scores.

Listening and Hearing

There is an adage that says that most people listen but few hear. Words assail us on all sides: Newspapers on the porch every day, magazines in the mail, books to be read, the omnipresent radio and televison sets, and the questions, advice, and endless prattle of friends, neighbors, relatives and teachers. It is a wonder that anyone hears anyone amidst the clatter. But the reporter must hear. His or her livelihood depends on it.

So many people are talking and so few listening with attention and courtesy that the reporter who trains himself or herself to hear will find people eager to talk to someone who cares about what they are saying.

To become a good listener:

• Cut down your ego. You are in an interview to hear what others say, not to spout your opinions.
• Open your mind to new or different ideas, even those you dislike.
• Grant the interviewee time to develop his or her thoughts.
• Rarely interrupt.
• Concentrate on what the person is saying and make secondary the person's personality, demeanor or appearance.
• Keep questions to the theme or to relevant ideas that turn up in the interview.
• Don't ask long questions.

Meticulous. The reporter notices the carefully ironed gown, the intensity of expression, the heavily veined hands of this 74-year-old woman who is readying herself for a meeting of the Ku Klux Klan in Kentucky. Photo by Greg Lovett.

Good listeners will have in their notes the quotations that give the reader or listener an immediate sense of the person being interviewed—what are known as high-quality quotes. Oscar Lewis, the anthropologist who wrote about Mexican and other Spanish-speaking peoples, began his article, "In New York You Get Swallowed by a Horse," (*Anthropological Essays,* New York: Random House, 1964, and *Commentary,* November 1964) about Hector, a Puerto Rican, this way:

We had been talking of this and that when I asked him, "Have you ever been in New York, Hector?"

"Yes, yes, I've been to New York."

"And what did you think of life there?"

"New York! I want no part of it! Man, do you know what it's like? You get up in a rush, have breakfast in a rush, go to work in a rush, go home in a rush, even shit in a rush. That's life in New York! Not for me! Never again! Not unless I was crazy.

"Look I'll explain. The way things are in New York, you'll get nothing there. But nothing! It's different in Puerto Rico. Here, if you're hungry, you come to me and say, 'Man I'm broke, I've had nothing to eat,' And I'd say, 'Ay, Benedito! Poor thing!' And I'd give you some food. No matter what, you wouldn't have to go to bed hungry. Here in Puerto Rico you can make out. But in New York, if you don't have a nickel, or twenty cents, you're worthless, and that's for sure. You don't count. You get swallowed by a horse!"

Me, Too. Studs Terkel, the master radio interviewer, has a way of making people feel at ease. "I'll say things like, 'Oh yeah, that happened to me.' If I bring some of my own stuff in, maybe that person will feel more akin."

The reporter may seem slightly passive in the interview, but he or she is working hard. The reporter is checking the incoming information against his or her preconceptions of the story. Is the source confirming or contradicting the reporter's ideas? Or is he avoiding them for some reason? Or is the source providing better thematic material? Just what does the source mean? What is he trying to say? Does he have any self-interest that affects his statements?

Some people will skirt a topic, and the reporter has to hear what is meant as well as what is said. The concealed meanings in every interview can be found by noting gestures, facial expressions, slips of the tongue, half-uttered remarks and the peculiar uses of words. Good listeners pick up the source's inconsistencies. And they are alert to the undercurrents that may be more important than the torrent of information the source seems only too willing to provide.

Taking Notes

Most interviews provide much more material than can be used. It is necessary to note only the salient facts and the high-quality anecdotes, quotes or incidents that will illustrate them. There is no way a reporter can keep up with the source's flow of information and still retain some control of the interview unless the reporter is constantly filtering the information.

As we saw in the discussion of how to write the longer story, the news story is an interplay between the general (the themes) and the specific (the buttressing material—quotes, incidents, anecdotes, illustrative detail). Any information not pertinent to theme or buttressing material is unnecessary.

After the Interview. Helen Benedict says that she goes to her typewriter immediately after an interview to write down everything her tape or note-taking did not catch: description of place, voice and the person; the way the subject said goodbye.

"I do this in story form, from the beginning." Benedict says. "Not only do I get good material for the story but often the lead."

A source, seeing the reporter stop his or her note-taking, may be discouraged from continuing. To avoid this, the reporter may want to seem to keep up note-taking while the source is supplying non-essential material. Actually, the reporter will be writing about the setting or the ideas he or she has from statements made earlier in the interview. With sources who inadvertently say more than they want to reveal, the reporter slows down note-taking or seems slightly disinterested so that the source does not take notice of the reporter's intensified interest.

Before leaving, or during the interview, the reporter may ask the source to repeat something in order to make certain the quotation is precise. If the reporter feels the source may want to retract a statement or will argue that he meant something else, the reporter will risk relying solely on his or her notes. Otherwise, the reporter must inform his or her source a retraction will not be honored.

Tape Recorder—Yes or No?

The tape recorder can provide large chunks of quotes, and the quotes will have the flavor of the person's speech. It also protects against charges of misquotation. However, some sources freeze in front of a recorder, or become so careful the interview is stilted.

One technique, suggested by a magazine interviewer for subjects who do not mind being taped, is to put the machine out of sight so that the subject is not conscious of the merciless machine with its ability to record every word.

"I tape, therefore I am," says Studs Terkel. Lillian Ross has no use for the machine and says flatly: "Do not use a tape recorder. The machine, surprisingly, distorts the truth. The tape recorder is a fast and easy and lazy way of getting a lot of talk down. . . . A lot of talk does not in itself make an interview. . . . A writer must use his own ears to listen, must use his own eyes to look."

First Impressions

The adage that first impressions are the best usually works for the reporter. Lillian Ross, the brilliant *New Yorker* writer whose profiles are studied for their understated yet incisive perceptions, says that "first impressions and first instincts about a person are usually the sound reliable ones that guide you to the rest of what the person has to offer." These early impressions can give the reporter a sense of the entire scene, the whole person, whereas the later impressions tend to be narrower, to focus on details and particulars.

The fresh observation is unimpeded by preconceptions. The reporter new on the scene will sometimes out-report the old timer who has formed notions and drawn conclusions after repeatedly seeing the same events and persons.

Off-the-Record Remarks

Sometimes a person being interviewed will suddenly stop and realize he has said something he does not want to see in print or hear on television or the radio.

"Please don't use that," he will say. "It's off the record."

Should the reporter honor that request? It depends: If the source is a good contact for the reporter and the material is not crucial to the story, the reporter probably will go along with the source's request, particularly if the source is not a public figure or official. If the source has said something important, or the information is of concern to the public, then the reporter will usually reply that since the source knew he was talking to a reporter, he cannot suddenly go off the record retroactively.

When Jessica Mitford was interviewing Bennett Cerf, one of the owners of the Famous Writers School, he let his guard down and chatted freely with the amiable but sharp-penned writer. In the middle of his discourse, Cerf realized he sounded contemptuous of the people who took the school's correspondence course.

Here is how Mitford describes what happened, in her July 1970, *Atlantic Monthly* article "Let Us Now Appraise Famous Writers":

> While Mr. Cerf is by no means uncritical of some aspects of mail-order selling, he philosophically accepts them as inevitable in the cold-blooded world of big business—so different, one gathers, from his own cultured world of letters. "I think mail-order selling has several built-in deficiencies," he said. "The crux of it is a very hard sales pitch, an appeal to the gullible. Of course, once somebody has signed a contract with the Famous Writers School he can't get out of it, but that's true with every business in the country." Noticing that I was writing this down, he said in alarm, "For God's sake, don't quote me on that 'gullible' business—you'll have all the mail-order houses in the country down on my neck!" "Then would you like to paraphrase it?" I asked, suddenly getting very firm. "Well—you could say in general I don't like the hard sell, yet it's the basis of all American business." "Sorry, I don't call that a paraphrase, I shall have to use both of them," I said in a positively governessy tone of voice. "Anyway, why do you lend your name to this hard-sell proposition?" Bennett Cerf (with his melting grin): "Frankly, if you must know, I'm an awful ham—I love to see my name in the papers!"

Here, Cerf spoke first, then requested that the material be excised from the reporter's notes. But when the source states beforehand that something is off the record and the reporter agrees to hear it on that condition, the material may not be used. Never? Well, hardly ever. Witness how Clifford D. May handled his source in this article, "Whatever Happened to Sam Spade?" in the August 1975, *Atlantic Monthly*. A private detective, Jeremiah P. Mc-Award, has been describing his difficulties in shadowing people:

> "It's harder than you'd think," McAward continues. "Don't print this, but I once lost a pregnant Indian who was wearing a red blanket and had a feather in her hair, in Macy's." I reply that he cannot tell me something like that and expect that I won't use it. "Really?" he asks. I nod. "All right, then." There is a pause and then he adds. "But she just evaporated. A two-hundred-pound Indian."

Many reporters cleanse the language of free-speaking sources before putting their quotes into stories. They also correct grammatical errors and ignore absurd and meaningless statements that are not central to the story.

The authors of a book about Clifford Irving, who hoaxed a major publisher into believing he had written an authorized biography of multimillionaire Howard Hughes, reported overhearing this conversation between a *Times* reporter and a lawyer for Hughes named Davis.

"Mr. Davis, I wanted to ask you if you have any comment on the things Mr. Maheu has been saying about you and your behavior in Las Vegas."

"It's just bullshit."

"But Mr. Davis, we can't put 'bullshit' in *The New York Times.*"

"Why not? You do it every day."

"No, I don't mean it in that sense. I mean it's a term we can't print."

"Oh, would you like it better if I said his remarks were utter nonsense?"

The next day, the authors say, the *Times'* story on the interview quoted Davis as saying Maheu's remarks were "utter nonsense."

To some sources, reporters sometimes apply the whip of literal quotations. They know the validity of the statement by Arnold Gingrich, editor-in-chief of *Esquire* magazine, "The cruelest thing you can do to anybody is to quote him literally."

In an interview with the chief of police of Providence, R.I., for the *Journal,* Christopher Scanlan quoted the chief as saying:

"Everyone knows you can stop crime if they gave the police the authority that they had. Nobody is going to tell me that you're going to stop crime by being nice to people. You have to push people around.

"I believe that if you have to take a guy around the corner and give him a couple of shots, maybe that's what we should do.

"If a guy commits a murder and we know he committed a murder, why don't they string him up the following day? That's my theory.

"Everybody is trying to rehabilitate. They want to rehabilitate these people. How can you rehabilitate an animal? You take a lion in the zoo they can't do anything with; what do they do with him after a while? They shoot him. That's realistic.

"In Providence we have the Puerto Ricans, we have the blacks, we have a lot of minority groups, and they're the toughest to control."

After Scanlan's story appeared, a black ministerial alliance asked the mayor to fire the chief. An arrangement was worked out whereby instructors from the Urban League and the National Association for the Advancement of Colored People would be on the teaching staff of the police academy.

Help Out. When the speaker said "incredulous" but obviously meant "incredible," the newspaper carried his word as spoken in a direct quote. *Winners & Sinners,* the in-house bulletin of the news of *The New York Times,* commented: "Of course we wouldn't doctor a quotation; that would be unethical. Nor would we insert 'sic'; it would be patronizing. But we should have removed the quotation marks and then, in a paraphrase, corrected the error. We prize direct quotes, but they're rarely worth embarrassing a speaker for a slip of the tongue."

Cautions. In writing an interview or profile story:

Link the person to an event; find a news peg.

Set the scene—in the lead or high up in the piece—so the reader knows where you and the subject are.

Keep descriptions tight, short, vivid.

Use plenty of quotes, but keep them short.

Here is a section from a piece in *The New Yorker's* "Talk of the Town." It is about a press conference attended by entrants in the Miss Universe beauty contest. Miss U.S.A. has just been introduced to reporters and is telling them that the Miss Universe contest has helped her express her feelings and widen her knowledge.

"For instance, Miss India has a red spot on her forehead. And do you know what? She says it's an Indian custom. . . .

"One of the experiences I've had was just this morning," Miss U.S.A says, "I'm rooming with Miss South Africa, and I just saw their money. You see people, but you never realize their money was different."

The reporters try to think of another question. Finally, one of them says, "What do you think of the feminist movement?"

"Oh, I think femininity is the best thing on this earth," she says.

"What about masculinity?"

"That's just as wonderful."

At this, says the magazine's reporter, the journalists decided to leave. "As the zoom lens pulls back from the Roma di Notte Restaurant, from Manhattan, from the Eastern Seaboard, the reporters retire to the nearby Clancy's Bar and attempt to drink themselves into insensibility."

A Television Interview

Let us watch a television reporter as he puts into practice some of the principles and techniques we have been discussing in the last two chapters on interviewing.

It is 6:30 a.m. and we are in an automobile with J. J. Gonzalez, a reporter for WCBS-TV, in New York City. Gonzalez and the crew are driving to Kennedy International Airport. Louis Treitler, the electrician, is at the wheel. Gonzalez is next to him. William Sinnott, the soundman, and Joe Landi, the cameraman, are in the back seat.

Gonzalez unfolds the typewritten note from the assignment editor and reads it again: "Go to Overseas National Headquarters at 175th St. off Farmers Blvd. (Right near the airport.) We will be able to get interviews with the passengers. Afterwards we were told that we would be able to get on the runway to film the boarding which has been delayed until 8:30 or 9. Crew should arrive 7:30 a.m."

The passengers the assignment refers to are airline personnel who had been on a DC-10 the previous week en route to the Middle East. The plane ran into a flock of seagulls on the runway, an engine ingested several of the birds, and before the plane could take off, one engine stopped turning over and dropped to the ground. The pilot managed to stop the plane and quickly ordered everyone out. Within seconds, the 10 crew members and 139 passengers

Burning Jetliner. Clouds of black smoke rise from the broken fuselage of a jetliner after the flight of the DC-10 was suddenly halted when a flock of seagulls was sucked into an engine. Gonzalez used some of the tape of the burning wreckage for his follow-up on the second attempt of the airline personnel to make their flight to Saudi Arabia. United Press International photo.

were spilling out of the exits and down the escape chutes. The plane caught fire and in five minutes was a charred hulk. No one was injured. But if those aboard had been the usual run of passengers, Gonzalez says, there might have been a catastrophe. The metropolitan editor had instructed Gonzalez to find out how the passengers felt about taking off a second time.

The Planning

It is a 45-minute drive to the airport, and Gonzalez and the crew have plenty of time to chat about the assignment. They will be going to three locations—first, to the airlines building where the passengers will be assembling, then to the airplane the passengers will board, and finally to a runway to watch the plane take off. Film of the plane heading off into the rising sun will make a good closing shot, they agree. But they are not sure that they will be allowed on a runway, and they discuss going to the airport control tower. Sinnott doubts that the tower will be available either, and they talk about using the public observation platform.

Gonzalez knows there is tape at the station that was shot of the burning plane the previous week. He will want to insert some of that dramatic tape into what he anticipates will be unexciting tape from today's assignment.

"This is really a bunch of talking heads," Gonzalez says. He means that the tape shot today will show individuals talking for the camera.

Gonzalez will need a number of transitions, or bridges, to move the viewer from one place to the next smoothly. Gonzalez begins to think of possible bridges—long shots of the airport, the passengers milling about.

Gonzalez makes mental note of the questions he will ask. If he is lucky, he will be able to interview the pilot of the plane that burned. He knows the pilot will not be on this morning's flight, but if he should happen to be around the airline office, an interview with him could liven up the story. It would also be useful as a transition to the tape of the burning plane and might even carry through as a voice-over (VO) of the firemen battling the flames.

On the Scene

Fortunately for Gonzalez, the pilot is there, and after chatting with him to obtain some background about the first flight, Gonzalez asks the pilot, "What went through your mind at this time?"

The pilot answers, "Basically, I thought we should be doing it some other way."

His reply makes everyone in the office laugh and it seems to break the tension.

"It's the understatement of the week," mutters one of the young women who was aboard the first flight. But when Gonzalez and the crew look toward her she has put on a sparkling smile, and in answer to Gonzalez's question about the mood of her fellow passengers she says that as professional airline people they are not too nervous.

Gonzalez is excited about his interview with the pilot. "This is the only real news here," he says. "No one else has had an interview with the pilot."

In his interviews, Gonzalez did not ask many questions. He knew that viewers are more interested in the interviewee than the interviewer. To keep from intruding when a source began to slow down in the interview, he would encourage the source with a smile or a headshake.

"I also use facial questions a lot," he remarked later. "When someone tells me something that is unclear or hard to believe, I will look incredulous or give the person a blank stare. This encourages them to go on and talk."

"Sometimes, the best question you can ask is one word, a simple, 'Why?' "

On the drive to the airport, Gonzalez had estimated the story to be worth "a pound and a quarter," a minute and 15 seconds. But it is Saturday, usually a dull news day, and there may not be many other local stories to compete with this story, so Gonzalez interviews several of the waiting passengers.

"How do you feel about taking the flight now? Uneasy?" he asks a young woman.

"No, I feel good," she answers as the cameraman shoots her reply. "I just want to get going."

Back in the newsroom, Gonzalez engages in another set of preparations. **In the Newsroom**
Before he writes his script, he jots down what he has on tape and the voices
that will accompany it. In one column, he lists the order in which he thinks
the tape will be put together and in another column, he indicates the lead-in
for the anchorman, his own voice and those of the interviewees.

Later, Gonzalez learns his hunch about the length of the story was correct. There are few breaking news stories, and CRASH, as he slugged it, is
given more than two pounds on the 7 o'clock news.

Cole, William, ed. *The Most of A. J. Liebling.* New York: Simon & **Further Reading**
Schuster, 1963.

Mitford, Jessica. *Poison Penmanship.* New York: Vintage Books, 1980.

Webb, Eugene J., et. al. *Unobtrusive Measures: Nonreactive Research
in the Social Sciences.* Chicago: Rand McNally, 1966.

CHAPTER SIXTEEN

Hunches, Feelings and Thinking Patterns

Preview

Reporters rely on hunches, intuition and feelings as well as rational, disciplined thinking for their reporting.

• Hunches and intuition spring from the application of the reporter's intelligence to the vast range of material the reporter has accumulated from reading, experience and general observations.
• Feelings and emotions can distort reporting. But they can also motivate a reporter to expose wrongs.
• Reporters seek relationships among apparently unrelated facts and events. The patterns the reporter discovers help readers move closer to the truth of events.

R eporters go about their work in a rational, almost scientific way. They assess events with detachment, breaking them down into facts that they weigh against each other and against their knowledge and the background of the event. They draw conclusions on the basis of their observations, not in accordance with their hopes and beliefs. Then they reconstruct these events into coherent, orderly stories.

Analysis and synthesis, the application of reason to experience—these are the processes underlying the reporter's work.

Yet, this summary is misleading. It ignores hunches and intuitions and emotional reactions that include feelings such as prejudice, hatred, friendship and love.

Hunches and Intuition

Every reporter has had the experience on assignment of intuitively sensing the meaning of the event, of suddenly seeing through the thickets of facts to the one idea that shapes the event. In fact, the process by which the news media determine what they will cover, and the thinking of the reporter as he or she selects the facts for use in a story probably are based as much on hunches as on reason.

Some reporters seem to possess extrasensory perception that enables them to detect stories. "I can smell something a mile away. It's just a fact of life," says Seymour Hersh, whose stories on the My Lai massacre and other investigative reports won numerous prizes.

Hunches, guesswork and intuition come into play as soon as a reporter is given an assignment. Before leaving the newsroom, before gathering a single fact, the reporter has ideas and feelings about the story that influence his or her coverage.

There is nothing wrong with this. The psychiatrist C. G. Jung said, "Feelings are not only reasonable but are also as discriminating, as logical, and as consistent as thinking." Even scientists admit the non-rational in their universe. Einstein wrote of the "underlying uncertainties of all knowledge and the function of intuition."

Hunches Lead to Stories

On a slow news day, a reporter decided to look into a proposal that had been made for a regional education plan for several Southwestern states. He wanted the comments of the governor of his state and he called the governor's office. The governor's secretary said the governor was on a brief vacation. Instantly, the reporter had a hunch something was amiss. He called a state official he knew was close to the governor, and when he was told that the official was "out of town" he was not surprised. Another hunch and the reporter called the state party chairman. The chairman's whereabouts were "unknown." A pattern was emerging, but what idea would put the pieces together?

Another hunch: The party was to be the host for a large gathering of western Republicans who were to discuss the various candidates for the party's presidential nomination. Assuming that the state party leaders were discussing arrangements for the conference, he was about to dismiss the affair as routine when his intuition—or reason—told him that the plans for secrecy were too elaborate for such a routine meeting.

The reporter knew that one of the issues the party faced—one that would probably surface at the conference—was what role Senator Joseph R. McCarthy should play in the presidential campaign. The reporter knew that the state chairman and the governor were disturbed by McCarthy's charges of subversion and treason against the Democratic administration which had caused turmoil within the country. An idea that linked or patterned his hunches and observations emerged: As host to the conference, the state's party leaders might be adopting a neutral position, or possibly one critical of McCarthy.

The reporter's hunches paid off. After many calls and some sleuthing, he managed to track down the state party officials. He learned that they were meeting to consider an anti-McCarthy statement.

When President Kennedy was assassinated in Dallas, the AP distributed an unconfirmed report that Vice President Johnson had been wounded. Tom Wicker, covering for *The New York Times,* was instructed by his desk to check. Wicker dismissed the report immediately because, he said later, he felt it was based on Johnson's holding his arm as he entered the hospital, and Wicker knew that the peculiar posture was a Johnson mannerism. It was an accurate hunch, fortunately for Wicker.

During the confusion that followed the shooting, Wicker and the other reporters heard reports they had no time to check. They had to make quick decisions. Wicker said rumors flew through the city and that he had to go on what he knew of the people he talked to, what he knew about human behavior, what two isolated facts added up to—above all on what he felt in his bones.

Wicker summed up, "in a crisis, if a reporter can't trust his instinct for truth, he can't trust anything."

Jerry Landauer, a superb investigative reporter for *The Wall Street Journal,* had a gut feeling when he first saw Spiro Agnew, then being nominated for vice president. "There was something too tanned, too manicured, too tailored for the guy to have been living on a governor's salary, with no other known source of income. So I started going down to Towson, seat of Baltimore County, the bedroom community where Agnew got his political start; talked to lawyers who frequently appeared to be on the losing side of zoning cases, to engineers who didn't seem to be getting a fair share of state business. After a couple of visits some started talking."

Experience as the Basis

We have seen a reporter who smells out stories (Hersh), and one who trusts his instincts (Wicker) to guide him in his coverage, and a third (Landauer) whose sense of proportion told him something was wrong.

Actually, what seems to be the play of intuition and hunches is the crystallization of experience. A hunch is the sudden leap from the reporter's storehouse of knowledge to a higher plane of insight. A new situation, fact, observation, statement suddenly fuses material from the storehouse. Reporters store thousands of facts about people, events, policies, and the various other elements of their daily experience. This vast storehouse is organized subconsciously. When a new piece of information strikes the reporter as important it seems to trigger the subconscious into releasing related material.

Hunches and instinct usually work for the good reporters, rarely for the talentless.

Ability plus experience equals excellence in all fields. During the 1982 hockey season, a talented young center for the Edmonton Oilers set records no one thought possible. Wayne Gretzky had fans comparing his feats with those in other sports. His goals, 82, and his assists, 120, for the season were the equivalent of a .425 batting average in baseball, 55 points a game over a basketball season, 3,000 yards gained in a season of professional football.

Still Better. Four years later, Gretzky did even better, breaking his 202 point total with 215 on 52 goals and 163 assists.

Pure instinct, say those who watch him. Not so, says Gretzky.

"Nine out of ten people think my talent is instinct," he said. "It isn't. It's all practice. I got it all from my dad."

When he was a 3-year-old in Brantford, Ontario, Gretzky's father iced down the backyard and had the youngster practicing. At the age of 10 he was skating five hours a day.

Good reporters make use of this same combination of talent and experience. The reporter who discovered the purpose of the meeting of the state's party leaders had more than intuition going for him. As he looked back on the event, he realized he knew from the voice of the governor's secretary that something was unusual about the governor's "vacation." Dozens of conversations with the secretary had given him a sense of her voice when routine matters were the subject. Her tone was different this time, and that triggered his hunch that something was happening.

Reporters who rarely develop good stories attribute the success of their colleagues to luck. It doesn't work that way. "Luck is what happens when preparation meets opportunity," says Raymond Berry, one of professional football's great players and the coach of the New England Patriots.

One of the biggest scoops of the 1980s was Dusko Doder's report to *The Washington Post* from Moscow that Yuri Andropov, the Soviet leader, had died. The *Post* put his story on page one in the first edition. Then the calls started coming. No one in government—not the foreign service, the White House or the CIA—had heard about Andropov's death. The *Post* pushed the story from page one to page nine in a later edition and gave it a cautious headline. The Kremlin confirmed the death the next day.

Doder says he knew the ailing Andropov had died because he saw lights burning unusually late in the KGB headquarters and the Ministry of Defense; also, Soviet radio played classical music instead of jazz. The same events had occurred 15 months before when Leonid Brezhnev had died, Doder knew. A call to a source indicated he was on the right track. Doder did not need official confirmation. All the facts led him to one inescapable conclusion.

The reporter's mind is like a computer in its capacity to store information. The mind, however, is able to make creative link-ups, as Doder did when he linked Andropov's illness, the late-burning lights and the classical music. This fusion of stored and new material is the reporter's highest achievement. It is accomplished through the application of logical thinking, inspiration and intuition to observations and background information.

Awed by a technological society in which computers and data processing machinery seem to minimize the human mind, reporters should retain their faith in the mind. "The largest computer now in existence lacks the richness and flexibility in the brain of a single honeybee," writes Peter Sterling, a brain researcher at the University of Pennsylvania Medical School.

Feelings

The reporter usually welcomes his or her hunches and intuitive guesses, but is less cordial toward feelings—that uncontrollable emotion that can hold the reporter captive without warning, lift him or her to ecstasy at a glance or a touch, and plunge its victims to bleakest despair with a word or a gesture.

This wilderness of feeling frightens most people, and it terrifies those who depend on their rationality, as reporters do. But reporters are human and must function within the limitations of the rationality of human behavior.

Feelings, in fact, can be an asset. "How can you write if you can't cry?" asked Ring Lardner. Feelings help develop value systems and keep them nourished. Moral indignation can direct a reporter to crowning achievements. The muckrakers, whose journalism may well have been the supreme journalistic achievement in this century, were propelled by a monumental moral indignation. Anyone who reads their work can sense the intensity of feeling behind it.

This same intensity drives most investigative reporters, who talk of their inability to tolerate wrongdoing. It is this strong emotional reaction to the abuses of power by public officials and the titans of commerce and industry that propels investigative reporters to their discoveries. The Teapot Dome scandal was exposed by a reporter for the *St. Louis Post-Dispatch* who spent years gathering evidence to prove that powerful oil interests had bribed the Secretary of the Interior in the Harding administration. The reporter, Paul Y. Anderson, was driven throughout his journalistic career by the need to expose wrongdoers.

Nevertheless, the reporter is right to check his or her emotions, for they can distort observations and impede the process of analysis and synthesis that is the foundation of reporting and writing.

A city hall reporter who finds the personal lifestyle and ideas of a councilwoman abhorrent may discover he is looking only for negative facts about her. A political reporter whose personal allegiance is to the Democratic Party may find she is overly critical of the Republican Party and its leaders. The idea of welfare payments to the able-bodied poor—or subsidies to farmers—might so violate a reporter's economic beliefs that his coverage is distorted.

Racial and religious loyalities and biases are especially powerful, and journalists are not free of their stranglehold.

Wishful Thinking. Following President Reagan's surgery for cancer of the colon, the ABC News and Washington Post Poll asked respondents whether they thought the President would develop cancer again before leaving office. Among those identifying themselves as Democrats, 40 percent said Reagan would have a recurrence of the disease; among Republicans, 28 percent said he would be struck again. Also: 48 percent of those who disapproved of the job Reagan was doing said cancer would recur, whereas 26 percent of those who approved of his presidency thought the disease would recur.

Race and Religion

When Louis Farrakhan, the leader of the Nation of Islam, spoke in Washington, *The Washington Post* carried two widely differing accounts. The first, by a reporter assigned to the event, described the speech as promoting an economic program for blacks. Two days later, a columnist reported that the most newsworthy part of the talk was the enthusiastic approval of the 10,000 people present to Farrakhan's mockery of the Holocaust and his attacks on "the wickedness" of the Jews.

A similar tale of varied coverage emerged in New York when Farrakhan spoke there. The story in the *Amsterdam News,* which has a black readership, carried this lead:

Minister Louis Farrakhan packed them in at a controversial rally held last Monday evening at Madison Square Garden despite a vicious campaign by city hall to discourage the general public from attending.

A *New York Post* reporter turned in this lead:

Black Muslim leader Louis Farrakhan turned Madison Square Garden into a mini-Nuremberg as he brought his message of hate to the city he called "the capital of the Jews."

The *Post* toned down the lead. The reporter, Peter Fearon, remarked in an interview with John Cassidy that "the outrageous aspects of the night were underplayed by most papers. All of the news media should have gone out of their way to say what a lot of outrageous nonsense this man is preaching. He represents a philosophy we have heard before. It is very close to being Hitlerite."

Not only are reporters victims of their feelings, newspapers and stations sometimes cater to what they construe to be the sensitivities of their audiences. The result often is that readers and viewers are denied essential information.

For some time, the press ignored facts about the appalling living conditions of the poor in minority communities apparently in the belief that such reporting would be seen as anti-minority. Consequently, policy makers had no public pressure to increase police protection for blacks and Hispanics, the major victims of crime. Little attention was paid to health conditions in these distressed areas, and the result was infant mortality rates two and three times greater than in middle-class white areas. The press is doing a better job of covering these matters now.

In Texas, the press was so restrained that it was possible for a small-town couple to dictate the kinds of textbooks children throughout the state could read. The couple claimed to speak for fundamentalists who wanted certain social, political and religious views presented in the public schools. Darwin thus became a non-person in science textbooks. The theory of evolution was treated gingerly, and "creation science," which holds that the earth and its inhabitants were created at once several thousand years ago, was included in science textbooks as a theory as valid as evolution. Texas could not adopt dictionaries because the couple found they contained obscene words.

Few newspapers wanted to take on the fundamentalists or seem anti-Christian until, in 1985, the attorney general ruled that "creation science" was not science but religion and its inclusion in textbooks violated the constitutional separation of church and state.

Auditing Feelings

The reporter's task is to audit his or her feelings about matters that have a high emotional content—for the reporter and for the reader and viewer. Here are some questions a reporter might ask himself or herself every so often:

Have I so committed myself to a person, an organization or an idea that I ignore negative information about the person or group?

Does my need for ego gratification—which runs high among journalists—lead me to see an event a certain way? (The blandishments of governors and presidents can lead to a journalism of cronyism and self-censorship. Clever sources know how to play to a reporter's need for praise.)

Does my need for immediate and frequent reward—a byline, a front page story—make me push a story so that I think it is ready to be written before all necessary facts are gathered? (The journalist often must write before every fact is in. Journalism is legitimately described as history in a hurry. But sometimes reporters make stories from skimpy material, particularly when they have not had a good story in a week or two.)

Is my competitive drive so great that I will ignore, underplay, or try to knock down another reporter's legitimate story on my beat?

No reporter can or should be neutral about life. But all reactions that swing to an extreme should be examined for their causes. The reporter should watch out for uncritical enthusiasm or unreasonable hostility.

Some reactions may be based on what the semanticists call "short-circuited responses," feelings that burst forth without thinking. A reporter may be positive about doctors or judges and negative about salesmen or plumbers without distinguishing among the individuals in these groups. This kind of knee-jerk thinking is known as stereotyping. It is a dangerous way to think, particularly for a reporter.

Stereotypes

Attitudes, fears, assumptions, biases and stereotypes are part of the baggage we carry with us from an early age. We see the world the way our parents, friends, schools and religious communities have defined it for us. We are also creatures of the culture that surrounds us—our jobs, the reading we do, the television programs we watch, and our government and economic system.

All these influence the way we think and how we see and hear. And the way we think, see and hear affects the accuracy of our journalism. In a famous experiment, journalism students were shown to have made more errors when they wrote stories about a report that was contrary to their biases and predispositions than they did when the report supported their feelings.

The journalist sees much of the world through lenses tinted by others. The maker of images and stereotypes, the journalist is also their victim.

Victim of Images

From Plato's time to the present, philosophers have speculated about how and what people see. In the "Simile of the Cave" in *The Republic,* Plato describes a cave in which people are shackled so that they can only look straight ahead at one of the walls in the cave. They cannot see themselves or each other. Outside, a fire burns, and between the fire and the cave dwellers there runs a road in front of which a curtain has been placed. Along the road are men carrying figures of men and animals made of wood, stone and other materials. The shadows that these figures cast up on the wall are all the cave dwellers can see.

"And so in every way they would believe that the shadows of the objects we mentioned were the whole truth," Socrates says of what the prisoners can see.

The parable is striking, almost eerie in its perception of image making. It takes little imagination to replace the cave with the movie theater or to visualize the shadows on the wall as the images on a television screen.

Plato goes still further with his insight into how images pass for reality. He examines what happens when the prisoners are "released from their bonds and cured of their delusions." Told that what they have seen was nonsense, they would not believe those who free them. They would regard "nothing else as true but the shadows," Socrates tells us. The realities would be too dazzling, too confusing.

Now let us jump some 2,250 years to the speculations of Walter Lippmann, whose classic description of how persons see is contained in his book, *Public Opinion* p. 81. Here is that description:

> For the most part we do not first see, and then define, we define first and then see. In the great blooming, buzzing confusion of the outer world we pick out what our culture has already defined for us, and we tend to perceive that which we have picked out in the form stereotyped for us by our culture.

Shadow Reality. A woman customer of a dating service that uses videotapes tells this story: She was reading the biographies of men in the service's reading room when she saw a young man who obviously was the man she was reading about. He seemed eminently suited for a young woman also in the room, and the woman whispered to the young man that he ought to introduce himself to the young woman. He did, and he spoke to the young woman for some time. When he suggested a date, she replied, "Oh no. Not until I see your videotape."

The Seduction of the Stereotype

Lippmann says that the "attempt to see all things freshly and in detail rather than as types and generalities is exhausting. . . ." Stereotypes allow us to fit individuals into categories defined for us, categories that are comfortable because they save time in a busy life and defend our position in society, Lippmann says. They also "preserve us from all the bewildering effects of trying to see the world steadily and see it whole," he writes.

But see it whole the reporter must. When a student movie reviewer at Barnard College saw a film made by Luis Buñuel, she wrote, in amazement, "How Buñuel at age 70 can still direct such marvelous, memorable, intelligent and worthwhile films is beyond me." Her comment illustrates one of the stereotypes common to youth, the belief that with age comes not wisdom but decrepitude.

Stereotypes are held by every age group, by religious groups, nationalities and the sexes.

Sexism

Sexual stereotypes are extraordinarily powerful. The stereotypes begin in infancy, carry through school and are retained in the workplace and home. Women are seen as weak, men as strong. Women are destined for jobs as secretaries, nurses, teachers, and when a woman becomes an engineer or a plumber, that is news. Obviously, journalists not only are victims of sexual stereotyping, they can also be its promoters.

Sexist writing identifies women through their relationship with men. Language itself often reflects male-centered thinking. The column on the left contains what is considered to be sexist language. The column on the right is preferable:

Sexist	Preferred
policeman	police officer
fireman	firefighter
postman	letter carrier

There are also inconsistencies in referring to men and women:

Wrong	Right
man and wife	husband and wife
men and ladies	men and women
Jack Parsons and Ms. (Miss, Mrs.) Sloan	Jack Parsons and Joan Sloan
Parsons and Joan	Jack and Joan
	Parsons and Sloan

On the Job. Women journalists contend that sexism is at work in keeping them from moving up to editorships. A study by Dorothy Jurney found that women held 12.4 percent of the editorships of all daily and Sunday newspapers in the U.S. in 1986.

Ten years ago, the percentage was 5.2, which led Jurney to conclude that unless the rate of increase changes, women will not achieve parity with male editors until 2055.

How to Tell a Businessman from a Businesswoman

An acute observer of the office scene compiled this telling commentary:

A businessman is aggressive; a businesswoman is pushy.

He is careful about details; she's picky.

He loses his temper because he's so involved in his job; she's bitchy.

He's depressed (or hung over), so everyone tiptoes past his office; she's moody, so it must be her time of the month.

He follows through; she doesn't know when to quit.

He's firm; she's stubborn.

He makes wise judgments; she reveals her prejudices.

He is a man of the world; she's been around.

He isn't afraid to say what he thinks; she's opinionated.

He exercises authority; she's bossy.

He's discreet, she's secretive.

He's a stern taskmaster; she's difficult to work for.

A news story grows out of the interaction between the reporter and the event. If the reporter sees the event in pre-fixed forms, he or she will pre-judge the event, making it conform to the stereotyped pictures carried in his or her head. Robert L. Heilbroner describes an experiment performed with college students that shows how powerful these pictures can be. The students were shown "30 photographs of pretty but unidentified girls, and asked to rate each in terms of 'general liking, intelligence, beauty' and so on," Heilbroner says.

"Two months later," he continues, "the same group were shown the same photographs, this time with fictitious Irish, Italian, Jewish and 'American' names attached to the pictures. Right away the ratings changed. Faces which were now seen as representing a national group went down in looks and still farther down in likability, while the 'American' girls suddenly looked decidedly prettier and nicer."

Stereotypes are, as the semanticist S. I. Hayakawa points out, "substitutes for observation," and reporters tend to fall back on them unless they are careful.

Journalists who settle for stereotyped responses to events might heed the warning of F. Scott Fitzgerald: "Begin with an individual and before you know it you have created a type; begin with a type and you have created—nothing."

Substitutes for Observation

Historical Note. In 1873, the Supreme Court ruled that a woman was not constitutionally entitled to practice law. The opinion of Justice Joseph B. Bradley stated: "The natural and proper timidity and delicacy which belongs to the female sex evidently unfits it for many of the occupations of civil life. The paramount destiny and mission of woman are to fulfill the noble and benign office of wife and mother. This is the law of the Creator."

Jews, Blacks and Hispanics

The most persistent stereotyping is directed at Jews, blacks and Spanish-speaking persons. Newspapers and broadcast stations have lent themselves to this stereotyping.

In the 1900s when mass migration brought many Jews to the United States, anti-Semitism spread rapidly, and newspapers were no deterrent. It was not unusual to see a criminal suspect described as a Jew or Jewish. The "Jew banker" and "Jew peddler" were common descriptions, as were "Jew store." Bargaining was known as "Jewing down."

Such language about Jews has disappeared from newspapers. But stereotyping for blacks and Hispanics remains, especially in descriptions of those involved with crime.

Patterns and Relationships

John Dewey said that "the striving to make stability of meaning prevail over the instability of events is the main task of intelligent human effort." These meanings are the patterns that establish relationships among facts and events. The great journalist of the muckraking period, Lincoln Steffens, said that his thinking about reporting was transformed by a prosecuting attorney during his investigation into municipal corruption in St. Louis.

"He was sweeping all his cases of bribery together to form a truth out of his facts," Steffens wrote later. "He was generalizing . . . he was thinking about them all together and seeing what they meant all together." Steffens said that this thinking led the prosecutor to conclude that the corruption was "systematic."

One of the most common patterns journalists form is the causal relationship. Here is an example of such a relationship. These are the first few sentences from a news story:

> Dozens of teen-agers threw bottles and rocks at a youth employment office today after the governor announced he was closing it and five others in the state to save money.
>
> Police said they dispersed the youths and made no arrests at Eighth Avenue and Essex Street.
>
> The incident followed an announcement yesterday by the State Director of. . . .

The story implies cause and effect: Because the governor closed the office, the youths demonstrated. The reporter did not visit the scene. He put two events into a pattern and established a causal relationship.

Cause and Effect. In a traffic fatality roundup in a San Francisco newspaper, the reporter made clear the causal relationship:

Ten lives in 10 hours. Such was the appalling toll yesterday of two head-on crashes that chalked up the grimmest period in Bay Area traffic history.

Not one person in the four cars involved survived. An entire family of five was snuffed out. That family, and a sixth individual, were innocent victims.

Speed was the killer. And liquor a confederate.

Three died in an explosive, flaming smashup on the Bay Bridge at 11:40 p.m. yesterday. The killer car was going 90 miles an hour.

Just 10 hours earlier, at 1:40 p.m., seven met death in a jarring smackup. . . .

Causal relationships are the result of thinking that goes this way: Because A preceded B, A caused B. The tip-off to such thinking often comes from the use of the words *after* or *following* in copy.

There are legitimate causal relationships. But when reporters do their job and move into Layer II to check out their assumptions about these relationships they often find the situation is more complicated than it appears at first glance. In the rock-throwing incident, if the reporter had questioned the youngsters it might have turned out that most of them were hot and bored that day and were angered when the supervisor bawled out a couple of youths who were lounging at the front door. The truth could well be that none of them knew of the governor's action.

Causal relationships are less certain in human affairs than they are in the world of mechanics and dynamics where physical forces have visible consequences. However, when a reporter has enough facts to indicate a relationship exists, he or she should be willing to make an inference on his or her own. The reporter will be cautious, for he or she knows that ultimate truths are rarely available to a reporter. Nevertheless, risks can be taken. In 1974, reporters for the *Minneapolis Tribune* came up with proof that the milk producers' lobby had channeled hundreds of thousands of dollars into the Republican Party treasury through dummy committees. Following these contributions, the reporters wrote, the White House decided to increase milk support prices.

There was no absolute proof that the contributions had caused the policy decision. But the reporters decided that the suggestion of a causal relationship was legitimate.

In the obituaries of Joe Pyne, a television and radio talk show host, and Hal March, a master of ceremonies on television quiz shows, *The New York Times* reported the men died of cancer. Then the stories noted that Pyne had been a "heavy smoker" and that "Mr. March had smoked two packs of cigarettes a day for many years." There was no proof their cigarette smoking had caused their lung cancer, but the data collected by the surgeon general's office had indicated a high probability of such a relationship, and the newspaper was willing to suggest the cause-and-effect for its readers.

Making causal relationships in print or on the air represents a certain risk to the reporter, but experienced reporters know when to take risks. In fact, risk-taking may be one of the marks of a successful journalist. The British mathematician G. B. Hardy remarked that high intelligence is not important to the success of most persons. No one, he said, can make the most of his or her talents without constant application or without taking frequent risks.

Knowing. "We do not simply store images or bits but become more richly endowed with the *capacity to categorize* in connected ways. . . .

"Human intelligence is not just knowing more, but reworking, recategorizing, and thus generalizing information in new and surprising ways."—Israel Rosenfield, "Neural Darwinism: A New Approach to Memory and Perception," *The New York Review of Books*, Oct. 9, 1986, p. 27.

Polar Alternatives

Another potentially dangerous line of thinking that is common among harried reporters is the polar alternative. For instance, the reporter may think: Either the Black Parents Association is right, or it is wrong in its stand on school books. This either-or thinking can save the reporter time and energy, but it can lead to superficial journalism.

Causes and actions are complex, a combination of many factors. The reporter who looks only for the black and white of situations will be limiting observations to the most obvious elements of the event. The world is hardly bilateral and the reporter should resist what is called bilateral consciousness by being aware of the infinite colors and shades between black and white.

Linking Facts

Confronting this multitude of facets, faces and facts is half the task. The reporter's most difficult job is to put them into some meaningful pattern, the story. But that is what journalism is about—linking facts to make stories.

Look back at the work of the reporter we watched as he tried to figure out the reason state GOP party leaders were meeting secretly. He was trying to link facts. But he had to provide the concepts to link his facts.

This kind of reporting takes us into the mainstream of contemporary journalism. It would have been Layer I journalism to have written that the governor had taken a vacation. Because of the reporter's hunch that there was more to the official's absence than a desire to try the Royal Coachman on a trout stream, the reader was taken closer to the truth. In other words, by digging for the significant relationship between the absence and the current political situation, the reporter moved into Layer II journalism.

We could say that the discovery came in an intuitive flash, a sudden insight. Reporters do make these sudden discoveries of the concept or idea that puts observations in a meaningful pattern. As we have seen, these leaps to significant relationships are actually launched from solid ground. They are based on experience and the logical thinking of the kind described by the philosopher Isaiah Berlin: "To comprehend and contrast and classify and arrange, to see in patterns of lesser or greater complexity is not a peculiar kind of thinking, it is thinking itself."

The technique of patterning is described by T. S. Eliot, the poet, this way: "The poet's mind is a receptacle for seizing and storing up numberless feelings, phrases, images, which remain there until all the particles which can unite to form a new compound are present together." In describing the emotion in a poem, he says it "is a concentration and a new thing resulting from the concentration, of a very great number of experiences which to the practical and active person would not seem to be experiences at all; it is a concentration which does not happen consciously or of deliberation."

There is not much difference in the ways poets and journalists think, indeed in the ways all creative people think. The ability to pattern observations and feelings is the mark of the thinking person, whether we look at a reporter covering a story or a composer at her piano.

Patterning is Organic. "As the cerebral cortex grew from apish dimensions through hundreds of thousands of years of evolution, it was forced to rely on tricks to enlarge memory and speed computation. The mind therefore specializes in analogy and metaphor, in a sweeping together of chaotic sensory experience into workable categories labeled by words and stacked into hierarchies for quick recovery."—Edward O. Wilson, professor of science and curator of entomology, Harvard University.

Famous Forecasts

No matter how brilliant the reporter's insights and intuition, he or she avoids making predictions. Forecasts have a way of turning sour. Witness these predictions from people in the know:

Sensible and responsible women do not want to vote.—Grover Cleveland, 1905.

Heavier than air flying machines are impossible.—Lord Kelvin, president of the Royal Society, 1895.

Who the hell wants to hear actors talk?—Harry M. Warner, Warner Bros. Pictures, 1927.

There is no likelihood man can ever tap the power of the atom.—Robert Millikan, Nobel Prize for physics, 1923.

Everything that can be invented has been invented.—Charles H. Duell, director, U.S. Patent Office, 1899.

Ruth made a big mistake when he gave up pitching.—Tris Speaker, outfielder, Cleveland Indians, 1921.

The good reporter has what the philosopher Alfred North Whitehead describes as an "eye for the whole chessboard, for the bearing of one set of ideas on another."

Reporters are always looking for facts that relate to each other. The obituary writer wants to know the cause of death, especially if the death is sudden, unexpected.

Finding the Links

A reporter covering such a death was given the explanation—accidental gunshot wound. But the reporter wonders: The death seems staged. Could it have been a suicide? That's playing games, he says to himself. Still, the death looks like that of a character in a novel. Thinking of this sort led the reporter to learn that Ernest Hemingway had killed himself, contrary to the explanation put out by the authorities, who had agreed to cover up the truth to save the family embarrassment.

A reporter assigned to write a year-end summary of traffic fatalities begins with the data the police department has supplied. As she scans the figures of deaths and injuries on city streets, she notices that pedestrian deaths and injuries are up 16 percent, whereas the overall increase over the previous year is 8 percent. She decides to concentrate on pedestrian accidents.

Further examination indicates that most of those killed and injured were 14 years old and under. The reporter recalls that some months ago a parents organization petitioned the city council to provide more play streets for the warm-weather months in areas where there is a heavy concentration of low-income families and few open spaces. She wonders whether the number of children who were killed and hurt in traffic accidents was high in the summer. She also checks the location of the accidents. A pattern is beginning to take shape. Now she must determine whether the facts support her ideas.

As she moves through the data, she notices the traffic department lists the times at which deaths and injuries occurred. She is surprised at the number of children who were killed or hurt in the evening. Well, she reasons, perhaps that is logical. Where else can kids play on hot summer evenings, especially youngsters from homes without air conditioning? She looks at her newspaper's clip file to check her recollections of the city council meeting. All this takes less than an hour. Next, she makes several telephone calls to gather additional information.

A reporter's approach to the story is as important as the fact gathering. She could have settled for Layer I reporting. Had she done so, her story might have begun this way:

> Pedestrian deaths and injuries in the city last year were 16 percent higher than the previous year, a year-end summary of traffic accidents disclosed today.

Instead, after her first hour of thinking and checking the clips, and another 45 minutes of calls, she is ready to write a story that she begins this way:

> For 10 of the city's children the streets they played on last summer became a death trap.

She then gives the total figures for all deaths and injuries to children under 14 and the total traffic deaths for the city. Then she works into her story the petition the parents had presented to the city council. Her finding that the evening hours were particularly dangerous for youngsters had not been discovered by the parents, who had asked for daytime restrictions on traffic. Before writing, the reporter calls the head of the parents group and tells her about the evening accident rate. The reporter is told that the group probably will renew its petitioning, this time with the request that in the summer some streets be permanently blocked off to traffic. This new material—the concept of 24-hour play streets—goes into the story, also.

The reporter not only turns out a meaningful story by linking up certain facts but performs a public service for her community as well.

Further Reading

Beveridge, W. I. B. *The Art of Scientific Investigation.* New York: Vintage Books, 1957.

Hayakawa, S. I. *Language in Thought and Action.* New York: Harcourt Brace Jovanovich, 1978.

Lippmann, Walter. *Public Opinion.* New York: The Free Press, 1965.

PART FIVE

A Reporter's Checklist

Photo by Anne Knudsen, *Los Angeles Herald Examiner.*

Introduction

The preceding chapters have described the processes that underlie reporting and writing. Now we are ready to move to specific stories. To help the new reporter handle these, we can devise a checklist of the necessary elements of any type of story.

For example: An obituary requires the name and identification of the deceased; the causes, time, place and location of death; the survivors; funeral and burial plans, and some background about the deceased. We can make similar lists of necessities for other story types.

In order to select the story types that most beginners encounter, many young reporters and veterans were canvassed for suggestions and for sample stories. The following chapters are the result.

Using the Checklist

When a reporter goes out on an assignment, the aim should be to gather information on the checklist, the essentials of the story. The checklist is only a starting point, however, a takeoff for imagination and enterprise. No rote learning of what to look for and how to structure a particular kind of story can substitute for creative journalism, just as no memorization of writing techniques can transmute slaglike prose into apples of gold.

The elements on the checklist are not in exact order. That is, any one of the elements could be made into a lead, depending upon the circumstances. Reporters must use their judgment to determine what constitutes the news angle or theme of the event. Not all of the elements will appear in every story, but most will.

Students should not look at the checklist as a cook approaches a recipe, first buttering the pan, then adding salt, stirring for six minutes, adding half a cup of flour. . . . This is a textbook, not a cookbook. Creative cooks always depart from the recipes, anyway. The reporter's task is to put his or her personal stamp on copy. The checklist will help point the reporter in the right direction if it is used carefully along with the reporting, writing and thinking processes that have been described in previous chapters.

Beats

The reporter starting on a beat tries to meet everyone—clerks, secretaries, typists, assistants as well as those in charge of the offices and agencies on the beat. A sound idea is to leave a card with name, address and phone number with all contacts and sources.

"Shoot the breeze," says an experienced beat reporter. "That's the way to develop sources and how you find good stories. People usually are happy to chat with a reporter.

"You need to establish a relationship of trust with sources. But you make no promises you cannot fulfill or that interfere with your responsibilities as a reporter."

CHAPTER SEVENTEEN

Accidents and Disasters

Preview

Local stories about accidents and disasters must include:

- Names and addresses of dead and injured.
- Time, location and cause of accident.
- Comments from eyewitnesses and authorities when possible.

Since these stories tend to read alike, an attempt should be made to find an aspect of the event that sets it apart from others like it. Eyewitness accounts can provide a unique perspective of the event that is useful for a lead and the main thread of the story. Usually, the number of dead and injured provides the theme.

Motor Vehicle Accidents

Motor vehicles kill, injure and maim an enormous number of people each year. News of collisions, of trucks and cars careening into trees and smashing into each other on fog-bound freeways is given good play in newspapers and on local radio and television news programs. Only the routine "fender benders," as reporters describe minor accidents, are ignored or summarized. Rare is the reporter who has never written a fatal, a story about an accident in which at least one person died. Most newsrooms make periodic checks with authorities so that they have the latest accident reports right up to deadline.

Four Dead, Three Hurt in Car Crash

Four men died and three others were critically injured when their speeding car smashed into a retaining wall in a residential section of Vallejo, police said yesterday.

Officers said six of the victims in the crash late Tuesday night were stationed at Mare Island Naval Base in Vallejo.

The dead civilian was identified as 23-year-old Patrick D. Hagen of Vallejo. The others, all in their early 20s and from the Mare Island Base were identified as Jonathon S. Cohen, Michael G. Williams and Manual Guitierrez.

The three injured men, who doctors at David Grant Hospital at Travis Air Force Base said are not expected to survive, were identified as Lucky V. Ramirez, Steve Criss and Conrad Anderson, also in their early 20s and stationed at the Mare Island Base.

Officers said the car carrying the men hit the retaining wall about a half-mile from the base at a speed of at least 70 miles per hour. Police described the road as narrow and twisted, with a posted speed of 25 miles per hour.

—San Francisco *Chronicle*

Accident stories tend to read alike. But the enterprising reporter can sometimes find an aspect of the event that sets his story apart from the flock. In this story from *The News-Gazette* in Champaign-Urbana, Ill., the location of the fatality was newsworthy:

DANVILLE—A 55-year-old Martinsville, Ind., man was killed Wednesday night as he was walking across the highway in the 2500 block of Georgetown Road.

Harold Owens was killed when he was struck by a car and a pickup truck while walking across Illinois 1 in the Hegler area south of Danville at 9:40 p.m.

That dark stretch of the road has been the scene of numerous fatal pedestrian accidents, according to Vermilion County Coroner Lyle Irvin.

Mr. Owens was with a logging crew that is working in the county. He was staying at a motel in the area and was walking across the road to a tavern, Irvin said.

The "dark stretch of road" has an ominous sound to it. We all know dangerous places like that. The story would have been more effective had that angle been worked into the lead.

Sometimes the remarks of the coroner or an official provide material for the lead, as in this story from the *Herald-Dispatch* in Huntington, W. Va.:

ELK CREEK, W. Va.—Two teen-agers died early yesterday when their car went off W. Va. 65, struck a tree and "practically disintegrated," a county official said.

The deaths were the second and third traffic fatalities in Mingo County in two days, said interim County Coroner Larry Wood.

He identified the victims as Jimmy Nichols, 16, of Varney, and Clyde R. Nichols, 18, of Columbus.

He said their car left the highway about 12:15 a.m., wrapped around a tree and "practically disintegrated."

Although wreckage was scattered over a wide area, evidence at the scene indicated that Jimmy Nichols was driving, the coroner said.

"From the appearance of the car and where it left the road, excessive speed probably caused the accident," said Deputy Bill Webb of the Mingo County Sheriff's Department.

There were no witnesses to the crash, he said. . . .

The accident story's importance is determined by the number of persons killed and injured and their prominence, the proximity of the accident to local readers or listeners and the circumstances of the accident.

____ Victims: Names, identification of dead and injured.
____ Type of vehicles involved.
____ Location.
____ Time.
____ Cause (from official source).
____ Names and identification of other drivers and passengers.
____ Cause of death, injuries.
____ Where dead taken.

Checklist: Motor Vehicle Accidents

_____ Where injured taken and how.
_____ Extent of injuries.
_____ Heroism, rescues.
_____ Latest condition of critically injured.
_____ Funeral arrangements if available.
_____ Damage to vehicles.
_____ Arrests or citations by police.
_____ Unusual weather or highway conditions.
_____ Accounts by eyewitnesses and investigating officers.
_____ Speed, origin and destination of vehicles.

Sources

State highway patrol; local, suburban police; sheriff's office; hospital; ambulance service; mortuary; coroner.

Cautions

Art Carey of _The Philadelphia Inquirer_ says that one of the first warnings he received while covering an accident was to be careful of inadvertently attributing blame when writing about the cause. Unless one of the drivers has been cited or arrested, it is best to avoid a detailed description of the cause. The reporter must be especially careful about saying which vehicle struck the other since such statements may imply responsibility.

Airplane Accidents

News of airplane accidents makes headlines. A motor vehicle collision in which two are killed will not receive the attention given the crash of an airplane with the same number of fatalities, probably because airplane accidents are infrequent. Airline crashes are big news. Local newspapers and stations will scan the casualty list carried on the wires for the names of local residents.

Checklist: Airplane Accidents

_____ Number of dead and injured.
_____ Time, location and cause of crash.
_____ Origin and destination of plane.
_____ Airline and flight number.
_____ Type of plane: Manufacturer, number of engines.
_____ Victims: Names and identification (including home town).
_____ Survivors by name.
_____ Condition of injured.
_____ Where dead and injured taken.
_____ Cause of death: Impact, fire, exposure.
_____ Altitude at time of trouble.
_____ Weather and flying conditions.
_____ Last words of pilot.
_____ Police, fire, rescue units at scene.
_____ Unusual incidents; heroism.

Midair. Resist the temptation to write that airplanes collided in midair, a word that has no meaning. Just write that they collided, says the AP. If they collide on the ground, say so in the lead.

____ Eyewitness accounts of survivors.
____ Eyewitness accounts of people on ground.
____ Comments by air controllers, officials, airline company.
____ Cost of aircraft.
____ Prominent people aboard.
____ Fire and other destruction as result of crash.
____ Direction aircraft heading before crash.
____ Flight recorder recovered?
____ If aircraft was missing, who found wreckage and how.
____ Funeral arrangements. (If available.)
____ Survivors of deceased. (If available.)
____ Official inquiry.
____ Previous crashes in area.
____ Previous crashes of same type of plane or same airline.

Sources

Airline; police, fire, and other rescue units; Federal Aviation Administration (which in many large cities has a special telephone number for accident information); air traffic controllers; airport officials; National Transportation Safety Board; hospital; mortuary; coroner; morgue.

Cautions

Eyewitnesses on the ground are notoriously inaccurate about aircraft crashes. Early reports of casualties tend to be exaggerated. Passenger flight lists can be erroneous; verify if possible.

Disasters

The line between accidents and disasters is difficult to draw. If the difference is the number of lives lost, the amount of property destroyed or damaged, then who would set down the numbers that distinguish the two? The fatal plunge of a school bus into a river that takes the lives of six children is a tragic accident in a metropolis, but to the residents of a town of 25,000 it is a disaster and much of the news staff will be mobilized.

Perhaps one definition of a disaster is that it is a situation that draws maximum coverage. Some define a disaster as massive, widespread death and destruction of the kind usually associated with the vagaries of nature—floods, earthquakes, hurricanes, storms and drought—a famine in Ethiopia, an earthquake in Mexico, a volcanic eruption in Colombia that takes 22,000 lives in one hellish night. But in actual usage, the word *disaster* covers large loss of life:

An American Airlines jetliner lost an engine and crashed shortly after takeoff from O'Hare International Airport this afternoon, killing all 272 persons aboard. It was the worst disaster in United States aviation history.

The National Guard is sometimes mobilized for disasters, and the Red Cross may dispatch units to help. Civil defense agencies may be present. State and federal agencies are often called upon to arrange access to the scene or to engage in rescue operations.

As in the accident story, the human toll is more important than the loss of property.

____ Dead.
____ Injured.
____ Total affected or in danger.
____ Cause of death.
____ Estimated death and injury toll.
____ Eyewitness accounts.
____ Property loss:
Homes.
Land.
Public utilities.
Permanent damage.
____ Rescue and relief operations:
Evacuations.
Heroism.
Unusual equipment used or unique rescue techniques.
Number of official personnel and volunteers.
____ Warnings:
Health department, public utility commission, police and highway department statements.
____ Looting.
____ Number of spectators.
____ Insurance.
____ Suits.
____ Arrests.
____ Investigations.

Checklist: Disasters

Action First. When several people are killed, most of the time the action that caused the deaths should come first, especially when the death toll is not high, the AP advises its correspondents.

So-so

Four teen-agers were killed when a World War II mine exploded in their classroom, police reported.

Better

A World War II mine exploded in a classroom and killed four teen-agers, police reported.

Sources

There is no dearth of sources for disaster stories. Statements may be issued by presidents and kings, generals and prime ministers, local police and priests. The destruction is so vast no one source can accurately assess the effect until the shock abates and human and property losses can be assessed.

Eyewitnesses Essential

Edward A. Mahar, a reporter and editor in New York City for many years, recalled his first big story as a cub reporter on the *Albany Argus*. It was the wreck of a New York Central train near Scotia, N.Y.

"On that big story I was fortunate enough to get one of the finest lessons a reporter can learn," Mahar recalled. "That is, to get your story, if you can, from someone who saw it happen.

"When I arrived at the scene about 1 o'clock on that cool, spring morning I saw bodies laid in a row alongside the wreckage. I thought I'd get sick, then and there. I got to the sheriff who admitted he knew little about the wreck. He pointed to a fellow sitting on the ground nearby.

" 'He saw it—talk with him,' he said, gruffly, over the din of the wreck crews.

"Though wide-eyed with shock, the fellow, a young farmer, told me how he had seen a freight pull out of a siding onto the main tracks right in front of a speeding passenger train. I took notes as fast as he talked.

"Finished with him, I counted the bodies and streaked off to a telephone, a half mile away. I had been sent to the scene merely to preempt a telephone and hold the line open for the star reporters coming later.

"I called the office and gave the city editor the farmer's eyewitness story and the count of the dead. Without knowing it, I had given the paper a good story for an 'extra.'

"Since then I have always stressed the importance of getting the story from someone who saw it happen—not second hand from a policeman or an ambulance driver."

Many disaster stories lack human interest because they focus on numbers of dead and injured, causes and costs. When a cold wave swept through the East over Christmas, it left seven dead in New Jersey. For his roundup of the disaster, Jim Dwyer chose five of the dead and began his story with vignettes: One man had in his pocket a 16-year-old newspaper clipping about his son's death; another was found dead in the front seat of a truck in which he had sought shelter the day before and from which he had been ejected.

A homeless man had dozed off under the Atlantic City boardwalk. "The temperature was basically warm when John went to sleep," said a friend, "but then it dropped rather drastically. In that drastic drop was when he died."

Hostage-Taking. Hardly an accident, and often not a disaster, the hostage story fits into a category of its own. From the murky politics of the Middle East to the main streets of the Midwest, hostages have been taken with as much an eye on publicity through the press as on pressuring authorities to meet the kidnappers' demands.

Hostage-takers frequently request press coverage, and the press usually obliges for fear of retaliation against the hostages. Many of these events are newsworthy, but even then questions arise because the event is orchestrated by the hostage-takers, as it was when a TWA airliner was taken over in Beirut. The U.S. hostages appeared on television to ask that their captors' demands be met. On their release, they pointed out that statements made with a gun against the temple are hardly given freely.

Press critics contend that hostage-taking is encouraged by enthusiastic press coverage. They say hostage-taking has become part of the politics of extremist groups and that the press must establish some guidelines for responsible coverage.

With stories of the dimension of a disaster the reporter is tempted to pull out every writing device he or she knows. Resist. If resistance is difficult, pause and reflect on the story—part fact, part fiction—told of the reporter from a Philadelphia newspaper sent to cover a mine disaster in Donora, Pa., where hundreds of miners were entombed dead or facing imminent death from mine gas. The mine was surrounded by weeping relatives, and when it was opened 200 bodies were taken out.

The reporter looked at this massive scene of death and grief and wired his newspaper the lead: "God sits tonight on a little hill overlooking the scene of disaster. . . ."

As these words came over the telegraph machine in the newsroom in Philadelphia, an editor shouted out, "Stop," and he handed the telegraph editor a message to send back to the reporter in Donora: "Never mind disaster interview God."

Writing Disaster Stories

CHAPTER EIGHTEEN

Obituaries

Preview

Obituaries are among the most frequently read sections of the newspaper. The obituary sums up the background and outstanding qualities of the individual. The obituary includes:

- Name, age, occupation and address of the deceased.
- Time, place and cause of death.
- Survivors.
- Funeral and burial plans.

The obituary usually centers on the person's most noteworthy accomplishment or activity. Useful information can be obtained from the newspaper library and from friends and relatives of the deceased. Increasingly, delayed leads are put on obituaries.

The obituary is a routine story that no reporter enjoys writing.

On the obituary page may be found the summing up of the glories, the achievements, the mediocrities, and the failures of a life which the rest of the paper chronicled day by day.

The first description is taken from a journalism textbook, the second from a veteran journalist's article about writing obituaries. Strangely, both summaries are accurate. Most obituaries in most newspapers are indeed routine, written by reporters who rigorously follow a formula so that only names, addresses, ages and the other vital statistics differentiate one obituary from another. However, the newspapers that ask their reporters to use their reportorial and writing skills on as many obituaries as possible find interested readers. Obituaries are among the best-read staples in the newspaper.

No reporter should approach any story with the intention of writing routinely. Of course, some stories are difficult to make interesting, but the obituary hardly falls into this category, for the reporter has a wide panorama from which to select material—a person's entire life. No life lacks drama, if the reporter has the intelligence and the time and the desire to look for it.

Even when the life is brief, the obituary can be interesting or moving. Here is an obituary of a 12-year-old boy written by a young reporter, James Eggensperger, for the *Sanders County Ledger* in Thompson Falls, Mont.

Goodbye, Ron

Ronald Laws, a rising star in Thompson Falls athletic competition, died Friday night doing one of the things he liked best, playing baseball. He was 12 years old.

Ron, as his friends and teachers and coaches called him, was batting in a Little League baseball game when he was hit in the chest by a pitched ball.

Then, according to one witness, he started running. After about 20 feet, he turned to the call of his coach, fell to the ground and never rose.

Spectators at the game rushed Ron to the Clark Fork Valley Hospital at Plains where the game was being played, but efforts there to start his heart failed.

His funeral was Monday in Thompson Falls. The Rev. Bruce Kline performed the service with special feeling because he had known Ron through Sunday school and liked him greatly. The Rev. Kline also performed graveside services at the Whitepine cemetery.

In fact, everyone who knew Ronnie liked him, teachers, classmates and teammates. He was a good sportsman and student and took pleasure in anything he undertook.

He left behind his parents, Mr. and Mrs. Larry Laws and two brothers, Larry Lee and Timothy, and a sister, Lori.

Fittingly, the Thompson Falls and Plains All Star baseball teams are planning a two-game fund raising baseball marathon for the 8th and 9th of July. Proceeds from the games will go to a memorial fund in Ron's name, a fund which will be used to support sports activities in both towns.

Other memorials for the fund may be sent to his parents.

Eggensperger recalls the day he took the call about the accident:

I remember feeling sick that such a thing should happen to such a good kid. But even more, that he had not had a chance to bloom into his potential and to enjoy all the things in life there are to enjoy. I put myself in his shoes and thought of all the memories, good and bad times, people and places I would have missed if I had not lived past 12, and the impact was overwhelming.

And in the back of my head was something I had been taught, which ran something like this: "An obit may be the only time a guy gets into the paper, and it's his last chance."

So I talked to some people and wrote what I felt.

Last Words. "At some point in writing each obit, the thought always crossed my mind that what I wrote would probably be the last words ever printed about the person. That's why I always worked hard to include something in that person's life of which he or she would have been most proud.

"I recall one woman who worked for years in the office of a candy factory. The part of her life she loved most was playing the violin at special Masses at St. Peter's and St. Paul's Churches in Dorchester. Or, for another example, there was a man who started as a busboy in a restaurant and later became the owner; after he became the owner, no job was too menial for him to handle. That clearly showed his character."—William Buchanan, *The Boston Globe.*

The Druggist
and the Laborer

Too Many. Across the country, 5,500 people die every day. In large cities 50 people die each day. To achieve an obituary of any length in metropolitan newspapers, said Alden Whitman, obituary writer for *The New York Times,* a person has to be "either unassailably famous or utterly infamous."

Deborah Howell, managing editor of the *St. Paul Pioneer Press,* says that "too many big-city dailies report just the deaths of important people—captains of industry and political leaders. That's a mistake. These newspapers ignore the woman who always feeds the ducks in the late afternoon at the city lake, the tireless youth worker at the neighborhood park, the druggist dispensing sage advice along with medicine for 50 years."

Howell recalled obituaries about ordinary people. A woman who died of cancer and who had asked for a party after her funeral was memorialized this way in the *Pioneer Press:*

The ladies sat in a circle of lawn chairs in the neatly clipped backyard, between the pea patch on the right and the tomatoes and cucumbers on the left, sipping their gentle scotches and bourbons and beers, while the mosquitoes buzzed around their ears, and the evening slowly faded without pain into the night.

When Tom Flaherty died in St. Paul, the paper was informed of his death by a friend of the family. "To most folks, Tom might have seemed quite ordinary," Howell said. "He worked his whole life as a laborer on the Great Northern Railroad, as did many of the Irish immigrants in St. Paul. At first, I worried how I was going to make an obit on Tom interesting. Then I decided that his life represented so much that is so Irish, so Catholic, so railroad, so St. Paul. When any Irish railroadman died, Tom was at the wake. At the St. Patrick's Day parade, Tom led the Flaherty section.

"I explained the kind of obit I wanted to one of our better writers. His obit began:

Tom Flaherty was an Irishman's Irishman, a John Henry of a man who for 50 years matched his mighty muscle against the hardest work the railroad had to offer.

"The trick is to make the dead person come alive again in an obituary, to remind family and friends and co-workers why someone was important.

"Too often reporters come away with just the basic facts about birth, education, marriage, vocation and perhaps a few war medals. Obituaries can be examples of the paper's best writing, meaning reporters must search for the kind of detail—the unusual facts—that makes any news story interesting to read."

Richard G. West, whose comments on the obituary appear in italics at the start of this chapter, says of the obituary: "Preparing an obituary is a delicate and exacting task, demanding the utmost diligence, insight and imagination. His obituary should be, as far as human judgment and ability may create it in the limits of a newspaper's space, a man's monument."

Monuments take time to carve, and the newspapers that attempt to carry an obituary for most of those who die within their circulation area cannot possibly devote much time or space to each. Still, some should be carefully prepared.

Beginning reporters usually are broken in by a stint of obituary writing. Most reporters consider it a dull assignment of little consequence.

"What nonsense. What an opportunity," says Joseph L. Galloway, who wrote his share of obituaries when he broke into newspaper work on a small Texas daily.

"The obits are probably read by more people with greater attention to detail than any other section of a newspaper," he says. "Nowhere else is error or omission more likely to be noticed.

"A good reporter gives each obit careful and accurate handling. He or she searches in the stack for the one or two that can be brought to life.

"Veteran of World War II, the funeral home sheet says. Did he make the D-Day landing on the beaches of Normandy? Taught junior high school English for 43 years? Find some former pupils who can still quote entire pages of Longfellow because somehow she made it live and sing for them."

The following items are required in all obituaries:

____ Name, age, occupation and address of the deceased.

____ Time, place and cause of death. (Some papers omit the cause as a matter of policy.)

____ Birthdate, birth place.

____ Survivors. (Only immediate family.)

____ Funeral and burial arrangements.

Survivors. The general rule is to include among survivors only the immediate family— widow, widower, children, brothers, sisters, parents. (A few newspapers will include surviving grandparents.) This sentence appeared in an obituary in *The New York Times:* "He is survived by his brother, Peter Rounds of Phoenix, and his companion, John Seidman." Not noted for innovations in matters of taste, the *Times* considered the companion a part of the immediate family.

Checklist: Obituaries

Many obituaries will also include:

____ Outstanding or interesting activities and achievements.
____ Memberships in fraternal, religious or civic organizations.
____ Service in the armed forces.
____ Anecdotes and recollections of friends and relatives.

Sources

First news of deaths can come from several sources. Many newspapers rely on the death notices mortuaries send newspapers to be placed in the classified advertising section. The news department is given a carbon. Some mortuaries will call in the death of a prominent person, and on some newspapers reporters regularly make the rounds of mortuaries by telephone. In the example from *The Fresno Bee,* the obituary form is supplied to mortuaries by the newspaper. Funeral home employees fill out the form and hand-deliver it to the newsroom.

The police and the coroner's office will have news of deaths caused by accidents. Wire service stories are scanned for the names of local people who may have been involved in disasters or accidents out of town.

Background material for the obituary is gathered from many sources. The starting point is the newspaper library. A check of the newspaper morgue for material about James S. Pope, the retired executive editor of *The Courier-Journal* and former president of the American Society of Newspaper Editors, turned up this interesting quotation from a speech Pope gave at the University of Georgia. It seemed to the reporter to sum up Pope's attitude toward journalism and it was placed high in the obituary:

> The good editor—and perhaps any good and useful leader—has to wake up angry every morning. He does not wait for the moment to crusade on a spectacular scale. He does not await an epidemic. He spots and cauterizes civic germs, regardless of the enemies it gets him, before an epidemic takes root.

Friends and relatives can provide information, some of it human interest material that makes an obituary interesting, and they can verify questionable or vague information. Here are the various sources:

- Mortuary.
- Relatives, friends.
- Newspaper clippings.
- References such as Who's Who.
- Police, coroner and other officials.
- Hospital.
- Attending physician.

Double Check. "The worst mistake I ever made in an obit was identifying the deceased as the same person who was shot and paralyzed in a holdup a few years earlier. I made that mistake because I didn't double check information that had been volunteered by a colleague with a reputation for accuracy."—Buchanan.

FUNERAL HOME DAVIS FUNERAL HOME   **Phone** 266-0666

(Please type or print. Use other side if necessary, but indicate on front.)

FULL NAME: Mr. Ms. Miss Mrs.

Greg Allen Bourne   **Age** 54

(Underline name known by)

Date of death 8/15/85   **Residence at death** Fresno   **How long resident of that city?** 20

Cause of death (natural, traffic, coroner's case?) Coroner's case

Birthplace Chicago, Ill.   **Previous valley residences and dates, if known** None

Occupation and employer Bartender and cook at John's Bar & Grill for 19 years.

Retired? No   **Date, if known** _____

Church Christian Science Church

Veteran? Yes   **(service branch and war)** Korean War - Army

Clubs, organizations, achievements, public offices Elk's Club, Veterans of Foreign WaRS, American Bartender's Association.

Deceased spouse's name _____ **Date of death** _____

SURVIVORS: put a check (√) over names with unusual spelling; list residence

Spouse Stephanie Bourne   **Marriage date:** _____

Parents _____ **City** _____

No. of sons 1   **Names** James Bourne of Los Angeles

No. of daughters 2   **Names** Janie Gillman of Florida

Marianne Bowen of Madera

No. of brothers 2   **Names** Robert Bourne of Illinois

Eric Bourne of New York

No. of sisters 1   **Names** Heather Bronson of Carmel

No. of grandchildren 5   **No. of great-grandchildren** 0

PRE-FUNERAL SERVICES None

(Rosary, Trisagion, wake, etc.)

FUNERAL SERVICES 10 a.m. Monday August 19 at Davis Funeral Home

DISPOSITION Holy Cross Cemetery   **Private?** No

(Burial, entombment, cremation, inurnment)

Visitation 9 a.m. to 5 p.m. Sunday August 18

Remembrances American Cancer Society or to donor's favorite charity

Family representative Stephanie Bourne   **Telephone** 234-5678

Obituaries are processed through the Metro Desk. The deadline is 6 p.m. For questions or corrections, call 441-6330.

Obituary Form. This form was filled out by the Davis Funeral Home and sent to *The Fresno Bee.* The story based on this information is on the next page.

Greg A. Bourne

Services for Greg Allen Bourne, 54, a local cook and bartender, will be at 10 a.m. Monday at Davis Funeral Home. Burial will be in Holy Cross Cemetery.

Mr. Bourne died yesterday following a heart attack.

He was born in Illinois and had lived in Fresno for 20 years.

He was a bartender and cook at John's Bar and Grill for 19 years.

He was a member of the Christian Science Church, the Elk's Club, Veterans of Foreign Wars and the American Bartenders' Association. He was a Korean War Army veteran.

Surviving are his wife, Stephanie; a son, James of Los Angeles; two daughters, Janie Gillman of Florida and Marianne Bowen of Madera; two brothers, Robert of Illinois and Eric of New York; a sister, Heather Bronson of Carmel, and five grandchildren.

Visitation will be from 9 a.m. to 5 p.m. Sunday at the chapel.

The family requests that any remembrance be sent to the American Cancer Society or to the donor's favorite charity.

Writing the Obit

Obituaries fall into two categories, depending on the circumstances of the death. When the death is accidental—as in a traffic accident, disaster or airplane crash—the lead emphasizes the cause of death. When death is anticipated—as it is for the elderly and persons who are seriously ill—the obituary concentrates on the person's background and achievements. In both cases, of course, the obituary will list the vital facts from the checklist.

Here are examples of the two types:

DE KALB, Tex.—Ricky Nelson, the singing idol who grew up on television in "The Adventures of Ozzie and Harriet," died in a plane crash yesterday that killed six other people, including his fiancee and his band members, authorities said.

Walter Lippmann, the retired columnist and author and the elder statesman of American journalism, died today in New York City at the age of 85.

As with any story, the obituary should concentrate on a major point or theme. Obviously, the overriding theme of all obituaries is the person's death. But that is not enough. The reporter must find the aspect of the person's life that is most noteworthy.

When Roger Maris died in Houston of lymphatic cancer, the theme was obvious. Maris, an outfielder with the New York Yankees in the 1960s, hit 61 home runs in 1961 to break Babe Ruth's record of 60. But Maris had to live with an asterisk in the record book:

*Hit 61 home runs in 1961 in a 162-game season.

Clearly, baseball wanted Ruth's record to remain, and the fans never took to Maris the way they had embraced Ruth. Maris was soured by this apparent rejection.

His obituary was framed around the theme of his bittersweet success.

When William H. Jones, managing editor of the *Chicago Tribune,* died at the age of 43 of leukemia, his professional accomplishments as an investigative reporter and an eminent editor were emphasized. The obituary noted his "tireless work, creative thinking and total integrity."

The obituary writer found in the newspaper files a story about a talk Jones gave to a graduating class at the Medill School of Journalism at Northwestern University. The reporter quoted from that talk in order to show Jones' philosophy of journalism. Jones had spoken about journalism as a career:

"It's a commitment to use your skills to improve your community, to speak loudly for the victims of injustice and to speak out against those who perpetuate it. Some of the best reporting begins with a single, voiceless citizen who seeks help from a newspaper that is willing to listen, and to dig out the facts."

Then the obituary quoted an investigator with the city's Better Government Association who worked with Jones on a series of stories that exposed widespread corruption in Chicago's private ambulance companies, which won Jones the 1971 Pulitzer Prize when he was 31. The investigator said, "Bill hated to see people abused, especially the helpless."

When Emma Bugbee, a pioneer woman reporter in New York, died, her obituary stressed the unique niche Bugbee filled in the days when women were a rarity on newspaper reporting staffs.

A founder of the Newspaper Women's Club of New York, Miss Bugbee was one of a handful of prominent female reporters who sought to expand the role of the women in what was the largely all-male world of journalism when she entered it in 1911.

Bugbee worked for *The New York Herald Tribune* for 56 years. For many of those years she was one of only two women reporters at the newspaper. They were not allowed to sit in the city room, the obituary recalled, "but had to work down the hall."

Delayed Leads

Not every obituary must lead with the news of the individual's death. Notice how Cary Stiff of the *Clear Creek Courant* of Georgetown, Colo., begins his story of the death of a prominent local citizen:

GEORGETOWN—When Tony Ricci was Georgetown's postmaster, he used to keep the Post Office open from 7 a.m. to 6:30 p.m.—seven days a week.

"Back in those days, the mail used to come in twice a day," his daughter, Irene Ricci Nelson, recalled Wednesday. "And he wanted to give the people good service."

Tony Ricci was proud of his appointment as the postmaster of Georgetown, perhaps because it proved that an Italian immigrant, a naturalized citizen, could amount to something in this big country of America.

The appointment was signed by the President of the United States himself— Franklin Delano Roosevelt, one of Ricci's heroes—and by the Postmaster General, James A. Farley.

And when Ricci died Monday in Denver just two months short of his 95th birthday, the document was still among his papers.

Funeral Story

For his story of the funeral of a slain civil rights leader, Charles Bailey of the *Minneapolis Tribune* began this way:

ARLINGTON, Va.—The humid haze of early summer lay hot and heavy on Washington, D.C., but here across the river, under the oak trees, the air was fresh and cool.

The little girl sat on a folding chair, her mother on one side and her older brother on the other. The child's face was blank and bemused, almost dazed. Around her stood a thousand others. Closer in, a score of men with cameras crept and scuttled and snapped their shutters at her.

The little girl, the story goes on to say, is the daughter of the dead man. The story continues, and still the man's name is not given. Here are the final two paragraphs:

Then the little girl and her brother and her mother were taken away, leaving their father and husband under the oak trees with the others who like him earned their right to lie there.

In a few weeks, he too will have a little headstone, with an inscription like all the thousands of others on the hills and in the hollows under the trees. His will say:

MEDGAR EVARS
MISSISSIPPI

Most obituaries read like the label on a bottle. The major ingredients are listed, but the reader has no idea of the actual flavor. The reporter's task is to help the reader to move close to the life of the person being written about. Few lives lack drama, if the reporter digs deeply enough to find it. This point was eloquently made by a reader of the *Lubbock* (Texas) *Avalanche-Journal* in a letter to the editor:

To the Editor,

A recent heading in the *Avalanche-Journal* read: "Relative of Ralls Negro found dead in an open chicken shack." Thin clothes, dirt floor, one quilt. Doctor gives probable cause of death as heart failure.

At ten degrees below zero, these conditions could stop a powerful heart in a young robust body. Still we wonder—what really caused death, a heart attack— or heartbreak? . . . Reckon how many bales of cotton Sam Jones picked in his lifetime? How many bales did Sam help grow? How many acres did he chop? How much profit did Sam's labor make for somebody the past sixty years? . . . Just before he died, he left a note asking to be buried near some cemetery. Sam was too modest to ask to be buried in a cemetery. . . .

In an obituary of Mrs. Helen Childs Boyden, who taught science and mathematics at Deerfield Academy, the reporter used several incidents from her life. When Mrs. Boyden had applied for work, the obituary reported, the principal was "not at all enthusiastic about the young applicant. But the school was too poor to insist on someone more experienced. He hired her on a temporary basis." She taught there for 63 years. The obituary continues:

. . . In a highly personal style she cajoled thousands of students through the intricacies of mathematics and chemistry.

Even in a large class she taught the individual, not the group. Her tongue was quick but never cutting. One boy, later a college president, recalls her telling him:

"Victor! When will you stop trying to remember and start trying to think?"

The Boy Is a Man. Some alert students at Syracuse University point out that the writer of the Boyden obituary has a "boy" doing the recalling in the second paragraph when obviously it is a man recalling something Boyden told him when he was a boy.

Here are some colorful paragraphs taken from obituaries:

Hyman G. Rickover—Washington (AP)—Adm. Hyman G. Rickover, the salty engineer who refused to go by the book and goaded the Navy into the nuclear era, died today. He was 86. . . . Rickover was a tiny, tidy man who was as demanding of himself as he was of others, suffering neither fools nor superiors—indeed, he often pronounced them one and the same.

Bill Stern, a radio and television sports announcer—While some radio and television critics and sportswriters contended that Mr. Stern's stories were sometimes taller than the highest infield fly, millions of listeners looked forward to his Sports Newsreel commentaries and anecdotes.

Use Human Details

Obituaries   399

Martin Gershen, a journeyman reporter—An intense, tenacious man, he made his search for news a personal quest and treated any withholding of information as a personal affront. As a result, his life and the news often ran together.

A wealthy retired business executive who lived on an estate—He knew the butcher, the baker, the news dealer and it was significant that he died in a moving-picture theater surrounded by a fireman, a policeman and the head usherette.

Duke Ellington, composer and musician—"Duke, he went all over the world after that, but nobody ever loved him better than we did," said an old-time tap dancer who goes by the name of Kid Chocolate.

Milton Bracker, a reporter for *The New York Times*—A restless, high-strung, energetic man whose unceasing productivity carried his work into just about every editorial corner of the *Times,* Mr. Bracker had a compulsion to write and his typewriter raced to appease his appetite for words.

The widow of a politician—She avoided the spotlight that focused on her husband through his long political career, but among teachers in local schools she was well-known as a tireless and cheerful volunteer who could be counted on to dry the tears of a newcomer to the first grade or to hand out graham crackers and milk at recess.

Sexist Obits

Most small- and medium-sized newspapers run at least a short item on everyone who dies in town. Metropolitan newspapers may run as few as one out of a dozen. Most of those selected are men. This is the consequence of the emphasis our society places on occupation and achievement. Traditionally, women have been housewives, clerks, typists and secretaries, not considered newsworthy occupations. But the perceptive reporter knows how important such tasks can be. There is as much drama—perhaps more—in the life of a woman who has reared three children or struggled to educate herself as there is in a man whose obituary is justified by the fact that he headed a local concern for 25 years.

Here is the beginning of an obituary in a Maine newspaper:

Mrs. Verena C. Hornberger, 92, died Tuesday at a Waldoboro nursing home. She was the widow of Hiester Hornberger.

She was born at Bremen, daughter of Franklin and Emma (Hilton) Chaney. . . .

Not only is the obituary routinely written, it finds Mrs. Hornberger's prominence to be in her relationship to her husband, which might be newsworthy if he is shown to be prominent. He is not. But the obituary does contain some clues that, if followed up, might have made a fascinating obituary. Look at the possibilities:

. . . She graduated in 1910 from Colby College where she was a member of Chi Omega sorority.

She was a teacher, first working in local schools. She also taught in Essex, Conn., and Verona, N.J., following graduate work in Germany at the University of Jena and Columbia's Teachers College.

Was she the last surviving member of the Class of 1910? Does the college have any information about her? She taught in local schools. Are there some stories from students about her? Was it unusual in those days for a woman to do graduate work abroad? And so on.

Here are answers to some questions about writing obituaries.

Frequently Asked Questions

Q. Does it make sense to prepare advance obituaries?

A. Yes, even before a prominent person is ill. Death is always sudden and often unexpected, despite the obituaries that report, as though unusual, that death came unexpectedly or suddenly. The AP keeps some 700 "biographical sketches" on hand, frequently brought up to date. A newspaper, depending on its size, may have a score or a handful. When a well-known person dies, the background, or B Matter, is ready so that all the reporter need write is a lead and the funeral arrangements.

Q. Must all second-day leads begin with the funeral or burial arrangements?

Second-Day Leads

A. Not necessarily. An enterprising reporter can turn up interesting and significant material although a competing newspaper or station may have had the first story on the death. Although many newspapers do require the standard second-day lead, nothing is as likely to discourage a reader from a story as the lead that begins: Services for (**name**) of (**address**) will be held at (**time**) tomorrow at the (**church or funeral home**). (**She/he**) died at (**her/his**) home (**date**).

Always Verify a Death

Q. Do I verify obituaries?

A. Always. Do so by telephoning relatives, the funeral home or mortuary, the police or hospital. Strange as it may seem, there are persons who call in reports of deaths, for revenge or because of some neurotic compulsion. Many reporters can recall experiences similar to that of a reporter who wrote an obituary only to find it was a hoax. This item had to be printed the next day:

> The Newark *News* yesterday printed an erroneous report of the death of James Barton of Westfield. The report, obviously a hoax, was received by the *News* in good faith from a source who purported to be an official of the company of which Mr. Barton is an executive. . . .
> The *News* regrets the error.

Embarrassing Material

Q. Should I omit material from a person's life that might offend some readers or embarrass survivors or friends?

A. Follow the policy of the newspaper or station. Generally, newspapers have become more frank since the 1930s when a new reporter for *The New York Herald Tribune* would be told by City Editor Stanley Walker that there were two rules for writing obits: "First, make sure he's dead. Second, if he's a rich drunk, call him a clubman and philanthropist."

We follow Walker's first rule by verifying reports of deaths. The second rule may be applied to a local businessman everyone in town knows was a heavy and habitual drinker in the last years of his life and lost most of his business because of his drinking. But when the novelist Jack Kerouac died in 1970, *The New York Times* said he had "increasingly eased his loneliness in drink." And a former member of the Federal Communications Commission who died in a rooming house in Miami was described by physicians in an obituary as a "chronic alcoholic." We are also frank about the subject's legal entanglements, personal beliefs and even his or her sexual preference.

Criminal activities from the person's past may be used. In the obituary of the FCC member, the lead described him as having been charged with plotting to fix the award of a television license. One obituary of Joseph P. Kennedy, the father of President Kennedy, reported that during the elder Kennedy's life there had been "whispers that Mr. Kennedy was anti-Semitic." Some of the obituaries of the writer W. Somerset Maugham referred to his homosexuality.

The taboos that once restricted such material are disappearing, and in time may completely vanish like the taboo against mentioning in an obituary that a person's death was a suicide. On smaller newspapers the tendency is to

Death from AIDS. More than 15,000 people have died from AIDS since 1981, "but nobody dies of AIDS in the obits," said a gay activist.

In a seven-month period, *The New York Times* listed only three AIDS-caused deaths. The news editor said the paper was "frustrated by close-mouthed survivors, doctors, hospitals and undertakers. Our goal is to deal with AIDS (and the conditions it aggravates) the same way we deal with heart disease or cancer: report all we can learn without browbeating the bereaved."

Few newspapers press survivors, but several are asking questions when the deceased is a young man.

look at the brighter side. However, incidents well known to the public cannot be disregarded. On the other hand, when a man or woman had led a useful life after making a mistake years past, no harm to truth is done by passing over the incident. The obituary of the former city treasurer who was sentenced to the penitentiary for graft 30 years before his death will be handled differently by different newspapers. Some will include his crime; others will not, on the ground that he paid for his mistakes and thereafter led a blameless life.

Q. When people request no flowers, what do I write?

Please Omit Flowers

A. Ask the caller if the family prefers that donations be made to an organization, scholarship or charity and name it. For example: The family requests that remembrances be sent to the Douglas County Heart Association.

Q. Do I always use the cause of death?

Cause of Death

A. The cause is given, unless policy is otherwise. For years, cancer—the country's second leading cause of death—was replaced in many obituaries by the euphemisms "long illness" or "lingering illness." For some reason, many people regarded cancer as a disease too horrible to name. Under the educational program of the American Cancer Society, newspapers have been encouraged to mention the disease. Cancer, cardiovascular diseases and the other leading causes of death should be mentioned whenever possible so that the public becomes aware of the major causes of death.

Sometimes, it is impossible to learn the cause. Relatives will not say, and physicians are not available or will give the answer, "heart failure." There are diseases that would embarrass relatives, such as cirrhosis of the liver, which often is the result of heavy drinking. If the person is prominent, the cause of death eventually will be revealed.

In an article in the *Nieman Reports,* "The Obituary as a Work of Art," June 1971, Michael Gartner recalls reading a New Hampshire weekly newspaper in which the "townsfolk had an unusual characteristic; they died of but two causes: a long illness or a short illness." He asked the editor why. The editor answered that most obituaries are submitted by funeral directors who presumably used the stock phrases to spare survivors distress. He went on, according to Gartner:

> They do present difficulties at times, as for instance recently when a man who resides here was found dead in a New York hotel room having fastened a noose and hanged himself from a peg on his bedroom door. We reported him as dead of asphyxiation under circumstances being investigated, which was the literal truth, but something less than the truth.

Cigarettes and Cancer. Some newspapers link death from lung cancer to its major cause, as the *Chicago Sun-Times* did in this lead to the obituary of one of its former staffers:

Martin Gershen, 60, author, journalism professor and a former *Sun-Times* reporter with an international reputation and a three-pack-a-day cigarette habit, died in Washington yesterday of lung cancer.

Cause and Effect. Studies have shown that the suicide rate increases after the publication of stories about suicides of well-known people. There is a "strong increase" in the number of suicides among teenagers, one study found. The copycat effect is known as the Werther effect, so named for the young man in a novel by Goethe who commits suicide. After the novel, *The Sorrows of Young Werther* was published late in the 18th Century, a wave of suicides among young people spread over Europe.

Suicide

Localizing Obituaries

Humorous Obituaries

As a matter of fact this belies your allegation that we have only two types of *causa mortis*. The real fun comes when a respected citizen meets his Maker not by way of long or short illness, but because of a very short illness in the form of suicide or homicide. In such cases, small town journalistic practice demands that the cause itself be passed over in one hasty sentence. We then proceed to describe the profusion of flowers at the funeral, the high esteem in which said citizen was held by his townsmen, etc.

Cause of death should always be listed—unless policy is otherwise—certainly when the deceased is relatively young, say under 60. Readers want to know.

Q. How do I handle suicides?

A. Follow the newspaper's policy. Most are frank; some avoid the word. The *Bangor* (Maine) *Daily News* uses the term "died unexpectedly," and the *Eagle-Tribune* in Lawrence, Mass., uses the words "short illness" for suicides. *The Morning Record and Journal* in Meriden, Conn., describes the cause of death in the final paragraph of the obituary, which allows the family to cut off the paragraph before preserving the story or sending it to others. Be careful to attribute suicide to an authority, the medical examiner or the coroner. Without such attribution, do not state suicide was the cause of death.

Q. Should I try to localize obituaries whenever possible?

A. Yes, if the person is a resident of your community and died elsewhere or was a former well-known resident. For example:

> John A. Nylic, 68, a retired maintenance worker at General Electric Co., died Friday night after suffering an apparent heart attack while visiting in Lebanon Springs, N.Y.
> Mr. Nylic, who lived at 78 W. Housatonic St. . . .
> —*The Berkshire Eagle*
> (Pittsfield, Mass.)

Q. Must the obituary always be solemn?

A. Most are and should be. Now and then the subject lends himself or herself to lighter treatment. When the screenwriter Al Boasberg died, the lead to his obituary shocked some readers. Others found it appropriate. Boasberg had written many of the gags that were used in the Marx Brothers movies.

Some of his most famous sequences involved death, such as the one of Groucho Marx posing as a doctor taking a patient's pulse and intoning: "Either this man is dead or my watch has stopped."

For the lead on Boasberg's obituary, Douglas Gilbert wrote:

The joke's on Al Boasberg. He's dead.

The Specialist

On most newspapers, obituaries are handled by beginners and feature and general assignment reporters who happen to be in the office. A few newspapers have writers whose specialty is obituaries. They are given wide latitude.

Alden Whitman, for years the master obituary writer for *The New York Times,* was allowed to comment on the personal habits and the accomplishments of his subjects. When he wrote the obituary of Mies van der Rohe, the prophet of an austere modern architectural style, Whitman noted that the architect chose to live on the third floor of an old-fashioned apartment house on Chicago's north side.

In his obituary of André Malraux, the French writer, Whitman wrote that he was "a chain smoker of cheap cigarettes." In his lengthy obituary of the American socialist, Norman Thomas, Whitman said Thomas' socialism "was to Marxism what Musak is to Mozart."

Further Reading

Mitford, Jessica. *The American Way of Death.* New York: Fawcett Crest, 1978.

Whitman, Alden. *Come to Judgment.* New York: Viking Press, 1980.

Whitman, Alden. *The Obituary Book.* New York: Stein and Day, 1971.

CHAPTER NINETEEN

Speeches, Meetings and News Conferences

Preview

• Speech stories include the name and identification of the speaker, the theme of the talk, the setting and ample quotations. When a prepared text is used for the story, it should be checked against the actual delivery.

• Meeting stories usually begin with the major action taken. They include the purpose of the meeting, background to the major action and quotations from those who spoke.

• A news conference story begins with the major point made at the conference unless a better lead turns up in the question-and-answer period. The story includes background and topics discussed in the question-and-answer period.

The Speech Story

"Ours is not to wonder why but to cover the speech or die," the reporter muttered as he put on his overcoat and stepped into the cold for a three-block walk to a downtown hotel where a testimonial dinner for the mayor was to be held. "I'll bet it's creamed chicken again," he said to himself.

The reporter's exasperation was caused as much by the fare he felt the speaker would offer as by the menu.

Speeches, hardly the most exciting stories a reporter covers, are a steady part of the journalist's day-to-day work. Realizing that not every speech can be covered, speakers and organizations deliver a prepared text to the newspaper and broadcast station ahead of time so that the story can be written in the office. (The reporter inserts the phrase, "In a speech prepared for delivery tonight . . ." or something similar.)

Speeches by prominent persons are usually covered, whatever the subject. Nothing could have been more mundane than the testimonial dinner set for Betty Ford, wife of President Ford, at the New York Hilton one warm June evening. She was to be honored at the dinner launching a $6 million fund drive for an American Bicentennial Park in Israel. Her remarks were expected to be routine. Indeed, as the evening wore on, reporters became restless. A few of them left, asking those who remained to cover for them should anything unusual turn up.

Naturally, the unusual did occur, and it was front page news in newspapers around the country.

As Mrs. Ford was being introduced, the president of the Jewish National Fund of America, who had just finished speaking, slumped down in his chair at the head table.

In the confusion, Mrs. Ford went to the microphone and spoke to the stunned guests: "Can we bow our heads for a moment and say a prayer for Rabbi Sage," she said. The New York *Daily News* began its story this way:

First lady Betty Ford led a stunned benefit dinner audience in prayer at the New York Hilton last night for a Zionist leader who collapsed at the affair honoring Mrs. Ford, and died of an apparent heart attack at a hospital a short time later.

Basics for the
Speech Story

Every speech story must include:

____ Who spoke—name and identification.
____ What he or she said—speaker's main point.
____ The setting or circumstances of the speech.

Any of these can provide the lead and theme of the story, although most speech stories emphasize what was said. All three must be included in the first few paragraphs, as in the story on the next page by Itabari Njeri in *The Greenville* (S.C.) *News*. Njeri began her story with a delayed lead and moved to the speaker's main point in the second paragraph.

The most important task the reporter faces is finding the theme. A tip-off to the theme may be the title of the speech. Often, speakers will use forensic devices to drive home their major points—pounding the podium, raising the voice, suddenly slowing down their delivery, the summary at the end.

When the reporter is unsure of the theme, it makes sense to interview the speaker after the talk. When combining material from a speech and interview, the journalist should tell the reader or listener where the information came from. Otherwise, those who attended the speech or heard it on radio or television will find the report puzzling.

Occasionally, a reporter will find a lead in what the speaker considers a secondary theme. Then, the reporter should lead with what he considers the most important element, but high in the story he should summarize what the speaker considers the major theme.

For example: The president of a large investment firm is speaking to a local civic club about "The Role of the Small Investor." The morning papers have a story from New York about a sudden selling wave on the stock exchange late yesterday that sent prices tumbling. The speaker sticks to his subject that noon, but in a digression predicts that the bottom of the market has not been reached. Obviously, the lead is his prediction of a continued decline. The reporter will probably want to nail the speaker after his talk for his comments on the market decline to give still more information to readers about his newsworthy prediction.

Fewer rules a goal, OSHA director says

By ITABARI NJERI
News staff writer

The three greatest lies, according to Dr. Eula Bingham, assistant secretary of labor: "The check is in the mail; Darling, I haven't looked at another woman in 27 years; and, I'm from the government and I'm here to help you."

The punchline got the desired laugh. But Dr. Bingham, who also directs the Labor Department's Occupational Safety and Health Administration, said she really is trying to help business and labor by eliminating or streamlining unnecessary government health and safety regulations.

Addressing the annual spring meeting of the South Carolina Occupational Safety Council, the former college professor and zoologist said: "We are attempting to revamp regulations that are burdensome and not meaningful. Our mandate is to protect the health, life and limb of working men and women. We are not interested in harassing or catching anybody."

Dr. Bingham said that when she was appointed to her position by President Carter in 1977 she came in with the bias of streamlining OSHA and giving businesses the flexibility to comply with health and safety regulations in a cost-effective manner. She said this is in keeping with the president's goal of a leaner, less inflationary government.

"We've taken 928 standards off the federal books and I have urged state programs to follow suit," she said. "Nine of those non-essential regulations accounted for 21,000 citations for OSHA violations being issued."

Dr. Bingham said that OSHA is currently rewriting its fire protection code which was 400 pages and will be 25 to 30 pages when it is completed in a few weeks.

"I hope to have that reduced to one paragraph of plain English," she said.

Dr. Bingham said that her agency must "speak to the needs of small businesses. It's not just General Motors that has safety difficulties."

She said OSHA provides on-site consultants to assist small businesses with safety problems.

"In an Alabama bakery employees were suffering from severe headaches. We sent a consultant there and discovered that the exhaust system was turned off after the bread was baked and carbon monoxide had built up in the bakery.

"In Tennessee, a paint shop was having problems with vapors from mixed solvents. Our consultant helped the company ventilate the shop at a very low cost," said the OSHA director. . . .

A speech consists of spoken words. So must the story. Unless there is an incident during the talk that would make the circumstances and the setting the most newsworthy item, the story should emphasize what was said with ample quotations at the top of the story. But resist the quote lead unless there is a highly unusual statement.

Now and then a reporter sits through an incoherent speech in which illogic and vagueness prevail. What should he or she do—confuse the reader with an accurate account? The reader will only blame the reporter. The reporter should seek out the speaker and attempt to clarify the confused points, ask others who know about the situation the speaker sought to discuss, and then write a short story.

The Fuzzy and the Funny Speech

John R. Hunt, who turned from prospecting in the wilds of northwestern Quebec to newspapering, has been covering the North country of Ontario for the *North Bay Nugget* for almost 30 years. "As a small-town newspaperman, I have covered hundreds of speeches," Hunt says.

"It is an interesting fact that a dull and boring speech can often become an interesting story. But I don't know of anything more difficult to write about than a funny speech." The best tactic is to use plenty of quotations and hope the humor carries through.

Off the Record

Speakers occasionally insist that reporters hold back on some of their statements. This request puts the reporter in a difficult situation, for at most speeches, the reporter is an invited guest. A reporter has the right to be present at an official and public meeting and to use all statements and actions there, but he has no legal right to attend a Rotary Club speech.

A reporter may have to leave if he or she refuses to go along with a request for off-the-record status of all or parts of a talk. But the reporter is under no compulsion not to report what he or she learns. A talk heard by dozens of persons cannot be kept confidential, and the reporter usually points this out to those making the request. He or she also points out that since those attending the session will talk to the reporter about the speech, the speaker may find the material somewhat garbled in the telling and should welcome an accurate report. This argument usually wins the reporter's battle.

Remember, the reporter is not bound by requests for off-the-record status of any item if the request is made after the information has been disclosed.

Washington Post **Policy.** In a large gathering—say 20 persons or more—but sponsored by a private organization, club, committee, where the reporter is present in his role as a reporter but also as an invited guest, he must protest vigorously any attempt by the speaker to go off the record. He should point out that the meeting was scheduled as open to the press and should declare that he will not be bound by the limitation.

Meetings

Meetings provide newspapers and broadcast stations with enormous amounts of news. Public bodies—school boards, city councils, legislatures, planning and zoning commissions—conduct much of their business at open meetings. Then there are the meetings of private groups—baseball club owners, the directors of corporations, protesting citizens.

The essentials of meeting stories are:

____ Purpose, time and location of meeting.

____ Items on the agenda.

____ Major business transacted: votes, decisions, adoption of policies.

____ Discussion and debate. Length of session.

____ Quotes from witnesses and experts.

____ Comments and statements from onlookers, authoritative persons and those affected by the decision that the reporter gathers after the meeting.

____ Background.

____ Unusual departures from the agenda.

____ Agenda for next session.

Not all meeting stories will contain every one of these items. Notice the items stressed in the first several paragraphs of this meeting story from The *Brattleboro Reformer* of Brattleboro, Vt. The reporter used a delayed lead to emphasize the unusually large number of people who turned out. The first paragraph sets the scene for the major business transacted by the town school board, which is described in the second paragraph:

Public Protests Budget Cuts in Elementary Programs

By Gretchen Becker

Nearly 300 people came to an emotional Brattleboro Town School Board meeting at Green Street School Tuesday night to protest proposed cuts in the elementary school art, music, and physical education programs.

Caught between the strong public opinion at the meeting not to make these cuts and a strong Town Meeting mandate to cut 5 percent from their budget, the school directors reluctantly approved almost $35,000 in budget reductions.

Approved were elimination of the elementary art instructor's position, the second physical education position, a part-time vocal instructor's position, the fifth and sixth grade basketball program, and rental of space at Centre Church.

Purpose
Time
Location

Major business
transacted

The board took no action on the administration's proposals to eliminate the instrumental music position and the part-time principal's position at Canal Street School. Approval of these cuts would have brought the total cuts to $46,000.

Salary Controversy

At Town Meeting March 22, the representatives voted to cut 5 percent, or $74,200, from the elementary budget. Those urging the cuts requested that teachers' salaries be frozen. However, WSESU Superintendent James Cusick has noted several times that the proposed budget included only $25,000 for increases in salaries. . . .

Background

Most often, the lead will focus on the major action taken at the meeting, as in this lead:

City Councilwoman Elizabeth T. Boskin persuaded council members to approve additional funds for the city police department last night.

Major action taken

The council had been cutting requested funds for the 1987–88 budget because of anticipated declines in tax revenues.

Purpose of meeting

But Boskin said violent crimes had increased 18 percent last year.

"The only way to handle this is with more police officers," she said.

Amplification of major theme that includes direct quote on theme

The department had asked for a 15 percent increase in funds over the current year's allocation for hiring an additional dozen officers.

Background

The council has been making cuts in the requests of city departments and agencies ranging from 10 to 20 percent.

Boskin's plea was persuasive, and the council voted unanimously to approve the request for an additional $87,000, an increase of 14 percent.

Amplification of theme

Then the council returned to wielding the hatchet. . . .

Transition to other actions

Sometimes a meeting continues past the reporter's deadline, and the reporter has to make do with what he or she has. It is possible, however, to catch the sense or drift of a meeting, as Robert T. Garrett did in this story in *The* Louisville *Courier-Journal:*

LEXINGTON, Ky.—The Fayette county school board appeared likely last night to reject the teaching of "scientific creationism" alongside the theory of evolution in local science classes.

Probable major action

The five-member board, which had been deadlocked 2–2 on the issue, heard opposing views from residents for several hours last night before a packed house at school headquarters.

Setting

The board had taken no vote as of 11:15 p.m.

But the fifth and previously undecided member of the school board, Harold Steele, hinted that he would vote against the proposed "two-model" science curriculum.

Buttressing of lead with quotes and paraphrases

Steele said he had concern that "very definite parameters will endure" that ensure the separation of church and state.

As the school board prepares to face the question of tuition tax credits in coming weeks, it must remember that public education "is not permitted to teach sectarian courses," Steele said.

Before last night's debate, school board Chairman Barth Pemberton and board member Carol Jarboe were on record opposing introduction of creationism in the schools.

Probable position of others on major action

Board members Mary Ann Burdette and David Chittenden had said they support the teaching of creationist views. Mrs. Burdette moved that the creationist proposal be adopted, and Chittenden seconded it.

Scientific creationism is a theory closely aligned to the biblical account of creation.

Background

It holds that man and the Earth were created by an outside force, such as God, in a short span of time less than 10,000 years ago and have changed little since. . . .

The school board did vote 3–2 to reject creationism in classrooms, as Garrett indicated it would.

The UPI Day Book, a listing of daily events used by New York City newspapers and broadcast stations as an aid in making local assignments, carried this item one Wednesday evening:

Manhattan District Attorney Robert Morgenthau holds news conference to produce evidence that confirms existence of ancient civilization in Israel between 2000–1500 B.C., 155 Leonard Street 10:30 a.m.

To local editors, it sounded like a good yarn. Moreover, many New Yorkers feel a kinship with Israel. Thus, when the district attorney began his conference, half a dozen reporters and two television crews were on hand.

The reporters were told that a Manhattan school teacher visiting Israel had taken a clay tablet out of the country. On trying to learn its value, the teacher had spoken to someone who discovered the tablet was an antiquity. Under Israeli law, no historical objects may leave the country, and the teacher was therefore in possession of stolen property, a criminal offense.

But the district attorney had decided not to prosecute. He had worked out an arrangement between the teacher and the Israeli government. Although all of this could have been announced in a press release, a news conference was called so that the district attorney could play midwife in the delivery of the tablet to an Israeli representative. The district attorney, an elected official whose office is financed through legislative appropriations, would appear to the public as a man of compassion and wisdom. The reporters would profit, too, for the story would get good play.

The incident illustrates the mutuality of interests that the news conference serves. It permits an individual, group or organization to reach many reporters at one time with an announcement that will receive more attention than a press release because of photo possibilities and the staging, and it is an efficient and economical way for the press to obtain newsworthy material.

The presidential news conference, originally an informal give-and-take, became televised during President Kennedy's administration. The result was greater exposure of the president to the public. But the televised news conference also became, says Wayne King of *The New York Times,* "a vehicle for self-promotion, a stage-managed political commercial imparting not information but image."

Usually, the news conference has a prescribed form. A prepared statement is read or distributed to the reporters beforehand. (See figure 19.1.) Then reporters ask questions.

At the district attorney's news conference, reporters wanted to know the size of the tablet, when it was discovered, how it was recovered and other facts. The news stories that appeared differed substantially from the press release.

News Conferences

Reluctant. The televised presidential news conference may have made presidents since Kennedy visible, but the device did not make them more accessible to the public. Average news conferences a month: Roosevelt, 6.9; Truman, 3.4; Eisenhower, 2; Kennedy, 1.9; Johnson, 2.2; Nixon, 0.5; Ford, 1.3; Carter, 1.2; and Reagan, 0.5.

DISTRICT ATTORNEY–NEW YORK COUNTY

For Release: November 20

Contact: Gerda Handler
732–7300
Ext. 603/4

Robert M. Morgenthau, District Attorney, New York County, announced today the recovery of a priceless antiquity from ancient biblical times. The object is a sherd–a fragment of a clay tablet–bearing a cuneiform inscription of unique archaeological significance.

Mr. Morgenthau today returned this antiquity, dating from between 1500 and 2000 B.C., to Amos Ganor, Acting Consul General of the State of Israel.

The sherd was originally found at the site of the archaeological excavation of the ancient city of Hazor, located about ten miles north of the Sea of Galilee in Israel.

It was removed from Israel in violation of that country's Antiquities Ordinance, which requires the finder of any antiquity to notify the Government of the discovery and afford it an opportunity to acquire the object. A complaint was filed with the District Attorney by the Government of Israel through Dr. Avraham Biran, former Director of the Department of Antiquities in Israel. An investigation was undertaken by the District Attorney which resulted in the recovery of the sherd.

The sherd records a case of litigation, conducted in the presence of the king, concerning real estate in Hazor. It is of great historical value because it confirms that the excavation, begun in 1955 near the Sea of Galilee, is the ancient city of Hazor. According to Professor Yigal Yadin, who headed a four year archaeological expedition at Hazor, the sherd is a major link in the identification of the excavation as the ancient city of Hazor, that was mentioned in the Egyptian Execration Texts of the 19th Century B.C., the Annals of the Pharaohs Thut–mose III, Amen hotep II and Seti I and in several chapters of the Bible.

Here is how Marcia Chambers began her account that appeared in *The New York Times*. Note that some material in the lead is not contained in the handout and was obtained through questioning. Also, the story stresses the action and places the district attorney in the third paragraph, whereas the press release begins with the district attorney's name:

A fragment of a clay tablet 3,500 to 4,000 years old that confirms the existence of the biblical city of Hazor in Israel was returned yesterday to the Israeli Government after a teacher who smuggled it out of Israel agreed to surrender it to avoid prosecution.

The odyssey of the 2-by-2-inch fragment, with a cuneiform inscription, began in 1963 when the young teacher was on his honeymoon. The teacher, an amateur archeologist, found the tablet at the site of an archeological excavation some 10 miles north of the Sea of Galilee.

It ended yesterday, at a news conference, when Robert M. Morgenthau, the Manhattan District Attorney, turned over the priceless piece to Amos Ganor, Israel's acting consul general here. . . .

News conference stories must include the purpose of the conference or the reason it was called. The atmosphere can be important when something unusual occurs or material is displayed.

Panel Discussions

In symposia and panel discussions, the presence of several speakers can pose a problem. But experienced reporters usually make their way through the tide of talk by emphasizing a thematic approach. They will find a basic theme and write a summary based on that theme:

Four members of the local bar agreed last night that probation is no longer a useful means of coping with criminal offenders.

Although the speakers disagreed on most matters at the symposium on "How to Handle Increasing Crime," they did agree. . . .

Even when there is little agreement, a summary lead is possible, for disagreement is a theme, too. Here is such a lead:

There was no accord at the College Auditorium last night as four faculty members discussed "Discord in the Middle East."

The political scientists and historians disagreed on the causes of unrest in that troubled area, and they disagreed on solutions.

All they agreed upon was that the situation is thorny.

"We really don't know whether peace will break out tomorrow, or war is in the offing," said Professor Walter. . . .

After the theme is developed for a few paragraphs, each speaker is given his or her say. Obviously, the more newsworthy statements come first.

When one of the speakers says something clearly more interesting than what the others are discussing, the newsworthy statement is the lead rather than a general theme. Here is how such a story runs:

A California research team may have found a potent opponent of the virus that causes the common cold sore.

The information was disclosed today at a discussion of bioscientists and physicians at the School of Public Health on the campus.

Dr. Douglas Deag, a naval biochemist, said that the enemy of the herpes simplex virus (types 1 and 2) may well be the popular seafood delicacy, seaweed. The red variety—known as Rhodophyta—contains a species that has an active agent that prevents the herpes virus from multiplying.

Herpes is responsible for keratitis—a severe eye infection—and a genital disease as well as the cold sore. But the research is in the early stages, Dr. Deag said.

He was one of five speakers who discussed "Frontiers of Medicine," which was concerned primarily with careers in the medical sciences. . . .

Stories involving several speakers will sometimes require multiple-element leads. However, it is generally best to avoid them since the number of speakers and multiplicity of themes can be confusing. Obviously, when necessary to the accurate retelling of the event, a multiple lead will be used.

Space exploration can be man's salvation, a physicist said today, but an astronomer worried that man might overreach himself and pollute the universe as well as his own planet.

The disagreement was voiced at a symposium last night, on "Space Travel," sponsored by the Science Club and held in the Civic Auditorium. More than 250 persons turned out, obviously drawn by the promise of hearing one of the speakers discuss Unidentified Flying Objects.

But if they came expecting to hear a defense of UFO's they were disappointed, for Dr. Marcel Pannel said flatly, "They do not exist.". . . .

Debate. A candidate for mayor of Woonsocket, R.I., makes a point about his opponent. The give and take of debate provides reporters with considerable news since the event usually cannot be controlled by the participants. Realizing this, some political candidates seek to duck debate and to rely on the orchestration that political advertising allows. Reporters will demand of such candidates why they avoid debate, and they will often insist that candidates answer relevant questions, whether put by an opponent or by the reporter. Photo by Bob Thayer, *The Providence Journal.*

CHAPTER TWENTY

The Police Beat

Preview

Police reporters cover a vast array of news. Their beat calls upon them to handle:

• Breaking stories—Accidents, crimes, arrests, fires.

• Features—Profiles of police personnel, criminals; stories about police investigations.

• Interpretative articles—Stories explaining law enforcement policies, significance of changes in departmental personnel and procedures.

• Investigative reporting—Examination of police activity such as false arrests, police–crime tie-ins, lax enforcement.

Police news is given prominent play in most newspapers because of its dramatic nature and the fact that so many people are affected by it. More than 35 million Americans are victims of crimes, only a third of which are reported to the police.

F ew beats produce as much news as the police beat, and few reporters are called upon to do as much as quickly as the police reporter. Each day, a dozen or more potential stories develop on the beat. The police reporter covers:

Crime—Reports of crime, investigation, arrest, booking, arraignment.

Accidents—Traffic, airplane, drowning, suicide, rescue.

Fires—Reports and on-the-scene coverage.

Departmental Activity—Coverage of police department personnel, policies, efficiency and accountability.

Departmental Integrity—Standards, policies and procedures for dealing with internal and external allegations, assumptions and attitudes about corruption, systematic or sporadic.

Other Law Enforcement Agencies—Sheriff's office, state highway patrol, suburban police departments.

The complexity of the police beat is no concern to editors who assign beginning reporters to the police station in the belief there is no faster way to test a reporter's ability and to teach him or her about the city.

The new police reporter immediately becomes acquainted with the organization of the police department and sets about making contacts with key officers. Survival depends on establishing a routine and developing good sources. Otherwise the police beat can become an impenetrable maze, and the reporter may be given only the information that the department deigns to hand out.

Police Department Organization

The police department is organized around the three police functions—enforcement of laws, prevention of crime, and finding and arresting criminals.

The department is headed by a chief or commissioner who is responsible to the mayor, director of public safety, or city manager. The chief or commissioner is appointed and although he makes departmental policy, broad policy decisions affecting law enforcement come from his superior and are often made in a political context. The chief's second-in-command may be an assistant chief or inspector. Commissioners have deputy commissioners under them.

The rest of the organizational chart depends upon the size of the city. In large cities, deputy inspectors are put in charge of various divisions or bureaus—homicide, detective, robbery, juvenile, rape, arson, traffic. The larger the city, the more bureaus. As the patterns of criminal activity change, organizational changes are made. These changes make good stories.

The next in command in large cities are captains, who are assigned to run precincts and are assisted by lieutenants. Sergeants are placed in charge of shifts or squads at the precinct house. The private in the organization is the police officer.

The beat reporter's day-to-day contacts are for the most part with sergeants and lieutenants. Reporters, trained to be suspicious of authority, are sometimes irritated by the para-military structure, secretiveness and implicit authoritarianism of the police department. But they learn to work with the system.

Bureaucrats with Guns. A professor of law at the University of California at Berkeley, Jerome H. Skolnick, says reporters focus too much on events in which the police are taking action and not enough on how the police departments operate as organizations. In his interviews with police chiefs, they complained that coverage of the department is superficial. David Johnson, a prize-winning reporter for the *Los Angeles Times*, says police generate "enormous mounds of paperwork that can be mined to learn much about how well the police protect and serve."

Making the Rounds

The police reporter usually is based at the police station, and coverage for most papers is extensive. *The Sacramento Bee,* a morning newspaper in California with a circulation of 250,000, has a police reporter on duty 17 hours a day. At 8 a.m., a reporter telephones 10 different agencies to check for news events that may have occurred after the newspaper was published. The California Highway Patrol, city and county fire agencies, the coroner's office, the city police, Sacramento County sheriff's office and other offices are called.

Then Mary Crystal Cage, the paper's chief police reporter, takes over the beat:

"My day begins at 10 a.m. After checking with the city editor, I begin the second round of calls to local police agencies and go to police and sheriff's headquarters to talk to detectives and review booking sheets and incident reports.

"If possible, I avoid dealing only with official department spokesmen because they are rarely directly involved with any incident I may want to cover. Some departments recognize that and routinely direct police reporters to senior field officers handling traffic accident investigations.

"I will talk to the department spokesman to get a general picture of what happened overnight or for a routine update on an ongoing case. But I always talk to the lieutenant or sergeant in key units, such as the homicide bureau, to get additional information.

Crime Reports

"At least an hour of my day is spent reviewing watch summaries that highlight notable incidents from the previous day. Those sheets generally contain the barest details and must be double-checked with officers for updates and accuracy. Sometimes police officers embellish reports with information that later proves to be inaccurate."

(*Note:* In many cities, these reports are inaccessible to the press. Called *dailies* in many cities, they are read to reporters by police officers.)

"When I review crime reports, I look for the penal code section that was violated, the name of the victim and the suspect, and whether anyone has been arrested in connection with the crime.

"The penal code is a number that refers to the specific crime that has been committed. In California, for example, a PC 211 is armed robbery; PC 187, homicide; and PC 261, rape. When I first took over the police beat, I always carried a small copy of the penal code, so I could tell the difference between a 459 (burglary) and a 187 (homicide).

"A reporter familiar with the city and its well-known residents can usually spot prominent persons by looking at the victim's name on the crime report. Another tip-off to prominence, if the name is not familiar, is the box that lists the victim's occupation or place of business. If I am still not sure about a name, I will check with the newspaper's library.

A New Language

"The police reporter has to learn more than penal code sections. He or she must also learn some legal terms and should become familiar with the court process. The reporter knows the difference between a suspect who is taken in for questioning and a person who has been arrested. He or she knows the difference between a person who is booked and a person who is charged with a crime. Each term has a specific meaning. A person who is booked into the jail may not be charged with a crime but can be held in connection with a particular crime.

Checking Reports. Mary Crystal Cage, police reporter for *The Sacramento Bee,* goes over police reports with an officer. She is looking for interesting details that will help her decide whether to follow up on a report. Photo by Matt Tully.

"The district attorney or local prosecutor officially charges a person with a crime. In California, the district attorney has 72 hours to file criminal charges against a person who has been arrested. If the district attorney decides the arresting agency does not have enough evidence the person must be freed.

Getting the Story

"Most newsrooms have police scanners that monitor law enforcement radio communications. Routine homicide stories frequently begin with a simple broadcast: Sheriff's deputies are responding to 4209 Sacramento Ave. where a possible homicide has occurred.

"The sheriff's press spokesman will usually go to the scene, talk to investigators and then will hold a mini–press conference to give reporters at the scene some of the basics—how many dead, the sex and approximate age of the victim, the name if it can be released at that time, when the death occurred and whether a suspect has been identified and captured.

"But that isn't the story. It is a starting point for the reporter to do his or her own investigation. I start knocking on doors, talking to neighbors, co-workers and friends. If there are any vehicles parked in the murder victim's driveway, I'll take down the license plate numbers and check them through the California Department of Motor Vehicles to find out ownership and home address. Sometimes, an owner turns out to be a friend and sometimes it turns out to be the murder suspect.

Enterprise

"The first murder story I covered was on a Christmas Eve. A man was shot in a quarrel over who was to be waited on first at a gasoline pump. The suspect wanted to use the pump, but the victim was already there so the suspect shot him. That's essentially how the police explained the murder. By adding a few comments from the shocked gas station attendant, I managed to write a six-inch story.

"There are about 100 homicides in Sacramento County every year. Many of the routine cases are treated as my Christmas Eve homicide was. The difference between a rookie reporter and a journeyman is knowing when to go beyond the official comments. For example:

"In May 1984, a usually quiet upper-middle-class neighborhood was shaken by the gunshot slayings of two residents. They were shot to death while they slept. Nothing was taken and there was no forced entry.

"They were found by the woman's son at 10 a.m. Eight hours later, Sacramento police arrested him for the deaths. A few days after his arrest, I got a phone call from a family friend who said the youth killed his mother and stepfather over money.

"His father, who worked for a railroad company, was killed in an on-the-job accident when the suspect was a child. His mother sued the railroad and got $185,000 as a settlement—some of which was held in trust for him, the tipster said. A check of probate records at the Sacramento County courthouse verified the tipster's information. The probate file made a good story.

"Police reporters use the courthouse to obtain the extra information that makes a difference between routine coverage and enterprise. Knowing how to use court documents can give the reporter information when officials won't talk or sources cannot verify information. Search warrants and arrest warrants are issued by the courts. To obtain them, detectives must explain in affidavits why they want to make a search or an arrest. Copies of these requests are kept at the courthouse and can lead to a story."

Next of Kin. The police reporter sometimes has to call a relative of a murder victim or traffic fatality. No reporter looks forward to the task. Surprisingly, the relative may want to talk.

"They want to talk about what kind of person their husband was, or their father," says Edna Buchanan, *Miami Herald* police reporter. "Also, it's probably the only time his name is going to be in the paper. It's their last shot. They want to give him a good sendoff."

Most crimes are committed by young men, and a growing number have involved teen-agers. Juveniles who are arrested are turned over to the juvenile court and their names are not released. In some states, in response to the rise in violent crime by youngsters, serious offenses, particularly murder, are by law handled by the regular court system. Newspapers usually name the accused, as an upstate New York newspaper did in the following crime.

The battered body of a 77-year-old man was discovered in his home at 11 p.m. by a neighbor who called the police. The neighbor said she saw two youths running from the scene. Police conducted an investigation and within five hours arrested a 16-year-old and a 14-year-old. The two were charged with second degree murder and at their arraignment entered pleas of not guilty.

The reporter for the local afternoon newspaper learns all this on his 7 a.m. check. He calls the coroner to obtain information about the cause of death, and he questions the police about the murder weapon and the motivation. He also asks where the youths are being held and the time they were arrested. With the information on hand, he calls his desk to report what he has and the city editor tells him to give the story 200 to 250 words. The dead man was not prominent.

The editor asks about the neighbor: Did she identify the youngsters, and if not how did the police learn their identities? The reporter says the police will not comment about the neighbor. The story will have to be a straight murder-and-arrest piece. Here is how the reporter wrote it:

> Two Saratoga youths were arrested early today and charged with the murder of 77-year-old Anthony Hay, a local fuel oil and coal dealer, whose battered body was found last night in his home.
>
> Police identified the youths as Arthur Traynor, 16, of 61 Joshua Ave., and John Martinez, 14, of 15 Doten Ave. Police said a neighbor saw two youths fleeing from Hay's residence at 342 Nelson Ave. The arrests were made within five hours of the slaying.
>
> The youths entered pleas of not guilty at their arraignment this morning on charges of second degree murder and were being held in the county jail pending a preliminary hearing.
>
> Hay's body was found at 11 p.m. in the business office of his home. He was "badly beaten about the head and face and had a fractured skull," Coroner Clark Donaldson reported. Police said they recovered the death weapon, a three-foot wooden club. They declined to give any motive for the slaying.

Arrest Stories

Who, Me? Photographer O. Gordon Williamson Jr. of *The Orlando Sentinel* chanced to see a bearded man make a getaway from a bank he had robbed. Williamson followed the man to a barber shop and while the identifying beard was removed Williamson called the police . . . and then took this picture of the arrest.

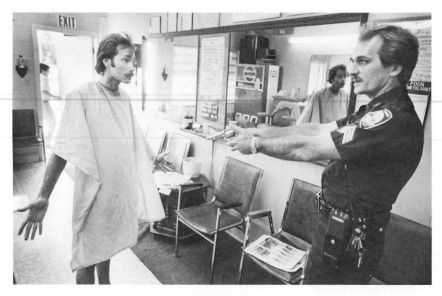

Victims

Traditionally, police reporting concentrated on suspects and arrests—the criminal. Now, reporters take equal interest in the victim. The same emphasis has been developing in stories about accidents. Reporters try to find out where the victims were going or where they had been when the accident occurred, how the accident affected the families involved. For fire stories, the reporter finds out where those burned out will sleep and what personal losses they suffered. Even suicides, long a taboo subject for newspapers and broadcast stations, and usually only briefly reported, are explored for human interest.

Checklist: Crime—Homicide

_____ Victim, identification.
_____ Time, date, place of death.
_____ Weapon used.
_____ Official cause of death or authoritative comment.
_____ Who discovered body.
_____ Clues. Any identification of slayer.
_____ Police comments. Motivation for crime.
_____ Neighbors', friends' comments.
_____ Any police record for victim; any connection with criminal activity.
_____ Consequences to victim's family, others.

Checklist: Arrest—Homicide

_____ Name, identification of person arrested.
_____ Victim's name; time, date, place of crime.
_____ Exact charge.
_____ Circumstances of arrest.
_____ Motive.
_____ Result of tip, investigation.

CRIME REPORT

FRESNO COUNTY SHERIFF'S DEPARTMENT

1. CASE NO: 76-0001

2 CODE SECTION	3 CRIME	4 CLASSIFICATION	5 REPORT AREA
Pc 211	Armed Robbery	Convenience Market—Handgun	Beat 2

6. DATE AND TIME OCCURRED - DAY: March 23 0400hrs.
7. DATE AND TIME REPORTED: March 23 0410
8. LOCATION OF OCCURRENCE: 5555 S. Blank Ave.

9. VICTIM'S NAME LAST, FIRST, MIDDLE (FIRM IF BUSINESS): DOE, John James
10. RESIDENCE ADDRESS: 2222 S. Elm Ave.
11. RES PHONE: 222-2223

12. OCCUPATION: Clerk
13. RACE - SEX: WMA
14. AGE: 30
15. DOB: 3-31-46
16. BUSINESS ADDRESS (SCHOOL IF JUVENILE): 2224 S. Elm Ave.
17. BUS PHONE: 485-2020

CODES FOR: V - VICTIM W - WITNESS P - PARENT RP - REPORTING PARTY DC - DISCOVERED CRIME
BOXES 20 AND 30

19. NAME - LAST, FIRST, MIDDLE
20. CODE: V
21. RESIDENCE ADDRESS
22. RESIDENCE PHONE

MODUS OPERANDI (SEE INSTRUCTIONS)

39. DESCRIBE CHARACTERISTICS OF PREMISES AND AREA WHERE OFFENSE OCCURRED:
Convenience market in low income, high crime residential area.

40. DESCRIBE BRIEFLY HOW OFFENSE WAS COMMITTED:
Suspect enters store, brandishes handgun and orders clerk to hand over money. Ties victim with rope and locks victim in storage area.

41. DESCRIBE WEAPON, INSTRUMENT, EQUIPMENT, TRICK, DEVICE OR FORCE USED:
Possibly .38-caliber revolver

42. MOTIVE - TYPE OF PROPERTY TAKEN OR OTHER REASON FOR OFFENSE:
Robbery--currency, checks

43. ESTIMATED LOSS VALUE AND/OR EXTENT OF INJURIES - MINOR, MAJOR:
$400

44. WHAT DID SUSPECT/S SAY - NOTE PECULIARITIES:
''This is a holdup, don't try anything or I will shoot you.''

45. VICTIM'S ACTIVITY JUST PRIOR TO AND / OR DURING OFFENSE:
Stocking shelves

46. TRADEMARK - OTHER DISTINCTIVE ACTION OF SUSPECT/S:
Suspect stuttered and seemed to walk with a limp.

47. VEHICLE USED - LICENSE NO. - ID NO. - YEAR - MAKE - MODEL - COLORS (OTHER IDENTIFYING CHARACTERISTICS)

48 SUSPECT NO.1 (LAST, FIRST, MIDDLE)	49 RACE - SEX	50 AGE	51 HT	52 WT	53 HAIR	54 EYES	55 ID NO. OR DOB	56 ARRESTED
unknown	WMA	30	5-9	155	Brn	Blu		YES ☐ NO ☒

REPORTING OFFICERS: Holmes

FURTHER ACTION ☐ YES ☐ NO   COPIES TO: ☐ DETECTIVE ☐ G11 ☐ JUVENILE ☐ PATROL ☐ DIST ATTNY ☐ OTHER ☐ SO/PD. ☐ OTHER

FRESNO COUNTY SHERIFF'S DEPARTMENT
Fresno, California

69. CASE NO.

70 CODE SECTION	71 CRIME	72 CLASSIFICATION
Pc 211	Armed Robbery	Conveniece Market—Handgun

73. VICTIM'S NAME - LAST, FIRST, MIDDLE (FIRM IF BUS.): DOE, John James
74. ADDRESS ☐ RESIDENCE ☐ BUSINESS
75. PHONE

RO responded to 5555 S. Blank Ave. where victim, Doe, advised he had been robbed by a man who tied him up and then locked him in a storage area. Victim said he managed to crawl to door where he continued to make noises until a customer entered the store and discovered him. Victim said the suspect did not touch anything during commisssion of crime and only said the words described on face sheet. Victim feels he could identify suspect if seen again. Advised victim detectives would be contacting him for follow-up.

REPORTING OFFICERS: Holmes

FURTHER ACTION ☐ YES ☐ NO   COPIES TO: ☐ DETECTIVE ☐ G11 ☐ JUVENILE ☐ PATROL ☐ DIST ATTNY ☐ OTHER ☐ SO/PD. ☐ OTHER

Crime Report. This report, filled out by the responding officer, describes an armed robbery of a grocery. There were no arrests at this time.

____ Officers involved in investigation, arrest.

____ Booking.

____ Arraignment. Bail, if any.

____ Suspect's police record (in states where it is not illegal to publish such information).

Burglary (B) is a crime against property, usually involving a home, office, or store break-in. Robbery (R) is a crime against a person, involving the removal of the person's goods or money with force or threat of force and is categorized as a violent crime.

Checklist: Crime—Burglary, Robbery

____ Victim, identification.

____ Goods or money taken. Value of goods.

____ Date, time, location of crime.

____ (R) Weapon used.

____ (B) How entry made.

____ (R) Injuries, how caused.

____ Clues.

____ Unusual circumstances. (Overlooked valuables, frequency of crime in area or to victim, etc.)

____ Statements from victim, witness.

_____ Name, identification of person arrested.
_____ Details of crime.
_____ Circumstances of arrest.

Note: Half or more of those arrested are not formally charged with the crime for which they were arrested. In St. Louis, no more than 35 percent of those arrested are charged, which led the *St. Louis Post-Dispatch* to change its policy of publishing the names of all persons who are detained. Now, the newspaper will name the person only after the prosecutor obtains a warrant for the arrest from a magistrate. There is no restraint on the press; the names can be used without worrying about legal action. The question is one of fairness.

Spot News

The police reporter spends much of his or her time thumbing through police reports and records. But now and then, the reporter speeds to the scene of a crime or some other activity involving the police. The police reports are usually fairly simple to handle, but reporting on the scene is often a challenge.

If the reporter is on deadline, one of the first tasks is to locate a telephone. Another early task is establishing location—police lines are usually set up to keep any but officers from crossing. In this case, the reporter stations himself or herself near someone in authority or next to an officer handling the police communications system.

When the full police contingents arrive, it is time to go back to the newsroom and use the telephone. For eyewitness accounts of the crime that the reporter has been unable to gather at the scene, the cross-indexed telephone directory will be used to call next-door neighbors.

The Arrest Process

The police reporter knows arrest procedures, and because on some smaller newspapers and on many radio and television stations the same reporter who covers an arrest might stay with the case through the trial, a knowledge of the criminal court process is necessary, too. Here, we will discuss the arrest process. In the next chapter, criminal court procedures are outlined.

A person may be arrested on sight or upon issuance of a warrant. Let us follow a case in which a merchant spots in his store a man he believes robbed him the previous week.

The store owner calls a police officer who arrests the man. The suspect is searched on the scene and taken to the station house. The suspect is then searched again in front of the booking desk. His property is recorded and placed in a "property" envelope. The suspect's name and other identification and the alleged crime are recorded in a book known to old-time reporters as a blotter. (The blotter supposedly takes its name from the work of turn-of-the-century police sergeants who spilled considerable ink in their laborious efforts to transcribe information and then had to sop up the splotches with a blotter.)

Catching the Drama. Close and direct observation of the event leads to better pictures and stories. For this picture of a suspected armed robber whose attempt to hold up a jewelry store went awry, Randy Piland of *The Macon Telegraph* edged through police lines. The man had threatened to shoot himself and held off police for 45 minutes before being talked into surrendering.

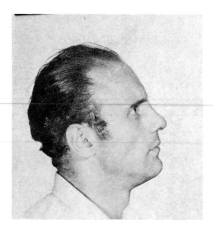
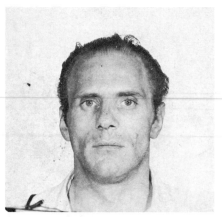

Mug Shot. After a person is arrested, booked and questioned, he or she is photographed. The picture, called a mug shot, goes into the person's file, which also contains his criminal record, known as a rap sheet. This is a photo of Joseph (Crazy Joe) Gallo, whose rap sheet showed a record of extortion, gambling and loan shark activity. Gallo reportedly had ordered the execution of a rival mob's leader, and a year later was gunned down himself by rivals as he celebrated his 43rd birthday in an Italian restaurant a block away from New York City police headquarters.

Little Effect. Studies have shown that in the 20 years since the Supreme Court ruled that a suspect must be informed of his right not to talk to police and his right to a lawyer, the Miranda warnings have had little or no effect on a suspect's propensity to talk. Most suspects waive their rights.

"Next to the warning label on cigarette packs, *Miranda* is the most widely ignored piece of official advice in our society," says Patrick A. Malone, a Washington, D.C., trial lawyer. Confession rates have remained unchanged since Miranda. "The compulsion to talk when one is accused of wrongdoing arises in part from the belief that silence is an admission of guilt," says Malone.

The police are required to tell a suspect at the time of arrest that he has the right to remain silent and to refuse to answer any questions. (This is called the Miranda warning.) He also has the right to consult an attorney at any time and is told that if he cannot afford a lawyer one will be provided. Unless the suspect waives these rights, statements obtained from him cannot be used against him at his trial.

The signed waiver permits the police immediately to interrogate the suspect about his actions, background and whereabouts in connection with the crime. If it is a homicide case, the practice is to call in an assistant prosecutor to insure the admissibility of any admission or confession.

The officer then prepares an arrest report, which is written in the presence of the suspect who also supplies "pedigree information"—age, height, weight, date and place of birth and other details. (See "Arrest Report: An Assault.")

The suspect may then be photographed and fingerprinted and be allowed to make a telephone call. A record is made of the number and person called and the suspect is returned to a detention cell to await arraignment. The arresting officer goes to the complaint room to confer with the victim and an assistant district attorney so that a complaint can be drawn up. The police officer may ask the complainant to identify the suspect again in a line-up.

The assistant district attorney has to decide whether the case is strong enough, the witness reliable, the offense worth prosecuting. The prosecutor must also decide whether to reduce a felony charge to a lesser felony or to a misdemeanor. He may reduce the charge if he feels the reduction would lead to a guilty plea.

The police officer may have to file additional reports. If he fired his weapon, he must file an "unusual incident report," as it is described in some jurisdictions, and if he shot someone he files an "inspector's report."

Arrest Report: An Assault

The form below is typical of arrest reports. In this arrest, the suspect, Roosevelt B. Thomson, a 19-year-old white male residing at 1870 Columbus Ave., was arrested for assaulting a 22-year-old male, Haywood Clarke, with a knife in an empty apartment at 159 W. 105th St. The time was 3:30 a.m. The police have their own abbreviations:

n/a—not available
a/o—arresting officer
A/C—according to Complainant
T/P/O—time and place of occurrence.

Thomson is accused of stabbing Clarke in the back, face and right side. He is arrested with someone else, presumably Miguel Negron about whom we know nothing. Why Clarke was in the empty apartment and what Thomson's motive may have been are not described in the police report. The arresting officer would have to be interviewed. But it appears that Clarke did not know his assailant because his identification is based upon photos shown him by officer John Vance.

On deadline, with no interviews possible, here is how an early lead might be written:

A 19-year-old unemployed plumber, described by police as a heroin addict, was accused today of the pre-dawn stabbing of a 22-year-old man apparently lured to an empty apartment on Manhattan's west side.

The victim, Haywood Clarke, stabbed in the back, face and side, was in serious condition at Logan Hospital. Police were interviewing Roosevelt B. Thomson and a companion, Miguel Negron, to try to establish a motive . . .

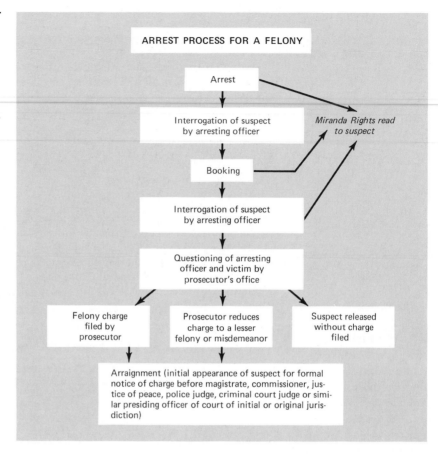

Figure 20.1 The Arrest Process. The police reporter is responsible for covering all aspects of the process, from arrest to arraignment. The reporter is aware that the original charge is often reduced by the prosecutor and that plea bargaining—the bartering of a lesser charge for a plea of guilty—frequently occurs. (See the next chapter for a discussion of plea bargaining.)

ARREST PROCESS FOR A FELONY

Arrest

Interrogation of suspect by arresting officer

Miranda Rights read to suspect

Booking

Interrogation of suspect by arresting officer

Questioning of arresting officer and victim by prosecutor's office

Felony charge filed by prosecutor

Prosecutor reduces charge to a lesser felony or misdemeanor

Suspect released without charge filed

Arraignment (initial appearance of suspect for formal notice of charge before magistrate, commissioner, justice of peace, police judge, criminal court judge or similar presiding officer of court of initial or original jurisdiction)

The fingerprints are checked in a central state agency to determine whether the suspect has a record, and the suspect's file is sent to the courts, which require the information before arraignment. The presiding judge decides whether bail should be set and the amount. A suspect with no record who is arrested for a minor crime may be released on his own recognizance, that is, without putting up bail.

Most large cities have overcrowded detention facilities and a backlog of untried cases. To cope, they may release suspects on low bail or none at all. Later, plea bargaining is arranged in which the defendant agrees to plead guilty to a lesser charge so that the case can be disposed of at arraignment (see Chapter 21).

Effect on Police

Plea bargaining may be the only way the judicial system can cope with many crimes and few judges and few cells, but it can lead to a disillusioned police force. A suspect whose arrest may have involved investigative work and some risk becomes the subject of plea bargaining and is out on the street the next day with a suspended sentence for petty theft. Eventually, police officers spend less time on the crimes they know will lead to plea bargaining and light punishment. Worse, citizens sometimes engage in vigilante activities or take the law into their own hands.

In some large cities, several types of non-violent crimes have been, in effect, decriminalized. Minor drug violations are ignored. Few small burglaries are investigated. Car theft is infrequently investigated and rarely prosecuted in metropolitan areas. In New York City during a recent year, 105,000 automobiles were stolen. The police arrested 9,000 persons on a charge of grand larceny motor vehicle theft. Nine were sent to prison. In many large cities, 80 percent of all felony arrests are either dismissed or plea bargained to misdemeanors or low-level felonies. Few of those convicted serve more than a year in prison.

In some cities, the district attorney's office has set up what are known as early case assessment bureaus or career criminal tracking systems. They enable prosecutors to single out the defendants they consider the most likely to commit further crimes. These few cases are prosecuted fully.

In the case of the robbery suspect whose arrest we are following, the assistant district attorney would not agree to plea bargain because, the store owner said, a gun was used and the defendant had a long criminal record.

Types of Felonies

There are seven types of felonies, which fall into two general categories, not including the so-called possessory felonies involving weapons and drugs.

Violent crime—murder, rape, robbery, aggravated assault.
Property crime—burglary, larceny-theft, motor-vehicle theft.

The FBI keeps crime data in these categories, as do local police. Ten percent of all felonies are violent and 90 percent are crimes against property.

Crime Rate

The amount of crime is proportionate to the size of the city. (See table 20.1.) In recent years, the FBI reports, serious crime is rising at a faster rate in the suburbs and rural areas than in large cities, although the crime rates are still highest in metropolitan areas. In the 58 core cities with populations of more than 250,000, the rape victim risk rate was 80 per 100,000 females in the 1980s. In rural areas, the rate was 30.

After two decades of increasing crime, the number of serious crimes declined in the mid 1980s. Still, some 35 million crimes are committed every year, 12 million of them reported to the police. A violent crime, 5.8 million in 1985, is committed every 25 seconds and a property crime every four seconds. Blacks are victims of violent crimes at a higher rate than whites or members of other minority groups. There is no significant difference in rates between blacks and whites for minor crimes.

Police reporters compare the crime rates of their city and nearby suburban areas with national data. The figures they use are taken from the annual report of the FBI, Crime in the United States, (Year of Publication), Uniform Crime Reports, which is available from the Superintendent of Documents, U.S. Government Printing Office, Washington, D.C., 20402.

Crime Victims. Violent crime victims are more likely to be men than women, young than elderly, black than white, Hispanic than non-Hispanic and to have low income.

The lifetime chances of being murdered are 1 in 131 for white males and 1 in 21 for black males. The risk of violent crime is highest among males 16 to 24.

Table 20.1 Crime Rate

	Metropolitan areas	Other cities	Rural
Murder	8.8	4.7	5.4
Forcible rape	41.1	20.9	17
Robbery	261.7	43.8	15
Aggravated assault	327.4	243.1	124.2
Burglary	1,424.3	967	610.2
Larceny-theft	3,120.9	2,988.1	905.1
Motor vehicle theft	533.1	183.4	97.6

Rate per 100,000 inhabitants.
These figures are based on the number of reported crimes, taken from the FBI's *Crime in the United States, 1984.*

The FBI report relies on local data, and some local police departments are inefficient, and sometimes they doctor figures. The police reporter must be aware of the tendency of the police to try to polish their images for a public angry over community crime. In Chicago, Pamela Zekman, an investigative reporter for WBBM-TV, showed that police were stamping "unfounded" on thousands of crimes, thereby wiping them off the books "as though they never happened." She found more than half the rape reports and a third of the burglary and robbery reports were suppressed. Another technique of doctoring the books is to claim that suspects arrested in one case had confessed to other crimes. This allows the police to raise the percentage of solved crimes.

Newsworthy Crimes

Over the next several pages five tables are presented. Local reporters might want to obtain data from their cities and states to make comparisons.

Table 20.2 shows the 10 cities with the highest crime rates in metropolitan areas. Sociologists say crime reflects social and economic conditions. The surge of crime in Florida is said to have been the result of the vast amount of drugs that enter the country through the state and the social turmoil caused by the influx of large numbers of Haitians and Cubans.

The appearance of Atlantic City in two of the categories parallels the legalization of casino gambling, which is said to have attracted drifters and undesirables to this once staid resort community.

Tables 20.3 and 20.4 show the 10 metropolitan areas and 10 states with the highest rates of murder and rape for 1984, according to figures compiled by the FBI, which defines a metropolitan area as "a core city or cities with a combined population of 50,000 or more inhabitants and the surrounding county or counties which share certain metropolitan characteristics."

The consequence of so much crime is that definitions of newsworthy crime have changed. A robbery is no longer news in a large city, unless the victim

Table 20.2 The Most Dangerous Cities in the United States

Total Crimes		Violent Crimes		Property Crimes	
Average for cities	**5,717**	**Average**	**639**	**Average**	**5,078**
1. Atlantic City	9,998	1. New York	1,631	1. Atlantic City	9,239
2. Miami	9,893	2. Miami	1,617	2. Lubbock	8,316
3. Lubbock, Tex.	9,121	3. Los Angeles/ Long Beach	1,186	3. Miami	8,276
4. W. Palm Beach/ Boca Raton, Fla.	8,253	4. Chicago	1,113	4. Ft. Worth/ Arlington	7,497
5. Savannah	8,247	5. Flint, Mich.	1,090	5. W. Palm Beach/ Boca Raton	7,287
6. Ft. Worth/ Arlington, Tex.	8,169	6. Baltimore	1,088	6. Stockton, Calif.	7,241
7. Detroit	7,997	7. Benton Harbor, Miss.	1,054	7. Portland, Ore.	7,184
8. New York	7,743	8. Memphis	1,041	8. Albuquerque	7,151
9. Fresno	7,682	9. W. Palm Beach/ Boca Raton	966	9. Odessa, Tex.	7,056
10. San Antonio	7,568	10. Detroit	964	10. Tucson	7,052

These figures are based on the number of reported crimes per 100,000 inhabitants of the cities in the tables. The figures are from the FBI's Crime in the United States, 1984.

Table 20.3 Murder and Non-Negligent Manslaughter

Metropolitan Areas		States	
Average	**8.8**	**Average**	**7.9**
1. Miami	23.7	1. Texas	13.1
2. New Orleans	22.5	2. Louisiana	12.9
3. E. St. Louis	19.2	3. Alaska	11.6
4. Houston	19	4. Florida	11.5
5. Savannah	19	5. Nevada	10.8
6. Dallas	17.9	6. California	10.6
7. New York	17.8	7. New York	10.1
8. Gary/Hammond	16.8	8. Michigan	9.7
9. Los Angeles/Long Beach	16.3	9. Alabama	9.4
10. Odessa, Tex.	16.3	10. Georgia	9.4

Rates per 100,000 inhabitants.

The End to Innocence. Police reporters say cynicism comes with the job. Things are seldom what they seem. A heartbroken father tells police a hitchhiker he picked up forced him out of his car at gunpoint and drove off with his two-year-old daughter in the back seat. A distraught mother reports her 4-year-old daughter and 2-year-old son disappeared in a department store on Christmas Eve. Newspapers and television carry the woman's prayer for the safe return of her children.

Two days after the hitchhiker story is played up by Canadian newspapers and television, the child's body is found in a garbage bin in an Ontario city. The father is charged with second degree murder; authorities say he left the child in the car on a hot day and she was asphyxiated.

Two days after the mother's tearful prayer, this lead appears on a story in a New York newspaper:

Two small Queens children whose mother had reported losing them in a crowded Flushing department store on Christmas Eve were found dead in a rubble-strewn lot in East Harlem last night, and the mother and a man with whom she lives were charged with the murders.

Table 20.4 Forcible Rape

Metropolitan Areas		States	
Average	**41.1**	**Average**	**35.7**
1. Benton Harbor, Miss.	117.3	1. Alaska	91.6
2. Memphis	97.7	2. Michigan	64.8
3. Anchorage	96.3	3. Nevada	60.7
4. Jacksonville, Fla.	87.7	4. New Mexico	55
5. Flint, Mich.	80.4	5. Florida	50.7
6. Reno	79.6	6. Washington	50
7. Saginaw/Bay City/Midland, Miss.	77.4	7. Delaware	48.9
8. Abilene, Tex.	75.3	8. Texas	45.9
9. Tacoma	73.7	9. California	45.7
10. Panama City, Fla.	71.3	10. Oregon	44.9

Rates per 100,000 inhabitants.

Rape. The National Crime Survey has found that victims of rape most often are unmarried women, 16 to 24, from low-income families. Rapists usually operate alone, at night and are unarmed and do not know the victim. Only about half the victims of rape or attempted rape report the assault to the police.

happens to be a justice of the Supreme Court of the United States. Even bank robberies, once good for major attention, now rate a few lines unless the amount is large or someone has been shot.

Murder, once sure to rate newspaper and broadcast station coverage, is now a frequent occurrence in several metropolitan areas. Ten cities have more than one murder a day, and three metropolitan areas—Chicago, Los Angeles and New York—have three or more murders a day. In these large cities, most homicides are disposed of in a few lines of type under a label headline.

The smaller the newspaper, the larger the amount of crime news published. Some small newspapers collect all police news for publication. The *Courier-Times* in New Castle, Ind., prints "all police news except for public intoxication," says the managing editor, Virginia Chambers. The *News-Gazette* in Champaign-Urbana, Ill., has a police and courts column that appears on page 2. One column reported theft from a trailer, the arrest of a man charged with urinating on a lawn and the arrest of a man charged with reckless conduct after he fired shots into an apartment.

In most cities, police coverage concentrates on individual crimes. But there is an increasing tendency for police reporters to examine patterns of crime, such as the growing amount of violence among young persons. Most violent crime is committed by those aged 16 to 25. A fifth of those arrested for violent crimes are under 18. Other patterns that can be examined include the relationship of the suspect and the victim (race, family ties, age); time, date and location of crimes; percentage of those arrested who are charged with a crime; percentage of those charged who plead guilty or are convicted. Trends can be ascertained. Robbery, say law-enforcement officials, can be used as an indicator of crime trends.

Table 20.5 Crimes on the Campus

Violent Crimes		Property Crimes	
University Maryland/College Park	53	Michigan State	2,041
North Carolina State Univ.	47	Ohio State	1,994
University of Calif. at Los Angeles	45	UCLA	1,984
Michigan State	45	University of Wisconsin/Madison	1,547
University of Florida	43	Indiana University/Bloomington	1,378
University of Oklahoma/Norman	42	Louisiana State University	1,270
University of Kansas	41	University of Arizona	1,246
Ohio State	39	University of Maryland/College Park	1,222
Boston College	30	University of Minnesota	1,206
Northeastern	29	Arizona State University	1,172
Southern Illinois University	29		

Number of offenses reported to police; from the FBI's Crime in the United States, 1984.

Table 20.6 Car Theft on the Campus

UCLA	419	University of California at Santa Cruz	69
University of Colorado/Boulder	155	University of Houston/Central Campus	59
Colorado State University	126	California State University at Long Beach	58
University of California/Santa Barbara	92	California State University at San Diego	57
California State University at Los Angeles	90	University of Illinois at Chicago	44

Number of offenses reported to police. From Crime in the United States, 1984.

Police Effectiveness

One measure of the effectiveness of a police force is the percentage of cases the prosecutor drops because of insufficient evidence or poor witness support. In Washington, D.C., the prosecutor drops about half of all arrests. Brian E. Forst, director of research for the Institute for Law and Social Research in Washington, says a major factor in these decisions is inadequate police work.

In Washington, a tenth of the police force accounted for half the convictions that followed arrests. "Clearly," Forst says, "some officers reveal a special skill in obtaining supportive witnesses, recovering evidence useful to the prosecutor, and in general making arrests with an eye to conviction. Most officers have no incentive for doing so, since police officers are not typically evaluated on the basis of what happens after arrest."

Another check of departmental activity can be made by examining the response to calls made to the police. A study of 2,000 calls to the St. Louis Police Department found that 25 percent of the calls were ignored. Of the 75 percent to which the police responded, arrests were made 50 percent of the time. Ten percent of those arrested went to trial, and 4 percent of those arrested were convicted.

Crime and Arrest. Most crimes are not cleared by an arrest. The FBI reports that murders are most frequently solved, motor vehicle theft least often:

Crime	Cleared by arrest
Murder	72%
Aggravated assault	58
Forcible rape	48
Robbery	24
Larceny-theft	19
Burglary	14
Motor vehicle theft	14

**Departmental
Activity**

Because of highly publicized inquiries into endemic police corruption in such cities as Albany, Boston, New York, Indianapolis and Denver, police reporters know that their editors and their readers expect them to dig into departmental integrity.

A reporter may be required to learn a new vocabulary to understand the underworld of deals, bribes and corruption. Some police officers have an "organized pad," by which they mean a secret list of underworld figures who pay them for protection. Most often, a pad contains the names of drug dealers and suppliers, vice operators and gambling operators.

The "grass eaters" are police officers who take small gratuities in connection with minor infractions, such as traffic violations, or who coerce merchants into gifts and free meals. The "meat eaters" are the corrupt police who take payoffs to release suspects, or who deal in drugs or perjure themselves on the witness stand.

Cautions

Garish details of rapes, homicides and assaults are considered unnecessary. Details essential to an investigation are not used, although there is no legal prohibition against using information obtained legally. Usually, police will not give reporters: confessions, statements, admissions, or alibis by suspects; names of suspects or witnesses; details of sex crimes against women. (Publication of a confession or statement can jeopardize a defendant's rights.)

All names, addresses, occupations should be double-checked against the city directory, telephone book and any other available source.

Beware of sudden clean-up drives for vice, gambling. Usually, they are designed for public consumption.

When the police arrest a suspect, reporters ask for his or her arrest record or rap sheet. In many cities and states the record may be denied or only a portion of it released. Sometimes the refusal is the result of state law. There has been a growing sensitivity among officials concerning the need to guarantee the accused a fair trial. Revelations about past crimes might compromise the defendant's rights.

Conviction data—information about a guilty plea, a conviction, or a plea of *nolo contendere*—usually can be used. Half the states make it illegal to use non-conviction data. Non-conviction material covers:

Acquittals and dismissals.

Information that a matter was not referred for prosecution or that proceedings have been indefinitely postponed.

Records of arrests unaccompanied by dispositions that are more than a year old and in which no prosecution is actively pending.

State laws that seal arrest records take precedence over sunshine laws. Where there are no explicit prohibitions against the use of such records, it is permissible to use them, whatever the disposition of the arrests. Reporters can use non-conviction information that they find in public documents that are traditionally open to the press: court records of judicial proceedings, police blotters, published court opinions, wanted announcements, traffic records.

Juvenile records usually are sealed, and family court rules almost always prohibit press coverage. But there are few state laws that make it illegal to identify a juvenile as a suspect or that prohibit stories about a juvenile's conviction. Generally, the press has gone along with the contention that such publicity could make rehabilitation of the young offender more difficult.

When a 9-year-old boy turned himself in to the FBI as a bank robbery suspect, newspapers and television stations gave the story huge play. The youngster, who took $118 from a teller, held what looked like a pistol.

The newspapers and stations were unhappy about using the story but said they had no recourse. It was "pointless" not to publish a picture of the youngster, said the metropolitan editor of *The New York Times,* that was already "on television all over town."

Fire Coverage

The police reporter monitors the police radio for reports of fires. If a fire is serious or involves a well-known building or downtown area, the reporter will go to the scene. Importance can be determined by the number of units dispatched, usually expressed in the phrase one alarm, two alarm, etc.

When a fire broke out in a downtown tire store at noon, it was too late for the staff of *The Anniston* (Ala.) *Star* to cover it for that day's newspaper. The presses had already started to roll. Because of the intensive radio coverage of the fire, the reporter assigned to the story knew that her piece for the next day's newspaper would have to feature some aspect other than the basic facts. Pam Newell Sohn found a feature angle and put a delayed lead on her story (see page 438).

On the jump page, Sohn wrapped up the details of the fire under this lead:

Virgil Coker Tire Service officials said today they are considering whether to rebuild a downtown Anniston warehouse blitzed by a spectacular fire Thursday.

Heroes

By PAM NEWELL SOHN
Star Staff Writer

They talked like it was all in a day's work.

. . . like anyone would work on a disabled, half-filled butane truck a few feet from a building burning out of control.

. . . like the expectation the truck might explode and level the entire block was of no more consequence than answering a ringing phone.

Their apparent attitude: It had to be done. And the handful of men did it.

WHILE POLICE were evacuating about 100 spectators from the scene of a savage fire Thursday at Virgil Coker Tire Service on Noble Street, and while firemen were trying to tame the flames, four men ignored warnings and made fast, makeshift repairs on the tank truck. Then they half-drove, half-dragged it out of immediate danger.

The four men were Anniston Police Sgt. Mike Fincher, wrecker driver Kenneth Garrett and brothers Lamar Crosson and Buford Crosson, both employees of Virgil Coker Tire Service.

The Southern Butane Co. truck, carrying about 400 gallons of highly flammable gas, was parked for repairs near the rear of the building when a fire broke out there at about 11:20 a.m.

The front-end of the truck was near a telephone pole and could not be moved forward. Two rear wheels and the drive axle had been removed from the truck. The empty wheel space was on the side of the burning building. Coker employees said work on the truck had reached a standstill waiting for the delivery of a new wheel hub.

WHEN IT BECAME apparent that the fire could not be extinguished quickly, some firemen and the four men began contemplating how to move the disabled truck.

Lamar Crosson said he heard mention of pulling the truck away from the blaze just as it stood. "But the (gas) valve was right there on the bottom and it could have broke and burned," said Crosson.

Crosson said that at about that time, the new hub was delivered and he and his brother began to reassemble the wheel hub and mount the tire, working between the truck and the burning building. They were assisted by fireman Jimmy Crossley, fincher and Garrett.

The men said they had to work "on and off" because of the intense smoke from the fire. And at times, according to Garrett, flames were as close as 10 feet away. When the smoke wasn't blinding and choking them, they were being doused with water from a fire pumper truck spraying cooling water on the butane tank, they said.

FINALLY, the men were able to secure one

(See Truck, Page 12A)

On the Scene. Good fire stories are written from on-the-scene observation. The reporter can find out about decisions made in controlling the fire and how rescue efforts are conducted. Bystanders can add information if they were on hand before the fire trucks arrived, and people from inside the burning structure can be interviewed. Photo by Jeff Widener.

Here are the beginnings of two fire stories that appeared in *The Tennessean* of Nashville:

A resident of an East Nashville rooming house suffered massive burns early today before fellow residents braved flames and yanked him to safety through a second-floor window.

The house at 256 Strouse Ave. was gutted by the blaze, which Metro fire officials have labeled "suspicious."

A 3-month-old Nashville girl asleep on a sofa-bed perished last night as her house went up in flames and relatives clawed in vain at an outside wall to rescue her.

The victim is the daughter of Janice Holt, who shares her 1925 16th Ave. N. home with several relatives, police said.

Firefighters arrived at the one-story dwelling off Clay Street shortly after the 6:45 p.m. call, and found the house consumed by flames, said Metro District Fire Chief Jordan Beasley.

If a fire is serious enough to merit a folo story, possible themes are the progress of the investigation into the cause and the condition of the injured. Another may be the cost of replacing the destroyed structure.

Checklist: Fires

_____ Deaths, injuries.
_____ Location.
_____ Cause.
_____ When, where started.
_____ How spread.
_____ When brought under control.
_____ Property loss: How much of structure damaged.
_____ Estimated cost of damage.
_____ Type of structure.
_____ Measures taken to protect public safety.
_____ If rescue involved, how carried out.

_____ Who discovered fire.

_____ Number fire companies, firefighters assigned. (How much water used.)

_____ Exact cause of deaths, injuries.

_____ Where dead, injured taken.

_____ Quotes from those routed. Effect on their lives.

_____ Comments of neighbors, eyewitnesses.

_____ Insurance coverage.

_____ Arson suspected?

_____ Any arrests.

_____ Unusual aspects.

_____ Fire chief, marshal, inspector.

Sources

_____ Police department.

_____ Hospital.

_____ Morgue, mortuary.

_____ Welfare agencies, rescue groups (Red Cross).

_____ City building, fire inspection reports.

Cautions

A New Jersey newspaper sent a young reporter to cover a fire in the business section. The fire had started in a hardware store, and the reporter asked one of the firefighters about the cause. "Looks like he had naphtha in the place," he replied, and the reporter wrote that. After the newspaper appeared, the store owner called the editor to complain that he never kept naphtha in the store. Statements about causes should be carefully handled. Only the chief, a marshal, or the fire inspector should be quoted about the cause.

Further Reading

Reiss, Albert. _The Police and the Public_. New Haven, Conn.: Yale University Press, 1971.

Wicker, Tom. _A Time to Die_. New York: Quadrangle/Times Books, 1975.

CHAPTER TWENTY-ONE

The Courts

Preview

Coverage of state and federal courts involves:

• Civil law—Actions initiated by an individual, usually a person suing another individual or an organization for damages. Many actions are settled out of court.

• Criminal law—Actions initiated by the government for violation of criminal statutes. The court reporter masters the legal process that begins with the arraignment of the accused and concludes with dismissal, a not guilty verdict or sentencing after a conviction. The reporter should be alert to the strategy and tactics of lawyers in covering trials.

Stories about the legal system interest readers:

• Plea bargaining.
• Sentencing patterns.
• Pretrial detention, probation, judges' efficiency.
• Politics and the courts.

New laws and regulations. A parade of defendants in the criminal courts. A barrage of lawsuits in the civil courts. The courts over the land are overwhelmed. They are at the confluence of a swollen tide of lawmaking, crime and litigation. Watching over all this, pencil poised, is the reporter.

What a dramatic image. The truth is that the courthouse reporter constantly struggles to keep from being engulfed. The only way the reporter maintains stability in this swelling tide of words—most of which are dense and arcane—is through knowledge of the judicial system, good sources and the ability to pick out the significant and interesting stories.

There are two judicial systems, state and federal. State systems differ **The Basics**
in detail but are similar in essentials. There are two kinds of law, criminal and
civil. In criminal law the government is the accuser, and in civil law an individual or group usually initiates the action, although the government can bring
an action in the civil courts. Because crime stories make dramatic reading,
the criminal courts receive the most media attention. Reporters cover the civil
courts for damage suits, restraining orders and court decisions on such issues
as taxes, business operations and labor conflicts.

These criminal and civil proceedings take place in state courts with a
variety of titles—district, circuit, superior, supreme. The lower-level courts of
original jurisdiction at the city and county levels—criminal, police, county,
magistrate and the justice of the peace courts—handle misdemeanors, traffic
violations and arraignments. The federal court system includes the federal
district courts, the circuit courts of appeals and the Supreme Court.

The county courthouse or court reporter covers state and local courts
and the office of the district attorney. The reporter assigned to the federal
courthouse covers the federal attorney, the federal commissioner and the federal courts. A key source is the commissioner who arraigns those arrested, sets
bail and arranges trial dates.

There are special state and local courts, such as the domestic relations
or family court, sometimes called juvenile or children's court; small claims;
surrogate's court (where wills are probated); and landlord-tenant court.

The court reporter's major emphasis is on the civil and criminal proceedings in the state courts of superior jurisdiction—district, superior, circuit
or supreme courts—and in the federal system.

Before we go into our examination of court coverage, a note of caution:
Reporting the courts has been the subject of considerable legal action. Certain
areas are off-limits—grand jury deliberations, certain activities of jurors—
and some have been hemmed in by judicial decree. Chapter 25 surveys the
continuing push-and-pull between journalists, who seek freedom to cover all
aspects of the judicial system, and the courts, which have sought to limit coverage on the ground that it sometimes compromises the defendant's right to
a fair trial. Many states have press-bar guidelines.

Civil law is divided into two major divisions, actions at law and equity **Civil Law**
proceedings.

These suits are brought for recovery of property, damages for personal **Actions at Law**
injury and breach of contract. The reporter who thumbs through the daily flow
of suits filed in the county courthouse singles out those in which large amounts
in damages are sought and those with unusual, important or timely elements.

The following story is about a lawsuit involving unusual circumstances and a large damage claim:

OREGON CITY—A 13-year-old who broke both arms during a Little League baseball game has filed a $500,000 suit in Clackamas County Circuit Court through his guardian. It charges the Lake Oswego School District and Nordin-Schmitz, Inc., a private corporation, with negligence.

According to the suit, plaintiff Martin K. McCurdy was injured when he fell into a ditch on the boundary between the school district and Nordin-Schmitz property as he was chasing a ball during a Little League game May 16.

Caution: Lawyers often file damage suits seeking vast sums. A $1 million lawsuit is commonplace. Most damage suits are settled for far less or tossed out of court. Relatively few go to trial. The reporter examines the suit to see whether it has newsworthy elements in addition to the amount sought. Here is the beginning of a 17-paragraph story that moved on the AP wires in South Carolina:

CHARLESTON--What probably is the largest wrongful death settlement in state history guarantees a 3-year-old Fayette County girl $5.95 million and assures her another $10.1 million if she lives to be 79, according to a lawyer who worked on the settlement.

Equity Proceedings

The courts have the power to compel individuals and organizations to do something or to refrain from action. When such an order is requested, the complainant is said to seek equitable relief. Reporters come across these legal actions in the form of injunctions and restraining orders. Here is a story about a restraining order from the radio news wire of the UPI:

PROVIDENCE, R.I.--A federal judge has issued a temporary order stopping efforts to put a reservist on active army duty because he refused to shave off his beard.
District Judge Edward Day in Providence, R.I., yesterday gave the army 10 days to answer a suit filed Friday by the American Civil Liberties Union....

Temporary injunctions, also known as preliminary injunctions, are issued before the case is heard on its merits in order to freeze the status quo until a court hearing can be scheduled. Thus, it makes no sense to write that the petitioner has "won" an injunction in such a preliminary proceeding (which is also called an "*ex parte* proceeding") since a permanent injunction cannot

Hold It. Temporary injunctions are sometimes issued in labor disputes to limit picketing. A court hearing follows the issuance of the temporary injunction in order to determine whether the order should be made permanent.

be issued until an adversary hearing is held in which both sides are heard. The respondent is ordered to show cause at the hearing why the temporary injunction should not be made final or permanent.

The show cause order is signed by the judge when he or she grants the temporary injunction, and the respondent is given a week to two weeks—or a shorter time, if necessary, as in strikes—to answer the show cause order:

It is further ordered that (the respondents) appear before this court in the Bernalillo County Courthouse, Albuquerque, New Mexico, at the hour of 1:30 p.m. on the 6th day of November, 1986, and then and there show cause, if any there be, why they should not be restrained and enjoined from using the premises and buildings located at (address) for the purpose of lewdness and assignation and in such a manner as to constitute a nuisance.

In the equity proceeding described below, a party asked the court to compel another party to take an action:

> The developers of a proposed shopping center and office complex at the intersection of Route 13 and West Trenton Avenue have asked Bucks County Court to order Falls Township to issue a building permit. . . .
> —*Bucks County Courier Times*

Pretrial and Trial

Documents filed in the clerk's office usually are privileged as soon as the clerk stamps the material received. The reporter is free to use privileged material without fear of libel because it has been given official status. Statements in court also are privileged.

A complaint lists the cause of action, the parties to the action, and the relief sought. The defendant has several alternatives. He or she may file a motion seeking to delay, alter or halt the action. He or she can ask for a change of venue, a bill of particulars or can file other motions. When the defendant is ready to contest the action, or if no motions to stop the action have been granted, he or she files an answer.

The case may then move to trial. Although there are more civil trials than criminal trials, few civil trials are covered. Reporters rely on records, lawyers and court personnel for information. Civil court stories are written on filing of the action and at the completion of the trial or at settlement.

Checklist: Civil Actions

_____ Identification of person or organization filing action.
_____ Background of plaintiff or petitioner.
_____ Defendant; respondent.
_____ Type of damage alleged.
_____ Remedy sought.
_____ Date of filing; court of jurisdiction.
_____ Special motivation behind action, if any.
_____ History of the conflict, disagreement.
_____ Similar cases decided by courts.
_____ Could suit lead to landmark decision? Is it a precedent?
_____ Possibility of an out-of-court settlement.
_____ Significance of action; effect on others.
_____ Lawyers for both sides; types of firms they are associated with.
_____ Date and presiding judge for trial, hearing.
_____ Judge's reputation with similar cases.

Should the reporter cover the trial, key points for reporting are: selection of the jury; relevant evidence; identification and expertise of witnesses; demeanor of witnesses on stand; judge's rulings; pertinent material from opening and closing statements of attorneys; the damages, if any are assessed, and whether the losing party intends to appeal.

Here are the essentials of verdict stories for civil actions:

___ Verdict. Damages, if awarded. (Same, less, greater than those sought.)

___ Parties involved.

___ Judge's statement, if any. Deviations by judge from jury's findings.

___ Summary of allegations by plaintiff.

___ Key testimony and attorneys' points.

___ Length of jury deliberations.

___ Comment by jurors on deliberations, verdict.

___ Any appeals or motions.

Checklist:
Verdict Stories

Private attorneys representing plaintiff and defendant; judges and their law clerks and clerks of the court; court stenographers; county courthouse clerk or assistant who is in charge of filing such actions. The clerk is usually the best source for tips on important cases.

Sources: Civil Actions

Negotiations between the sides often will continue even after a trial begins, and the reporter should be aware of the possibility of a sudden settlement. In many damage suits, the plaintiff threatens to go to court to support his or her demand for a certain sum or other remedy. In turn, the defendant appears to be unconcerned about the possibility of a court battle. In reality, neither side welcomes the inconvenience, cost and unpredictability of a trial. The judge, too, wants a settlement. The civil courts are overwhelmed.

Attorneys for the losing side usually indicate an appeal will be filed. Do not overplay these assertions, but when an appeal is filed it can be a good story.

Cautions

Whether it is night court where the sweepings of the city streets are gathered, or a high-panelled district courtroom where a woman is on trial for the murder-for-hire of her wealthy husband, the criminal courts offer endless opportunities for coverage.

The assumption that underlies the criminal justice system is that an injury to the individual affects the general public. Crimes are therefore prosecuted in the name of the state as the representative of the people.

The public prosecutor, an elected official, is usually known as the district attorney, state's attorney, county attorney or people's attorney. In the federal system, the prosecutor, a presidential appointee, is called the United States attorney.

Criminal Law

The criminal court system goes into operation shortly after the arrest. The system consists of pretrial and trial periods.

The pretrial period can be divided into four phases, arraignment, preliminary hearing, grand jury action and jury selection. Usually, these are accomplished in line with the constitutional provision: "In all criminal prosecutions, the accused shall enjoy the right to a speedy and public trial. . . ."

Criminal Court Process

Arraignment

At arraignment, the defendant is advised of the charges and of his or her right to an attorney. If the defendant cannot afford a lawyer, the court assigns one. Arraignments are held in courts of original or least jurisdiction. These courts are empowered to try only misdemeanors and violations, such as gambling, prostitution, loitering and minor traffic offenses. In a felony case, the court will determine bail. The prosecutor is present at arraignment, and he or she may decide to dismiss or lower the charge. If a felony charge is lowered to a misdemeanor, the case can be disposed of then and there.

The arraignment court, often called the criminal or city police court, acts like a fine-necked funnel, allowing only those felonies to pass through that the district attorney considers serious. Others are reduced to violations and misdemeanors and handled forthwith.

At the arraignment, the defendant may plead to the charge. If the defendant pleads guilty to a misdemeanor, the court can sentence immediately. If the defendant pleads guilty to a felony charge, the case is referred to a higher court.

If a plea of not guilty is entered to a misdemeanor, the judge can then conduct a trial or preliminary hearing. For felony not-guilty pleas, the case is referred to the appropriate court for a preliminary hearing. If the preliminary hearing is waived, the defendant is then bound over to the grand jury for action.

Checklist: Arraignments

___ Formal charge.
___ Plea.
___ Bail. (Higher, lower than requested; other conditional release.)
___ Behavior, statements of defendant.
___ Presentation, remarks of prosecutor, defense lawyer, judge.
___ Summary of crime.

Preliminary Hearing

Determination is made whether there are reasonable grounds, or probable cause, to believe the accused committed the offense and whether there is sufficient evidence for the case to be bound over to the grand jury. If the presiding judge considers the evidence insufficient, he or she can dismiss the charge. Also, bail can be increased, eliminated or reduced at the hearing.

Since the defendant is represented by an attorney, he or she has another opportunity to seek to have the charge lowered through plea bargaining. Some attorneys handling criminal cases prefer to have their clients plead guilty and receive probation or a light sentence rather than risk a trial and a lengthy sentence. Also, the bulk of crimes involve low-income defendants who are represented by overworked public defenders, who cannot devote much time to a single case.

The prosecutor usually goes along with plea bargaining, but if the crime is serious, the defendant has a long record, or the presiding judge is convinced there is reason to believe a serious crime was committed, the case will be sent to a grand jury for action.

Here is the beginning of a story of a preliminary hearing in the federal system:

BOSTON, Dec. 24—A Harvard Law School student, who allegedly enrolled under separate identities twice in the last seven years, was ordered yesterday bound over to a United States grand jury on charges that he had falsified a federal student loan application. . . .

United States Magistrate Peter Princi found probable cause yesterday that the student falsified applications for $6,000 in federally insured loans, which helped to see him through 2½ years of law school. . . .

A jury of citizens, usually 23 (of which 16 is a quorum), decides whether the evidence is sufficient for a trial on the charges brought. If 12 jurors so decide, an indictment, known as a *true bill,* is voted. If not, dismissal, known as a *no bill,* is voted. Only the state's evidence is presented to the jury.

Many states and the federal criminal justice system use the grand jury, but several states have a two-track felony prosecution system that permits the prosecutor either to file a felony *information* in the court without the interposition of a grand jury or to present the case to the grand jury. Following the filing of an information, the defendant is entitled to a hearing to determine whether there are reasonable grounds for the information.

Here is the beginning of a grand jury indictment story:

A Champaign County grand jury yesterday indicted a Champaign woman on charges of felony theft for allegedly defrauding an elderly nursing home resident of several thousand dollars.

Alice C. Donovan, 32, of 90 Belle Vista Ave., turned herself in to authorities June 19 after a warrant had been issued for her arrest.

According to Champaign Police detective Richard Nelson, Donovan is alleged to have stolen "in excess of $10,000 from a 90-year-old resident. . . ."

—The Champaign-Urbana *News-Gazette*

After the grand jury indictment, the defendant is again arraigned, this time before a judge empowered to try felony cases. If he pleads not guilty, a date for trial is set.

Grand Jury Action

Prosecutor Power. Since the defendant is not represented before a grand jury, some state courts have ruled the procedure unfair and allowed the defendant a preliminary hearing following indictment at which the accused's lawyer is present. In California, the result has been the near-abandonment of the grand jury indictment and use of the information.

Rearraignment

For example:

Feb. 11 Trial Date Set In Slaying of Coed

Superior Court Judge William T. Low yesterday set a Feb. 11 trial for Ellis Lee Handy Jr., 21, who is charged with murder in the death of San Diego State University coed Tanya Yvonne Gardini, 18.

Handy, a sailor from the helicopter carrier New Orleans, was arraigned on a grand jury indictment and pleaded innocent. He is represented by attorney Thomas Ryan.

On recommendation of Deputy Dist. Atty. Joseph Van Orshoven, Low ordered Handy held without bail. However, at Ryan's request, Low set a bail review for Dec. 30.

Miss Gardini's body was found in her dormitory suite Dec. 2 by her roommate. According to the coroner, she died from strangulation. Superficial stab wounds and bruises also were found and she had been sexually assaulted, a coroner's aide said.

—*The San Diego Union*

Plea bargaining continues at the rearraignment following grand jury indictment. Felonies, which usually are classified by degree—Class A, B, C, D and E—can be adjusted downward, a Class A felony moving down to a C or D, a Class C or D being negotiated down to a misdemeanor.

Plea Bargaining

Plea Bargain. LOS ANGELES—The father of singer Marvin Gaye pleaded no contest today to voluntary manslaughter in the shooting death of his son during an argument on April 1.

The charge was reduced from first-degree murder on a plea bargain. The father could be sentenced to up to 13 years in prison, but his lawyer said he hopes to persuade the judge not to send his client to prison.

If every arrest were to be followed by a plea of not guilty and the accused granted the speedy trial promised by the Bill of Rights, the court system in every large city would collapse. The only way the courts can cope with the crush is to permit or to encourage arrangements whereby the defendant and the prosecutor agree that in return for a lowered charge the defendant will plead guilty. The nature of the sentence is often explicitly promised by the judge as a condition to the defendant's agreement to plead guilty.

No reporter can cover the criminal justice system without understanding plea bargaining. In Milwaukee County, Wis., the district attorney estimated that 70 to 75 percent of the cases handled by his office involved plea bargaining. The figures are even more startling for cities with high crime rates. In Manhattan, about 15 percent of those indicted and 3 percent of those charged with a felony go to trial.

Even serious crimes such as murder and rape are the subject of plea bargaining. In New York City, three-fourths of all murder arrests are plea bargained, and in Philadelphia three-fifths are plea bargained. Prosecutors defend the practice by saying that plea bargaining is necessary to cut down the backlog of cases in the courts. In Philadelphia, the backlog was cut from 20,000 to 13,000 through plea bargaining.

Some critics say the judicial system has become administrative rather than adjudicative. Prosecutors say they are willing to plea bargain most cases so they have time for cases involving hard-core criminals.

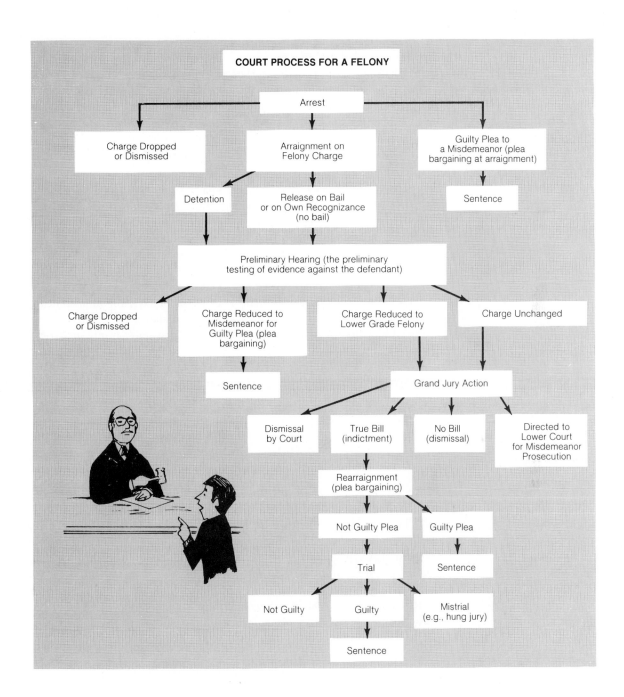

COURT PROCESS FOR A FELONY

Arrest

- Charge Dropped or Dismissed
- Arraignment on Felony Charge
- Guilty Plea to a Misdemeanor (plea bargaining at arraignment)

Arraignment on Felony Charge →
- Detention
- Release on Bail or on Own Recognizance (no bail)

Guilty Plea to a Misdemeanor → Sentence

Preliminary Hearing (the preliminary testing of evidence against the defendant)

- Charge Dropped or Dismissed
- Charge Reduced to Misdemeanor for Guilty Plea (plea bargaining)
- Charge Reduced to Lower Grade Felony
- Charge Unchanged

Charge Reduced to Misdemeanor for Guilty Plea → Sentence

Grand Jury Action

- Dismissal by Court
- True Bill (indictment)
- No Bill (dismissal)
- Directed to Lower Court for Misdemeanor Prosecution

True Bill (indictment) → Rearraignment (plea bargaining)

- Not Guilty Plea
- Guilty Plea

Guilty Plea → Sentence

Not Guilty Plea → Trial

- Not Guilty
- Guilty
- Mistrial (e.g., hung jury)

Guilty → Sentence

As a result of the criticism of plea bargaining, the practice has been dropped in Alaska and in a number of cities and counties—New Orleans; El Paso; Blackhawk County, Iowa; Maricopa County, Ariz.; Oakland County, Mich., and Multnomah County, Ore. The elimination and the restriction of plea bargaining in these areas has led judges toward greater leniency in sentencing, the Justice Department has shown.

Pretrial Motions

After the defendant has been formally accused, several kinds of motions can be filed:

Motion to quash the indictment: The defendant can challenge the legality of the indictment. If the motion to dismiss is granted, the indictment is quashed. The prosecutor can appeal the quashing. He can also draw up another indictment if the grand jury again hands up a true bill, even if the first has been quashed, because the constitutional protection against double jeopardy does not apply.

Motion for a bill of particulars: When the defense attorney wants more details about the allegations against the accused, such a motion is filed.

Motion to suppress the evidence: Evidence shown to be seized or obtained illegally may not be used in the trial if the court grants such a motion.

Motion for a change of venue: A defendant who believes he or she cannot receive a fair trial in the city or judicial area where the crime took place may ask that it be transferred elsewhere. Such motions are also filed to avoid trials before a particular judge.

Jury Selection

When a case emerges from the pretrial process and has been set for trial, a jury is usually empanelled. (The accused may waive the right to jury trial, in which case the judge hears the evidence.) Jurors are drawn from a wheel or jury box in which the names of all jurors on a jury list are placed. The list is made up of men and women drawn from the voting lists in the judicial area.

Twelve jurors and several alternates are selected in a procedure during which the defense attorney and prosecutor are permitted to challenge the seating of jurors. There are two types of challenges: *peremptory,* when no reason need be given for wanting a person off the jury; *for cause,* when a specific disqualification must be demonstrated. The number of peremptory challenges allotted each side is usually set by statute. A judge can set any number of challenges for cause.

"Most trials are won or lost in jury selection," says Larry Scalise, a trial lawyer who served as attorney general of Iowa. The attentive reporter can spot the strategy of the prosecution and the defense during the questioning of potential jurors. Jury selection is so important, it has spawned an industry—jury consultancy. Behavioral consultants advise attorneys how to select sympathetic jurors and how to use psychological techniques to persuade juries.

Few Trials. A study of felony charges in 12 cities indicated that no more than a fifth of the charges result in criminal trials. Charges are dropped and reduced to misdemeanors, defendants plead guilty, and judges dismiss most of the remainder. Here are some percentages of felony charges that go to trial:

Washington	11
Los Angeles	13
Detroit	19
New Orleans	19
Indianapolis	21

During the selection of a jury for one of the Watergate defendants, defense lawyers asked potential jurors about their favorite movie actors and their religious preferences. Those who said they liked John Wayne and attended Mass regularly were sought as jurors by the defense, which obviously wanted jurors who would be inclined to believe authorities.

The Trial

A reporter cannot attend all the trials conducted in the courthouse he or she covers. A reporter may sit through opening and closing statements and key testimony, but only the most celebrated cases are covered from opening statement to verdict and sentence. Reporters cover most trials by checking with the court clerk, the prosecutor and the defense attorney.

Because the reporter is dependent on sources who often have a stake in the trial, court transcripts are used in important trials if they can be obtained in time for publication. A friendly court stenographer can quickly run off key testimony in an emergency.

The trial procedure follows this pattern:

1. Opening statements by prosecuting attorney and the defense attorney outline the state's case, the defense or alibi of the defendant and give a general preview of the evidence.

2. The prosecution presents its case through testimony of witnesses and evidence. At the end of the presentation, a judge can direct a verdict of acquittal if he or she finds that the state has not established what is called a *prima facie* case, which occurs when the state fails to present sufficient proof of the crime that is charged. The questioning by the prosecutor of his or her witness is called direct examination.

3. The defense attorney may cross-examine the state's witnesses. For example:

Direct examination

The prime witness in the case against suspended Treasurer Bruce Knapp testified last night that in a routine audit he discovered Oakland had failed to pay the federal government taxes withheld from the paychecks of municipal employes.

Joseph W. Davis, the borough auditor, itemized his findings as he was led by Borough Atty. William DeLorenzo through most of the 17 counts of financial irregularity charged against Knapp.

Cross-examination

Defense attorney Richard DeKorte later hammered away at Davis's testimony, chiefly by challenging his expertise in tax and accounting procedures. . . .
—*The Record*
(Hackensack, N.J.)

4. Redirect examination is permitted the prosecutor should he want to re-establish the credibility of evidence or testimony that the defense's cross-examination has threatened.

5. The defense may make a motion for a directed verdict of acquittal or of dismissal based on its contention the state did not prove its case. For example:

An Evergreen man charged with murdering his wife and setting her and his house on fire to disguise the crime was acquitted Tuesday in Golden District Court.

Jerome Joseph Downer, 38, was found innocent of second degree murder and first degree arson by Dist. Judge George C. Priest.

The decision came after the prosecution had rested its case in the week-old trial and defense attorney Jay Gueck moved for acquittal by the judge.

In not allowing a jury verdict, Priest said Dist. Atty. Nolan Brown "didn't have much of a case."

He said the evidence presented "wasn't of sufficient quality and quantity to persuade a reasonable man the defendant is guilty beyond a reasonable doubt."

—*Rocky Mountain News*
(Denver, Colo.)

6. The defense may call witnesses to rebut the state's case. The defendant may or may not be called, depending on the defense attorney's strategy. The prosecutor is not permitted to comment on the defendant's failure to take the stand.

7. The prosecutor may cross-examine the defense witnesses.

8. Should the state seem to weaken the defense's case through its cross-examination, the defense may engage in redirect examination of its witnesses.

9. Rebuttals are offered on both sides. Witnesses may be recalled. New rebuttal witnesses may be called, but new witnesses ordinarily cannot be presented without the judge's permission after a side has rested its case.

Note: At any time during the trial the defense may move for a mistrial, usually on the basis that some irregularity has made a fair verdict by the jury impossible. If the judge grants the motion, the jury is discharged and the trial is stopped. Since double jeopardy does not apply in such situations, the defendant can be tried again.

Mistrial Story. NEW ORLEANS (AP)—Defense attorneys who refused to ask for a mistrial for a former Tulane basketball player changed their minds today, asked for a mistrial and got it.

Judge Alvin Oser declared the mistrial and scheduled a new trial for John Williams on sports bribery charges. . . .

(Williams was found not guilty in the new trial.)

10. Closing arguments are offered by the defense and the state in which the case is summarized for the jurors. These presentations, known as summations, provide reporters with considerable news. Attorneys sometimes make dramatic summations before the jury.

11. The judge charges or instructs the jury before it retires for its deliberations. The judge may review the evidence, explain the law that should be applied to the facts of the case and explain the verdicts that can be reached. The jury must accept the judge's explanation of the law but is the sole judge of the facts in the case.

12. Jury deliberations may be short or extended. In important trials, the reporter may want to stay with the jury until deadline because verdicts make headlines. A jury may ask for further instructions on the law, or it may wish to review certain material from the trial. Stories can be written speculating on the meaning of lengthy deliberations or the questions the jury asks the judge.

13. The verdict in criminal trials must be unanimous. After being discharged, jurors may report their discussions in the jury room to the press unless the judge gags the jurors. (In most states, the judge does not have the power to gag jurors, and the First Amendment would seem to forbid its use anywhere.) A jury may return a verdict of guilty or not guilty. If the jury reports it is hopelessly deadlocked, the judge declares a mistrial because of the so-called hung jury. After a verdict of guilty, the defense may file to set aside the verdict, or it may make a motion for a new trial. The motion usually is denied but the decision can be appealed.

A Superior Court jury Friday acquitted Cheshire building contractor Guy E. Michaud, on trial for threatening two people with a pistol in an early-morning incident on a Lanesboro back road in January.

The jury deliberated less than two hours before returning at 12:10 p.m. with not-guilty verdicts on the two counts of assault with a dangerous weapon.

Michaud, 31, who lives in the Pine Valley Trailer Park, had been arrested Jan. 17 for the assault on Richard J. De-Groat and a passenger in his auto, Patricia A. MacHaffie, both of Pittsfield. . . .

—*The Berkshire Eagle*
(Pittsfield, Mass.)

14. The sentence may be pronounced immediately after the verdict or later, pending a probation report. State laws usually set ranges—minimum and maximum sentences—that may be imposed. Convictions on more than one count can lead to concurrent or consecutive sentences. A judge may also issue a suspended sentence, place the defendant on probation, or levy a fine. Here is a story about a sentence of probation:

Sentencing

HOUSTON—A judge ruled yesterday that a teen-ager who took LSD at a Grateful Dead concert could not go to any more of the group's concerts for five years.

State District Judge Woody Densen sentenced Sean Foley, 17, to five years

probation and fined him $500. The youth, from McLean, Va., said he had planned to follow the group around the country for two years after his high school graduation.

A majority of offenders in all states are placed under community supervision of some kind rather than confinement. In 1981, 526,408 adults were confined and 1,445,798 were under supervision.

In sentencing, a judge may comment about the offender or the crime. The judge's comments can be an important part of the story:

The organizer of a forgery ring which cashed more than $16,000 in phony State of Colorado checks, is going to prison despite the pleas of several prominent Denver residents.

Judge Robert Fullerton of Denver District Court Thursday afternoon refused to grant probation to Ralph Brown George and indicated the court wasn't overly impressed by the testimony and letters of George's friends.

The friends, who urged that George be given another chance and placed on probation, included State Sen. George Brown, the Democratic candidate for lieutenant governor, and Elvin Caldwell, a Denver city councilman.

"Other people who come before me don't have the acquaintances you have," Fullerton said before ordering George to serve an indeterminate term, not to exceed 10 years, in the Colorado State Penitentiary in Canon City.

"For this reason, I can't give a great deal of weight to their comments.

". . . there also is the implication that people who have friends such as these will get better treatment. I don't want that implication left in this case.". . .

—*The Denver Post*

In a story about a sentencing that followed plea bargaining, John Katzenbach of *The Miami Herald* began with the sentence, gave the circumstances of the crime, and described the defendant's demeanor as he heard his sentence of life in prison:

Emilio Cabrera, the accused killer of three—a suspected drug dealer, a man whose body he sawed into eight pieces, and his own son—pleaded no contest to murder charges Tuesday and was sentenced to life in prison.

Cabrera peered out from behind thick black-rimmed eyeglasses as Dade Circuit Judge Bruce Levy sentenced him to three concurrent life terms. The 47-year-old former owner-operator of La Union Cafeteria will serve a mandatory 25 years, according to the plea negotiated by Assistant State Attorneys Jeff Swartz and David Waksman and defense attorney John Thornton.

Cabrera showed little emotion. As part of the plea, the state reduced the charges from first-degree murder to second-degree murder in two cases: the deaths of alleged drug dealer Andres Doreuit, 48, last Feb. 14, and of his own son, Emilio Cabrera Jr., 24, a month later.

Cabrera then pleaded guilty to first-degree murder in the March 1981 death of Cecilio Hernandez, whose chopped and burned body was dumped into Biscayne Bay.

Later in the story, Katzenbach tells the reader why the prosecutors decided to plea bargain these heinous crimes.

Prosecutors said they offered Cabrera the plea out of fear they might lose the entire case. They said evidence on the murder of the son was weak, since his wounds were "contact" wounds, which could have been interpreted as suicide.

"With everything considered the jury could have found him not guilty," Swartz said. If convicted, however, Cabrera could have been sentenced to death.

In reporting a sentence, indicate along with the minimum and maximum terms when the defendant will be eligible for parole. In some states, in trials involving the possibility of a death sentence, the jury decides the sentence following conviction, or a new jury is empanelled to decide.

Many states are following the lead of California, Illinois, Indiana and Maine in turning away from the indefinite sentence to the definite or determinate sentence. Under the new system, sentences are fixed by law with no judicial latitude possible and no parole.

Studies indicate that only 15 percent of those arrested are first-time offenders; 60 percent are recidivists—criminals who had served time in prison—and 25 percent had convictions but were given probation. In some states, law requires a stiff sentence for a frequent offender.

Almost half of the recidivists entering prison in 1979, says a federal study of state prisons, would have been in prison at the time of their offense if they had served the maximum term of their last sentence.

A follow-up to a sentencing can make a good story. The victim of the crime is asked whether he or she thinks the sentence matches the severity of the crime. Here is a story from *The Miami Herald:*

Officer Decries Sentence for Man Who Shot Him

By John Katzenbach

His voice is thick; one bullet split his tongue. His right thumb, fractured by another slug, won't bend. His spleen is gone, surgically removed, along with 20 inches of intestines. He spends much of his time visiting doctors as he re-orders his life.

Metro Officer Richard Wentlandt's freedom has been curtailed, as much by the memory of his shooting as by his wounds.

Tuesday, Wentlandt watched the man who shot him lose his freedom.

Bernard Pratt, a 23-year-old Miami man, pleaded guilty to the attempted first degree murder of Wentlandt and the kidnap-rape of a young woman. Pratt, who had been scheduled for trial when he entered the plea, was sentenced by Dade Circuit Judge Fredricka Smith to 90 years in prison. He must serve at least nine years before he can be considered for parole.

Wentlandt gripped his wife Wendy's hand tightly as Pratt stood before the judge.

The policeman was asked by the judge if he had anything to say. "I wish he would be in jail for a while," Wentlandt said.

He told the judge that after the May 29 shooting he spent eight days in Parkway Hospital. His life probably was saved by a bullet-proof vest he wore when he came upon Pratt and the woman victim in a car parked in a deserted area adjacent to Florida Memorial College.

When he ordered the pair from the rear seat of the car, Pratt came out shooting a .357 Magnum revolver, hitting Wentlandt in the jaw, back and hand.

Judge Smith also asked the rape victim if she had anything to say. Trembling with emotion, the young woman said: "He raped me. It affected my life. He should be locked up because he might do it to somebody else. I have a little daughter. He might do it to her."

The victim paused, then added in a barely audible voice, "He took away my pride."

Pratt, sitting next to defense attorney Jesse McCrary, didn't react. He seemed reluctant to make the plea—a plea that was offered by Judge Smith, not by prosecutors Rabin and Pat Ewing.

Pratt, a thin, wiry man with a scant black moustache and wispy beard, huddled with a half-dozen family members discussing the offer. At one moment he could be heard saying, "I don't want to do any time!"

But he faced a possible life term on each count, if convicted. When he finally agreed to the deal, he replied to Judge Smith's questions in a soft, monotonal voice.

Outside the courtroom, Wentlandt said that he wants to remain a police officer, but that he couldn't take working the streets again. He hopes to go into administration or teaching, he said. Considered disabled by the force, he said that more than five months after the shooting, he continues to see doctors.

"Maybe now we can get on about our lives," his wife said.

Asked about Pratt's sentence, Wentlandt said, "I feel it should be more time, but I know the way the system works. It should be a lot more time, but it can't be.

"Our system stinks."

Checklist: Criminal Cases

A story written at any one of the 14 points in the process should include: the charge, full identification of the defendant, the circumstances surrounding the charge, summary of the preceding developments.

In covering trials, find material that gives the trial individuality. It may be the behavior of the defendant or of the defense attorney, or unusual testimony. Drama is enhanced by describing the setting, the reactions of spectators and the reactions of jurors. Stories about testimony can be written using the question-and-answer technique.

Reporters understand the necessity of finding patterns of strategy and tactics during a trial. Every prosecutor has a plan, and every defense attorney keys his presentation to a theme. Each witness, every bit of evidence is presented with a purpose. The reporter's job is to discover the design of each side in this adversary proceeding. Strategy and tactics shift with the evidence, requiring the reporter to be alert during each day's testimony. The reporter should always ask himself or herself: What is the purpose of this line of questioning, this witness, this piece of evidence?

This kind of coverage gives the reader, listener, or viewer a sense of the movement and direction of the trial. All other coverage is episodic.

Court Records. With the docket number of a case, various records may be obtained, such as: the police complaint, the affidavit filed by the complainant, the felony complaint, the disposition if a plea was made at the arraignment or preliminary hearing, the amount of bail. If there has been an indictment and a trial has been held, this may be kept in another file, again by docket number.

Sources

Private attorneys; prosecutor's office, which includes assistant prosecutors, investigators and bureau heads; legal aid attorneys; law clerks of the judges; clerks of the court; court stenographers; bailiffs and security guards; police officers; probation department; state parole office, and trial judges, many of whom like to chat with reporters. Clerks also can tip reporters to important motions, hearings and trial dates.

Stories About the System

Courthouse reporters are increasingly being asked to take an overview of their beats. Editors want stories about trends in the handling of criminal cases, how Supreme Court decisions affect the local judicial system, plea bargaining, new investigative techniques by the prosecutor's office, politics and the courts. Some editors want their reporters to do accountability pieces: Does the system work; are some judges giving unusually light sentences to mobsters or drug pushers; are judges efficient in clearing caseloads; are white-collar criminals being treated leniently?

Some of the most sensitive issues in setting crime control policy are bail and pretrial detention. Denial of bail resulting in detention deprives the defendant, presumed not guilty, of freedom, limits his or her participation in preparing a defense and deprives the person of earnings. Pretrial release, however, makes it possible for the defendant to commit crimes.

The court reporter can write profiles of prosecutors and defense attorneys. Diane M. Goldie began her portrait of a 41-year-old prosecutor this way in the *News/Sun-Sentinel* of Ft. Lauderdale, Fla.:

Before the sun has even considered rousing itself and before most of us get our motors running each morning, Palm Beach County Assistant State Attorney Michael Gersten is setting the wheels of justice in motion.

At 5 a.m., on many weekday mornings, Gersten can be found telephoning police officers to alert them that the deadline for filing a case is that day.

Observant reporters may spot trends in the way cases are being handled. Prosecutors may be throwing the book at the defendants charged with violent crimes and almost ignoring property crimes so that some types of crime have become, in effect, decriminalized.

Elected or appointed, the judiciary has a deep involvement in politics. Mayors, governors, senators and the president reward party members and campaign supporters, despite their campaign promises of appointments to the bench " strictly on the basis of merit without any consideration of political aspect or influence," as Jimmy Carter put it during his campaign for the presidency in 1976.

Even before he was elected, acording to *The Nation* magazine, Carter made a deal with Sen. James Eastland, chairman of the Senate Judiciary Committee. "The administration would agree not to challenge senatorial patronage prerogatives for selection of district court judges and U.S. attorneys in exchange for the establishment of presidentially appointed panels to select circuit court judges," *The Nation* said. This kind of trade-off is natural to the political system.

In many areas, the path to the bench begins with a political apprenticeship, either in a campaign or in a party post. Or it may be paved with contributions to a campaign. A vacancy on the Sixth Circuit, which includes Kentucky, Ohio, Michigan and Tennessee, was considered a Tennessee seat and priority was given to Sen. James Sasser of that state. He favored Gilbert Merritt, a contributor to Sasser's campaigns. (Three contributions of $1,000 each were made to Sasser by three of Merritt's children, the oldest 12 years of age.) Merritt was given the appointment as a federal judge.

Detainees. In a study of eight cities, 15 percent of all defendants were detained prior to trial. Of the 85 percent released, 15 percent were rearrested for additional crimes and another 15 percent fled. A federal study has shown that almost half of the nation's jail population consists of pretrial detainees, men and women who were not convicted of the crimes for which they were charged.

The Courts and Politics

Switch. Sen. Slade Gorton of Washington opposed Daniel Manion, a Reagan nominee to the federal appeals bench. But when the White House promised Gorton a nominee of his own, the senator switched his vote. Manion was approved 50–49, but Gorton paid a high price.

The *Seattle Post-Intelligencer* said that "Gorton failed the test" of standing up to his conscience. Gorton, a Republican, lost his Senate seat three months later to the Democratic candidate.

When President John Kennedy wanted congressional action on key legislation he found it bogged down in the Senate, blocked by Sen. Robert Kerr. A Kennedy aide called Kerr and asked why, and Kerr answered, "Tell him to get his dumb (expletive) brother to quit opposing my friend Ross Bohannon for a federal judgeship in Oklahoma." (Kennedy's brother, Robert, was attorney general.) Kennedy thereupon called up his brother, Bohannon was confirmed as a federal judge and Kennedy soon had Senate action on his bill.

During Ronald Reagan's first term, he appointed more than 200 district and circuit court judges, almost all of them adherents of the president's conservative political philosophy. Appointees were screened on their attitude toward abortion, affirmative action and First Amendment rights. One of the private screening organizations, the Center for Judicial Studies, "is said to have the cooperation and financial support of the Moral Majority Foundation and other right-wing groups interested in perpetuating their conservative agenda through the courts," reported James Reston in *The New York Times*.

The consequence of the Reagan screening: 98 percent of his first-term judicial appointments were Republicans, 93 percent white, 92 percent men and more than 20 percent millionaires.

During his second term, Reagan continued to seek out candidates for the bench who favored a strict interpretation of the Constitution on such issues as busing, school desegregation and the death penalty.

Judicial posts are elective in 39 states. In some, campaigns are becoming political, and costly. This has meant that some candidates have to seek campaign contributions from lawyers and others who may appear before them in the courts. It has also meant that some qualified candidates refuse to consider appointment because of the costs of a campaign. The Fund for Modern Courts has found that among elected—as opposed to appointed—judges there is an imbalance in the number of women and minorities.

Good judges have come out of the political system. Some of the great justices on the Supreme Court of the United States owed their appointments to political considerations. The reporter who examines the system of election and appointment to the bench must be careful not to predict performance.

The Grand Jury

The grand jury may initiate investigations as well as act on charges brought by a prosecutor. It can look into the administration of public institutions and the conduct of local and state officials and investigate crime. In some states, grand juries must be empanelled to make periodic examinations of specific state institutions and official bodies.

Special grand juries can be appointed to look into matters such as mistreatment of patients in a state hospital or a tie-in between the police vice squad and organized crime. The district attorney or the attorney general's office directs the inquiry, although the governor may appoint a special prosecutor to direct the investigation.

When a grand jury initiates action on its own and hands up a report on offenses, the report is known as a *presentment*. A presentment may be a statement of the jury's findings or it can charge a person with a crime.

Grand jury deliberations are secret and any publication of the discussions is treated severely by the courts. However, reporters are free to write about the area of investigation, and witnesses can talk to the press about their testimony. Reporters often will try to learn who is testifying by stationing themselves near the jury room. Knowing the identity of witnesses, reporters are free to speculate. But the morality of publishing the names of witnesses is questionable, since the grand jury may question witnesses not directly involved in wrongdoing, and even those under suspicion are not to be considered guilty.

One way reporters have learned about witnesses is by watching for motions to dismiss subpoenas issued to require an appearance before the grand jury. Such motions are usually part of the public record and thereby provide the reporter with a document that can be reported.

In covering grand jury matters, as any pretrial proceeding, the danger is that publicity may harm innocent persons or impair a defendant's right to a fair trial. Several verdicts have been reversed because of newspaper and broadcast coverage. The reporter must balance the right of the individual with the public's need to know what its official bodies are doing. Once the grand jury takes formal action, the report can be publicized.

Trouble Areas

Some reporters knowingly violate or skirt the laws in obtaining information about grand jury investigations. They act in the belief that there will be no prosecution of their deeds. Sometimes they are mistaken, as the managing editor, city editor, and two reporters for *The Fresno Bee* learned after their newspaper published material from a sealed grand jury transcript. They refused to reveal their source and were charged with contempt of court.

The reporter should check the laws of his or her state, particularly when assigned to the police or court beats. Here are some actions that violate the laws of many states:

- Publishing confidential grand jury information leaked by someone in the prosecutor's office. (It is legal to use information provided by a witness as to what he has told the grand jury.)
- Using documents or property stolen from the police or an individual.
- Using confidential records transmitted or sold by the police.

In these instances, the reporter becomes an accomplice to a criminal act and can be prosecuted.

Court Terms

The judicial system has a language of its own that lawyers, judges and clerks use with exactitude. The beginning reporter should learn these terms and add to them through reading and experience.

Officers of the Court

attorneys Prosecutors and defense lawyers whose duties are to represent their clients; the attorney's role is partisan; he or she is an advocate; it is not unusual, therefore, for an attorney to try to sell his case to the press. The press should be skeptical of statements outside the courtroom.

bailiff Keeps order in courtroom; takes charge of the jury; sees to it no one talks to jury.

court clerk Calls the court to order before each stage of the proceedings and administers the oath to witnesses; clerk's office contains records of all judicial proceedings. (This office is an excellent source of news.)

court reporter Records the courtroom proceedings; unless records are sealed, transcripts can be purchased; price varies from court to court and state to state.

judge Presides over trial, rules on points of law dealing with trial procedure, evidence and law; the jury determines the facts.

Court Terms

acquit A verdict of not guilty. The legal and formal certification of innocence of a person charged with a crime.

adjudicate To make a final determination through legal action.

adversary proceeding An action that is contested by opposing parties.

alibi Used in criminal law; to be elsewhere, in another place.

allegation The assertion, declaration or statement of a party to an action; an assertion of what is expected to be proved.

arraign In criminal practice, the formal calling of a prisoner to the bar of the court to answer charges in the indictment or to give information as to whether he is guilty or not guilty. Suspect is acquainted with charge against him following arrest; bail set at arraignment.

arrest The deprivation of a person's liberty by authority of the law.

autopsy The inspection and dissection of a body to learn the cause of death.

bail The security given for the release of a prisoner. Cash or a bond is placed in the court to guarantee that the person held in legal custody will appear at the time and the place the court sets. Defendants are usually entitled to be set at liberty on bail unless charged with an offense punishable by death, and even sometimes in these instances. The judge or magistrate sets bail. The Constitution prohibits excessive bail.

beneficiary One for whose benefit a trust is created.

booking The process whereby a suspect's name, address and purported crime are entered into a book in the police precinct or police headquarters.

bribery The receiving, offering or soliciting by or to any person whose profession or business involves the administration of public justice or has other official status in order to influence his or her behavior. Giving or taking a reward in connection with voting also constitutes bribery.

brief A written document prepared by counsel to serve as the basis for argument. It embodies the points of law that the counsel desires to establish.

burglary Breaking and entering the house or other property of another with intention of committing a felony, whether the felony is committed or not. Burglary does not involve a crime against a person, which is **robbery.**

chambers The private room or office of a judge.

charge In criminal law, an accusation.

code A collection, compendium or revision of laws.

complainant A person who brings a criminal or civil action.

concurrent In a prison sentence, terms that are to be served together (not in succession). In judges' action or opinion, an agreement.

conspiracy In criminal law, an agreement between two or more persons for the purpose of committing some unlawful act.

contempt A willful disregard of public authority.

contract A promissory agreement between two or more persons that creates, modifies or destroys a legal relation.

cross-examination The practice whereby an opposing lawyer questions a witness at a hearing or trial.

de facto In fact or actually. Usually refers to a situation or an action that has the appearance of legality and is generally accepted as such but is actually illegal.

de jure Rightful, legitimate, legal.

defendant A person in a criminal or civil action who defends or denies the allegations.

dissent The explicit disagreement of one or more judges with the decision passed by the majority in a case before them.

eminent domain The power to take private property for public use by paying for it.

evidence Concrete objects for the purpose of inducing belief in the minds of the trial judge or jury presented at trial through witnesses, records, documents.

exculpatory Clearing or tending to clear from alleged guilt.

extradition When one state (or nation) surrenders to another state an individual accused or convicted of a crime outside its territory.

felony A crime of a graver or more atrocious nature than one designated as a misdemeanor. Usually, punishable by more than one year in a penitentiary.

grand jury A jury of inquiry whose duty is to receive complaints and accusations in criminal cases, to hear the evidence presented by the state and to find bills of indictment when the jury is satisfied a trial ought to be held.

homicide The killing of a human being.

indictment An accusation handed up to the court by a grand jury.

indigent A poor person. In court, an indigent is usually defended by legal aid or an attorney in the public defender's office.

information A formal accusation of a crime by the appropriate public official such as the prosecuting attorney. In some states, accused persons may be brought to trial by an information—a sworn, written accusation that leads to an indictment without a grand jury investigation.

jury The court-approved individuals—twelve for criminal cases and six or eight for civil cases depending on the attorneys' stipulations—who decide the guilt or innocence of defendant(s) in a trial; their verdict in a criminal case must be unanimous. (Referred to as petit juries in criminal and civil cases.)

manslaughter The unlawful killing without malice of another human being.

misdemeanor Offenses lower than felonies and generally punishable by fine or imprisonment in other than a penitentiary.

nolo contendere "I will not contest it." The defendant does not contest the facts. The plea has the same legal effect as a plea of guilty, but it cannot be used as an admission of guilt elsewhere, as in a civil suit.

parole The conditional release of a prisoner from confinement. The condition usually is that if the prisoner meets the terms of the parole he or she will be given an absolute discharge from the remainder of the sentence. If not, the prisoner is returned to serve the unexpired term.

plea A response to the court made by the defendant himself or herself or his or her representative either answering the charges or showing why he or she should not be required to answer.

plea bargaining The arrangement between prosecutor and defendant whereby the state offers to reduce the charges against the defendant in return for a guilty plea.

preliminary hearing Follows arraignment; evidence is heard to determine if a crime has been committed. The judge may dismiss the case if he feels the evidence against the suspect is insufficient or was illegally obtained. If he believes the evidence is sufficient, he will bind the case over to the grand jury for possible indictment. If an indictment ensues, the case is transferred to a higher court.

presentment The written action by a grand jury without an indictment; a presentment usually seeks to change the nature or operation of a particular institution that permitted offenses against the public.

probation Allowing a person convicted of a criminal offense to stay out of jail under a suspension of sentence during good behavior and generally under the supervision or guardianship of a probation officer.

search warrant A court order authorizing an officer or a citizen to search a specified house or other premises for evidence, stolen property or unlawful goods.

stay An action that stops or arrests a judicial proceeding by order of the court.

suspended sentence A sentence withheld or postponed by the judge. In most cases, the suspension is indefinite and depends upon satisfactory probation reports.

term Used in some jurisdictions to denote the ordinary session of court.

unconstitutional An action or law that is contrary to the Constitution or to state constitutions. (Do not confuse with illegal.)

venue The place or county in which an injury or crime is said to have been committed.

voir dire The preliminary examination that the court or lawyers may make of a prospective juror to determine whether he or she is acceptable to decide a case as a juror.

CHAPTER TWENTY-TWO

Sports

Preview

Sports news is, after the local news, the most heavily read section of the newspaper. Television coverage of baseball, basketball and football games draws millions of viewers. The nation is made up of fans, many of them experts on the sports they follow.

The sports reporter handles a variety of assignments:

• Game stories—Coverage of high school, college and professional sports. Game stories require score, key plays and players, effect of game on standings, turning point of game and post-game interviews.

• Profiles—Personality stories on newly acquired players, athletes having outstanding seasons, game stars, coaches, owners of professional teams. Profiles require: backgound of individual, plenty of quotations, the individual in action.

• Sports as business—The emergence of billion-dollar television contracts for baseball, multi-million-dollar salaries, unions for athletes and the movement between cities of professional teams have added a new dimension to sports reporting.

• Illegal and improper activities—Payoffs to college players, drug use among athletes.

Television, said the sages of journalism, will cause a drastic change in the way newspapers cover sports. Why would anyone want details about a game he or she had seen on television? Sportswriters would emphasize investigative and feature articles on subsidies for college athletes, the stars' personal lives and the economics of professional sports.

A glance at the sports pages of any newspaper proves the prophets part right, part wrong. Depth coverage has increased in many papers, but radio and television have whetted readers' appetites for details of the game.

When Susan V. Hands went to her first job to cover sports for *The Charlotte Observer* she was anxious to investigate the growth of participant sports and to promote the development of women's athletics. Hands, the *Observer's* first woman sportswriter, quickly shifted gears.

"I learned that people buy the morning paper to find out what happened in last night's football or basketball game. And our readers would be angry if, instead of finding the highlights and statistics of yesterday's North Carolina State basketball game, there was an investigative piece on the lack of athletic training available to girls in Charlotte high schools," she says.

Readers do want to see the score, and they want to savor the important plays again, despite having seen them twice—once as they unfolded, and once again, courtesy of instant replay. The assumption that readers have seen the game on television may no longer be valid, says Frank Barrows, executive sports editor of the *Observer*. With so many games available to television viewers, the reporter cannot presume that the reader saw any particular game.

"Game results sell newspapers," says Hands.

The sports pages encompass more than they did a couple of decades ago—more analytical stories, more interviews with players. New areas of coverage have developed, such as the commercialization and sometimes corruption of college sports, the increasing amount of international and women's competition and the use of drugs by athletes.

Participant sports have grown enormously. Hunting and fishing columns are regular features in most newspapers. Local tennis and golf tournaments attract local coverage. A young journalist who fancies a sportswriting career would be wise to learn about these sports as well as all the local high school and college games.

Fans want details with the scores. They turn to the sports pages to find out why the Syracuse coach pulled his quarterback in the second half, the strategy by which Missouri managed to hold Kansas State to five points in the last six minutes of play. They look for the explanations and facts that the broadcast—indeed their own attendance at the game—may not have revealed. Game stories must give the fan what happened and also how and why.

More and more, reporters are looking at the man and woman behind the tennis racket and under the shoulder pads. The personal lives of athletes, sports reporters have learned, can make interesting stories.

Jerry Tipton of the *Herald-Leader* in Lexington, Ky., wrote a moving profile of George Adams, a University of Kentucky tailback, from interviews with the football player and his friends and family. Tipton began his story with the player's mother:

> When Ruth Adams, mother of nine, sits in the living room of her Lexington home, she can look at nine photographs of her children. Five of them are of her younger son, George.
>
> "The others get on me for having so much about George," she said. "I love them all, the grandchildren, too. But George has a special place."

Expanded Coverage

Economic Forces. The sportswriter moves over a wider range than ever. Because of increased agricultural, industrial and housing activity in the U.S. and Canada, more than half the original prairie wetlands in the U.S. and a third of the grasslands in western Canada have disappeared. By 1985, the breeding population of ducks and geese declined from 62 million a decade before to half that number. To save the birds, and to make hunting possible, the U.S. and Canada are trying to conserve breeding areas, a running story for readers and viewers.

Personal Lives

Tipton develops his story slowly, and the picture that emerges is of a family that has survived many difficulties. Adams' father drank. A brother and a sister have served time in jail. Another, the mother said, is "in trouble."

"George never gave me no kind of trouble," she said, breaking a long pause. "He always brought good things home from school. He made me happy."

When others caused so much trouble, why didn't George?

"He saw so much pain in his mother's eyes," said Donnie Harville, who coached Adams in basketball at Lafayette High. "And he decided he wouldn't make his mother suffer more."

Tipton delves into the family's problems:

> Adams can remember seeing his father walking unsteadily down a street. The son would cross to the other side to avoid a face-to-face meeting. . . .
>
> "When I was young, it hurt a lot," Adams said. "I mean a whole lot. I told myself I'm not going to be like that."

Adams had a dream for his mother. "If I can play pro football, the first thing I want to do with my first contract is buy my mother a house." he told Tipton.

Adams was drafted by the New York Giants in the first round of the professional football draft. He signed a four-year contract for $1.5 million, and he did buy the house his mother had dreamed of.

Sources

Since professional sports thrive on newspaper and broadcast coverage, owners usually are generous to reporters, providing everything from athletes for interviews to statistics, ballpoint pens, hot dogs, and even full-course meals in the press boxes. Many colleges, which field highly professional teams despite their amateur status, are equally helpful.

High school sports coverage is another matter. Coaches often are busy with physical education classes and are inaccessible. Players are unavailable, except during and after games. There is little assistance in the high school press box, no paid publicity personnel as at college and professional games.

For participant sports, bowling lane managers and tennis and golf professionals will call in unusual scores and the results of tournaments and matches. Although these callers may be self-serving, they do turn in newsworthy material.

One day, the *Times-Union* of Rochester, N.Y., was called by the manager of a bowling center and told that a league bowler had bowled 299. A reporter interviewed the bowler and found he was a plumber who was bowling on his day off. A 183-average bowler, his 299 had helped his team move into first place by two points. The human interest story was a switch from the usual sports page emphasis on baseball, basketball and football.

Sources are cultivated by the local reporter. He or she attends sports banquets, drops by the pro shops at the golf and tennis courts, chats with the unsung athletes on the high school swimming, soccer, wrestling and track teams. The high school and college athletes who may go through a season never playing before more than a handful of spectators make for good stories. Not many readers understand why a youngster will run 10 to 20 miles a day to prepare for a cross-country meet, what it is like to engage in a non-contact sport in which the only adversary is the athlete's own mind and body. The runners, the javelin throwers, the swimmers, the gymnasts, the fencers and the wrestlers should not be overwhelmed by the glut of basketball and football coverage.

Young Pro. The personal-professional life of a young athlete makes a good story. Handled like a Live-In, the story can provide an insight into the many frustrations and few successes that mark the lives of most beginners.

Karen Stabiner tells the story of a 16-year-old tennis pro, Debbie Spence, in her book, *Courting Fame: The Perilous Road to Women's Tennis Stardom* (New York: Harper & Row, 1986). Debbie's talent is not enough to make her a marketable commodity in the commercial tennis world. She is slightly overweight, "not a classic beauty," an agent says.

Debbie's world is made up of budget motels; subsidies from her father, a junior high school teacher; burgers on the run, and loneliness.

On most newspapers, a reporter will cover several sports and has a list of key contacts who can supply background quickly and accurately. Usually, the first name on the reporter's list is the athletic director or the publicity director. For high school sports, the coach is the major source.

Fans, especially the armchair expert who has made his avocation following one of the local teams, can be excellent sources. The "sports nut" as some reporters call this person, has at his or her fingertips records, statistics, and standings going back years.

Close and Too Close

Ron Rapoport, sportswriter for the *Chicago Sun-Times,* says sportswriters are probably closer to their sources than are other reporters. "They cover the same people day after day, often travel with them and spend a huge amount of time with the people they write about. This can have both a good and a bad effect," he says.

"On the one hand, sportswriters get to know the people they're writing about quite well and this can be useful in writing about their personalities and in getting tips for other stories. How are you going to find out that former baseball team owner Bill Veeck, who lived in Chicago, went all the way to Milwaukee to see major-league games because he was feuding with the ownership of both the Cubs and the White Sox? You hear it from a friend of Veeck's who casually drops the information in the dugout at Wrigley Field before a game one day.

"The perils of such close proximity, however, must be guarded against. If age is finally catching up with perhaps the least talented, but hardest-working man ever likely to be named to the Hall of Fame (as it did with Maury Wills in 1972), can the reporter keep the personal sadness out of his stories? If he's honest, he can.

"The team must not become 'we.' The player you had breakfast with must not have excuses made for his errors. It is impossible to spend so much time with a team and not have personal favorites. Political reporters have theirs, too. The sports reporter has to guard against letting his prejudices show, just as does the political reporter."

Wanted: Writers

Sports fans tolerate almost any kind of writing so long as they are given the correct scores, accurate details of the game, interesting anecdotes and inside information about teams and players. The result is that sportswriting has been described by Roger Kahn, a sportswriter, as "the best and the worst writing to be found in the American newspaper today." Kahn says that at first glance "sports appears to be the shallow end of the American sea: puerile speeches at the letter club banquet, the hustling of transparent con men, simple adults pursuing childhood activities, amiable anecdotes repeated on old-timer's day. The same man who demands harsh film criticism and likes his political reporting merciless accepts a pabulum view of sport. . . ."

But this is changing. The sports pages are no longer the exclusive reading of the fan whose consuming passion in life is the Dallas Cowboys or the Fresno High School basketball team. Sports appeal to a wide range of readers and viewers, and many of them appreciate good writing as well as information.

Internal pressures also move sports reporters to work at their writing. Conscious of the criticism of sports as the slag heap of journalism, they can, and do, point out that some of the country's best writers graced the country's sports pages. Sportwriters are heirs to a splendid heritage—Ring Lardner, Westbrook Pegler, Heywood Broun, Red Smith—and many, like Kahn, are serious guardians of that tradition.

Good writing does not mean sportswriters have to turn the colorful and exciting language of sports into the homogeneous prose that infects most newspaper and television writing. Russell Baker, a columnist for *The New York Times,* bemoaned the decline of baseball talk that, he wrote, once "crackled with terseness, vibrancy and metaphor." He had heard a television sportscaster say, "Ryan has good velocity and excellent location." He meant, wrote Baker, that Ryan "is throwing very fast and putting the ball where he wants to."

This kind of impoverished writing, while sports are flourishing, is the result of sports "going through a period of highbrow pretension, brought on perhaps by the hordes of college men cluttering up the locker rooms and the advent of high-falutin' sportswriters too self-conscious about their master's degrees in creative writing to risk playing a kid's game at the typewriter," Baker wrote.

The situation makes a sports fan long for Dizzy Dean, the St. Louis Cardinals pitcher and then sports announcer who was known for his picturesque language. Once he was struck on the toe while pitching and a doctor examined him on the mound, "This toe is fractured," the doctor said. To which Dean replied, "Fractured hell. The damn thing's broken."

Sportswriters have written some memorable lines, such as this one about a midwestern quarterback who was a wizard on the field, a dunce in the classroom: "He could do anything with a football but autograph it." (The line came back to some sportswriters when they wrote about a football player at UCLA who was arrested for killing his drug dealer. The player, it turned out, could not read—the product of the win-at-any-price philosophy of big-time sports.)

Red Smith was a master writer. Of a notorious spitball pitcher, he wrote that "papers needed three columns for his pitching record: won, lost and relative humidity." Look at this lead he wrote about Buck Leonard, a black first baseman whose career ended before baseball was integrated:

Wearing a store suit, horn-rimmed glasses, and a smile that could light up Yankee Stadium, a sunny gentleman of 64 revisited his past yesterday and recalled what it was like to be the black Lou Gehrig on a food allowance of 60 cents a day.

Rise of the South. The South is the breeding ground for the nation's most skilled football players, says Professor John F. Rooney of Oklahoma State University, who devised a formula for measuring the states that send players to 136 college football powers.

Mississippi is first, Louisiana second, and Alabama, Georgia, and South Carolina are also in the top 10. Twenty years ago Ohio was the major breeding ground with Pennsylvania and New Jersey also prominent.

Sports, says Rooney, are part of the South's "macho culture. . . . The South has put a single-minded emphasis on football, building a one-sport culture while the rest of the country has widened its variety of sports."

The last few words chill an otherwise warm recollection. They sum up a period of American life in a phrase.

Anecdotes

Good sportswriters have memories that go back to the details of the first high school basketball game they covered. They are insatiable collectors of anecdotes to be stored away and used at the appropriate moment.

When an imaginative boxing promoter was trying to schedule a match between Muhammad Ali, who had made a friendly visit to Arab countries, and Mike Rossman, who carried the nicknames the Jewish Bomber and the Kosher Butcher, James Tuite of *The New York Times* recalled in his story a similar ethnic promotion. Years before, Irish Eddy Kelly and Benny Leonard, a Jewish fighter, were in the ring. Leonard was battering Kelly. Finally, in a clinch, Kelly whispered to Leonard. "Hub rachmones. (Yiddish for "take pity.") I'm really Bernie Schwartz."

Rossman, Tuite pointed out, was born Mike DePuano and took to wearing the Star of David on his trunks along with his new name to help sell tickets. The Ali-Rossman match was laughed out of the ring by pieces like Tuite's.

Young sportswriters sometimes try too hard. They press language, reach for words and phrases. When this happens, the result is sawdust and shavings. Here is a lead that tries so hard to invest sports with some higher value that it is tasteless:

> Martin Luther King had a dream. John McKay, Sr., had a plan. Both men were persecuted in their attempts to overcome adversity. Only McKay lived to tell how difficult it was to succeed, but there were times when he, too, felt he was going to die. Coaching the Tampa Bay Buccaneers had not been easy.

Direct, slender, purposive prose flows naturally from the event. Sports lead easily to good writing, for they have built-in essentials of drama—conflict, leading characters, dramatic resolution. There are enough incidents and examples to highlight the event; anecdotes that illustrate the situation, and high-quality quotations that reveal the nature of the individual and the event.

Let 'em Talk. The writer's technique of letting a source talk works well for sports stories. In a piece about Billy Williams, a Chicago Cubs outfielder for many years and later its batting coach, Frederick C. Klein of *The Wall Street Journal* quotes him on hitting:

"You hear fans saying that this star or that one was a 'natural,' but 99 percent of the time they're wrong. Sure, you gotta have ability, but you also gotta work, and every good hitter I knew worked hard to get that way. You have to practice your swing all the time, just like a golf pro. And if you think golf's hard, try it sometime with a guy throwing the ball at you."

Checklist: Game Coverage

_____ Result: Final score, names of teams, type of sport (if necessary to explain that it is high school, college, professional). League (NFL, AFC, Big Eight, Ivy League, NHL).

_____ Where and when game took place.

_____ Turning point of game; winning play; key strategy.

_____ Outstanding players.

_____ Effect on standings, rankings, individual records.

_____ Scoring. (Details of important baskets, goals, runs, etc.; summaries of others.)

_____ Streaks, records involved, by team or player.

_____ Post-game comments.

_____ External factors; weather; spectators.

_____ Size of crowd.

_____ Injuries and subsequent condition of athletes.

_____ Statistics.

_____ Duration of game when relevant.

The game story usually begins with a combination of an interesting or significant situation (and usually a key play or player) and the score.

DAYTON, Ohio (AP)—Scott Skiles scored, passed and even helped to coach his Michigan State teammates to an 80–68 victory over Georgetown today in second-round play of the National Collegiate Athletic Association tournament at the University of Dayton.

Sometimes, the victory involves a record, and this goes into the lead:

IOWA CITY (UPI)—Iowa today captured its ninth straight NCAA wrestling title, tying a record.

Leads

Pigskins, Horsehides, Hoops and Three Baggers

The sportswriter has greater writing freedom than any other member of the news staff, but does not use it when he or she:

• Uses the trite words and phrases of the trade—hoop, netminder, pigskin, split the uprights, gave it the big try—and the scores of others that infect sports pages.

• Plays the expert by using technical language to persuade the reader he or she is savvy.

• Follows formulas: _____ (passed, ran) for _____ touchdowns as _____ (outscored, manhandled, held off) _____ Saturday, _____ to _____ .

• Tries too hard.

Growing Popularity.
Television has given greater visibility to sports like golf and tennis, and sports pages have responded with more coverage of the big tournaments and local matches. The major golfers and tennis players have become publicity-wise and vie for space and viewer time. Some golfers have attracted followers as devoted and as vociferous as football and baseball fans. The antics of some of the temperamental tennis players have forced sports reporters to consider a new element in what had been regarded as a sport for the cultivated gentleman and gentlewoman. Photo by Joel Strasser.

The score may not be in the lead, but it should be high up in the story:

PONTIAC, Mich. (AP)—It didn't take Kelly Tripucka long to get well and the Knicks paid for it last night.

Tripucka came out of a shooting slump with 21 points as the Detroit Pistons defeated the Knicks 112–89.

Story Structure

As in any other type of story, the structure of the sports story follows the themes established by the lead. Look at the lead and second paragraph in the basketball story from Pontiac. What ran through the reporter's mind after he wrote the lead?

He knew he had to say more about Tripucka's shooting slump, and he did. Here are the next few paragraphs, all about Tripucka:

After going 2 of 16 from the field against Indiana Wednesday night, Tripucka came out firing against the Knicks, hitting 9 of 13 attempts.

"That was tough, mentally. I never had a night like that one against Indiana," Tripucka recalled. "Fortunately, I hit my first shot tonight. Once I did that, I just felt the old confidence coming back."

Tripucka was especially effective in the third quarter when Detroit moved from a 53–49 halftime lead to an 84–72 advantage after three periods.

Tripucka hit five of Detroit's first seven baskets after intermission, and once the Knicks switched their defense to concentrate on Tripucka, the rest of the Pistons got into the act.

Notice the last paragraph. The last section of it is a transition. The reporter sets up a new theme with the transition, scoring by other players:

Four other Pistons scored in double figures: Bill Laimbeer with 18, Isiah Thomas and Tony Campbell with 15 each and Vinnie Johnson with 12.

The third paragraph is as deep as the writer should go into the piece before giving the score. A reporter was so captivated by the final game in the U.S. Tennis Open in which Ivan Lendl defeated John McEnroe that he took six paragraphs to get to the score in his story.

Advice From a Pro: Try Again, and Again

Red Smith was always helpful to young writers. When a college student sent Smith columns he had written for his school newspaper, Smith replied:

> When I was a cub in Milwaukee I had a city editor who'd stroll over and read across a guy's shoulder when he was writing a lead. Sometimes he would approve and sometimes say gently, "Try again," and walk away.
>
> My best advice is, try again. And then again. If you're for this racket, and not many really are, then you've got an eternity of sweat and tears ahead. I don't mean just you; I mean anybody.

Charles McCabe of the San Francisco *Chronicle* wrote a column shortly after Smith's death in which he said:

> Red was nearly always the last man to leave the press room. Like Westbrook Pegler, he was a bleeder. I well remember him at the Olympic Games in Squaw Valley in 1960. When everyone else left and was up at the bar, Red sat sweating, piles of rejected leads surrounding him. He hadn't really even started his story yet. But when the lead came he wrote fluently and always met his deadline.

Smith once remarked, "The English language, if handled with respect, scarcely ever poisoned the user."

Favorites. A poll by *USA Today* of its readers' favorite sports found that 57 percent favored baseball, followed by 35 percent football and 8 percent basketball.

Covering a Baseball Game

Vinny DiTrani covers baseball for *The Bergen Record*. He covers a lot of games in a season, almost as many as the full schedule.

"In baseball, where there are 162 games each season, often the game itself can be submerged in favor of a personality piece, or an overall situation piece concerning a player or a team's status. In football, where there are only 16 games, I think more attention must be focused on the actual contest."

DiTrani was assigned to cover a game between the Minnesota Twins and the New York Yankees. The Twins pitcher was Jerry Koosman, who had pitched for the New York Mets for 11 years before being traded. It was clear to DiTrani that his story would have to focus on Koosman, since many of his readers had followed the Mets and Koosman. He wanted to give the readers a "status report," he said.

"Luckily, in this case, the game result fit perfectly into the personality piece." When he was with the punchless Mets, Koosman lost many close games. Now, with the Twins, he was still losing them. Here's how DiTrani began his piece:

NEW YORK—Some things just never change for Jerry Koosman. He still gets a thrill when he sees the bright lights of New York City. He still can't get over the hustle and bustle that goes on beneath those bright lights. He still thinks of the whole New York scene as home.

And he still manages to lose one-run ball games.

"Those things happen to every pitcher at one time or another," rationalized the veteran lefthander, who nevertheless collected more than his share of wasted efforts while pitching for the Mets. Last night, however, it was the Twins who did the wasting, dropping a 3–2 decision to the Yankees in Koosman's homecoming game.

It was the fourth straight setback for the 35-year-old Koosman, who started the year with a team-record seven consecutive victories. Three of the four losses have been by one run, and Koosman's earned run average has dwindled from 4.23 to 3.64 during that stretch.

DiTrani says that before writing a game story he asks himself: "What do the fans want to know about this game? In this case, I thought they most wanted to know about Koosman. In another, it may be the mechanics around a certain play, or the overall effect of the game on a team's outlook, its standing, and so on."

He described the game story as a "challenge, to create a story the reader will not pass over as just another of 162 installments."

Since fans usually are experts in the sports they follow, the sports reporter has to know more than his or her readers or viewers. When Andrea Sachs, a journalism student, was assigned to interview a jockey at a horse track on Sunday, she was worried. Sachs had never been to a track and, as she put it, "I did not know the difference between a horse and a goat.

"That night, I bought a copy of *The Daily Racing Form* and two track magazines at a newsstand. I asked the man behind the counter if he knew anything about racing. He suggested that I talk to the customer standing next to me.

"The customer was able to give me the names of the top jockeys at the track, and he explained a little about racing.

"I called the publicity office at the track and asked if I could speak to one of the apprentice jockeys. I made several other calls and worked out appointments.

Losers. Good stories—sometimes the best pieces—can come from the defeated. One of the greatest interviews in sports was by Murray Kempton of Sal Maglie, the losing pitcher when Don Larsen pitched his no-hit game in the 1956 World Series. Maglie had pitched well, allowing the Yankees five hits. He had the misfortune to run into the rarest of the rare—the perfect game.

Quick Learning

Youngster at the Big A. Apprentice jockey Robbie Davis on the way out of the saddling enclosure to the starting gate at the Aqueduct Race Track in New York. New York Racing Authority photo.

"Before I went to the track, I read the racing section of the newspaper. I discovered that a race was being televised that Saturday and bought another *Racing Form* and watched the race. That provided me with background knowledge and some conversation openers for my interviews."

Sachs left early for the track to watch the horses being exercised. She wandered around the track, chatting with jockeys and trainers. At the coffee

From Pocatello to New York.
Davis describes his quick rise
from riding in county fairs to
riding with the best jockeys in
the world. New York Racing
Authority photo.

stand, she asked a man to explain the betting system. Finally, it was time to interview her jockey, Robbie Davis, a youngster from Pocatello, Idaho, who had just won his first race at the track.

"He was amazingly open and willing to answer any questions. I spoke to him several times during the afternoon."

Her article for her class assignment began:

Robbie Davis' first race at Belmont was a young jockey's dream.

The shy 21-year-old apprentice jockey from Pocatello, Idaho, had driven to New York a week earlier from Louisiana Downs, where he had been riding since May. After exercising horses for a few days at Aqueduct, Davis went to Belmont in early September for the first time.

He was to ride Comanche Brave in a mile-and-an-eighth claiming race with experienced jockeys such as Angel Cordero and George Martens.

Davis recalls his feelings: "I didn't know the track at all . . . it was the biggest track I'd ever seen."

Comanche Brave went off at 20–1 odds, on a muddy track. Davis, who was used to shorter tracks, said that he watched "real close, trying to save as much horse as I could, because I knew it was a long straightaway."

The strategy worked. The next thing he knew, Davis was sitting in the winner's circle. "I couldn't believe it."

Encouraged by her instructor, Sachs sold the article to Davis' hometown newspaper, *The Idaho Journal.*

Coverage Preparation

Game stories can be difficult to handle because of the pressure to meet a deadline and because of the essential similarity of the stories—one team wins, the other loses. The reporter copes with deadlines with careful preparations. This may mean arriving at a high school gym well ahead of the game to find a telephone that will be available late in the evening so that the story can be called in to the sports desk.

"With starting times constantly being pushed back—all World Series games are now played at night, for example—and deadlines always being moved forward, you simply can't have too much in your notebook too soon," says Rapoport. What seemed like a stroke of luck for Rapoport after the first game of the 1985 World Series was actually foresight. Rapoport decided to do a column on Kansas City pitcher Charlie Liebrandt, and he interviewed the pitcher before he was to start in the first game. "I sent it to the newspaper just as Liebrandt was losing the game despite pitching brilliantly," Rapoport said. "After the game, a distraught Liebrandt wouldn't talk to reporters. Only those who had interviewed him before, and those who had covered him all year, knew enough about him to write anything interesting."

When she covered high school games out of town, Hands would trade information with local reporters. The exchange turned up nicknames, personal information about the players and the detail that gives a game story an individual touch.

Keeping Statistics

One way to avoid trouble about game facts is to keep statistics of the event. Let us watch Hands cover a high school football game.

When she arrives at the field, she checks the program to make sure the numbers on the players' jerseys are the same as those on the program. Then she sets up her scoring sheet.

"Every sportswriter has developed his own method of keeping a play-by-play and statistics, and of course, each sport lends itself to a different method," she says. "It's a good idea for a beginner to check with his or her editors or other sportswriters and to try a few out on radio or TV games before trying the first one at a game. It's necessary because you can't count on being able to remember the sequence of plays, and you'd better not count on anybody else keeping statistics.

"You have to keep all the statistics you can because you can never tell what's going to be important. The game may be decided by punting. It may be decided by return yardage (which is not included in total offense). The key to the game may be one player's ability to set up tackles.

"If you can bring along a friend to spot tackles while you keep offense, that's great. Sometimes you can trade off with another sportswriter in the press box. I've never seen anybody who can keep offense and defense at the same time, but I'm told there are a couple.

"Use halftime to tally up. Sometimes it is surprising to see what the statistics reveal. They don't always match the appearances."

Perspective. Sports fans inhabit a world of their own. When a Chicago Bears football game on television was interrupted with a bulletin about the collapse of a summit talk between the US and Russia, irate fans flooded the station with angry calls.

Mike Ditka, coach of the Bears, was scornful. "This is only a pigskin," he said. "The other thing can blow us up."

From the Players' Perspective

To see the game the right way, look at it the way the players do. The advice is given by Thomas Boswell, a sportswriter for *The Washington Post,* in his book *Why Time Begins on Opening Day* (New York: Doubleday, 1984). Boswell writes about baseball, but his suggestions apply to most sports that reporters cover:

Judge slowly. "Never judge a player over a unit of time shorter than a month . . . you must see a player hot, cold, and in between before you can put the whole package together."

Assume everybody is trying reasonably hard. ". . . giving 110 percent . . . would be counterproductive for most players. . . . Usually something on the order of 80 percent effort is about right."

Forgive even the most grotesque physical errors. "It's assumed that every player is physically capable of performing every task asked of him. If he doesn't it's never his fault. His mistake is simply regarded as part of a professional's natural margin of error."

Judge mental errors harshly. "The distinction as to whether a mistake has been made 'from the neck up or the neck down' is always drawn."

Pay more attention to the mundane than to the spectacular. "The necessity for consistency usually outweighs the need for the inspired."

Pay more attention to the theory of the game than to the outcome of the game. Don't let your evaluations be swayed too greatly by the final score. "If a team loses a game but has used its resources properly . . . then that team is often able to ignore defeat utterly. Players say, 'We did everything right but win.'"

Keep in mind that players always know best how they're playing. "At the technical level, they seldom fool themselves—the stakes are too high."

Stay ahead of the action, not behind it or even neck and neck with it. "Remember that the immediate past is almost always prelude."

Hands says she does not mind doing most press box chores herself. "That way, I'm never at the mercy of PR men. I'm glad to have them help me, but I don't have to count on it," she says.

Reporters hang on to these statistics and their score cards. They come in handy. Rapoport was watching the Los Angeles Dodgers one evening when the game pattern began to seem familiar. Al Downing was pitching for the Dodgers and his infielders seemed to be booting as many grounders as they fielded. "It came to me that I had seen something like this before, and I began to flip through the pages in my score book," Rapoport says. "The last time Downing had pitched, the Dodgers had made several errors and he had lost. And twice before that as well.

"A quick recapitulation of those losing games along with the day's score and a wry quote from Downing made for a fairly decent start to an otherwise routine game story."

A survey of sports readers by the Sports Committee of the Associated Press Managing Editors Association indicated that readers depend on the newspaper for tabulated detail: box scores, racing entries and results, football summaries and the other data. More than half the readers always read baseball box scores, and two-thirds always read the football summaries.

Game Details

Unless a game is exciting or important, Rapoport says he tends not to include much detail.

"Usually a couple of paragraphs are enough to sum up the key plays. I prefer to use the space to concentrate on one or two or three of the most interesting things that happened and to tell what the players involved or the manager thought about them.

"Often, a game story will be built around somebody who had a large effect—positive or negative— on the outcome." Rapoport says. "It is almost mandatory that we hear from this key player and, though there are some spontaneous talkers who begin at the sight of a notebook, it is almost always better to have a question in mind. This sounds simple enough, but often takes some thought. The right question will often do wonders.

"I also like to listen to what's being said by the players—not to reporters—but to each other. They often have funny conversations when they've won, sympathetic ones when they've lost. Good dialogue can dress up a story."

William Perry, the Chicago Bears' 300-pound-plus defensive lineman who was nicknamed the "Refrigerator," created a stir during the 1985 season when he lined up in the offensive backfield and began scoring touchdowns. Rapoport recalls a locker room incident: "After a game in Green Bay when Perry became the National Football League's widest receiver and caught a scoring pass, Bear defensive tackle Steve McMichael sneaked up on him in the locker room and began singing in his ear, 'They always call him Mr. Touchdown.' You have to listen for things like that."

The small moves, the slight shift in position, a change in the way a guard plays his man—these details that the observant reporter picks up often mean the difference between victory and defeat. Watch a center fielder play each batter differently. Keep an eye on the way a forward moves to the basket in the second period after all his shots missed or were blocked in the first period.

Listening. Bob Gibson, premier pitcher for 17 seasons for the St. Louis Cardinals, tells of a game in which Tom Seaver, then of the Mets, threw at him three times. On the third brushback, Gibson shouted, "You got better control than that, buddy." Seaver replied, "So do you." Gibson says that Seaver remembered that in spring training Gibson had hit Mets outfielder John Milner to keep him from crowding the plate.

Gibson said that Milner was "trying to take away my bread and butter by positioning himself in a way that gave him an advantage."

Gibson says he pitched the brushback, knockdown and hit-batter pitches to keep his advantage. When Gibson broke Duke Snider's elbow with a pitch, he recalled, "there was no point in apologizing since I was only doing my job."

High School Sports

Most beginners on the sports beat are assigned to local high school basketball and football coverage. To the young reporter who can quote the pass completion percentage of all the quarterbacks in the National Football League, being assigned to cover a Friday night high school football game may seem a comedown.

Richard H. Growald, the UPI's national reporter, noted that "despite the growth in popularity of such attractions as professional football, local high school sports remains a dominant civic factor. An American may not be too familiar with the workings of his city hall, but he knows his high school football team lineup."

High school sports are the major sports interest in most towns and cities because they are the only local spectator sports available to these fans. For every Ohio State enthusiast, there are a dozen high school fans in the state.

"It's not uncommon in North and South Carolina for 10,000 people to watch a regular season high school football game," says *The Charlotte Observer's* Susan Hands. "And every one of those 10,000 is a potential reader of the sports page, if his or her hometown high school hero's name is in the paper."

In fact, Hands says, the most widely read stories in the *Observer* are high school sports. Hands was responsible for covering 116 high school teams in the Carolinas. She handled most of the coverage by telephone and covered one game a week.

In Danville, Ill., the *Commercial-News* covers two local high schools and 30 area high schools as well as a local junior college and Big Ten sports at the University of Illinois and Purdue. Fowler Connell, the sports editor, says that during the school year, "football and basketball on the local scene are king, although the other sports are covered also.

"We feel we are obligated to do more for our readers than any big-city paper can possibly do. Danville and our area towns belong to 'us' and, conversely, we like to think they want us in their homes," he says.

The paper covers all home and away games of the local teams and each of the other 30 high schools at least once. If an area team is in contention for the state playoffs, the newspaper will cover it several times.

The newspaper also runs roundups of the area teams Tuesdays, "Player of the Week" features during football and basketball seasons Wednesdays, pre-game advances and an area roundup of coming games on Thursdays. Illinois and Purdue are given the big play Fridays for their Saturday games. Friday nights the staff is out covering high school games, and Saturday's newspaper is dominated by the results of these games.

With demands such as these on his staff, everyone has to be able to cover several sports. "No one is wedded to any one team or any one sport," says Connell.

Women Sports Reporters

"I think women belong in the kitchen," said the owner of the San Francisco 49ers football team, Edward DeBartolo Jr. He was commenting after a federal judge ruled that the National Football League team had to grant equal access to its locker room to a female sports reporter for *The Sacramento Bee*.

Characters like DeBartolo and his coach are rarities these days in professional sports. By now, women sportswriters are an accepted part of the sports scene. The victory was hard won. Not until 1975 were women admitted to locker rooms of professional basketball and hockey teams for post-game interviews.

In 1976, a female reporter for *Sports Illustrated* was denied access to the Yankee Stadium clubhouse and filed suit in federal court. She won, and baseball teams opened their locker rooms and clubhouses.

Most athletes no longer care whether they are interviewed by a male or a female sportswriter. The story is told about a female sportswriter in the San Diego basketball team's locker room following a game. As Randy Smith started to pull off his uniform, a fellow player cautioned him, "Randy, there's a lady in the room." Smith replied:

"That's no lady. That's only a writer."

Partisanship

"Sportswriting has survived because of the guys who don't cheer," said Jimmy Cannon, a gifted New York sports columnist. He was friendly with some of the players whose teams he covered, but was never a cheerleader. In broadcasting, the premier announcer in radio's palmiest days was Red Barber, and his credo was non-partisanship. In a warm southern drawl, he described the Brooklyn Dodgers with no greater affection than the visiting Giants or Cubs. His love was the game, not the team. His ability to call the shots impartially may have cost Barber his job when local sports coverage on television turned to the gee-whiz crowd and the rooters.

The partisanship of broadcasters has become so obvious that it gave rise to the word "homer" to describe the hometown bias of the sportscasters. The exceptions are rare. Ed Westfall, a former hockey player who does the color for New York Islanders games, saw an Islander defenseman cross-check an opponent, and called it that way. But the referee gave both men two-minute penalties. Westfall showed the incident on replay and commented: "I might offend some people if I say something. But really, look at this. You see? Oh well, they each get two minutes, Morrow for giving, Franceschetti for receiving."

Reporters do cover local teams from the point of view of the hometown fans. This is fair. But the reporter is not supposed to cross the line between reporter and rooter, as some journalists in Kentucky did when competing reporters exposed illegal payments to college athletes.

Hoopla in Kentucky

Drugs on the Diamond.
When two small newspapers printed stories about possible drug use by Philadelphia Philly baseball players, Philadelphia newspapers attacked the reporters who wrote the stories. Five years later, a more serious drug scandal erupted, and this time the press held back nothing. A federal grand jury investigating cocaine distribution in Pittsburgh turned up the names of several star baseball players as users: Lonnie Smith, Jeff Leonard, Dale Berra, Keith Hernandez, Enos Cabell, Joaquin Andujar, and Dave Parker, among others. Even the television announcers, most of whom are selected or approved by the baseball clubs, referred to the investigation. (The baseball commissioner fined the seven 10 percent of their salaries and ordered them to do 100 hours of community service a year for two years.)

In 1985, the *Lexington Herald-Leader* published a series of articles describing cash payments by boosters to basketball players at the University of Kentucky. The players also received up to $1,000 each for their complimentary tickets. A guard said he made $8,400 selling tickets to a lawyer. Another player said he made eight to a dozen talks at $150 each, and some said they were paid as much as $500 for a talk.

All this, the newspaper said, took place during the period Joe B. Hall coached the team. The reporters, Jeffrey Marx and Michael York, interviewed 33 players, 31 of whom said they knew of violations of the rules of the National Collegiate Athletic Association; 26 admitted receiving cash or some other kind of improper benefit during their playing careers at Kentucky.

The reaction was swift, and angry. Kentucky has, in York's words, "the winningest of all college basketball programs, and basketball has been called the most widely practiced religion in the Bluegrass state."

Fans cancelled subscriptions. The newspaper received bomb threats. York was offered a bullet-proof vest by a member of the police department. What was especially galling was the reaction of some radio and television journalists, most of whom "lined up behind the university." An ABC affiliate said the stories were evidence of the newspaper's "self-serving sensationalism."

The reporters were awarded the Pulitzer Prize for investigative reporting in 1985.

The reporter-turned-rooter may see only the excitement and drama of the sport he or she is covering and ignore the cheap shots, the drug use, the sordid deals and the crass commercialism of the sport.

Distance Best

Young reporters sooner or later have to decide whether to handle sports as entertainment or as news, and how to treat athletes. Stanley Woodward, sports editor of *The New York Herald Tribune,* used to shake his head at the veneration of athletes that seeped through copy. "Will you please stop godding up these ball players," he would tell his staff.

Red Smith, like Cannon, had many friends among the athletes, but he wrote with distance and some bemusement about sports. "I've tried not to exaggerate the glory of athletes," he said.

The sports reporter who becomes too deeply involved in his or her coverage might chat with the political reporter, who usually can provide ample evidence of what partisanship can do to a working journalist.

"Only politicians lie more than football coaches," Cannon once observed.

Involvement can lead to dislike as well as admiration, but sportswriters usually manage to control these feelings. However, if the athlete is the beneficiary of often-unmerited admiration, perhaps the balance should be struck with an occasional insight into the reality of the athlete's life.

Here is what a *New York Post* sports columnist wrote about a baseball player:

> Graig Nettles doesn't like me even a little bit. The feeling is mutual. Just so I would know how he feels about me last week in St. Petersburg he decided to call me a "backstabbing Jew bleeper." He said it three times, so I would get the point.
>
> . . . Graig is too vicious for me. On two occasions he has treated official sources with whom he disagreed foully enough to make your stomach turn. . . .

Sports reporting, like any other kind of coverage, responds to changing situations. Two major changes have swept through sports in the past four decades: The increasingly important role of money in amateur as well as professional sports and the inclusion of blacks and women in activities that had been closed to them.

Sports is a commercial enterprise, whether the game is played in the Astrodome or on a college football field. Once, says Gerald Eskenazi of *The New York Times,* "an athlete was revered by the American public, placed on the same pedestal reserved for generals, Medal of Honor winners, movie stars, aviators. . . ." Today, the pedestal is gone, and alongside the athlete in the public's mind are agents, lawyers, and financial advisers.

In the 1970s, the average major league baseball player earned $35,000 a year. In 1986, the average was $412,250. In the old days, players stayed with one team for their entire career. Now, they move to the call of the highest bidder, and teams are likely to trade away athletes with high salaries. Historian Henry Steele Commager noted the shifting about and commented, "We have nothing to be loyal to."

At the college level, football and basketball are million dollar enterprises, much of the fuel coming from booster clubs. The average big-time sports school receives more than $500,000 a year for the athletics department.

Changes

Take That. Pittsburgh Pirates third baseman Bill Madlock shows what he thinks of umpire Gerry Crawford's third-strike call. Photographer Robert Pavuchak caught this detail for *The Pittsburgh Press*. In covering sports, reporters and photographers are alert for the details that highlight the game. Photo by Robert J. Pavuchak.

Big Money. Football can generate up to $10 million a year in income; the 1986 Rose Bowl netted $12 million for the teams and their conferences from TV and attendance. The 1986 bowl games made $40 million.

Big money leads to recruiting violations, says William Gildea of *The Washington Post* sports staff. At Texas Christian, a high school player was spirited to a motel, entertained with meals and prostitutes until he signed a letter of intent. During his four seasons with the TCU team, he was paid $27,100, Gildea says.

Tates Locke, a former Clemson basketball coach, says sports reporters must have been aware of such practices. "You guys are in the locker room. And when I say, 'What's going on?' and you reply, 'I don't know; I didn't see anything,' that's a lie. You see what kind of clothes he wears, you see his car, you've been to his room. And he comes from the Pulpwood city limits—you gotta be kidding."

While these contributions have kept many athletic programs from dropping into the red, they also have caused considerable turmoil on and off campus. Frederick C. Klein of *The Wall Street Journal* found that many "in college sports regard the necessity of raising large sums of money from boosters as unfortunate. . . ." One of the consequences is an increase in "the already-enormous pressure for victory in those 'revenue' sports. . . ."

Boosters are hard to control. Of the 70 penalties the NCAA handed down from 1980 through 1985, 45 involved improper activities by boosters. Harry Edwards, associate professor of sociology at the University of California at Berkeley and a specialist in the sociology of sports, says players have been offered "cars, clothing accounts, lucrative no-work jobs, thousands of dollars in cash . . . and thousands more under the table once they have enrolled." Southern Methodist University boosters paid a high school recruit more than $10,000 and offered cash and cars to others. At Texas Christian University, a running back said he was paid $600 a month by a regent in the late 1970s. In 1982, University of Southern California boosters paid large sums for players' complimentary tickets. Arizona State University was given a two-year NCAA football probation partly as the result of improper payments to athletes and coaches by a local booster club. The University of San Francisco dropped varsity basketball after it found it could not control student-aid violations by alumni. The situation has led to new kinds of stories. Hero worship has been replaced by exposé.

Reporters regularly dig into the role money plays in luring top high school athletes to many colleges and universities, even those who James H. Wharton, chancellor of Louisiana State University, says "read at the fourth-, fifth- or sixth-grade level." Many of the athletes Wharton refers to are black and are lured to campuses where they are kept eligible as long as possible, then sent packing. Edwards says universities have bent and broken the rules in recruiting and enrolling black athletes.

Some journalists had made gentleman's agreements with college officials not to dig into what everyone knew was a scandal. The pressure to produce winning teams extended to the local press. The hands-off agreement was no credit to sportswriters, who had turned themselves into boosters.

But by the mid-1980s, the excesses had grown so great the system exploded. Sports reporters turned to investigative reporting.

ATLANTA—A federal court jury today found that a University of Georgia instructor had been dismissed illegally in retaliation for opposing favored treatment for athletes.

The instructor, Jan Kemp, had refused to change failing grades for five athletes. She said university officials had intervened in 1981 to enable nine football players to pass a remedial English course they had failed. A non-athlete who had also failed was dismissed from the university.

The Macon Telegraph & News won a Pulitzer Prize the year before the Kemp trial for digging into the university sports program; it noted that only 17 percent of Georgia's black football players had earned degrees over the previous 10 years.

Similar stories have been written at other universities. Memphis State University, for example, graduated only four of 38 basketball players from 1973 to 1985; two were black.

The graduation rate for black athletes in U.S. colleges and universities is 25 percent; three-fourths of those who graduate have degrees in physical education. The attitude toward black athletes by some college officials was seen to have been summed up by an attorney for the University of Georgia during the Kemp trial. He defended the university's athletic program for blacks by saying: "We may not make a university student (out of an athlete). But if we can teach him to read and write, just maybe he can work for the post office rather than as a garbage man."

The scene, the Montreal Expos baseball stadium. The event, a playoff game. It is fall, evening. It is cold, and snowflakes occasionally swirl across the field. Hardly baseball weather.

The baseball commissioner sits resolutely, the only man visible who is not wearing an overcoat. The commissioner is trying to prove a point.

Exception. When a North Carolina State basketball player pled guilty to breaking and entering (he had previously been convicted of assaulting a woman student) it was found he had a combined score of 470 on his SAT, 70 more than a test-taker is given for signing his or her name.

Exploitation

The Faithful. During the Kemp trial, the university athletic department held its annual fund-raising drive. It took in a record $4.2 million.

Lowest in Big Ten. Figures compiled by the Big Ten in 1986 show that University of Minnesota male athletes had the lowest graduation rate in the league for those who entered the university between 1973 and 1978—28 percent graduated within five years of entering school. For the basketball team, two of 23 entering freshmen graduated within the five-year period.

Why No Soccer?

The point is that it is fine to play baseball at night; the weather is no problem.

What this is all about is money. The playoffs and the World Series must be played at night in order to capture the audience. Advertisers won't pay top dollar for a weekday daytime game. And so baseball, summer's game, the game that was once played on grass on warm afternoons, has moved into the evening. Should the Chicago Cubs go into the playoffs, the league ruled, they would have to play their games elsewhere. Wrigley Field has no lights.

Some sports have had rules changed, timeouts added in order to make room for commercials. Why no soccer on commercial television? Because, says one reporter, the world's most popular game is continuous. There is no time for a commercial. A bastardized version of the game was tried, with timeouts, but nobody would look at it. Fans wanted the real game.

New Players

On April 15, 1947, Jackie Robinson ran out of the Brooklyn Dodger dugout and became the first black in modern history to break the color line. Since then, blacks have been the dominant figures in many sports.

In baseball, over a recent dozen-year period, 22 of the 24 National and American League stolen-base leaders were black, as were half of the batting champions. Every rushing leader in the National Football League since 1963 has been black, and in the National Basketball Association only a few white players have led the league in scoring since 1960 and only two in rebounding since 1957.

Women have also entered sports. In college and the commercial sports, women make news. Their exploits in track, tennis and golf are chronicled by sports pages and network television.

An Overview

Roger Kahn—who wrote a fine book about baseball, *The Boys of Summer*—has a basic approach to his reporting. Most good sportswriters do. Here, from one of Kahn's columns in *Esquire,* is how he describes his approach to his beat:

> Sports tells anyone who watches intelligently about the times in which we live: about managed news and corporate policies, about race and terror and what the process of aging does to strong men. If that sounds grim, there is courage and high humor, too. . . .
> . . . I find sport a better area than most to look for truth. A great hockey goalie, describing his life on ice, once said, "That puck comes so hard, it could take an eye. I've had 250 stitches and I don't like pain. I get so nervous before every game, I lose my lunch."

NCAA: Probation to TV Blackout

For the two years from Sept. 1, 1983, through Aug. 31, 1985, the National Collegiate Athletic Association imposed the following public penalties on colleges and universities. The date of penalty and its nature is included:

Sept. 1, '83–Aug. 31, '84

1. **West Virginia University**—9/20/83—public reprimand and censure, men's basketball.
2. **Wake Forest University**—10/31/83—public reprimand and censure, men's basketball.
3. **University of Wisconsin, Madison**—11/22/83—one year probation, no live televison in football, one representative disassociated.
4. **University of Kansas**—11/21/83—two years probation, no postseason play or live television in football for one year, one former assistant football coach disassociated for three years.
5. **Jackson State University**—12/9/83—public reprimand and censure, football.
6. **San Diego State University**—1/7/84—one year probation, no postseason play or live television in men's basketball, grant cuts.
7. **Western Kentucky University**—4/25/84—public reprimand and censure, men's basketball.
8. **Southern University, Baton Rouge**—4/26/84—public reprimand and censure, grant cuts in football.
9. **Alcorn State University**—5/1/84—public reprimand and censure, women's basketball.
10. **Oregon State University**—5/14/84—one year probation, return $342,634.62 from 1982 Division I Men's Basketball Championship, deletion of the university's record of participation in the 1980–81–82 NCAA basketball championships.
11. **University of Alaska, Anchorage**—5/25/84—two years probation, grant cuts in men's basketball.
12. **Florida State University**—6/12/84—public reprimand and censure, football.
13. **University of Illinois, Champaign**—7/26/84—two years probation, no postseason play or live television in football for one year, grant cuts, no off-campus recruiting by head football coach as well as one assistant, assistant football coach's salary frozen until 3/7/87 and head football coach's salary frozen for 1984.

Sept. 1 '84–Aug. 31, '85

1. **Austin Peay State University**—9/12/84—public reprimand and censure, certification of eligibility and financial aid procedures.
2. **Middle Tennessee State University**—9/12/84—six-month probation, basketball.
3. **University of Arizona**—9/14/84—one men's assistant basketball coach prohibited from engaging in any recruiting activities for one year.
4. **University of Akron**—9/26/84—two-year probation and no postseason competition and grant cuts in the sport of men's basketball for one year.
5. **University of Georgia**—1/3/85—and 5/21/85—one-year probation, grant cuts in sport of football, no off-campus recruiting by men's basketball coaching staff for one year; $238,200 returned to the Association from the 1985 National Collegiate Division I Men's Basketball Championship.
6. **University of Florida**—1/13/85—three-year probation; no postseason competition or live television appearances for two years, and grant cuts for two years.
7. **Tennessee State University**—2/7/85—one-year probation; $80,052.80 returned from the 1981 and 1982 National Collegiate Division I-AA Football Championship.
8. **University of Southern Mississippi**—2/7/85—one-year probation and a reduction to 60 in the number of official visits in the sport of football for one year.
9. **Arizona State University**—2/18/85—$9,000 returned from participation in the 1983 and 1984 National Collegiate Division I Baseball Championships and 1984 National Collegiate Division I Wrestling Championships; adoption of conference action that precluded postseason competition in baseball for one year, and grant cuts in baseball, men's gymnastics and wrestling.
10. **Alabama State University**—4/4/85—20-month probation, restriction of off-campus recruiting activities by head football coach for one year, and requirement to develop procedures to ensure proper application of eligibility standards.
11. **Idaho State University**—6/19/85—two-year probation; no postseason competition or live television appearances for one year, and disassociation of the head men's basketball coach from the intercollegiate athletics program.
12. **Cheyney University of Pennsylvania**—7/1/85—one-year probation, and development and implementation of educational and monitoring programs for staff members in women's basketball.
13. **San Francisco State University**—8/7/85—public reprimand and censure in the sport of men's basketball; $522.80 returned to the Association from participation in the 1984 National Collegiate Division II Men's Basketball Championship.
14. **Southern Methodist University**—8/16/85—three-year probation; no postseason competition and grant cuts in football for two years; no live television appearances for one year; elimination of representatives from any recruiting activities during probationary period.
15. **American University**—8/25/85—public reprimand and censure, men's basketball.

Double Standard. In a talk to the Associated Press Managing Editors convention, sportswriter Howard Cosell asked sportswriters to "bring true journalism to sports, not glorification to the victor and hearts and flowers to the loser."

Cosell said that *The Boston Globe* withheld a story about drug use by New England Patriot football players until the team played in the Super Bowl.

"Yet, the *Globe,* along with *The Washington Post* and *The New York Times,* published the Pentagon Papers at a time when some people felt it impinged on the national security."

He said newspapers should be covering the effect devotion to sports is having on society.

Show Business: 'Let's Go to the Videotape'

Almost a million people in the New York area watch him at 6 p.m. He draws $600,000 a year for doing two four-minute sports shows five days a week. He never goes to sports events, and team officials say he almost never calls for information. He is Warner Wolf, whose show one sportswriter describes as "the MTV of sports."

Wolf's four minutes are videotapes of exciting seconds in the games of the last 24 hours. On Wolf's 11 p.m. show, Gerald Eskenazi of *The New York Times* said he counted 14 baskets by three teams, three goals and two fights in a hockey game. "It really is show business," says Wolf's producer. "That's the way Warner views it."

"Some football players," I said to the goalie, whose name is Glenn Hall, "say that when they're badly scared, they pray."

Hall looked disgusted, "If there is a God," he said, "let's hope he's doing something more important than watching hockey games." Offhand I can't recall a better sermon.

Red Smith, who was writing his sports column for *The New York Times* until a few days before he died in 1982, said of sports:

Sports is not really a play world. I think it's the real world. The people we're writing about in professional sports, they're suffering and living and dying and loving and trying to make their way through life just as the bricklayers and politicians are.

This may sound defensive—I don't think it is—but I'm aware that games are a part of every culture we know anything about. And often taken seriously. It's no accident that of all the monuments left of the Greco-Roman culture, the biggest is the ball park, the Colosseum, the Yankee Stadium of ancient times. The man who reports on these games contributes his small bit to the history of his times.

Rapoport takes what he calls a practical view of sports coverage. "If you can't find something light or something that will make the reader smile or laugh, at least remember and try to show, in style or substance, that these are games these people are involved in, not foreign policy discussions," he says.

"However, dramatic things do happen and when they do the reporter shouldn't be afraid to haul out the heavy artillery. The day a young player left his career on a cyclone fence in the outfield, the lead was:

Bobby Valentine sat in center field,
facing the fence the ball had just gone over,
staring down at the grotesque sight the
broken bone was making beneath the skin,
trying not to scream, not to think, not to
do anything.

When the veteran Rico Carty was cut from the Toronto Blue Jays training camp, Alison Gordon, who covered the team for the *Toronto Star,* described Carty's reaction:

Gold chains and medallions glittered
at his neck, but he looked battered and
confused, like a boxer who had defended
his title in one too many fights.

Further Reading

Anderson, David, ed. *The Red Smith Reader.* New York: Random House, 1983.

Berkow, Ira. *Red: A Biography of Red Smith.* New York: Times Books, 1986.

Kahn, Roger. *The Boys of Summer.* New York: New American Library, 1973.

Smith, Red. *Strawberries in the Wintertime.* New York: Quadrangle Times Books, 1974.

CHAPTER TWENTY-THREE

Business Reporting

Preview

Business and economic activity affects everybody. It affects the cost and quality of the goods we buy, whether some people will buy or rent a home, what kind of car can be purchased, even the college a high school graduate can afford to attend. The business reporter handles:

• Local spot news stories—Store openings and closings, company personnel changes, new construction, changes in the business climate, annual reports of local companies.

• Features—New products developed by local enterprises, profiles of company officials and working people.

• Interpretative stories—Effects of national and international economic developments on local business, the power of local business leaders on municipal policies such as the tax structure.

Business reporters read widely for background—business newspapers and magazines, books on business and economics and the wide array of pamphlets and reports put out by private and government groups.

News about business and economics has become everybody's personal business. Most of us want to know about the cost of living, job possibilities, how high or low interest rates may go, whether layoffs are imminent in local industries and the value of a bond or stock that we or our parents own.

Our food, clothing and shelter are produced by business enterprises, and their quality and the prices we pay for them are largely the result of business decisions. Even the quality of the air we breathe and the water we drink is affected by decisions made by the business community. We have a large stake in those decisions, and we want to be informed of them and to know how they are made.

News about commerce is as old as the newspaper itself. The gazettes and newsletters of the 17th century were established in the business centers of Europe for the emerging commercial class. Though it seems obvious that everyone would have a great interest in pocketbook news—news of the economy—editors came lately to the realization.

One of the causes of this awakening was the consumer movement in the 1970s that resulted in a new kind of coverage for television and for many newspapers—consumer journalism. Reacting to what appeared to be an attitude of *caveat emptor* (let the buyer beware) among U.S. businesses, newspapers and broadcast stations went into the marketplace to find out why the quality of goods and services was declining while prices were steadily rising.

Curiosity, if not skepticism, about business was strong. Consumers were irritated by products that fell apart too soon and too often, and they were infuriated by the indifference of manufacturers, sellers, repairmen and mechanics.

The environmental movement also turned public attention, and then media attention, to the board rooms of corporations. Journalists concluded that their job was to make corporate power accountable. Tom Johnson, publisher of the *Los Angeles Times,* said, "Business news has become page one news because of the emergence of highly controversial issues in which there is an obvious potential for conflict between the corporate and the public interest."

John Morton, a former reporter who is a newspaper analyst with an investment firm, says journalists are giving business and financial news increased attention because newspapers realized readers want this kind of information and that advertisers are "eager to reach those readers." He said, "The world of business and finance has become the source of major stories involving scandal, fascinating personalities and the uses and abuses of power."

Business and economic reporting on television has exploded. From the boring nightly reading of the Dow Jones industrial average and a few other statistics, it has grown to an imaginative and innovative branch of television journalism. One of the reasons for the growth is the availability of computer technology, which has made it possible to draw graphs and charts quickly. The station artist can draw multidimensional figures that tumble, move back and forth and fade.

Friday night, Tom and Ann Ryan sit down after dinner to make a decision. The birth of their second child means they will need another bedroom. They must decide whether to rent a larger apartment or buy a house.

They reread a story in their local newspaper's business section about mortgage rates. The prospect is that rates probably will go down slightly over the next six months. But they are still too high for the Ryans, who decide to rent until the rate falls some more.

Interest rates also are a concern of the Goldensohn family. Robert, a high school senior, wants to attend a private college. The tuition is high and he must have a student loan. The family income meets the necessities and little more. Robert may have to borrow at least $5,000 a year.

TV Too. The programs on television are affected by business decisions. Since women make at least 80 percent of all consumer purchases, they are the target of advertisers, and advertisers pay the freight in television. One of the results, say news directors, is an emphasis in news programs on lifestyle reporting, women's medical news and how-to-cope features.

The Scope of Business News

If they cannot handle the loan, Robert will have to attend a community college. Their newspaper carries a story on the latest information about student loans and interest rates. The Goldensohns decide Robert will go to the community college.

In homes in every part of the city, people look to business stories for information that affects them. Workers whose contracts are tied to the cost of living watch the papers and television to see how their paychecks will be affected by the latest figures from Washington. Farmers follow the livestock and commodity markets. Vacationers search through the list of foreign exchange rates to see what the dollar is worth abroad before deciding where to spend their vacations. Residents north of the city hear that a new shopping center will be built there; they look through the business pages to find out more about it.

The Beat

The business reporter ranges widely. In the morning, he or she interviews local service station dealers on a price war, and that afternoon the reporter localizes a story about the new prime rate and the failure of the coffee crop in Brazil.

Local stories include:

- Store openings, expansions and closings.
- Real estate transactions. New products from local enterprises. Construction projects planned.
- Plants opened, expanded, closed. Personnel changes, awards, retirements. Layoffs, bankruptcies.
- Annual and quarterly business reports. Annual meetings.

If the newspaper or station has no labor reporter, the business reporter covers labor-management relations and the activities of labor unions.

In addition to these spot news stories, the business reporter is aware of trends and developments in the community and area. The business reporter knows the relationship between the prime rate and the local housing market and understands how the city's parking policies affect downtown merchants.

Here is how Bob Freund of *The Times-News* in Twin Falls, Idaho, began a story that blended local and national business and economic activity and trends:

TWIN FALLS—As spring turned into summer, the brightest news for the Magic Valley economy was coming from consumers.

They climbed into new cars at an accelerated pace, and sought credit both to pay for the new wheels and for improvements at home.

They benefited from a vicious war of price cutting and couponing among area grocery stores.

Indicators compiled by The Times-News for the second quarter ending June 30 show some momentum in the Magic Valley economy, but also some significant drags.

Despite lower mortgage rates and a national surge in homebuying, the biggest consumer of all, the home buyer, still is not pounding down the doors at Magic Valley real estate agencies.

Agriculture, the underlying financial pump for the valley economy, remains grounded by low commodity prices.

Of course, the Magic Valley is not alone in these problems. Idaho's economy generally is weak, and with trade imbalances pressing more and more on manufacturing, the U.S. is wavering in a twilight zone between recession and growth.

Nationally, economists are calling the situation a growth recession. The economy is growing, but it is not gaining enough strength to cut unemployment substantially.

The Times-News surveyed the cattle industry and came up with stories that described the plight of a major section of the economy. A story by Freund began:

TWIN FALLS—Cattle market observers are waiting for cattle prices to hit the bottom with a solid thud. When that happens, ranchers, feedlot owners, packing companies and the businesses that depend on them at least will know that the next direction is up.

But, after drifting downward for months, cattle prices have taken a headlong plunge in the past four weeks, and they've found only open air below.

"Every time it drops a few dollars, somebody quotes it as being the bottom," says Stenson Clontz, associate manager of the Twin Falls Livestock Commission. "We've got to find the bottom somewhere."

The cattle industry throughout the country slowly is starving. It keeps pushing more beef to supermarkets and restaurants for consumers to eat, but it doesn't get back enough cash to fill its financial gut.

Then Doug Wright's piece showed the consequences to an individual farmer:

TWIN FALLS—Times have been tough in recent years for Mark Kunzler.

After farming successfully in the Rupert area for almost 25 years, Kunzler was forced into filing for bankruptcy last November.

Now he's losing everything he owns—his livestock, his equipment, his land, his house. Because of his age, 48, he's even having problems finding another permanent job.

"I'm at the point where I either go on public welfare, or my family scrounges by through my wife and kids working," he says.

But Kunzler insists that he and his family are not "a bunch of deadbeats." He's had 30 years experience in the farming business, his children do well in school and the two oldest would even like to go to college, he says.

So how was Kunzler, who had a successful, solvent dairy in the 1970s and early 1980s, reduced to what he calls "a welfare state?"

He lost his financial backing because he suffered several consecutive years of bad weather, he says. The U.S. Farmers Home Administration, which had formerly financed his mortgage and operations, decided to cut off his credit, which forced him out of business.

Kunzler, however, is not alone. A large number of farmers in the Magic Valley, the state, and the nation are suffering from similar financial problems.

A recent study conducted by the University of Idaho and commissioned by Gov. John Evans predicts that the state may lose 10 percent of its 24,600 farmers within the next several years.

Measurements of Idaho farmers' debt/asset ratios, which are probably the best indicators of financial stress, paint a bleak picture for Idaho agriculture in the near future.

The study shows that 10.8 percent, or about 2,680 Idaho farmers, have debt/asset ratios exceeding 70 percent, meaning that they probably won't survive in the farming business more than two years.

Notice how Wright blends the particular (Kunzler's problems) with the general (the state situation—declining numbers of farmers, causes).

The more the newspaper or station stresses local news, the more detailed business stories will be. In small communities the line between news and free advertising is so narrow it approaches invisibility. A large department store that is opening in the center of town will be covered by the biggest newspapers. But a drugstore opening will not. The smaller newspaper or station probably will carry the drugstore opening, and might cover the enlargement of a hardware store.

Here is the beginning of an 11-paragraph story that appeared in *The Berkshire Eagle:*

For 10 years, tailor Frank Saporito plied his trade with Davis & Norton Inc. on North Street here, where he was in charge of all alterations. When that business closed last month, Saporito was out of work—but not for long.

Saporito landed on his feet and decided to go into business for himself at 251 Fenn St., just across the street from the post office. He's been open there a little more than a week.

"I wanted to try it by myself," Saporito said. "I think it's a good move. I sure hope so."

Puff Pieces

Merchants want news stories of this kind, and sometimes enthusiastic advertising sales people promise an advertiser a story about a store expansion or about the cashier who has spent 25 years behind the Hamburger Heaven checkout counter. When the publisher orders a story, the piece is known as a BOM (business office must). Even on larger newspapers or stations, advertisers pressure the news staff to run—or not to run—stories about them. Newspaper executives, themselves important business people in the community, may order stories to be run because of their own interests.

Increasingly, media critics have condemned these stories as free advertising, and few newspapers are willing to risk censure. Still, it could be argued that some of these events can make good stories. The perceptive business reporter sent to interview the hardware merchant who is enlarging his store might find that the store owner is staking his last dime on this gamble to keep from losing business to the franchise hardware dealer in the big shopping center. And the Hamburger Heaven cashier could become a human interest story.

Let's look at some stories that appear on the business page:

Story Types

The *Rockford* (Ill.) *Register Star*—New car sales for the first two months of the year in northern Illinois show a 29 percent drop from the preceding year.

Chicago Tribune—A profile of Charles T. Grant and the Fort Dearborn Paper Co., the $17 million-a-year paper converting firm Grant purchased through the Minority Enterprise Small Business Investment Companies Act. The firm is one of the 10 largest black-owned businesses in the United States.

The Nevada State Journal—Union Carbide's proposed Glad Bag plant in Stead will probably employ a large number of workers, but officials are not yet saying how many.

The Salt Lake Tribune—A comprehensive economic development plan is proposed to bring industry to Salt Lake City.

The Wichita Eagle-Beacon—A record number of bankruptcies were filed last year.

The business reporter is a specialist, with a detailed knowledge of a specific area or beat. Many business reporters prepared for their careers by studying economics and finance in college, and all have read in their field.

The business reporter feels at home with numbers and is not frightened by lengthy reports and press releases, many of which contain rates, percentages, business and consumer indexes and the jargon of the business world.

Morton says that a knowledge of accounting is helpful to the business reporter—"an ability to analyze a profit-and-loss statement and a balance sheet." He advises students interested in a career in business journalism to take a college-level accounting course. "Many of the secrets of the world of finance are buried in financial statements, and it is important for reporters to know how to pull apart the statements to get them."

Beyond this, little detailed training is necessary beyond the basic journalistic skills. "After all," he says, "a good reporter's expertise lies in making the complex seem simple and easy to understand, and highly specialized training can blunt if not obliterate that skill."

Among the skills and attitudes the business reporter takes to the job is the recognition of the power business exerts. Along with this, the reporter has a healthy skepticism that keeps him or her from being in awe of the muscle and money that business power generates.

The business reporter approaches the money managers and manipulators with the same objectivity and distance that any reporter takes on an assignment. In his profile of a corporate raider, Michael A. Hiltzik of the *Los*

The Reporter's Requirements

Required. Reporters who want to cover economic affairs need two qualifications, says Gardner Ackley, former chairman of the President's Council of Economic Advisers. They must take a course in economics, and they should pass it.

Two Types of Companies

Publicly held—Company owned by investors who bought its stock. Stock is traded on exchange or market where its price or market value is determined by what investors pay to own it. Must file documents with SEC and publish annual reports, which are sources of information for reporter.

Privately or closely held—Company is usually controlled by a small group or a family. Stock is not publicly traded on an exchange. Value is set by owners. Information is difficult to obtain. Company may be regulated by state or federal agency, which will have some information about it.

Angeles Times was able to find sources and anecdotes to get to the heart of his subject, Irwin L. Jacobs of Minneapolis. Jacobs acquires and merges companies, usually at great profit.

Jacobs usually would pledge to operate rather than to dismantle the firms "on the insight that Americans lionize industrialists and not liquidators," Hiltzik says. For his piece, Hiltzik was able to show that Jacobs dismantled one firm in 17 days, despite his promise to operate Mid American Bancorporation of Minnesota "for his children and his children's children," the story said. Jacobs' profit: an estimated $4 million.

"As I do my research," Hiltzik says, "I find that newspaper and magazine writers tend to return to the same formulas in profiling financiers: brilliant minds, stern taskmasters, frightful antagonists and so on. I see I've used the same conceits myself, but I've tried in each case to describe a couple of key deals to show there is more to it than the kinds of character traits that newspapers rely on."

Specialist though he or she may be, the business reporter must know much more than the world of finance. When Hiltzik was assigned to cover the tribulations of a precious metal investment firm, he had to look through court documents with the same scrupulous and knowledgeable attention a courthouse reporter gives the records. In fact, Hiltzik found in one of the documents a human interest lead to his story about the complicated activities of the firm.

He began his lengthy account of Monex International Ltd. with the story of Kathleen Ann Mahoney, a professional singer who was living in Newport Beach, Calif., when she bought $10,000 worth of silver through Monex. The price of silver went up, and Hiltzik reports, she "invested another $12,000, then another $10,000, and then her last $13,000, relying on what she says were her Monex salesman's contentions that silver prices were rising so fast they might earn $100,000 for her over a year's time." The price of silver reached $50 an ounce.

"Four days later, Mahoney was wiped out. Silver had plunged to $28, and the crash had taken most of her investment with it," Hiltzik wrote.

This technique of showing the consequences of business machinations gone sour, or sweet, is used by reporters to reveal the consequences of business and economic activity. When the stock market soared in 1986, people who never thought of themselves as well-to-do suddenly found themselves holding stocks worth a lot of money. Reporters interviewed these people, and their stories put flesh on the Dow Jones averages.

Sources of Information

The business reporter has a harder job digging for information than most journalists. Most reporters deal with public officials who live in a goldfish bowl. Laws and a long tradition have made the public sector public.

The business world, however, is generally private, secretive and authoritarian. The head of a company can order his employees not to talk to reporters, and that's that. Since business people usually are in competition, secrecy is a natural part of business life. True, businesses are required to file many kinds of reports with various governmental agencies, and these are excellent sources of information. But in the day-to-day coverage of the beat, the business reporter must rely on human sources.

Human Sources

Good contacts and sources can be made among the following:

Bank officers, tellers.
Savings and loan officials.
Chamber of Commerce secretaries.
Union leaders and working people.
Securities dealers.
Real estate brokers.
Trade organization officials.
Teachers of business, economics.
Transportation company officials.
Federal and state officials in agencies such as the Small Business Administration, Commerce Department, various regulatory agencies.

On first contact with a reporter, the business source is likely to be wary, says James L. Rowe Jr., New York financial correspondent of *The Washington Post*. "As a result, it is often difficult to gain the source's trust.

"But if the reporter does his or her homework, learns what motivates business people, is not afraid to ask the intelligent questions but doesn't have to ask the dumb one, more than enough sources will break down."

In developing these sources, the reporter will want to find people who can put events into perspective and who can clarify some of the complexities the reporter cannot fathom. Caution is important. Not only must the sources be dependable, they must be independent of compromising connections and affiliations. Obviously, such sources are hard to find. The traditional independent source was the academician, the cloistered professor who had no financial stake in the matters he would comment about. But no more. Academicians now serve on the boards of banks, chemical companies and pesticide manufacturers. The alert reporter makes certain that background information from such sources is neither biased nor self-serving.

Sources are used in two ways—for quotations and for background information. When quoting a source, note all of the person's business affiliations relevant to the story. In a banking story, it's not enough to say that Professor Thomas Graham teaches economics at the state university. His membership on the board of directors of the First National Bank should also be included.

The background source is rarely quoted, and so readers and viewers cannot assess the information in terms of the source's affiliations. Since background sources influence reporters by providing perspective, the independence of these sources is essential. Good background sources can be found without leaving the office. The accountants, marketing people and the legal adviser to the newspaper or station can figure out some of the complexities of reports and documents. They also are close to the business community.

The business office has access to the local credit bureau and the facilities of Dun and Bradstreet, which can provide confidential information. These can be helpful in running a check on a local business.

Chris Welles of *Business Week* says, "By far the most important sources on company stories are former executives. Unconstrained by the fear of being fired if word gets out that they talked to you, they can be extremely forthcoming about their former employer." Welles is cautious about the information from former employees, which he says is mostly negative. Competitors are another good source, as are suppliers, the managers of investment portfolios, bankers and others who are likely to know the company's financial situation.

In interviews, Welles will share his problems obtaining material. "Most people are predisposed to respond favorably to someone who, in a non-threatening way, asks for a little help." Welles says he listens "with great interest and sympathy." He says that "sources have a great deal of trouble terminating a conversation with someone who seems to be hanging on their every word."

Welles finds sources for company stories often request anonymity. He is willing to grant it, and he sticks to his word. Those who don't find their sources soon clam up. Speak to a lot of people, he says. Look through as many documents as possible. In short, he says, "Work your tail off."

Physical Sources

At the local level, reporters should know how to use city and county tax records. The city and county keep excellent records of real estate transfers, and the assessor's office has the valuation of real property and of the physical plant and equipment—whatever is taxed. The sales tax shows how much business a firm is doing. Many local governments issue business licenses on which the principals involved are named and other information is given.

State governments also issue business licenses. There are scores of state boards that license barbers, engineers, cosmetologists, doctors, morticians, lawyers, accountants and others. These agencies usually keep basic information about the businesses they oversee.

The state corporation commission or the secretary of state will have the names, addresses and sometimes the stock held by directors of corporations incorporated in the state and of firms that do a large amount of business in the state. The company's articles of incorporation and bylaws are also on file.

Federal Records

For companies with $1 million in assets and at least 500 stockholders, the Securities and Exchange Commission requires regular reports. Some 10,000 companies file such reports, listed in the annual Directory of Companies Required to File Annual Reports. To obtain the directory and other reports write: Public Reference Section, Securities and Exchange Commission, 450 Fifth St. N.W., Washington, D.C. 20549. For general information, call 202 272-2650.

Among the SEC reports available is the 10-K, which many reporters use because it includes the company's finances, ownership, major contracts, management history, salaries and other monies paid the major officers.

Turner and CBS: The Deal that Soured

When Ted Turner made a spectacular offer to buy the CBS network, Hiltzik put the deal in perspective. Hiltzik had read the documents accompanying Turner's offer and had found the Turner Broadcasting System had lost money in three of the preceding five years. ("I always look for the parentheses in a report. They indicate losses.") This and other material indicated to Hiltzik the offer made little sense to CBS stockholders. He began his story:

NEW YORK—Atlanta cable television entrepreneur Ted Turner, taking an audacious gamble to realize his dream of running a major TV network, Thursday offered to acquire CBS without paying any cash.

Instead, he offered CBS shareholders a risky package of notes, bonds and stock in his Turner Broadcasting System that he valued at $175 a share, or $5.2 billion. The plan drew immediate skepticism on Wall Street, where the consensus was that Turner would fail.

Hiltzik's careful examination of the documents led him to write:

Among the risks, according to Turner's own registration statement filed with federal authorities, is the prospect that a merged CBS-Turner Broadcasting System will be unable to pay interest on the more than $5 billion in debt the merger would require. Turner said that that debt would have to be reduced after merger by selling off pieces of CBS.

The deal collapsed after such stories as Hiltzik's.

The Bottom Line. Turner paid an estimated $1 billion for the 3,800-film library of MGM, and in what he described as a move to "protect my investment," he added color to about 100 of the movies, including the classic "The Maltese Falcon." The film's director, John Huston, was furious, and one commentator said the action "trashes" a part of American history.

Tinting the black and white film, said one director, "makes Bogart's toupee look like a toupee, makes the sets look like sets and makes everything look fake."

Welles, who has been writing about business and economics for 25 years, says that when he is to write about a company the first step he takes is to obtain three basic documents: the 10-K, the annual report and the proxy statement. Like the 10-K, the other two are available from the SEC.

Welles describes the annual report as "a kind of public relations version of the 10-K." He says that "no single body of information is more crucial to the understanding of a corporation than its financial statements." We will be looking at the annual report in detail later in this chapter.

The proxy statement, an SEC-mandated document, is sent to all stockholders before an annual meeting. It contains the salaries and stockholdings of most senior executives. The statement also lists any deals between the firm and its management or directors.

Other useful documents are the 8-K, which is filed monthly for important company activities such as a merger, and the 10-Q, a quarterly report with information like that in the annual 10-K.

Non-profit organizations must file Form 990 with the Internal Revenue Service. The report includes information on the income and expenses of officials of the organizations. The expenses can be illuminating. Often, a small part of the money raised by the organization is used for charity or for whatever other purpose the organization raises money.

SEC material can be obtained from regional SEC offices. Companies usually send on request their 10-K, proxy statement and annual report.

The Bureau of the Census issues many economic reports, some of them covering city and county business activity. Major economic censuses are taken every five years, for the years ending in 2 and 7. Also, there are annual surveys. The Bureau has a vast publications program. For a general guide to what the Bureau does and what data it makes available, write to the U.S. Department of Commerce, Bureau of the Census, Washington, D.C. 20233, and ask for the Guide to the 1982 (or 1987) Economic Censuses and Related Statistics.

Daily reading of *The Wall Street Journal* is necessary for the business reporter. Written for business people and those with some involvement in financial matters, the stories nevertheless are written in layman's language. The newspaper is both record-keeper for the business community and its watchdog. Its investigative reporting is among the best in the country.

Reading

Business Week, a weekly business news magazine, is staffed by journalists with a good command of business, finance and economics. The magazine concentrates on the major industries and companies. Its long articles are aimed at the men and women who are in executive posts in business.

Forbes is addressed to investors, people who own stock in companies. The *Journal, Business Week,* and *Forbes* are pro-business. Though they do go after the bad apples in the barrel, they never question the barrel, the system itself, as former *Journal* staffer Kent MacDougall puts it. The most pro-business publication is *Nation's Business,* which is published by the U.S. Chamber of Commerce and the National Association of Manufacturers.

There are 5,000 trade publications, magazines and newspapers that cover a particular business or trade. The reporter who specializes will be a regular reader of the trade publications in his or her field.

"Because trade journalists write for people who know the industry," says Professor Warren Burkett of the University of Texas at Austin, "the facts, figures and quotations generally will be accurate. It's the interpretations of the material that you must watch out for. These often are given in light of what is best financially for most companies, as the editors see it.

"This does not invalidate the use of these publications as sources for the facts, figures and quotations."

References

A good local library or any business school library at a college or university will have the following references that business reporters find useful:

Dun and Bradstreet Directories—One covers companies with capital under $1 million; another is for those whose capital exceeds $1 million. (Address, corporate officers, sales, number of employees.)

Who Owns Whom—To find the parent company of a firm you are checking.

Standard & Poor's Register of Corporations, Directors and Executives.
Moody's Manuals.

Regulatory Agencies

All levels of government regulate business. Local laws prescribe health, fire and safety regulations to which businesses must adhere. The city grants franchises and checks to see that the provisions are followed, such as those requiring public access to the local cable television company. Regional and county governments set standards for factory emissions.

Note: Some of these agencies may take their cases to court. The business reporter should know how to use the documents in civil, criminal and bankruptcy courts.

The state regulates some banks, savings and loan institutions, insurance companies and public utilities. State agencies handle rate applications and oversee operational procedures of utilities. Basic information about these businesses is available to the journalist.

State licensing boards also regulate the trades and professions they license. Usually, they have the power to investigate complaints and to hold hearings. Although most of these boards are creatures of the businesses and professions they regulate, occasionally a board will act decisively. Failure to take action is an even better story, as one reporter learned when the board regulating veterinarians failed to hold a hearing for a veterinarian who was the subject of a number of complaints by pet owners whose dogs and cats had died in his care.

Although most federal regulatory agencies are in Washington and too distant for personal checking, a local business reporter can ask the newspaper's Washington bureau or the AP or UPI to run something down. These agencies compile considerable material about companies and individuals seeking permission to operate interstate. Some agencies:

Interstate Commerce Commission (ICC)—regulates trucking companies, railroads, freight carriers, oil pipelines and express agencies.

Federal Communications Commission (FCC)—regulates radio and television stations. Ownership and stock information are available.

National Labor Relations Board (NLRB)—is concerned with labor disputes.

Literacy. *Q:* If you were to become business editor of your local newspaper and were able to make one major change in content or direction, what would it be?

A: I'd give my staff an economic literacy test. I'd ask them to define the difference between earnings and revenues, profits and profitability, ownership and management. If they failed the test, I'd give them the choice of taking a good course in business economics or moving on. . . . You can't write about football unless you know the difference between a fourth-down punt and a field goal. And you can't write about business unless you understand it and master its vocabulary.—Herbert Schmertz, vice president, Mobil Oil Corporation.

Business pumps out vast quantities of information for newspapers and broadcast stations, some of which is useful to the business and economics reporter. The business reporter also has to dig deeper for news.

Don Moffitt, a veteran business journalist, says that business reporters "should consider that they have a license to inquire into the nuts and bolts of how people make a living and secure their well-being.

"For a local paper, the fortunes of the community's barbers, auto mechanics, bankers and public servants are business stories. Business is how people survive.

"If people are falling behind in their mortgage payments, show how and why they are falling behind, how they feel about it and what they're trying to do about it," he says.

"Local government financing and spending is, in part, a business story. Who's making money off the local bond issues, and why? Is the bank keeping the county's low-interest deposits and using the cash to buy the county's high-yielding paper? Who suffers when the township cuts the budget, or can't increase it? Show how they suffer."

Always go beyond the press release, business reporters say. When a $69 million reconstruction job at a shopping center was announced, the developers sent out stacks of press releases. By asking why so much money was being spent, a reporter learned that sales at the center had sharply declined recently—a fact not mentioned in any of the releases.

Steve Lipson, business news writer for *The Times-News,* developed ideas for stories by a simple technique—keeping his eyes open. "I read ads, I notice changes in the businesses where I shop. I count the number of cars in a car dealer's lot, and I look at what people wear, eat and drink," Lipson says.

"I look for unique stories," he says. He did one on the growing popularity of potato-skin appetizers. "This big boost to potato consumption would land someone in the Idaho Hall of Fame if anyone knew who was responsible. Alas, my story found no one really knows why the dish suddenly became chic."

Lipson knows that local merchants usually put a good face on business conditions. "So I asked a team of Yellow Page ad salesmen for their summary of the local business mood after they finished a 10-week selling blitz in the area and had talked to virtually every retailer in town." Here is the beginning of Lipson's story:

TWIN FALLS—Before people can let their fingers do the walking, Mountain Bell sends salesmen through town selling those advertisements found in the Yellow Pages.

The salesmen, instead of relying on their fingers, do most of their work by car, foot and phone. Yet by the time they finish, their fingers have a good feel for the local business pulse.

The Mountain Bell directory sales crew spent about 10 weeks in Twin Falls during November, December and January. The salesmen visited more than 1,000 businesses while preparing the directory. What they found is that the pulse remains strong, although the patient is weaker.

Enterprise

Newsletters. Among the vast quantities of material the business reporter receives are the newsletters and reports of various trade associations. These can be good sources for enterprise stories.

Jim Toland developed an interesting story about beer consumption in California for the San Francisco *Chronicle* by picking up a trade association report. His story began this way:

The race to win California's beer drinkers is tightening up.

Adolph Coors is still leading the derby but Anheuser Busch is making steady gains to capture the No. 1 spot.

Big Business Journalism. The concentration of ownership of newspapers and its implications are infrequently examined. The largest of the chains, Gannett Co., owned 93 newspapers at the end of 1986, eight television stations and 16 radio stations. John Morton, a newspaper analyst, predicts that "acquisitions will continue until all newspapers of much consequence are owned by a few large companies."

Handout-Watchout

Here are the beginnings of three press releases. What do they have in common?

United States Steel Corp. today announced a series of moves designed to insure that its steel sector will continue as a major force in world steel markets for the balance of the century and beyond . . .

Greenbelt Cooperative Inc.'s Board of Directors unanimously approved a plan to strengthen the organization's financial position and continue expansion . . .

W & J Sloane, the retail furniture company long noted for its reputation for quality, style and trend-setting furniture, is once again taking the lead in the furniture industry . . .

If you found the companies about to report high earnings or an expansion, go to the rear of the class. The firms were all announcing bad news. U.S. Steel cut 15,600 jobs and closed plants in several cities. Greenbelt closed its co-operative supermarkets and gas stations. And W & J Sloane closed a store and sharply reduced its range of furniture in other stores. All this was in the releases—buried.

Consumer Price Index

Another resource that can be put to good use by the business reporter is the Consumer Price Index (CPI), a statistical measure of changes in prices of goods and services issued monthly by the Bureau of Labor Statistics. The index represents price changes for everything people buy and pay for—food, clothing, automobiles, rent, home furnishings, fuel and energy, recreational goods, fees to doctors, beauty shops and so on.

The Bureau calculates monthly indexes for the country and for five major areas. Bimonthly indexes are published for 23 areas. When the CPI goes up, it means that the dollar is buying less. In January 1986, in the northeast, the index stood at 323.1, which meant that $32.31 was required to buy what $10 purchased in January 1967, which is used as the base period. (1967=100.)

Honesty and Realism

In journalism's old days, newspapers turned away from unpleasant business news. The business news pages practiced boosterism. The credo was: If you can't boost, don't knock. But the professionalization of journalism has led journalists to give the same careful scrutiny to business as to other news.

When a recession hit many areas of the country, newspapers looked deeply at the consequences. "With declining neighborhoods, declining population, and all the attendant problems, we decided to look at the Buffalo of the future," said Murray Light, the editor of the *Buffalo Evening News*. The view was not pleasant. The first article of the five-part series began:

Buffalo will never again be what it once was.

Light said that the newspaper "drew a good deal of heat" from the Chamber of Commerce and other local business boosters. But, he added, "it demonstrated to our readers that we cannot bury our heads in the sand and that it isn't all bad to be a smaller city."

Many students are attracted to journalism because it is concerned with people and how they get along with each other. These students are interested in the qualitative aspect of life. Journalism, with its feature stories and its emphasis on human interest, can use the talents these students take to the job. But much of what we know about the world—and people—is derived from quantitative studies.

Numbers and More Numbers

The student who is thinking about a career in business journalism—and this is one area of journalism that never seems to have enough reporters and editors—cannot manage without an ability to deal with numbers. If business is the bottom line on a balance sheet, then the student thinking of becoming a business reporter has to know what to make of the numbers on the line.

The ability to blend the qualitative and the quantitative is essential to the business journalist. Numbers alone do say a lot, but when these barometers are matched with human beings, they take on dramatic significance. When home loan applications go down (quantitative), the reporter finds a family like the Ryans we met a while back and shows why this family decided to rent rather than to buy (qualitative).

Let's look at an example of a story the business reporter handles that is concerned primarily with figures. In our list of stories with which the business reporter deals we mentioned annual reports, the yearly accounting of publicly owned companies.

Annual Reports

Newspapers usually run a summary of the annual reports of industries and businesses in their readership area. Readers want to know the economic health of the companies that employ local people, and some may own stock in these firms. Many readers also want to know about the status of the well-known firms that have large numbers of shares of stock distributed nationwide—IBM, Kodak, General Motors, Polaroid, AT&T, Ford, General Electric. These readers may be shareholders—more than half the adult population owns stock—or they may be planning to invest in stocks. The business reporter must be able to swim through a sea of figures toward the few pieces of essential information in the report.

What to Look For

First off, read the auditor's report, which is usually at the back. "Generally, if the Auditor's Report is two paragraphs long, the financial statements have been given a clean bill of health," says the American Institute of Certified Public Accountants. "Anything longer—an extra paragraph or so—and normally that's a red flag alerting you to look further."

Jane Bryant Quinn, CBS business commentator, says the words "subject to" in the auditor's report are a warning signal.

"They mean the financial report is clean *only* if you take the company's word about a particular piece of business, and the accountant isn't sure you should," she says.

The CPA Institute has a general caution about the auditor's report: "All it means is that the financial statements are fairly presented in conformity with generally accepted accounting principles." It doesn't mean that the company is in great financial shape, or even in adequate condition. All it means is that the books are kept properly.

Next, skim through the footnotes, says Quinn. Sometimes they explain the figures that seem surprising, even alarming. Earnings might be down. But the footnote may explain that the company has applied a policy of accelerated depreciation on plants and other equipment. "This," says the CPA Institute, "could reduce earnings, while a slower depreciation rate could boost earnings."

Next, look at the letter from the chairman or the president's report in front of the annual report. It usually is frank—if it adheres to the standards set by the CPA Institute. Usually, the statement is a candid summary of the past year and of prospects.

The Figures

The figure in which most people are interested is "earnings per share," also called "net income per common share." (See table 23.1.) This is the bottom line, a sign of the company's health. It is, in effect, the profit the company has made. It is computed by dividing the total earnings by the number of shares outstanding. The CPA Institute says that slight year-to-year changes can be ignored. Look for the trend in the five- and ten-year summaries. "If the EPS either remains unchanged or drops off, this may pinpoint trouble ahead," it says.

Be careful about earnings per share. A sudden increase can come from selling a plant or cutting advertising or research, says Quinn. The footnotes will explain unusual increases if they have unusual causes. A sudden decrease can come from a change in the number of shares, a stock split or a new issue—which is also noted in the report.

Next, look for the figures on working capital. "This is regarded as an important index of a company's condition because it reports whether operations generate enough cash to meet payroll, buy raw materials and conduct all the other essential day-to-day operations of the company," says the CPA Institute.

After all the expenses have been met, the company uses part of its net income to pay dividends. These are paid from net working capital, and if this figure (net working capital) shrinks consistently from year to year, even quarter to quarter, it is a sign the company may "not be able to keep dividends growing rapidly," says Quinn.

Table 23.1 Net Income per Common Share: NRW Enterprises

	1986	1985	% Change
Net sales from continuing operations	$671,227,000	$601,960,000	+ 11.5
Income from continuing operations	$36,031,000	$43,685,000	− 17.5
Income from discontinued operations	—	$1,112,000	—
Gain on sale of discontinued operations	$5,300,000	—	—
Net income	$41,331,000	$44,797,000	− 7.7
Net income per common share: Continuing operations	$2.62	$3.18	− 17.6
Discontinued operations	—	$.08	—
Gain on sale of discontinued operations	$.39	—	—
Net income per common share	$3.01	$3.26	− 7.7
Dividends per common share	$1.14	$1.03	+ 10.7
Cash dividends paid	$15,251,225	$13,736,454	+ 11.0
Capital expenditures	$27,535,000	$20,722,000	+ 32.9
Stockholders' equity	$259,668,000	$233,529,000	+ 11.2
Equity per common share at year end	$18.91	$17.02	+ 11.1
Outstanding common shares at year end ...	13,730,288	13,720,186	—

Net income per common share is a sign of the company's health. Business reporters look for this figure in annual reports.

Look over the record of dividends as well as the current dividend. Is there a trend? Here is a five-year period of dividends of NRW Enterprises:

Dividends per common share	**1986** $1.14	**1985** $1.03	**1984** $1	**1983** $.99	**1982** $.91

This firm shows a steady climb in dividends over the past five years. However, the business reporter will note that although the 1986 dividend is larger than the previous year's dividend, the company's net income per share was down—from $3.18 to $2.62. (See table 23.1.) In other words, the company plowed less of its earnings back into the firm in 1986 than it did in 1985 in order to keep the dividends on an upward course.

The business reporter writes to companies in his or her area to be placed on their mailing list for annual and quarterly reports. If these reports raise questions, he or she calls the company for clarification. If the report indicates the company is in trouble, it is necessary to obtain comments from company officials, the accountants, shareholders, and any public agencies that may be involved.

Business Terms

assets These are anything of value the company owns or has an interest in. Assets usually are expressed in dollar value.

balance sheet A financial statement that lists the company's assets, liabilities and stockholder's equity. It usually includes an *Earnings* or *Income Statement* that details the company's source of income and its expenses.

calendar or **fiscal year** Some companies report their income or do business on the regular calendar year. Others do it on a fiscal year that could run from any one month to the same month a year later. Always ask if the companies do business on a fiscal or calendar year. If the answer is fiscal, ask the dates and why. You might find out something unusual about the company.

capital expenditures This is the amount of money a company spends on major projects, such as plant expansions or capacity additions. It is important to the company and the community as well. If the company is expanding, include it in the story. Frequently, such plans are disclosed in stock prospectuses and other SEC reports long before the local paper gets its press release.

earnings Used synonymously with profit. Earnings can be expressed in dollar terms (XYZ earned $40) or on a per-share basis (XYZ earned $1 per share for each of its 40 shares of stock). When used as an earnings figure, always compare it to the earnings for the same period in the prior year. For example, if you want to say XYZ earned $1 a share during the first quarter, half or nine months of 1986, compare that with the 50 cents per share the company earned in the first quarter, half or nine months of 1985. That would be a 100 percent increase in profit.

liabilities These are any debts of any kind. There are two types of liabilities—short term and long term. Companies consider anything that has to be paid off within a year a short-term liability and anything over a year a long-term liability.

sales or **revenues** These terms are used synonymously in many companies. A bank, for example, doesn't have sales. It has revenues. But a manufacturer's sales and revenues frequently are the same thing, unless the company has some income from investments it made. Always include the company's sales in a story with its earnings. If you say a company earned $40 in 1986 compared to $30 in 1985, you also should tell the reader that the profit was the result of a 100 percent increase in the company's sales, from $100 in 1985 to $200 in 1986. Use both sales and earnings figures. Don't use one and not the other.

stockholder's equity This is the financial interest the stockholders have in the company once all of its debts are paid. For example, say XYZ company has assets of $1,000 and total debts of $600. The company's stockholder's equity is $400. If that figure is expressed on a per-share basis, it is called *book value*. (If XYZ had issued 40 shares of stock, each share would have a book value of $10.)

This material was prepared by Jim O'Shea for *The Des Moines Register.*

A number of organizations study and rate companies. Value Line, for example, keeps track of 1,700 companies. It summarizes on a single page the relevant financial data about each of these companies. Standard & Poor's and Moody's also publish useful investment advisories.

Some tips:

• Well-managed companies should have at least twice the amount in current assets as they have in current liabilities.

• Avoid advising readers to buy or sell any particular stock. This is called "touting," and to offer such advice you must be registered with the SEC, as some advisory services are. Some reporters who have given such advice have been fined.

• Be careful of press releases about new products or developments. These may be planted to drive up the price of a certain stock. After a while, says Warren Burkett, a business reporter learns which are the trustworthy and responsible sources and which are trying to use the media.

For further information about how to read an annual report, write the CPA Institute, 1211 Avenue of the Americas, New York City, N.Y., 10036, and ask for the booklet, "What Else Can Financial Statements Tell You?"

Stock Tables

The business reporter sometimes needs to check the current price or the dividend of a stock listed on one of the exchanges. Here are a few stocks listed on the New York Stock Exchange and a guide to understanding the symbols:

High	Low	Stock	Div.	Yld %	P-E Ratio	Sales 100s	High	Low	Close	Net Chg.
[1]	[2]		[3]							
33¼	29	ATT	1.20	3.8	16	10740	31½	30	31½	+1
				[4]	[5]					
83½	79½	Gannett	1.68	2.0	24	1833	83	81¼	83	+¼
		[6]				[7]				
66	56	GMot **pf**	5	7.7	. . .	7	65½	65	65	. . .
							[8]			
38½	24⅛	Greyhound	1.32	3.9	14	1190	34¼	33	34⅛	+¼
									[9]	
13	7	Wendy's	.20	1.7	14	140	12⅞	11¾	11¾	− 1

On the Floor. A trader checks the latest selling price of a stock on the floor of the New York Stock Exchange where trading activity during the mid-1980s exceeded 100 million shares a day. New York Stock Exchange photo.

1. The highest and the lowest price the stock has sold for in the past 52 weeks.

2. Abbreviated name of the corporation that lists the stock. Stocks are common stocks unless an entry after the name indicates otherwise.

3. The annual dividend. When a letter follows the dividend, a box at the bottom of the stock table is consulted as a reference.

4. Yield is the dividend paid by the company expressed as a percentage of the current price of the stock. A stock that sells for $50 at the current market value and that is paying a dividend at the rate of $2 a year is said to return or to have a yield of 4 percent. In the example of Gannett, the dividend of $1.68 divided by the price of 83 results in the yield percentage of 2.0.

5. P-E Ratio stands for the price-earnings ratio. The price of a share of stock is divided by the earnings per share over a 12-month period. A stock selling for $50 a share with annual earnings of $5 a share is selling at the price-earnings of 10 to 1. The P-E ratio is 10.

6. *pf* following the name indicates a preferred stock. Usually, preferred stock entitles stockholders to a specified rate of dividends, here $5 a year. Holders of preferred stock are entitled to a claim on the company's earnings before dividends may be paid to holders of common stock.

7. The number of shares traded this day for the stock, listed in 100's. Here, 700 shares of General Motors preferred stock were sold.

8. The highest price paid for this stock during the day's trading was $34.25. The lowest price paid was $33.

9. The closing price, or the price of the stock on the last sale of the trading day. Here, the closing price was $11.75 a share. The closing price was down $1 from the closing price of the previous day.

Annual Meetings

The annual meetings of most companies are prosaic affairs. Often held in some out-of-the-way place to discourage small shareholders from asking troublesome questions, the meetings are well-programmed. The news story is usually based on an announcement by the president, chairman or chief executive officer.

At annual meetings, mergers are voted on. Also, dissident shareholders can voice their displeasures with the way the company is being run—which can give the observant reporter a good insight into the company.

Depth Reporting

The best kind of business reporting blends spot news with trend, depth and investigative reporting. Business journalism has emerged from the days of puffery and is no longer a handmaiden to every local merchant who seeks space. It has also done a good job exposing the bad apples in the business community. But it has not done so well examining the way business affects government (in the U.S. and abroad), how it prices its goods and services and the consequences of the exchange of business and government personnel.

The Founding Fathers were concerned about the dangers of a strong central government. They could not have imagined the power that business would acquire. International banks and the conglomerates exercise enormous influence over the lives of people everywhere, and this power is worthy of scrutiny by the press in its role as watchdog.

Such examination starts at the local level. How much power does the local real estate business have over planning and zoning decisions? What role does money play in local, county and state elections? Does local government really have to give businesses and developers tax write-offs and abatements as an incentive? Is the tax structure equitable, or does it fall too heavily on families, working people, homeowners? In states with natural resources, is the severance tax properly balanced with other taxes, or are the extractive industries penalized or given preferential treatment?

Budgets and Trade Balances

One way business reporters can help their listeners, readers and viewers is to localize one of the most important stories of all—the federal budget. Left to Washington correspondents and network television financial experts, the story rarely shows the direct impact on the people who have to carry the burden of the budget through their taxes.

When the government spends more money than it takes in, it has to borrow money, just as anyone else with a cash shortage. The United States had a national debt of $930 billion in 1981. Four years later, because of huge borrowing, the debt zoomed to $1,680 billion.

Where does the government obtain the money to keep going? From lenders. How does it find these lenders? The same way any borrower does— by offering high interest rates for its notes and bonds. One of the country's biggest sources of money has been foreign investors who could obtain better interest rates in the United States than in their own countries.

The government has been paying about $130 billion a year in interest on these loans. This is added to the budget, and it grows as borrowing increases.

Now let's take a closer look at these foreign investors. The U.S. government sells bonds to purchasers with dollars, not yen, marks or pesos. This means foreign investors or lenders have to buy dollars with their own currencies in order to buy U.S. bonds. This demand sends the price of the dollar higher in terms of the currencies of foreign countries. The result, in the terminology of the business pages, is a "strong dollar." From 1980 to 1984, the dollar increased its value about 60 percent against the currencies of the 10 countries with which the United States does most of its trading.

In Canada, for example, the dollar has gone as high as $1.42 Canadian. This means a Canadian would have to spend $1.42 of his money to buy one U.S. dollar.

That sounds fine for the United States. But the local reporter can find some consequences that are not so pleasant.

When the U.S. dollar buys so much abroad, businesses buy from foreign countries—onions from Canada instead of from upstate New York growers, wheat from Argentina instead of from Kansas. Also, businesses will find it harder to sell their products abroad, since the cost of producing their goods is paid with U.S. dollars, strong dollars. The U.S. goods must compete with goods made much more cheaply abroad.

In short, U.S. exports are overpriced and imports are underpriced.

Eastman Kodak Company was severely affected by the strong dollar and decided to tell its 183,000 stockholders the extent of the injury. It had lost $1 billion in earnings since 1980 as a result of the strong dollar, the company said. The firm said:

> The strong dollar has resulted in a decrease of several percentage points in U.S. economic growth, helped to produce a trade deficit of $123 billion in 1984 and, according to some, eliminated more than 2 million manufacturing jobs. At Kodak alone, some 20,000 jobs depend upon exports.

It's possible that companies in the United States may find it more advantageous to become marketing firms for products made abroad, the direction in which the auto industry seems to be heading.

At first glance, it would seem that consumers benefit from this situation, since cheap foreign goods mean less money spent by the shopper. But if increasing amounts of material are made abroad, local plants are shut down and local merchants find their customers have no money for washing machines, cars and stereo sets.

One of the reactions by affected industries, farmers and businesses is to seek restrictions on imports through tariffs and quotas. Not many economists favor this method, although Congress is susceptible to this kind of pressure.

The antidote favored by many economists is less borrowing, which means a pared down federal budget—lower expenditures, higher taxes. The former antagonizes the hundreds of affected groups from the poor to farmers on subsidies; the latter course is bitter medicine for most people.

The reporter has a major role in explaining all of this through local references. It can be done. Too much explaining has been left to national correspondents and to various pressure groups. The local business reporter, independent of self-interest, is best suited to the task.

Up and Down. When the dollar was strong, Kodak had a hard time meeting foreign competition, especially that of Japanese companies, and the company announced it would lay off 12,900 people.

When the dollar started to decline in 1985, a headline in the business section of *The Wichita Eagle-Beacon* read: Kansas Exporters Cheer Dollar's Decline.

Further Reading

Daniells, Lorna. *Business Information Sources.* 2nd ed. Berkeley, Calif.: University of California Press, 1985.

Galbraith, J. Kenneth. *The Affluent Society.* Boston: Houghton Mifflin, 1958.

Mintz, Morton. *At Any Cost.* New York: Pantheon Books, 1985.

Moffitt, Donald, ed. *Swindled: Classic Business Frauds of the Seventies.* Princeton, N.J.: Dow Jones Books, 1976.

Silk, Leonard. *Economics in the Real World.* New York: Simon & Schuster, 1985.

Smith, Adam. *The Money Game.* New York: Random House, 1976.

CHAPTER TWENTY-FOUR

Covering Local Government

Preview

The local government reporter covers the actions of agencies and departments in ongoing municipal affairs and the interplay of special interest groups and government. Some special areas of coverage are:

- Budgets, taxes and bond issues.
- Politics—The activities of candidates and elected officials.
- City planning and zoning.
- Education—The financing of the school system, curriculum decisions. (This is often made a separate beat.)

Local government reporters cover government as a process. They cover the daily interaction of the public, pressure groups and city government and report how the consequences affect residents of the community.

Newspaper readers, television viewers and radio listeners are more interested in local events than in any other kind of news. They want to know what the ambulance was doing around the corner, why the principal of the Walt Whitman High School was dismissed and the background of the new city manager.

Newspapers and stations respond to this interest by assigning their best reporters to key local beats, and usually the best of the best is assigned to city hall, the nerve center of local government. From city hall, elected and appointed officials direct the affairs of the community—from the preparation of absentee ballots to the setting of zoning regulations. They supervise street maintenance and construction; they issue birth and death certificates; they conduct restaurant inspections, collect waste and dispose of it, and they make parking meter collections.

The city hall reporter is expected to cover all these activities. To do this, the reporter must know how local government works—the processes and procedures of agencies and departments, the relationship of the mayor's office to the city council, how the city auditor or comptroller checks on the financial activities of city offices.

The city government engages in many essential activities that the reporter must scrutinize:

1. Authorization of public improvements, such as streets, new buildings, bridges, viaducts.

2. Submission to the public of bond issues to finance these improvements.

3. Adoption of various codes, such as building, sanitation, zoning.

4. Issuance of regulations affecting public health, welfare and safety. Traffic regulations come under this category.

5. Consideration of appeals from planning and zoning bodies.

6. Appointment and removal of city officials.

7. Authorization of land purchases and sales.

8. Awarding of franchises.

Most of the city government's activities are routine. But a significant number affect many residents and businesses. The city government sets the direction and pace of growth and expansion. The city is a major buyer of goods and services, and usually one of the city's largest employers. Its decisions can enrich some businesses as the beginning of this story by Josh Getlin of the *Los Angeles Times* indicates:

During the last year, Los Angeles Councilman Howard Finn and his wife enjoyed a free weekend in Newport Beach and Councilwoman Peggy Stevenson was wined and dined at some of New York's finer restaurants.

In both cases, Group W Cable TV officials were wooing council members to round up votes for the East San Fernando Valley franchise that could be worth $75 million.

Lavish entertaining is just part of a multimillion dollar campaign by six firms to win the city's last major cable franchise . . . .

The starting point in understanding municipal government is the fact that the city is the creature of the state. The state assigns certain of its powers to the city, enabling the city to govern itself. The city has the three traditional branches of government—a judicial system, an executive and a legislative arm. These vary from city to city. In some cities, the executive is a powerful mayor who has control over much of the municipal machinery. In others, the mayor's job is largely ceremonial and the mayor may not even have a vote on the city council.

Legislative branches differ, too. But for the most part the city council or commission has the power to act in the eight areas outlined above.

The council or commission takes action in the form of resolutions and ordinances. A resolution idicates the intention or the opinion of the legislative branch. Or it may grant permission to take an action. An ordinance is a law. An ordinance is *enacted* and a resolution is *adopted*.

Forms of Local Government

The city council–mayor system is the most common form of local government. In large cities, the mayor is usually a powerful figure in city government, the centerpiece of what is called the strong mayor system. In this system, the mayor appoints the heads of departments and all other officials not directly elected. This system enables the mayor to select the people he or she wants to carry out executive policies.

One way to classify local government is by the strength of the office of the mayor, the power the chief executive has to initiate and carry out programs and policies. The two systems have variations:

Weak Mayor	**Strong Mayor**
Commission	Council–mayor
Commission–manager	Mayor–manager
Council–manager	

The weak mayor systems and the creation of the post of city manager were reactions to the misuse of power by strong mayors and their inability to manage the bureaucracy. To be elected and to hold office, the mayor must be an astute politican, not necessarily an able administrator. The wheelings and dealings of the strong mayors—exposed by such muckrakers as Lincoln Steffens—caused a repulsion from a system that some critics said encouraged corruption. A movement toward less-politicized and more efficient local government developed early in the 20th century. It took the form of the council–manager system.

The manager, who is hired by the council, is a professionally trained public administrator who attends to the technical tasks of running the city government—preparing the budget, hiring, administering departments and agencies. While the manager does increase the managerial efficiency of local government, the system has been criticized as insulating government from the electorate by dispersing responsibility and accountability. Several cities have returned to the strong mayor system in an effort to place responsibility in an identifiable, elected official.

An offshoot of the council-manager system has been the mayor-manager plan. This combines the strong mayor, politically responsive to the electorate, with the trained technician who carries out executive policies and handles day-to-day governmental activities.

In weak mayor systems, elected commissioners serve as the legislative branch and the executive branch. The comissioners are legislators and also head various municipal departments—finance, public works, public safety, planning, personnel. Often, the commissioner of public safety also serves as mayor, a largely ceremonial post in this system.

The commission form has been criticized for blurring the separation of powers between the legislative and executive branches. In the commission system, there is no single official that the electorate can hold responsible for the conduct of local affairs.

Livable Cities. Nine factors are used by Rand McNally for its listing of the most livable cities in the country—economy, climate, crime rate, housing, education, health care, recreation, transportation and the arts.

MAYOR-MANAGER FORM

(A strong mayor system)

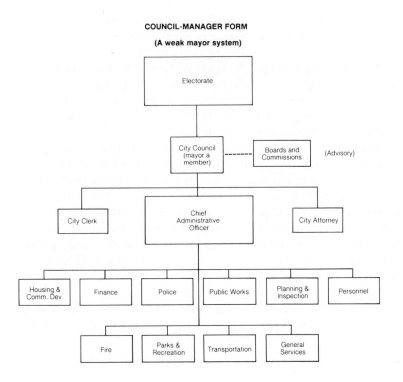

```
                    Electorate

    Comptroller      Mayor         Council

                               Office of      City Clerk
                               Budget
                               Review

                    Manager

Planning Dept.  Office of    Fire Dept.  Police Dept.  Public Works  Personnel
                Management
                and Budget
```

Figure 24.1a The mayor appoints most department and agency heads and the City Manager who is responsible for day-to-day operations.

COUNCIL-MANAGER FORM

(A weak mayor system)

```
                    Electorate

            City Council         Boards and      (Advisory)
            (mayor a             Commissions
            member)

    City Clerk      Chief             City Attorney
                    Administrative
                    Officer

Housing &   Finance   Police   Public Works  Planning &   Personnel
Comm. Dev.                                   Inspection

        Fire    Parks &    Transportation  General
                Recreation                 Services
```

Figure 24.1b The mayor, who is separately elected, serves as a member of the City Council. The mayor's powers are mostly ceremonial. Major appointments are made by the council.

The council-manager and the mayor-manager systems are the most prevalent in the country. The commission system, once strong in cities of less than 500,000 population, appears to be giving way to the commission-manager.

The Public Interest

As we saw, the city manager plan was initiated during a period of reform as a means of taking politics out of local government. Other means have been advanced: The non-partisan ballot, extension of the merit system and the career services to protect city jobs from being used for patronage, the payment of low salaries to mayors and council or commission members to take the profit out of public service. Many cities have been the battleground between the good government groups and their opponents, who disdainfully describe the good government people as the goo-goos. Some contend that the result of taking power from party leaders and elected officials is its transfer to non-governmental groups and bureaucracies.

There are few identifiable public interests that most people agree upon. There can be a public consensus on such matters as public safety and national defense. But the great majority of issues resolve into a contest among differing special interests. The political process involves much more than the nomination and election of candidates. We can define the political process as the daily interaction of government, interest groups and the citizenry.

Participants in the Political Process

Professors Wallace S. Sayre of Columbia University and Herbert Kaufman of Yale put the political process in terms useful to the government reporter. They describe the participants as actors in a contest for a variety of goals, stakes, rewards and prizes. The police officer on the beat whose union is seeking to fend off reductions in the police force is an actor in the contest, as is the mother of three who is urging her school's Parents Association to speak out for more crossing guards at the elementary school. They are as much a part of the political process as the mayor who journeys to the state capital to seek a larger slice of the state's funds for welfare and health, or who decides to seek re-election and lines up backing from unions and ethnic groups.

We can group the participants in the city's political process as follows:

The political party leaders—The leaders and their organizations have a strong hand in the nominating process, but the other participants have increased their power and influence recently, while the party has declined in importance. Insurgents sometimes capture nominations, and the leaders must compromise their choices for the highest offices in the interest of finding a candidate who can win.

Elected and appointed officials—The mayor, members of the city council or commission and their administrators occupy key roles in governing the city. As the party has declined in importance, the mayor and the visible elected and appointed officials have become independent decision makers.

Balancing Act. Professor Martin Shefter of Cornell University says local government officials try to balance two sets of goals:

1. Getting elected and preserving civil harmony.

2. Nurturing the local economy and maintaining the city's ability to pay its bills.

To line up large constituencies for election, a mayoral candidate may make promises to groups (1) that could compromise the city's credit rating, which would make it difficult to sell bonds and to borrow from banks (2).

Interest (pressure) groups—Every aspect of city policy making is watched by one or more of the political interest groups. Business groups are especially interested in the budget process: real estate interests will want a low property tax rate, larger and more efficient police and fire departments; the banks scrutinize the debt policies since they are the buyers of bonds and notes; contractors urge public improvements. The bar associations watch the law enforcement agencies and the legal department as well as the judiciary.

Religious groups and educational organizations are interested in schools. Medical and health professions examine the activities of the health department. The nominating process and the election campaigns attract ethnic and labor groups as well as the good government groups.

Interest groups compete with each other to influence the city leadership and its bureaucracy, and this limits their influence. Sometimes, however, an interest group may control the decision making of a department or agency, as when, for example, the real estate interests take over the planning and zoning department or the banks and bond market control decisions about the sale of bonds.

Organized and professional bureaucracies—City employees have become independent of the party organization as the merit system, unionization and the professionalization of city service have increased. Police, firefighters and teachers have been among the most active in influencing the political process.

Other governments—The city government is in daily contact with a variety of other governmental units: the county, the state, the federal government, public authorities and special assessment districts. These governments are linked by a complex web of legal and financial involvements. State approval is often necessary for certain actions by the city. State and federal governments appropriate large amounts of funds for such city services as education, health and welfare. City officials are almost always bargaining with other governmental units, as are the other participants in the city's political process.

The press—"The communication media provide the larger stage upon which the other participants in the city's political contest play their parts with the general public as an audience," says Kaufman. But, he continues, the media "do more than merely provide the public stage." They also take a direct part in the process. Having its own values, emphasis, stereotypes and preoccupations, the press is not an exact mirror or reporter, he says. The media highlight personalities, are fond of exposés, are prone to fall for stories about new public works, are too zealous in looking for stories about patronage crumbs—and are too skeptical of officials and party leaders, he says.

Lewis W. Wolfson, a professor of journalism at American University, says that the press too often depicts government "not as a process, but as a succession of events, many of them in fact staged for the media." He suggests that the press "tell people more about how government works, how it affects them, and how they can influence it."

Kaufman says the press does keep officials alert and helps to raise the level of behavior of the participants in the political process. But it omits important aspects of the process, and it contributes to the caution, timidity and delay of the participants in decision making, he says.

Politics

Politics Defined. Ambrose Bierce defined politics as "a strife of interests masquerading as a contest of principles," and John Kenneth Galbraith said, "Politics is not the art of the possible. It consists in choosing between the disastrous and the unpalatable."

Many issues are decided in a public setting—through discussion and debate. Others are settled by elections. The task of the reporter covering politics is to make clear to readers and viewers the issues that define and separate the candidates so that an informed choice may be made.

Despite appearances, campaigns are carefully planned, sometimes on the basis of significant issues. Ralph Whitehead at the University of Massachusetts says, "It is possible to read a campaign.

"Assume every decision is made for a reason. Hence, a campaign can be decoded. A reporter's job is to do this decoding." The plan is rarely divulged. Unless a reporter identifies the plan, he or she cannot put the campaign into perspective, he says.

David Broder, who covers politics for *The Washington Post,* says the reporter's job is to cull from campaign rhetoric "those few words, incidents and impressions that convey the flavor, the mood and the significance of what occurred." This means selectivity, Broder says, "the essence of all contemporary journalism. And selectivity implies criteria. Criteria depend on value judgments, which is a fancy term for opinions, preconceptions and prejudices. There is no neutral journalism."

Key Elements. David Yepsen of *The Des Moines Register* says there are four elements to a political campaign— the candidate, the money, the issues and the organization. Coverage of each involves:

Candidate—profile, interviews with friends, associates.

Money—political fundraisers, campaign disclosure reports, advertising program.

Issues—candidate's platform, public's input.

Organization—key figures, campaign plans.

One of the journalist's biases, or values, is that candidates are obligated to address the issues. When the reporter's reading of the campaign reveals a candidate is avoiding the issues that the reporter considers important and relevant, then it is the reporter's obligation to place the issues on the political agenda by asking the candidate for opinions on these issues.

Important as partisan politics is, reporters spend too much time on the give-and-take of campaigns at the expense of time spent on the way politics works. How is an ordinance enacted; what are the politics behind the adoption of the property tax; how does the mayor push through a police reorganization plan that some council members oppose? The reporter who shows the way the system works informs and educates readers and listeners. These stories also make good reading and listening—everyone wants to know what goes on behind the curtains.

Some Tips on Campaign Coverage

Campaigns are confusing at best, no matter how ably run. The nature of politics is such that no one can predict their form and shape from day to day. A political reporter needs some general steering points.

Candidates go where the votes are. This is applicable to candidates for local and state offices, less so to candidates for the major national offices since television takes their campaigns into homes everywhere. The reporter covering a mayoral or gubernatorial campaign who watches the candidates' schedules for the week can make some informed conclusions, says Whitehead.

Where does the candidate go, how often and on what terms? When a Jewish candidate spends most of his time in the Catholic areas of town, one conclusion may be drawn. If he gives a large part of his time to appearances at synagogues and Jewish organizations, another conclusion may be drawn.

Another tip: Watch the media purchases. If the candidate is buying television spots near daytime soap operas, he or she is looking for the homebound woman's vote.

Whitehead suggests a rule of thumb: "The larger the electorate, the more likely a candidate will run a rational and intelligent campaign." The larger the electorate, the more money a candidate is allowed to raise and spend, and the skilled professionals in the campaign management business are attracted to the big spenders. When a small-town candidate runs a skilled and well-financed campaign, chances are that a foundation is being built for future campaigns for higher office.

Most candidates run to win, but sometimes a candidate runs to raise an issue, or is being used as a strawman or stalking horse for other interests. If an Irish candidate is running against a candidate of Polish descent, the Irishman may field another candidate of Polish descent to split the Polish vote. The subsidized candidate is known as a stalking horse.

All of these suggestions are aimed at making the reporter competent at digging beneath the handout and the press release, the prepared text and the television appearance. The purpose of a reporter's coverage should be to learn precisely what the candidate is trying to do and who he or she is, and to reveal that to the electorate.

If voters are to cast ballots intelligently rather than on the basis of paid television spots—which surveys indicate are an important basis of voting behavior—then reporters must direct their questions and coverage to what they consider the issues candidates should speak to. This is nothing unusual for the journalist. Every reporter who goes out on a story draws up questions for sources. The political reporter is no different. He or she has a sense of the important matters facing the community, state or nation, and these become the substance of questions directed to the candidates. Their answers can provide the voters with more information than the source-originated handout, speech or television commercial provide.

Too many reporters have more interest in the politics of government than in its substance. The result is that many reporters are unable to make judgments about substantive matters and must rely on the so-called experts, some of whom have vested interests in the issues. James Fallows, the Washington editor of *The Atlantic* and a contributing editor of *The Washington Monthly,* says that emphasizing "the business of winning elections and gaining points in the polls" does readers and viewers a disservice. In his article, "The President and the Press" in the October 1979 *Washington Monthly,* Fallows says, "We all love a horserace. All they (reporters) leave out is the *what*—what he's saying, what happened when that approach was tried before, what effect this proposal will have on the permanent culture of the government or the national culture outside.

Surprise. When a Republican candidate for governor of New Mexico devoted 75 percent of his time to campaigning in Democratic strongholds, few reporters drew the obvious inference: The Republicans felt the Democratic candidate was highly vulnerable in areas Democrats took for granted. Not only did reporters fail to perceive the strategy—neither did the Democrats. In that election, the Democrats lost the statehouse for the first time in 20 years when the Republican candidate picked up almost half of the registered Democratic vote and 80 percent of the much smaller Republican vote. Reporters were surprised by the result.

Vigilance. The Democratic Party in Illinois was thrown into chaos when two candidates from the party of Lyndon LaRouche won Democratic nominations for state office. The candidate for governor, Adlai Stevenson Jr., refused to run on the ticket with them, citing the LaRouche group's extreme positions—the party contends Queen Elizabeth, Henry Kissinger and others are part of a drug conspiracy; it is anti-black, anti-Semitic.

Some politicians blamed an indifferent electorate, but a study showed that none of the state's major newspapers, nor television stations, pointed out the presence of LaRouche candidates on the ballot.

Chastened, in later congressional elections, the press ferretted out these candidates and none of the 85 LaRouche party candidates won a primary race.

Campaign Contributions.
Most states and some cities require candidates to file contribution reports. At the state level, they are usually filed with the secretary of state.

Candidates for federal office file with the Federal Election Commission, 1325 K St., NW, Washington, D.C. 20510. Telephone 1–800 424–9530.

Presidential candidates file in the states in which they spend money.

"The *what* is missing because most reporters still lack either the interest or the confidence to judge the substance of government as acutely as they judge politics."

Equality is one of the major issues that face the country. It is being debated at every level of government. The United States has a greater commitment to political equality than any other developed nation, political scientists say. But it has adopted policies that have produced one of the lowest levels of economic opportunity among developed countries.

"Even the least egalitarian leaders of Sweden, those of big business, are considerably more egalitarian not only than their business counterparts in the United States but also than the most radical American groups," say Sidney Verba and Gary R. Orren in their book *Equality in America: The View from the Top* (Cambridge, Mass.: Harvard University Press, 1986).

There is considerable agreement that there should be legal prohibitions against discrimination, that there should be equality of opportunity. But there is no consensus that there should be equality of result in housing, employment, income. The consequence has been that many communities face vast social and economic problems—ghettoes, illiteracy, teen-age pregnancy and disease and early death—that fall to a minority population. The politics of race and class underlie many of the issues the reporter has to confront.

Political decisions affect people, as the beginning of this story by Lisa Austin in *The Wichita Eagle-Beacon* indicates:

Legacy. The Urban Institute, a private research organization, concludes that although the Reagan administration dismantled much of the federal domestic apparatus, state and local governments moved in by increasing their spending on housing, health care, welfare and other programs so that "in a real sense his stamp appears to have been canceled—not fully but partially—by state and local policies and actions."

Planning next year's local budget, the city of Hays is expecting to do without the federal government's $150,000 contribution to this year's budget. And officials say the town can get by without special federal grants, like this year's $400,000 to replace water mains.

"We may just do without a piece of equipment or make an older piece last another year," says City Manager Ken Carter, knowing there's stretching room in the capital budget that uses $77,000 of that $150,000 in federal funds. And landing the water-main grant was a stroke of luck and long-term planning anyhow.

But replacing the $73,000 cut for social programs comes tougher.

"Now, especially, perhaps even more money is needed," said Carter, who oversees the northwest Kansas community of 16,000. "We need to be doing more socially . . . .

Cutting Through the Rhetoric

The banner across the window of campaign headquarters read, "Your congressman is there when you need him." The theme was repeated in the congressman's campaign for re-election. No one bothered to ask what it meant. Emboldened by the acceptance of slogans and generalities, politicians and office-seekers generate empty catch-phrases by the bushel.

The political reporter should see through these slogans. They are substitutes for the specific. They are the calculated devices by which the candidate or the official avoids taking a position. It is impossible to hold a public official accountable for his rebounding promise: "I pledge to work for you." Nor is the public a whit more informed after being told the candidate "cares" and that he intends to "listen to you."

The political reporter must bring the high-flying orator back to earth by asking questions about issues. The alternative is to permit the candidates to trivialize the campaign.

Pretense and sham pervade politics. Candidates blur issues, try to appear as cosy as the television advertising pitchman. And reporters sometimes fall for this. "Our great democracies," said the philosopher Bertrand Russell, "still tend to think that a stupid man is more likely to be honest than a clever man, and our politicians take advantage of this prejudice by pretending to be even more stupid than nature made them."

Cynicism

Reporters who cover government are so trained to find the malfunctions and the excesses and failures that they become cynical about government. They forget that the tasks of government often reflect the demands citizens make on it. They join a skeptical public in what Felix Frankfurter, a distinguished former justice of the Supreme Court of the United States, has described as "the paradox of both distrusting and burdening government." He said that this state of mind "reveals the lack of a conscious philosophy of politics."

A reporter needs to define for himself or herself some approach to the job of covering the interaction between those who govern and those who are governed. Cynicism disables the reporter in his or her task of helping the public to articulate its demands on its officials. The cynic believes that the process is futile or the actors in it are hopelessly corrupt or so inefficient that nothing can work. The reporter who acts as stenographer to officialdom is equally useless since he or she deprives the public of the informed intelligence of the reporter in helping to set the agenda for public debate. The reporter must understand that for individuals to lead fruitful lives there must be systematized cooperation between the governed and those who govern and that the journalist helps to bring this about by pointing to the necessary interdependence of all the actors in the public drama.

Political PR. "We construct events and craft photos that are designed for 30 seconds to a minute so that it can fit into that 'bite' on the evening news. . . . We'd be crazy if we didn't think in those terms."—Michael Deaver, aide to Ronald Reagan.

The Budget

Covering local government—indeed, covering all levels of government—requires a knowledge of how money is raised and how it is spent. Money fuels the system. The relationship between money and the workings of government can be seen in the budget process.

"I've had to learn how to cover five governmental units, and I find the single best way to learn what they are doing is to attend budget hearings," says David Yepsen, political reporter for *The Des Moines Register*. "They let you know the current situation, what the problems are, the proposed solutions and where government is headed."

The Many Tasks of Government. Local governments collect trash, maintain roads and public transit, clean graffiti off public buildings and attend to the hundreds of other tasks that citizens ask government to perform. A major job of the reporter is to present the unlimited demands of the public on government and its limited resources. This conflict reaches its most visible level during budget discussions. Cable car photo by Joel Strasser; others by Miriam Wieder.

"Follow the buck," says the experienced reporter. The city hall reporter follows the path of the parking-meter dime and the property tax dollar as they make their way through government. The path of these dimes and dollars is set by the budget.

The budget is a forecast or estimate of expenditures that a government will make during the year and the revenues needed to meet those expenses. It is, in short, a balance sheet. Budgets are made for the fiscal year, which may be the calendar year or may run from July 1 through June 30 or other dates. The budget is made by the executive branch (mayor, governor, president, school superintendent) and then submitted to the legislative body (city council, state legislature, Congress, board of education) for adoption.

The budget is the final resolution of the conflicting claims of individuals and groups to public monies. This means that the conscientious reporter watches the budgeting process as carefully as he or she examines the finished document. Aaron Wildavsky of the University of California at Berkeley describes the budget as "a series of goals with price tags attached." If it is followed, he says, things happen, certain policy objectives are accomplished.

The budget is hardly an impersonal document. It is a sociological and political document. As Prime Minister William Ewart Gladstone of Britain remarked more than 100 years ago, the budget "in a thousand ways goes to the root of the prosperity of the individuals and relation of classes and the strength of kingdoms."

Appropriations in the budget can determine how long a pregnant woman waits to see a doctor in a well-baby clinic, how many children are in a grade school class, whether city workers will seek to defeat the mayor in the next election.

Here is the beginning of a budget story by Paul Rilling of *The Anniston* (Ala.) *Star:*

A city budget may look like a gray mass of dull and incomprehensible statistics, but it is the best guide there is to the plans and priorities of city government.

Rhetoric and promises aside, how the city council decides to spend available money says what it really sees as the city's top priorities.

Tuesday, the Anniston City Council will consider for formal adoption the proposed city budget for fiscal . . . .

City hall, education, county and legislative reporters handle budget stories on a regular basis. Reporters on these beats begin to write stories several months

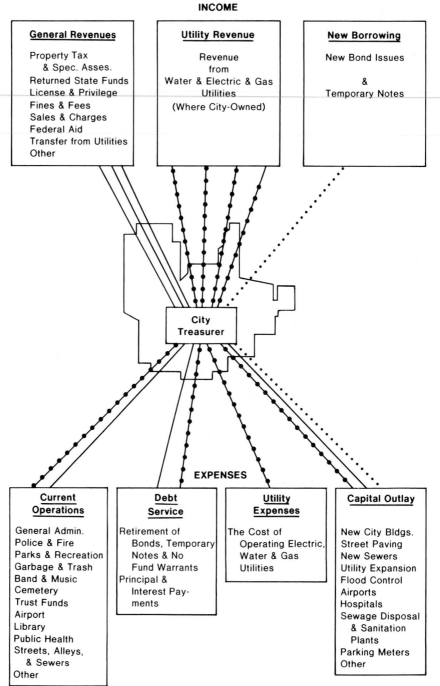

INCOME

Figure 24.2 A City's Money Flow. Here are the major sources of revenue and the major areas of expenditures in an average city. Note the specific uses to which income may be put by following the different types of lines to and from the city treasurer.

General Revenues

Property Tax
    & Spec. Asses.
Returned State Funds
License & Privilege
Fines & Fees
Sales & Charges
Federal Aid
Transfer from Utilities
Other

Utility Revenue

Revenue
from
Water & Electric & Gas
Utilities
(Where City-Owned)

New Borrowing

New Bond Issues

&

Temporary Notes

**City
Treasurer**

EXPENSES

**Current
Operations**

General Admin.
Police & Fire
Parks & Recreation
Garbage & Trash
Band & Music
Cemetery
Trust Funds
Airport
Library
Public Health
Streets, Alleys,
    & Sewers
Other

**Debt
Service**

Retirement of
    Bonds, Temporary
    Notes & No
    Fund Warrants
Principal &
    Interest Pay-
    ments

**Utility
Expenses**

The Cost of
    Operating Electric,
    Water & Gas
    Utilities

Capital Outlay

New City Bldgs.
Street Paving
New Sewers
Utility Expansion
Flood Control
Airports
Hospitals
Sewage Disposal
    & Sanitation
    Plants
Parking Meters
Other

before the new fiscal year begins so that the public can be informed of the give-and-take of the process and participate early in the decision making. In a six-week span, beginning in February, Bill Mertens, city hall reporter for *The Hawk Eye,* wrote more than a dozen stories. Here are the beginning paragraphs of two of them:

School crossing guards may be one of the programs lost if Burlington city councilmen intend to hold the new budget close to the existing one.

The city council has asked Burlington fire department heads to cut $30,000 from their budget request.

Most of the dozen-plus stories were enterprised by Mertens. Knowing the budget process and having good sources, Mertens was able to keep a steady flow of interesting and important copy moving to the city desk. In his stories, Mertens was always conscious of the human consequences of the belt-tightening. By writing about possible cuts in such areas as school crossing guards and the fire department, Mertens alerted the public. Residents could, if they wished, react by informing their council members.

Types of Budgets

Two types of governmental expenses are budgeted—funds for daily expenses and funds for long-range projects. At the local governmental level, these expenses are included in two kinds of budgets:

Daily Expenses

1. *Expense or executive budget.* This budget covers costs of daily expenses, which include salaries, debt service and the purchase of goods and services. Expense budget revenues are gathered from three major sources:
   a. Taxes on real estate—the property tax—usually the single largest source of income.
   b. General fund receipts, which include revenues from fines, permits, licenses, and taxes such as the income, corporation, sales and luxury taxes. (States must give cities permission to levy taxes.)
   c. Grants-in-aid from the federal and state governments.

Long-Range Projects

2. *Capital or construction budget.* This budget lists and gives the costs of capital projects to be built and major equipment and other long-range products to be purchased. The borrowing period is 10, 20 or 30 years. Capital budget funds are raised by borrowing, usually through the sale of bonds pledged against the assessed valuation of real estate in the governmental

unit. Bonds are approved by the voters and then sold to security firms through bidding. The firms then offer them for public sale. The loan is paid back much like a homeowner's payments on a mortgage. Principal and interest are paid out of current revenues and are listed in the expenditures column of the expense budget as "debt service," which should run under 10 percent of the total budget for the city to be on safe economic footing.

Here is the beginning of a story by Bob Freund of the *Times-News* about an election to approve the sale of bonds to finance construction of a city swimming pool.

Clarification. The reason the tax increase is $5.60 for the home valued at $50,000—and not $9.50—is that in Twin Falls, and many cities as well, the assessed value of a piece of property is set at the market value minus exemptions. (When the figures do not make sense in any tax story, the reporter must clarify them for the reader.)

TWIN FALLS—A voter would have to be living underwater to miss the publicity splash about the April 23 bond election that will float or sink a new pool in Twin Falls.

On Saturday, 174 youngsters from schools, sports teams, clubs and community hung leaflets on doorknobs from one end of town to the other.

A phone campaign also is starting. Volunteers are dialing phones throughout the city, reminding residents about the vote and taking an attitude survey.

The third wave washes into local mailboxes just before the pool goes to the polls. A letter will ask registered voters to cast their ballots . . . .

The April 23 election will ask city voters to approve a $700,000 bond issue paid by property taxes. That money and $500,000 worth of reserves in the city's capital improvement budget will build the pool. The yearly property tax increase would be about 19 cents for every $1,000 of market value or $5.60 for a house valued at $50,000.

Making the Budget

Most budgets are adopted in this series of steps:

1. Budget request forms go out to all department heads, who must decide on priorities for the coming year and submit them to the budget officer, mayor or school superintendent.

2. Meetings are held between budget officer and department heads to adjust requests and formulate a single balanced program.

3. Submission of the budget, sometimes accompanied by a narrative explaining the requests, to the city council or commission, the board of education or other legislative arm of the governmental unit.

4. Study by the legislative body and adoption of budget items for each department.

5. Public hearings. (See *Budget Session* news story.)

6. Adoption of the budget.

The reporter can cover each stage of this process. Good reporters describe the behind-the-scenes bickering, dickering and politicking as well as the formal activities of the various department heads, executives and the legislators. All sorts of pressures are brought to bear on the budget-makers. Property owners and real estate interests want the budget held down, for increased

Budget session 7 tonight

A Budget Hearing. This precede from *The Hawk Eye* prepares Burlington residents for the major issues at the hearing.

A contingent from the League of Women Voters is expected to be among the crowd of objectors at tonight's public hearing on the Burlington city budget proposal. The hearings start at 7 p.m. on third floor of city hall, and is the only business on the agenda.

The questions are expected to be varied, but the League has a special interest in the budget decisions. Its members have followed the local use of general revenue sharing (GRS) in the past two years, and is interested in the planned use during the fiscal year beginning July 1.

In its monthly letter, "The Burlington Voter," the League has listed six objections to the planned use of the funds:

● No open meeting for citizen input was held.

● Most GRS monies have been and are being used for capital expenditures — machinery, etc. — or for general governmental expenditures.

● Funding for the Library has not been correctly reported.

● There are no provisions for "people" programs.

● The council ignored requests from groups that wanted to apply for funding.

● The material on Equal Employment Opportunity cannot be verified because the forms, due Dec. 31, 1975, have not been submitted to Washington.

In the existing budget, revenue sharing funds totaling $548,000 were earmarked for the following expenditures: operation of city-school swimming pool, $65,989; Port of Burlington, $75,000; ambulance operation, $49,928; city's share of county health operation, $65,823; Public Library, $160,580; and $42,000 for some costs in the property maintenance and vehicle maintenance departments.

The council has budgeted $237,000 of revenue sharing funds in the $10.6-million proposal for 1976-77 for operation of the city-school pool, the Library and the city summer recreation program.

The city only budgeted for funds to be received before the end of 1976, since renewal of revenue sharing has not been approved by Congress, although extension is expected. If so, the city would receive another $158,000 during the first of 1977, if funding levels remain the same.

Also, the city is proposing the transfer of $287,583 from the revenue sharing reserve to the general fund to meet working capital reserves needs for the first quarter of the new fiscal year. That would leave a balance of revenue sharing funds, as of June 31, at $70,837, according to city officials also.

Burlington has received more than $1 million through the program since its inception in 1972.

---

expenditures usually mean higher property taxes. The business men and women who rely on selling goods and services to the city seek to keep the money flowing to the departments and agencies they serve. Inside government, employees want salary increases, more generous fringe benefits and more lines in the budget for promotions. Politicians seek to reward constituencies and to fulfill campaign promises in order to advance their careers and their party's future.

| Checklist: | _____ Amount to be spent. |
| Budget Adoption | _____ New or increased taxes, higher license and permit fees and other income that will be necessary to meet expenditures. |

Checklist:
Budget Adoption

_____ Amount to be spent.

_____ New or increased taxes, higher license and permit fees and other income that will be necessary to meet expenditures.

_____ Cuts, if any, to be made in such taxes, fees or fines.

_____ Comparison with preceding year(s).

_____ Justification for increases sought, cuts made.

_____ Rate of current spending, under or over budget of previous year.

_____ Patterns behind the submission and subsequent adjustments, such as political motives, pressure groups, history.

_____ Consequences of budget for: agencies, departments, businesses, the public.

Checklist:
Budget Follow-Up

_____ Per-person comparison of costs for specific services with other cities or school districts of the same size.

_____ Check of one or more departments to see how funds are used, whether all funds were necessary.

Sources

There are five major interest groups that seek to influence budget-making and are sources:

1. *Government*—Chief executive, who submits the budget: mayor, governor, school superintendent, president; city manager; head of budget bureau or budget director; department heads; finance and taxation committees of the city council or commission; council members. (Party leaders outside government are sometimes helpful.)

2. *Money-providing constituencies*—Local real estate association; property owners association; chamber of commerce; taxpayer organizations; merchant and business groups; banks; savings and loan associations.

3. *Service-demanding groups*—Lobbyists for education, health, welfare and other services.

4. *Organized bureaucracies*—Public employees, municipal unions, civil service associations and the public employees' retirement fund manager.

5. *Independent groups*—League of Women Voters; National Municipal League; National League of Cities; U.S. Conference of Mayors; Advisory Commission on Intergovernmental Relations. (Addresses usually can be obtained from the state university's political science or government department, which itself may have a municipal study organization.)

Cautions

Tax money is the source of great passion in the political marketplace, and politicians often seek to impress the public with promises of parsimony to avoid angering the money-providing constituencies.

The truth is that many items in the budget are mandated costs that no one can shift or eliminate. The mandated funds include salaries, debt service, pensions, matching funds that localities must produce to meet state and federal grants, particularly for such services as health, welfare and education.

When the city accepts grants from the state or federal government, it must abide by the rules and regulations that often necessitate expenditures.

The actual maneuvering room in most budgets is not great, especially since salaries, which represent the largest single expense item, are set by contract in many cities. Only about 10 percent of the budgets for most large cities is discretionary because of mandated costs.

Costs can be reduced if commitments to the poor, the elderly and the ill were cut back. However, this would antagonize the service-demanding constituencies. Maneuvering room could be created by changing earmarked funds, such as those for education, to general funds. Again, groups that benefit from the status quo would object.

The competition for free-floating general funds is always intense, and the perceptive reporter will examine this contest during the budgetary process. In this competition, the administrator finds it necessary to trade off the demands of various groups. The trade-offs make good stories.

A little skepticism helps in assessing budget requests. Departments and agencies usually exaggerate their needs, and pressure groups seek deeper cuts than are feasible. The reporter must realize that budget-making is a give-and-take process and that despite the agonized pleas or the dire warnings of the participants, the city, state or nation usually survives.

Hidden Motives

Some aspects of the process are hidden from view. The reporter must dig them out and learn the constituencies involved, the motives of the participants. Are political debts being paid by building a school in one section of the city or by increasing salaries in a particular agency? Have cuts been made in the department of a critical or independent administrator?

The fiscal balance that the final budget represents is the result of a political as well as a financial balancing act—the adjustments among groups, organizations and classes that seek more money and services and those that resist the taxes and other costs necessary to meet these needs and demands. One of the few independent spectators of this balancing act is the reporter.

Budget Politics

During a legislative session, Gov. Malcolm Wilson of New York, a Republican, proposed a new formula for the distribution of state aid to local school districts that reflected the demands of big-city school officials. A few days later, a group of Republican state senators and assemblymen from Long Island met with the governor, who was facing re-election. Following the meeting, the governor's aid formula was changed to give more aid to suburban school districts, especially to Long Island.

"What happened at the gathering," reported *The New York Times,* "was summed up later by Joseph M. Margiotta of Uniondale, the powerful Nassau County Republican leader, who related that the Long Island delegation had simply delivered to Mr. Wilson the stern message that without more state education aid, Long Island property taxes would skyrocket in September and Mr. Wilson's campaign would sink in October."

When Mayor John Lindsay of New York "dropped the broom and picked up the nightstick"—the graphic phrase the *Daily News* used to describe the shift in budget priorities from clean streets to public safety—it was widely interpreted as Lindsay's recognition that law and order would make a more attractive national issue than sanitation. Lindsay had presidential ambitions.

Budgeting, says Wildavsky, deals with the many and diverse purposes of man.

Property Tax

The property tax is the largest single source of income for municipalities, counties, special districts, and school systems and affects more people than any other local tax but the sales tax. Considerable local, county and school coverage centers on the action of the council, commission or board in setting the property tax. The reporter should know the formula for figuring the property tax. The tax is formally known as the mill levy. A mill is .1 cent (1/10¢), and the property tax technically is expressed in terms of mills levied for each dollar of assessed valuation of property. Here is the formula:

Mill levy = (Taxes to be collected) ÷ (Assessed valuation)

Let us assume budget officials estimate that $1 million will have to be collected from the property tax and that the assessed valuation of real estate in the city or school district is $80 million. Here is how the tax is figured:

Mill levy = ($1 million) ÷ ($80 million)

Mill levy = $1 ÷ $80 = $.0125

Mill levy = 1.25 cents on each $1 of assessed valuation

Since mill levies are usually expressed against $100 or $1,000 in assessed valuation, the levy in this community would be $1.25 for each $100 in valuation, or $12.50 for each $1,000 in valuation.

Here is a paragraph from a reporter's story in which these figures are used to describe the municipal budget in a medium-size Kansas community:

Last year, the commission budgeted $1,161,313 of which $641,135.25 was to be raised from property taxes. These taxes, based on the assessed valuation of property, were based on a 20.91 mill levy, or $20.91 for each $1,000 property valuation. The total assessed valuation was $30,661,583.

Reporters should always apply the mill levy to representative home values. But they must note that the mill levy is applied to assessed valuations, not to actual value as determined in the marketplace. Assessed value is usually a percentage of market value. The tax levy of $20.91 per $1,000 in the story from the Kansas newspaper made greater impact on readers because the reporter later noted that the property tax on a home with an assessed valuation of $10,000 would be $209.10. (The $20.91 multiplied by 10.)

Here is the beginning of a story on a school board budget by Art Carey:

The Pennsbury School Board adopted a $21.7 million budget last night which will cost residents another six mills in property taxes . . . .

The new budget means the tax rate in the Pennsbury School District stands at 108.5 mills . . . .

Those living in homes assessed at $5,000 can expect to pay $542; those living in $10,000 homes, $1,085; those living in $15,000 homes, $1,627; and those living in $20,000 homes, $2,170.

—*Bucks County Courier Times*
(Levittown, Pa.)

Since the property tax is levied against ownership of the property, the third paragraph would have been more accurate had it stated, "Those *owning* homes assessed at . . . ."

Christine Rouvalis of the *Pittsburgh Post-Gazette* began a story about the county budget this way:

Democratic county Commissioners Tom Foerster and Pete Flaherty united yesterday to approve a real estate tax increase of 2¼ mills to support a $410.7 million budget for 1986.

Despite the 7.76 percent increase for a total of 31¼ mills, the commissioners voted to spend $11.5 million of the county's emergency reserve funds to balance the budget. They also abolished most of the county Probation Department and imposed a hiring freeze.

The increase will cost the owner of a $60,000 home an extra $33.75 a year. The total bill for a home with a market value of $60,000—and thus an assessed value of $15,000—will be $468.75.

The tax increase—the first in four years—will provide an additional $14.1 million in revenue for the county. Each mill raises about $6.5 million.

Republican Commissioner Barbara Hafer, who opposed any tax increase, voted against the budget.

When asked what cuts she would make to prevent a tax increase, Hafer said, "Not cuts, priorities. County government has always been a bottomless pit. There should be more scrutinizing of the books."

Hafer also criticized the budget because it "eats up half of the reserves."

Flaherty, who in his seven years as mayor of Pittsburgh never raised taxes, said he had to vote for a county real estate tax increase in order to continue providing essential county services.

Foerster said the spending plan—which passed about 13 hours before the state-mandated deadline—was the most difficult one he has worked on during his 18 years as commissioner . . . .

Notice the use of the two commissioners in the lead. Rouvalis decided that their decision to vote for the tax increase made it possible for the measure to pass. Also, notice the way the reporter includes comments on the action after she explains what the new tax will mean to the homeowner whose property is assessed at $15,000.

Remember that the property tax is a major source of revenue for several governmental units. When covering the action of one unit in setting a tax rate, it is necessary to inform the reader that this particular property tax is not the only one the property owner will pay. Often overlooked by reporters are the property taxes levied by special assessment districts, which can add a large chunk to the tax bill. There are almost 30,000 special districts, and they account for 11 percent of all local government expenditures, about $35 billion. The special districts construct and maintain services such as power and water lines, hospitals, sewage systems and community development projects. Each district has the power to levy taxes on property within the district.

Property valuations are made by the tax assessor and are public record. The tax rate is set each year, but valuations on individual pieces of property are not changed often. Total assessed valuation does change each year because of new construction and shutdowns that add to or subtract from the tax rolls. The taxing district must establish the total assessed valuation each year before a new tax rate can be set.

When the assessor does make new valuations, the intensity of feeling is considerable, as revealed in this story:

SPRING VALLEY, N.Y., Dec. 12— Listening to people here, a visitor would almost think that someone was stalking the streets, sowing horror and destruction.

But it is only the tax assessor, equipped with a collapsible 10-foot measuring stick, a set of appraisal cards, a practiced eye that can tell the difference between a toilet and a water closet and experience that tells him which adds more value to a house.

This village of 22,450 persons, 2,219 dwellings and 109 commerical properties is nearing the end of a year-long reappraisal. . . .

The assessor sometimes is politically motivated in establishing assessments. In some cities, residential properties are consistently underassessed in order to placate homeowners. In Philadelphia, tax officials assessed residences at 40 percent of market value, whereas commercial property was assessed at 54 percent and industrial property at 59 percent. In the Chicago area, the political machine of Mayor Richard J. Daley underassessed large corporations and industries. At election time, these beneficiaries of the assessor could be counted on for large campaign contributions.

Governments cannot meet their needs out of current revenues. Most cities **Borrowing** need seasonal funds to tide them over while waiting for taxes or grants. There is also a need for money to finance major construction projects. Sometimes at the end of the fiscal year or during the year an emergency will come up and quick cash is needed.

There are two ways of coping with these needs for cash. For seasonal borrowing or for emergencies when small amounts are needed, the city may issue anticipation notes that the city sells to banks. Future tax collections and anticipated grants-in-aid are pledged as security. Usually, the state must approve. Most large borrowing is done through the sale of bonds.

The idea behind the sale of bonds is that the costs of such long-range **Bonds** projects as schools, hospitals, streets, sewage plants and mass transit should be borne by those who use them over the anticipated life of the project.

There are three major types of bonds. They differ as to the type of security pledged to repay them:

General Obligation: Most frequently issued. Security is the general taxing power of the city. Bonds are retired by taxes on all property in the city.

Special Improvement: For construction of sidewalks, sewers and similar public works. Taxes are levied on the property owners who will benefit from the construction. Charges levied on the property are called special assessments. Special assessment districts are set up to levy and collect the taxes.

Revenue Bonds: To pay for the acquisition, construction, improvement of such properties as college dormitories and public utilities. Pledge is a lien on earnings, which are used to redeem the bonds. These earnings come from room charges in dormitories, water, gas and electric collections from utility customers, toll charges on bridges and highways.

Bonds are paid off in two ways:

Term Bond: The securities are retired at the end of the specified term, 10, 15, 20 years. Meanwhile, money is set aside regularly in a sinking fund and invested to be used to retire the bonds at the end of the term.

Serial Bond: Most common. A portion is retired each year.

In writing bond stories, the reporter should make sure to include the cost of the bonds to taxpayers. Some readers will be astonished to learn how much a seemingly small rate of interest can amount to over 10 or 20 years.

Many units of government maintain bank accounts that draw little or no interest at the same time they issue bonds at rates higher than their savings are drawing. This incongruity can be the basis of excellent stories about mismanagement.

Anticipation Notes

Short-term low-interest borrowing consists of three types of anticipation notes—revenue, tax and bond. All must be repaid in a year.

Grants-in-aid are an important part of the governmental unit's income or revenue. But these federal and state payments for such items as education, welfare, health and other services usually do not arrive in time to meet the payroll or the demands of vendors to be paid for their goods and services. The city, county or school district may have to borrow money for a short time, then pay it back when the grants arrive. This borrowing is in the form of revenue anticipation notes (RANS) sold to banks.

Some local taxes are not collected until late in the year, and the anticipated income has to be made up for by short-term loans, which are made by issuing tax anticipation notes (TANS).

Bond anticipation notes (BANS) are sold in anticipation of revenue from the sale of bonds. Here is the beginning of a story from *The Daily Register* of Red Bank, N.J., about a school board borrowing money in anticipation of income from the sale of bonds:

> MONMOUTH BEACH—The Board of Education is borrowing another $150,000 at 5½ percent interest from Colonial First National Bank to finance the Griffin St. school addition.
>
> The money is being borrowed against the $1,422,750 bond issue approved by voters in March. The board has been waiting for a favorable bond market before selling the bonds . . . .

City Clerk

In most medium-sized and small cities the city clerk is a career public official who knows local government inside and out. In Fresno, Calif., the present city clerk took office in 1963. Her predecessor held office for 25 years. Through changes in administration and even changes in governmental systems, the city clerk usually is the survivor necessary to handle the thousand-and-one matters that keep government functioning.

The city clerk, who usually is appointed by the council or commission, serves as secretary to the legislative branch, issues city licenses, keeps all records and statistics and registers voters. The city clerk draws up the agenda for the council or commission, records ordinances and resolutions and keeps minutes of meetings. The city clerk can be one of the reporter's major sources.

Wherever public money is involved there is an overseeing agency that checks to see that the money is spent properly. Most governmental units undergo internal checks made by agency auditors, and these make good stories. Here is the beginning of a story by Jayne Garrison of the San Francisco *Examiner:*

OAKLAND—A Social Services Department audit says mismanagement and internal squabbling are so severe that clients would be better off if the agency were dismantled.

Cities, states and the federal government have a department or office independent of the executive that checks the financial activities of all agencies within government. At the federal level, the Government Accounting Office does this work. At the state level, the state auditor or comptroller is the watchdog, and at the city level an elected official, also known as the auditor or comptroller, examines the financial records of city offices.

A regular or pre-audit examination is made of purchase orders and vouchers. This audit determines whether there is money to pay for the goods, whether there are certified receipts for the delivered goods, whether there has been competitive bidding when required by law, whether the prices are reasonable.

Increasingly, auditors and comptrollers are conducting performance audits, which check the efficiency of the services, the quality of the goods and the necessity for purchasing them.

Pre-audit example: A state official claims travel reimbursement for an official trip between Boulder and Denver. The auditor will determine whether the 39 miles claimed on the official's expense account attached to a pay order is the actual distance and will see whether the 19 cents a mile is the standard state payment.

Performance audit example: The comptroller has decided to make a check of welfare rolls to see whether money is going out to ineligible persons. The office makes a computer check of the welfare rolls against (a) death lists; (b) marriage certificates (if a person receiving aid to dependent children has married, the working spouse is obligated to support the children); (c) children in foster care homes still listed as at the residence; (d) city and state payrolls to determine if any employed persons are receiving welfare.

Journalists make their own checks as well as using the work of the auditor and comptroller. They regularly look through vouchers and pay orders in the auditor's office, and they look at the cancelled checks in the treasurer's office.

When a governmental unit wants to buy something, it sends a purchase order to the comptroller or auditor's office, which makes a pre-audit. The order is given approval and sent to the vendor. Records are kept by the number of the purchase order, the agency involved and often by the name of the vendor.

On delivery of the goods or services, a voucher is made up with the accompanying bill, and this starts the payment to the vendor. The payment is made in the form of a check, a warrant.

When Christopher Scanlan of *The Providence Journal* was examining vouchers of the Providence Housing Authority he came upon payments of $3,319.59 made to restaurants in Providence and Warwick for "authority meetings." On checking, he learned that members of the authority had been meeting over meals for years.

"The restaurant tabs were paid from authority funds, the majority of which are derived from rents paid by low income tenants at the city's 14 public housing projects and from federal subsidies," Scanlan wrote. After the story ran, the authority members agreed to hold meetings in the housing projects it manages.

An examination of vouchers and warrants enabled George Thiem, a reporter for *The Chicago Daily News*, to expose a multimillion dollar corruption scheme by the Illinois state treasurer. Thiem could see that a number of checks were endorsed by typewriter. Interviewing some of those who supposedly were paid by these checks for work done for the state, he learned that the persons listed on the checks had never done state work; nor had they received the checks. The treasurer went to prison as a result of Thiem's investigation.

The Shoebox Papers

While she was gathering material for an article about the effects of federal budget cuts on the poor, Carol Matlack of the *Arkansas Gazette* spoke to a church worker who told Matlack about an elderly man and his wife who had lost their home through foreclosure.

"She told me there was something suspicious about it," Matlack says.

"She gave me a bundle of the man's papers—he had recently died—that had been stored in a shoebox in his house.

"The documents proved the key to the story."

With the papers and from records in the county courthouse and through interviews Matlack was able to piece together the story of an interlocking relationship between a private investment firm and a special assessment district in a poor neighborhood that cost residents their homes through foreclosures.

Her series began this way:

Hosie and Clover Mae Willis were stunned when they got a letter ordering them to move out of their home. It was their first notice that their modest frame house on College Station's Frazier Pike had been sold for nonpayment of $62 in special improvement taxes several years earlier.

After describing the couple's improvements to the property, in which they had reared three children, Matlack disclosed that Southern Investment Co. of Little Rock had purchased the property from Water Improvement District 74 for $124.71 in taxes and penalties.

Had the Willises inquired further, they would have learned that the commissioners of Water Improvement District 74 who sold their property—W. J. White, Jack Barger and Marcelite Cook—all were affiliated with Southern Investment.

They would also have learned that at least two dozen College Station residents have lost their property in similar fashion because of a failure to pay taxes—sometimes as little as $20—to one of five water improvement districts in the predominantly poor, black community south of Little Rock Airport.

Residents said they had never been told their taxes were delinquent. Nor were they notified their land was being sold. In some cases, residents continued to receive tax bills and to pay property taxes years after their land had been sold.

Why all the activity in a poor, black neighborhood? Matlack answers the question in her third article that begins:

"Little nuggets of gold." That's how Pratt Remmel Sr., a Little Rock businessman, describes a string of weed-choked lots he owns along a potholed road in College Station.

Matlack points out that a highway will soon go by the area, carrying "one of the heaviest traffic volumes in Arkansas." An interchange is to be built north of College Station, and the area will have hotels, restaurants, motels and an industrial park.

Follow the buck. The paper trail Matlack followed led from the simple homes of poor folk to the offices of wheelers and dealers.

Postscript: In its next session, the General Assembly of Arkansas reformed procedures for delinquent tax notification.

Zoning and Planning

For centuries, the mentally ill had been locked up. The reasons seemed logical: Isolated, the mentally ill could be healed more rapidly; free in society, their conditions worsened, they menaced others and they were a danger to themselves. Gradually, the truth seeped out. Journalists showed these institutions were snake pits where the patients were treated inhumanely. Few were cured. With the development of tranquilizing drugs and other treatment, it became possible to offer outpatient care. But there had to be a transition, a halfway house to help the patient adjust after his or her institutionalization.

In New Jersey, the Catholic Diocese of Trenton decided to administer several such houses. The state intended to de-institutionalize its mental patients, and the diocese sought to help. The diocese found a structure in Willingboro that fit its needs. But it needed permission from the zoning board since the building was in a residential area.

The Willingboro zoning board, like thousands of other such boards, carries out the community's planning goals, which are usually set by the planning commission. The zoning boards divide an area into zones or districts and designate them residential, commercial or industrial. The boards then grant building and construction permits consistent with these designations.

The boards also regulate the use of land and buildings within these zones. They regulate the height of buildings, lot size, yard dimensions and other aspects of construction. The city council enacts the ordinances that the zoning board enforces.

Zoning can be restrictive, a way of keeping someone out of an area. By requiring that new construction be of single-residence homes on one-acre lots, a zoning regulation will effectively keep out of the area all but the well-to-do. When Laura King, who covered Willingboro on her suburban beat, attended the zoning board meeting at which the diocese requested a variance for its halfway house, she was struck by the hostility of the spectators. King decided that the opposition to the house was the story.

When the New Jersey Supreme Court ruled that a city must provide its "fair share" of low- and moderate-income housing and must change its zoning ordinances to provide for that kind of housing, King wrote a feature that began:

March 24, 1975 may well go down as the day the carefully built walls of such upper class suburban meccas as Mount Laurel and Moorestown began to crumble.

It was the day the New Jersey State Supreme Court struck down exclusionary zoning practices in the sprawling bedroom community of Mount Laurel.

And it was a victory not just for low-income people but for as much as 60 percent of the present South Jersey population, according to Carl Bisgaier, attorney for the successful plaintiffs in the Mount Laurel case.

Here is the beginning of a story about a planning and zoning board action written by Pat Marcantonio of the *Times-News* in Twin Falls, Idaho:

TWIN FALLS—A request to operate a trout processing plant three miles west of Buhl was approved Thursday by the Twin Falls County Planning and Zoning Board.

Mark Lupher requested a conditional use permit to use an existing building on 40 acres to process about 5,000 pounds of trout a week.

The site of the property, owned by Richard Kelly, is located in an agricultural zone.

Board member Lyle Fuller said he was concerned about the potential odor from the plant.

Lupher argued that his operation, comparatively smaller than surrounding fish processors, needed a chance to survive. He had planned to sell the fish to markets, such as Washington D.C. and Atlanta, Ga., not reached by the larger producers.

Lupher also said he had the means to control odor.

"The only way to prove it is to do it," he told the board.

Another board member, Lyle Frazier, told Lupher that if the smell becomes a nuisance, the county will close the operation.

Neighborhood Stories

City hall reporters spend too much of their time in city hall, says a veteran municipal government reporter. He recommends that they make regular trips out of the protected environs of the municipal building and venture into the neighborhoods of the community to see what is on the minds of people, to check how city programs and policies have been carried out. Here is the beginning of a neighborhood story by Garrison of the *Examiner:*

OAKLAND—In the heart of the Oakland flatlands, the moms and pops of small business are plotting to sweep out the rubble: dope, litter and boarded buildings.

About 35 merchants meeting in churches and stores the last few weeks have organized a voice they hope will boom across town to City Hall—the Central East Oakland Merchants Association.

This is the first time in more than a decade that merchants along central East 14th Street have tried to wield clout to-gether. The odds against them are steep. They have little political pull and even less money. They face absentee landlords who own some boarded storefronts, and youths who have no work outside the drug trade.

But they do have determination.

"You see that red church down there?" said Al Parham, nodding toward a tall brick steeple half a block past Seminary Avenue on East 14th Street. "They just built that. So people are coming back into the community. And they're going to church. They care."

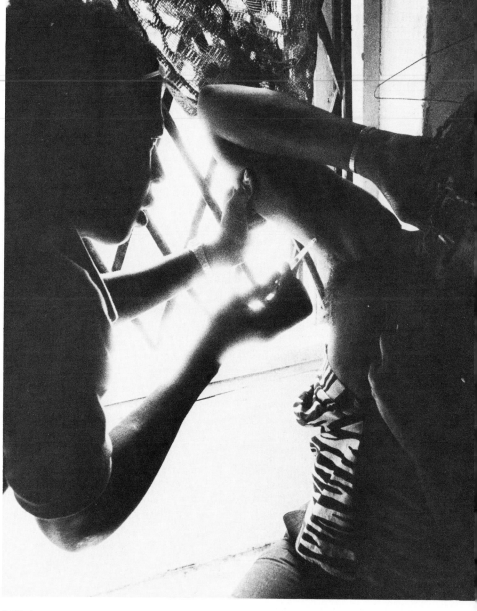

City Scenes. Reporters who seek out stories in the areas described by one sociologist as "dreadful enclosures" will find people who feel ignored and unwanted. A longtime resident of a Philadelphia community lives behind three deadbolt locks. "Ain't like it used to be," she said. "Everybody's scared." Photo by Larry C. Price of *The Philadelphia Inquirer*.

A Hit. In apartments and abandoned tenements drug addicts buy heroin and rent the equipment for their injections. The needles are often passed from user to user without being disinfected. Intravenous drug users are major victims of AIDS. The police usually are too busy with violent crimes to raid these shooting galleries. Photo by Mel Finkelstein, copyright New York News, Inc.

Communities spend more money on public education than on any other single tax-supported activity. Free public education has a long history in the United States. In 1642, the Massachusetts Bay Colony made education compulsory in the primary grades and required towns to establish public schools. The cost is borne by all in the community, whether the individual has children in the public school or not. The reason was given succinctly by Thaddeus Stevens to the Pennsylvania state legislature in 1835 when some legislators objected to the general financing of the schools.

"Many complain of the school tax," Stevens said, "not so much on account of its amount, as because it is for the benefit of others and not themselves. This is a mistake. It is for their own benefit, inasmuch as it perpetuates the government and ensures the due administration of the laws under which they live, and by which their lives and property are protected."

The faith in education as the underpinning of democracy is a constant theme in American life, along with the belief that it paves the way to a good job. Education pervades the life of most families because they have children in school.

The interest in schools—which really means a concern for the community's children—led *The Fincastle Herald* in Virginia to run a banner across page one when the Scholastic Aptitude Test (SAT) scores for the county were made public. "Low SAT scores surprise school officials," read the headline. The story was accompanied by a large box comparing county scores with those in Virginia, southern states and the nation. The story by Edwin McCoy begins:

Botetourt County students scored at least 20 points below the state and national averages on both parts of the Scholastic Aptitude Test (SAT), according to figures provided by the county school system this week.

McCoy says that education is the "focal point in the community. Basically, what happens in the schools affects a lot of people, and it takes tax dollars. People and the pocketbook—these two criteria make education a primary news subject." He says the story was important because the "quality of education is important to industrial or commercial development because developers are interested in the quality of life in any area they choose to expand in or move to."

Covering the Schools

Complaints. School superintendents complain:

• Reporters emphasize events rather than trends, thus failing to give the public a rounded view of the system.

• Writers do not go to schools and classrooms enough. They give too much attention to the views of administrators, not enough to those of teachers.

• Reporters overlook the impact on education of changes in children such as their defiance of authority, sexual precocity, their expectation of constant entertainment and frequent shifts in subject matter—changes, officials say, that have been brought about by television.

Structure of the System

The school system is based in school districts that are usually contiguous with city boundaries. The schools are independent of municipal government and are subject to state regulations through a state board of education. School boards, usually with five to seven members, are elected in non-partisan elections, though in some cities board members are appointed by the mayor. The board hires a superintendent of schools who is responsible to the board.

Reporters covering the education beat tend to center their attention on the administration of the system. Stories from the board and the superintendent's office involve such subjects as changes in the curriculum and personnel, teacher contracts, the purchase of new equipment, aid to education, teacher certification, school dates for opening, closing and holidays and the vast area of school financing that includes budgeting and the issuance of bonds.

The school administration can provide material for assessing the performance of the system and its schools. Dropout and truancy records are kept, as are the results of standardized tests. Reporters can compare the community-wide scores with those of other cities. Comparisons can also be made of schools within the system. Do the students in the low-scoring schools come from economically depressed areas with serious social and economic problems? Is there a correlation between these factors? Historical comparisons can also be made: Are students in a relatively stable school district doing as well as or worse than their parents did in reading and writing?

A check of high school graduates would indicate what percentage is going to college from each school. Interviews with the students may uncover information just as revealing as the students' test scores. This takes us to the primary responsibility of the education reporter.

School Financing. When the Miami school board found it was $27 million short in revenues for its $760 million budget, the board members agreed to approve larger classes for the coming school year.

With more students in classes, fewer teachers would be needed, and the board estimated a $9.7 million saving from the cut of 290 teachers.

In the Classroom

The education reporter's responsibility is to hold the school system accountable to parents and to the community. The United States has committed itself to an educational system that will turn out large numbers of people educated beyond the level that the country demanded only of its educated elite a century ago. How well is it doing this?

The best way to begin to find out is to visit the classroom, to look at what is happening day after day and to check these observations against test scores and the assessments of parents and educators. When Bob Frazier of the *Register-Guard* in Eugene, Ore., covered education he would fold his 6′4″ frame into a grade schooler's chair and sit in class. The stories he wrote were much more significant than any release from the superintendent's office.

School visits will tell the reporter whether the principal has a sense of mission and exerts strong leadership. They will reveal the professional level of teachers, whether they are given respect and give students respect and attention. The school environment is checked: Is the school safe? Is there a strong code of behavior, and are violators punished?

Other checks the education writer makes include an examination of the attendance rate. Is truancy increasing or declining? Records can be examined for the frequency, number and type of discipline problems and vandalism.

Does the high school have various tracks for its students, such as academic, vocational and general, and if so, what percentage of students is in each? In the early 1960s, one of 10 students nationally was in the general track; by 1980, the figure was more than four of 10. (The general track usually gives credit for physical and health education, work experience outside school, remedial English and mathematics and developmental courses such as training for adulthood and marriage.)

How much homework is being given? Educators agree that there is a relationship between good school performance and assigned homework. William Cohan's story for *The Raleigh Times* that half the state's students in the sixth and ninth grades do less than three hours of assigned homework a week was given banner play on page one.

In another story, Cohan interviewed teachers about their salaries. He began a two-part series with the economic problems of a fifth grade teacher:

This summer, as in years past, Betty White has sold sportswear at Hudson Belk for the minimum wage, earning about $135 a week. She will continue working there part-time in the fall after she resumes teaching fifth grade at North Ridge Elementary.

"Teachers are not paid enough money to do the kinds of things we would like to do for ourselves and our family," Mrs. White said in an interview. "Not extraordinary things, just things that help us get by."

Mrs. White is at the top of the teacher pay scale in Wake County. She earns $19,930 a year . . . .

The educational system has been passing through still another crisis, one brought about by social and economic factors affecting students and teachers. The majority of students in public schools in 23 of the 25 largest cities in the United States are minority-group youngsters. Some teachers are patronizing toward these children and expect less of them. One of the consequences is an illiteracy rate among minority children that is said to be higher than 40 percent.

Decline's Causes. A panel appointed by the College Board to study the decline in national test scores of high school seniors reported the following causes:

Expansion of electives and a decline in enrollments in academic courses.

Automatic promotion.

Homework cut in half, and not as demanding.

Grade inflation.

Textbooks for junior and senior classes written at the junior high school level.

Less thoughtful and critical reading demanded, and less careful writing asked of students.

The situation over the next decade will be even more strained, for the grade school–age population has been steadily growing. The new baby boom is different from the post-World War II population growth, reports *The Wall Street Journal:*

> . . . because of high black and Hispanic birth rates, heavy Hispanic immigration, the epidemic of teen-age pregnancies and the growth in female-headed families, the coming new schoolers will be more heavily than ever poor, minority children—particularly difficult to teach, discipline, keep from dropping out.

Remedial Courses

Education writers have localized national issues such as the expansion of remedial courses at the college level and the censorship of textbooks.

Community college or selective four-year college, remedial classes are proliferating. "There are a lot of people who aren't clear about what a sentence is when they arrive here," said Eugene R. Hammond, director of freshman English at the University of Maryland. John E. Roueche, of the University of Texas, has found about half the freshmen entering college are "poorly prepared" for college work. Eighty percent of all colleges offer remedial instruction, and most give credit toward graduation for such course work.

Should colleges raise their entrance requirements? If not, will they become what Michael R. Winston, vice president for academic affairs at Howard University, said Howard's college of liberal arts had become—"a basic skills development center"? This national dilemma—to accept the low-scoring high school graduate and offer remedial work or to turn the student down—can be localized.

Textbooks

Improvement. A group of educators who reviewed 31 of the most frequently used high school and junior high school history textbooks in 1986 concluded that the "dumbing down" of the books has eased up. The contents have improved by not avoiding "recognizable blemishes," although the treatment of Hispanics, Asians and American Indians is still inadequate.

In Texas, high school science textbooks gave scant space to the theory of evolution and skirted around naming one of the greatest scientists in history, Charles Darwin—the result of the strenuous work of a small-town couple. Because Texas adopts few textbooks in each subject, it orders large numbers of books, and this affects the textbook industry. Textbook publishers made their authors include creative science—a religious, not a scientific, theory—in biology and general science books. As a consequence, some states found it almost impossible to adopt science textbooks that did not distort the subject.

History textbooks have been blamed for ignoring or skimming over women, fascism, racism, the Holocaust, the Civil War and other topics that publishers have for some reason considered controversial.

The education writer, who sometimes considers himself or herself a consumer reporter in that coverage is devoted to determining the quality of the product, can also play the role of book reviewer. Textbooks should be examined every so often, especially during the adoption period.

Some of the issues education reporters find relevant: Key Issues

Survival of the public school system: Today, less than 30 percent of the population sends children to public schools; 20 years ago, it was 40 percent.

Teacher preparation: Every system admits to a shortage of quality instructors. Some systems want to use merit pay to stimulate good teaching. About 20 states give teachers examinations to test their competence. Some states found that many graduates of schools of education failed the tests.

Financing schools: The public seems unwilling to pay higher taxes that would raise teacher salaries, allow for smaller classes, build up libraries, laboratories and the physical plants. At the same time, the public is asking the schools to take on many roles—music and driver eduction, interscholastic sports activities, psychological and career counseling, breakfast and lunch programs, pre-kindergarten classes, after-school activities.

There are other issues the education reporter examines: integration of the schools and the teaching force, year-round schooling, drug use, racial tensions in the classroom and on school grounds, bilingualism, church-state confrontations, conflicts over the curriculum, the use of vouchers. These arouse passions and generate acrimony in the community. Intelligent reporting can aid in the resolution of some of them.

Most of these issues are argued and resolved, sometimes only temporarily, within a political context.

The conventional wisdom is that education is "above politics." The proof: The administration of the schools is separated from city government and placed in an independent board whose members are chosen without regard to party affiliation, usually in elections set apart from the partisan campaigning of the regular local election. Politics and Education

The truth is that education is inextricably bound up with politics. Politics enters the scene because, to put it simply, people differ in their notions of how youth should be trained, who should pay for it, who should control it. These differences are resolved in a political context. The conflict and its resolution should be at the heart of much of the reporter's coverage. The political debate runs from the White House to the local school board that meets in the little red schoolhouse.

To take one example, financing: Since the 1940s, the pattern of school financing has changed drastically, moving away from local sources to the states and the federal government. The local property tax can no longer sustain the schools. Fifty years ago, the local taxpayers provided 70 percent of the money for running the public schools. Today, the federal and state governments provide the majority of the funding.

The financing of the schools is made by politicians subject to the pressures of interest groups in a charged political atmosphere. Classic confrontations result—taxpayers anxious to hold down taxes versus teachers worried about salaries; state legislators and congressmen concerned over budget deficits facing up to the powerful teachers' unions and parents' organizations.

Making Eye Contact. A youngster is comfortable talking to someone at eye level rather than looking up, especially when the child is being asked a lot of questions. Beth Hughes of the San Francisco *Examiner* kneels to interview a little girl. Photo by Chris Hardy, San Francisco *Examiner*.

Visiting Elementary Schools

1. As soon as you enter a classroom, sit in a chair; better still, kneel so that you can talk to children comfortably and look them in the eye.
2. Let children come to you. Most children are shy, but almost all are curious. Letting them take the initiative will create a more natural atmosphere.
3. Don't patronize children. Children usually want to be taken seriously. Treat them like intelligent human beings and you will get the story you seek.

Rachel Theilheimer, who made these recommendations, says principals are often uncomfortable about allowing reporters into schools, fearing they might "get a bad impression." She suggests reporters ask the teacher to persaude the principal to allow a visit.

Although reporters tend to stress the financial conflicts, there are other issues just as important. Debate is intense among school and parent groups about the curriculum. The relationship of church and state, its roots deep in Western history, is always in tension. In many communities, the school system is a major source of jobs, and politicians seek to use it for patronage and to reward businessmen and merchants. In big cities, school authorities face serious problems integrating classes and schools. One solution—busing—has aroused intense feelings that are worked out in a political setting.

In the 1980s, conservative religious groups became politicized, and one of their targets was the public school. They sought to have prayer and instruction in creationism introduced into the school, and they opposed books, curriculums, even the showing of certain plays and movies. (In Hillsboro, Mo., a parents group fearing "secular humanism" protested the showing in school of the movie "Romeo and Juliet," and in Cobb County, Ga., the school superintendent circulated a memo to teachers that restricted classroom discussions of evolution, communism and other topics.)

In 1984, organizations such as the Moral Majority and the Pro-Family Forum succeeded in inserting the phrase "secular humanism" in an amendment to the Education for Economic Security Act. The act prohibits the use of federal magnet school funds for "any course of instruction the substance of which is secular humanism." The phrase, which has no formal definition, has become a rallying cry for those who feel that the school is anti-God, anti-family, even anti-American.

Ban. In 1985 there were 126 incidents of attempted censorship of books in 44 states.

School board meetings are often political battlegrounds where these issues are fought out. Here is a guide to covering board meetings.

Information to have in mind before meeting:

Checklist: Board of Education Meeting

____ Names of board members and areas they represent if elected by subdistricts.

____ Names of superintendent and top aides.

____ Number of students in district, geographical area it covers. Demographic data on school district, if relevant.

For story about meeting:

_____ Exact wording of actions taken.

_____ How each member voted. If there is no formal vote but an informal consensus, get nods of heads or any other signs of approval or disapproval. Ask if uncertain.

_____ The size and makeup of audience.

_____ Reaction of audience to proposal(s).

_____ Position of groups or organizations with a position on the issue. (Obtain beforehand if possible.)

_____ Arguments on all sides.

_____ Statements from those for and against proposal on what the decision of the board means.

Checklist: A New Educational Program

Many meetings of school boards are concerned with new programs. Here is a checklist of items for the reporter:

_____ Source of the idea.

_____ The superiority to the present program as claimed by sponsors.

_____ The cost and the source of funding the program.

_____ The basic philosophy or idea of the program.

_____ Other places it has been tried and the results there. (Make an independent check of this, if possible. How well is it working there; its cost.)

_____ Whether it has been tried before and discarded.

_____ How does it fit in with what the system is doing now. How it fits with trends in the area, state, nation.

_____ If someone is suggested to head it, who the person will be.

_____ Arguments pro and con, naming those involved.

Further Reading

Adrian, C. R., and C. Press. *Governing Urban America.* 5th ed. New York: McGraw-Hill, 1977.

Cremin, Lawrence A. *Transformation of the School: Progressivism in American Education.* New York: Random House, 1964.

Rosten, Leo. *The Washington Correspondents.* New York: Harcourt, Brace, 1937.

Sayre, Wallace S., and Herbert Kaufman. *Governing New York City.* New York: Norton, 1965.

Shefter, Martin. *Political Crisis/Fiscal Crisis: The Collapse and Revival of New York City.* New York: Basic Books, 1985.

Wildavsky, Aaron. *The Politics of the Budgetary Process.* 2nd ed. Boston: Little, Brown, 1974.

PART SIX

Risks and Responsibilities

Photo by John Harte, *The Bakersfield Californian*.

CHAPTER TWENTY-FIVE

Reporters and the Law

Preview

The laws of libel and privacy limit what reporters may write. Stories that damage a person's reputation can be libelous, unless the material is privileged or can be proved to be true. Stories about an individual's personal life can invade the person's right to privacy.

• Libel—Most libelous stories are the result of careless reporting. All material that might injure someone should be double-checked. The courts protect journalists who libel public figures or public officials; but recent court decisions have limited these exceptions.
• Privacy—The right to privacy is protected by law. The personal activities of an individual can be reported if the written material is about a newsworthy person and is not highly offensive.

O ne of the most dangerous areas for the journalist is libel. To the beginner, the region is a land of mystery in which all the guideposts read *Don't*. To the experienced reporter, it is a cautionary presence in the newsroom.

Broadly speaking, libel is published defamation of character. That is, it is writing or a picture that exposes a person to hatred, shame, disgrace, contempt or ridicule, or that injures his reputation or causes him to be shunned or avoided, or that has a tendency to injure him in his occupation.

Of course, many articles and pictures do libel individuals. In most cases, the defamatory material may be safe for publication if it is privileged. By this we mean that the article is a fair and accurate report of a judicial, legislative, or other public official proceeding, or of anything said in the course of such sessions, trials or proceedings. The contents of most public records are privileged. Those who made our laws recognized that open debate of serious issues would be impeded unless the public had full access to official actions.

Another defense against libel is truth. No matter how serious the defamation may be, if the statement can be proved to be true and to have been made without malice, the defamed individual cannot successfully bring legal action.

A third defense, fair comment and criticism, most often involves the writing of editorial writers and reviewers. So long as the comment or criticism is directed at the work and not at the individual, the writing is safe.

In summary, the libel laws hold that a reporter is not in danger if the material is from a privileged proceeding (public *and* official) or if the material is substantially accurate or constitutes fair comment.

For broadcast journalists, defamatory statements made from a prepared script fall under libel, whereas extemporaneous defamatory remarks are treated as slander, which can be defined as oral or uttered defamation.

Grounds for Libel Suits

Matter that might be held libelous by a court would have to:

1. Imply commission of a crime.
2. Tend to injure a person in his or her profession or job.
3. Imply a person has a disease, usually a loathsome disease that might lead to the individual's ostracism.
4. Damage a person's credit.
5. Imply a lack of chastity.
6. Indicate a lack of mental capacity.
7. Incite public ridicule or contempt.

For years, libel was a great weight on the shoulders of the press, particularly for newspapers that handled controversy and emphasized investigative reporting. The press associations had special concerns, for libel law was state law and was beyond the protection of the Constitution. What was legal in one state might have been libelous in another.

In effect, libel laws restrained the press, as the Supreme Court recognized in an epochal decision in 1964 that was to lighten the burden on the press. The court ruled that defamatory statements could have First Amendment protection. Our seven danger points are still to be watched, but the press now has much stronger defenses, thanks to the Supreme Court. To understand that decision—and to understand the organic nature of the law—we must travel back in time to Montgomery, Ala.

An Incident on a Bus

When Mrs. Rosa Parks boarded the Cleveland Avenue bus in December 1955, she spotted an empty seat toward the rear, just behind the section reserved for whites. Tired from a day's work in a downtown department store, she eased into the space, only to be ordered to move. Seats were needed for white passengers.

Mrs. Parks, a quiet, reserved woman, refused to give up her seat. She was taken off the bus and arrested. That weekend, plans were made by the black community to boycott Montgomery's buses.

Martin Luther King Jr., a black minister who helped plan the boycott, recalled how he awoke early Monday morning to see whether Montgomery's black residents would heed the word that it was better to walk in dignity than to ride in shame. The bus line that passed by the King home carried more blacks than any other line in the city. The first bus went by at 6 a.m. It was empty. Another, 15 minutes later, was empty, too.

That was the beginning of the boycott. Some 42,000 Montgomery blacks said they would walk to and from work or use volunteer vehicles and black-owned taxis until the bus system altered its seating arrangements and hired black drivers for buses along the predominantly black routes.

For 381 days they stayed off the buses rather than be told to move to the back. Many persons went to jail for violating the state's anti-boycott laws, including Mrs. Parks and Dr. King. Finally, the Supreme Court ruled bus segregation illegal.

Tension Mounts

To some blacks, the action of Mrs. Parks and others was more significant than the decision of the Supreme Court the year before that prohibited the segregation of public schools, for in Montgomery blacks had brought about change by themselves. This effort accelerated the mass movement of non-violent resistance to discrimination among blacks. It was to develop slowly in the 1950s and to spread in the early 1960s in marches, lunchroom sit-ins, Freedom Rides and picketing throughout the South, in which some communities openly defied the 1954 school desegregation ruling.

Tensions mounted. In 1963, Medgar Evers, a black civil rights worker, was murdered in the doorway of his home in Jackson, Miss. The following year, three young civil rights workers were murdered in Philadelphia, Miss.

Newspapers and television stations sent waves of reporters to the South to report the conflict. Viewers saw fire hoses, police dogs and cattle prods used on blacks in Birmingham, and they saw the clubs of state troopers in Selma. The press reported the cry of blacks for an end to humiliation, economic exploitation, segregation in schools and discrimination at the polls.

It was also obvious the South was hardly budging. The border areas, yes. Portions of Tennessee and Kentucky, and metropolitan communities like Atlanta and Richmond accommodated. But not the towns and parishes of the Black Belt—Selma, Plaquemines, Yazoo City. Here, non-violence met intractable resistance. Blacks might wait patiently outside the courthouse in Selma to register to vote. But the doors would stay closed to them, unless they were broken down by the federal government and the courts.

Press Coverage Increases

Because of the intensive coverage in the press, a consensus was developing outside the Black Belt. Most of the nation saw the anguish of the blacks who were hurling themselves against the wall of segregation, and some believed the nation was heading toward a race war.

In 1963, President Kennedy, aware of the developing conflict, declared that the struggle of blacks for civil rights was a "moral issue." Then four girls attending Sunday school in the black Sixteenth Street Baptist Church in Birmingham died in a bomb blast at the church.

The press stepped up its coverage. In some northern newspapers and on network television, the South was presented as a forbidding region of racism, its law officers openly defiant of the law, its white citizens unwilling to adjust to the changing times. Southerners were dismayed by the coverage, and some whites assaulted reporters covering civil rights demonstrations. The retaliation also took the form of suits against the press and television.

A Legal Club

Millions of dollars in damages were being claimed by officials, who asserted they had been defamed by press and television. By 1964, libel suits seeking $300 million in damages were pending against news organizations covering the racial story. One of the largest suits was brought against *The New York Times* by five officials in Alabama who contended that they had been inferentially damaged in an advertisement in the *Times* in 1960 that sought to raise funds for the civil rights movement. The advertisement, headlined "Heed Their Rising Voices," attacked the treatment of blacks in the South. The five officials brought suit for a total of $3 million.

The first case to be tried involved L. B. Sullivan, a Montgomery city commissioner responsible for the police department. At the trial, it was evident that the advertisement contained errors and exaggerations. An Alabama state court jury awarded Sullivan the $500,000 he had sought from the *Times,* although the advertisement had not named him but had made erroneous statements about the Birmingham police.

In a headline over the story about the suits against the *Times,* a Montgomery newspaper seemed to reveal the motives behind the libel suits: "State Finds Formidable Legal Club to Swing at Out-of-State Press."

The Court Acts

It was in this atmosphere that the Supreme Court considered the appeal of the *Times* from the state court decision. The case of *The New York Times v. Sullivan* (376 US 254) in 1964 was to mark a major change in the libel laws. But more important, by granting the press wider latitude in covering and commenting on the actions of public officials, the decision gave the press greater freedom to present issues of public concern, like the racial conflict that was tearing the country apart.

The Supreme Court realized the unique nature of the appeal. The Court commented: "We are required for the first time in this case to determine the extent to which the Constitutional protections for speech and press limit a state's power to award damages in a libel action brought by a public official against the critics of his official conduct."

Politic Action. The Sullivan case, like the school desegregation case 10 years before and the Nixon tapes decision 10 years later, reflected the need for a unanimous court decision in order to show the nation that certain issues were beyond debate.

The Sullivan decision supported a searching, vigorous and free press; *Brown v. Board of Education, Topeka* said the 14th Amendment guaranteeing equal protection under the laws made school segregation unconstitutional.

The Watergate tape decision came at a time the president was under grave suspicion and a crisis of leadership threatened the nation. The decision, said an editorial writer for *The New York Times*, "ultimately drove Richard Nixon from the White House" because it allowed the special prosecutor to gather evidence of Nixon's culpability in covering up the break-in.

"Throughout history," said the *Times* writer, "the Court has been a vital factor on the political scene, even when trying to float majestically above it."

No Absolute Immunity. Justices Hugo Black and Arthur Goldberg wrote concurring opinions in *Sullivan* but disagreed with the concept of actual malice. Justice William O. Douglas joined them in their concern. Justice Black wrote: "The requirement that malice be proved provides at best an evanescent protection for the right critically to discuss public affairs and certainly does not measure up to the sturdy safeguard embodied in the First Amendment." Black said he read the Constitution as "granting the press an absolute immunity for criticism of the way public officials do their duty." Black's views have never commanded a majority of the Supreme Court.

In its decision, the Supreme Court took from the states their power to award damages for libel "in actions brought by public officials against critics of their official conduct." The Constitutional protections for free speech and free press would be seriously limited by state actions of the kind the Alabama court took, the Court said.

Justice William J. Brennan wrote: "The Constitutional guarantees require, we think, a federal rule that prohibits a public official from recovering damages for a defamatory falsehood relating to his official conduct unless he proves that the statement was made with 'actual malice'—that is, with knowledge that it was false or with reckless disregard to whether it was false or not."

The Court apparently agreed with the argument of Herbert F. Wechsler, who wrote in a brief for the *Times:* "This is not a time—there never was a time—when it would serve the values enshrined in the Constitution to force the press to curtail its attention to the tensest issues that confront the country or to forgo the dissemination of its publications in the areas where tension is extreme."

Justice Brennan noted in his opinion that the Supreme Court had seen in the use of such legal concepts as "insurrection," "contempt," "breach of the peace," "obscenity," and "solicitation of legal business," attempts to suppress the open discussion of public issues. Now it was libel.

In the Sullivan libel case, the Court extended the First Amendment in order to accomplish a social-political purpose: The protection of dissident voices in a repressive atmosphere.

The decision, establishing what became known as the Times Doctrine, noted that the "Constitutional safeguard was fashioned to assure unfettered interchange of ideas for the bringing about of political and social changes desired by the people." To accomplish this, there must be "maintenance of the opportunity for free political discussion to the end that government may be responsive to the will of the people and that changes may be obtained by lawful means, an opportunity essential to the security of the Republic. . . .

"Erroneous statement is inevitable in free debate," Brennan said. Running through the decision is the belief that free discussion will lead to a peaceful settlement of issues. Free expression, he was saying, has social utility. The Court seemed to be addressing itself to the millions of Americans in trauma because of the racial conflict.

In summary, the decision in the case makes it clear that under the Constitution no public official can recover damages for defamation in a newspaper article or "editorial advertisement" concerning his or her official conduct unless he can prove the article is defamatory and false and also show that:

1. The publication was made with the knowledge that it was false; or
2. The statement was made with reckless disregard of whether it was false.

Items 1 and 2 constitute the Court's concept of "actual malice."

The decision is the law in every state and takes precedence over federal and state laws, state constitutions and all previous state and federal court decisions.

In the decade following the enunciation of the Times Doctrine, the Court went beyond applying it to public officials and included public figures, then private individuals involved in matters of public concern. In a significant case, a businessman lost a libel suit that involved a clear case of error by a radio station.

A distributor of nudist magazines was arrested while delivering the magazine to a newsstand. The Philadelphia, Pa., police reported the incident to a local radio station, which broadcast an item about the distributor's arrest on a charge of selling obscene materials. Further, the station stated that the magazines were obscene. In a subsequent trial, the distributor was acquitted. The distributor said he had been defamed by the radio station and sued. A jury awarded him general and punitive damages.

The radio newsman had violated one of the first rules a beginner learns: Never state as fact what is only charged and therefore subject to determination in the courts.

However, the reporter and his station were fortunate. The Court of Appeals reversed the lower court verdict, and in 1971 the Supreme Court upheld the reversal on the distributor's appeal (*Rosenbloom v. Metromedia, Inc.*, 403 US 29). The Court ruled:

> We thus hold that a libel action, as here by a private individual against a licensed radio station for a defamatory falsehood in a newcast relating to his involvement in an event of public or general concern may be sustained only upon clear and convincing proof that the defamatory falsehood was published with knowledge that it was false or with reckless disregard of whether it was false or not.
>
> Calculated falsehood, of course, falls outside the "fruitful exercise of the right of free speech."

Rosenbloom was neither public official nor public figure. But he was involved in an event of "public or general concern," and ordinary citizens so involved can successfully bring a libel action only by a showing of actual malice, the Court stated.

Rosenbloom might have been luckier had his troubles occurred later, for the Supreme Court in 1974 reversed directions and did so again in 1976 and 1979. The rulings significantly narrowed the category of "public figure." By doing this, the Court made it possible for many more libel plaintiffs to collect damages for defamatory falsehoods, since for private citizens the proof of defamation may be negligence or carelessness, not the actual malice necessary for public figures to prove.

Extension and Contraction of Times Doctrine

A Change in Directions

In the 1974 case of *Gertz v. Robert Welch, Inc.,* (418 US 323) the Supreme Court suddenly ceased the steady expansion of First Amendment protection to publications in libel actions. Elmer Gertz, a civil rights lawyer in Chicago, had been defamed by *American Opinion,* a monthly magazine published by the John Birch Society. The magazine described Gertz as a "Communist-fronter" and said he had designed a national campaign to discredit the police. Although the trial judge had found no evidence the magazine had published recklessly, a jury awarded Gertz $50,000. The magazine appealed.

The Supreme Court ruled that as a private citizen Gertz did not have to show "actual malice" but was entitled to damages if he could prove the material was false and defamatory and that it had been the result of negligence or carelessness by the publication. The Court returned to an emphasis on the plaintiff's status rather than the subject matter.

In 1976, the Court altered slightly the definition of a "public figure" in a case involving *Time* magazine, which had appealed a Florida court decision awarding $100,000 in damages in a libel suit brought by Mary Alice Firestone. *Time* had incorrectly reported the grounds on which Mrs. Firestone's husband had been granted a divorce. *Time* contended Mrs. Firestone was a public figure, which would have required her to submit proof of "actual malice" by *Time.* Mrs. Firestone had not submitted such proof. But the Court ruled that although Mrs. Firestone was a well-known socialite she "didn't assume any role of especial prominence in the affairs of society. . . ."(409 US 875).

In 1979, the Court further constricted the definition of a public figure. The cases, decided 8 to 1, were *Hutchinson v. Proxmire,* (443 US 111), and *Wolston v. Reader's Digest Assn., Inc.,* (443 US 157). The Court said there are two kinds of public figures: "A small group of individuals" who occupy positions of "persuasive power and influence" and people who have "thrust themselves to the forefront of particular public controversies in order to influence the resolution of the issues involved" and have, therefore, become public figures for the limited purpose of comment on their connection with these controversies.

In *Hutchinson,* the Court ruled against Sen. William Proxmire, who, in bestowing one of his Golden Fleece awards, had belittled a project by Ronald R. Hutchinson, a scientist who had used monkeys in an effort to find an objective measure of aggression. Several of the federal agencies that had granted Hutchinson $500,000 were cited by Proxmire as wasting public money. Hutchinson brought a libel action against Proxmire, seeking $8 million for mental anguish and loss of income. A lower federal court ruled against Hutchinson in two areas. It said that by soliciting and receiving federal grants Hutchinson had become a public figure and that Proxmire had legislative immunity.

The Supreme Court rejected the defense contention that Hutchinson was a public figure. The Court said that the scientist "did not have the regular and continuing access to the media that is one of the accoutrements of having become a public figure." As for Proxmire's immunity, the Court said that the

Footnote. In an important footnote to *Hutchinson,* Chief Justice Warren Burger wrote that "proof of actual malice calls a defendant's state of mind into question. . . ." This became the central issue in *Herbert v. Lando* (441 US 153). (See page 580.)

Golden Fleece award was made known by the senator's newsletter and press releases, and these do not enjoy the same protection as words on the Senate floor. The court rejected the assertions of House and Senate leaders that Proxmire's public relations activities were part of the "informing function" of Congress. Proxmire settled out of court with a payment of $10,000 to Hutchinson.

In the other 1979 case, Ilya Wolston contended he was libeled by *Reader's Digest* when it falsely listed him in a book as being a Soviet agent. The book used an erroneous FBI document as its source. In 1958, Wolston had failed to appear before a grand jury investigating a spy ring. He later pleaded guilty to contempt and was given a suspended sentence.

The Wolston situation attracted considerable attention, but the Court ruled that Wolston did not "voluntarily thrust" or inject himself into the controversy over the inquiry. "It would be more accurate to say that Wolston was dragged unwillingly into the controversy," Justice William H. Rehnquist wrote.

"A private individual is not automatically transformed into a public figure just by becoming involved in or associated with a matter that attracts attention," the justice wrote. A person who engages in criminal conduct does not automatically become a public figure. "To hold otherwise would create an 'open season' for all who sought to defame persons convicted of a crime," Rehnquist said.

Suspects and Defendants— Not Public Figures

Bruce W. Sanford, a libel lawyer, described Rehnquist's remarks as "unbelievable language. Reporters and editors don't go hunting for people (least of all criminals) to defame." The Court, he said, had made a "startling" ruling by rejecting—here Sanford quotes the Court—the "contention that any person who engages in criminal conduct automatically becomes a public figure for purposes of comment on a limited range of issues relating to his conviction." This is a significant shift in the Court's views since *Rosenbloom*. Sanford states the decision means the criminal suspect or defendant "now will probably not be classifiable as a public figure."

Richard Schmidt, general counsel of the American Society of Newspaper Editors, found in a footnote in *Hutchinson* a remark by Chief Justice Warren E. Burger that would "throw out the window" summary judgments in libel cases and force them to go to trial before "juries which will stick it to the press if they can."

In another footnote, Chief Justice Burger notes that the category of public official "cannot be thought to include all public employees, however." Sanford said that this footnote on public officials "undercuts the public official test and with it the whole rationale underlying the Court's own finding in *The New York Times*—that the press should be allowed to encourage robust debate about public affairs."

Since most journalism is concerned with the activities of officials and public figures, the Court's definitions of such persons made reporters cautious in their assumptions about the law.

Summary Judgments. In 1986, the Supreme Court addressed Schmidt's concern by ruling that libel suits filed by public officials and public figures in federal courts must be dismissed before trial unless the evidence indicates they can prove libel with "convincing clarity." This ruling, in a case involving a suit by Liberty Lobby Inc. against Jack Anderson, saves newspapers costly trials.

In order to defeat a pretrial defense motion for a summary judgment, the Court ruled, the plaintiff's evidence must meet the same "clear and convincing" standard that would apply at the trial stage.

Courts Differ

The Washington Post escaped a libel judgment when a federal district court ruled a police informant was a public figure and had to prove actual malice. The *Post* had incorrectly stated the informant was a drug user. But three months later a federal judge in Maryland ruled that a police informant was a private individual and thus need only prove that the Baltimore *News-American* was careless in mistakenly stating he had broken into a lawyer's office to steal documents for the police.

In state courts, a Kansas judge ruled that a lawyer appointed to defend a penniless criminal defendant was a public official. Two months later, a Michigan judge said that an attorney appointed to represent an impoverished defendant was neither public figure nor public official.

Caution: Events that are the subject of gossip or public curiosity and have no significant relation to public affairs usually do not confer on the persons involved in them the status of public figures. This means that no matter how public a person's marriage rift may be that person is not therefore a public figure. Nor does the usual kind of crime or violence confer on the person involved the status of public figure.

If the reporter can prove that an event relates to public affairs or an important social issue, then the persons involved may be classified as public figures. For example: If a physician or a lawyer injects himself or herself into a controversy over a local bond issue, then the person has made himself or herself a public figure for news about the bonds, but not about his or her personal life.

Repeating a Libel

In a story about neighborhood politics, a student newspaper reporter wrote and the newspaper printed the paragraph:

A member of Board 9, who asked not to be identified, charged that Lawrence and Fine were involved in a kickback scheme in which the district manager, who is the board's paid administrator, pushed along projects beneficial to Chevra in return for an unspecified kickback.

Asked if he knew that the allegation about kickbacks is clearly libelous since accepting a kickback is a crime, the student replied, "But I attributed it." His instructor could only shrug in exasperation. A reporter can be held liable if he or she repeats a libelous statement or quotes someone making such a statement unless the original material is privileged.

However, if the assertion is made in court or at an official meeting the statement—even if untrue—would be privileged and the privilege would be a defense against claims for damages.

Conditional and Absolute Privilege

The privilege to those participating in court cases and legislative sessions is an "absolute privilege," meaning the participants—the judge, lawyers, witnesses—cannot be held legally accountable even for malicious and deliberately false statements that are made within the scope of their participation in the proceedings. A newspaper or station, however, cannot use absolute privilege as a defense in libel suits. Their protection is known as "conditional" or "qualified privilege." The newspaper must present full, fair and accurate reports that are free of actual malice to be granted privilege.

A candidate for re-election to Congress who says of his opponent, "That man is a swindler" on the floor of the House of Representatives can make the statement with impunity, and a reporter can publish the accusation. (Obviously, the reporter would also carry the accused's reply.) But should the congressman make the charge in a political rally and the reporter's newspaper print the allegation, both are in trouble, unless the reporter can prove the man is indeed a swindler, and this would require proof of the man's conviction on that charge.

Warning: These protections do not cover proceedings, meetings, or activities that are private in nature. The news story must deal with a judicial, legislative or other official proceeding. Also, they do not cover records that are sealed by law or court order.

Dangerous Words

Swindler is just one of many words that alert the careful reporter to the possibilities of libel. Any word that is associated with the seven danger areas listed at the outset of this chapter is carefully examined to see that it is (1) privileged or (2) provably true, by which we mean that a document (not someone's assertion) supports the charge. Here are some dangerous words in the danger areas on the list, "Grounds for Libel Suits" at the beginning of this chapter.

1. Thief, loan shark, shoplifter, gangster—implies commission of a crime.
2. Incompetent, failure, quack, shyster, slick operator—injures a person in his or her profession.
3. Wino, leper, has VD, AIDS—implies a loathsome disease.
4. Unreliable, bankrupt, gambler, failure—damages a person's credit.
5. Loose, seducer, B-girl, stud, immoral, mistress, hooker, streetwalker—implies a lack of chastity.

6. Screwy, nutty, incompetent, strange, out-of-it—indicates a lack of mental capacity.

7. Phony, coward, hypocrite—incites public ridicule or contempt.

The danger is not avoided by preceding these words, or others like them, with the words *alleged* or *reported*.

Some federal courts have adopted the concept of "neutral reporting," which allows a newspaper to report a defamatory charge—in effect to repeat it—if the charge is made by a responsible organization and is accurately reported. The concept emerged in *Edwards v. National Audubon Society* [556F. 2d 113(1977)] in which *The New York Times* was sued by three scientists whom a Society spokesman accused of misusing bird counts to suggest that DDT did not harm birds. The Second Circuit Court of Appeals ruled unanimously that the "First Amendment protects the accurate and disinterested reporting" of charges "regardless of the reporter's private views of their validity." The Supreme Court refused to review the case.

**Time Copy
Not Exempt**

The Supreme Court has been generous to reporters who make mistakes under pressure of deadline. But reporters who have time to check material may not fare so well under the Court's distinction between "hot news" and "time copy." The differences were spelled out in two companion cases decided in 1967, *Curtis Publishing Co. v. Butts* and *Associated Press v. Walker* (both 388 US 130), involving public figures.

Edwin Walker was a former Army general who had become involved in the civil rights disputes in the South and had taken a position against desegregation. He was on the campus of the University of Mississippi in September 1962 when it erupted over the enrollment of James Meredith, a black student.

The AP moved a story that Walker had taken command of a violent crowd and had personally led a charge against federal marshals on the campus. The AP said Walker had encouraged rioters to use violence and had instructed white students how to combat the effects of tear gas. He sued for $800,000 in damages. Walker testified that he had counseled restraint and peaceful protest and had not charged the marshals. The jury believed his account and awarded him the sum he sought. The trial judge cut out the $300,000 in punitive damages because he found no actual malice in the AP account.

Wally Butts was the athletic director of the University of Georgia in 1962. He was employed by the Georgia Athletic Association, a private corporation, and so, like Walker, he was a private citizen when, according to *The Saturday Evening Post,* he conspired to fix a football game between Georgia and Alabama in 1962. An article in the magazine said an Atlanta insurance salesman had overheard a conversation between Butts and Bear Bryant, coach of the Alabama football team, in which Butts outlined Georgia's offensive strategy in the coming game and advised Bryant about defending against the plays.

Fight Back. Newspapers are countersuing lawyers for court costs and legal fees when they bring losing libel suits. Papers in Florida and West Virginia have won such suits by claiming they had no merit but were brought to throttle criticism.

Butts sued for $5 million in compensatory damages and $5 million in punitive damages. The jury awarded him $60,000 on the first charge and $3 million on the second, which was subsequently reduced to $460,000.

The Curtis Publishing Co., publishers of *The Saturday Evening Post,* and the AP appealed to the Supreme Court. Butts won his appeal, but Walker lost. The Court ruled that the evidence showed that the Butts story was not "hot news," but that the Walker story was. The *Post*'s editors, the Court stated, "recognized the need for a thorough investigation of the serious charges" but failed to make the investigation.

In the Walker case, the Court noted: "In contrast to the Butts article, the dispatch which concerns us in *Walker* was news which required immediate dissemination. . . . Considering the necessity for rapid dissemination, nothing in this series of events gives the slightest hint of a severe departure from publishing standards. We therefore conclude that Walker should not be entitled to damages from the Associated Press."

In its opinion in the Butts case, the Court said that stories involving investigation and research require greater care and attention than spot news. In a ruling that bears on the work of the investigative reporter, the Court found *The Saturday Evening Post* had sought to expose Butts, which required considerable care.

Oily Waters

One of the most ominous libel rulings of the 1980s was the decision of a three-judge panel of the United States Court of Appeals for the District of Columbia Circuit against *The Washington Post,* which had been sued for libel by the president of the Mobil Oil Corporation. In affirming the district court ruling against the *Post,* the panel by a 2–1 vote held that a newspaper's emphasis on "hard-hitting investigative stories" could, with other evidence, support the inference that the newspaper was inclined to publish reckless falsehoods.

Judge J. Skelly Wright, who dissented, found the majority to have revised libel laws by counting as an element of actual malice a newspaper's reputation for investigative journalism. He wrote that the majority "appears to criticize what it takes to be the general climate in journalism today" and to show a "deep hostility to an aggressive press."

The *Columbia Journalism Review* said of the opinion that it is "not that the judges were ignorant of investigative journalism, but that they knew what it was, did not care for it, and were looking for ways to circumscribe it." The majority judges, the *Review* continued, "appeared to evince the fear and loathing that investigative journalism has aroused in the years since Watergate." The ruling is not only a "disturbing departure in libel law," the magazine said, "but also a ratification of the political agenda that would undermine freedom by setting up the press as a disloyal opposition and a target for chastisement and restriction."

Libel Insurance. Newspapers are covered by libel insurance policies, but as the result of the number and the cost of suits in the last few years premiums have escalated and the companies have set large deductibles. Also, some insurance companies set limits on the damages they will cover, and some firms will not guarantee payments for punitive damages.

All Speech Not Equal

In another decision that worried some journalists, the Supreme Court in 1985 ruled that punitive damages can be awarded without the plaintiff's proving actual malice if the libelous material is not a matter of "public concern." The case, decided in 1985 by a vote of 5–4, arose from an erroneous credit report by Dun & Bradstreet about a firm, Greenmoss Builders. The court let stand a $300,000 award for punitive damages.

"We have long recognized that not all speech is of equal First Amendment importance," wrote Justice Lewis E. Powell in his opinion. "It is speech on 'matters of public concern' that is 'at the heart of the First Amendment's protection.' . . . Speech on matters of purely private concern is of less First Amendment concern."

The court did not define "public concern," and this worried journalists and their lawyers, who were also concerned by the court's decision not to apply what is known as the Gertz rule, which prohibits the award of punitive damages when there is no showing of actual malice. The court said the Gertz rule does not apply on matters of non-public concern.

The Consequences

A study by the Libel Defense Resource Center of 63 trials held between 1982 and 1984 found that papers and stations lost more than half (54 percent) of libel cases that went to trial and that the average initial award to the defendant was $2 million. In post-trial rulings, the study found that the media do well. On appeal, 68 percent of judgments adverse to the media were reversed, and most of the large awards were reduced.

But the cost of defending these cases can be high, which has led many newspapers and stations to settle out of court. The average cost of a libel trial is $150,000. Henry R. Kaufman, general counsel to the libel center, said that because judges have failed to dismiss "meritless libel claims" prior to trial "additional and concerted efforts for legal reform must be pursued."

The standards developed in the Times Doctrine have been weakened so that they "no longer provide any meaningful protection to the media in a defamation action," said Irving R. Kaufman, of the U.S. Court of Appeals for the Second District, who is considered a First Amendment absolutist. The reason, he said, is that juries do not understand the complexities of the doctrine. They are, he said, "lost upon even the most conscientious jury."

CBS and Time

Following massacres of Palestinians in Beirut in 1982, *Time* magazine reported that Gen. Ariel Sharon of Israel had encouraged the killings. Sharon sued for $50 million. The case reached the court in 1984 and was decided in 1985.

In his instructions to the jury, Federal District Court Judge Abraham D. Sofaer said that under the Sullivan Rule for public figures three conditions would have to be met:

1. The material was defamatory.
2. The material was false.

3. The material was published with actual malice; the publication knew that the charge was false or had serious doubts about its truth but printed it anyway; the publication of the material was reckless or deceitful.

The jurors found *Time* had defamed Sharon and that the charge it made was false. The reporter, the jury said, acted negligently and carelessly. But it said that *Time* had met the third test for protection under the Sullivan Rule—it had not acted with actual malice.

The legal fees to Sharon and *Time* amounted to $3 million.

In another protracted and highly publicized libel trial, Gen. William C. Westmoreland, who had sued CBS for $120 million, called it quits after 18 weeks of the trial. Westmoreland, U.S. troop commander in Vietnam from 1964 to 1968, said he was libeled by CBS's assertion that his command had underreported enemy strength in a conspiracy to withhold information that might have caused the public to call for an end to the war. The suit cost both sides a total of $2 million.

Westmoreland said later:

> The chilling effect of a libel suit on journalistic enterprise is a valid concern. . . . The route of the libel suit is not good, either for the plaintiff or defendant. In many cases, the legal costs alone are prohibitive. . . . The rules of evidence, the legalisms of the court system, do not promote open and free debate.

Just what has been the effect of the growing number of libel suits and their cost?

Michael Massing, author of an excellent summary of the libel situation, "The Libel Chill: How Cold *Is* It Out There?," in the May/June 1985 *Columbia Journalism Review,* found that "a chill has indeed set in." He interviewed 150 reporters, editors and media lawyers, and he concluded that journalists are aware that danger lurks behind every critical word in a story. Officials are using the apparent willingness of juries to punish the press to file what seem to most observers to be frivolous suits. The consequence, Massing says, is intimidation and harassment.

To Lyle Denniston, the Supreme Court reporter for *The Sun* of Baltimore, the Supreme Court has changed from a "strong pro-press majority" to a "new, conservative, and often unsympathetic majority." In the decade after the Brennan decision establishing the Times Doctrine, he said, the "press lost more of the *Sullivan* protections against libel, found that the right of access to courts was not as complete as it had hoped, discovered that the right of access would not be expanded readily to other parts of government, learned anew that broadcasting would remain a Constitutional stepchild, and saw the recently revived right of commercial speech seriously threatened."

That's Half a Billion. Dr. Elliot Gross, chief New York City medical examiner and the subject of a *New York Times* series documenting allegations of mishandling autopsies, has filed a $512 million libel suit against the newspaper.
—*Editor & Publisher*

The Chill

Some Warmth. Despite the setbacks, the press has far greater protection from libel suits now than it did before the Sullivan case. There has been steady progress from the days when a plaintiff could win a libel suit simply by proving that a statement damaged his reputation, the common law the United States inherited from England.

Gradually, the courts began to recognize truth as a defense. But the defendant was required to prove the truth of the material. Following the Sullivan ruling, public figures have had the burden of proving that statements about them are damaging, false and made with actual malice.

Burden. Private figures also carry the burden of proof, but they need only show that the defendant acted negligently or carelessly; they do not have to prove actual malice. To win punitive damages, however, private figures must prove actual malice if the matter is "of public concern."

Denniston, whose comments appeared in "The Law Giveth, the Law Taketh Away," *The Quill,* November 1984, said that the one victory in the period, *Bose v. Consumers Union* (466 US 485), 1984, confirmed prevailing doctrine. *Bose* was the first libel case won by the press before the Supreme Court in a decade. By a 6–3 vote, the Court ruled that the consumer publication could not be found to have libelled Bose when the magazine contended that the company's speakers were inferior, whatever the actual quality of the speakers, because the assessment was not published with reckless disregard of its truth or falsity.

Privacy

Constitutional. Privacy is not protected by the U.S. Constitution, but 10 states do list the right to privacy: Alaska, Arizona, California, Florida, Hawaii, Illinois, Louisiana, Montana, South Carolina and Washington. Several states have laws protecting privacy.

While truth is the strongest defense against libel, it is the basis of invasion of privacy suits. Invasion of privacy is said to occur when an individual is exposed to public view and suffers mental distress as a consequence of the publicity. Unlike defamation, which has deep roots in the common law, the right to privacy is a fairly new legal development, and one in which there is even less certainty for the reporter than in the area of libel.

The balance must be struck by the courts between the public's right to know—a right commonly accepted though not in the Constitution—and the individual's right to privacy.

Three categories of privacy concern the reporter:

1. Publicity that places a person in a false light in the public eye. The Times Doctrine applies, provided the matter is of public interest.

2. Public disclosure of embarrassing private facts about an individual. If the facts are in an official document, they can be published, but not if they are private acts of no legitimate concern to the public.

3. Intrusion by the journalist into a private area for a story or a picture without permission—eavesdropping or trespassing. The use of electronic devices to invade a home or office is illegal. Newsworthiness is not a defense.

Except for intrusion, the newsworthiness of the event is a defense against invasion of privacy suits. A public event cannot have privacy grafted on it at the behest of the participants. However, the reporter cannot invade a person's home or office to seek out news and make public what is private. Nor can he or she misrepresent the purpose of reporting to gain access to home or office. There is no prohibition against following and watching a person in a public place, but the reporter cannot harass an individual.

Privacy Forfeited. Three persons who were pictured in scanty costumes at the San Francisco Erotic Ball by *Penthouse* magazine lost their $10 million privacy suit when the California Court of Appeals ruled that they had surrendered their right to privacy because the ball was open to thousands of people and was covered by the media.

Although the law of libel and the right of privacy are closely related, they involve distinctive legal principles and are fundamentally different. Libel law is designed to protect a person's character and reputation. The right of privacy protects a person's peace of mind, his or her feelings, spirits and sensibilities. Generally, privacy guarantees an individual freedom from the unwarranted and unauthorized public exposure of the person or his affairs in which the public has no legitimate interest.

The right of privacy is the right of the person to be let alone unless he or she waives or relinquishes that right, the UPI tells its reporters. Certain persons, defined by the federal courts as "newsworthy," lose their right to privacy, but the material published about that person cannot be "highly offensive."

In making rulings on the claim of invasion of privacy, the Supreme Court has applied the Times Doctrine. That is, even when the claimant can prove that the report was false, if it were a matter of public interest the person bringing the action would have to show the error was made "with knowledge of its falsity or in reckless disregard of the truth."

"Calculated Falsehoods"

In one case, decided in 1974 by the Supreme Court, such disregard of the truth was proved by a claimant. The Court in *Cantrell v. Forest City Publishing Co.* (419 US 245) upheld a $60,000 award against *The* Cleveland *Plain Dealer* on the ground that a reporter's story about a visit to the home of the claimant "contained significant misrepresentations." Although the woman was not at home when the reporter visited, the article said she "will talk neither about what happened nor about how they were doing. . . ." He wrote that the widow "wears the same mask of nonexpression she wore at the funeral." A lower court jury awarded her $60,000 to compensate for the mental distress and shame the article caused. An appeals court reversed the verdict, and the woman appealed to the Supreme Court, which found the reporter's statements implying that the woman had been interviewed were "calculated falsehoods."

The decision was 8–1. Some months later in March 1975, in another 8–1 decision, the Supreme Court ruled on the second category involving privacy—the rights of private persons to keep their personal affairs from public disclosure. In this case, the Court nullified a Georgia law that made it a misdemeanor to print or broadcast the name of a rape victim. The case involved the father of a young woman who had been raped and killed in 1971 by a gang of teen-age boys. An Atlanta television station had used the victim's name, and the state court had ruled in favor of the father under the state law. The station appealed this ruling.

In setting aside the Georgia law, the Supreme Court stated that "once true information is disclosed in public court documents open to public inspection, the press cannot be sanctioned for publishing it." The Court stated (in *Cox Broadcasting Corp. v. Martin Cohn,* 420 US 469):

> The commission of crimes, prosecutions resulting therefrom, and judicial proceedings arising from the prosecutions are events of legitimate concern to the public and consequently fall within the press' responsibility to report the operations of government.

In both cases, the Supreme Court cautioned against broad interpretations of its rulings. Nevertheless, the first case clearly indicates that the press must take care in publishing material about individuals that is false, and the second indicates the Court will not extend the right of privacy to private persons involved in actions described in official documents.

Pictures. The picture was stark and it led to a suit for invasion of privacy. The photo in *Today* of Cocoa, Fla., showed a woman covered only by a towel as she fled from a house where her estranged husband had kept her hostage. A lower court jury awarded her $10,000 in damages, but the state supreme court upheld an appeals court decision that overturned the verdict. The appeals court said the law is clear "that when one becomes an actor in an occurrence of public interest, it is not an invasion of privacy to publish her photograph with an account of such occurrence. . . . The published photograph is more a depiction of grief, fright, emotional tension and flight than it is an appeal to other sensual appetites."

Secret Taping

A quick guideline in matters of privacy is provided by a case involving a surfer who was interviewed by *Sports Illustrated* and then sued because the published report contained unflattering material about his personal life along with information about his surfing activities. A federal appeals court ruled that the public had a legitimate interest in him and that the facts reported were not so offensive as "to lose newsworthiness protection." The guideline:

> A reporter or publication that gives publicity to the private life of a person is not subject to liability for unreasonable invasion of privacy if the material is (1) about a newsworthy person—who need not be an elected official or a celebrity—and (2) is not "highly offensive to a reasonable person, one of ordinary sensibilities and is of legitimate public concern."

The use of hidden electronic mechanisms for newsgathering may result in trouble if stories are based on the material gathered by hidden cameras and microphones. A federal court in California ruled in 1972 (*Dietemann v. Time, Inc.,* 449 F. 2d 245) that a man who was healing people with herbs, clay and minerals could sue for invasion of privacy because of the tactics used by employees of *Life* magazine in gathering information. The reporter, who posed as someone needing help, had a radio transmitter in her pocketbook. The transmitter relayed to other reporters the healer's conversation as he examined her in his home. Also, a picture was taken with a hidden camera; the picture was later published in the magazine.

The ground rules of journalism require reporters usually to tell sources when they are being photographed, taped or quoted. The television journalist, for example, should inform his or her source when the camera is on, unless it is made clear beforehand that anything and everything may be filmed and recorded. But such full disclosure usually is impossible in investigative reporting, said the attorneys for *Life* in their defense. However, the appeals court ruled that intrusion had occurred. The court stated:

> We agree that newsgathering is an integral part of news dissemination. We strongly disagree, however, that the hidden mechanical contrivances are "indispensable tools" of newsgathering. Investigative reporting is an ancient art; its successful practice long antecedes the invention of miniature cameras and electronic devices. The First Amendment has never been construed to accord newsmen immunity from torts or crimes committed during the course of newsgathering. The First Amendment is not a license to trespass, to steal, or to intrude by electronic means into the precincts of another's home or office. . . .

Note: There is an ethical as well as a legal aspect to privacy. Some journalists and many readers question the moral right of reporters to pry into the personal affairs of individuals, even when they are public figures or hold public office.

When Anne M. Burford, head of the Environmental Protection Agency during the Reagan administration, was accused of being soft on polluters, her home was staked out by reporters. Asked one morning outside her home if she were preparing to resign, she replied, "I'm getting ready to go to work, gentlemen. And it's becoming increasingly difficult when I have press people peering through my windows while I'm trying to get dressed."

Stakeout journalism, as this peering and prying is known, raises ethical questions. Whenever privacy is invaded the moral question is whether the information to be gained is essential to public understanding, even when there is no doubt that the invasion of privacy is legal.

Avoiding the Dangers

The guide in libel and invasion of privacy suits seems fairly clear. Caution is necessary when the following are *not* involved—public officials, public figures, public events. When a private individual is drawn into the news, the news report must be full, fair and accurate. Of course, no journalist relies upon the law for loopholes. He or she is always fair and accurate in coverage.

The reporter who follows the guidelines in Chapter 2 on the basic components of the news story need not worry about being hauled into court.

Libel suits usually have been the result of the following:

- Carelessness.
- Exaggerated or enthusiastic writing.
- Opinions not based on facts.
- Statements of officials or informants made outside a privileged situation.
  - Inadequate verification.
  - Failure to check with the subject of the defamation.

When a libel has been committed, a retraction should be published. Although a retraction is not a defense, it serves to lessen damages and may deprive the plaintiff of punitive damages.

The Reporter's Rights

The press carries a heavy burden. It has taken on the task of gathering and publishing the news, interpreting and commenting on the news, and acting as watchdog in the public interest over wide areas of public concern. The burden of the press has been lightened by the foresight of the Founding Fathers through the guarantee in the First Amendment of the Constitution that Congress shall make no law abridging freedom of speech or of the press. This has meant that the press has the right to publish what it finds without prior restraint.

To journalists, it also came to mean that they had the freedom to gather and prepare news and that the processes involved in these activities were shielded from a prying government and others. Also, journalists understood that their sources, their notes, their thoughts and their discussions with sources and their editors were protected.

They had good reason to believe all this. State legislatures and the courts had interpreted the concept of press freedom to cover these wide areas of newsgathering and publication. In 1896, for example, the state of Maryland passed a law allowing reporters to conceal their sources from the courts and from other officials. The concern of the public traditionally has been that the press be free and strong enough to counterpose a powerful executive. This sensitivity to central government began with the revolution against the British Crown. It was reinforced by the generations of immigrants who fled czars, kings, dictators and tyrants.

Old as the story of the abuse of power may be, and as frequent as the exposures of its ruinous consequences have been by the press, the dangers implicit in centralized government are always present, as the Watergate revelations taught U.S. citizens. This tendency of government to excessive use of its power was foreseen by the American revolutionaries who sought to make in the press a Fourth Estate outside government control and free to check on government.

There is, however, no clear-cut constitutional statement giving the press the privileges it had come to consider immutable. Absolute freedom of the press has never been endorsed by a majority of the Supreme Court, but the federal courts usually have been sympathetic to the rights of the press. However, in the 1970s following Watergate, as the press started to dig and check with growing tenacity, a former ally in its battles with governmental power—the judiciary—began to render decisions the press found to be increasingly restricting. Many of these decisions—particularly those of the Supreme Court—convinced the press that its assumptions about its privileges were false. The press, the courts ruled, has no greater rights than any citizen of the land.

To the press, some of the rulings appeared almost vindictive. To the judiciary, they were necessary to balance constitutional rights. In its decisions, said Justice William J. Brennan, the Supreme Court must weigh the First Amendment's protection of the "structure of the communicative process against a variety of social interests." The press's ability to gather and publish the news may be outweighed "by society's interest in the enforcement of criminal law," Brennan said in explaining two decisions—*Branzburg* and *Zurcher*—that the press found hobbled its freedom to protect sources.

In its balancing of the public right to know against individual rights to privacy and the accused's rights to a fair trial, the courts denied the confidentiality of sources, the protection of unpublished material and the privacy of the editorial process. The courts gradually limited the press's access to information, and some newsgathering was specifically prohibited.

These restrictive rulings continued into the 1980s, and they seemed to be welcomed by the public. Polls showed that the public was becoming disenchanted by the press because of what it saw as the press's unresponsive power and its inaccuracies and unfairness. Also, some people were angered by what they perceived as a liberal orientation of the press.

The love affair between the press and the public inspired by Watergate was dim history. The public wanted the press harnessed, it appeared.

Newsgathering

There are, of course, still wide areas of newsgathering open to the press. Generally, the actions of official bodies are accessible to journalists. Judicial, legislative and executive activities can be freely covered—with exceptions. A reporter has the right to cover a city council meeting, except for executive sessions. But the reporter has no legal right to sit in on a meeting of the board of the American Telephone & Telegraph Co., a private company. In a Florida court case involving a newspaper that sought to examine the records of a disciplinary proceeding that had been held by a bar association for a lawyer who later became a public official, the ruling went against the newspaper because the lawyer had been in private practice at the time of the proceeding and the alleged infraction was not a criminal matter. Criminal matters following arrest, charge or indictment are public record. Had the infraction involved the lawyer in his official activities, the matter would have been open to the press.

Journalists have rights—along with all citizens—to vast areas of official activities. The Supreme Court has ruled (*Branzburg v. Hayes*) that the press has protection in some of its newsgathering activities. The Court stated that "without some protection for seeking out the news, freedom of the press would be eviscerated."

But the Court ruled that a reporter cannot protect information a grand jury seeks, and grand jury proceedings are closed to the press. When *The Fresno Bee* published material from a grand jury inquiry and its staff members refused to tell the court how they had obtained the information, they were sent to jail for contempt of court.

Executive sessions of public bodies may be closed to the press, but the reason for holding closed-door sessions must not be trivial. Usually, state laws define what constitutes an executive session. Reporters are free to dig up material discussed at these meetings.

Material of a confidential and personal nature held by such agencies as health and welfare departments is not available to the press. A reporter has no legal right to learn whether a certain high school student was treated for gonorrhea by a public health clinic. But the reporter is entitled to data on how many were treated last month or last year, at what cost, how many persons the clinic has on its staff and so on. Nor are there prohibitions against a reporter interviewing a clinic user who is willing to talk about his or her treatment, just as a person who appears before a grand jury may tell reporters about his testimony to the jury.

Most of these limits have been in existence for some time, and reporters generally have recognized them. But in the 1970s the limitations were extended. In 1978, the Supreme Court ruled that the press has no "special privileges" of access. A sheriff had kept reporters and photographers from entering a California county jail to follow through on an investigation reporters had made of the sheriff's activities. The Court said the sheriff could keep the gates closed to the press.

The most serious constrictions of access to information have occurred in the coverage of the courts. In the 1970s, the courthouse doors seemed to be closing for pretrial coverage, but during the 1980s a series of Supreme Court rulings widened them.

Free Press— Fair Trial

In his survey of rulings in 1978, an attorney wrote that "whenever pretrial publicity is substantial, trial judges will not hesitate to hold closed hearings." His remarks were prophetic, for the following year, 1979, the Supreme Court handed the press a major blow. It ruled that closing pretrial hearings to the press does not violate the Constitution.

The restrictive 1979 Supreme Court decision came in *Gannett v. DePasquale* (443 US 368). Judge Daniel A. DePasquale had ordered reporters to leave his courtroom during a hearing on a pretrial motion to suppress evidence in a murder trial.

Judges contend that some news can prejudice jurors and thus compromise a defendant's Sixth Amendment "right to an impartial jury," making a fair trial impossible. An increasing number of criminal convictions in lower courts had been set aside because of such publicity.

Pretrial hearings do involve material that is potentially prejudicial. At these hearings, decisions are made as to whether a confession is voluntary, whether a wiretap violates constitutional safeguards, whether the defendant is competent to stand trial, whether a search leading to physical evidence was conducted with constitutional protections.

A judge may toss out a confession. He or she may rule that certain evidence cannot be admitted—the issue before Judge DePasquale. News reports of the matters before the court at the pretrial hearing might be heard or read by jurors who would not be allowed to hear such information at the trial.

Since 80 to 90 percent of all criminal cases are disposed of prior to trial through dismissal and plea bargaining, pretrial closure orders put most cases beyond the scrutiny of the press and the knowledge of the public. Thus, little can be known of police conduct, of the prosecution's activities or of judicial conduct.

There seems to be little question that pretrial publicity does influence jurors. Studies of actual and simulated jury trials have indicated that when jurors have been given pretrial publicity about prior criminal records and information about confessions the jurors are prone to find guilt. Jurors not exposed to such pretrial material are less likely to find the defendant guilty.

Nevertheless, the traditional position of the judiciary had been, in the words of an opinion of the Third Circuit Court of Appeals, that "secret hearings—though they be scrupulously fair in reality—are suspect by nature. Public confidence cannot long be maintained where important legal decisions are made behind closed doors and then announced in conclusive terms to the public, with the record supporting the court's decision sealed from view."

Judges do have ways to protect the defendant from damaging publicity that would compromise the defendant's right to a fair trial. In *Nebraska Press Association v. Stuart* (427 US 539), the Supreme Court discussed changing the location of the trial, adjourning the trial until pretrial publicity that may be prejudicial has dissipated, careful questioning of jurors during the voir dire (jury empaneling), sequestering the jury and other methods.

Gannett v. DePasquale

In their brief before the Supreme Court, the Gannett lawyers said that closing pretrial proceedings "may mask collusion among the participants harmful to the defendant and of which he is personally unaware. Alternatively, a closed proceeding may unduly benefit a criminal defendant to the detriment of the public interest."

The attorney for Judge DePasquale argued that while the public has the right to know, "without an impartial jury, any other right granted to the accused is meaningless." He pointed out that the judge did not enjoin the media from publishing information about the case. There was no gag order, no prior restraint. There was only a denial of access, which he contended was legal.

Gag orders against the press clearly violate the Constitution. The *Nebraska Press* case classified a gag order as prior restraint. Reporters could publish whatever they could find out about matters before the court. But closures—denials of access—had been upheld, and it was this area of the law that the Supreme Court was being asked to rule on in the *Gannett* case. Could a pretrial proceeding be closed to the press despite the phrase in the Sixth Amendment about a "public trial"?

When the ruling was issued in July 1979 it stunned everyone. The Sixth Amendment does not create the right of access to pretrial proceedings for the public and press, the Court said. The opinions of the majority seemed to go well beyond the issue before the Court and appeared to show an antipathy to the press.

One of the justices, Rehnquist, concurring with the majority in the 5–4 decision, said the majority reasoning was broad enough to authorize court-clearing orders in most cases without giving "any reason whatsoever" to outsiders.

Judges immediately interpreted the ruling to mean that criminal trials, even sentencing, could be carried out in secrecy. Reporters, but not other spectators, were thrown out of several courtrooms. The situation was such that Chief Justice Burger took the unusual step a month after the ruling was handed down to comment that the ruling referred only to pretrial hearings, not to trials or sentencing.

Less than a year after *Gannett* there were 239 motions to bar the public and the press from criminal justice proceedings. At least 37 of these were motions to close actual trials and sentencing proceedings. More than half the attempts at closure were successful.

The Court Acts

Aware of the confusion of its ruling in *Gannett,* the Court in 1980 took up the issue of whether criminal trials must be open to the public.

In *Richmond Newspapers, Inc. v. Virginia* (448 US 555), the Court decided 7–1 that "openness" is essential to the criminal trial and that media representatives should enjoy the same right of access as does the public. In his opinion, Chief Justice Burger wrote:

> People in an open society do not demand infallibility from their institutions, but it is difficult for them to accept what they are prohibited from observing. . . .
>
> Plainly it would be difficult to single out any aspect of government of higher concern and importance to the people than the manner in which criminal trials are conducted. . . .
>
> What this means in the context of trials is that the First Amendment guarantees of speech and press, standing alone, prohibit government from summarily closing courtroom doors which had long been open to the public at the time that amendment was adopted. . . .
>
> Absent an overriding interest articulated in findings, the trial of a criminal case must be open to the public.

TV in Court. In 1981, the Supreme Court reversed a finding it had made in the 1960s when it ruled that televising trials was prejudicial and "foreign to our system." The 1981 ruling stated that states may permit cameras in the courtroom without violating the defendant's Sixth Amendment right to a fair trial. As a result, 41 states permit some form of television coverage. In 13 states, the defendant in a criminal case may veto camera coverage. Most states leave the decision about camera coverage to the judge. Cameras are prohibited in federal courtrooms.

But what of pretrial hearings? Although the press at first welcomed *Richmond* as opening these hearings, a close examination of the decision led to despair. The Court clearly did not reverse its ruling in *Gannett v. DePasquale.* Pretrial hearings in criminal cases could, it appeared, still be closed.

In 1982, the Court did allow a California court to bar the press from jury selection in a criminal trial. But two years later, the Court unanimously in *Press-Enterprise v. Superior Court of California* (104 S.Ct. 819) overturned a California court order barring the press from jury selection. The Court appeared to imply that jury selection is part of the trial rather than a pretrial proceeding. The Court did suggest that such proceedings can be closed if it is made clear that the defendant's right to a fair trial cannot be protected any other way and if the privacy of potential jurors and those not party to the suit cannot be protected otherwise.

The *Press-Enterprise* of Riverside, Calif., was involved in another significant Supreme Court decision affecting access to pretrial proceedings. The newspaper had been barred from covering the 40-day preliminary hearing for a nurse who was charged with murdering 12 persons. The county court judge ruled that press coverage would endanger the nurse's Sixth Amendment right to a fair trial, and two state appellate courts agreed. They ruled that no constitutional right of access to preliminary hearings exists.

The Supreme Court disagreed. It ruled 7–2 in 1986 that the press has a qualified right to attend such hearings, even over the objection of the defendant. It said the First Amendment bars closing preliminary hearings in criminal cases unless the action is "essential" and no "reasonable alternatives to closure" are available.

Chief Justice Burger noted that in California most defendants plead guilty after their preliminary hearings so that these hearings are the only chance for the press and public to hear the detailed evidence in the case. Openness of pretrial proceedings, he wrote, plays a "positive role in the actual functioning of the process."

The press hailed the decision, *Press-Enterprise Company v. Superior Court of California* (known as Press-Enterprise II to distinguish it from the 1984 case), as a great victory for access to criminal proceedings.

Gannett Decision Made Irrelevant

Reporters often encounter information that would be prejudicial to a defendant on trial. Such material includes reports of confessions and information about the prior record of the defendant. Federal law enforcement officials recommend that limits be placed on the access to criminal records or "rap sheets." Some states expunge all details about arrests that did not result in convictions. Others prohibit access to criminal records, and some states limit what police may release. A few make use of rap sheet material a misdemeanor.

Reporters are able to track down criminal records since they are kept by a variety of sources—police, the courts, the prosecutor's office, probation officers. Reporters should first learn their newspaper's policy and the laws of their state and then decide in each case whether usage is justified.

For confessions, many reporters write: The arrested person (or the defendant) made statements to the police about the crime. Few details will be given.

Rap Sheets

Protecting the
News Process

Events become news stories by way of dozens of decisions by editors and reporters. Journalists contend that these decisions are made rationally, against a set of criteria that are as objective as possible. But they also concede that there is a good deal of imprecision, guesswork and intuition. The delicate nature of this process was opened to public exposure by the Supreme Court in 1979 in a ruling that journalists say makes the decision-making process even more difficult.

The Court ruled that the First Amendment does not grant journalists immunity from answering questions about the process put by litigants who claim to have been injured by the news. The Court's logic was that since an official or a public figure in a libel suit must prove "actual malice" he or she should be able to determine this by inquiring into the editorial process (*Herbert v. Lando,* 441 US 153). Malice, the logic goes, is obviously a state of mind, and it can only be proved by evidence from the alleged defamer's thoughts and newsroom conversations with colleagues.

Barry Lando, a producer for CBS, had produced a program about Col. Anthony Herbert, who had accused the Army of covering up reports of civilian deaths in Vietnam. The program questioned Herbert's role in Vietnam and was disparaging. Lando also wrote an article about the program, titled "The Selling of Colonel Herbert," for *The Atlantic.* Herbert sued Lando, *The Atlantic* and television reporter-interviewer Mike Wallace for $44 million. He said he had been libeled.

Faced with the prospect that the courts can make judgments about their editorial decisions, journalists may make only safe decisions. Since confidential, unedited and unused material may be exposed in libel cases, a process that is complicated enough has been made even more difficult. The threat of government looking over journalists' shoulders is, to news workers, ominous.

The counter-argument is that the press cannot escape responsibilities for what it publishes and broadcasts. If it makes errors, it must be held to account, just as the rest of us are.

But the press is by nature a risk-taker, and it will err, as Justice Brennan said in the Sullivan decision. Indeed, a centuries-old tradition tells us that the best path to truth is through the dissemination of a variety of doctrines, ideas, explanations, theories. A press concerned that it could be held accountable in court for its thoughts might not have published the Pentagon Papers, exposed the disasters of Vietnam, or dug into Watergate.

Case Dismissed. Herbert's suit was dismissed in 1986 by a circuit court of appeals, which found that CBS had presented sufficient evidence to defend its view of Herbert, even though some of its assertions remained in dispute. The action dismissing the suit before trial heartened journalists, who said it could encourage other judges to dismiss libel cases without long and costly trials. The Supreme Court ruling that journalists do not have First Amendment protection for their thoughts and newsroom conversation stands.

In 1978, a year before the *Herbert* decision, the Supreme Court limited the rights the press claimed for itself to resist the intrusion of government. *The Stanford Daily* had run stories and pictures of a campus demonstration and the police obtained a search warrant for them. The student newspaper went to court, and two federal courts ruled that a search warrant could not be issued against a newspaper if the employees were not suspected of criminal activity. The material would have to be obtained through a subpoena, the federal courts ruled.

These rulings helped the newspaper, and the press in general, because a subpoena can be contested in court by a motion to quash the subpoena. Search warrants are requested by law enforcement officials in *ex parte* proceedings—hearings at which only one side is represented. Unlike the subpoena, which requires notice to the party to turn over the requested material, the purpose of a search warrant is surprise.

The lower court rulings were appealed to the Supreme Court and in *Zurcher v. Stanford Daily* (436 US 547) the Court ruled 5–3 that people not involved in a crime—"seemingly blameless" third parties—have no greater rights to resist a search for evidence of a crime than those directly implicated.

The only question, then, is the method by which law enforcement agencies may obtain evidence. To require a subpoena, the Court said, "could easily result in the disappearance of the evidence, whatever the good faith of the third party."

The *Columbia Journalism Review* found the majority opinion of Justice Byron R. White to be "redolent of indifference or malice toward the press." The *Review* characterized as an "offhand judgment" Justice White's assurance that searches authorized by warrant will not deter "normal editorial and publication decisions."

Congress then stepped in and passed the Privacy Protection Act. Overwhelmingly, it voted that federal, state and local law enforcement officers could not, except under limited circumstances, use a search warrant for notes, films, tapes or other materials used by those involved in broadcasting and publishing. The authorities would have to obtain a subpoena, which would give news organizations the chance to oppose the request in court.

Confidentiality Requires Protection

Newspapers and broadcast stations contend that confidentiality is essential to freedom of the press. The press points out that the power of the government to punish people involved in unpopular causes led the courts to safeguard anonymity in many areas. The courts have come to recognize the doctor-patient and lawyer-client relationship as generally beyond legal inquiry. Journalists have sought the same protection for their sources.

If the press is to be the watchdog of government, as the press believes the Founding Fathers intended, then the press must be free to discover what public officials are doing, not merely to print what officials say they are doing. In order to ferret out these activities, insiders and informants are necessary. These informants usually must be promised anonymity.

Reporters contend that their notes—which may include the names of confidential sources as well as the reporters' own investigative work—should be treated as confidential. State shield laws grant the reporter this protection unless in a criminal case the defense can prove that the notes are relevant and that alternative sources of information have been exhausted.

But some state shield laws have been struck down, and some courts have indicated that reporters may not hold back the identity of their sources should a trial judge require such identification.

The New York Times appealed a $285,000 fine and the jailing of one of its reporters for refusing to give investigating officers his notes. In turning down the arguments of the *Times,* the New Jersey Supreme Court said shield laws must give way to the constitutional right under the Sixth Amendment to a fair trial. As for the First Amendment argument, that appears to have been lost in the 1972 *Branzburg v. Hayes* (408 US 665) decision when the Court denied that the First Amendment automatically grants reporters the privilege to withhold sources and other information in legal proceedings. News reporters, *Branzburg* stated, have no greater rights than other citizens.

As a result, the press decided to raise in the courts, state by state, the question of privilege and to seek a qualified privilege under the First Amendment. This would require a showing of (1) a high degree of relevance, (2) materiality and (3) exhaustion of alternate ways to obtain the same information before a reporter would be required to testify or produce notes.

The press strategy paid off, and a number of state courts and most federal circuit courts have granted the qualified privilege. In 1983, for example, the court of appeals in the state of Washington held that newspapers have a

No Shield. A Boston television reporter was sentenced to three months in jail for contempt of court for refusing to identify a source who told her he saw police officers loot a pharmacy in a nearby city. The case was being looked into by a grand jury. A prosecutor told the judge his office was stymied in its inquiry and that the witness's testimony was vital. Massachusetts, like 23 other states, has no shield law.

qualified privilege under common law to protect their sources but that judges may make a "balancing test" with the defendant's right to a fair trial. If the information the defendant seeks is found to be crucial to the case, then the information may not be withheld.

In 1986, the Court of Appeals for the Third Circuit affirmed the constitutionality of a Pennsylvania law allowing reporters to keep the names of their sources confidential. The federal court made the ruling in a libel case in which a Philadelphia police officer sought information about a source used by KYW-TV. The court ruled that the officer's right to reputation was outweighed by "the state's interest in maintaining a free and uninhibited press and the vital role that the shield law plays."

In its pursuit of the malefactors in public life, the press has been seen as a critic not only of sacred cows but of sacred institutions. "Nothing to be left untouched" may have been an excellent guide for the reporter, but it disturbed those who want and need ideals and heroes, men and women to look up to, to be loyal to. Few individuals or institutions can stand up under the scrutiny to which the press subjects them.

Causes and Consequences

The public reaction has been to resort to the ancient technique of destroying the messenger.

Tyrone Brown, a law clerk to Chief Justice Earl Warren in the 1960s, then general counsel for Post-Newsweek Broadcasting and later a member of the Federal Communications Commission, said the Court's rulings reflect public antagonism toward the press.

"All those so-called absolute principles like the First Amendment are functions of the time when they're decided," Brown says. "The Justices' role is a process role—making accommodations between various power groups in the country at various times. The Warren Court balanced competing interests more in favor of the First Amendment." The Burger Court, he said, appeared "to be doing otherwise."

Whatever the cause, most observers agree that the turnabout began with the *Branzburg* decision in 1972.

The key finding of *Branzburg* was that the First Amendment has to move aside before "the general obligation of a citizen to appear before a grand jury or at a trial . . . and give what information he possesses."

Joel M. Gora, author of the book, *The Rights of Reporters* (New York: Avon Books, 1974), saw *Branzburg* as a "severe setback in the campaign to secure constitutional protection for the newsgathering process in general and, in particular, for the right of reporters to safeguard their sources of information.

"For the first time, the Supreme Court explored the nature of the newsgathering process and the reporters' need for a Constitutional right to protect confidential sources. The reporters lost."

In several decisions affecting the press, Justices White and Burger suggested that the Times Doctrine be re-examined. They asserted that subsequent rulings for the press have permitted the press to abuse privacy and to be held exempt from responsibility for its articles. With the appointment of Antonin Scalia to the Supreme Court and the elevation of Justice Rehnquist to chief justice, there was concern among journalists that the desire to overturn the Times Doctrine could some day command a majority of the justices of the Supreme Court.

Summing Up

In his book on the rights of reporters, Gora tells reporters to know their rights and to assert them. He notes:

• The police cannot arbitrarily deny a press pass to a reporter.
• Except for reasonable restrictions on access to events behind police lines, the police cannot interfere with a reporter engaged in newsgathering activities in public places.
• Reporters cannot be denied access to open meetings of legislative or executive bodies.
• The reporter can try to use state law to open certain hearings of public bodies that have been closed as "executive sessions." But there is no constitutional right to attend. Several states have adopted "sunshine laws" that require public agencies to have open meetings and open records.
• Reporters do not have a constitutional right to documents and reports not available to the general public. (The Supreme Court has equated the press's right to access with the right of access of the public.) There are, however, state and federal laws granting access to official information.

Reporters:

• Have no special right of access to news.
• Should be careful about what they print about the records of criminal defendants.
• May be asked to divulge the thoughts they had before they wrote a story.
• Can have their files examined by police.
• Cannot guarantee sources confidentiality.
• May be required to give testimony or documents to a grand jury.
• Should be careful about telling sources the press and the source are protected by a state shield law.

Help. The Reporters Committee for Freedom of the Press runs a Legal Assistance Hotline from Washington, D.C. The telephone service assists those who run into government censorship, receive subpoenas for confidential sources, are threatened with libel and privacy suits or prior restraints on publication. The number is 202–466–6313.

Cater, Douglass. *The Fourth Branch of Government.* New York: Vintage, 1959.

Chaffee, Zechariah Jr. *Free Speech in the United States.* Cambridge, Mass.: Harvard, 1948.

Denniston, Lyle. *The Reporter and the Law.* New York: Hastings House, 1980.

Hand, Learned. *Liberty.* Stamford, Conn.: Overbrook Press, 1941.

Oran, Daniel. *Law Dictionary for Non-Lawyers.* St. Paul, Minn.: West Publishing Co., 1975.

Pember, Don R. *Mass Media Law.* 3d ed. Dubuque, Iowa: Wm. C. Brown, 1984.

Sanford, Bruce W. *Synopsis of the Law of Libel and The Right of Privacy.* New York: World Almanac Publications, 1981.

CHAPTER TWENTY-SIX

Taste—Defining the Appropriate

Preview

Material that is obscene, vulgar or profane offends readers and listeners. But it can be informative, and sometimes the reporter risks offending to move closer to the truth of the situation.

Decisions on usage depend on:

• Context—If the event is significant and the material essential to describing the event, offensive material may be used.

• Nature of the audience—A publication for adults or a special-interest group will contain material that a mass medium may not.

• Prominence of those involved—Public officials and public figures lead public lives. What would be prying into the life of a private individual may be necessary reporting of the activities of a public personality.

Two Cornell University astronomers had an idea for the Pioneer 10 spacecraft flight. For its journey beyond our solar system it would carry a drawing of a man and a woman as well as information about the planet Earth. Should the spacecraft then nuzzle down on some distant civilization the inhabitants could visualize what earth man and woman looked like.

The National Aeronautics and Space Administration accepted the suggestion, and when Pioneer 10 was launched in February 1972, a gold-plated aluminum plaque engraved with a sketch of the Earth and its solar system and a drawing of a naked man and woman standing next to each other was aboard. NASA released the drawing to newspapers, thereupon confronting many editors with a dilemma. The picture was newsworthy, but would its publication be in bad taste? (See figure 26.1.)

The *Chicago Sun-Times* published the drawing in an early edition after an artist had removed the man's testicles. In a later edition, the rest of the genitals obviously were erased. *The Philadelphia Inquirer* did even more brush work: The male had no genitals and the nipples had been removed from the woman's breasts. The *Los Angeles Times* ran the drawing untouched. "Filth," a reader wrote in protest.

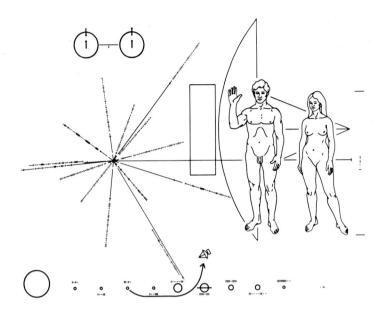

Now, more than a decade later, the assertions of bad taste and the editors' anxieties seem as obsolete as the embarrassment pregnant women once were made to feel in the male-oriented society. (The word *confinement* to describe the term of pregnancy goes back to this period because pregnant women were kept at home to hide their supposed shame.) But no matter how liberated we may think ourselves, matters of taste still concern the reporter.

How, for example do the media cover a hearing of the Senate Commerce, Science and Transportation Committee that is concerned with what some groups insist is record-album pornography? The committee is considering whether the First Amendment gives free-speech rights to rock groups that sing about rape, suicide, murder, sado-masochism and sex. The hearing attracts hundreds of spectators and a large complement of reporters. Four-letter words and sexually explicit lines explode from the rock videos they watch.

The reporters quote Sen. Ernest Hollings: "It is outrageous filth and we must do something about it." And they quote John Denver, Dee Snider and Frank Zappa, who oppose censorship.

But they do not use the words or lines of the music in their stories.

The New Republic, a weekly journal of opinion and commentary on politics and the arts, does not have to be circumspect. It quotes from Prince's "Jack U Off," and from "Darling Nikki" it quotes a verse beginning, "I knew a girl named Nikki/I guess you could say she was a sex fiend." It quotes from Judas Priest's song "Eat Me Alive."

A Paradox. Some reporters pointed to the paradox of newspapers filtering and censoring words that 12- and 13-year-olds heard on their Walkmans. Newspapers, their editors replied, follow (distantly)—not lead—the popular culture.

No one wants to write a story that offends readers or viewers. Nor—in the case of broadcast journalists—is there much sense in offending the Federal Communications Commission, which has rules about obscenity, indecency and profanity on the air. But how do we draw the lines that separate obscenity and profanity from revelation? How does a reporter or an editor decide when to risk giving offense in order to give essential information? Just what is the "good taste" that journalists are supposed to exercise?

Taste is Relative

Taste is usually defined as a set of value judgments in behavior, manners, or the arts that is held in common by a group or class of people. Generally, these values help to keep society stable, to insulate it from sudden and possibly destructive change. Those who advocate strict controls on pornography, for example, argue that such material stimulates anti-social behavior.

The values that determine decisions about taste are not absolute. They change with time, place and context. The word *rape* was taboo in many newspapers until the 1950s. Wedding announcements have consisted of platitudes. But when the wedding of Prince Charles, heir to the British throne, and Lady Diana Spencer was announced, the Knight-Ridder News Service ran this:

> She has been forced to submit to a discreet but thorough gynecological examination to be proclaimed fertile enough to deliver royal heirs to the House of Windsor. No such results have been announced for the prince.
>
> Questioned by reporters in the weeks after the engagement announcement, her uncle, Lord Fermoy, assured the public that the bride is indeed a virgin. It has been generally understood, in true double standards, that Prince Charles, 12 years older than Diana, is not.

Time

The Washington Post tells its reporters that "society's concepts of taste and decency are constantly changing. A word offensive to the last generation can be part of the next generation's common vocabulary."

In 1939, the public was scandalized when in the movie *Gone With the Wind,* Rhett Butler turned to Scarlett O'Hara and said, "Frankly, my dear, I don't give a damn."

In 1948, a New York newspaper's obituary of an elderly woman who had owned a world-famous house of prostitution referred to it as a "seraglio" and buried in the fifth paragraph a reference to her and her sister as "madams." Twenty years later not much had changed. When the Yale University School

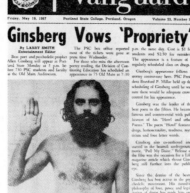

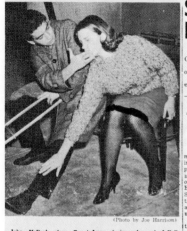

the Vanguard

Friday, May 19, 1967   Portland State College, Portland, Oregon   Volume 22, Number 34

Ginsberg Vows 'Propriety'

By LARRY SMITH
Entertainment Editor

Beat poet and psychedelic prophet Allen Ginsberg will appear at Portland State Monday at 3 p.m. before 730 PSC students and faculty in the Old Main Auditorium.

Allen Ginsberg will appear in Old Main auditorium 3 p.m. Monday.

Eligibility, Disapproval Narrow List . . .

Faculty Rate Mosser Money Co

By BOB MEYER
Acting News Editor

Senate Examines Club

By HUNTLY GOODHUE
Managing Editor

Touching Bottom

"ARCHIE AND Mahasthel," with Gay Mathis, will open at the Idea Theater Thursday at 9 p.m.

Vol. 40—No. 7   VILLANO

Forty Seniors At

(Photo by Joe Harrison)

John McPeak slaps Bonnie Lucas during rehearsal of Belle Masque production of "Mask of Angels" (see below for details).

College Papers Cause Problems. During the 1960s, many college newspapers deliberately sought to expand the boundaries of the acceptable, and they ran into trouble. Even when they did not seek confrontations they had problems with suspicious advisers: At Villanova University, the adviser added a hemline to a picture. But at Portland State College, the student journalists deliberately sought a confrontation over their right to print what they wished. The half-nude photo of poet Allen Ginsberg, infuriated the college president; the following week the newspaper ran a picture of a scantily clad student actress. The newspaper was shut down.

of Drama sent out an advertisement that included the title of the opening play in its season, John Ford's 17th century tragedy, " 'Tis Pity She's a Whore," New Haven and Hartford newspapers reached for the red pencil.

The New Haven Register elevated her morals and retitled the play, " 'Tis Pity She's Bad." *The Hartford Courant* made it, " 'Tis Pity She's." Explained the *Courant*'s advertising manager to incredulous university officials, "We try to run a clean newspaper."

In the 1970s the culture had adapted to explicitness. By the 1980s movies, theater, books and magazines left little to the imagination. For those with exotic tastes, a $7 billion a year pornography industry catered to every conceivable fantasy, with not much legal interference. In time, journalism moved, too, though not very far.

Yes and No. Before Rock Hudson's death, readers had to "guess what the hell was going on," says Steve Findlay of *USA Today.* To John M. Langone, senior medical editor at *Discover* magazine, the reticence was "ridiculous. The media cover the most horrible crimes and yet in matters of sex there's still prudery. There are words you can't use." When WNBC-TV used the term *anal intercourse* on the air, the station received calls from outraged listeners.

Few newspapers followed the lead of *Los Angeles Times* medical writer Harry Nelson who, in 1983, gave the facts in a straightforward manner: AIDS "is associated with passive (receptive) anal intercourse," he wrote. He wrote that the AIDS agent is present in "the semen of the active partner which in turn is transmitted to the passive partner's bloodstream through breaks in the rectal membranes."

Context

Television, radio and newspapers remain convinced that their audiences are sensitive to explicit language and to graphic descriptions of sexual activities. This was evident in the coverage of the sudden appearance of AIDS.

Reporting the full dimension of the disease and its prevention necessitated describing the sexual activities of homosexuals and the practices of intravenous drug users. It was not difficult to describe how the addicts contracted the disease: A drug user could be infected if he or she used a needle that an addict with AIDS had used. Homosexuals transmit the disease through blood and semen when they engage in anal intercourse. Newspaper and broadcast editors concluded they could not describe such intercourse or other homosexual practices. Some also found it difficult to describe what health authorities suggested as "safe sex" for homosexuals—the use of condoms—thus failing in their role as carriers of essential information.

When Rock Hudson, the movie star, died in 1985 of AIDS, news magazines, *People,* the *Star, National Enquirer* and other publications all played up Hudson's death. But only *Time* used the word *condom* in describing safe sex, according to Ron Dorfman, a media critic. Dorfman added that few publications and no networks accept advertisements for condoms, which, he said in his October 1985 column in *The Quill,* "also would slow the spread of herpes, hepatitis, syphilis, gonorrhea and probably a few other serious diseases, not to mention that their widespread use could affect the rates of unwanted pregnancy, abortion and single parenthood."

Taste changes with place. Behavior appropriate in a football stadium would be boorish in an opera house. Language inoffensive to most residents of San Francisco would be tasteless, if not worse, to residents of Salt Lake City. The *San Francisco Chronicle* publishes classified advertisements for "escort services" that include "Call A Girl," "Playmates—for the discreet," "Fanny's—We do please" and "Euphoria." In 1986, Peoples Drug Stores and Southland Corp. pulled *Penthouse* and *Playboy* magazines from their shelves.

Taste also is a function of the context in which the material is used. A story in *Rolling Stone* would contain language and references abhorrent to a reader of *The Christian Science Monitor.* Here is a sidebar to an article in the *Columbia Journalism Review:*

Meeting Mr. Scaife

Richard Scaife rarely speaks to the press. After several unsuccessful efforts to obtain an interview, this reporter decided to make one last attempt in Boston, where Scaife was scheduled to attend the annual meeting of the First Boston Corporation.

Scaife, a company director, did not show up while the meeting was in progress. Reached eventually by telephone as he dined with the other directors at the exclusive Union Club, he hung up the moment he heard the caller's name. A few minutes later he appeared at the top of the Club steps. At the bottom of the stairs, the following exchange occurred:

"Mr. Scaife, could you explain why you give so much money to the New Right?"

"You fucking Communist cunt, get out of here."

Well. The rest of the five-minute interview was conducted at a rapid trot down Park Street, during which Scaife tried to hail a taxi. Scaife volunteered two statements of opinion regarding his questioner's personal appearance—he said she was ugly and that her teeth were "terrible"—and also the comment that she was engaged in "hatchet journalism." His questioner thanked Scaife for his time.

"Don't look behind you." Scaife offered by way of a goodbye.

Not quite sure what this remark meant, the reporter suggested that if someone were approaching it was probably her mother, whom she had arranged to meet nearby. "She's ugly, too," Scaife said, and strode off.

K.R.

The *Review*'s editors wanted to show its readers the full dimension of Scaife's personality. Since most of the readers are journalists, the editors knew this brief exchange would enlighten rather than offend them.

A vulgarity uttered by the president may be essential to the story, whereas an offhand obscene remark by an athlete may be unnecessary. During the negotiations with steel companies about price increases, President Kennedy said, "My father always told me businessmen were sons-of-bitches." *The New York Times* printed the president's remarks as made. But almost 20 years later the *Times* in-house bulletin, *Winners & Sinners,* was unhappy about a sports story that quoted Reggie Jackson, then with the New York Yankees, saying, "I can say this because George can do nothing to me. He can do nothing because I can hit the baseball over the wall. But when I can't hit, they'll screw me too. I know they'll screw me the same way they screwed Rosen." *Winners & Sinners* commented:

> Depending upon one's broad-mindedness, *screw* is either obscene or vulgar. Our stylebook, citing the 1974 precedent of the Watergate transcripts, says we use such language "only when the printing of the objectionable word or words will give the reader an insight into matters of great moment—an insight that cannot be otherwise conveyed." It adds that "most such instances would almost certainly involve a person of high standing—a president, perhaps."

A Guideline

The most important guide to the use of questionable subject matter and explicit language is that the event must be significant and the questionable material essential to the story to justify its use. *The Washington Post* advises reporters to "avoid profanities and obscenities unless their use is so essential to a story of significance that its meaning is lost without them."

We must immediately qualify this guideline in two ways. There are legitimate differences of opinion as to what constitutes significance or importance, and place must be considered in the application of the guideline. When

Charles Alexander, the editor of *The Journal Herald* in Dayton, Ohio, decided his readers should have the fullest possible account of a quarrel between two agents with the Treasury Department, he approved the following quotation:

"Gibson God damn it, you are fucking with my family. You are fucking with my future. I am not going to let you do it. I'll kill you first."

The paper was quoting agent Casper Carroll Gibson's account of the quarrel. Gibson said the other agent then started to pull a gun out of his pocket. Gibson grabbed the gun, it went off and his colleague fell dead.

Alexander's bosses found the use of the words indefensible for Dayton readers. When Alexander would not back down and apologize, he was fired.

"It's a matter of truth," Alexander said. "To me, the telling of that message from an incident in real life, including in one instance the raw vulgarity used by a man blind with rage, is a lesson that every man, woman and child should perceive in all its dimensions. It is shocking—it surely should be. . . ."

Alexander lost his job in 1975. Four years before, *The Record* in Bergen County, N.J., across the Hudson River from New York City, carried a story about a Democratic party official's reaction to being told she could not attend a party meeting at the home of the state chairman. She went anyway. When she arrived, the chairman told her she would have been welcome but for the language the men used in their discussions. To which she replied, "I don't give a shit what kind of language you use."

The Record quoted her as saying just that. (The men then told her she could attend.)

Apparently, the editors of *The Record* decided their readers were ready in 1971 to see explicit language in print, whereas four years later the management of the *Journal Herald* in Dayton presumed their readers would be offended by explicit language.

Changing Standards

Standards in taste traditionally have been set by the upper class and the respected elders of the community. Although these groups still carry some weight, their power has significantly diminished since World War II. As a consequence, taste-by-edict has been replaced by a more realistic and pragmatic set of guidelines. In two areas, sex and death—the ageless taboos—the boundaries for the press are expanding, and graphic language that had been presumed to be vulgar, obscene or profane, however it was used, is now appearing in newspapers and is heard on television and radio. The transformation has been startling, and the changes bother those who regard the loosening of standards for language and subject matter as a threat to the social fabric.

Journalists realized that the country had moved through a series of divisive and traumatizing events since 1945 and that old presumptions were subject to re-examination. The profanities and the obscene acts that accompanied the country's crises were symbols of the collapse of the old order. The civil rights struggles of the 1950s, the liberation movements of the 1960s, and the increasing power of the young in social, economic and political affairs upset the old balances. The battles and the new balances were decisively changing the culture, and they had to be reported.

The increasing activity and power of the young (18-year-olds were given the right to vote in 1971) were obviously newsworthy, and although some of the more conservative members of the community considered the young to be the modern counterparts of the barbarians at the gates, the young unquestionably were causing significant changes in society. But to report the full dimensions of these activities—the language and slogans—the press would risk censure by the upholders of order in the community, the very people upon whom the newspaper depends for its survival. Radio and television station managers had less leeway. The FCC, they said, required them to conform to contemporary community standards.

In 1968, the turmoil that was afflicting the country over Vietnam seemed to focus on Chicago where the Democratic presidential convention was being held. Anti-war demonstrators—many of them young—were congregating in Chicago to try to persuade the party to pledge an early end to the war by picking an anti-war candidate. There, in the summer's heat, they were met by Chicago police. The clash between police and demonstrators was bloody, violent and vicious. Profanities and blows were exchanged.

An inquiry by the National Committee on the Causes and Prevention of Violence was graphic in its descriptions and quotations—so much so that the Government Printing Office refused to publish it unless deletions were made. The director refused, saying that the obscenities by the police and the demonstrators were essential and that deletions would "destroy the important tone" of the report.

A number of private publishers rushed into the vacuum created by the GPO, and one newspaper organization, *The Courier-Journal* and *Times* in Louisville did carry some of the graphic language of the report. On looking back at what his newspaper had done, the executive editor of the papers, Norman Isaacs, had misgivings. Although the younger members of the staff were pleased with the newspaper's frankness, the community was not.

"In my considered judgment we have made a grievous error in misjudging our own community," Isaacs said. "A newspaper under conditions of monopoly that exist in 95 percent of the American cities is no longer a free agent.

"It must have a community ethic. We can understand standards only in terms of community conscience," he said. "A family newspaper should not use language that some people find objectionable," he continued. Isaacs apologized to churchmen who were angered by the publication.

ACID RAIN LINKED TO U.S. EMISSIONS BY REAGAN'S AIDE

—*The New York Times*

His humming rear end is a major distraction

—*Toronto Sun*

Double Meanings. The journalist must be alert to hidden meanings in stories, headlines and photographs. This photograph, which appeared in *The Plain Dealer,* outraged members of the World Association of Women Journalists, who were attending a conference in Cleveland. They contended that it was in bad taste, that the way some of the members were posed in front of the statue had an obscene suggestiveness.

In their effort to compress stories into a few words, headline writers sometimes imply meanings that are in questionable taste, as in these headlines from *The New York Times* and *Toronto Sun.*

The incident raises several questions journalists have to consider in making decisions about matters of taste. Does a monopoly newspaper or broadcast station have responsibilities that differ from publications and stations with competition? To some degree, yes. The responsibility is to carry controversial material, not to screen it out, for unless the single paper or station in town uses the material the public will be uninformed.

Next, what is the community conscience or ethic, and who defines it? The answers, never simple, were becoming more difficult. Youth, women and blacks had rarely been consulted. Isaacs' churchmen, who were offended by the Chicago riot report, had become less influential in the community, and their voices were by no means unanimous in matters of taste.

The community was in flux. Years of racial strife and urban crises, the consequences of the women's movement, the disenchantment with political and business leaders as a result of Vietnam, Watergate and business scandals had made the standard-setters suspect, for had not the best and the brightest of them led us into the Vietnam quagmire, and had not some of them defended Nixon?

The awareness that journalists themselves could define taste was inevitable. Events had made it imperative that the press describe the changes, and to describe them accurately a new sense of the appropriate in language and subject matter was necessary.

The Turning Point

In 1960, during a school integration demonstration in New Orleans, the AP quoted some of the women who were shouting at the leader of the school sit-ins, "Jew bastard, nigger lover." In answer to many protests that the use of such words was in bad taste, the AP said it "judged them essential to establishing the temper and the mood of the demonstrators."

Gradually, pertinence or significance was becoming the guideline in determining whether an obscenity or profanity should be included in news accounts. The turning point may have been reached during Watergate when the tapes of the White House conversations revealed a profusion of vulgarities and profanities. As a West Coast journalism review, *feed/back,* put it, the "Nixon administration made inoperative the detente that existed in the daily press against words once excised by editors."

The words *shit* and *fuck,* used in the White House, appeared in such papers as *The Washington Post,* the *St. Paul Dispatch* and *Pioneer Press,* the Atlanta *Journal,* the *Kansas City Star* and *The Seattle Times.*

It would have been impossible, many editors felt, to have changed the emphatic language of a statement by President Nixon from the key tape of March 22, 1973:

> I don't give a shit what happens. I want you all to stonewall it, let them plead the Fifth Amendment, cover up or anything else if it'll save the plan. That's the whole point.

The AP made a survey of newspapers using the Watergate material and found nearly 30 percent of them printed all or nearly all of the obscenities without alteration. Slightly more than half sanitized the word *shit* or other words, and 15 percent of the papers completely edited out the vulgarities and profanities by paraphrase or deletion.

One of the newspapers that did not use Nixon's language was the Huntington (W. Va.) *Herald-Dispatch* and *Advertiser,* whose executive editor said, "In this very Fundamentalist market, we came to the conclusion that there was no reason to offend unnecessarily."

Turning away from some kinds of reality while daily parading man's most obscene acts—murder, torture, terrorism—seems an act of hypocrisy to some editors. Another kind of hypocrisy—the discrepancy between private and public morality—is revealed by an incident involving television station WGBH in Boston. The station decided to do a program a few days after the 1968 student demonstrations on the Harvard campus. It invited people from the community to have their say. One of those who showed up took the microphone at the beginning of the program and shouted, "What I have to say is fuck Harvard and fuck Pusey [Harvard's president] and fuck everybody." David Ives, the president of the public TV station recalled, "I was upstairs, and you have never seen so many telephone calls. The most interesting thing about them was the quality of what they said.

"One woman said, 'I just want you to know that no language like that has ever been permitted in this house.' And in the background you could hear a man saying, 'You know God damn well it has.' The prize came from a man who called and said, 'I'm just not going to have any of that kind of shit in my living room.'"

Public Outrage, Private Delight. When it was discovered that Miss America was being displayed in the nude in *Penthouse* magazine, (the photos had been taken before she won the title), the public was outraged and the pageant took away her crown. The issue with the photos sold 6 million copies, twice its normal circulation.

As language that had been deemed unfit to print was gradually working its way into newspapers and magazines, subject matter once considered taboo for the mass media became acceptable.

Here is the beginning of a story that was published in *The Sacramento Bee,* circulation 225,000:

Necrophiliac Takes Stand

By Jaime Diaz
Bee Staff Writer

Confessed necrophiliac Karen Greenlee, looking drawn and tense, took the stand before a jury in Sacramento Superior Court Friday and quietly admitted climbing into coffins to have sexual contact with corpses.

Under questioning by attorney Leo O'Connor, Greenlee, 23, said she had sexual contact in an embalming room and in other locations at the Sacramento Memorial Lawn mortuary, where she was an apprentice embalmer in late 1979.

She also admitted she drank heavily in her apartment at the mortuary during her employment there.

Greenlee and the mortuary are defendants in a suit by Marian Gonzales, who contends she suffered severe emotional distress when Greenlee stole the body of her son, John Mercure, 33, in a mortuary hearse Dec. 17, 1979.

The hearse containing Greenlee and the corpse were recovered the next day near Alleghany in Sierra County. After surrendering herself, Greenlee attempted suicide by swallowing pain relievers.

Greenlee pleaded guilty to interfering with a burial and illegally driving a hearse, and spent 11 days in jail and was fined $255 and placed on two years probation, with medical treatment recommended. She is now living ...

Mort Saltzman, weekend editor of the *Bee,* used the story because the arguments for its use outweighed those against it:

Pro:
1. It's interesting.
2. It deals with a human being and with another facet of our complicated lives.
3. Freedom of the press.
4. It touches on the subject of necrophilia, a subject about which little is known and, more importantly, little is published or examined. Informative.
5. It's happening in our community.

Con:
1. Bad taste.
2. Who needs to know?
3. Lacks regard for the woman involved, shows a lack of compassion and sensitivity and ignores journalistic ethics.
4. Panders to the public's lust.
5. Not newsworthy or significant.

"What it really boils down to is that this story is extremely interesting, is being talked about by most folks in town and is being handled in what I consider good taste," Saltzman said.

The ombudsman for the *Bee*— its internal critic—said he had received no more than five complaints about the story and said he thought that coverage had been handled with "good taste."

Prominence a Determinant

In 1976, on a flight from the Republican presidential convention, a *Rolling Stone* reporter overheard and described in the magazine a conversation among John Dean, the singer Pat Boone and a member of President Ford's cabinet. Boone says to the cabinet member:

"John and I were just discussing the appeal of the Republican party. It seems to me that the party of Abraham Lincoln could and should attract more black people. Why can't that be done?"
The cabinet member replies:
"I'll tell you why you can't attract coloreds. Because coloreds only want three things: first, a tight pussy; second, loose shoes; and third, a warm place to shit. That's all."

Rolling Stone ran the quotes in full but without attribution. The wire services and newspapers picked up the story. UPI handled the offensive comments with the paraphrasing "good sex, easy shoes and a warm place to go to the bathroom." *The Washington Post* made it: ". . . Coloreds only want three things . . . first, a tight (woman's sexual organ); second, loose shoes; and third, a warm place to (defecate)." The quote was attributed to Earl Butz, secretary of agriculture.

AP paraphrased the statement in its story and used it in full in a note for editors. Later, it used language much like the *Post*'s.

A UPI survey showed that one newspaper, *The Capital Times* of Madison, Wis., had used the full quote. The fury of the public led to Butz's resignation, and then *The* Toledo *Blade* used the original comments. The *Blade* received eight calls, six protesting, two approving. The Erie, Pa., *Morning News* told readers in a front page editor's note that Butz's comments were in poor taste but that adult readers could see them in the newspaper office. More than 100 persons did just that. In Lubbock, Texas, the *Avalanche Journal* made a similar offer, and 350 persons showed up, including a farmer and his wife who drove 70 miles into town, copied the material to show their neighbors, and drove back.

The managing editor of *The Capital Times,* Robert Meloon, said, "We think readers have the right to know exactly what Mr. Butz said and to judge for themselves whether the remarks were obscene and racist in character; the paraphrasing we've seen doesn't carry off the same meaning as the actual words."

When the UPI quoted Billy Carter, the president's brother, saying of Jews who had protested his ties with the leaders of Libya, "They can kiss my ass," there were some protests. The UPI replied that its decision was "based on the reality that members of the president's family are public figures and we have to chronicle their excesses, verbal or otherwise."

Thus, the prominence and importance of the persons involved in news events as well as the importance of the event and the relevance of the explicit language to the event bear on the use of obscenity or profanity.

Limits on Broadcasting

The FCC is empowered to enforce federal statutes and the decisions of the courts in the area of obscenity, indecency and profanity. The FCC can fine a station or revoke its license if it finds that it violated section 1464 of the federal Criminal Code, which provides for penalties for uttering "any obscene, indecent or profane language by means of radio communication." ("Radio" includes television.)

But even broadcasters and the FCC have changed with the times. In 1960, NBC censored the use of the initials *W.C.* on the Jack Parr show, the nightly televised network talk program that was a predecessor to the Johnny Carson show. *W.C.* stands for water closet, which in Britain means *toilet.* A dozen years later, the Public Broadcasting Service showed an "education entertainment" called the "V.D. Blues." There were no protests about the initials, and there were surprisingly few objections to some of the language in such songs as "Don't Give a Dose to the One You Love Most" and "Even Dr. Pepper Won't Help You," which was about the futility of douching as a contraceptive practice.

Although some stations made cuts, and stations in Arkansas and Mississippi did not carry the program, the majority of public broadcast stations decided that the program was a public service. When "V.D. Blues" was followed by a 2½ hour hotline on the New York City station, 15,000 persons called with questions about venereal disease. One of the city's V.D. clinics reported the next day that the number of persons seeking blood tests went up by a third.

The program obviously was aimed at teen-agers, whose venereal disease rate is epidemic. But stations must be careful about children in the audience.

In 1973, in a broadcast in the early afternoon over station WBAI (FM) in New York City, George Carlin gave a comedy monologue entitled, "The Seven Words You Can't Say on Radio and Television." Carlin said his intent was to show that the language of ordinary people is not threatening or obscene. The station later said in its defense that the broadcast was in the tradition of satire. In the broadcasts Carlin had said:

"Filthy Words"

> I was thinking one night about the words you couldn't say on the public airwaves . . . and it came down to seven but the list is open to amendment and in fact has been changed. . . . The original seven words were shit, piss, fuck, cunt, cocksucker, motherfucker and tits. . . .

He repeated the tabooed words several times in what he said later was a purposeful "verbal shock treatment."

There was one complaint, and the FCC investigated. In 1975, it issued a declaratory order finding that the words were "patently offensive by contemporary community standards for the broadcast medium and are accordingly 'indecent' when broadcast by radio or television. These words were broadcast at a time when children were undoubtedly in the audience."

The station was not prosecuted under the federal statute. Nor was a fine imposed. The finding was, however, to be part of the station's file. It was, in effect, probation for the station.

The station appealed to the federal courts, and many stations and civil rights advocates joined the appeal against what was seen as a threat to freedom of expression. The case reached the United States Supreme Court, and in 1978 the Court ruled 5–4 that radio and television stations do not have the constitutional right to broadcast indecent words. It said that the government has the right to forbid such words because of the broadcast medium's "uniquely pervasive presence in the lives of all Americans." The Court stated that "of all forms of communication, it is broadcasting that has received the most limited First Amendment protection."

The Supreme Court emphasized the limits of its ruling:

> It is appropriate, in conclusion, to emphasize the narrowness of our ruling. . . . The Commission's (FCC) decision rested entirely on a nuisance rationale under which context is all important. . . . The time of day was emphasized by the Commission. . . .

Nevertheless, the Court's ruling was seen as a setback in the attempt by broadcasters to gain the same kind of freedom granted the print media.

Obscenity and The Law

On matters of obscenity, indecency and profanity, which are not constitutionally protected, *Miller v. California* in 1973 (413 US 15) is the standard for determining whether a printed work is obscene. The Court for the first time set community rather than national standards. It said, "Diversity is not to be strangled by the absolutism of imposed uniformity." The test is whether:

a. The average person, applying contemporary community standards, would find that the work, taken as a whole, appeals to the prurient interest.

b. The work depicts or describes in a patently offensive way, sexual conduct specifically defined by the applicable state law.

c. The work, taken as a whole, lacks serious literary, artistic, political or scientific value.

For the work to be ruled obscene all three elements must be present.

In the Carlin-WBAI case, which became known as the "Filthy Words Case," the FCC defined indecent language as "language that describes, in terms patently offensive as measured by community standards for the broadcast medium, sexual or excretory activities and organs." The Commission also stated that when children are likely to be in the audience indecent language "cannot be redeemed by a claim that it has literary, artistic, political or scientific value."

As for profanity, the FCC said that the legal test is whether the words indicated "an imprecation of divine vengeance or implying divine condemnation, so used as to constitute a public nuisance." In other words, the FCC will not act when profanities clearly are not intended to be taken literally.

Although the courts have ruled that obscenity is not constitutionally protected, they have been reluctant to rule against printed material, even the pornographic publications that are sold at newsstands.

Several of Carlin's Seven Filthy Words were used with dramatic impact in a film documentary, "Scared Straight," broadcast on television six years later. The documentary was aimed at young viewers. It described a prison program designed to show youngsters the consequences of crime. The cameras followed a group of youths as they toured the Rahway State Prison in New Jersey.

"You think you're tough or something? You think this is a fucking joke," says one of the lifers to a smirking youngster.

To another youth who wondered about life in prison, a murderer says: "We have sexual desires. Who do you think we get, and don't tell me each other. We get young, dumb motherfuckers just like you."

The program was given an Oscar at the 1979 Academy Awards for the best feature-length documentary of the year.

Unlike the Carlin broadcast, which was planned and deliberate, the language on "Scared Straight" was spontaneous, a distinction that the Supreme Court had made in the Carlin case.

Sexual Matters

The taboos against explicit reference to the sex act have been eased at a much slower pace than other prohibitions. Still, there have been changes, hardly surprising in view of the vast alterations in society over the past three decades. If journalism is the mirror held to life, then a journalism that is prohibited from chronicling changes in how we live is worse than useless; it is misleading and irresponsible.

The press has followed the arts, which journey wherever the imagination soars. Fiction, the movies, magazines had flung off the fig leaf and discarded the asterisk and dash years ago. The press lagged, and this failure to keep up, some press critics say, led to a public uninformed on such issues as sex education, venereal disease and the role of sex in behavior.

But some publications gradually became aware of the necessity to report these matters and their consequences. They began to report fully such issues as family planning, abortion, birth control, homosexuality, sex education, teenage sex, family relationships, venereal disease and laws affecting sexual behavior.

The pioneering work into human sexual behavior, Alfred C. Kinsey's *Sexual Behavior in the Human Male,* had been treated gingerly by the mass media when it was published in 1948. In 1966, another important work on sexual activity was published, *Human Sexual Response,* by Dr. William H. Masters and Virginia E. Johnson. The result of a detailed 11-year study of

Freud on Language. "Anyone who considers sex as something mortifying and humiliating to human nature is at liberty to make use of the more genteel expressions 'Eros' and 'erotic.' I might have done so myself from the first and spared myself much opposition. But I did not want to, for I like to avoid concessions to faintheartedness. One can never tell where that road may lead; one gives way first in words, and then little by little in substance too. I cannot see any merit in being ashamed of sex. . . ."—Sigmund Freud, *Group Psychology and the Analysis of the Ego* (1921).

sexual physiology, the work was too important to be ignored. The question was not whether to run a news story—times had changed—but how the story was to be written. The study was based on the direct observation of sexual intercourse and masturbation and was published to give those treating problems of sexual inadequacy information based on scientific observations.

Offensive Words

The story that appeared in the April 18, 1966, issue of *The New York Times* used the words *vagina, vaginal lubrication, intravaginal diaphragms, orgasm,* and other sexually explicit words. As the story was being edited, a problem came up on the desk.

As the event is recounted by a *Times* copy editor, the desk noticed the frequent and explicit references to the female sex organ (six times before the continuation) and only euphemistic references (two) to the male organ—"genital organ" and "the organ." The question was referred to an assistant managing editor who served as the arbiter of language and taste at the *Times.* He decreed *vagina* for the woman and *organ* for the man as proper.

Two years later, the *Times* was more forthcoming in its use of explicit language. Reporting the changes *The Washington Post* and *Chicago Tribune* had made in a review appearing in their Sunday book review supplement, "Book World," the *Times* reported that the newspapers had called back a press run of the supplement to delete a section that "consisted of a paragraph containing reference to the penis in a discussion of the sexual behavior of primates."

The paragraph that so offended the sensibilities of decision makers at the *Post* and *Tribune* that they called back a million copies of the press run at a cost of $100,000 began:

> Many a cocktail party this winter will be kept in motion by this provocative chit chat; man is the sexiest primate alive; the human male and not the gorilla possesses the largest penis of all primates. . . .

The *Post* and *Tribune* were clinging to the concept of the newspaper as family reading, though *Life* and *Newsweek* had used the word in their stories about the book, *The Naked Ape* by Desmond Morris, and though it was commonplace among millions of nursery school children, who had been told to call a penis a penis.

In the 70s, birth control devices were distributed on college campuses. Women talked openly about their sexual needs. Abortion, once a hush word, was frequently in the news because of the suits brought by groups urging repeal of abortion laws, and the counter-drive waged by various groups to retain the measures. Venereal disease was reported as a serious health hazard.

Just a Girl. In its profile of an assistant district attorney who is in charge of the city's Sex Crimes Prosecution Unit, the *Daily News* magazine quotes her about her personal life:

"Naturally, as a single woman I go out with my fair share of assholes, but the job certainly hasn't turned me off to men. If anything, I'm one of those slightly old-fashioned women who doesn't mind being referred to as a 'girl.' "

Sexual Abuse. For their frankly written series on sexual abuse of children, Rebecca Mabry and Mike Howie were explicit. One story in their series in *The News-Gazette* of Champaign-Urbana, Ill., began:

As a teen-ager, Jan tried three times to get help in stopping her father.

The first time was when she was 13, and although her father had been molesting Jan since she was about 5, he had never before attempted intercourse with her.

Jan recalls he held a knife to her throat and told her that if she ever told anyone what he had done, she would never speak again.

In 1975, the *Argus Leader* in Sioux Falls, S.D., carried a streamer across the top of page one:

At Least 14 Sexually-Transmitted Diseases Spreading In Epidemic Proportions

Right above the headline and under the newspaper flag was the newspaper's motto, "A Newspaper for the Home." The decision to play the story this way may have been influenced by one of the quotes in the AP's account:

"The public would panic if any other disease were advancing at the rate gonorrhea is," declares Dr. Bruce Webster of New York Hospital-Cornell University Medical College.

For years, reporters had ignored the alcoholism of public officials. With the exception of Drew Pearson, a Washington columnist, no one wrote stories about senators and representatives who were drunk in Congress or committee, despite their obvious inability to function.

In 1975, the escapades of Rep. Wilbur Mills, one of the most powerful men in Congress, with a burlesque dancer catapulted him and the issue of alcoholism to the front pages. Mills confessed he was an alcoholic. This admission, wrote Jack Anderson, Pearson's successor, caused reporters to ask one another "whether they should write more about the drinking habits of Washington dignitaries."

The answer by some journalists is that they should if the drinking affects the official life of the public figure. Clearly, conduct in office is an appropriate subject for journalism, particularly if the conduct incapacitates the official.

There is less agreement about coverage of the public but unofficial activities of officials and prominent persons. A movie star's nightlife may be subject to coverage as that is the world of the public personality, the star's allure. But is the nightlife of a mayor or governor a fit topic for coverage? Most reporters would say it is only if the hangovers incapacitate him for work.

But then, suppose most people in town know that the mayor has an eye for women and an insatiable thirst. Does not that public knowledge justify reporting? Most would say no. When Louisiana Gov. Edwin W. Edwards gambled large sums of money at Las Vegas casinos, that was news because of federal charges against him. Almost all would agree that what a public figure

Personal Lives

'Wife Beater.' Managing Editor Norman Pearlstine of *The Wall Street Journal* said he "agonized a couple of weeks" over the report. The story going the rounds in Washington was that the director of enforcement at the Securities and Exchange Commission had been accused of beating his wife. Other papers heard the report but didn't bother pursuing it. The *Journal* did. And it published its findings on page one. The official resigned.

There was no evidence that the official's personal problems were affecting his official life, an important test to decide whether material should be used. However, argued Michael Kinsley, editor of *The New Republic*, the official was a law-enforcement officer. After the *Journal* published the story, other newspapers carried it.

does in the privacy of his or her home—or apartment, or motel—is that person's own business. But not all. The sexual dalliances of another powerful congressman, Rep. Wayne Hays, were exposed by *The Washington Post* in 1976. The newspaper ran the revelations of Elizabeth Ray, a $14,000 a year employee of Hays. Her real job, the 27-year-old clerical worker said, was to serve as the congressman's mistress. Hays, chairman of the House Administration Committee, denied the allegations at first, then admitted them.

Three years later, another test of the propriety of publicizing the personal life of public figures emerged that seems to have established new guidelines for writing about the private lives of public officials.

The Rockefeller Heart Attack

Nelson Rockefeller, for many years governor of New York, an aspirant to the presidency and vice president to Gerald Ford, died in the company of a young woman while ostensibly working on an art book. A spokesman released the information about Rockefeller's fatal heart attack. But where Rockefeller died, when he died and the circumstances of his death were, the press learned, garbled by the spokesman.

The truth, as it was pieced together over the next several days, made increasingly vivid reading. There seemed little doubt that the 25-year-old woman who was with him in his townhouse at the time he was stricken (not in his office as the spokesman had announced) was more than simply Rockefeller's assistant. Although their relationship was never made explicit, there was no need. The usually staid *New York Times* took the lead in uncovering the details, among which was the fact that the young woman—whose salary was $60,000 a year—was clad in what appeared to be a black evening gown of some kind.

Although the other two New York City newspapers also covered the story, some journalists had misgivings. After all, Rockefeller was no longer a public official. Clearly, he was a public figure, but his notoriety was not that of a rock star or a movie idol whose reputation as a stud may be carefully cultivated.

A New York City television journalist, Gabe Pressman said press accounts of the death were an "effort to pander to the people of New York." He called the play the story received "salacious" in its use of "innuendoes and smears."

In their defense, editors pointed out that the first account of Rockefeller's death given by a family spokesman was almost completely erroneous. The press, sensitive to coverups after Watergate, dug into the story when the spokesman's account began to crumble, and once the ferreting began it was unlikely to be halted by a sudden surge of second thoughts about propriety.

A case can be made for intrusion into the personal lives of public officials, even after they have left office. It is made effectively by Sanford Levinson, who teaches in the department of politics at Princeton University. In an article in the May/June 1979 issue of the *Columbia Journalism Review,* Levinson justifies the Rockefeller coverage because of the spokesman's attempt to "make Rockefeller's death exemplary . . . to elevate it to the status of a public spectacle, and, so to speak, to invite the press to witness it after the fact." The spokesman sought to have Rockefeller die to rave notices, much like any public relations agent tries to orchestrate an event. Rockefeller had throughout his public career enjoyed excellent press coverage. He was rarely held to account by the New York press, Levinson says. And so the spokesman "can be excused for expecting one last act of cooperation from the press."

But some of the press refused to go along with the Rockefeller spokesman for the "one last act of cooperation." Their stories amounted to, in Levinson's words, "a rejection of the power that wealth has to transform reality in this society."

The official, sanitized version of the Rockefeller death was accepted by some journalists. Two days after Rockefeller died, James Reston led off his column in the Sunday *New York Times* with this observation.

It should particularly be remembered that Nelson Rockefeller died at his desk late on a Friday night after almost everybody else had gone home for the weekend. He was a worker, a yearner, and a builder to the end.

In an article, "Letter to Jimmy Carter," that appeared in the July/August 1979 issue of *The Washington Monthly,* Charles Peters wrote: "Unlike Edward Kennedy, you do not get drunk, nor do you have to worry about explaining from whose bed you may be called at the moment of nuclear decision." In response to many protests, Peters said that the personal life of Sen. Kennedy was appropriate for discussion because the senator was considered a candidate for the presidency. Peters had made explicit what other journalists had been alluding to in their profiles of the senator for several years.

The personal life of the public official or the private individual involved in public policy matters was considered relevant by *The Minneapolis Star.* Late in 1979, after an extensive inquiry, it published articles quoting prostitutes who said that many of the men who made and enforced laws against prostitution were their customers. The men were named and included a state district judge, a state senator, the United States Attorney for Minneapolis and St. Paul and the chief lobbyist for the Minnesota Catholic Conference, who argued for legislation against prostitution.

The politician who seeks our trust, and votes, because he proclaims himself virtuous must in truth be what he declares himself. It may be that the fury with which some reporters responded to the White House lies and cover-ups during Watergate was a declaration of anger and anguish that they had been had, that they had been party to a gigantic pseudo-event, the buildup of shallow, ruthless men.

After all, it was Richard Nixon in one of his famous debates with John Kennedy in 1960 who said of Harry Truman's cussing:

> . . . whoever is president is going to be a man that all children look up to or look down on, and I can only say that I am very proud that President Eisenhower restored dignity and decency and, frankly, good language to the conduct of the presidency of the United States.
>
> And I can only hope, should I win this election, that I could approach President Eisenhower in maintaining the dignity of the office and see to it that whenever any mother or father talks to his child, he can look at the man in the White House and, whatever he may think of his policies, he will say, 'Well, there is a man who maintains the kind of standards personally that I would want my child to follow.'

Journalists, hardly paragons of virtue themselves, do not expect saints to occupy public office. But they want the right to report the language and deeds of those who pass themselves off as white knights.

Pictures

After her revelations in the Wayne Hays caper, Elizabeth Ray reappeared in the news. The AP transmitted to its clients a photograph of Ray from *Playboy* magazine in which she was shown lying on what seemed to be a couch, bare-breasted, her arms upraised, her fingers running through her hair.

The photo committee of the APME was interested in how many editors thought the AP should have transmitted the photo. Of 138 who replied, 98 said yes, the AP did the right thing. But only 24 said they used the picture, 20 of them cropping the photo to avoid showing Ray's breasts. Clearly, editors are not ready—or believe their readers are not—for nudity.

Outrage. Henry McNulty, the Reader Representative for *The Hartford Courant*, concluded after taking more than 5,000 telephone calls on his job that pictures arouse more response than stories. Readers may be "appalled at a news story, but they are shocked and outraged at a news photo."

But readers and television viewers are apparently ready for some pictures that once were considered offensive. Bodies of accident and murder victims are regularly shown on television. The breakthrough came during the Vietnam War. It made no sense for war coverage to hide war's consequences. Some writers believe that the frank coverage by television of death and disaster may have caused the eventual public disillusionment with the war that led to U.S. withdrawal.

Not long after the Elizabeth Ray photo was distributed by AP Photo, another photograph containing offensive material was moved by AP Photo. This one pictured Nelson Rockefeller, then vice president, chortling as he "gave the finger" to hecklers at a political rally. Taken by Don Black of the Binghamton *Press* and *Sun-Bulletin,* it ran on page two of Black's newspaper but was given page-one display over three, four and five columns, in newspapers from *Newsday* on Long Island to the *Chronicle* in San Francisco, from the *Herald* in Portsmouth, N.H. to the *Democrat* in Tallahassee.

Black said he disagreed with the decision of his editors to put the picture on page two, but he understood "the reluctance of the editor to give front page display to an obscene gesture, no matter who had made it."

The picture was prominently displayed on page one of the *Knickerbocker News* in Albany, where Rockefeller was governor for 15 years. Executive editor Bob Fichenberg said of his use of the photo, "Either we put ourselves in the position of protecting the vice president from his own actions or we report it pictorially, as well as in text, and let the public know. We decided to let them know."

Pueblo Prisoners. When AP Wirephoto distributed this picture of men from the captured intelligence ship Pueblo in 1968, it ran an editor's advisory: "Your attention is called to the possible obscene nature of the fingers in this picture." *The New York Times* ran the picture and in the caption stated, "The defiant finger gesture by three of the men seems to have eluded the North Korean photographer." Photo from Wide World Photos.

Death

Despite the heavy toll traffic accidents take, newspapers have been reluctant to use photos of traffic fatalities. They will show the photograph of a plane crash in another state but are reluctant to use the picture of a sheet-draped body of a local motorist killed on a highway.

Claude Cookman was working on the photo desk of *The Miami Herald* when a decision had to be made involving pictures of Haitians who had drowned attempting to reach the United States and whose bodies had been washed up on Florida's shores. The newspaper used the photos.

Cookman says that in deciding about photo use, these questions must be resolved:

1. What do the pictures really show?

2. What are the readers likely to add or read into their interpretation of the photos' content?

3. What are the circumstances under which the photographs were obtained?

4. How compelling is the news situation out of which the photos arose?

5. How compelling or significant are the photos in terms of what they teach us about the human experience?

6. Do the positive reasons for publishing the photos outweigh the almost certain negative reaction they will elicit from a sizable portion of the readership?

Suicide. A series of photographs taken by Stewart Bowman of a distraught woman jumping off a building in Louisville was not used by *The Courier-Journal* on the ground that the woman was not a public figure and that the incident had only minimal news value. *The Courier-Journal*'s sister newspaper, the *Times,* used one of the pictures.

Claude Cookman, then photo editor of the *Times,* argued for its use. "In the first place, these were extremely powerful pictures, and they made me think about my own death.

"I think that we should show the entire range of human experience. We always run pictures of people singing and dancing. That's part of life, but death is, too. If we don't show suffering, then we aren't giving a complete view of life."

Compare the incidents—the Louisville suicide (above), the Bakersfield drowning (p. 610) and the drowned Haitian—in terms of Cookman's guidelines.

In the drowning, the attempt of Haitians to reach the United States was a running news story. This was not an isolated death. Many others had drowned in the incident. The news situation (No. 4) was strong.

The news value of the woman's suicide was negligible. She was not prominent. This was not the one case that set a record for the city or county's number of suicides. Clearly, the pictures were dramatic. But that is not reason enough.

Intrusion or Warning? The photograph of a family mourning over a drowned child appeared in *The Bakersfield Californian* and quickly became one of the most disputed photographs of the 1980s. More than 400 persons called the newspaper to protest, and 500 wrote to protest the intrusion into the family's grief. Eighty readers cancelled subscriptions, and there was one bomb threat, which led to the evacuation of the newspaper building. The newspaper responded by apologizing three times in print, and in a memo to the staff, Managing Editor Robert Bentley said, "We make mistakes—and this clearly was a big one."

Bob Greene, a columnist for the *Chicago Tribune*, described the picture as "a gross invasion of privacy." Afterwards the picture was distributed by the AP and many newspapers used it. Reader response was angry wherever it was used. The *Press-Telegram* in Long Beach, Calif., ran 70 column inches of letters in response.

The photographer, John Harte, has no apologies for taking the picture, or for his paper's running it, and he disagrees with the newspaper's apologizing for its use. "Our general policy is not to run photos of deceased persons, and we pay special attention to the sensitivities of both our subjects and our readers. But special circumstances prevailed that led to the running of this photo.

"One, our area is plagued by an unusually high number of drownings annually. During the week this photo was taken, there were four drownings, two that day, in our area's public waters. Two, by having a policy of not running these pictures except for special circumstances, we hoped that by running this one our readers would have gotten the message that we felt it was important they witness the horror that can result when water safety is taken lightly.

"As horrible as it was, there was a message in that photo."

What do you think?

Cookman made the point that there is something that transcends news values—the human value, you might call it. If so, question No. 5 could be applied to the suicide as follows: The pictures of a 71-year-old woman leaping to her death show us that old age, ill health and loneliness take their toll in many ways that this youth-oriented culture prefers to turn its back on.

Number 6 was used in defense of the publication of the Bakersfield drowning picture.

Nora Ephron, a media critic, says of pictures of death:

"I recognize that printing pictures of corpses raises all sorts of problems about taste and titillation and sensationalism; the fact is, however, that people die. Death happens to be one of life's main events. And it is irresponsible—and more than that, inaccurate—for newspapers to fail to show it."

A sensitivity to personal feelings is essential to the journalist, not because invasions of privacy are illegal but because compassion is a compelling moral demand on the journalist. The photograph can be as callously intrusive as the television crew at the scene of a disaster poking camera and microphone in the faces of the bereaved. Yet, death is part of reality, and it is possible to be overly sensitive to it.

Death has provided the press with almost as many problems as has sexual material. We cringe from confrontation with our mortality. Morticians try to make death resemble life. Wakes are no longer fashionable. Black for the bereaved is a past practice. Children are kept from funerals by solicitous relatives. Death is said to be the last taboo.

Young reporters sometimes go to the other extreme. Carried away by the drama of violence, they may chronicle the details of death—the conditions of bodies strewn alongside the airliner, the mutilated homicide victim, the precise plans of the youngster who committed suicide in the garage.

This enthusiasm is as tasteless as prurient sexual interest, for it uses the tabooed subject as the means to shock readers, to call attention to the reporting rather than to the subject. Death can be terrible and horrifying. But its terror and horror are best made known through understatement. In sensitive areas, the whisper speaks louder than the shout.

Guidelines

Reporters are often told that on matters of taste the decision as to what will be used will be made by an editor or the copy desk. Nevertheless, reporters should set criteria for themselves. Obviously, what the reporter sees and how he or she sees it is influenced by his or her attitudes and values. A censurious reporter may block out relevant material. A prurient reporter may overindulge his or her fantasies. An open attitude toward the matters we have discussed is a corrective to the natural propensity to be guided, and consequently victimized, by impulse and sentiment.

By their nature, editors are conservative. Like libel lawyers, when they are in doubt they tend to throw out questionable material. A reporter learns early in his or her career to fight for stories. The reporter who has a set of standards from which to argue his or her story past the desk will be better able to do a good job of presenting to readers and listeners the world of reality.

The self-appointed guardians of good taste no longer have the power to issue dicta. Now, it's the journalist who decides what is essential and what is offensive and unnecessary. Guidelines are essential for responsible use of this power. Here are some:

1. Is the questionable material essential to a story of significance? If so, there is compelling reason to use it.

2. Use depends on the kinds of readers and listeners who use the medium. But care should be taken to see to it that all are considered, not just those who are most vociferous.

3. The tone of the publication or station is a consideration.

4. The private as well as the public actions of public officials and public figures are the subject of journalism if they bear on matters of public concern.

The Morality of Journalism

Newspapers, broadcast stations and press organizations have adopted codes of ethics and guidelines that:

- Prohibit journalists from accepting anything of value from sources.
- Limit activities that may pose conflicts of interest.
- Stress the journalist's responsibility to society and the obligation to be accurate, impartial and free of conflicts of interest.

The reporter should also adopt a personal code that stresses the reporter's:

- Compassion for the poor, the handicapped, the different.
- Moral indignation when the powerless are victimized.
- Willingness to place responsibility for the failures of policies and decisions on those who made them.
- Commitment to the improvement of his or her skills.

I don't mean to seem unfriendly," the fragile old man said, "but I just don't want people to see any stories about me." He looked down for a moment and then back to his visitor, Kevin Krajick, a reporter for *Corrections* magazine. Krajick was on assignment to interview elderly prisoners, and during his stop at the Fishkill, N.Y., state penitentiary he had been told about one of the oldest, Paul Geidel, 84 years old and in his 68th year behind bars for murder.

Geidel offered to make toast and tea for Krajick, and he accepted. Geidel had turned away many reporters before, but a guard had suggested Krajick try anyway, and he had led the young reporter to Geidel's 10 X 10 room in the prison infirmary.

With the gentleness of his age, Geidel said he understood that Krajick's job was "to get a story." He respected that calling, he said, but he really didn't want to talk about himself.

"I began slipping in questions about his past, his feelings about his life," Krajick recalled, "He answered several of them, but he said several times, he did not want 'any story.'"

"He had tried to live in solitude and repentance, he said, and any notoriety upset him. He wanted to die in obscurity." A reporter had visited him a few years before and had promised that no story would come out of their conversation, Geidel told Krajick.

"I thought they would leave me alone, but then one day I pick up the paper, and oh, there's my name and my picture splattered all over the front page."

Geidel, the son of an alcoholic saloon keeper, was put in an orphanage at seven. At 14, he quit school and worked at menial jobs. When he was 17 he broke into a hotel room in New York, stuffed a chloroformed gag in a guest's mouth, grabbed a few dollars and fled in a panic. The victim suffocated. Geidel was sentenced to life in prison for second-degree murder.

It was all in the newspaper, again, 60 years later.

"It was terrible, just terrible," Geidel said.

"I had decided at that point that I would not put him through the pain of printing a story about him," Krajick said. "I told him that I would not. I figured there were plenty of interesting elderly prisoners who wouldn't mind being written about."

The two chatted about an hour and parted good friends.

"Then I learned that Mr. Geidel had served the longest prison term in U.S. history. I started to waver. I checked the files and found that several magazines and television stations had run stories on him when he refused parole at the age of 81. I then called the state corrections and parole authorities to find out how Geidel had been held for such an incredible term—a point that had not been made clear in the previous articles.

"It turned out that he had been classified as criminally insane on what turned out to be a pretty flimsy basis and then totally forgotten about. He had not stood up for himself during all those years and had no one on the outside to do it for him.

"This obviously was a story of more significance than I had first thought. It was the most dramatic demonstration possible of the abuse of power under the boundless mental commitment statutes that most states have. What could be more moving than the story of the man who had spent the longest term ever, whom everyone acknowledged as meek and repentant and who, under other circumstances, would have been released before he reached the age of 40?

"The public clearly had reason to know about this man's life. It would be difficult to justify leaving him out since I was writing what was supposed to be a definitive article on elderly prisoners for the definitive publication on prisons."

Krajick faced a moral dilemma. Were the reasons for publishing his story sufficiently compelling to outweigh his promise to Geidel and the pain that the article would certainly inflict on the old man?

Critical. Surveys show that among the major complaints against reporters is their supposed lack of concern about whether their stories hurt people. The studies report the two other major criticisms are sensationalism and invasion of personal privacy.

The Morality of Journalism 613

"I was anxious not to hurt a man who had, as prison records and he himself said, spent his life in mental anguish. I was sympathetic with his wish to remain obscure."

In his work, Krajick had faced situations in which people had been imprudently frank with him and had asked to be spared publicity. Those decisions had not been hard to make. He had reasoned that those who are hurt or embarrassed by the truth usually deserve to be. But Geidel deserved neither society's curiosity nor its condemnation. He had paid his debt to society.

In the balance Krajick was striking—a balance of conflicting values—were two other factors: Articles had already been written about Geidel, and the fact that he had become a statistic in the Guinness Book of World Records would soon draw other reporters whose articles, Krajick felt, would be more flamboyant and less accurate than his.

"On this basis, I decided to print the article, though not without misgivings," Krajick said. "I realized that if Mr. Geidel were to see the article he would be distressed, and he would feel betrayed by the young man who was nice to him but ended up lying. I only hope those around him have the sense not to show him the article. That would be the only escape for my conscience."

The piece appeared in the magazine under the title, "The Longest Term Ever Served: 'Forget Me.'" The concluding paragraph of the article reads:

As his visitor left, he offered to write to Geidel. "Oh, no, please," he said. "Please. I don't mean to seem unfriendly. But please don't write. Forget me. Forget all about me." A distressed look crossed his face and he turned and hobbled down the hall to clean the teapot.

Solicitude for people is fairly new to journalism. If there had been a practical guide for reporters it could well have been, "The story's the thing." For many years, outsiders had urged on the press a sense of responsibility, a caution that the First Amendment was not a license for money-making and sensation-mongering. In the 1970s, the press began to heed these criticisms, and this self-scrutiny included an examination of ethical problems.

This self-examination led to the adoption of codes and standards that call for accuracy, impartiality and avoidance of conflicts of interest and that proscribe certain activities, such as the acceptance of gifts from sources. But the codes do not help to resolve problems like the one Krajick faced. By examining a variety of ethical problems journalists have encountered we shall try to construct a series of ethical signposts that will supplement the codes and will help the journalist to set a general direction for his or her journalism.

Without some kind of moral framework, journalism is reduced to a repetitive chase after disconnected stories, and this becomes for the journalist a life empty of meaning and dignity.

James C. Thomson, Jr., a former curator of the Nieman Foundation, noted in an article in the Winter/Spring 1978 issue of the *Nieman Reports* that during the previous five years there had been a "sharply increasing preoccupation both inside and outside the media, with journalistic ethics: the values and behavior of news organizations and individuals."

Some journalistic practices were embarrassing. *The Detroit News* made a study of the gifts staff members had received in 1972. The watches, offers of free travel, Christmas hams and poinsettia plants added up to $56,000. The newspaper decided that gift-givers should be put on notice that gifts would either be returned or given to charitable organizations.

Free travel was an embarrassment. In 1972, three-fourths of the newspapers surveyed said they accepted free travel for staff members. A dozen years later, after attention had been called to the practice, three-fourths said they generally did not accept free or subsidized trips for staff members. Here are the changes through the years:

	'72	'74	'77	'84
Would accept free travel from tax-supported agencies.	78%	32%	25%	28%
Sportswriters accept free transportation to travel with team.	—	38	25	16
Editors accept free travel on airlines' inaugural flights.	—	37	19	13

As journalists continued to examine their practices, similar declines were reported in the acceptance of gifts and the holding of part-time jobs that created conflicts of interest with the journalists' full-time jobs.

Two major journalism organizations adopted codes and a third revised its code during the 1970s. Many newspapers and broadcast stations drafted codes of their own. By the early 1980s, three out of four newspapers and stations had adopted codes of ethics. These codes have been effective in correcting abuses by the press that compromised its claim to be the conscience of the community.

The codes of the 1970s trace their lineage to the report of the Commission on Freedom of the Press in 1947, which sought to establish standards of responsibility for the press. The study team was headed by Robert M. Hutchins, then chancellor of the University of Chicago. Hutchins summed up the report in its preface: "This report deals with the responsibilities of the owners and managers of the press to their consciences and the common good for the formation of public opinion."

Causes for Concern

No Thanks. When Donald Bluhm, travel writer for *The Milwaukee Journal,* learned he had won second place in a contest about "the image of Mexico" abroad, he was delighted. When he learned he had won $12,500, he was astonished. The Pulitzer Prize, journalism's most prestigious award, is $1,000.

The *Journal* learned that the contest had been sponsored by the Mexican tourist industry, which, the paper said, "gives the appearance of a conflict of interest that compromises the newspaper's credibility." Bluhm agreed with his editors and turned down the award.

Codes of Conduct

None Censured. The code of the Society of Professional Journalists pledges to "actively censure" those who violate the code. In the 13 years since the code's adoption, no one has been censured. A review process suggested in 1984 to establish a procedure for censure was rejected by the Society.

The study was the culmination of extensive criticism of the U.S. press as insular, often sensational and sometimes irresponsible. It was carried out in a period of change. The United States had emerged from World War II as the leading world power. Vast social changes had occurred. The members of the Commission—most of them prestigious faculty members at leading universities—concluded that the press had not been "adequate to the needs of society."

The reaction was mixed. Some newspapers supported the findings, but others ignored the recommendations when they did not assail the Commission, possibly because the Commission consisted of outsiders, and the press does not take kindly to being told what to do by any but the brethren, if by them.

Still, the Commission recommendations were a persistent reminder to the press of its shortcomings. During the 1950s and 1960s, one recommendation was particularly pertinent—that the press had failed to give "a representative picture of the constituent groups in the society." Vast segments of society had been ignored by the press, particularly the young and the aged, racial minorities, the poor and women. Gradually, the press became more responsive to external criticism. Journalists themselves became outspoken, and their criticisms began to appear in the various press reviews that sprang up around the country. Journalists began to take their trade more seriously—possibly because of the steady infusion of college-trained reporters who were questioning some of the assumptions of the craft. The climate was established for journalists to codify good practices, to set lines between the acceptable and the morally indefensible.

The codes established ethical norms for a craft with aspirations to professional status. The problems these codes address have tainted journalism with a grubbiness inconsistent with the standards of professional conduct. But they do not address many of the problems that grew out of the concerns Thomson cited in his article. To do so, Thomson writes, is not easy. Journalists have to "tangle with a number of ambiguities about journalism, news and the U.S. Constitution," he says.

Limitations of the Codes

"What codes, standards, or models could—or should—encompass the extraordinarily wide varieties of practitioners in, and avenues of approach to journalism?" he asked. Then there is the definition of news. It is "undefinable," says Thomson. The news organization is "both a private, profit-making business and, simultaneously, a constitutionally-protected semi-public service. Such outfits are therefore operating both To Make Money (at the least, not to lose it) *and* To Do Good (or expose iniquity, and thereby to improve society). Therefore, a first and unresolvable tension is between greed and idealism."

Finally, the "difficult fact, for journalists, is that the Constitution, its amendments, and its judicial interpreters have recognized and guaranteed several other citizens' rights" in addition to the free-press portion of the First Amendment.

Thomson describes these ambiguities as "too endemic and ineradicable," and journalism's "domain too wide and infinitely varied" for a code to cover.

"What code can be written for such a special craft other than those of the philosophers and saints who have tried to teach men how to coexist?" he asks.

Even if journalists were to find specific guidelines to codify, there seems scant chance that such a disputatious group as journalists could agree to any but the most general admonitions, injunctions and exhortations. In 1974, the National Conference of Editorial Writers, concerned that some syndicated columnists had undisclosed conflicts of interest, entertained a motion that the columnists "should be censured." After considerable debate, the group changed the wording to "subject to criticism."

The codes define unethical behavior. But most of the dilemmas journalists must resolve require choices between what journalists consider to be conflicting moral or ethical actions.

Krajick had to choose between what he saw as two positive ends. To print the story would reveal some truths about a system that crushed one prisoner and may still be affecting others. It would be morally right to use Geidel to illustrate the inadequacy of the mental competency process, he believed. Not writing about Geidel would also be a moral action because then Geidel would be spared the further agony of public exposure. Surely, a man who has spent 68 years behind bars deserves our compassion. Moreover, there was Krajick's promise not to use the material. Can a public need justify the reporter's going back on his word?

Looking to codes for guidance, we find in one of them, that of the Society of Professional Journalists, that the journalist should "serve the general welfare." Krajick would serve the general welfare with publication. The same code stresses "respect for the dignity, privacy, rights and well-being of people encountered in the course of gathering and presenting the news." Clearly, respect for Geidel would mean heeding his plea not to write about him. The codes are no help here.

Most of the criticism of the press is addressed to what is printed or broadcast—the vast number of pseudo-events orchestrated by people in power and the disconnected tidbits of news and entertainment that are only of momentary interest. The major sins of the press may well be those of omission—ignoring the significant actions of the powerful and the travails and the longings of vast numbers of powerless people.

No code can make a journalist a person of good conscience. Only a personal commitment to a journalistic morality can determine that.

Greed. The discovery was almost too good to be true—a trove of volumes that constituted Hitler's diaries. It was a publisher's fantasy come true, for interest in the Nazi tyrant has never waned.

Without checking their authenticity thoroughly, the West German magazine *Stern* spent $8.6 million on the material, and Rupert Murdoch bought the rights for his News International.

When the diaries proved a clumsy hoax, Murdoch shrugged off the news of their fraudulence: "After all, we are in the entertainment business."

Newsweek had some doubts, but went ahead and put the story on its cover. To play it safe, the magazine ended its piece: "Now the appearance of Hitler's diaries—genuine or not, it almost doesn't matter in the end—reminds us of the horrible reality on which our doubts about ourselves, and each other, are based."

Newsweek's declaration that truth does not matter has come to represent the counting-house mentality of journalism.

Sins of Omission

No code led *The Charlotte Observer* to address the fact that North Carolina's leading income producer, its tobacco crop, is the source of the single greatest cause of lung cancer, which is responsible, health authorities say, for 1,000 deaths a day. It was the conscience of the *Observer's* management and editors that caused the newspaper to examine the issue in detail in a special section.

Morality Underlies Journalism

Morality is basic to the theory and practice of journalism. The free press justifies its existence in terms of moral imperatives; it rationalizes much of its behavior with moral declarations.

If public consent freely given is essential to the proper functioning of a democracy, then for the consent to be meaningful the public must be adequately informed by a press free of government or any other control. Thomas Jefferson expressed this simply: "Where the press is free and every man able to read, all is safe." The First Amendment makes this consensual system possible. Although neither the Constitution nor any laws require that the press carry out its essential role in the system, the press does take on itself responsibilities and obligations. The decision to offer thorough coverage of those in power—even at some risk—is a moral decision. Some publishers and station owners obviously choose otherwise, to maximize profits by offering vast quantities of entertainment—splashy color photos, news tidbits, profiles of singers and TV actors—and crowding the remaining news with advertising.

The highest praise in journalism goes to the reporter, the newspaper or the station that engages in public service journalism. Journalists are expected to be socially conscious, to have "at their heart a touch of anger," as Richard L. Strout, veteran Washington correspondent of *The Christian Science Monitor,* puts it. At what is their anger directed? Here is a list of awards made by the Associated Press Managing Editors organization:

The Atlanta *Constitution:* Examining practices used to deny voting rights to blacks.

The Jackson, Miss. *Clarion-Ledger:* Detailing the plight of poor farmhands in the Mississippi Delta.

The Long Beach *Press-Telegram:* Exposing police brutality.

The Seattle Times: Reporting that freed a man wrongfully convicted of rape.

The Worcester, Mass. *Evening Gazette:* Describing the plight of elderly people forgotten by their friends, family and society.

The Albuquerque Tribune: Uncovering the extensive dumping of dangerous wastes in New Mexico.

The Columbia (Mo.) *Daily Tribune:* Investigating Missouri's hospital for the criminally insane.

The Greeley (Colo.) *Daily Tribune:* Revealing inadequate care in some nursing homes.

The Mission. "The newspaper that is true to its highest mission will concern itself with the things that ought to happen tomorrow, or the next month, or the next year, and will seek to make what ought to be come to pass . . . the highest mission of the press is to render public service."—Joseph Pulitzer.

The *Longmont* (Colo.) *Daily Times-Call:* Covering the fatal shooting of two Hispanics by local police in what began as a routine traffic stop.

The *Salisbury Post,* Salisbury, N.C.: Revealing how the high cost of medical care has affected health.

The Ledger and *Enquirer* of Columbus, Ga.: Examining an ignored killer—infant mortality.

Pulitzer Prizes have been awarded to the Jackson (Miss.) *Clarion-Ledger* for its campaign to reform the state's public school system, to Loretta Tofani, a reporter for *The Washington Post,* for her investigation of rape and sexual assault in the Prince George's, Md., detention center, to Mark J. Thompson of *The Fort Worth Star-Telegram* for reporting that showed that 250 U.S. servicemen had lost their lives as the result of a design problem in helicopters, and for reporting by *The Philadelphia Inquirer's* William K. Marimow that showed city police dogs had attacked 350 innocent people.

These stories grew out of the understanding by reporters and their editors that journalism is a moral enterprise.

In his book, *Deciding What's News,* Herbert J. Gans describes a set of "enduring values" that he says "can be found in many different types of news stories over a long period of time. . . ." These values, he says, "affect what events become news, for some are part and parcel of the definition of news." Among these are the desirability of economic prosperity; the undesirability of war (which does not extend to certain wars, Gans points out); the virtues of family, love and friendship, the necessity of honest government, and the ugliness of hate and prejudice.

Gans also lists eight "clusters" of values that influence news decisions: ethnocentrism, individualism, altruistic democracy, responsible capitalism, moderatism, social order, small-town pastoralism and national leadership. Journalists see news in terms of deviations from these values. The belief in altruistic democracy, for example, is revealed, says Gans, in the "stories about corruption, conflict, protest and bureaucratic malfunctioning." The news stories about these deviations imply "that politics should follow a course based on the public interest and public service."

In their reporting and editing, journalists are always making choices: What to report, whom to interview, what to put in the story, what to leave out. Selection, the heart of journalistic practice, is guided by news values, and these values reflect the prevailing concerns and value system of the society and are rarely disputed.

There are, however, disputes when the choice is between alternative actions, each of which has some claim to principle. This is no different from the decision-making most of us face in our daily lives. "The world that we encounter in ordinary experience," says the philosopher Isaiah Berlin, "is one in which we are faced with choices between ends equally ultimate and claims equally absolute, the realization of some of which must inevitably involve the sacrifice of others. . . . If, as I believe, the ends of men are many, and not all of them are in principle compatible with each other, then the possibility of conflict—and of tragedy—can never be wholly eliminated from human life, either personal or social. The necessity of choosing between absolute claims is then an inescapable characteristic of the human condition."

Life as Referent

Can the journalist refer to some universal values as guides to choice, or is decision subject to particular circumstances and individual decisions—what the philosophers call a situational ethic? Traditionally—perhaps instinctively—mankind has sought absolutes as guides. And as often as the priest or the guru has supplied them they have been found to be so general as to be impractical. Or they have been discovered to be a way of keeping a religious, political, economic or social system in power.

Even so, we may find in these searches for an ethic to live by some suggestions for a useful journalistic morality. The concern for the good life, the properly led life, is almost as powerful as the need for sustenance. We may find some guides from religion and philosophy, from the Prophets and Plato, from the guru who traces his ethic to the Bhagavad-Gita and from contemporary philosophers.

"Life is the referent of value," says Allen Wheelis, a psychiatrist, who writes about ethics. "What enlarges and enriches life is good; what diminishes and endangers life is evil." If we define life as physical survival and apply Wheelis' referent to one of the immediate problems of industrial societies, we can conclude that factories and automobiles that poison the air, water and earth are bad. To preserve an atmosphere we can breathe is good. Industries that endanger the lives of their workers or nearby residents are bad. Safety procedures—or plant closures if this cannot be accomplished—are good.

Journalists have revealed many of these unsafe and life-threatening conditions. Water supplies contaminated by industrial waste and land that is permeated with toxic materials have been the subject of diligent journalism.

But the factory and plant owners and the automobile manufacturers have opposed strict environmental protection standards. To clean up a plant, to make a car that does not emit pollutants, to make a process safe in the factory would be costly, so costly the price of the car would have to be increased or so expensive the plant might have to shut down, owners have said. This means unemployment, a loss of taxes to the local community, a decline in business where the plant or factory is located. No wonder that workers often oppose proposals for safety, clean air and clean water.

Is it the responsibility of the journalist to continue to point out that the factory is poisoning the air? Or does the reporter turn elsewhere? If so, jobs may be saved, the profits of the company assured and taxes kept low.

Money v. Life. Smoking is blamed for an estimated 350,000 deaths a year in the United States. As a result, the American Medical Association's House of Delegates proposed laws to ban tobacco advertising.

The American Newspaper Publishers Association and the Magazine Publishers Association told the AMA: "Products that can be legally sold in our society are entitled to be advertised; if it is legal to sell a product, it should be legal to advertise it." Only six newspapers and the *Reader's Digest, Saturday Evening Post* and *Good Housekeeping* do not accept cigarette advertising.

Sam Zagoria, the ombudsman of *The Washington Post,* asked, "Is there any media group for social responsibility? Are there any more companies for corporate responsibility?"

Tobacco advertising amounts to $2.6 billion a year.

A Religious Perspective

Peter Brown, *professor of classics and history at the University of California at Berkeley*—"The deep religious anger of the Prophet Muhammad at what he saw around him, wealth squandered, the weak oppressed, the insensitive pride of the well-fed. The Prophet's clear and chilling message: The possible perfection of a human being, living at ease with his fellows."

Abraham Heschel, *an Old Testament historian*—The prophets were "intent on intensifying responsibility." They were "impatient of excuse, contemptuous of pretense and self pity." They "felt fiercely" and were "attuned to a cry imperceptible to others."

Will Campbell, *an activist minister with the Committee of Southern Churchmen*—"Jesus judges us by what we do to the children, the prisoners, the whores, the addicts, the scared and the bewildered—to the 'least of them.' "

Genesis, *Chapter 18*—The Lord tells Abraham that he will destroy Sodom and Gomorrah for their sins. "Wilt thou also destroy the righteous with the wicked?" asks Abraham. No, the Lord replies,"I will not destroy it for ten's sake." But ten righteous men could not be found. (The point is the same one that philosophers have made through the generations: The individual has an inescapable moral obligation to society. On him or her may depend its salvation and survival.)

The dilemma is not new. The playwright Henrik Ibsen describes it in "An Enemy of the People." Dr. Thomas Stockman, medical officer of the municipal baths, a considerable tourist attraction, discovers that the baths—the source of the town's economic resurgence—are being poisoned by the nearby tanneries. He wants to close them as a menace to public health.

But the community leaders and the local newspaper editor point out that any revelation about the pollution will lead people to shun the baths, and this will cause economic problems, among them unemployment and higher tax rates for property owners. Dr. Stockman is reviled as an enemy of the people.

The practical concerns of a money-based society have occupied many writers. Dickens' novels cry out against the "cash-nexus" as the "only bond between man and man," as one literary critic put it.

"Breathe the polluted air," Dickens says in *Dombey and Son.* "And then, calling up some ghastly child, with stunted form and wicked face, hold forth on its unnatural sinfulness, and lament its being, so early, far away from Heaven—but think a little of its being conceived, and born, and bred, in Hell!"

If "life is the referent of value," what other choice has the professional whose reason for being is service to the public than to see and to speak out so that others may see and understand. In the calculus of values, life means more than the bottom line on a ledger sheet. Joseph Conrad said: "My task which I am trying to achieve is, by the power of the written word, to make you hear, make you feel—it is, before all, to make you see. That—and no more, and it is everything."

Harold Fruchtbaum, a Columbia University social scientist, describes as "one of the intellectual's primary functions" the task of placing "responsibility for the failures of our society on the people and the institutions that control the society." Translated into a moral concern for the journalist, this is the task of holding power accountable, whether the power be held by a president or a school superintendent.

Communal Life

In holding power accountable to the people, the journalist takes to his or her job a sense of communal life. That is, the reporter has a set of values that tell him or her when power is being abused so that the quality of life in the community suffers. Philosophers through the ages have talked about the "good life," which has its starting point in a communal life whose underpinnings are freedom, tolerance and fairness. In such a society, individuals have basic rights that neither the state nor other individuals may violate, and the individual has, in turn, obligations to the community.

In writing about the American philosopher John Dewey, Sidney Hook said that Dewey believed

> . . . the logic of democracy requires the elimination of economic, ethnic, religious and educational injustices if the freedom of choice presupposed by the ethos of democracy is to be realized.
>
> One man, one vote is not enough—if one man can arbitrarily determine the livelihood of many others, determine where and under what conditions they can live, determine what they can read in the press or hear on the air.

Dewey also believed that the community has the responsibility for eliminating hunger and poverty, that political power must be harnessed to solve the problems of group and individual welfare. Economic conditions must be such, he wrote, that the equal right of all to free choice and free action is achieved.

"Democracy means the belief that humanistic culture *should* prevail; we should be frank and open in our recognition that the proposition is a moral one—like any idea that concerns what *should* be," Dewey wrote.

Communal life is an unfolding process in which the experienced past and the desired and anticipated future are considered in making the present. The journalist plays a key role in this process. The reporter describes the immediate and distant past and shows the possible future in his or her work every day. The reporter gives voice to those who seek change to bring about some result, and the reporter describes the activities of those who seek to carry the past into the future by maintaining present policies.

Compassion for All. In the good community, there is concern for the sick, the elderly and the impoverished. Newspapers and stations reinforce communal values by calling attention to those who need special attention and help. (Left) Photo by Stephen Gross, *The Anniston Star*. (Right) Photos by Bob Thayer, *The Providence Journal*.

The Good Life

When moral philosophers speak of the good life they mean a life in which people can read, speak and choose freely, that they need not live in fear of want, and that they can count on shared values such as those Gans describes—the desirability of equal opportunity, the undesirability of crime, and so on.

Journalists enrich and promote these values through the values and assumptions that they take to the job. For example: A journalist is told that at the local university the political science department is promoting Marxism, that instructors are doing more than describing the ideology; they are endorsing it. To check on the charge, the reporter disguises herself as a student and attends classes. In her story, she describes her experiences, quoting class lectures and discussions, using the names of students and instructors. The charge is found to be groundless.

We do know that posing and using disguises are generally not acceptable in society. Let us strike a balance in deciding whether the use of a disguise by the reporter is ethical.

The benefits: An irresponsible allegation is proved false. The reporter was able to do first-hand reporting, which is more persuasive and closer to truth than transcribing the instructors' denials.

The costs: Deception must be revealed to the readers as a journalistic method. Privacy has been violated.

We can broaden this example and cite some actual cases of questionable reportorial tactics:

• A *Toronto Sun* reporter posed as a psychology student interested in doing volunteer work at the Queen Street Mental Health Centre.
• The *Lexington Herald-Leader* reporters who uncovered a basketball scandal at the University of Kentucky taped telephone calls to some former players without their knowledge, which is permissible under Kentucky law.
• The *Anchorage Daily News* used grand jury material its reporters picked out of a courthouse trash can.

We will examine these matters in detail later in this chapter, but now we can say that the costs of some of these actions—no matter how well intended—outweigh the benefits if we keep in mind that the good life is the healthy communal life. What kind of community will we have if we cannot speak freely and openly to one another in class because we fear our words may be broadcast or published? What kind of community will we have when all of us must fear peering eyes so much that we must shred our garbage?

There may well be exceptions to the shared value of the right to privacy, of the abhorrence most of us feel at people posing, of our belief that the classroom should be a forum where everyone can discuss ideas without fear of being quoted in a news story. We will look at some of these exceptions later. (Certainly, those in power cannot claim privacy for their official acts.)

Actions that hurt people or disrupt the community are immoral, unless justified by powerful moral considerations. A story about a convicted rapist will hurt the rapist; but we justify the story because punishment of those who commit crimes shows the community that society does not tolerate and will punish crimes. Crime unpunished can lead to the breakdown of the community.

Survival and the good communal life. Are there additional guidelines, more specific guidelines that we can find that are of use to the journalist in helping him or her to make choices? Through an examination of a few of the practical problems reporters face we may find some.

In the six weeks of a libel trial against the San Francisco *Examiner* for $30 million, there was minimal coverage by the Bay Area news organizations. There was one brief spot on KPIX-TV, another on a local public televison news show and a feature in the San Francisco *Chronicle,* which ran four weeks after the trial began. Why so little coverage?

"It wasn't a terribly good television story," the news director of one television station said. It could not be squeezed into the station's 90-seconds-per-story format, she said. The *Chronicle's* city editor said the story was of greater interest to reporters than to the general public.

One of the defendants gave another reason. "The story was sensitive and complex—and it didn't include the raciness of the stories they like." It was also embarrassing to the *Examiner.* The suit involved a story alleging illegal actions by law enforcement officers in a murder case.

When he was a columnist for the *Chicago Sun-Times,* Mike Royko was arrested on charges of speeding and driving while intoxicated. The story was carried by the *Chicago Tribune,* local television stations and the UPI's national wire. The *Sun-Times* did not carry the story because of "simple news judgment," according to the newspaper's editor.

The news shocked the people of Missoula. The 21-year-old daughter of a well-known couple in the Montana community had been stabbed to death outside her Washington, D.C., apartment house. She had been a high school honor student and an accomplished musician and had won a scholarship to Radcliffe.

Less than a week later, the managing editor of *The Missoulian,* a 32,500 circulation daily in the city, had an even more shocking story on his desk: The young woman had been a streetwalker in Washington, "a $50-a-trick prostitute" who "used to talk freely about her work and bragged about being 'a pro,' " according to a story *The Washington Post* planned to run the next day under the headline, "A Life of Promise that Took a Strange and Fatal Turn." The *Post* had learned she had returned to Missoula after dropping out of Radcliffe and one night in a bar she had been approached by a man who asked her to return with him to the East. He was a pimp who recruited young women around the country.

Rod Deckert, the managing editor of *The Missoulian,* was confronted with a difficult decision. If he ran the story, the family would suffer new anguish. If he did not, he would be suppressing news that was bound to be known since the *Post* was moving the story on its news service wire and papers distributed in Missoula and nearby might carry the dramatic story of a small-town girl come to a sordid end in the East. It was, Deckert said, "the most painful day in my 11 years of life in the newsroom." Jack Hart and Janis Johnson recount the story in "Fire Storm in Missoula" in the May 1979 *Quill.*

To Print or Not to Print

Public or Private? A city councilman has AIDS. A candidate for governor is known as a womanizer. Newsworthy?

Some guidelines provided by Carl Sessions Stepp in his article "When a Public Figure's Private Life Is News" in the December 1986 *Washington Journalism Review:*

• Verify the report.

• Does it affect the person's public performance?

• If the fact is well known, no good is served by keeping it out of print.

• The competitive situation. If a competing station or paper uses it, the fact is now public.

• Leonard Downie, managing editor of *The Washington Post*—use it "when the private conduct of a public figure is symptomatic of a societal problem."

Deckert reasoned that the young woman's experience could be a warning to other young women in the university community. However, he had to weigh this against the pain it would cause the family and friends.

Deckert decided to run an edited version of *The Washington Post* story with some locally gathered inserts. Deckert played the story on page 12 with no art under an eight-column headline. The last paragraph reads:

"She was a pretty nice girl," said Officer Geary Scott, who arrested (her) under the name Mika Jenson, and charged her with soliciting for prostitution November 9, 1977. She was convicted the following December.

The Silent College Daily

Traditionally, college health services had been charged with a lack of concern for the needs of students—aspirin was a favorite prescription, according to students. In the 1970s, the health services began to become important treatment centers for sexual and psychiatric problems. Sex counseling, contraception, abortion referral and venereal disease treatment were provided. Some colleges set up gynecological clinics.

There was little opposition at most schools, but at the University of Michigan, the student journalists at *The Michigan Daily* were concerned that the Board of Regents might object if publicity were given to the new services. The *Daily* decided not to run a story on the contraception clinic.

Sylvia Porter, a financial columnist with an estimated 31 million readers in 350 newspapers, admitted in one column that she had information about internal problems in the financial community that could have had damaging consequences to it and that she had held back on printing the information for fear she might start "a panic."

To criticism that her job as a journalist required that she go into the matter, she replied, "If you're going to be an analyst and a columnist on economic life, don't you think you have a responsibility not to bring the whole structure down?"

In preparing the obituary of a local businessman, the reporter noticed that 30 years before, when he was a county official, he had been convicted after a fund shortage was discovered in his office. He was given six months probation. Since then, he had married, raised a family and had become a respected businessman. His life for 30 years apparently had been exemplary. Should the conviction be included in the obituary? *The* Louisville *Courier-Journal* decided to put it in.

In the mid-1970s, a Boston physician was convicted of manslaughter after he performed an abortion in the second trimester of a woman's pregnancy. The story aroused national interest. Race and religion figured in the legal situation, as well as the volatile issue of abortion. Here are the comments of H. L. Stevenson, editor-in-chief of the UPI in answer to a criticism of the UPI story:

> Several letters have taken us to task for failing to make clear that Dr. Kenneth C. Edelin, involved in the Boston abortion case, is black. The jury which convicted him was all-white and predominantly Roman Catholic, another fact subordinated in our stories on the verdict.
> There was no deliberate attempt to suppress these facts.
> Our feeling—and those involved in the coverage have been advised—is that the racial and religious identification was pertinent to this sensitive story. These facts should have been reported more prominently.

In 1961, *The New York Times* decided to eliminate from its story about an impending U.S.-sponsored invasion of Cuba to overthrow Fidel Castro the expected date of the invasion and the fact that it had been largely financed and directed by the Central Intelligence Agency. The story was given a four-column headline on page one, but the publisher and managing editor changed that to a one-column headline. The news editor and assistant managing editor, who made up the page, told the managing editor that the *Times* had never before changed its front-page play for reasons of U.S. policy.

In another international issue columnist Jack Anderson came into possession of letters and memoranda said to be from the internal files of the International Telephone & Telegraph Company that showed the firm's effort to enlist the U.S. government's support to prevent Salvador Allende, a Marxist, from taking office as president of Chile. The publication would have embarrassed the United States in Latin America. Anderson printed the information.

A correspondent in Central America sent stories to *The Christian Science Monitor* from Nicaragua detailing U.S. cooperation with the Somoza dictatorship. The foreign editor was concerned that the articles would feed growing anti-U.S. sentiment in the area and considered not publishing the material. Finally, the editor agreed that the stories merited publication, despite their implications. (The editor's worries were justified. The stories were picked up by some Latin American newspapers to prove that the United States was an opponent of political, social and economic reform in Latin America.)

National Security

The Progressive magazine, which has described the concept of national security as the government's way of stifling debate about matters such as the arms race, in 1978 approved an idea for an article about the hydrogen bomb. The free-lance writer, Howard Morland, said he wanted to show that the so-called "secret" of the construction of the bomb was no secret. Morland had been an economics major at Emory University, then a Vietnam War transport pilot (he flew aluminum coffins across the Pacific) and then an anti-nuclear activist. Morland visited plants where the components of the bomb are put together, and he read about the subject.

The Progressive scheduled Morland's article for the April 1979 issue under the title "The H-Bomb Secret: How We Got It, Why We're Telling It."

His point, Morland said, "is that the myth of secrecy is used to create an atmosphere in which public debate is stifled and public criticism of the weapons production system is suppressed. I hope to dramatically illustrate that thesis by showing that what many people considered to be probably the ultimate secret is not really a secret at all. The information is easily available to anyone who wants to acquire it."

The editor of *The Progressive,* Erwin Knoll, knew that the penalty for publishing restricted information is severe—prison and a fine. He sent the piece to the Department of Energy, which found that it contained restricted data and said all the drawings and 20 percent of the article would have to be removed.

Knoll had to choose between two courses of action that seemed to him legitimate: To publish and expose the vast "nuclear warhead assembly line," as Morland put it, or to accede to the government and not risk the further proliferation of nuclear weapons by divulging possibly secret information.

Knoll decided on publication. The government asked for a restraining order (which was granted), the first injunction to suppress publication of an article in American history and the first case of prior restraint since the Pentagon Papers case eight years before, in 1971. (Knoll later said he regretted not having gone ahead with publication and risking prison instead of first seeking clearance.

The press was divided on Knoll's attempt to publish the article. Many newspapers said that the case was not important enough to risk having the Supreme Court put serious restrictions on the press. But most opposed the government's seeking and the court's granting a gag order. The magazine appealed the prior restraint. During the trial before the circuit court the government suddenly dropped its case. The piece was finally published, and most scientists concluded what the government's prosecutors apparently had come to see—there was a negligible security risk.

What would you have done had you the responsibility for deciding these matters? We will be returning to these cases in a few pages. Here, to help you draw some guidelines, are some ethical dilemmas with comments.

When David Kennedy, a son of Robert Kennedy, died in Florida of a drug overdose, reporters converged on the scene. The Kennedy family tried to close some medical records, documents that by state law were open to the press. The press won access to most of what it sought, but an ethical issue evolved when more than 30 reporters covered the wake at the family home in Virginia.

"Why were we there?" asked Eric Schmitt of *The New York Times* in an article he later wrote for *The Quill* ("Absence of Pity," July/August 1984). "It shocked my sense of civility that the press or the public believed it had a rightful place there. Instead of what should have been a private moment for the family, the press declared the sad gathering of Kennedys a newsworthy event."

H. Eugene Goodwin, a professor of journalism at the Pennsylvania State University, described the press coverage as an invasion of privacy. "I am talking here, of course about invasion of privacy in the ethical sense. It was not illegal for the press to cover the Kennedy wake—no privacy suit could be successfully brought by that coverage. But the question is: 'Was it ethical?' "

His answer provides some guidelines about privacy. Reporters and editors should first determine whether "the publication or broadcast of the private facts (is) justified by the public interest." That is, "Does the public need to know these private facts for some clear reason?"

Professor Goodwin would then ask, "How much harm is apt to result from invading someone's privacy in a news story?" And: "How much long-term good is apt to result from publicizing private facts?"

The White House spokesman was furious. Details of the federal budget began to appear five days before it was scheduled for release. This was the third year in a row that information about the budget, which had been embargoed—or marked hold for release—had been revealed early. The finger pointed to *The New York Times*. Once it began to carry stories about the budget, other newspapers and the AP felt obligated to move the story. Some reporters said they were able to obtain material from sources inside the Reagan administration.

Unless the news organizations agreed to some kind of code, a White House spokesman said, "it's going to be a jungle out there."

Embargoes are useful for complicated material because reporters usually need time to prepare stories of this sort. So the embargo serves the press. It also serves the source, who is able to release material for maximum media exposure. In other words, the embargo generally pleases everyone. The public is well served, too, because it will have thoughtful rather than hastily written information.

No law prevents a reporter from breaking a hold-for-release date. The issue is an ethical one.

Private or Public?

Request Granted. The press responded differently to the death of Christa McAuliffe, the teacher who died in the explosion of the space shuttle Challenger in 1986. It respected the request of the family for privacy. Coverage was confined to the public ceremonies.

Hold for Release

Few reporters will turn away from a source willing to give them a story. After all, the journalist's job is to write stories, all the better if the story is an exclusive.

Newspapers compete with broadcast stations and the wire services and each other. The scoop has always been sought, and those reporters who can break stories before their competitors are prized.

Nevertheless, when a reporter or his or her news organization participates in a news event that is embargoed, it is morally bound to adhere to the release date. And most of the time this is done.

Race

The young woman was attacking her boyfriend with a knife, and police said they were unable to stop her. Fearing she might kill the man, they shot her. In the story, the woman's arrest record—petty larceny, loitering, prostitution—was included along with the autopsy finding that her blood alcohol level was .15, beyond the point at which a person is legally drunk.

The reaction in the black community was immediate and angry. The woman was the daughter of a black leader in the community. At a public meeting, the newspaper was condemned for "executing" the woman. In response, the editor wrote a column saying that in obituaries the criminal record of the deceased usually is not included, but in this story her record was necessary because of the nature of the event.

The black community remained dissatisfied, and in a meeting with the newspaper's editors it accused the paper of being anti-black. Again, the editor responded in print, this time with an apology for "unbalanced and insensitive" coverage. The staff was furious at what it considered the editor's capitulation.

The story was uncomplimentary, and clearly it could add fuel to the fires that burn in the mind of the bigot. But the newspaper cannot have one policy for whites and another for blacks. Nor can it ignore events that are likely to become known. When they are, the newspaper stands convicted by the public of a cover-up.

Let's now examine some of the incidents that were reported a few pages back. We will try to draw some guidelines.

A Few Conclusions

Clearly the journalist speaks to all, for all. That is, the journalist's concern is the public, not the special interest. On matters that require the balancing of the press's self-interest (the San Francisco *Examiner* libel case) or the interest of a special group (Sylvia Porter's financial community) against the general interest, the latter should prevail. Defining the general interest is not easy, for, as some maintain, there is no public interest but a melange of special interests. But there are concerns shared by most people, and access to information is one of the basic needs of a democratic society.

The journalist with an overly acute sense of responsibility is sometimes as dangerous as the recklessly irresponsible reporter. When *The Courier-Journal* printed the conviction of the deceased former county official, it did disregard a personal interest (the family's) for the general interest. Yet what was the general interest that was served? Disclosure of a minor crime committed 30 years before by a person who is dead seems to serve no end at all but the purpose—often sound enough—of full disclosure. If our goal is truth, and truth is served by presenting all the facts, then certainly we are on sound moral ground if we include this unsavory but factual detail in the obituary. But the journalist knows that he or she can never hope to learn everything about an event. Moreover, the journalist is forced to select for use from this limited stockpile of information the few facts that can be fitted into the restricted time and space allocations. In this selection process, the journalist applies to the material the tests of utility, relevance and significance within a value system. (Several days after the obituary appeared, the editor apologized to the family.)

Many agencies and groups do take on themselves the task of providing full disclosure. The *Congressional Record,* minutes of council meetings, court transcripts and the like are available. But the journalist must summarize, condense, select. And he should be understanding—the man appeared to redeem himself. Although redemption is handled by another calling, journalists should consider compassion in their work.

Had the crime been well known at the time of the man's death, the journalist could not ignore it. What the public knows the press cannot skip over without risking charges of covering up information. This could also apply to the Missoula case. There was no way the community would remain ignorant of the death of the young woman. Had the newspaper failed to run some story, accusations could have been made that the newspaper showed partiality to a middle-class family while day after day it chronicles the troubles of others less affluent and influential. The newspaper might have handled the story with an editor's note admitting its dilemma. Then the violent reaction—the newspaper's editorial writer condemned the story and scores of people protested by calls and cancellations—might have been avoided or alleviated. (Krajick's dilemma might have been less intense had he considered such an editor's note. Although readers usually need not be told the reporter's problems, situations such as these can be less troublesome with full disclosure.)

Suppose the Missoula newspaper alone had learned that the young woman died a prostitute. Should it have included the fact in its story? If her work had been an inextricable part of the crime, there would have been no way to avoid it. But she had been found dead near her apartment house, the victim of an unknown assailant. No newspaper dredges up every aspect of an individual's past, whether for an obituary or a straight news story.

However, as it turned out later, her work was part of her death, for the man charged with her murder was her pimp. The sordid affair would have to have been told when her murderer was arrested and charged.

Postscript: Eight months after the *Missoulian* published the story of the young woman's murder, a late model Chrysler New Yorker rolled into Missoula and the four occupants went to work. Two cruised bars, and two went to the high schools. Within hours, the police were told by an alerted public.

The four men were arrested and convicted of criminal trespass and soliciting for prostitution.

In the first draft of this section, the young woman's name was used, the instinctive reaction of a journalist to supply basic information. Surely, in a book that seeks to examine a subject in detail, the name would seem to be relevant. But is it? What does it add to the information necessary to understand the situation? Nothing, it would seem. It would appear to be information for the sake of information, which has some merit. But balance this against the damage revelation could cause. This textbook is used at the University of Montana and it could be the inadvertent cause of grief to the family. Still, there is a principle no journalist can turn from: What the public knows or will learn, the journalist cannot ignore. Surely, after the newspaper ran the story, most people in town knew the identity of the young woman. But the story is now several years old.

The argument can continue indefinitely. Unlike the philosopher, who may spin out syllogisms for a lifetime, the journalist must act quickly. The decision in this case was against disclosure.

The principle that what the public will learn itself the journalist must tell if the event is significant could apply to the University of Michigan newspaper's decision to ignore the health clinic story. An event of considerable magnitude in the community soon becomes common knowledge, and the newspaper ignores the event at its peril. This is a pragmatic argument, but it has theoretical validity in that the journalist tends toward disclosure because publication usually serves a community better by preventing rumor mongering.

Racial Issues

There will always be people who over-react to the word. The reporter who writes straightforward accounts of events may indeed feed the fires of bigotry and violence. Not to print important news on occasion may seem responsible at first glance. But such decisions corrode the journalist's moral injunction to be the carrier of information, bad as well as good. In the area of racial news, much has changed since newspapers gingerly approached news of racial and ethnic groups.

In a roundup on the ways the press was handling racial news in the 1970s, *The Wall Street Journal* summarized the journalist's dilemma:

> If the press hews to its ideals and holds a mirror up to society, reflecting all its evils, cankers and tensions as well as its virtues, it runs the risk of stirring dangerous passions. But if it deliberately distorts the image or blots out the parts that might inflame, it casts itself in the dubious role of censor and judge.

Some newspapers and stations, the *Journal* reported, had taken on self-censorship. Some agreed to arrangements whereby news of racial disturbances would be delayed. Most said they strove to be careful in handling sensitive racial news but would not limit coverage. "It is the public, not the press, that must in the end find a way out of racial crisis—and the public can't be expected to do that unless the press gives it an accurate picture of society, warts and all," the *Journal* stated.

Still, some newspapers approach racial matters with exteme care, as did the Rochester newspaper in its handling of the incident involving the black leader whose daughter was shot by police. A book by Thomas H. Landess and Richard M. Quinn, *Jesse Jackson and the Politics of Race,* (Ottawa, Ill.; Jameson Books, 1985) argues that Jackson is given kid-glove treatment by the press because he is considered a spokesman for blacks. The authors argue that when Jackson referred to Jews as "Hymies" and New York City as "Hymietown" he was treated "delicately" by the press compared with the treatment Earl Butz received after his remarks about blacks.

The black poet Langston Hughes remarked that he would know television—and society—had matured when TV shows could portray a black as a liar, a cheat or a criminal.

Progress is being made. In Salt Lake City, the National Association for the Advancement of Colored People (NAACP) condemned a state health department film on teen-age pregnancy—not because it portrayed minority teen-agers having illegitimate children, but because it did not.

"All the actors are white. Minority teens get pregnant too," the president of the local NAACP chapter said.

National Security

Stories involving national security pose complicated questions about the responsibilities of the press. Clearly, the experience of the press during periods of crisis following World War II destroyed the unspoken alliance between journalists and the government. Reporters learned that the government had systematically misled or lied to them on crucial issues. The government, reporters found, not only misled them about the facts but covered up by pulling the cloak of national security over matters of legitimate public concern. In so-called national security matters, only one voice is heard—that of the state.

Clearly, the government cannot disclose all it knows. But who is to decide what protects the state and what protects the policy maker, what secrets are crucial to survival of the nation and what undisclosed truths protect an administration in office? The state says it shall decide. The press says history indicates that as irresponsible as the press may well have proved itself at times, press disclosure is the least dangerous alternative in a democracy. Support of South Korea or a Marcos, the nuclear arms buildup and arms pacts are debatable policy. But without disclosure of all information there can be no informed debate. The logic and the morality of democracy call for publication.

Color Blind. The following dialogue took place at a regional conference sponsored by the American Society of Newspaper Editors:

White editor: I felt it was racist when we reported that a black Baptist minister wore elaborate jewelry and drove a Mercedes.

Black editor: Don't be afraid of color in a story. If someone wears flashy jewelry, report it.

A Journalist's Moral Framework

• **Loyalty to the facts.** "You inevitably develop an intense sense of revulsion or a mild attachment for one candidate or the other," said Joseph Alsop Jr., a political writer. "But you have to be loyal to the facts or lose your reputation." John Dewey put it this way: "Devotion to fact, to truth, is a necessary moral demand."

• **An involvement in the affairs of men and women** that requires experiencing or witnessing directly the lives of human beings. Involvement generates compassion, accuracy and fairness, which are the foundations of an ethical journalism.

• **The ability to distance one's self from experience** to generate understanding. Antonio Gramsci, an Italian writer imprisoned by Mussolini for his commitment to freedom, said he had to learn the necessity of being "above the surroundings within which one lives, but without despising them or believing one's self superior to them."

• **A reverence for shared values, rules, codes, laws and arrangements** that give a sense of community. Such concern causes the journalist to keep careful watch for any action that can divide people into hostile groups, classes or races.

• **Faith in experience** when intelligently used as a means of disclosing some truths.

• **An avoidance of a value-less objectivity.** This kind of objectivity can lead to what philosopher Stuart Hampshire describes as an "ice age of not caring." He writes that such an attitude can mean the end of civilization "not in a flurry of egotism and appetite leading to conflict . . . but in passivity and non-attachment, in a general spreading coldness. . . ."

• **A willingness "to hold belief in suspense,** the ability to doubt until evidence is obtained, the willingness to go where the evidence points instead of putting first a personally preferred conclusion; ability to hold ideas in solution and use them as hypotheses instead of dogmas to be asserted; and (possibly the most distinctive of all) enjoyment of new fields for inquiry and of new problems."—John Dewey.

• **An awareness of our limitations and responsibilities.** The story can never equal the whole truth. A concern for the consequences, the impact of what we write. A firm understanding of the line between fact and fiction.

• **Belief in the methods of journalism**—the gathering of relevant material and evaluation of those facts through analysis; the synthesizing of them in the story. Conviction that this method will lead to some kind of truth worth sharing.

• **A moral vision of the future.** "If you don't have that vision," says the Indian writer Ved Mehta, "sooner or later the system will collapse." Without a moral vision, the journalist's compulsion may be power, profit and place in society.

Taping, Posing, Trashing

In the section headed "The Good Life" some pages back, we looked at some questionable ethical acts by three newspapers.

The *Lexington Herald-Leader*'s reporters taped calls to basketball players without telling the athletes their conversations were being recorded. The reporters, Michael York and Jeff Marx, described their action as "the prickliest ethical issue" involved in their reporting. Most of the former players were told their comments were being taped, and those who were interviewed personally saw the tape player. But a few were secretly taped.

The reporters received permission to violate the newspaper's rule requiring the source's permission to tape interviews because "we thought there was a chance that some players would develop . . . 'amnesia' after the story appeared," York said. Anyway, he commented, "There's very little difference between the use of a tape recorder and shorthand notes from which a complete transcript of the interviewee's answers could be reproduced." In other words, so long as a source is speaking to a reporter, the source must presume the reporter is taking notes, whatever the method.

So long as the interviewer makes it clear that the interview is for use by the newspaper or broadcast station, the method of transcription is irrelevant.

The *Anchorage Daily News* defended its violation of grand jury secrecy by saying that it used material in a wastebasket from 23 pages of handwritten notes taken by the jury clerk because "this situation goes back to the basics of journalism, and that is you learn things and you tell them to your readers," as Howard Weaver, the managing editor of the paper put it. (The paper could not be prosecuted because state laws require secrecy of jurors and court officials but of no others.)

Howard Simons, curator of the Nieman foundation, said dipping into the trash can was satisfactory journalism because the "trash contains things that other people throw away" and no law was violated.

True enough. But legality is no test of morality. There is no law against lying, no law against a political reporter working for a candidate for office, no law against accepting a fur coat from a Mafia leader. The question is whether trash-bashing is moral.

When the *National Enquirer* published a story based on the findings in the trash of a secretary of state, the ombudsman of *The Washington Post* was moved to comment that trash-picking is "indefensible—both as a journalistic practice and as civilized behavior. It is a question first of all of the way decent people behave in relation to each other, a question of how we permit one another to live. There are certain basic conditions, certain vulnerabilities, to all our lives—public and private figures alike—that we must be able to assume others will not take unfair advantage of."

If we all must monitor our garbage, we are consigned to live in a community of distrust and fear. The fact that the press is the cause of our uneasiness is as unsavory as the sight of a journalist fingering garbage.

The reporter for the *Toronto Sun* who posed as a psychology student was criticized by the Ontario Press Council. "Deception should be used only as a last resort to obtain a story that is in the public interest," the Council stated. We will look in some detail at poses and disguises and other dubious practices next.

The Pose and the Disguise

Deception has had a long and, until recently, an honorable journalistic history. In 1886, a young and ambitious reporter who called herself Nellie Bly feigned insanity to enter a mental hospital and exposed inhuman conditions in the hospital. Ninety years later, a reporter from *The Washington Post* gained admission to St. Elizabeth's, a federal hospital in Washington D.C., with the same ruse.

Early in this textbook, we saw how a reporter posed as a woman worried that she was pregnant in order to expose an abortion mill. One of the most revealing and dramatic books about life for blacks in the South, *Black Like Me,* was written by a white man, John Howard Griffin, who darkened his skin to pass as a black.

Reporters have disguised themselves as priests and policemen, as doctors and distraught relatives to get stories. Some of the great coups in journalism have come through deception. Although many of the questionable methods are used for laudable ends—usually the exposure of corruption—questions have been raised about their use.

Is there a dividing line we can locate between permissible deception and irresponsible impersonation? Is the line located at the point where an adversary press checks power to serve the legitimate public interest?

The Mirage Watering Hole and Pub

In 1978, *Chicago Sun-Times* reporters won several prizes for their exposé of abortion mills that were endangering women's lives. The reporters posed as women in need of abortions. A complex subterfuge was worked by the same newspaper when it purchased a bar, staffed it with reporters and photographers and set out to gather proofs of payoffs and corruption. The series led to reforms of the city inspection system. But when the articles were recommended for a Pulitzer Prize by the Prize jury, some members of the advisory board considered the operation of the Mirage Bar dishonest.

Benjamin Bradlee, the executive editor of *The Washington Post* and a Pulitzer Board member, asked, "How can newspapers fight for honesty and integrity when they themselves are less than honest in getting a story?" Eugene C. Patterson, another board member, said that the *Sun-Times* reporters should have interviewed bar owners. "That would have been the hard way to get the story," he said, implying that deception was the easy way out. (The Pulitzer board did not award a prize to the *Sun-Times*, although it stated it did not reject the series on the ethics issue because it did not want to set a precedent for future entries.)

Interviewing bar owners—if they would have talked, which seems unlikely—does not provide the physical evidence investigative reporters always seek to support their stories. The accounts of human sources are never as convincing as physical evidence. But the requirements of journalism, as we have seen in the case of the San Francisco television station that could not fit the libel trial into its format, do not weigh heavily in balancing moral choices.

The Public Says No. In a major study of media credibility, the researchers found that more than half of those polled disapprove of reporters posing as someone other than journalists, of recording conversations without telling people they are being recorded and of quoting unnamed sources.

Is Bradlee's point—that the consequences of deception are damaging to the press—valid? One of the basic tests of an action is its consequences. If the action would have damaging consequences to individuals, it should probably not be taken. But in this case, the damage is to the press, and journalists are supposed to take risks to publish truths. Bradlee's argument does have validity in that no one can claim exemption from the rules that he or she would set for others. In the case of the poses to expose Chicago bar inspectors or abortion mills, this moral balancing could be struck:

1. If we adopt a disguise, we can help to reform the city inspection system or close down abortion mills that endanger the lives of women. It may not be a moral tactic, posing, but the ends justify the means. We are acting morally because we are trying to right a wrong in our exposé.

2. To pose is wrong. It misleads individuals who may take us into their confidence to tell us things they would not if they knew we were reporters. It treats people as means. A corollary to the principle of life as a referent is that we may not treat a person as a thing to be used for our purposes. Here, for a story, we would be treating people as things. But not to pose would mean we might not dig up the story, and if our function is to expose wrong then we are immoral in not acting.

If we use life as the referent for testing the moral validity of actions, then posing to gain access to health clinics is morally defensible since lives are involved. But the adoption of poses for routine stories would appear unjustified. The reporter who disguises himself as a health seeker to gain access to the tent of a faith healer may have greater claim to moral justification than the reporter who poses as a customer to expose a massage parlor as a front for prostitution.

One of the time-tested guides to behavior is Immanuel Kant's categorical imperative: "Act as if the maxim from which you act were to become through your will a universal law of nature."

Kant had another imperative: "So act as to treat humanity, whether in your own person or that of another, in every case as an end in itself, never as a means." The imperatives of Kant, a major figure in the history of philosophy, may appear old fashioned at first glance, but his prescriptions can help to resolve some of the sticky moral questions journalists face.

In a sense, people are always means to the journalist's end, which is the news story. Even when deception is not used, the reporter maneuvers and manipulates sources to his or her end. The reporter justifies this on the ground that such actions serve useful purposes, even for the source, since the individual is a member of the society that is being served by the reporter.

Illegal. A reporter for a Virginia newspaper was fined $500 and given a six-month suspended jail sentence for impersonating a law enforcement officer in order to enter a maximum security prison to interview an inmate on death row.

The Heifetz of the Telephone

One line of thinking that has allowed reporters an escape hatch from the moral dilemma presented by disguise, posing and deception is this: A reporter need not identify himself or herself as a reporter, and if a source presumes the person talking to him is not a reporter, so be it. An intentional disguise or pose would be deceptive and therefore unethical, but a telephone call asking for information need not be preceded by the reporter's identifying himself as a reporter. Harry Romanoff of the defunct *Chicago American* went a giant step beyond this questionable tactic.

Romanoff was known as "the Heifitz of the telephone" for his flawless performances. His greatest act of virtuosity was his coverage of the mass murder of eight student nurses in Chicago. Romanoff, who never left his desk to cover a story, extracted the details of the crime from a policeman by pretending to be the Cook County Coroner. He was also able to write a story about the suspect by convincing the suspect's mother that he was her son's lawyer.

Romanoff and others who have used deception to gather information usually do not disclose their tactics in their stories. Now it is considered responsible journalism to make full disclosure in the copy. Then the journalist can be held responsible for his or her tactics by an informed reader. A useful guideline: If the reporting technique cannot be described in the story, then it should not be used.

There are some practical guidelines for the use of deception. Gary Seacrest, a lawyer for the Gannett newspapers, says "Reporters have to be very careful about how they obtain a story or a photograph. The use of deception is very risky. Journalists should identify themselves for what they are—reporters on assignment. This is crucial when a journalist invades a private place, but less important when operating in the public arena. Judges are often harsh on the imposter's technique."

Dishonesty

Imposters come in different guises. The reporter who poses as a priest or a detective to reach a grieving widow is one form. The reporter who claims the work of a colleague as his or her own is another.

During the past decade, plagiarism and fabrication seemed to increase. Some reporters used the work of syndicated columnists as their own. A reporter for a Chicago newspaper invented a bar in Texas and quoted characters he invented. A reporter for *The Washington Post* invented an 8-year-old heroin addict and wrote a harrowing tale that won the author a Pulitzer Prize in 1981.

In their defense, some of these reporters contend their work should be judged like any creative writing—imaginative in detail but true in ultimate meaning. They say they have poetic license. Unfortunately for them, journalism issues no such licenses.

Others say they have been swept up in the headlong drive of journalism for ever-more-fanciful writing. This does not exempt them from responsibility for their unethical actions, but there may be some legitimacy to this defense.

Some editors want clever writing above all else. They pressure their reporters to gloss over the facts that do not quite fit, to burnish the dull quotation so that it glistens. All of this is dishonest, and, says Roy Peter Clark of the Poynter Institute for Media Studies, "Dishonest writing is bad writing, no matter how beautiful the style.

"We cannot tolerate self-indulgent over-writing, the creation of stereotypes, composite characters, improved quotations, rearranged facts, invented authorial presence or the omniscient looking into minds.

"If information is important it often needs attribution because we have a responsibility to let our readers know not only our knowledge, but the limits of our knowledge.

"Good writing is not just a veneer to coat the facts. It is not style without substance. It is clarity, relevance, humanity and hard work."

Composites, reconstructed dialogue, descriptions of what people think, concealment of sources and locations. These techniques have attracted journalists over the past two decades since Truman Capote's successful "nonfiction novel," *In Cold Blood*. They have been trumpeted by the New Journalists and have helped sell magazine articles as well as books. But they are taboo for the journalist. The philosophy behind their use was inadvertently revealed when a magazine editor said he had permitted an author to make readers believe a prostitute named "Redpants" was an actual person instead of a composite. He had edited out the fact the character was a composite, he said, because "it got in the way of the flow."

That is, technique was placed above truth. It is permissible to change names and disguise places where the truth can cause trouble for a source. But the story must say so, high up in the piece.

Carl Bernstein says that while digging into the Watergate story he needed cooperation from the chief investigator for the Dade County (Fla.) state's attorney. To obtain it, Bernstein promised to dig up the military records of a man running against the state's attorney. A source in the Pentagon agreed to look for material about mental illness, arrests or homosexuality. Bernstein says he did not have to transmit the information because the state's attorney decided he did not need it.

Jack Anderson describes how he turned over information to Sen. Joseph McCarthy. In his book, *Confessions of a Muckraker* (New York: Random House, 1979), Anderson says that shortly after the senator made his famous speech in Wheeling, W. Va., in which he asserted he had names of 205 Communists who were "shaping policy in the State Department," McCarthy asked Anderson's help. McCarthy had been challenged to produce the names. He did not have them, and he called on Anderson to gather some names.

Fact and Fiction. Alastair Reid, a long-time *New Yorker* writer, told students in a seminar at Yale that he fabricated people, sometimes invented scenes and created conversations for some of his pieces. These embellishments, he said, made his articles more accurate.

Reid and some other journalists talk of a "subjective truth" that is more revealing than "objective truth."

John Hersey, another long-time *New Yorker* writer, has said there is one sacred rule of journalism: "The writer must not invent. The legend on the license must read: None of this was made up. The ethics of journalism, if we can be allowed such a boon, must be based on the simple truth that every journalist knows the difference between the distortion that comes from subtracting observed data and the distortion that comes from adding invented data."

The Quid Pro Quo

Abysmal/Good Journalism. To obtain an interview with the Palestinian terrorist accused of planning the hijacking of the ship the Achille Lauro, on which a U.S. citizen was murdered, NBC News had to promise not to reveal his identity. (He was under indictment by a U.S. grand jury.)

The *Chicago Tribune* described the deal as "an abysmal disgrace to journalism." In *The Quill*, columnist Ron Dorfman defended the arrangement because the man was not "merely a criminal" but a "political or military figure," because he was "newsworthy."

What do you think?

"As I recall, the decision to help McCarthy was almost automatic," Anderson says. "I went to our files and pulled out what was the most promising." He said he told McCarthy the material was unsubstantiated. McCarthy found the material "terrific." Anderson did not tell his boss, Drew Pearson, what he was doing but when Pearson decided to attack McCarthy as a witch hunter, Anderson tried to talk him out of it.

"He's our best source on the Hill," Anderson said.

"He may be a good source, Jack," Pearson said. "But he's a bad man."

Anderson stopped leaking to McCarthy, and soon began investigating the senator. Two years later he wrote a book condemning McCarthy.

Many reporters swap information with their sources. But this puts the reporter into a provocative role as the supplier of confidential information or publicity the source could not otherwise obtain. This is a dangerous role for a journalist to play, and an unethical one as well.

Some working reporters might contend that anything that helps to develop a good story should not be rejected too hastily. Granted, so long as in choosing between irreconcilably opposed moral claims, the decision can be defended with honor and dignity. The sociologist Max Weber said that when a man "is aware of a responsibility for the consequences of his conduct and really feels such responsibility with heart and soul he then acts by following an ethic of responsibility and somewhere he reaches the point where he says, 'Here I stand; I can do no other.'"

Knowledge as a Value

The journalist cannot in conscience be passive about a threat to public awareness. "If you are among brigands and you are silent, you are a brigand yourself," a Hungarian poem tells us. The brigands come in all shapes and sizes. Some are treated leniently by the press because they appear innocently misguided, censoring books and movies for what they believe is the public welfare. Others play on that part of us that fears knowing too much.

But the journalist must recognize these as threats to an immanent value, the necessity of knowing, of having information that will liberate us from ignorance, prejudice and the limitations of time and place. Information becomes memory, and memory, says the Polish writer Czeslaw Milosz, "provides a foundation for values" by which a society lives.

This does not mean that journalists use everything they can find. All facts are not equal, and other values come into play in the selection of what is to be published and broadcast. But when the source is closed the possibility of knowing is denied.

The open society is a perilous one. When all the winds of doctrine are set loose, the turbulence can be overwhelming. The world since 1945 has seen democratic nations that were born in optimism succumb to the tyrant who promises order. The journalist hardly contributes to order, for the journalist's task is to broadcast competing ideas and doctrines. It is also the journalist's task, some journalists believe, to maintain an adversary relationship to centers of power.

How a reporter approaches power determines much of the reporter's coverage. James Reston, a long-time Washington correspondent and columnist for *The New York Times,* said in a series of lectures before the Council of Foreign Affairs that "the rising power of the United States in world affairs, and particularly of the American president, requires not a more compliant press, but a relentless barrage of facts and criticism, as noisy but also as accurate as artillery fire. . . .

"Our job in this age, as I see it, is not to serve as cheerleaders for our side in the present world struggle, but to help the largest possible number of people to see the realities of the changing and convulsive world in which American policy must operate. . . ."

Increasingly, governments seek the cooperation, even the compliance, of the press. The reaction of the American Society of Newspaper Editors at its 1980 convention indicated the distance editors seek to put between their newspapers and the government. When the head of the Central Intelligence Agency, the U.S.'s spy service, told editors he reserves the right to enlist journalists in secret missions, the editors protested that this would endanger reporters' lives and would make questionable the integrity of their reports. Reporters need to be what they represent themselves as, independent seekers after information for the public, editors said. In response to the charge that such a position is unpatriotic, *The New York Times* stated in an editorial:

There is no higher service for a free press than to operate openly and independently to inform all Americans, including the intelligence agencies. That, too, is serving the nation. As Justice Hugo Black once observed, the press is "one of the very agencies the Framers of our Constitution thoughtfully and deliberately selected to improve our society and keep it free. That worthy ideal cannot be pursued if the line between the American press and the American government is so dangerously blurred."

Adversary Journalism

Questioning Power. John F. Kennedy said, "Those who create power make an indispensable contribution to the nation's greatness, but [those] who question power make a contribution just as indispensable . . . for they determine whether we use power, or power uses us."

The comment of the Italian journalist Oriana Fallaci may seem to trivialize the choice between adversary journalism and compliance with power, but it actually gets to the heart of the matter. She said, "Almost every time I have tried to absolve even partially some famous son-of-a-bitch, I have been bitterly sorry." After *The New York Times* had gone along with "national security" interests to play down President Kennedy's secret plans to invade the Bay of Pigs in Cuba in 1961, it confessed its decision had been wrong.

Journalists make these decisions with care and concern. They realize that leadership is essential, that strong leadership is important. They understand that people need to have faith in their leaders, and they fear feeding the stereotype that politicians are crooked, corrupt or stupid.

They are also aware of the attacks on the press that adversary journalism stimulates:

"The real threat to freedom, the real threat to freedom of speech and the real threat to our constitutional system is on our TV screens every evening and on the front pages of our newspapers every day."— Sen. Jesse Helms of North Carolina.

"We're trying to build up America, and the press is trying to tear down America."—Dr. George Keyworth, President Reagan's science adviser.

Secretary of State George Shultz wondered why reporters were not clearly "on our side" but "always against us" after reporters asked questions about the invasion of Grenada.

And so journalists worry about their traditional role as adversaries to power. But they are more concerned about the uses of power by the state and its functionaries. The powerful state, says Milosz, "like a crab, has eaten up all the substance of society." The society versus the state, he says, "is the basic issue of the twentieth century." Anthony Lewis wrote in *The New York Times* that during Reagan's first term the press had held back "from giving an unvarnished picture of the president." Why the hesitation by reporters? He answered his question:

"They care about their country, and they find it too upsetting to acknowledge—to the public or to themselves—that the enormous power of its leadership is in such hands."

The last word on adversary journalism goes to Richard Nixon, who once described the press as delighting in giving him a "going over." Ten years out of office, Nixon said: "There has to be an adversarial relationship between the press and whoever is in office."

The journalist who is committed to the open society, to democratic values, has a moral structure from which to work, an alertness to institutions and their activities that threaten the right of everyone to take part justly, equally and freely in a meaningful community life. Any word or deed that denies this way of life to people because of their sex, age, race, origin, religion or position in society must be revealed by the journalist.

When *Times* columnist Anthony Lewis learned that the Nixon administration had made a deal with Vice President Spiro Agnew for his resignation in return for the promise of a non-prison sentence on his plea of "no contest" to a felony, he wrote that this was the correct action. It was right, Lewis said, on "political grounds: the need to investigate the president's wrongdoing without having as his potential successor someone who was himself under indictment."

But Lewis then had second thoughts. They followed the sentencing to prison of two businessmen whose confession of corrupt payments had led to Agnew's resignation from the vice presidency. "So they go to prison," Lewis wrote, "while the sleazy felon who soiled our politics earns $100,000 in his new career as 'business broker.' " Instead of trusting the democratic institutions of law and politics to work, Lewis wrote, the attorney general had made personal policy.

"That unhappy precedent was carried further in the pardon of Richard Nixon," he wrote. "Of course, Watergate is not alone in examples of law applied unequally. It is commonplace, and terribly damaging to our system of criminal justice, for the powerful to go free while the little wrongdoers go to prison."

The journalist's passion for decency among people and nations sometimes impels him or her to speak out, to drop the cloak of detached observer. When Edward R. Murrow was reporting World War II for CBS radio he visited the death camp at Buchenwald. His report stunned listeners:

> MURROW: There were two rows of bodies stacked up like cordwood. They were thin and very white. Some of the bodies were terribly bruised, though there seemed to be little flesh to bruise. Some had been shot through the head, but they bled but little. It appeared that most of the men and boys had died of starvation. They had not been executed. But the manner of death seemed unimportant. Murder had been done at Buchenwald.
>
> I have reported what I saw and heard, but only part of it. If I have offended you by this rather mild account of Buchenwald, I'm not in the least sorry.

The Democratic Commitment

Responsibility to the Journalist

A young reporter who was asked to describe what journalistic ethics meant to her said the organization for which she worked had "only one type of morality—making money." The staff was too small to cover the community, she said. Most of the reporters were, like her, young, inexperienced and underpaid.

"The newspaper had no library to speak of and a small staff," she said. She was distressed by the coziness of some editors with the community power structure.

"Most reporters covered their stories through press releases and over the phone. They were rarely out on the street.

"No one cared."

At the *Trenton Times,* the newspaper president established this philosophy of news coverage after a reporter had been fired for rewriting a press release: "We do not feel an obligation to print what we think readers ought to know, but what they want to read. Some people think a newspaper is a hallowed institution. A newspaper is a product, like a candy bar. You have to package it to be attractive to the reader. You have to put in the ingredients they want. You have to market it properly."

The newspaper or station that does not carry out its obligations to its staff—a decent salary, adequate staffing of reportorial and editing positions, full support for penetrating journalism, intelligent and independent leadership—cannot demand the loyalty of the staff. When he was dean of the School of Journalism at Columbia University, Edward W. Barrett advised students to have a "go-to-hell fund," a few dollars squirreled away that would enable the discouraged journalist to take off should he or she find the newspaper or station irresponsible.

A Personal Credo

"Not to decide is to decide," says Harvey Cox, a writer on religion. To put off making the choice between difficult decisions is irresponsible. For every story a reporter covers, there are two the reporter never sees because he or she has not developed a moral sensitivity.

Young journalists might consider the adoption of a personal set of values as guidelines in their work. From a variety of sources—from the Greek philosophers to police reporters—the following emerge as suggestions for consideration:

• A belief in and a commitment to a political culture in which the cornerstone is restraint in the use of power.

• Moderation in life and behavior.

• A secular, scientific attitude toward the work at hand. Knowledge is allowed to speak for itself. The professional does not believe on the basis of hope but of evidence.

• An openmindedness that seeks out and tries to comprehend various points of view, including those in conflict with those the reporter holds.

• Responsibility to one's abilities and talent. To leave them fallow, to fail to labor to develop them through indolence or want of seriousness of purpose demeans the self and punishes the society whose betterment depends on new ideas vigorously pursued. In Homer, the good was the fulfillment of function. For Aristotle, the good was living up to one's potential, and for Kant the development of one's talents was a duty, and adherence to "duties" constitutes the moral life. The reporter who fails to report and write to his or her potential is immoral.

• An understanding of and a tolerance for the ambiguities involved in most important issues, and the ability to act despite these uncertainties and doubts. The willingness to take responsibility for these actions.

• The willingness to admit errors.

• A capacity to endure solitude and criticism, the price of independence.

• A reluctance to create heroes and villains to the rhythm of the deadline.

• A knowledge of the pathfinders in fields of knowledge, including journalism.

• A commitment to work.

• A sense of the past. "Let us remember that though great artists of the past could not change the course of history, it is only through their work that we are able to break bread with the dead, and without communion with the dead, a fully human life is impossible."—W. H. Auden.

• Resistance to praise. Humility. "You have to fight against the praise of people who like you," says I. F. Stone, the crusading journalist. "Because you know darn well it wasn't good enough." He tells the story of the great conductor Arturo Toscanini who was engulfed by admirers after a concert. "Maestro, you were wonderful," one said. Toscanini knew the oboe had not come in at the right point and that the violins were off. And Toscanini burst into tears because he knew it had not been good enough.

• Duty. "If a man is burdened with an idea, he not only desires to express it; he ought to express it. He owes it to his conscience and the common good. The indispensible function of expressing ideas is one of obligation—to the community and also to something beyond the community, let us say to truth."—John Dewey.

• Avoidance of the desire to please. Self-censorship is a greater enemy than outside censorship. Pleasing an editor, the publisher or the source is commonplace. Setting one's values to the "pragmatic level of the newsroom group," as Warren Breed puts it, can lead to timid, status-quo journalism.

Compassion. To learn something about the way reporters work for his role in "The Mean Season," Kurt Russell accompanied a reporter and photographer for The Miami Herald to the crime scene where he watched the photographer shoot a crying baby being carried from the house where he had lain in the blood of his parents. Russell was as appalled by the photographer's seeming insensitivity as he was by the scene. Then the photographer told Russell: The baby "is the real victim here," and readers "have a right to see that." Russell said later,"These are very caring people. They may be callous about how they do their jobs, but they're not callous about people."

• André Maurois, the French writer and political activist, warns the writer to beware making words an end in themselves:

> Power, Glory and Money are only secondary objects for the writer. No man can be a great writer without having a great philosophy, though it may often be unexpressed. A great writer has respect for *values*. His essential function is to raise life to the dignity of thought, and he does this by giving it a shape. If he refuses to perform this function he can be a clever juggler and play tricks with words such as his fellow writers may admire, but his books will be of little interest to anybody else. If, on the contrary, he fulfills it, he will be happy in his writing. Borne aloft by the world as reflected in himself, and producing a sound echo in his times, he helps to shape it by showing to men an image of themselves which is at once true and disciplined.

Summing Up

Reporters should seek to give voice to all groups in society, not to report solely those who hold power.

The public's need to know is an immanent value.

In determining what shall be reported and what shall be included in a news story, the reporter should consider the relevance of the material to the real needs of the audience.

If the reporter cannot disclose in the story the tactics and techniques used to gather information for the story, such tactics should not be used.

The reporter should:

• Be wary of treating people as a means.
• Believe on the basis of facts, not hope.
• Be committed to a value system but be free from ideologies and commitments that limit thought.
• Be wary of promising to help or give information to a source in return for material.

In balancing moral alternatives, the choice can be made on the basis of:

• The importance of the possible actions to life. (Life is the referent of value.)
• The public interest as against the private interest.
• The extent of knowledge of the event. If it is public knowledge or is likely to become so and the material is significant and relevant, the information should be used.
• Serving the needs of society. If the material assists people in participating justly, equally and freely in a meaningful community life, then it should be used.

(The codes of the Society of Professional Journalists, Associated Press Managing Editors and the American Society of Newspaper Editors are in Appendix D.)

The Adversary Press. St. Petersburg, Fla.: The Poynter Institute for Media Studies, 1983. (Discussion of ethics by 19 editors, publishers and scholars at an Institute seminar.)

Bagdikian, Ben H. *The Effete Conspiracy and Other Crimes by the Press.* New York: Harper & Row, 1972.

Frye, Northrop. *The Morality of Scholarship.* Ithaca, N.Y.: Cornell University Press, 1967.

Gerald, J. Edward. *The Social Responsibility of the Press.* Minneapolis: University of Minnesota Press, 1963.

Hulteng, John. *Playing It Straight.* Chester, Conn.: The Globe Pequot Press, 1981.

Ibsen, Henrik. *An Enemy of the People.* 1882. (Available in many anthologies and collections.)

McCulloch, Frank, ed. *Drawing the Line.* St. Petersburg, Fla.: The Poynter Institute for Media Studies, 1984.

Reston, James. *The Artillery of the Press.* New York: Harper & Row, 1960.

Smith, Z. N., and Pamela Zekman. *The Mirage.* New York: Random House, 1979.

Swados, Harvey. *Years of Conscience: The Muckrakers.* New York: The World Publishing Co., 1962.

Further Reading

A Personal Word

At this point, some of you may be thinking about the future, the kind of journalism you want to do, the station or newspaper that is the best place to launch a career in journalism.

Years ago, a reporter who had worked on several newspapers around the country advised a journalism student:

"Find a small newspaper or station where you can keep learning, where you will be assigned to everything—schools, local politics, the courthouse, police, the city council and the Kiwanis Club," he said.

Such advice is still given, and it's still sound. Why a small newspaper or station? Let Eugene Roberts, executive editor of *The Philadelphia Inquirer,* answer the question. Roberts, who has his pick of job applicants, says he has a prejudice "in favor of the reporter who cut his professional teeth doing everything under the sun on a small newspaper.

"If you're on a paper of, say, less than 20,000 circulation, during the run of the year you're probably going to cover every conceivable type of story—trials and floods and politics and crime and breaking news and nonbreaking news and features."

Not every small newspaper or station is worth your time. Some are understaffed, and editors and reporters have no time to help a newcomer. These newspapers do little more than slap at the news. But there are many good ones, and it isn't difficult to find out which they are.

These are the newspapers and stations that win awards for their reporting. The duPont-Columbia and George Foster Peabody Awards honor broadcast journalists; the Pulitzer Prizes and the Associated Press Managing Editors awards are for newspaper journalists. Many honors exist for print and broadcast journalists, such as the George Polk Awards and the Sigma Delta Chi Awards.

Reading through professional publications like *Broadcasting* and *Editor & Publisher* you will come across pieces about the good work being done by the smaller staffs. Ever hear of the Winter Haven *News Chief,* circulation 15,000? Probably not. This small central Florida daily newspaper was the subject of a long article in *Editor & Publisher. The News Chief* revealed that inadequate background checks were made of Florida teachers and as a result more than 35 convicted child molesters, rapists, drug sellers and other criminals were teaching children. Following the stories, a state law was adopted requiring more extensive background checks of applicants. Newspapers over the country followed the lead of the small Florida daily.

649

Pulitzers. Here are the names of some newspapers that were finalists or won Pulitzer Prizes:

California: *The Mercury-News*, San Jose; Colorado: *The Denver Post*; Georgia: *The Macon Telegraph and News*; Iowa: *The Des Moines Register*; Kentucky: *The Herald-Leader*, Lexington; Minnesota: *St. Paul Pioneer Press Dispatch*; Montana: *The Independent Review*, Helena; North Carolina: *The Greensboro News & Record*, the *News & Observer*, Raleigh; Ohio: *The Journal*, Lorain; Pennsylvania: *The Pittsburgh Press*; Texas: *The Dallas Morning News*, the *Ft. Worth Star-Telegram*; Virginia: *The Virginian-Pilot*, Norfolk; Wisconsin: *The Daily Herald*, Wausau; Wyoming: the *Star-Tribune*, Casper.

Other good newspapers have been mentioned throughout the textbook.

There are plenty of newspapers like *The News Chief* that beginners can look into, newspapers and stations that take pride in public service journalism.

These newspapers and stations are the first step on the ladder. The next jump is to a medium-sized newspaper or station, and then, if you are interested in metropolitan journalism or foreign correspondence, the big stations and newspapers.

Some newspapers regularly figure in lists of the country's best newspapers. At the head of the list, invariably, is *The New York Times,* the nation's newspaper of record. It has a large Washington and foreign staff, and its national correspondents span the continent. Right behind are *The Washington Post* and *Los Angeles Times,* both likely to do more investigative reporting than *The New York Times. The Wall Street Journal* is considered the best-written newspaper of all. Much more than a daily chronicle of business, the *Journal* offers excellent Washington coverage and has an enterprising staff of digging reporters. *The Miami Herald* is considered to offer the best coverage of Latin America. It is one of the crown jewels in a string of excellent newspapers operated by the Knight-Ridder newspaper chain.

The Philadelphia Inquirer, another Knight-Ridder newspaper, has stressed investigative journalism and has won many Pulitzer Prizes. *The Boston Globe, Newsday, Chicago Tribune, The Milwaukee Journal, The Christian Science Monitor, The Courier-Journal* (Louisville, Ky.), and *St. Petersburg Times* are also mentioned as among the nation's best.

Here are the call letters of radio and television stations that have won prizes for outstanding reporting over the past several years:

WJZ-TV, Baltimore; WBRZ-TV, Baton Rouge, La.; WGBH-TV, Boston; WBBM-TV, WMAQ-TV, WTTW-TV, Chicago; WFFA-TV, Dallas; KPRC-TV, Houston; WJXT-TV, Jacksonville, Fla.; KAIT-TV, Jonesboro, Ark.; KNXT-TV, Los Angeles; WHAS, Louisville; WPLG-TV, Miami; WCCO-TV, WTCN-TV, Minneapolis; WSM-TV, Nashville; WWL-TV, New Orleans; KMTV-TV, Omaha; KYW and WCAU-TV, Philadelphia; KDKA, Pittsburgh; KSL-TV, Salt Lake City; KGO-AM and KRON-TV, San Francisco; KCTS-TV, Seattle; KGUN-TV, Tucson; KTUL-TV, Tulsa; WDVM-TV, Washington, D.C.; KWWL-TV, Waterloo, Iowa.

Salaries

Salaries on small stations and newspapers are low for beginners—$250 a week for radio and television stations in small markets; $250–$300 a week for small and medium-size newspapers.

For the talented, the large markets and the big newspapers beckon. Here, salaries can go to $700 a week for a radio news director and $2,000 a week for a television anchorperson. For a skilled reporter on a metropolitan newspaper, salaries of $500–$800 a week are offered. For the gifted, those who are courted, there is no limit.

Good Luck.

Stylebook

addresses Abbreviate *Avenue, Boulevard, Street* with specific address: *1314 Kentucky St.* Spell out without specific address: *construction on Fifth Avenue.*

Use figures for the address number: *3 Third Ave.; 45 Main St.* Spell out numbers under 10 as street names: *21 Fourth Ave.; 450 11th St.*

age Use figures. To express age as an adjective, use hyphens: a *3-year-old girl.* Unless otherwise stated, the figure is presumed to indicate years: *a boy, 4, and his sister, 6 months.*

Further guidelines: *infant:* under one year of age; *child:* the period between infancy and youth, ages 1 to 13; *girl, boy:* under 18; *youth:* 13–18; *man, woman:* over 18; *adult:* over 18, unless used in specific legal context for crimes such as drinking; *middle-aged:* 35–55; *elderly:* over 65; avoid when describing individuals.

a.m., p.m. Lowercase with periods.

amendment: Capitalize when referring to specific amendments to the U.S. Constitution. Spell out for the first through ninth; use figures for 10th and above: *First Amendment, 10th Amendment.*

anti- Hyphenate all but words that have their own meanings: *antibiotic, antibody, anticlimax, antidote, antifreeze, antihistamine, antiknock, antimatter, antiparticle, antipasto, antiperspirant, antiseptic, antiserum, antithesis, antitoxin, antitrust.*

bi, semi When used with periods of time, the prefix *bi* means every other; *semi* means twice. A biannual conference meets every other year. A semiweekly newspaper comes out twice a week. No hyphens.

brand name A non-legal term for a trademark. Do not use them as generic terms or as verbs: *soft drink* instead of *Coke* or *coke; photocopy* instead of *Xerox.*

capitalization Generally, follow a down style.

Proper nouns: Use capitals for names of persons, places, trademarks; titles when used with names; nicknames of persons, states, teams; titles of books, plays, movies.

century Lowercase, spelling out numbers less than 10, except when used in proper nouns: *the fifth century, 18th century,* but *20th Century-Fox* and *Nineteenth Century Society,* following the organization's practice.

chairman, chairwoman Use *chairman* or *chairwoman* instead of *chair* or *chairperson; spokesman* or *spokeswoman* instead of *spokesperson* and similar constructions unless the *-person* construction is a formal title.

Use *chairman* or *spokesman* when referring to the office in general. A neutral word such as *representative* often may be the best choice.

co- Use a hyphen when forming nouns, adjectives and verbs that indicate occupation or status: *co-star, co-written.* No hyphen for other constructions: *coeducation, coexist.*

congress Capitalize when referring to the U.S. Senate and House of Representatives. The term is correctly used only in reference to the two legislative branches together.

Capitalize also when referring to foreign governments that use the term or its equivalent.

Constitution, constitutional Capitalize when referring to the U.S. Constitution, with or without the *U.S.* modifier. When referring to other constitutions, capitalize only when preceded by the name of a nation or state. Lowercase *constitutional.*

court names Capitalize the full proper names of courts at all levels. Retain capitalization if *U.S.* or a state name is dropped.

dates *July 6, 1957,* was her birth date. (Use commas.) *She was born in July 1957.* (No comma between month and year.)

Abbreviate month with specific date: *Feb. 19.* Spell out all months when standing alone. With dates, use abbreviations: *Jan., Feb., Aug., Sept., Oct., Nov., Dec.* Spell out *March, April, May, June, July.*

directions and regions Lowercase *north, south, northeast,* etc. when they indicate compass direction: *Police followed the car south on Route 22.*

Capitalize when they refer to regions: *Southern accent; Northeastern industry.*

With names of nations, lowercase except when they are part of a proper name or are used to designate a politically divided nation: *tourism in southern France,* but *South Korea* and *Northern Ireland.*

Lowercase compass points when they describe a section of a state or city except when part of a proper name (*South Dakota*) or when they refer to a widely known region (*Southern California; the East Side of New York*).

Capitalize when combining with a common noun to form a proper noun: *the Eastern Hemisphere; the North Woods.*

entitled Does not mean *titled. Citizens 18 and older are entitled to vote,* but *the book is titled "News Reporting and Writing."*

ex- No hyphen for words that use *ex* in the sense of *out of: excommunicate, expropriate.* Hyphenate when using in the sense of *former: ex-husband, ex-convict. Former* is preferred with titles: *Former President Gerald R. Ford.*

fireman Use *firefighter* since some women hold these jobs.

fractions Spell out amounts less than 1, using hyphens: *one-half, two-thirds.* Use figures for amounts larger than 1, converting to decimals whenever possible: *3.5* instead of *three and one-half* or *3½.*

Figures are preferred in tabular material and in stories about stocks.

gay Do not use as a noun to refer to a homosexual unless it is within quoted matter or in the name of an organization. *Gay* may be used as an adjective meaning *homosexual.*

historical periods and events Capitalize widely recognized periods and events in anthropology, archeology, geology and history: *the Bronze Age, the Ice Age, the Renaissance.*

Capitalize widely recognized popular names for eras and events: *the Glorious Revolution, the Roaring 20s.*

holidays and holy days Capitalize them. In federal law, the legal holidays are New Year's, Martin Luther King's Birthday, Washington's Birthday, Memorial Day, Independence Day, Labor Day, Columbus Day, Veterans Day, Thanksgiving and Christmas.

States are not required to follow the federal lead in designating holidays, except that federal employees must receive the day off or must be paid overtime if they work.

Jewish holy days: Hanukkah, Passover, Purim, Rosh Hashana, Shavuot, Sukkot and Yom Kippur.

in- No hyphen when it means *not: invalid; inaccurate.* Mostly used without hyphen in other combinations, but there are a few exceptions: *in-house; in-depth.* Consult a dictionary when in doubt.

-in Always precede with a hyphen: *break-in; sit-in; write-in.*

initials Use periods and no space: *H.L. Mencken; C.S. Lewis.* This practice has been adopted to ensure that initials will be set on the same line.

like- Follow with a hyphen when used to mean *similar to: like-minded; like-natured.*

-like No hyphen unless the *l* would be tripled: *lifelike,* but *shell-like.*

mailman Use the term *letter carrier* since women hold some of these positions.

man, mankind *Humanity* is preferred for the plural form. Use *a person* or *an individual* in the singular. A phrase or sentence usually can be reconstructed to eliminate any awkwardness.

nationalities and races Capitalize the proper names of nationalities, peoples, races, tribes, etc. Lowercase *black, white, red,* etc. Lowercase derogatory terms such as *honky* and *nigger.* Use them only in direct quotations.

See *race* for guidelines on when racial identification is pertinent in a story.

National Organization for Women. Not *National Organization of Women.*

nobility Capitalize *king, queen, duke* and other titles when they precede the individual's name. Lowercase when standing alone: *King Juan Carlos,* but *the king of Spain.*

non- Hyphenate all except the following words, which have meanings of their own: *nonchalance, nonchalant, nondescript, nonentity, nonsense, nonsensical.*

numerals Spell out *one* through *nine,* except when used to indicate age or with dates. Use figures for *10* and above.

Spell out a number when it begins a sentence: *Fifteen members voted against the bill.* Use figures when a year begins a sentence: *1980 began auspiciously.*

Use figures for percentages and percents.

For amounts of $1 million and more, use the *$* sign and figures up to two decimal places with the *million, billion, trillion* spelled out: *$1.65 million.* Exact amounts are given in figures: *$1,650,398.*

When spelling out large numbers, separate numbers ending in *y* from next number with a hyphen: *seventy-nine; one hundred seventy-nine.*

people, persons Use *person* when referring to an individual. *People* is preferred to *persons* in all plural uses.

People also is a collective noun that takes a plural verb when used to refer to a single race or nation: *The Philippine people are awaiting their parliament's decision on the election.* In this sense, *peoples* is the plural form: *The peoples of Western Europe do not always agree on East-West issues.*

percentages Use figures—decimals, not fractions—and the word *percent,* not the symbol: *2.5 percent; 10 percent.* For amounts less than 1 percent, place a zero before the decimal: *0.6 percent.*

When presenting a range, repeat *percent* after each figure: *2 percent to 5 percent.*

policeman Use *police officer* instead.

political parties and philosophies Capitalize the name of the party and the word *party* when it is used as part of the organization's proper name: *the Democratic Party.*

Capitalize *Communist, Conservative, Democrat, Liberal,* etc. when they refer to the activities of a specific party or to individuals who are members of it.

Lowercase the name of a philosophy in noun and adjective forms unless it is derived from a proper name: *communism; fascist.* But: *Marxism; Nazi.*

In general, avoid the terms *conservative, radical, leftist* and *rightist.* In casual and popular usage, the meanings of these terms vary, depending on the user and the situation being discussed. A more precise description of an individual's or a group's political views is preferred.

post office Should not be capitalized. The agency is the U.S. Postal Service.

prefixes Generally, do not hyphenate when using a prefix with a word starting with a consonant.

Except for *cooperate* and *coordinate,* use a hyphen if the prefix ends in the same vowel that begins the following word: *re-elect,* not *reelect.*

Use a hyphen if the word that follows is capitalized: *pan-American; anti-Catholic.*

Use a hyphen to join doubled prefixes: *sub-subclause.*

presidency Always lowercase.

president Capitalized only as a title before an individual's name: *President Ronald Reagan,* but *The president said he would spend New Year's at his California ranch.*

presidential Lowercase unless part of a proper name: *presidential approval,* but *Presidential Medal of Freedom.*

race Race, religion and national origin are sometimes essential to a story but too often are injected when they are not pertinent. When in doubt about relevance, substitute descriptions such as *white, Baptist, French.* If one of these descriptions would be pertinent, use the original term.

religious references DEITIES: Capitalize the proper names of monotheistic deities, pagan and mythological gods and goddesses: *Allah, the Father, Zeus.* Lowercase pronouns that refer to the deity: *he, him, thee, who,* etc.

Lowercase *gods* when referring to the deities of polytheistic religions. Lowercase such words as *god-awful, godlike, godsend.*

LIFE OF CHRIST: Capitalize the names of major events in the life of Jesus Christ in references that do not use his name: *the Last Supper; the Resurrection.* Lowercase when the words are used with his name: *the ascension of Christ.* Apply the same principle to events in the life of his mother.

RITES: Capitalize proper names for rites that commemorate the Last Supper or signify a belief in Christ's presence: *the Lord's Supper; Holy Eucharist.* Lowercase the names of other sacraments.

HOLY DAYS: Capitalize the names of holy days: *Hanukkah.*

OTHER WORDS: Lowercase *heaven, hell, devil, angel, cherub, an apostle, a priest,* etc.

rock'n'roll Not *rock and roll.*

room numbers Use figures and capitalize *room: The faculty met in Room 516.* Capitalize the names of specially designated rooms: *Oval Office; Blue Room.*

saint Abbreviate as *St.* in the names of saints, cities and other places except *Saint John* (New Brunswick) to distinguish it from St. John's, Newfoundland, and *Sault Ste. Marie.*

seasons Lowercase *spring, summer, fall, winter* and their derivatives. Capitalize when part of a formal name: *St. Paul Winter Carnival; Summer Olympics.*

self- Always hyphenate: *self-motivated; self-taught.*

senate, senatorial Capitalize all references to specific legislative bodies, regardless of whether the name of the nation or state is used: *U.S. Senate; the state Senate.*

Lowercase plural uses: *the Iowa and Kansas state senates.* Lowercase references to non-governmental bodies: *the student-faculty senate.*

Senatorial is always lowercase.

sexism Avoid stereotyping women or men. Be conscious of equality in treatment of both sexes.

When writing of careers and jobs, avoid presuming that the wage-earner is a man and that the woman is a homemaker: *the average family of five* instead of *the average worker with a wife and three children.*

Avoid physical descriptions of women or men when not absolutely relevant to the story.

Use parallel references to both sexes: *the men and the women,* not *the men and the ladies; husband and wife,* not *man and wife.*

Do not use nouns and pronouns to indicate sex unless the sex difference is basic to understanding or there is no suitable substitute. One way to avoid such subtle sexism is to change the noun to the plural, eliminating the masculine pronoun: *Drivers should carry their licenses,* instead of *Every driver should carry his license.*

Personal appearance and marital and family relationships should be used only when relevant to the story.

state names Spell out names of the 50 U.S. states when they stand alone in textual matter.

The names of eight states are never abbreviated: *Alaska, Hawaii, Idaho, Iowa, Maine, Ohio, Texas, Utah.*

Abbreviate other state names when used with a city, in a dateline or with party affiliation. Do not use Postal Service abbreviations.

Ala.	*Kan.*	*Nev.*	*S.D.*
Ariz.	*Ky.*	*N.H.*	*Tenn.*
Ark.	*La.*	*N.J.*	*Vt.*
Calif.	*Md.*	*N.M.*	*Va.*
Colo.	*Mass.*	*N.Y.*	*Wash.*
Conn.	*Mich.*	*N.C.*	*W.Va.*
Del.	*Minn.*	*N.D.*	*Wis.*
Fla.	*Miss.*	*Okla.*	*Wyo.*
Ga.	*Mo.*	*Pa.*	
Ill.	*Mont.*	*R.I.*	
Ind.	*Neb.*	*S.C.*	

statehouse Capitalize all references to a specific statehouse, with or without the state name. But lowercase in all plural uses: *the New Mexico Statehouse; the Arizona and New Mexico statehouses.*

suspensive hyphenation The form: *The 19- and 20-year-olds were not served alcoholic beverages.* Use in all similar cases.

Although the form looks somewhat awkward, it guides readers, who may otherwise expect a noun to follow the first figure.

syllabus, syllabuses Also: *memorandum, memorandums.*

teen, teen-ager(noun), **teen-age** (adjective) Do not use *teen-aged.*

telecast (noun), **televise** (verb)

temperatures Use figures for all except *zero.* Use the word *minus,* not a minus sign, to indicate temperatures below zero. *The day's high was 9; the day's low was minus 9.*

Temperatures are higher and lower, rise and fall but do not become warmer or cooler.

Third World The economically developing nations of Africa, Asia and Latin America.

time Exact times often are unnecessary. *Last night* and *this morning* are acceptable substitutes for *yesterday* and *today.* Use exact time when pertinent, but avoid redundancies: *8 a.m. this morning* should be *8 a.m. today* or *8 o'clock this morning.*

Use figures except for *noon* and *midnight. 12 noon* is redundant.

Separate hours from minutes with a colon: *3:15 p.m.*

titles

ACADEMIC TITLES: Capitalize and spell out formal titles such as *professor, dean, president, chancellor, chairman,* etc., when they precede a name. Lowercase elsewhere. Do not abbreviate *Professor* as *Prof.*

Lowercase modifiers such as *journalism* in *journalism Professor John Rist* or *department* in *department chairwoman Kim Power,* unless the modifier is a proper name: *French Professor Jeannette Spear.*

COURTESY TITLES: Do not use the courtesy titles *Miss, Mr., Mrs.* or *Ms.* on first reference. Instead, use the person's first and last name. Do not use *Mr.* unless it is combined with *Mrs.: Kyle Scott Hotsenpiller; Mr. and Mrs. Kyle Scott Hotsenpiller.*

Courtesy titles are used on second reference for women. Use these guidelines:

Married women: On first reference, identify a woman by her own first name and her husband's last name: *Betty Phillips.* Use *Mrs.* on first reference only if a woman requests that her husband's first name be used or her own first name cannot be determined: *Mrs. Steven A. Phillips.*

On second reference, use *Mrs.* unless a woman initially identified by her own first name prefers *Ms.: Rachel Finch; Mrs. Finch* or *Ms. Finch.*

If a married woman is known by her maiden last name, precede it by *Miss* on second reference unless she prefers *Ms.: Sarah Wilson; Miss Wilson* or *Ms. Wilson.*

Unmarried women: Use *Miss* or *Ms.* on second reference, according to the woman's preference.

For divorced and widowed women, the normal practice is to use *Mrs.* on second reference. Use *Miss* if the woman returns to her maiden name. Use *Ms.* if she prefers it.

If a woman prefers *Ms.*, do not include her marital status in a story unless it is pertinent.

Note: A number of newspapers drop *Mrs., Miss* and *Ms.* as well as *Mr.* on second reference. In 1985, the AP stylebook added: If the woman says she does not want a courtesy title, refer to her on second reference by last name only.

GOVERNMENTAL TITLES: Capitalize when used as a formal title in front of a person's name. It is not necessary to use a title on second reference: *Gov. Fred Florence; Florence.* For women who hold official positions, use the courtesy title on second reference, according to the guidelines for courtesy titles: *Gov. Ruth Arnold; Miss Arnold, Mrs. Arnold, Ms. Arnold.* (Some newspapers do not use the courtesy title on second reference.)

Abbreviate *Governor* as *Gov., Lieutenant Governor* as *Lt. Gov.* when used as a formal title before a name.

Congressional titles: Before names, abbreviate *Senator* as *Sen.* and *Representative* as *Rep.* Add *U.S.* or *state* if necessary to avoid confusion.

Short form punctuation for party affiliation: Use abbreviations listed under **state names** and set off from the person's name with commas: *Sen. Nancy Landon Kassebaum, R-Kan., and Rep. Charles Hatcher, D-Ga., attended the ceremony.*

Capitalize and spell out other formal government titles before a person's name. Do not use titles in second references: *Attorney General Jay Craven spoke. Craven said. . . .*

Capitalize and spell out formal titles instead of abbreviating before the person's name only in direct quotations. Lowercase in all uses not mentioned above.

OCCUPATIONAL TITLES: They are always lowercase: *senior vice president Nancy Harden.* Avoid false titles: *bridge champion Helen P. George* should be: *Helen P. George, Sioux Falls bridge tourney winner.*

RELIGIOUS TITLES: The first reference to a clergyman, clergywoman or nun should include a capitalized title before the person's name.

On second reference: for men, use only a last name if he uses a surname. If a man is known only by a religious name, repeat the title: *Pope Paul VI* or *Pope Paul* on first reference; *the pope* or *the pontiff* on second reference. For women, use *Miss, Mrs.* or *Ms.*, according to the woman's preference.

Cardinals, archbishops, bishops: On first reference, use the title before the person's first and last name. On second reference, use the last name only or the title.

Ministers and priests: Use *the Rev.* before a name on first reference. Substitute *Monsignor* before the name of a Roman Catholic priest who has received this honor.

Rabbis: Use *Rabbi* before a name on first reference. On second reference, use only the last name of a man; use *Miss, Mrs.* or *Ms.* before a woman's last name, according to her preference.

Nuns: Always use *Sister* or *Mother: Sister Agnes Mary* in all references if the nun uses only a religious name; *Sister Ann Marie Graham* on first reference if she uses a surname, *Sister Graham* on second.

TITLES OF WORKS: For book titles, movie titles, opera titles, play titles, poem titles, song titles, television program titles and the titles of lectures, speeches and works of art, apply the following guidelines:

Capitalize the principal words, including prepositions and conjunctions of four or more letters.

Capitalize an article or word of fewer than four letters if it is the first or last word in a title.

Place quotation marks around the names of all such works except the Bible and books that are primarily catalogs of reference material, including almanacs, directories, dictionaries, encyclopedias, handbooks and similar publications.

Translate a foreign title into English unless a work is known to the American public by its foreign name.

Do not use quotation marks or italics with the names of newspapers and magazines.

TV Acceptable as an adjective but should not be used as a noun.

upstate, downstate Always lowercase.

venereal disease *VD* is acceptable on second reference.

versus Abbreviate as *vs.* in all uses.

vice Use two words, no hyphen.

vice president Follow the guidelines for **president.**

war Capitalize when part of the name for a particular conflict: *World War II; the Cold War.*

well- Hyphenate as part of a compound modifier: *well-dressed; well-read.*

wide- Usually hyphenated: *wide-eyed.* Exception: *widespread.*

words as words When italics are available, italicize them. Otherwise, place in quotation marks: *Rep. Ellen Jacobson asked journalists to address her as* "congresswoman."

years Use figures. Use an *s* without the apostrophe to indicate spans of centuries: *the 1800s.* Use an apostrophe to indicate omitted numerals and an *s* to indicate decades: the *'80s.*

Years are the only figures that may be placed at the start of a sentence: *1959 was a year of rapid city growth.*

Punctuation

Keep a good grammar book handy. No stylebook can adequately cover the complexities of the 13 punctuation marks: apostrophe, brackets, colon, comma, dash, ellipsis, exclamation point, hyphen, parenthesis, period, question mark, quotation marks, semicolon. The following is a guide to frequent problems and usages:

Apostrophe Use for (1) possessives, (2) to indicate omitted figures or letters and (3) to form some plurals.

1. *Possessives:* Add apostrophe and *s* ('s) to the end of singular and plural nouns or the indefinite pronoun unless it has an *s* or *z* sound.
   The woman's coat. The women's coats.
   The child's toy. The children's toys.
   Someone's pistol. One's hopes.
   If the word is plural and ends in an *s* or *z* sound, add apostrophe only:
   Boys' books. Joneses' farm.
   For singular common nouns ending in *s*, add an apostrophe and *s* ('s) unless the next word begins with s:
   The hostess's gown. The hostess' seat.
   For singular proper nouns, add only an apostrophe:
   Dickens' novels. James' hat.
2. *Omitted figures or letters.* Use in contractions—*Don't, can't.* Put in place of omitted figure—*Class of '88.*
3. *To form some plurals:* When figures, letters, symbols and words are referred to as words, use the apostrophe and *s.*
   a. Figures: *She skated perfect 8's.*
   b. Letters: *He received all A's in his finals.*
   c. Symbols: *Journalists never use &'s to substitute for the ands in their copy.*

Caution: The pronouns *ours, yours, theirs, his, hers, whose* do not take the apostrophe. *Its* is the possessive pronoun. *It's* is the contraction of it is.

Note: Compound words and nouns in joint possession use the possessive in the last word:

- Everybody else's homes.
- His sister-in-law's book.
- Mondale and Kennedy's party.

If there is separate possession, each noun takes the possessive form:

Carter's and Kennedy's opinions differ.

Brackets Check whether the newspaper can set them. Use to enclose a word or words within a quote that the writer inserts: *"Happiness [his note read] is a state of mind."* Use for paragraph(s) within a story that refer to an event separate from the datelined material.

Colon The colon is usually used at the end of a sentence to call attention to what follows. It introduces lists, tabulations, texts and quotations of more than one sentence.

It can also be used to mark a full stop before a dramatic word or statement: *She had only one goal in life: work.* The colon is used in time of day: *7:45 p.m.;* elapsed time of an event: *4:01.1,* and in dialogue in question and answer, as from a trial.

Comma The best general guide for the use of the comma is the human voice as it pauses, stops and varies in tone. The comma marks the pause, the short stop:

1. He looked into the hospital room, but he was unable to find the patient.
2. Although he continued his search on the floor for another 20 minutes, he was unable to find anyone to help him.
3. He decided that he would go downstairs, ask at the desk and then telephone the police.
4. If that also failed, he thought to himself, he would have to give up the search.

Note that when reading these sentences aloud, the commas are natural resting points for pauses. The four sentences also illustrate the four principles governing the use of commas:

1. The comma is used to separate main clauses when they are joined by a coordinating conjunction. (The coordinating conjunctions are: *for, nor, and, but, or.*) The comma can be eliminated if the main clauses are short: *He looked into the room and he froze.*
2. Use the comma after an introductory element: a clause, long phrase, transitional expression or interjection.
3. Use the comma to separate words, phrases or clauses in a series. Also, use it in a series of coordinate adjectives: *He was wearing a long, full cape.*
4. Set off non-essential material in a sentence with comma(s). When the parenthetical or interrupting non-restrictive clauses and phrases are in the middle of a sentence two commas are needed: *The country, he was told, needed his assistance.*

Other uses of the comma:

Use a comma with full sentence quotes, not with partial quotes: *He asked, "Where are you going?" The man replied that he was "blindly groping" his way home.*

To separate city and county, city and state. In place of the word *of* between a name and city: *Jimmy Carter, Plains, Ga.*

To set off a person's age: *Orville Sterb, 19, of Fullerton, Calif.*

In dates: *March 19, 1940, was the date he entered the army.*

In party affiliations: *Bill Bradley, D-N.J., spoke.*

Caution: The comma is frequently misused by placing it between two main clauses instead of using the period or semicolon. This is called comma splice:

WRONG: The typewriter was jammed, he could not type his theme.

RIGHT: The typewriter was jammed. He could not type his theme. The typewriter was jammed; he could not type his theme.

Dash Use a dash (1) to indicate a sudden or dramatic shift in thought within a sentence, (2) to set off a series of words that contains commas and (3) to introduce sections of a list or a summary.

The dash is a call for a short pause, just as are the comma and the parenthesis. The comma is the most often used and is the least dramatic of the separators. The parenthesis sets off unimportant elements. The dash tends to emphasize material. It has this quality because it is used sparingly.

1. He stared at the picture—and he was startled to find himself thinking of her face.
   The man stood up—painfully and awkwardly—and extended his hand in greeting.
2. There were three persons watching them—an elderly woman, a youth with a crutch at his side and a young woman in jeans holding a paperback—and he pulled her aside out of their view.
3. He gave her his reasons for being there:
   —He wanted to apologize;
   —He needed to give her some material;
   —He was leaving on a long trip.
   (*Note:* This third form should be used infrequently, usually when the listing will be followed by an elaboration.)

The dash is also used in datelines.

Ellipsis Use the ellipsis to indicate material omitted from a quoted passage from a text, transcript, play, etc.: *The minutes stated that Breen had asked, "How many gallons of paint . . . were used in the project?"* Put one space before and one space after each of the three periods. If the omission ends with a period, use four periods, one to mark the end of the sentence (without space, as a regular period), three more for the ellipsis.

The ellipsis is also used by some columnists to separate short items in a paragraph.

Do not use to mark pauses, shifts in thought, or for emphasis.

Exclamation point Much overused. There are reporters who have gone through a lifetime of writing and have never used the exclamation point, except when copying material in which it is used. The exclamation point is used to indicate powerful feelings, surprise, wonder. Most good writers prefer to let the material move the reader to provide his or her own exclamation.

When using, do not place a comma or period after the exclamation point. Place inside quotation marks if it is part of the quoted material.

Hyphen The hyphen is used (1) to join words to express a single idea or (2) to avoid confusion or ambiguity.

1. Use the hyphen to join two or more words that serve as a single adjective before a noun: *A well-known movie is on television tonight. He had a know-it-all expression.*
   Caution: Do not use the hyphen when the first word of the compound ends in *ly* or when the words follow the noun: *He is an easily recognized person. Her hair was blonde black.*
2. (a) Avoid ambiguity or (b) an awkward joining of letters or syllables by putting a hyphen between prefixes or suffixes and the root word.
   a. He recovered the chair. He re-covered the chair.
   b. Re-enter, macro-economics, shell-like.

Parenthesis Generally, avoid. They may be necessary for the insertion of background or to set off supplementary or illustrative material.

Use period inside closing parenthesis if the matter begins with a capital letter.

Period Use the period at the end of declarative sentences, indirect questions, most imperative sentences and most abbreviations.

The period is placed inside quotation marks.

Question mark The question mark is used for direct questions, not indirect questions.

DIRECT: Where are you going?
INDIRECT: He asked where she was going.

The question mark goes inside quotation marks if it applies to the quoted material: *He asked, "Have you seen the movie?"* Put it outside if it applies to the entire sentence: *Have you seen "Guys and Dolls"?*

Quotation marks Quotation marks set off (1) direct quotations, (2) some titles and nicknames and (3) words used in a special way.

1. Set off the exact words of the speaker: *"He walked like a duck," she said. He replied that he walked "more like an alley cat on the prowl."*
2. Use for book and movie titles, titles of short stories, poems, songs, articles from magazines and plays. Some nicknames take quotation marks. Do not use for nicknames of sports figures.
3. For words used in a special sense: *An "Indian giver" is someone who gives something to another and then takes it back.*

Punctuation with quotation marks:

The comma—Use it outside the quotation marks when setting off the speaker at the beginning of a sentence: *He said, "You care too much for money."* Use inside the quotation marks when the speaker ends the sentence: *"I just want to be safe," she replied.*
The colon and semicolon—Always place outside the quotation marks: *He mentioned her "incredible desire for work"; he meant her "insatiable desire for work."*
The dash, question mark and exclamation point—inside when they apply to quoted matter only; outside when they refer to the whole sentence: *She asked, "How do you know so much?" Did she really wonder why he knew "so much"?*

For quotes within quotes, use single quote mark (the apostrophe on typewriter) for the inner quotation: *"Have you read 'War and Peace'?" he asked.* Note, no comma is used after the question mark.

Semicolon Usually overused by beginning reporters. Unless there is a special reason to use the semicolon, use the period.

Use the semicolon to separate a series of equal elements when the individual segments contain material that is set off by commas. This makes for clarity in the series: *He suggested that she spend her allowance on the new series at the opera, "Operas of the Present"; books of plays by Shaw, Ibsen and Aristophanes; and novels by Tolstoy, Dickens and F. Scott Fitzgerald.*

Grammar

In grandfather's day, students stood at the blackboard and diagrammed sentences. They broke down sentences into nouns, verbs, pronouns, adjectives, adverbs, prepositions, conjunctions and interjections. From there, they went into phrases—verbal, prepositional, participial, gerund and infinitive. Then they examined clauses—main and subordinate. This is the way they learned how sentences are constructed. Today, most students learn through the study of a foreign language. For a journalist, this is inadequate training.

One way the beginning journalist can cope with this inadequacy is to invest in a handbook of grammar. It will not only solve grammatical problems quickly, but it will also expand the student's writing range. Some journalists stick with a limited style because it is all they can handle. No matter what the story, it is written with the same flat sentence structure the reporter used on the blues-singer interview yesterday and the bus-truck collision the day before that.

Think of the humiliation a *New York Times* reporter experienced when he saw in print this sentence he had written:

> While urging parents to remain loving, the program, which is controversial in that it's techniques are considered questionable by a good number of experts, advises them to stop being intimidated and manipulated by their misbehaving children.

Contorted as this sentence is, the one error that shouts for attention is the misuse of *it's*.

The following guide will help you to avoid grammatical errors that frequently turn up in student copy.

Agreement

A verb must agree in number with its subject. Writers encounter trouble when they are unsure of the subject or when they cannot decide whether the subject is singular or plural.

Uncertainty often arises when there are words between the subject and the verb:

WRONG: John, as well as several others in the class, were unhappy with the instructor.

RIGHT: John, as well as several others in the class, was unhappy with the instructor.

The subject is *John,* singular.

WRONG: The barrage of traffic noises, telephone calls and similar interruptions make it difficult to study.

RIGHT: The barrage of traffic noises, telephone calls and similar interruptions makes it difficult to study.

The subject is *barrage,* singular.

A collective noun takes a singular verb when the group is considered as a unit and a plural verb when the individuals are thought of separately:

RIGHT: The committee usually votes unanimously.
RIGHT: The family lives around the corner.
RIGHT: The family were gathered around the fire, some reading, some napping.

The pronouns *anybody, anyone, each, either, everyone, everybody, neither, no one, nobody, someone* and *somebody* take the singular verb.

A pronoun must agree in number with its antecedent.

WRONG: The team has added two players to their squad.
RIGHT: The team has added two players to its squad.
WRONG: Everyone does their best.
RIGHT: Everyone does his or her best.
WRONG: Each of the companies reported their profits had declined.
RIGHT: Each of the companies reported its profits had declined.

Dangling Modifier

Another trouble spot is the dangling modifier—the word, phrase or clause that does not refer logically or clearly to some word in the sentence. We all know what these look like:

Walking through the woods, the trees loomed up.

The italicized phrase is a dangling participle, the most common of these errors. There are also dangling infinitive phrases:

To learn to shoot well, courses in markmanship were offered.

The way to correct the dangling modifier is to add words that make the meaning clear or to rearrange the words in the sentence to make the modifier refer to the correct word. We can easily fix the two sentences:

Walking through the woods, *the runaway boy* felt the trees loom up at him.

To learn to shoot well, *the police* were offered courses in markmanship.

Related parts of the sentence should not be separated. When they are **Misplaced Words** separated, the sentence loses clarity.

Adverbs such as *almost, even, hardly, just, merely, scarcely, ever* and *nearly* should be placed immediately before the words they modify:

VAGUE: He only wanted three keys.
CLEAR: He wanted only three keys.
VAGUE: She nearly ate the whole meal.
CLEAR: She ate nearly the whole meal.

Avoid splitting the subject and verb:

AWKWARD: She, to make her point, shouted at the bartender.
BETTER: To make her point, she shouted at the bartender.

Do not separate parts of verb phrases:

AWKWARD: The governor said he had last year seen the document.
BETTER: The governor said he had seen the document last year.

Avoid split infinitives:

AWKWARD: She offered to personally give him the note.
BETTER: She offered to give him the note personally.

Note: Watch long sentences. Misplaced clauses and phrases can muddy the intended meaning. Read the sentence aloud if you are unsure about the placement of certain words. Generally, the problem can be solved by placing the subject and verb of the main clause together.

The parts of a sentence that express parallel thoughts should be bal- **Parallel** anced in grammatical form: **Construction**

UNBALANCED: The people started to shove and crowding each other.
BALANCED: The people started to shove and crowd each other.
UNBALANCED: The typewriter can be used for writing and to do finger exercises.
BALANCED: The typewriter can be used for writing and for doing finger exercises.

A pronoun should agree with its antecedent in number, person and gender. **Pronouns** The most common errors are shifts in number and shifts in person.

WRONG: The organization added basketball and hockey to their winter program.

RIGHT: The organization added basketball and hockey to its winter program. (The pronoun *its* agrees in number with its antecedent, *the organization.*)

WRONG: When one wants to ski, you have to buy good equipment.

RIGHT: When one wants to ski, he or she has to buy good equipment. (The pronouns *he* and *she* agree in person with the antecedent, *one.*)

A common error is to give teams, groups and organizations the plural pronoun:

WRONG: The team played their best shortstop.

RIGHT: The team played its best shortstop.

WRONG: The Police Department wants recruits. They need 1,500 applicants.

RIGHT: The Police Department wants recruits. It needs 1,500 applicants.

Sentence Fragments

A phrase or a subordinate clause should not be used as a complete sentence:

FRAGMENT: The book was long. And dull.

CORRECT: The book was long and dull.

FRAGMENT: The score was tied. With only a minute left to play.

CORRECT: The score was tied with only a minute left to play.

FRAGMENT: He worked all night on the story. And then collapsed in a heap.

CORRECT: He worked all night on the story and then collapsed in a heap.

Note: Sometimes writers use a sentence fragment for a specific writing purpose, usually for emphasis: *When in doubt, always use the dictionary. Always.*

Sequence of Tenses

One of the most troublesome grammatical areas for the beginning journalist is the use of tenses. Improper and inconsistent tense changes are frequent. Since the newspaper story is almost always told in the past tense, this is the anchoring tense from which changes are made.

WRONG: He *looked* into the briefcase and *finds* a small parcel.

RIGHT: He *looked* into the briefcase and *found* a small parcel.

Not all changes from past to present are incorrect. The present tense can be used to describe universal truths and situations that are permanently true:

> The Court *said* the Constitution *requires* due process.

When two actions are being described and one was completed before the other occurred, a tense change from the past to the past perfect is best for reader comprehension:

> The patrolman *testified* that he *had placed* his revolver on the table.

Broadcast writers, who tell most of their stories in the present tense, can handle similar situations with a change from the present tense to the present perfect:

> The company *denies* it *has paid* women less than men for comparable work.

In the course of the story, the tense should not make needless shifts from sentence to sentence. The reader is directed by the verb, and if the verb is incorrect, the reader is likely to be confused:

> Moore said he *shot* the animal in the back. It *escaped* from the pen in which it was kept.

The reader wonders: Did the animal escape after it was shot, or did it escape and then it was shot? If the former, inserting the word *then* at the start of the second sentence or before the verb would help make it clear. If the animal escaped and then was shot, the second sentence should use the past perfect tense to indicate this:

> It *had escaped* from the pen in which it was kept.

Spelling

Good spellers use the dictionary. Poor spellers do not. Every editor knows that some writers cannot spell well. Editors accept this, but they do not accept excuses for misspelled words. They expect all their reporters to use the dictionary.

The first step in improving spelling is to diagnose the particular spelling problem. One frequent cause of misspellings is mispronunciation. We usually spell as we pronounce, and if we pronounce *goverment, sophmore, Febuary, athalete* and *hinderance,* this is how we will spell these words—incorrectly.

Sometimes we are fooled by words that sound alike or nearly alike but have different meanings:

accent, ascent, assent   formally, formerly
accept, except   irrelevant, irreverent
advice, advise   later, latter
affect, effect   loose, lose
allusive, elusive, illusive   moral, morale
altar, alter   precede, proceed
capital, capitol   prophecy, prophesy
choose, chose   respectfully, respectively
complement, compliment   stationary, stationery
decent, descent, dissent   who's, whose

One way to overcome a spelling problem is to keep a list of words you often misspell. Poor spellers usually assume they are spelling correctly, which is one reason poor spellers give for not using the dictionary. To start your list, here is a compilation of 50 commonly misspelled words. Look them over. If any surprise you, jot them down.

accommodate   environment   occurrence
a lot   exaggerate   parallel
already   exhilarate   possess
altogether   exorbitant   precede
arctic   February   prejudice
athlete   finally   privilege
calendar   forty   restaurant
career   governor   separate
cemetery   grammar   sophomore
commitment   harass   strictly
competent   hindrance   tragedy
consensus   immediately   truly
dependent   indispensable   undoubtedly
descendant   lightning   vacuum
ecstasy   mathematics   villain
eighth   nickel   weird
embarrass   nuclear

The dictionary is a guide to meaning as well as to spelling. Use it to **Usage** distinguish between words of similar sound and spelling such as the following words that are frequently confused. They are not synonymns.

anticipate, expect	lay, lie
because, since	lighted, lit
boycott, embargo	like, as
compose, comprise, constitute	majority, plurality
convince, persuade	misdemeanor, felony
due to, because of	pretense, pretext
fewer, less	rack, wrack
flaunt, flout	ravage, ravish
imply, infer	rebut, refute
last, latest	rifle, riffle

Avoid using the specialized terminology of the sciences, arts and aca- **Jargon** demic disciplines. Jargon is unintelligible to lay people, and when it comes into common usage, as has much computer terminology, it is pretentious.

JARGON: As a caterer, she interfaces with many of the city's most prominent business people.

BETTER: As a caterer, she meets many of the city's most prominent business people.

JARGON: Many people have been losing money in the bear market.

BETTER: Many people have been losing money as prices on the stock market have declined.

What were once brilliant metaphors and figures of speech are now so **Clichés** commonplace that they are bankrupt of meaning. Don't rely on clichés such as these to describe a situation or to present an image: *an eye for an eye, a far cry, nose to the grindstone, beast of burden, high time, water under the bridge, when the chickens come home to roost.*

Because these sentences and phrases are heard everywhere, all the time, writers have them imprinted in their memory banks, and in the struggle to find an apt expression they pop out. Shove them back in again.

George Orwell advised writers to be wary of using any phrase they are accustomed to seeing in print.

Wordiness

Good writing is crisp and clear. Each word contributes to the meaning of the sentence. Flabby writing can be improved by trimming useless words. Usually this means letting nouns and verbs do the work.

One way to tighten a sentence is to use the positive form for assertions. The positive form not only shortens the sentence, but also can replace adjectives or verb phrases with active verbs.

WORDY: Mrs. Jones said she would not buy the company's products because it advertises on television programs that portray violence.

BETTER: Mrs. Jones said she would boycott the company's products because it advertises on television programs that portray violence.

WORDY: In a campus poll, 35 percent of freshmen said they do not trust politicians.

BETTER: In a campus poll, 35 percent of freshmen said they distrust politicians.

A change from the negative to the positive form emphasizes the meanings of subject complements:

WEAK: Three of the six council members were not present at last night's meeting.

STRONGER: Three of the six council members were absent from last night's meeting.

WEAK: Professor Smith does not care about his students' complaints about homework.

STRONGER: Professor Smith is indifferent to his students' complaints about homework.

Writers who make each word count avoid the use of qualifying adjectives and adverbs like *very, rather, quite, kind of, sort of* and *somewhat.* A play that is very good is simply good—unless it is excellent. A man who is rather tall is tall—or he towers. Someone who is rather tired is either tired or exhausted.

The use of modifiers also leads to another symptom of muddy writing: redundancies.

Editor & Publisher carried this cutline:

The Associated Press staff in Santiago, Chile, goes back to work after armed gunmen from the Manuel Rodriguez Patriotic Front raided the office.

If the raiders were gunmen, obviously they were armed.

The use of adjectives and adverbs leads to these absurdities:

totally destroyed	successfully docked
first annual	fatally killed
serious crisis	

Here is a list of the most common redundancies seen in newspaper copy. It was compiled by the Minnesota Newspaper Association:

absolutely necessary	important essentials
advance planning	necessary requirements
ask the question	open up
assemble together	other alternative
at a later day	patently obvious
attached hereto	plain and simple
at the present time	postpone until later
canceled out	reasonable and fair
carbon copy	redo again
city of Chicago	refer back
close proximity	refuse and decline
consensus of opinion	revert back
continue on	right and proper
cooperate together	rise up
each and every	rules and regulations
enclosed you will find	send in
exactly identical	small in size
fair and just	still remain
fall down	temporarily suspended
first and foremost	totally unnecessary
friend of mine	true facts
gathered together	various and sundry
honest truth	

Sometimes redundancies and other useless words come in the form of prepositions added to verbs:

start up	pay out
send off, send over	end up
go out	shout out
call up	drop off

WORDY: She immediately called up her doctor.
BETTER: She immediately called her doctor.
WORDY: The couple paid out $30,000 in back taxes.
BETTER: The couple paid $30,000 in back taxes.
WORDY: Doc's Diner's sales have dropped off 15 percent since the campus grill opened up in October.
BETTER: Doc's Diner's sales have dropped 15 percent since the campus grill opened in October.

Another way to tighten your writing is to combine sentences:

WORDY: Mitch Ellington is the youngest player to make a hole-in-one on the course. He is 13.
BETTER: Thirteen-year-old Mitch Ellington is the youngest player to make a hole-in-one on the course.

Public Opinion Polling Checklist

Reporters should satisfy themselves on each of the following points before making extensive use of any poll:

Date. When was the poll taken? Later polls are more accurate than earlier ones in political races as people have less time to change their minds.

Interviews. How many were made? How were they conducted? Face-to-face interviews at home are best; telephone polls are quicker and cheaper. Mail surveys achieve small returns and those answering may be non-representative.

Methods. Does the pollster divulge the methods used and allow reporters to see computer breakdowns that are the basis of the pollster's conclusions? How have those who "don't know" been handled in adding up the final percentages? What was the technique used to estimate those who are eligible to vote and those likely or unlikely to vote? How big is the subsample of groups that are being broken out for specific analysis?

Disclosure. What part of the data is disclosed and what part is not? If the data are released by sources other than the pollster, does the material have the approval of the pollster? Is the material self-serving?

Sample. Who were interviewed and how were they selected? Was a probability sample used? (Did everyone eligible have an equal likelihood of being interviewed?) If a probability sample was used, how was the list selected from which the sample was drawn? The population that was sampled should be made clear. A check should be made to make sure the poll claims no more than the persons in the sample are qualified to say.

Questions. Is the exact wording of all questions provided? Questions can be slanted to favor a predetermined result. (A national mail survey asking who voters favored for the Republican nomination for president offered only the names of conservative candidates.) The questions may be unclear. Are the questions of the generally accepted type for the purpose? If not, were they pretested?

Interviewers. Who are they? Survey interviewers are supposed to be trained for the task. Campaign workers and reporters often are not. (Most reputable newspaper and television polls are conducted by professional organizations.)

Sponsor. Is it clear who paid for the poll and who made it? Polls made by candidates and political parties should be scrupulously examined.

Accuracy. Does the information include the error allowance or margin of error that will allow the results to be set within the actual limits of reliability? All polls should include this information, and the reporter should include it in the story. A pollster or a politician cannot claim that a 51–49 result is conclusive if the margin of error is the usual 3 percentage points in a national poll. Readers and listeners should know this. (See "Margin of Error.")

Saliency. Do opinions reflect subject matters of importance to respondents? Do respondents have enough information to understand the question?

Interpretation. What does the pollster or source distributing the results claim? Has the poll been fragmented in the interpretation so that only favorable results are used? Does the pollster or source claim more than the results indicate? Sometimes a segment of a poll will be used to assert that a certain part of the population favors a candidate when the actual sample of that part of the population is too small for the claims. The smaller the sample, the larger the margin of error.

Early Polls

Polls taken some time—a month or more—before an election say more about the state of the campaign at that precise moment than about the possible outcome. The closer to election day, the less time for voters to change their minds. But voters are often undecided even as they enter the voting booth.

The release of early polls by a candidate may be intended to influence the election. The press itself may accomplish the same result with its own early polling, although there is no clear evidence that the "bandwagon influence" is any more real than the "underdog influence." Certainly, the victory the newspapers and everyone else forecast for Thomas E. Dewey in 1948 turned out to be almost as sour a prediction as the Landon victory in 1936. One newspaper, the *Chicago Tribune,* went so far as to banner Dewey's victory across page one in an early edition. One of the most famous political photographs shows a beaming Harry Truman holding the *Tribune* the day after election.

There is no question that a strong start helps a candidate and that early polls showing strength can affect donations and press coverage. Cash tends to follow success. A potential donor may divert a contribution from what appears to be a losing cause. The press also takes cues from early polls. A third or fourth finisher in a preprimary poll will not be given as much coverage as the leaders. Thus, a self-fulfilling prophecy is brought about: The polls say Bettinger is trailing; we will not spend much time covering his primary campaign, which guarantees the public will know little of Bettinger. Without adequate press coverage, Bettinger cannot compete equally, and he loses.

Margin of Error

If a poll were to be made of everyone in a group that we want to learn something about, our conclusions would be completely reliable. But because of such practical considerations as time and cost, population samples must be used, and this leads to sampling error—the difference between what we would have learned from the entire group (called the *universe* in polling parlance) and what we found out from the sample.

The more persons interviewed, the smaller the margin of error. At a 95 percent confidence level—which means that in 95 of 100 surveys the data will be within the limits of margin of error stated—the error will be:

Number Interviewed	Margin of Error
50	± 14 percent
200	± 7
600	± 4
1500	± 3
9600	± 1

If we wanted the maximum confidence (99 percent) and the minimum margin of error (plus or minus 1 percent), we would have to interview 16,590 persons. In national polls, a 95 percent confidence level with a 3 percentage point margin of error is usually accepted as meaningful.

By the time a national pollster has conducted a number of polls on the same question, his cumulative totals sometimes approach the numbers that give maximum confidence and minimum margin of error.

The margin of error should be applied to all polling results so that they do not seem to be more exact than they are. Here is how the margin of error is applied:

With a 3 percent margin of error, a candidate's percentage can move up or down 3 points, which is a 6 percent range or spread. Thus, polling results that are close cannot be said to favor one or the other of the candidates. With a 3 percent margin of error, any results that are separated by 6 percentage points or fewer are too close to call.

A poll that shows Jackson leading Torrance by 53–47 could actually be a nip-and-tuck race, 50–50 (subtracting 3 percent from Jackson; adding 3 percent to Torrance). Or it could be decisively for Jackson, 56–44 (adding 3 percent to Jackson and subtracting 3 percent from Torrance).

If the poll showed Jackson leading Torrance 52–48 with a 3 percent margin of error, the actual result might be Torrance ahead 51–49 (subtracting 3 percent from Jackson and adding 3 percent to Torrance).

Even these margins do not tell the full story. Five times out of 100 (the confidence level) our poll can be off target. Also, these are the lower limits of possible error. There are problems that exist beyond the statistical area, such as the human errors made during polling and the mistakes made in interpreting the results.

Stories about polls should include the margin of error. Predictions about the results must be measured against the limits set by these statistical necessities. The reporter should tell the whole story, including what he or she does not know.

Polls and surveys are useful additions to the standard reporting techniques. There is nothing magical, nothing fraudulent about polls. Used within the limits of their capabilities by discerning journalists, they extend the reporter's eyes and ears beyond the traditional interviewing process.

Newspapers should describe how they conduct their polls. One way to do this is to run a short piece next to the main story explaining the polling methods used. Here is a piece that could serve as a model:

This poll is based on telephone interviews November 18 through 23 with 600 adults who live in the city.

The telephone numbers were chosen in such a way that all sections of the city were represented in proportion to population. Numbers were formed by random digits, thus permitting access to unlisted and listed numbers.

The results have been weighted to take account of household size and to adjust for variations in the sample relating to race, sex, age and education.

In theory, it can be said that in 95 cases out of 100 the results based on this sample differ by no more than four percentage points in either direction than from what would have been obtained by interviewing all adults in the city.

The theoretical errors do not take into account a margin of additional error that could result from the several practical difficulties in taking any survey of public opinion.

Subgroups

Pollsters make groupings on the basis of religion, occupation, sex, region, race and income. The generalized assumption of the pollster is that persons with particular characteristics will vote in ways that differ significantly from the voting patterns usually evident among persons with other characteristics.

This has led to such generalities as: Jewish areas vote more Democratic than the overall average; Lutherans vote more Republican; factory workers vote more Democratic; farmers vote more Republican. When such groups behave differently, change their normal voting proportions, there is a story in the shift.

However, journalists should be cautious about drawing conclusions from such data. The way a person votes is a reflection of a variety of influences. Also, patterns change as old ethnic neighborhoods break up or as workers become more affluent. As the culture becomes more diverse, it is increasingly difficult to establish a cause-and-effect relationship. Beware of single-cause explanations.

How to Use the Freedom of Information Act

**Who Can Make
a Request?**

The FOIA permits "any person" to request access to agency records.

In practice, this includes U.S. citizens, permanent resident aliens, and foreign nationals, as well as corporations, unincorporated associations, universities, and state and local governments and members of Congress.

**How Quickly Will an
Agency Respond?**

The FOIA requires an agency to respond to an initial request within 10 working days and to an administrative appeal within 20 working days.

An agency may take an additional 10 days to respond to either the initial request or the administrative appeal in "unusual circumstances" involving the agency's need to obtain records from field facilities, process separate and distinct records, or consult with another agency or two or more of its own components having a substantial interest in the request.

If the agency fails to comply with the applicable time limit requirements, the requester is deemed to have exhausted his administrative remedies and may seek satisfaction in court. In such a case, however, if the agency can show that "exceptional circumstances" exist and that it is exercising due diligence in responding to the request, the court may retain jurisdiction and allow the agency additional time to complete its review of the records.

Otherwise, upon any determination by an agency to comply with a request, the FOIA requires that the records "shall be made promptly available" to the requester.

Where to Write

The first order of business in making an FOIA request is to determine which agency should receive it.

If you are uncertain about which agency may have the information you seek, go to the library and check records you want, and find out the specific mailing address for its FOIA office.

The FOIA simply requires that a request must "reasonably describe" the records being sought. This means that the description must be sufficiently specific so that a government employee who is familiar with an agency's filing system will be able to locate the records within a reasonable amount of time. There is no requirement that you explain why you are seeking the information, but such an explanation might be necessary if you want the agency to waive its fees or comply more fully with your request. The more precise and accurate the request, the more likely you are to get a prompt and complete response, with lower search fees. If you do not give a clear description of the information that is being requested, the agency will contact you for clarification.

Describing What You Want

- Try to limit your request to what you really want. If you simply ask for "all files relating to" a particular subject (including yourself), you may give the agency an excuse to delay its response and needlessly run up search and copying costs.
- If you know that the request involves a voluminous number of records, try to state both what your request includes and what it does not include.
- Try to be specific about the "search logic" you want the agency to follow. Use *and/or* to describe the different subject matters under request. By using the word *and* between different topics (for example, "mail openings *and* surveillance"), you may receive information that falls into both categories but receive none of the documents which relate *only* to "mail openings" or *only* to "surveillance."
- If you want material released to you in an order of specific priorities, inform the agency of your needs; for example, you might want to have materials reviewed and released to you in chronological or geographical order, or you may simply not want to wait for *all* of the records to be reviewed before any are released.
- Decide whether you want to write a local or regional office of a given agency instead of (or in addition to) the headquarters. Headquarters will ordinarily have policy-making information, plus information of a more general nature than the local officials have chosen to report; the field offices ordinarily have the working files.

Plan Your Request Strategy

- If there are published accounts—newspaper clips, articles, congressional reports, etc.—of the material requested, these should be cited specifically. If they are brief, it may also be helpful to enclose copies of relevant sections.
- If you know that portions of the requested records have already been released, point this out. (It may eliminate or reduce search fees.) Give information, if possible, to identify that release (i.e., date, release number, original requester).
- If you know the title or date of a document, who wrote it, the addressee, or the division or field office of the agency in which it originated, such information should be included.

Identify What You Want as Clearly as Possible

Sample Request Letter

Tele. No. (business hours)
Return Address
Date

Name of Public Body
Address

To the FOI Officer:

This request is made under the federal Freedom of Information Act, 5 U.S.C. 552.

Please send me copies of *(Here, clearly describe what you want. Include identifying material, such as names, places, and the period of time about which you are inquiring. If you wish, attach news clips, reports, and other documents describing the subject of your research.)*

As you know, the FOI Act provides that if portions of a document are exempt from release, the remainder must be segregated and disclosed. Therefore, I will expect you to send me all non-exempt portions of the records which I have requested, and ask that you justify any deletions by reference to specific exemptions of the FOI Act. I reserve the right to appeal your decision to withhold any materials.

I promise to pay reasonable search and duplication fees in connection with this request. However, if you estimate that the total fees will exceed $_____ , please notify me so that I may authorize expenditure of a greater amount.

(Optional) I am prepared to pay reasonable search and duplication fees in connection with this request. However, the FOI Act provides for waiver or reduction of fees if disclosure could be considered as "primarily benefiting the general public." I am a journalist *(researcher, or scholar)* employed by *(name of news organization, book publishers, etc.)*, and intend to use the information I am requesting as the basis for a planned article *(broadcast, or book). (Add arguments here in support of fee waiver)*. Therefore, I ask that you waive all search and duplication fees. If you deny this request, however, and the fees will exceed $_____ , please notify me of the charges before you fill my request so that I may decide whether to pay the fees or appeal your denial of my request for a waiver.

As I am making this request in the capacity of a journalist *(author, or scholar)* and this information is of timely value, I will appreciate your communicating with me by telephone, rather than by mail, if you have any questions regarding this request. Thank you for your assistance, and I will look forward to receiving your reply within 10 business days, as required by law.

Very truly yours,

(Signature)

Included here are the Code of Federal Regulations (CFR) citations. The **FOIA Addresses**
Code of Federal Regulations lists the policies for each agency and may be
helpful in your research. The CFR can be found in any law library and many
public libraries.

Central Intelligence Agency
Information and Privacy Coordinator
Washington, DC 20505
phone: (703) 351–2083

Appeals
same address

32 CFR Part 1900

Civil Rights Commission
Solicitors Office, Rm. 710
1121 Vermont Ave. NW
Washington, DC 20425
phone: (202) 254–3070

Appeals
same address

45 CFR Part 704

Consumer Product Safety Commission
Freedom of Information Office
Washington, DC 20207
phone: (202) 492–6800

Appeals
Chairman of Commission
Consumer Product Safety Commission
Washington, DC 20207

16 CFR Part 1016

Department of Agriculture
Office of Information
14th and Independence SW
Rm. 458A
Washington, DC 20250
phone: (202) 447–7454

Appeals
Dept. of Agriculture
Office of the General Counsel
Office of the Inspector General
Rm. 8-E
14th and Independence SW
Washington, DC 20250
phone: (202) 447–6979

7 CFR Part 1

Department of Commerce
Office of Information Policy and
    Management Division
Rm. 6622
Washington, DC 20230
phone: (202) 377–4217

Appeals
Office of the General Counsel
Rm. 5870
14th and Constitution Ave. NW
Washington, DC 20230

15 CFR Part 4

Department of Defense
Office of the Secretary of Defense
Public Affairs
Director for Freedom of Information
    and Security Review
Rm. 2C757, Pentagon
Washington, DC 20301
phone: (202) 697–4325

Appeals
same address

32 CFR Part 286

**Department of Health and Human
    Services**
Central Information Center
Dept. H.H.S.
Health Building
330 Independence Ave. SW
Washington, DC 20201

45 CFR Part 5

Food and Drug Administration
Freedom of Information Office
Rm. 12 A-12
5600 Fishers Lane
Rockville, MD 20857
phone: (301) 443–6310

Appeals
Assistant Secretary for Health
Dept. of Health and Human Services
200 Independence Ave. SW
Washington, DC 20201

21 CFR part 20

Department of Housing and Urban Development
Program Information Center
451 7th St. SW
Washington, DC 20410
phone: (202) 755–6420

Appeals
Assistant General Counsel,
  Administrative Law
Office of The General Counsel
451 7th St. SW
Washington, DC 20410

24 CFR Part 15

Department of Justice
Freedom of Information and Privacy
  Acts
Referral Unit
Rm. B-113
10th and Constitution NW
Washington, DC 20530
phone: (202) 633–2353

Appeals
Department of Justice
Office of Information and Privacy
550 11th St. NW
Washington, DC 20530
phone: (202) 724–7400

28 CFR Part 16

Department of State
Information and Privacy Staff
Rm. 1239
2201 C St. NW
Washington, DC 20520
phone: (202) 632–1267

Appeals
Asst. General Counsel for Public Affairs
same address

22 CFR Part 6

Department of the Treasury
Freedom of Information Office
Room 5423
Main Treasury
Washington, DC 20220
phone: (202) 566–0770

Appeals
same address

31 CFR Part 1

Department of the Treasury
Internal Revenue Service
Public Service Branch
Director of Disclosure and Security
  Division
PO Box 388
c/o Ben Franklin Station
Washington, DC 20044
phone: (202) 566–3359

Appeals
Chief Counsel
Internal Revenue Service
PO Box 929
c/o Ben Franklin Station
Washington, DC 20044

26 CFR Part 601, subpart G

Environmental Protection Agency
Freedom of Information Office
A 101
401 M St. SW
Washington, DC 20460
phone: (202) 382–4048

Appeal
same address

40 CFR Part 2

Equal Employment Opportunity Commission
Headquarters
Office of Legal Counsel
Legal Services
2401 E St. NW
Washington, DC 20506
phone: (202) 634–6690

Appeal
Chairman
EEOC
2401 E St. NW
Washington, DC 20506

29 CFR Part 1610

Federal Bureau of Investigation
Chief Freedom of Information and
  Privacy Act
10th and Pennsylvania Ave. NW
Washington, DC 20525
phone: (202) 324–5520

Appeals
Attorney General
Office of Legal Policy
Dept. of Justice
Office of Information and Privacy
Washington, DC 20530

28 CFR Part 16

Federal Trade Commission
Freedom of Information Request
Deputy Executive Director's Office
Rm. 692
6th and Pennsylvania Ave. NW
Washington, DC 20580
phone: (202) 523–3640

Appeal
Freedom of Information Appeal
Office of General Counsel
Federal Trade Commission
6th and Pennsylvania Ave. NW
Washington, DC 20580

16 CFR Section 4.11

Nuclear Regulatory Commission
Director, Division of Rules and Records
Office of Administration
Washington, DC 20555
phone: (202) 492–8133

Appeals
depends on denial; they will tell you to
    whom you should write your appeal.

10 CFR Part 9

Selective Service Systems
Office of Administration
National Headquarters
1023 31st St. NW
Washington, DC 20435
phone: (202) 724–0828

Appeal
Director of Selective Service Systems
1023 31st St. NW
Washington, DC 20435

32 CFR Part 1662

Small Business Administration
Freedom of Information Office
1411 L St. NW
Washington, DC 20416
phone: (202) 653–6460

Appeal
same address

13 CFR Part 102

Veterans Administration
McPherson Square Bldg.
Rm. 950
Washington, DC 20420
phone: (202) 389–5120

Appeal
Veterans Administration
Administrator
810 Vermont Ave. NW
Washington, DC 20420

38 CFR section 1.500

The material in this section was made available by the Center for National Security Studies, 122 Maryland Ave. NE, Washington, D.C. 20002, and was compiled by Allan Adler and Ann Profozich.

APPENDIX D

Codes of Ethics

Adopted by the Society of Professional Journalists, Sigma Delta Chi, 1973

The Society of Professional Journalists, Sigma Delta Chi, believes the duty of journalists is to serve the truth.

We believe the agencies of mass communication are carriers of public discussion and information, acting on their Constitutional mandate and freedom to learn and report the facts.

We believe in public enlightenment as the forerunner of justice, and in our Constitutional role to seek the truth as part of the public's right to know the truth.

We believe those responsibilities carry obligations that require journalists to perform with intelligence, objectivity, accuracy, and fairness.

To these ends, we declare acceptance of the standards of practice here set forth:

RESPONSIBILITY: The public's right to know of events of public importance and interest is the overriding mission of the mass media. The purpose of distributing news and enlightened opinion is to serve the general welfare. Journalists who use their professional status as representatives of the public for selfish or other unworthy motives violate a high trust.

FREEDOM OF THE PRESS: Freedom of the press is to be guarded as an inalienable right of people in a free society. It carries with it the freedom and the responsibility to discuss, question, and challenge actions and utterances of our government and of our public and private institutions. Journalists uphold the right to speak unpopular opinions and the privilege to agree with the majority.

ETHICS: Journalists must be free of obligation to any interest other than the public's right to know the truth.

1. Gifts, favors, free travel, special treatment or privileges can compromise the integrity of journalists and their employers. Nothing of value should be accepted.

2. Secondary employment, political involvement, holding public office, and service in community organizations should be avoided if it compromises the integrity of journalists and their employers. Journalists and their employers should conduct their personal lives in a manner which protects them from conflict of interest, real or apparent. Their responsibilities to the public are paramount. That is the nature of their profession.

3. So-called news communications from private sources should not be published or broadcast without substantiation of their claims to news value.

4. Journalists will seek news that serves the public interest, despite the obstacles. They will make constant efforts to assure that the public's business is conducted in public and that public records are open to public inspection.

5. Journalists acknowledge the newsman's ethic of protecting confidential sources of information.

ACCURACY AND OBJECTIVITY: Good faith with the public is the foundation of all worthy journalism.

1. Truth is our ultimate goal.

2. Objectivity in reporting the news is another goal, which serves as the mark of an experienced professional. It is a standard of performance toward which we strive. We honor those who achieve it.

3. There is no excuse for inaccuracies or lack of thoroughness.

4. Newspaper headlines should be fully warranted by the contents of the articles they accompany. Photographs and telecasts should give an accurate picture of an event and not highlight a minor incident out of context.

5. Sound practice makes clear distinction between news reports and expressions of opinion. News reports should be free of opinion or bias and represent all sides of an issue.

6. Partisanship in editorial comment which knowingly departs from the truth violates the spirit of American journalism.

7. Journalists recognize their responsibility for offering informed analysis, comment, and editorial opinion on public events and issues. They accept the obligation to present such material by individuals whose competence, experience, and judgment qualify them for it.

8. Special articles or presentations devoted to advocacy or the writer's own conclusions and interpretations should be labeled as such.

FAIR PLAY: Journalists at all times will show respect for the dignity, privacy, rights, and well-being of people encountered in the course of gathering and presenting the news.

1. The news media should not communicate unofficial charges affecting reputation or moral character without giving the accused a chance to reply.

2. The news media must guard against invading a person's right to privacy.

3. The media should not pander to morbid curiosity about details of vice and crime.

4. It is the duty of news media to make prompt and complete correction of their errors.

5. Journalists should be accountable to the public for their reports and the public should be encouraged to voice its grievances against the media. Open dialogue with our readers, viewers, and listeners should be fostered.

PLEDGE: Journalists should actively censure and try to prevent violations of these standards, and they should encourage their observance by all newspeople. Adherence to this code of ethics is intended to preserve the bond of mutual trust and respect between American journalists and the American people.

Adopted by the Associated Press Managing Editors, 1975

This code is a model against which newspaper men and women can measure their performance. It is meant to apply to news and editorial staff members and others who are involved in, or who influence, news coverage and editorial policy. It has been formulated in the belief that newspapers and the people who produce them should adhere to the highest standards of ethical and professional conduct.

Responsibility

A good newspaper is fair, accurate, honest, responsible, independent and decent. Truth is its guiding principle.

It avoids practices that would conflict with the ability to report and present news in a fair and unbiased manner.

The newspaper should serve as a constructive critic of all segments of society. It should vigorously expose wrongdoing or misuse of power, public or private. Editorially, it should advocate needed reform or innovations in the public interest.

News sources should be disclosed unless there is clear reason not to do so. When it is necessary to protect the confidentiality of a source, the reason should be explained.

The newspaper should background, with the facts, public statements that it knows to be inaccurate or misleading. It should uphold the right of free speech and freedom of the press and should respect the individual's right of privacy.

The public's right to know about matters of importance is paramount, and the newspaper should fight vigorously for public access to news of government through open meetings and open records.

Accuracy

The newspaper should guard against inaccuracies, carelessness, bias or distortion through either emphasis or omission.

It should admit all substantive errors and correct them promptly and prominently.

Integrity

The newspaper should strive for impartial treatment of issues and dispassionate handling of controversial subjects. It should provide a forum for the exchange of comment and criticism, especially when such comment is opposed to its editorial positions. Editorials and other expressions of opinion by reporters and editors should be clearly labeled.

The newspaper should report the news without regard for its own interest. It should not give favored news treatment to advertisers or special-interest groups. It should report matters regarding itself or its personnel with the same vigor and candor as it would other institutions or individuals.

Concern for community, business or personal interests should not cause a newspaper to distort or misrepresent the facts.

The newspaper and its staff should be free of obligations to news sources and special interests. Even the appearance of obligation or conflict of interest should be avoided.

Conflicts of Interest

Newspapers should accept nothing of value from news sources or others outside the profession. Gifts and free or reduced-rate travel, entertainment, products and lodging should not be accepted. Expenses in connection with news reporting should be paid by the newspaper. Special favors and special treatment for members of the press should be avoided.

Involvement in such things as politics, community affairs, demonstrations and social causes that could cause a conflict of interest, or the appearance of such conflict, should be avoided.

Outside employment by news sources is an obvious conflict of interest, and employment by potential news sources also should be avoided.

Financial investments by staff members or other outside business interests that could conflict with the newspaper's ability to report the news or that would create the impression of such conflict should be avoided.

Stories should not be written or edited primarily for the purpose of winning awards and prizes. Blatantly commercial journalism contests, or others that reflect unfavorably on the newspaper or the profession, should be avoided.

No code of ethics can prejudge every situation. Common sense and good judgment are required in applying ethical principles to newspaper realities. Individual newspapers are encouraged to augment these APME guidelines with locally produced codes that apply more specifically to their own situations.

Adopted by the American Society of Newspaper Editors, 1975

PREAMBLE: The First Amendment, protecting freedom of expression from abridgment by any law, guarantees to the people through their press a constitutional right, and thereby places on newspaper people a particular responsibility.

Thus journalism demands of its practitioners not only industry and knowledge but also the pursuit of a standard of integrity proportionate to the journalist's singular obligation.

To this end the American Society of Newspaper Editors sets forth this Statement of Principles as a standard encouraging the highest ethical and professional performance.

ARTICLE I—RESPONSIBILITY: The primary purpose of gathering and distributing news and opinion is to serve the general welfare by informing the people and enabling them to make judgments on the issues of the time. Newspapermen and women who abuse the power of their professional role for selfish motives or unworthy purposes are faithless to that public trust.

The American press was made free not just to inform or just to serve as a forum for debate but also to bring an independent scrutiny to bear on the forces of power in the society, including the conduct of official power at all levels of government.

ARTICLE II—FREEDOM OF THE PRESS: Freedom of the press belongs to the people. It must be defended against encroachment or assault from any quarter, public or private.

Journalists must be constantly alert to see that the public's business is conducted in public. They must be vigilant against all who would exploit the press for selfish purposes.

ARTICLE III—INDEPENDENCE: Journalists must avoid impropriety and the appearance of impropriety as well as any conflict of interest or the appearance of conflict. They should neither accept anything nor pursue any activity that might compromise or seem to compromise their integrity.

ARTICLE IV—TRUTH AND ACCURACY: Good faith with the reader is the foundation of good journalism. Every effort must be made to assure that the news content is accurate, free from bias and in context, and that all sides are presented fairly. Editorials, analytical articles and commentary should be held to the same standards of accuracy with respect to facts as news reports.

Significant errors of fact, as well as errors of omission, should be corrected promptly and prominently.

ARTICLE V—IMPARTIALITY: To be impartial does not require the press to be unquestioning or to refrain from editorial expression. Sound practice, however, demands a clear distinction for the reader between news reports and opinion. Articles that contain opinion or personal interpretation should be clearly identified.

ARTICLE VI—FAIR PLAY: Journalists should respect the rights of people involved in the news, observe the common standards of decency and stand accountable to the public for the fairness and accuracy of their news reports.

Persons publicly accused should be given the earliest opportunity to respond.

Pledges of confidentiality to news sources must be honored at all costs, and therefore should not be given lightly. Unless there is clear and pressing need to maintain confidences, sources of information should be identified.

These principles are intended to preserve, protect and strengthen the bond of trust and respect between American journalists and the American people, a bond that is essential to sustain the grant of freedom entrusted to both by the nation's founders.

Glossary

These definitions were provided by the press associations and working reporters and editors. Most of the brief entries are from the *New England Daily Newspaper Study,* an examination of 105 daily newspapers, edited by Loren Ghiglione (Southbridge, Mass.: Southbridge Evening News Inc., 1973).

Print Terms

add An addition to a story already written or in the process of being written.

assignment Instruction to a reporter to cover an event. An editor keeps an assignment book that contains notations for reporters such as the following:
Jacobs—10 a.m.: Health officials tour new sewage treatment plant.
Klaren—11 a.m.: Interview Ben Wastersen, possible Democratic congressional candidate.
Mannen—Noon: Rotary Club luncheon speaker, Horlan, the numerologist. A feature?

attribution Designation of the person being quoted. Also, the source of information in a story. Sometimes, information is given on a not-for-attribution basis.

background Material in a story that gives the circumstances surrounding or preceding the event.

banger An exclamation point. Avoid. Let the reader do the exclaiming.

banner Headline across or near the top of all or most of a newspaper page. Also called a line, ribbon, streamer, screamer.

B copy Bottom section of a story written ahead of an event that will occur too close to deadline for the entire story to be processed. The B copy usually consists of background material.

beat Area assigned to a reporter for regular coverage; for example, police or city hall. Also, an exclusive story.

body type Type in which most of a newspaper is set, usually 8 or 9 point type.

boldface Heavy, black typeface; type that is blacker than the text with which it is used. Abbreviated bf.

break When a news development becomes known and available. Also, the point of interruption in a story continued from one page to another.

bright Short, amusing story.

bulldog Early edition, usually the first of a newspaper.

byline Name of the reporter who wrote the story, placed atop the published article. An old-timer comments on the current use of bylines: "In the old days, a reporter was given a byline if he or she personally covered an important or unusual story, or the story was an exclusive. Sometimes if the writing was superior, a byline was given. Nowadays, everyone gets a byline, even if the story is a rewrite and the reporter never saw the event described in the story."

caps Capital letters; same as upper case.

caps and lower case Initial capital in a word followed by small letters. See **lower case.**

clip News story clipped from a newspaper, usually for future reference.

cold type In composition, type set photographically or by pasting up letters and pictures on acetate or paper.

column The vertical division of the news page. A standard-size newspaper is divided into five to eight columns. Also, a signed article of opinion or strong personal expression, frequently by an authority or expert—a sports column, a medical column, political or social commentary, and the like.

copy Written form in which a news story or other material is prepared.

copy flow After a reporter finishes a story it moves to the city desk where the city editor reads it for major errors or problems. If it does not need further work, the story is moved to the copy desk for final editing and a headline. It then moves to the mechanical department.

correction Errors that reach publication are retracted or corrected if they are serious or someone demands a correction. Libelous matter is always corrected immediately, often in a separate news story rather than in the standard box assigned to corrections.

correspondent Reporter who sends news from outside a newspaper office. On smaller papers often not a regular full-time staff member.

crony journalism Reporting that ignores or treats lightly negative news about friends of a reporter. Beat reporters sometimes have a tendency to protect their informants in order to retain them as sources.

crop To cut or mask the unwanted portions, usually of a photograph.

cut Printed picture or illustration. Also, to eliminate material from a story. See trim.

cutline Any descriptive or explanatory material under a picture.

dateline Name of the city or town and sometimes the date at the start of a story that is not of local origin.

deadline Time at which the copy for an edition must be ready.

edition One version of a newspaper. Some papers have one edition a day, some several. Not to be confused with issue, which usually refers to all editions under a single date.

editorial Article of comment or opinion usually on the editorial page.

editorial material All material in the newspaper that is not advertising.

enterprise copy Story, often initiated by a reporter, that digs deeper than the usual news story.

exclusive Story one reporter has obtained to the exclusion of the competition. A beat. Popularly known as a scoop, a term never used in the newsroom.

feature Story emphasizing the human or entertaining aspects of a situation. A news story or other material differentiated from straight news. As a verb, it means to give prominence to a story.

file To send a story to the office, usually by wire or telephone, or to put news service stories on the wire.

filler Material used to fill space. Small items used to fill out columns where needed. Also called column closers and shorts.

flag Printed title of a newspaper on page one. Also known as logotype or nameplate.

folo Story that follows up on a theme in a news story. When a fire destroyed a parochial school in Chicago, newspapers followed up the fire coverage with stories about fire safety precautions in the Chicago schools.

free advertising Use of the names of businesses and products not essential to the story. Instead of the brand name, use the broad term camera for Leica or Kodak.

futures calendar Date book in which story ideas, meetings and activities scheduled for a later occurrence are listed. Also known as a futures book. Kept by city and assignment editors and by careful reporters.

good night Before leaving for the day, beat reporters check in with the desk and are given a good night, which means there is nothing further for the reporter from the desk for the day. On some newspapers, the call is made for the lunch break, too. Desks need to know where their reporters are in case of breaking stories.

graf Abbreviation for paragraph.

Guild Newspaper Guild, an international union to which reporters and other newspaper workers belong. Newspapers that have contracts with the Guild are said to be "organized."

handout Term for written publicity or special-interest news sent to a newspaper for publication.

hard news Spot news; live and current news in contrast to features.

head or headline The display type over a printed news story.

head shot Picture featuring little more than the head and shoulders of the person shown.

HFR Abbreviation for "hold for release." Material that cannot be used until it is released by the source or at a designated time. Also known as embargoed material.

insert Material placed between copy in a story. Usually, a paragraph or more to be placed in material already sent to the desk.

investigative reporting Technique used to unearth information that sources often want hidden. This type of reporting involves examination of documents and records, the cultivation of informants, painstaking and extended research. Investigative reporting usually seeks to expose wrongdoing and has concentrated on public officials and their activities. In recent years, industry and business have been scrutinized. Some journalists contend that the term is redundant, that all good reporting is investigative, that behind every surface fact is the real story that a resourceful, curious and persistent reporter can dig up.

italics Type in which letters and characters slant to the right.

jump Continuation of a story from one page to another. As a verb, to continue material. Also called runover.

kill To delete a section from copy or to discard the entire story; also, to spike a story.

lead (pronounced leed) First paragraph in a news story. In a direct or straight news lead it summarizes the main facts. In a delayed lead, usually used on feature stories, it evokes a scene or sets a mood.
Also used to refer to the main idea of a story: An editor will ask a reporter "What's the lead on the piece?" expecting a quick summary of the main facts.
Also: A tip on a story; an idea for a story. A source will tell a reporter, "I have a lead on a story for you."

localize Emphasizing the names of persons from the local community who are involved in events outside the city or region: A local couple rescued in a Paris hotel fire; the city police chief who speaks at a national conference.

lower case Small letters, as contrasted to capitals.

LTK Designation on copy for ''lead to come.'' Usually placed after the slug. Indicates the written material will be given a lead later.

makeup Layout or design. The arrangement of body type, headlines and illustrations into pages.

masthead Formal statement of a newspaper's name, officers, place of publication and other descriptive information, usually on the editorial page. Sometimes confused with flag or nameplate.

morgue Newspaper library.

mug shot See **head shot.**

new lead See **running story.**

news hole Space in a newspaper allotted to news, illustrations and other non-advertising material.

obituary Account of a person's death; also called obit.

offset Printing process in which an image is transferred from a printing plate to a rubber roller and then set off on paper.

off the record Material offered the reporter in confidence. If the reporter accepts the material with this understanding, it cannot be used except as general background in a later story. Some reporters never accept off-the-record material. Some reporters will accept the material with the provision that if they can obtain the information elsewhere they will use it. Reporters who learn of off-the-record material from other than the original source can use it.
No public, official meeting can be off the record, and almost all official documents (court records, police information) are public information. Private groups can ask that their meetings be kept off the record, but reporters frequently ignore such requests when the meeting is public or large numbers of persons are present.

op-ed page Abbreviation for the page opposite the editorial page. The page is frequently devoted to opinion columns and related illustrations.

overnight Story usually written late at night for the afternoon newspapers of the next day. Most often used by the press services. The overnight, or overnighter, usually has little new information in it but is cleverly written so that the reader thinks the story is new. Also known as second-day stories.

play Emphasis given to a news story or picture—size and place in the newspaper of the story; typeface and size of headline.

P.M. Afternoon or evening newspaper.

pool Arrangement whereby limited numbers of reporters and photographers are selected to represent all those assigned to the story. Pooling is adopted when a large number of persons would overwhelm the event or alter its nature. The news and film are shared with the rest of the press corps.

precede Story written prior to an event; also, the section of a story preceding the lead, sometimes set in italic.

press release Publicity handout, or a story given to the news media for publication.

proof Reproduction of type on paper for the purpose of making corrections or alterations.

puff or puffery Publicity story or a story that contains unwarranted superlatives.

quotes Quotation marks; also a part of a story in which someone is directly quoted.

rewrite To write for a second time to strengthen a story or to condense it.

rewriteman Person who takes the facts of stories over the telephone and then puts them together into a story and who may rewrite reporters' stories.

roundup A story that joins two or more events with a common theme such as traffic accidents, weather, police reports. When the events occur in different cities and are wrapped up in one story, the story is known as an "undated roundup."

rowback A story that attempts to correct a previous story without indicating that the prior story had been in error or without taking responsibility for the error.

running story Event that develops and is covered over a period of time. For an event covered in subsequent editions of a newspaper or on a single cycle of a wire service, additional material is handled as follows: New lead— important new information; Adds and inserts—less important information; Sub—material that replaces dated material, which is removed.

sell Presentation a reporter makes to impress the editor with the importance of his or her story; also, editors sell stories to their superiors at news conferences.

shirt tail Short, related story added to the end of a longer one.

short Filler, generally of some current news value.

sidebar Story that emphasizes one part of another nearby story.

situationer Story that pulls together a continuing event for the reader who may not have kept track as it unfolded. The situationer is helpful with complex or technical developments or on stories with varied datelines and participants.

slant To write a story so as to influence the reader's thinking. To editorialize, to color or misrepresent.

slug Word or words placed on all copy to identify the story.

source Person, record, document or event that provides the information for the story.

source book Alphabetical listing, by name and by title, of the addresses and the office and home telephone numbers of persons on the reporter's beat and some general numbers—FBI agent in charge in town, police and fire department spokesmen, hospital information, weather bureau.

split page Front page of an inside section; also known as the break page, second front page.

stringer Correspondent, not a regular staff member, who is paid by the story or by the number of words written.

style Rules for capitalization, punctuation and spelling that standardize usage so that the material presented is uniform. Most newspapers and stations have stylebooks. The most frequently used is the common stylebook of the United Press International and the Associated Press. Some newspapers stress the "down" or "lower case" style, by which is meant that most titles are lower case. Some newspapers capitalize (upper case) frequently. Also, the unique characteristics of a reporter's writing or news delivery.

stylebook Specific listing of the conventions of spelling, abbreviation, punctuation, capitalization used by a particular newspaper, wire service. Broadcast stylebooks include pronunciations.

sub See **running story.**

subhead One-line and sometimes two-line head (usually in boldface body type) inserted in a long story at intervals for emphasis or to break up a long column of type.

text Verbatim report of a speech or public statement.

tight Full, too full. Also refers to a paper so crowded with ads that the news space must be reduced. It is the opposite of the wide open paper.

tip Information passed to a reporter, often in confidence. The material usually requires further fact gathering. Occasionally, verification is impossible and the reporter must decide whether to go with the tip on the strength of the insider's knowledge. Sometimes the reporter will not want to seek confirmation for fear of alerting sources who will alter the situation or release the information to the competition. Tips often lead to exclusives.

trim To reduce or condense copy carefully.

update Story that brings the reader up to date on a situation or personality previously in the news. If the state legislature appropriated additional funds for five new criminal court judges to meet the increased number of cases in the courts, an update might be written some months later to see how many more cases were handled after the judges went to work. An update usually has no hard news angle.

VDT Video display terminal; a part of the electronic system used in news and advertising departments that eliminates typewriters. Copy is written on typewriter-like keyboards and words appear on attached television screens rather than on paper. The story is stored on a disk in a computer. Editing is done on the terminals.

verification Determination of the truth of the material the reporter gathers or is given. The assertions, sometimes even the actual observation, do not necessarily mean the information is accurate or true. Some of the basic tools of verification are: the telephone book, for names and addresses; the city directory, for occupations; Who's Who, for biographical information. For verification of more complex material, the procedure of Thucydides, the Greek historian and author of the *History of the Peloponnesian War,* is good advice for the journalist: "As to the deeds done in the war, I have not thought myself at liberty to record them on hearsay from the first informant or on arbitrary conjecture. My account rests either on personal knowledge or on the closest possible scrutiny of each statement made by others. The process of research was laborious, because the conflicting accounts were given by those who had witnessed the several events, as partiality swayed or memory served them."

wire services Synonym for press associations, the Associated Press and United Press International. There are foreign-owned press services to which some newspapers subscribe: Reuters, Tass, Agence France Presse.

Broadcast Terms

actuality An on-the-scene report.

audio Sound.

closeup Shot of the face of the subject that dominates the frame so that little background is visible.

cover shot A long shot usually cut in at the beginning of a sequence to establish place or location.

cue A signal in script or by word or gesture to begin or to stop. Two types: incue and outcue.

cut Quick transition from one type of picture to another. Radio: A portion of an actuality on tape used on broadcast.

cutaway Transition shot—usually short—from one theme to another; used to avoid jump cut. Often, a shot of the interviewer listening.

dissolve Smooth fading of one picture for another. As the second shot becomes distinct, the first slowly disappears.

dolly Camera platform. Dolly-in: Move platform toward subject. Dolly-out: Move platform away.

dub The transfer of one videotape to another.

establishing shot Frequently a wide shot; used to give the viewer a sense of the scene of action.

FI or fade in A scene that begins without full brilliance and gradually assumes full brightness. **FO** or **fade out** is the opposite.

freeze frame A single frame that is frozen into position.

graphics All visual displays, such as art work, maps, charts and still photos.

jump cut Transition from one subject to a different subject in an abrupt manner. Avoided with cutaway shot between the scenes.

lead-in Introductory statements to film or tape of actual event. The lead-in sets up the actuality by giving the context of the event.

lead-out Copy that comes immediately after tape or film of an actuality. The lead-out identifies the newsmaker again so listeners and viewers will know whom they just heard or saw. Used more often in radio. Also known as tag lines.

long shot Framing that takes in the scene of the event.

medium shot Framing of one person from head to waist or of small group seated at table. Known as MS.

mix Combining two or more sound elements into one.

montage A series of brief shots of various subjects to give a single impression or communicate one idea.

O/C On camera. A reporter delivering copy directly to the camera without covering pictures.

outtakes Scenes that are discarded for the final story.

panning or pan shot Moving the camera from left to right or right to left.

remote A taped or live broadcast from a location outside the studio; also, the unit that originates such a broadcast.

segué An uninterrupted transition from one sound to another; a sound dissolve. (Pronounced seg-way.)

SOF Sound on film. Recorded simultaneously with the picture.

SOT Sound on tape. Recorded simultaneously with picture on tape.

trim To eliminate material.

V/O Reporter's voice over pictures.

VTR Video tape recording.

zooming Use of a variable focus lens to take closeups and wide angle shots from a stationary position. By using a zoom lens an impression can be given of moving closer to or farther away from the subject.

Computer Terms

These definitions were provided by Merrill Perlman of *The New York Times*.

access Locating and processing material in storage is called accessing.

busy light or working light Tells the user that the computer is working on the function requested. Most computer systems prevent any other functions being performed while the light is on.

change case Usually a key that allows a lowercase letter to be turned into an uppercase letter. The function is particularly useful when the user has forgotten to unlock the shift key.

control, command, supershift Usually a key that allows an extra function to be programmed onto a single key. For example, an x will yield a lowercase x with no extra key pressed, an uppercase x when the shift is pressed and perhaps a + mark when the supershift key is pressed. The control key also may act as a safety key that must be pressed simultaneously with another function key to, for example, erase an entire story.

crash The system "locks up" and the terminals stop functioning. This is the bane of computerized newsrooms, since in most cases all the copy that was on the screen when the system crashed is either lost or frozen. Most computer systems have a key or function that allows the user to protect or save copy from crashes by taking it off the screen for a moment so it can be entered into computer memory.

CRT Cathode ray tube.

cursor The square of light that indicates the place in the copy where the changes will be made. The user positions the cursor using directional keys before adding or deleting matter.

delete Just that. Most computer systems have keys for deleting characters, words, sentences, lines, paragraphs or blocks of copy that are defined by the user.

directory, file, basket Designations for the storage of stories, notes, memos, etc. The computerized equivalent of a file holder. Each reporter will have a file or directory; the copy desk will have another, etc.

disk drive A device or a system that reads material from a storage disk or sends information to it.

downtime The period a computer is malfunctioning.

file A grouping of related material.

film Terminology on some computer systems for setting a story into type.

format A specific set of instructions telling the computer to do something. Many systems have common formats built in; others require the user to format each story individually. The formats usually consist of the type size, the leading, the type face, the column width and any special instructions, such as cut-ins for the copy, to allow for half-column graphics or other special typographical set-ups. In some systems, formatting is called styling.

hardware The terminals, computers and other equipment of the system. (See **software**.)

home In most systems, a single key allows the user to return the cursor "home" to the top left-hand corner of the screen, or to the start of the text, depending on how the system is programmed.

hyphenate and justify Usually a function key on most systems, this takes the story, removes it from the screen for a bit and returns it to the screen with the words lined up and hyphenated in the proper column width, just as they will appear in type.

interface Equipment that permits different electronic devices to function with each other.

keystroke Pressing one key one time. Functions are often expressed in terms of a keystroke.

load When the computer terminal is being programmed, either by the user or by the systems people, this is called loading.

mainframe A powerful system that can handle considerable processing and storage. (See **minicomputer**.)

menu A list of material that can be called up on the screen or put into the system.

minicomputer A computer that can process and store but has less power than a mainframe.

off-line Equipment not in direct contact with the central processor of the system. **On-line** refers to devices that are in contact with the computer system.

program To give instructions to the computer. Also, the plan that enables the computer to perform routines or to solve a problem. Keys on various systems are programmable as well, so often-used functions or phrases can be entered into them. For example, a programmable key may have "By The ASSOCIATED PRESS" programmed into it, so the person working at the terminal can press just the programmed key to get all those characters.

scope Jargon for video display tube or terminal.

scroll To move the text on the screen up or down, to bring the next lines into view. Most computer systems allow users to scroll through the entire story; some limit scrolling to a certain number of characters.

software The programs that make it possible for the computer to do specific jobs.

terminal An individual work station.

tube Jargon for video display tube or terminal.

VDT Video display tube or video display terminal.

Credits

Chapter 1

pp. 7–8   News story from *Anniston (Ala.) Star*. Used with permission.

p. 11   Excerpt from news story from *The Wall Street Journal*. Copyright © by the Dow Jones Co., Inc. Reprinted with permission of *The Wall Street Journal*.

p. 20   News story from the *Daily News*. Used with permission.

Chapter 2

p. 31   Excerpts from news stories from *The Milwaukee Journal*. Reprinted by permission.

p. 32   News story from the *Associated Press*. Used with permission.

pp. 32, 33   News story from the *Associated Press*. Used with permission.

p. 39   News story from the *Daily News*. Used with permission.

pp. 42–43   Excerpts from news story from *The New York Times*. Copyright © by *The New York Times*. Reprinted with permission.

p. 45   Quotes and picture from the *Atlanta Constitution*. Used with permission.

p. 46   Excerpt used with permission of *The Washington Post*, copyright © 1978, from *The Washington Post Deskbook on Style*, edited by Robert A. Webb. New York: The McGraw-Hill Book Company.

p. 51   News story from *The New York Times*. Copyright © by *The New York Times*. Reprinted with permission.

Chapter 3

p. 63   Front page of *Rocky Mountain News* (Shuttle Extra edition). Reprinted with permission.

Chapter 5

p. 107   News story from *The Charlotte (N.C.) Observer*. Used with permission.

pp. 111–12   News story from the *Daily News*. Used with permission.

pp. 112–13   News story from *The New York Times*. Copyright © by *The New York Times*. Reprinted with permission.

Chapter 6

p. 125   Story from the *El Paso Herald-Post*. Used with permission.

p. 127   News story from the *San Francisco Chronicle*. Copyright © 1975, The Chronicle Publishing Co. Used with permission.

pp. 127–28   Excerpt from news story from *The Wall Street Journal*. Copyright © by the Dow Jones Co., Inc. Reprinted by permission of *The Wall Street Journal*.

Chapter 7

p. 158   Material by Jon Franklin of *The (Baltimore) Evening Sun*. Used with permission.

pp. 166–67   Excerpt from the book *Working: People Talk About What They Do All Day and How They Feel About It*. Copyright © 1972 by Studs Terkel. Reprinted with permission of Pantheon Books, a division of Random House, Inc., New York City.

p. 168   Excerpt from news story from *The Philadelphia Bulletin*. Used with permission.

p. 172   Excerpt from news story from *The Miami Herald*. Used with permission.

p. 173   Part of front page from the *Daily News*. Used with permission.

p. 175   News story from *The State Journal* (Topeka, Kan.). Used with permission.

p. 176   Excerpt from news story from *The Wall Street Journal*. Copyright © by the Dow Jones Co., Inc. Reprinted with permission of *The Wall Street Journal*.

Chapter 8

pp. 185–88   Excerpts from story from *The Lexington Herald-Leader*. Used with permission.

pp. 188–89   Excerpts from news stories from *The Charlotte (N.C.) Observer*. Used with permission.

pp. 190–91 News story from the *Houston Chronicle*. Used with permission.

p. 191 Excerpt from news story from *The Miami Herald*. Used with permission.

pp. 191–92 News story from the *Houston Chronicle*. Used with permission.

p. 193 News story from the *Houston Chronicle*. Used with permission.

pp. 196–97 Excerpts from news story from *The Lexington Herald-Leader*. Used with permission.

pp. 197–99 Excerpts from news story from *The (Baltimore) Evening Sun*. Used with permission.

p. 199 Excerpt from news story from *The Wall Street Journal*. Copyright © by the Dow Jones Co., Inc. Reprinted with permission of *The Wall Street Journal*.

pp. 200–201 From the series "The Feminization of Poverty," in the *Globe-Gazette*. Used with permission.

Chapter 9

p. 216 Material from *The Associated Press*. Used with permission.

Chapter 10

p. 242 Excerpt from article from the *Village Voice*. Copyright © by the Village Voice, Inc., New York City. Reprinted with the permission of the *Village Voice*.

pp. 243–45 Excerpts from *UPI Reporter* are from *United Press International*. Used with permission.

Chapter 11

p. 266 Excerpt from news story from *The New York Times*. Copyright © by *The New York Times*. Reprinted by permission.

p. 269 News story from *The Albuquerque Journal*. Used with permission.

p. 270 News story from *The New York Times*. Copyright © by *The New York Times*. Reprinted by permission.

Chapter 12

p. 288 Portion of front page from *The Wall Street Journal*. Copyright © 1975 by the Dow Jones Co., Inc. Reprinted with permission of *The Wall Street Journal*.

Chapter 13

p. 295 Excerpt from news story from *The New York Times*. Copyright © by *The New York Times*. Reprinted by permission.

p. 310 Excerpt from news story from *The Philadelphia Bulletin*. Used with permission.

p. 312 Excerpt from *Let Us Now Praise Famous Men*. Copyright © 1941 by James Agee and Walker Evans. Reprinted with the permission of Houghton Mifflin Company, Boston.

Chapter 14

p. 318 Excerpt from news story from the *Record* (Bergen County, N.J.). Used with permission.

p. 324 Excerpts from the *Times-Standard*, Eureka, Calif. Used with permission.

pp. 324–25 Excerpt from news story from *United Press International*. Used with permission.

p. 325 Excerpt from news story from *The Wall Street Journal*. Copyright © by the Dow Jones Co., Inc. Reprinted with permission of *The Wall Street Journal*.

pp. 326–29 Excerpts from news stories from *The Providence Journal-Bulletin*. Used with permission.

p. 330 Page of newspaper from *The Bulletin* (Bend, Ore.). Used with permission.

p. 339 News story from *The Providence Journal-Bulletin*. Used with permission.

p. 342 Excerpt from the book *Confessions of a Muckraker*. Copyright © 1979 by Jack Anderson and James Doyd. Reprinted with the permission of Random House, Inc.

Chapter 15

p. 351 News story from the *El Paso Herald-Post*. Used with permission.

p. 352 Excerpts from news story from *The New York Times*. Copyright © by *The New York Times*. Reprinted with permission.

p. 355 Excerpt from *Anthropological Essays*. Copyright © 1964 by Oscar Lewis. Reprinted with permission of Random House, Inc., New York City.

p. 358 Excerpt from the article "Let Us Now Praise Famous Writers," in *Atlantic Monthly*. Copyright © 1970 by the Atlantic Monthly Company, Boston. Reprinted with permission.

p. 358 Excerpt from "Whatever Happened to Sam Spade," in *Atlantic Monthly*. Copyright © 1975 by the Atlantic Monthly Company, Boston. Reprinted with permission.

p. 359 Excerpt from news story from *The Providence Journal-Bulletin*. Used with permission.

p. 360 Excerpt from "Talk of the Town," in *The New Yorker*. Copyright © 1975 by the New Yorker Magazine, Inc. Reprinted by permission.

Chapter 17

p. 382 News story from the *San Francisco Chronicle*. Copyright © 1975, The Chronicle Publishing Co. Used with permission.

p. 383 Excerpt from news story from the *Herald-Dispatch* (Huntington, W. Va.). Used with permission.

Chapter 18

p. 391 News story from the *Sanders County Ledger*. Used with permission.

p. 398	Excerpt from obituary from *Clear Creek (Colo.) Courant*. Used with permission.
p. 398	Excerpt from news story from the *Minneapolis Tribune*. Used with permission.
p. 399	Excerpt from a letter to the editor from the *Avalanche-Journal*. Used with permission.
p. 404	Excerpt from obituary column from the *Berkshire Eagle*. Used with permission.

Chapter 19

p. 407	Excerpt from news story from the *Daily News*. Used with permission.
p. 408	Excerpt from news story from *Greenville (S.C.) News*. Used with permission.
pp. 410–11	Excerpt from news story from the *Reformer* (Brattleboro, Vt.). Used with permission.
p. 412	Excerpt from news story from *The Louisville Courier-Journal*. Used with permission.
p. 415	Excerpt from news story from *The New York Times*. Copyright © by The New York Times. Reprinted with permission.

Chapter 20

| p. 438 | Excerpt from news story from *Anniston (Ala.) Star*. Used with permission. |

Chapter 21

p. 444	Excerpts from news stories from the *Associated Press*. Used with permission.
p. 446	Excerpt from news story from *Bucks County Courier Times*. Used with permission.
p. 450	News story from the *San Diego Union*. Used with permission.
p. 453	Excerpt from news story from *The Record*. Used with permission.
p. 454	News story from the *Rocky Mountain News*. Used with permission.
p. 455	Excerpt from news story from the *Berkshire Eagle*. Used with permission.
p. 456	Excerpt from news story from the *Denver Post*. Used with permission.
p. 456	Excerpt from news story from the *Miami Herald*. Used with permission.
pp. 457–58	News story from the *Miami Herald*. Used with permission.

| pp. 462–65 | Court terms based on definitions in *Black's Law Dictionary*, revised fourth edition, 1968. Published by West Publishing Co., St. Paul, Minn. Reprinted with the permission of the publisher. |

Chapter 22

| pp. 467–69 | Excerpts from news stories from *The Lexington Herald-Leader*. Used with permission. |
| p. 481 | Excerpt from *Why Time Begins on Opening Day* by Thomas Boswell. Copyright © 1984 by Thomas Boswell. Reprinted by permission of Doubleday and Company, Inc. |

Chapter 23

| p. 507 | Excerpt from news story from *The Times-News* (Twin Falls, Idaho). Used with permission. |

Chapter 24

p. 529	News story from *The Anniston (Ala.) Star*. Used with permission.
p. 533	Part of news story from *The Hawk Eye* (Burlington, Iowa). Used with permission.
p. 537	Story by Cristine Rouvalis of the *Pittsburgh Post-Gazette*. Used with permission.
p. 540	Excerpt from news story from *The Daily Register*. Used with permission.
pp. 542–43	Story excerpts from the series by Carol Matlack of the *Arkansas Gazette*. Used with permission.
p. 547	Part of story from *The Fincastle Herald*. Used with permission.

Chapter 26

pp. 590–91	News story from *The Columbia Journalism Review*. Used with permission.
p. 596	Excerpt from news story from *The Sacramento Bee*. Used with permission.
p. 649	Excerpts from a speech by Gene Roberts, used with permission of Gene Roberts, executive editor of *The Philadelphia Inquirer*.

Index